Gulf War

Air Power Survey

Volume I

Planning

and

Command and Control

Washington, D. C.
1993

Library of Congress Cataloging-in-Publication Data

Gulf War Air Power Survey
 p. cm.
 Gulf War Air Power Survey directed by Eliot A. Cohen.
 Includes an unnumbered summary report by Thomas A. Keaney and Eliot A. Cohen.
 Includes bibliographical references and indexes.
 Contents: v. 1. Planning and Command and Control -- v. 2. Operations and Effects and Effectiveness -- v. 3. Logistics and Support -- v.4. Weapons, Tactics, and Training and Space Operations -- v. 5. A Statistical Compendium and Chronology.
 1. Persian Gulf War, 1991--Aerial operations. American. 2. United States. Air Force--History--Persian Gulf War, 1991. I. Cohen, Eliot A. II. Gulf War Air Power Survey (Organization : U.S.). III. United States. Dept. of the Air Force. IV. Title: Gulf War Air Power Survey. Summary Report.
DS79.724.U6G85 1993
956.7044'248--dc20   93-30601
                                                                              CIP

For sale by the U.S. Government Printing Office
Superintendent of Documents, Mail Stop: SSOP, Washington, DC 20402-9328
ISBN 0-16-042909-9

Gulf War Air Power Survey

Staff

Dr. Eliot A. Cohen, *Director*

Col. Emery M. Kiraly	*Executive Director*
Lt. Gen. Robert E. Kelley (Retired, USAF)	*Senior Military Advisor*
Dr. Wayne W. Thompson	*Senior Historical Advisor*
Mr. Ernest D. Cruea	*ANSER Program Manager*
Maj. Joseph W. Patterson	*Executive Officer*
Mr. Lawrence J. Paszek	*Publishing Manager*
Lt. Col. Daniel T. Kuehl	*Chief, Statistics*
Lt. Col. Robert C. Owen	*Chief, Chronology*
Dr. John F. Guilmartin	*Chief, Weapons, Tactics and Training*
Mr. Richard A. Gunkel	*Chief, Logistics, Space, and Support*
Dr. Thomas C. Hone	*Chief, Command, Control, and Organization*
Dr. Alexander S. Cochran	*Chief, Strategy and Plans*
Mr. Barry D. Watts	*Chief, Operations and Effects*
Dr. Thomas A. Keaney	*Chief, Summary Report*

Gulf War Air Power Survey

Review Committee

Hon. Paul H. Nitze, *Chairman*
Diplomat in Residence
Paul H. Nitze School of Advanced International Studies

Gen. Michael J. Dugan (USAF, Retired)
Multiple Sclerosis Society

Adm. Huntington Hardisty (USN, Retired)
Center for Naval Analyses

Dr. Richard H. Kohn
The University of North Carolina
 at Chapel Hill

Dr. Bernard Lewis
Princeton University

Mr. Andrew W. Marshall
Office of the Secretary of Defense

Mr. Phillip Merrill
Former Assistant Secretary General
 for Defense Support, NATO

Dr. Henry Rowen
Stanford University

Hon. Ike Skelton
U.S. House of Representatives

Gen. Maxwell Thurman (USA, Retired)
Association of the U.S. Army

Maj. Gen. Jasper A. Welch, Jr. (USAF, Retired)
Former Assistant Chief of Staff (Studies
 and Analysis)

Dr. James Q. Wilson
University of California at Los Angeles

Foreword

From 16 January through 28 February 1991, the United States and its allies conducted one of the most operationally successful wars in history, a conflict in which air operations played a preeminent role. The Gulf War Air Power Survey was commissioned on 22 August 1991 to review all aspects of air warfare in the Persian Gulf for use by the United States Air Force, but it was not to confine itself to discussion of that institution. The Survey has produced reports on planning, the conduct of operations, the effects of the air campaign, command and control, logistics, air base support, space, weapons and tactics, as well as a chronology and a compendium of statistics on the war. It has prepared as well a summary report and some shorter papers and assembled an archive composed of paper, microfilm, and electronic records, all of which have been deposited at the Air Force Historical Research Agency at Maxwell Air Force Base, Alabama. The Survey was just that, an attempt to provide a comprehensive and documented account of the war. It is not a definitive history: that will await the passage of time and the opening of sources (Iraqi records, for example) that were not available to Survey researchers. Nor is it a summary of lessons learned: other organizations, including many within the Air Force, have already done that. Rather, the Survey provides an analytical and evidentiary point of departure for future studies of the air campaign. It concentrates on an analysis of the operational level of war in the belief that this level of warfare is at once one of the most difficult to characterize and one of the most important to understand.

The Survey was directed by Dr. Eliot Cohen of Johns Hopkins University's School of Advanced International Studies and was staffed by a mixture of civilian and military analysts, including retired officers from the Army, Navy, and Marine Corps. It was divided into task forces, most of which were run by civilians working temporarily for the Air Force. The work produced by the Survey was examined by a distinguished review committee that included scholars, retired general officers from the Air Force, Navy, and Army, as well as former and current senior government officials. Throughout, the Survey strived to conduct its research in a spirit of impartiality and scholarly rigor. Its members had as their standard the observation of Mr. Franklin D'Olier, chairman of the United States Strategic Bombing Survey during and after the second World War: "We wanted to burn into everybody's souls that fact that the survey's responsibility . . . was to ascertain facts and to seek truth, eliminating completely any preconceived theories or dogmas."

The Survey attempted to create a body of data common to all of the reports. Because one group of researchers compiled this core material while other task forces were researching and drafting other, more narrowly focused studies, it is possible that discrepancies exist among the reports with regard to points of detail. More importantly, authors were given discretion, within the bounds of evidence and plausibility, to interpret events as they saw them. In some cases, task forces came to differing conclusions about particular aspects of this war. Such divergences of view were expected and even desired: the Survey was intended to serve as a point of departure for those who read its reports, and not their analytical terminus.

This first report in this volume deals with the genesis and development of the plan for the air campaign of the Gulf War as executed in Operation Desert Storm; the second report explains how the United States air forces were organized, what challenges faced the command and control process, and how the commanders dealt with them.

Acknowledgments

The Survey's members owe a great debt of gratitude to Secretary of the Air Force Donald B. Rice, who conceived of the project, provided it with resources, and set for it the highest standards of independence and objectivity. Many organizations and individuals gave generously of their resources and time to support this effort. Various branches and commands of the Air Force were particularly helpful in providing material for and, in some cases, personnel to conduct the study. The United States Navy, Marine Corps, and Army aided with this study in different ways, including the sharing of data pertaining to the air war. A number of the United States' coalition partners also made available individuals and records that were vital to the Survey's work. Many participants in the war, including senior political officials and officers from all of the Services were willing to speak with the Survey and share their recollections of Desert Shield and Desert Storm. Private students of the Gulf War also made available their knowledge of the crisis and conflict. Wherever possible and appropriate such assistance has been acknowledged in the text.

The Survey's independence was its reason for being. Each report is the product of the authors who wrote it and does not necessarily represent the views of the Review Committee, the Air Force or the Department of Defense.

Security Review

The Gulf War Air Power Survey reports were submitted to the Department of Defense for policy and security review. In accordance with this review, certain information has been removed from the original text. These areas have been annotated as [DELETED].

Gulf War Air Power Survey

Summary Report

Volume I:

    Part I: Planning Report

    Part II: Command and Control Report

Volume II:

    Part I: Operations Report

    Part II: Effectiveness Report

Volume III:

    Part I: Logistics Report

    Part II: Support Report

Volume IV:

    Part I: Weapons, Tactics, and Training Report

    Part II: Space Report

Volume V:

    Part I: A Statistical Compendium

    Part II: Chronology

Contents

Foreword v

Acknowledgments vii

Security Review viii

List of GWAPS Reports ix

Part I: Planning

Index to Planning Report

Part II: Command and Control

Glossary

(**Note:** Each of the two reports retained pagination independent of the other. Accordingly, the table of contents for each report accompanies each report independently of this table of contents).

Glossary

Part I

Planning

Part I

Planning

Task Force Chief

Dr. Alexander S. Cochran

Principal Authors

Dr. Alexander S. Cochran
Mr. Lawrence M. Greenberg
Mr. Kurt R. Guthe
Dr. Wayne W. Thompson
Mr. Michael J. Eisenstadt

Principal Contributors

Capt. John R. Glock
Maj. Mark Clodfelter
Lt. Col. Allan W. Howey

Contents

Report Acknowledgments xi

Introduction xiii

1 The Air Campaign Plan of 16 January 1991:
      An Overview 1

2 Pre-Crisis Air Planning for the Persian Gulf 17

3 Iraq: The Road to War 55

4 Policy Objectives, Restraints, and Constraints 83

5 Instant Thunder and Desert Shield 105

6 Evolution of the Offensive Air Campaign Plan 143

7 Intelligence for Air Campaign Planning 191

8 Planning the Gulf War Air Campaign: Retrospective 223

Appendix

A Military Organization Glossary 233

B USCINCCENT Regional Plans .... [DELETED]

Index 235

Tables

1 Coalition Campaign Objectives 7

2 CENTAF Target Categories (Sets)-December 1990 10

3 USCINCCENT OPLAN 1002-88 Force Requirements 22

4 USCINCCENT OPLAN 1002-88 Key Assumptions 25

5	USCINCCENT OPLAN 1002-90 Milestones	26
6	USCINCCENT OPLAN 1002-90 Concept of Operations Force Requirements and Deployment Schedule	28
7	USCINCCENT OPLAN 1002-90 Concept of Operations Key Assumptions	30
8	Draft USCINCCENT OPLAN 1002-90 (July 90) Force Requirements and Deployment Schedule	33
9	Comparison of USAF Aircraft In-Theater OPLAN vs Desert Shield	34
10	Draft USCINCCENT OPLAN 1002-90 (July 90) Key Assumptions	36
11	Evolution of USCINCCENT OPLAN 1002	39
12	Exercise Internal Look 90 Participants	45
13	USCENTAF Internal Look 90 Target List: 15 June 1990	48
14	Internal Look 90 (for OPLAN 1002-900 Target Lists	50
15	Planned U.S. Aircraft Beddown-April 1990	52
16	Prioritized USCENTAF Mission List Exercise Internal Look 90	53
17	Force Requirements and Deployment Schedule U.S. Central Command Preliminary Planning	130
18	USCINCCENT Preliminary Planning Assumptions	131
19	Target Growth by Category	146
20	Target Growth by Category	185

21	ATO Targets Planned for Attack by Day	189
22	CENTAF Target Sets by OPLAN 1002-90 Objectives	193
23	CENTAF Target List-15 June 1990	193
24	CENTAF and CENTCOM Target Lists	199
25	Known Iraqi Targets by GAT Category-2 August 1990	201
26	Estimates of Iraqi Ground Forces-16 January 1991	203
27	Iraqi Pre-War Ground Order of Battle	204
28	Iraqi Air Force as of 2 August 1990	207
29	Known Iraqi AIF Targets by Category: 16 January 1991	212
30	Growth of Known Iraqi AIF Targets by GAT (CENTAF) Category Before and After Operation Desert Storm	216
31	Growth of GAT Target Sets Before and After Operation Desert Storm	217
32	Overall Growth of Known Iraqi AIF Targets by GAT Category	219
33	Percentage of Total Targets by Category	226
34	Military Organization Glossary	233
35	USCINCCENT Regional Plans Summary	[DELETED]

Figures

1	D-Day Sequence	8
2	G-Day Sequence	8

3	Warning and Deployment Timelines	31
4	Crisis Planning Assumptions vs Actual Response	37
5	Anticipated Iraqi Attack	43
6	Iraqi Ground Force Deployment in the KTO: 16 January 1991	76
7	Extract from "THE" Target List Provided to CINC, CJCS, SECDEF	89
8	D-Day Plan (ATO-Bravo) Proposed Targets	138
9	Punishment ATO Attack Plan	141
10	Concept to Execution Planning	144
11	Attack Plan First Day, AM-Night	176
12	Attack Plan First Day, AM-Night	177
13	Attack Plan First Day, PM-Day	178
14	Attack Plan First Day, PM-Night	179
15	Attack Plan Second Day, AM-Night	180
16	Attack Plan Second Day, AM-Day	181
17	Attack Plan Second Day, PM-Day	182
18	Attack Plan Second Day, PM-Night	183
19	ATO Targets by Category	190
20	CENTAF Iraqi Target Study-Kuwait	195
21a	CENTAF Iraqi Target Study Attack Plan-Iraq	196
21b	CENTAF Iraqi Target Study Attack Plan-Iraq	196
21c	CENTAF Iraqi Target Study Attack Plan-Iraq	197
21d	CENTAF Iraqi Target Study Attack Plan-Iraq	197

22 Iraqi Ground Force Deployment in the KTO:
            16 January 1991 205

23 Intelligence Estimates of Iraqi Scud Missiles 210

24 Growth of Iraqi AIF Targets by Category,
            July 1990 - July 1991 221

Report Acknowledgements

The primary author of this report was Dr. Alexander S. Cochran; major portions were written by Lawrence Greenberg, Kurt Guthe, Wayne Thompson, and Michael Eisenstadt. Mark Clodfelter, John Glock, and Al Howey provided significant input. Richard Kohn, a member of the Review Committee, Abe Shulsky from the Office of the Principal Deputy Undersecretary of Defense for Strategy and Resources, and Michael Hayden from the Office of the Secretary of the Air Force offered significant comments that were gratefully incorporated into the study. The views on planning presented in the volume, however, are those of the primary author.

Introduction

The focus of air planners was to envision the use of air power in achieving coalition objectives and military strategy. This report begins with the genesis of that plan with some background to place it within an historical perspective and traces its development through what existed on 16 January 1991.

The planning task force addresses three specific questions. First, what were the origins of the air campaign plan that was developed prior to the outbreak of the Gulf War in late July 1990? In brief, there were two: one, a series of contingency plans, the 1002 family of plans developed by planners for the region. In early August, however, the plan proved unable to provide the answers to the Iraqi invasion of Kuwait and threatened attack of Saudi Arabia. The second set of origins was the scenario rehearsed during Exercise Internal Look, a Central Command (CENTCOM) wargame conducted only days before the Kuwaiti invasion. Though time prevented planners from implementing solutions to problems encountered, the exercise did focus their attention on the Gulf and provided them with a precursor of the final air campaign.

In addressing the second question, why did planners of the air campaign develop the plan as they did from August 1990 through January 1991? What were the determinants? Five positive influences are identified. First were the national objectives along with constraints and restraints prescribed by the President early in the crisis. Washington clearly outlined the goals and expectations of the air campaign plan, and its planners maintained them in the forefront throughout their efforts. Second was the overall concept for Instant Thunder, a plan for an independent offensive air campaign proposed by air planners in early August and remained the sole offensive option available to Gen. H. Norman Schwarzkopf, Central Command commander, during the first month of the crisis. Even after it was overcome by the arrival of additional resources, air planners used it as the basic blueprint for the final air campaign plan. Third were the various defensive plans made to support Desert Shield, the defense of Saudi Arabia, which remained the focus of U. S. concern through October. Air planners' efforts here, particularly in target selection and tactical development, facilitated their expansion of the Instant Thunder concept into the Desert Storm plan. Fourth was the overall theater campaign plan in which CENTCOM planners from the outset had featured air power as the essential element. Even after additional ground forces were added in October and the final phases of the offensive operation were developed, they retained air power as the key to all phases. And lastly, there was the planning process used by CENTAF planners in outlining just how they would use air power within the overall construct of the theater campaign and the concept of operations suggested by Instant Thunder to achieve national objectives. From the outset they followed a logical procedure that linked centers of gravity to specific target sets.

There were also several factors which, in retrospect, limited the planners in their development. Most significant here was the less than satisfactory relationship between intelligence analysts and planners. Intelligence analysts often lacked detailed or timely information on Iraq, while operational planners excluded them from much of the planning process. Air planners made faulty assumptions about such important issues as the Iraqi employment of mobile Scuds as well as expectations on availability of bomb damage assessment essential to the development of their plan. Operational planners did not ask the right questions; neither did intelligence analysts anticipate them.

The final question posed here dealt with the final plan as planners turned it into an execution order on January 16, 1991. Just what was that plan? What were the expectations of its planners? Here authors discovered several points. First, planners had put forth an extraordinary amount of work on the first phase of the air campaign plan–the strategic air campaign–particularly the first forty-eight hours. However, they had devoted surprisingly little detailed planning for the last two phases of Desert Storm. Second, planners' selection of total numbers of targets within target categories remained remarkably similar to those first proposed in the Instant Thunder plan. Both of these suggest the degree to which air planners remained convinced that air power alone could achieve the overall objectives.

The focus of this report is the air campaign plan; that is, the plan for using air power throughout the entire Desert Storm campaign. From November 1990 CENTCOM planners expected an air campaign of approximately one month. The time frame for developing the plan lasted from August 1990 through January 1991, which proved to be an extraordinarily long period for planners. Likewise, they were assured from mid-September of having in theater all air power resources needed to execute the plan.

This investigation focuses on the substance as well as the process of the plan, with emphasis on the former, and it views "a plan" as the simple expression, written or otherwise, of implementing strategy and using military resources to achieve objectives. It consists of a statement of intentions–normally expressed as mission–a vision to be realized, sometimes referred to as a "concept of operations," and tasks for subordinate elements that may or may not be specific in nature, but from which orders flow. Included also is a sense of priorities for these subordinate tasks, particularly if they are to be sequenced or if resources are limited, and an established system of command and control: who works for whom. Implicit in such statements are a sense of measurement, of success–a reference by which the plan may be determined to have succeeded or overtaken by events, a point at which victory may be proclaimed or another plan required.

The planning section of this report is organized into three parts. The first provides background for the discussion of the plans themselves. It does not deal with the logistical build-up or requirements for support of air operations; these are outlined in the GWAPS report on logistics. Chapter One presents an overview of the air campaign plan that planners translated into the order for Operation Desert Storm on 16 January 1991. Chapter Two outlines American planning for the Gulf Region prior to the invasion of Kuwait including the wargame, Internal Look. In Chapter Three, the report investigates the Iraqi perspective on the Kuwait invasion, the period between the invasion and the coalition offensive and the situation on the eve of Desert Storm.

The second part of planning, the major effort, concentrates on the actual plans, while details of the planning process have been left to the GWAPS report on Command and Control, which appears as Part II of this volume. Likewise, the consideration of the day-to-day training and operational activities of the U.S. Air Force from September 1990 through January 1991 in preparation for the air campaign can be found in the other volumes of GWAPS. Chapter Four describes the formation of national policy objectives, restraints, and constraints that shaped the overall theater campaign. Instant Thunder is described in Chapter Five, as are the various air plans, both defensive and offensive, formulated from August through December 1990 for the defense of Saudi Arabia, Chapter Six deals with the evolution of the final air campaign plan for Desert Storm. The role that intelligence played–both in theory and in reality–in the formulation of these plans is discussed in Chapter Seven.

The final section of the planning report returns to the questions initially introduced and expands them with particular reference to the air campaign plan in mid-January 1991.

The authors encountered several matters during their research and analysis of planning that deserve mention at the outset—in particular sources, perspective, and precedent. To the greatest degree possible, this study is based upon research in primary sources. The GWAPS effort has been blessed with massive amounts of records on the conduct of the Gulf War. With regard to air campaign planning at the U.S. Air Force level to include CENTAF and the Ninth Air Force, this is particularly true. Frequently, however, the authors encountered both "too much" and "too little" at the same time. Thanks to the copying machine, in many instances, planning documents—to include very sensitive and highly classified ones—were reproduced in numbers and placed in varied files. Thus, at first blush a researcher is happily confronted by cubic feet of files, only to discover that the majority were merely copies of copies. Often they proved difficult to trace or date. On the other hand, there were many decisions or substantive discussions that the GWAPS researchers simply could not document. Some may have been recorded in informal minutes or notes still classified; others could only be derived from interviews and oral histories; many remain locked in individual memories.

The authors also encountered references that may be confusing to readers and which should be brought to their attention. The reference "day" used in the *Gulf War Air Power Survey* in many instances is based on Greenwich Mean Time (GMT), known in the U.S. military as "Zulu" or "Z" time. In other references of the *Survey*, however, the time period may be expressed in local time, which of course varies from GMT. Key local time conversions are derived in the following manner: Eastern Standard or Daylight Savings Time (Z - 5 or Z - 6 hours) and Saudi Arabian as (Z + 3 hours). Thus, if an event occurred at 1700L (Local) time in Riyadh, it may be reported as having occurred at 1400Z. A detailed comparison of reference days for air tasking orders appears as Table 176, "ATO Reference Dates," in *A Statistical Compendium*, Volume V of the *Gulf War Air Power Survey*.

U.S. military messages are cited throughout the GWAPS reports by their distinguishing date-time group (DTG). Normally appearing at the head of all U.S. military messages, a DTG indicates the time of initial transmission. Thus, a DTG of 032100 Nov 90 indicates that a message was transmitted on 3 November, 1990, at 2100 hours.

Gulf War planners may have been the first in history to record their concepts and decisions on briefing slides and scripts instead of written operation plans and meeting minutes. While conducting research, the authors found it essential to understand the misleading nature of "bullet slides" and blandness of "canned scripts" as well as the purpose of "back-up slides" that may or may not have been used.

This study is close in time to the event. After a year of research, the report's authors continued to find new documentation that altered their analysis. One can only assume that such revelations will continue as new planning documents are opened for official research and more senior decision makers reveal their own roles and attitudes.

Throughout, the authors were conscious that the World War II U. S. Strategic Bombing Survey, the GWAPS model, produced no report that dealt with the planning effort *per se*. Thus, they had no precedent; neither did they have a standard against for comparison. Lacking such guidance, the authors based the study upon judgment that the plan for the Gulf War air campaign was worthy of close study and detailed analysis. As with all human endeavors, it had its virtues, and it had its weaknesses. This report deals with both.

1

The Air Campaign Plan of 16 January 1991: An Overview

The Desert Storm Campaign Plan

Planners for the Gulf War air campaign plan of 16 January 1991 relied upon the "U.S. eyes only" theater operation plan for Desert Storm that had been published on 16 December 1990. Coalition planners delayed publishing their own version of the offensive plan until 17 January 1991 for reasons that will be discussed in greater detail in this report. In both of these documents, U.S. and coalition planners laid out the purpose of their offensive plan–to counter Iraqi aggression and secure and restore ("provide for the establishment of") the legitimate government of Kuwait.[1]

The mission for both U.S. and coalition military forces flowed from these purposes. Planners saw Operation Desert Storm as an offensive operation to be executed when directed by higher authorities. Coalition forces viewed their objectives as twofold: (1) eject Iraqi forces from Kuwait and (2) be prepared to secure and defend Kuwait. The CENTCOM plan for U.S. forces was more detailed, though noting that their job was "in concert with coalition forces." U. S. forces were to neutralize Iraqi National Command Authority, eject Iraqi armed forces from Kuwait, destroy the Republican Guard, destroy Iraqi's ballistic missile, nuclear, biological and chemical warfare capabilities as early as possible, and assist in the restoration of the legitimate government of Kuwait.[2]

---

[1] Information used in this chapter was taken primarily from the following two Operation Plans: (S) OPLAN USCENTCOM, Riyadh, HQ Joint Forces/Theater of Operations, Riyadh, *(S) Combined OPLAN for Offensive Operations to Eject Iraqi Forces from Kuwait,* 17 Jan 91, GWAPS NA-106, hereafter cited as (S) Coalition *Combined OPLAN*; and (S/NF) USCINCCENT, *U.S. OPLAN Desert Storm,* 16 Dec 1990, GWAPS, CHC 18-2, hereafter cited as (S/NF) USCINCCENT *OPLAN Desert Storm.*

[2] (S) Coalition *Combined OPLAN,* p 3; (S/NF) USCINCCENT *OPLAN Desert Storm,* p 9.

Central Command, as well as coalition planners made use of the concept of "centers of gravity." Defined by the 19th century philosopher of war, Carl von Clausewitz as "the hub of all power and movement, on which everything depends . . . the point against which all our energies should be directed," this notion had gained acceptance in military thinking and planning over the past decade.[3] As this report (and others in GWAPS) will make clear, both political decisionmakers and their military planners differed on just what constituted centers of gravity for this war.[4] U.S. and coalition planners for the Gulf War offensive identified Iraq as having three "primary centers of gravity": (1) leadership, command and control (U.S. planners were even more precise here, identifying Saddam Hussein); (2) chemical, biological, and nuclear capability; and (3) forces of the Republican Guard. There also was agreement that "these will be targeted throughout . . . to ensure destruction, neutralization, elimination or degradation as soon as possible."[5] With one exception to be noted, planners did not attempt to quantify or further define tasks such as "destruction, neutralization, elimination, degradation, or attrit."

From the overall mission and centers of gravity came specific objectives. U.S. planners first stated the U.S. national objectives that had been central to their efforts for the past five and a half months were to achieve the immediate, complete, and unconditional withdrawal of Iraqi forces from Kuwait; restore the legitimate government of Kuwait; and remain committed to the restoration of security and stability of the Arabian Gulf. Both sets of plans then laid out "operational campaign objectives": (1) destroy Iraq's military capability to wage war (U.S. planners were more precise here, saying "neutralize Iraqi leadership and command and control"); (2) gain and maintain air supremacy; (3) cut Iraq supply lines (the U. S. document added the word "totally"); (4) destroy Iraq's chemical, biological, and nuclear capability; (5) destroy Republican Guard forces; and 6) liberate Kuwait City with Arab forces.[6]

---

[3]Clausewitz, Carl, *On War*, ed Michael Howard and Peter Paret, etc, pp 595-6. Clausewitz wrote a single center of gravity; however Central Command planners assumed that there could be several.

[4]For further discussion on this matter, see GWAPS report on Effects and Effectiveness.

[5](S) Coalition *Combined OPLAN*, p 4; (S/NF) USCINCCENT *OPLAN Desert Storm*, p 9.

[6](S) Coalition *Combined OPLAN*, p 2; (S/NF) USCINCCENT *OPLAN Desert Storm*, p 5.

Early Target selection for an offensive, Strategic Air Campaign by Air Staff's Planning Group in Washington.

Planners of the Gulf War offensive, Desert Storm, worked from several key assumptions. The first was that this plan was the logical extension of their earlier plans to "deter further Iraqi aggression" and "defend critical port and oil facilities." Second, they assumed "application of overwhelming air, naval, and ground combat power" and "contribution of many nations' forces." And last–here again U.S. planners were more precise–offensive operations would be followed by "security of Kuwait . . . as a result of the offensive campaign or a political settlement, . . . regional security . . . (through) conflict termination, . . . (and) strategic redeployment of designated U.S. force."[7]

Desert Storm planners envisioned an offensive operation in four phases, each with its own separate set of objectives and time estimates. The operation was to commence with

> . . . an extensive strategic air campaign . . . against targets in Iraq focusing on enemy centers of gravity. The air campaign will progressively shift into the KTO (Kuwait Theater of Operations) to reduce the effectiveness of Iraqi defenses and isolate the KTO (U.S. planners again were more precise here adding 'inflict maximum enemy casualties'). On order, a multi-axis ground, naval, and air attack will be launched . . . to create the perception of a main attack in the east. The main effort . . . will be in the western KTO.[8]

They noted that "execution of the phases is not necessarily discrete or sequential; phases may overlap as resources become available or priorities shift."[9]

They entitled Phase I "Strategic Air Campaign." The designation "strategic" had different connotations for air planners and their ground counterparts, but remained undefined throughout the plan. Interestingly, in some cases it was introduced in capital letters while in other instances it was "lower-cased," perhaps avoiding the issue. Regardless, the campaign's objective was clear in the U.S. plan:

---

[7](S/NF) USCINCCENT *OPLAN Desert Storm*, pp 3-4.

[8](S) Coalition *Combined OPLAN*, pp 4-5; (S/NF) USCINCCENT *OPLAN Desert Storm*, pp 9-10.

[9](S) *Ibid.*

... attack Iraq's strategic air defenses, aircraft/airfields, strategic chemical, biological and nuclear capability; leadership targets; command and control systems; RGFC (Republican Guard Force Command) forces; telecommunications facilities; and key elements of the national infrastructure, such as critical LOCs (lines of communications) between Baghdad and the KTO, electric grids, petroleum storage and military production facilities.[10]

Planners expected this phase to last six to nine days, anticipating "disruption of Iraqi command and control, loss of confidence in the government, significant degradation of Iraqi military capabilities and isolation and destruction of the RGFC."[11]

The phase was to be both joint and coalition as special operation forces were to destroy intercept operations centers on the Iraq-Saudi border, resistance forces were to disrupt key communication sites in Kuwait and Iraq, while naval forces were to initiate sea control and countermine operations in the Gulf. And finally, under the cover of the air campaign, ground forces were to move into attack positions for the final phase of Desert Storm, a move that planners estimated would take fifteen days.[12]

Exactly when planners expected Phase II, Air Supremacy in the KTO, to begin was not clear, though they noted that "the phase will be initiated coincident with, or immediately following, the strategic air campaign." They also noted that "as strategic air campaign objectives are met, . . . Phase II begins with priority of air effort shifting to the KTO to roll back Iraqi air defenses and sever supply lines."[13] Specific attack objectives included aircraft, airfields, air defense weapons, and command and control systems in Iraq and Kuwait "to provide an environment in which B-52s, tactical air and attack helicopters can operate effectively in subsequent phases." They expected this phase to last from one to two days.[14]

---

[10](S/NF) USCINCCENT *OPLAN Desert Storm*, p 12.

[11](S) Coalition *Combined OPLAN*, p 5; (S/NF) USCINCCENT *OPLAN Desert Storm*, p 12.

[12](S/NF) USCINCCENT *OPLAN Desert Storm*, p 12.

[13]*Ibid*, p 11.

[14]*Ibid*, p 12.

Phase III, Battlefield Preparation, was to be an extension of Phase II, with increased attacks against "Iraqi ground combat forces and supporting missile/rocket/artillery units." Planners directed a shift to "tactical air and naval surface fires" to interdict supply lines and destroy command, control, and communications systems in southern Iraq and Kuwait. Planners projected this phase to last eight days. The purpose of this effort was "to open a window of opportunity for initiating ground offensive operations by confusing and terrorizing Iraqi forces in the KTO and shifting combat force ratio in favor of friendly forces." The desired effects were to cut the Iraqi supply lines (the U.S.-only plan specified this as "totally"), and reduce Iraqi combat effectiveness in the KTO by at least fifty percent.[15]

As will be discussed in this report, just what planners meant by fifty percent was never clear; indeed it varied widely by component and level. The U.S.-only plan specified the percentage as "particularly the RGFC," noting also destruction of Iraqi chemical, biological, and nuclear capabilities. They also anticipated that this phase might commence during the short Phase II, if air defense systems had been degraded.

If all went as envisioned, planners estimated that Phase IV, Ground Offensive Operations, would commence approximately three weeks after the launching of Desert Storm. The objectives for this phase were to liberate Kuwait, cut critical lines of communication into southeast Iraq, and destroy the Republic Guard. The main attack was to be conducted along the western border of Kuwait to "destroy Republican Guard forces," It was to be a ground attack, "combined with continuous B-52 strikes, TACAIR (tactical air) attacks, and attack helicopter operations." Planners envisioned four secondary attacks, by coalition, U.S. Army, and the U.S. Marine forces along with a series of feints, demonstrations and amphibious operations. In anticipation for the main attack, "the bridges, roads and rail line immediately south of Basra will be cut to block withdrawal of RGFC and to form a kill zone north of Kuwait."[16] Though the planners did not specify in writing exactly how long they expected this phase to last, a graphic in the U.S.-only plan indicated: "Republican

---

[15](S) Coalition *Combined OPLAN*, p 6; (S/NF) USCINCCENT *OPLAN Desert Storm*, p 13.

[16](S) Coalition *Combined OPLAN*, pp 6-7; (S/NF) USCINCCENT *OPLAN Desert Storm*, pp 13-14.

Guard destroyed, establish defense SE Iraq and Kuwait" by G+6 Day, thus assuming that Phase IV would be completed within a week.[17]

U.S. and coalition planners included two matrixes in the Desert Storm plan. The first as shown below outlined specific objectives along with the phases during which they were to be accomplished:

Table 1
Coalition Campaign Objectives

Military Objective	Phase			
	I	II	III	IV
Military capability to wage war	■	■	■	■
Air supremacy	■	■		
Cut supply lines	■	■	■	■
Destroy RGFC	■		■	■
Liberate Kuwait City				■

Source: (S) Coalition *Combined OPLAN*, 17 Jan 91, Riyadh, p 4.

Planners did not include in this matrix the objective to "destroy Iraq's chemical, biological, and nuclear capability." The second matrix was one that aligned the specific phases and selected tasks along a time line, as noted in Figures 1 and 2. As these charts made clear, planners expected Desert Storm to last a month or less.

---

[17](S/NF) USCINCCENT *OPLAN Desert Storm*, Appendix 17 to Annex C, np.

Figure 1
D-Day Sequence

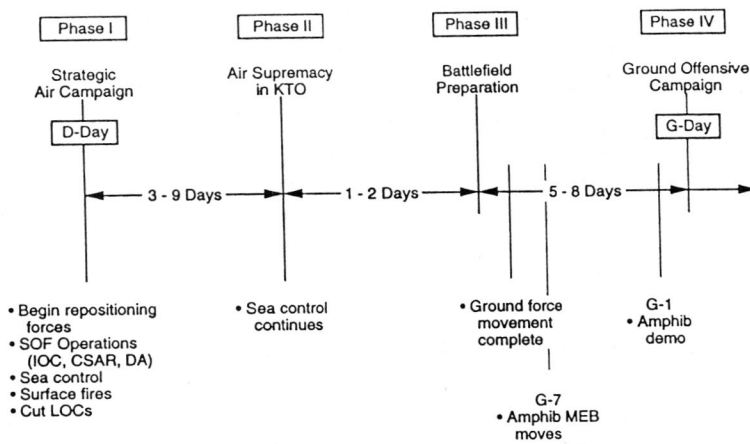

Source: USCINCCENT *OPLAN Desert Storm*, Appendix 17 to Annex C, np; Coalition *Combined OPLAN*, p 6.

Figure 2
G-Day Sequence

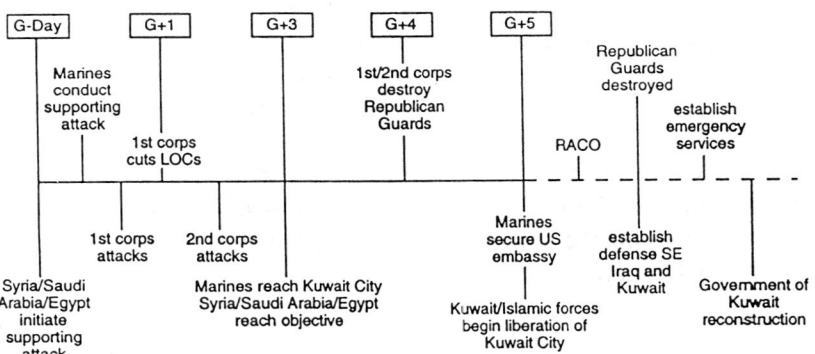

Source: USCINCCENT *OPLAN Desert Storm*, Appendix 17 to Annex C, np.

The key–indeed in some phases the critical–role in the overall operation plan as well as individual phases was to be played by air power. In the U.S.-only plan, the Commander U.S. Central Command Air Force (COMUSCENTAF) was designated "Joint Force Air Component Commander for the USCENTCOM AOR (Area of Operations)." Included were responsibilities to "plan, coordinate, allocate and task sorties . . . direct coordination . . . to ensure integration of the air campaign . . . (and) integrate supporting maritime air resources."[18] While the coalition plan was not that specific, these planners did direct COMUSCENTAF to accomplish tasks including "prepare an air campaign plan to destroy Iraq's military capability to wage war . . . in coordination with Commander, Royal Saudi Air Force."[19]

Both plans gave COMUSCENTAF tasks that were specifically tied to the phases already discussed, such as "cut bridges, roads and rail lines immediately south of Basra to block withdrawal of RGFC forces and block reinforcement and/or resupply of Iraqi forces from the west and to isolate Iraqi forces in the KTO . . . (and) be prepared to assist in securing and defending of Kuwait City."[20] These served to emphasize the tasks outlined.

The Desert Storm air campaign plan

From the outset of the Gulf War crisis, theater planners had relied upon air power, featuring it initially in defensive and then in offensive theater campaign plans that evolved as will be discussed in detail in this report. Early in this crisis, CENTAF planners produced a plan that followed the classic "five paragraph field order" format (situation, mission, execution, administration and logistics, and command and signal) format.[21] However, for reasons that are not clear, planners of the Gulf War air campaign in their subsequent efforts turned to different formats to outline and detail the specifics of the air plan for the Gulf War for both decisionmakers and operators.

---

[18](S/NF) USCINCCENT *OPLAN Desert Storm*, p C-2.

[19](S) Coalition *Combined OPLAN*, p 10.

[20](S) *Ibid*, pp 9-10.

[21](S) OpOrd, COMUSCENTAF Offensive Campaign-Phase I, 2 Sep 90, GWAPS files.

The initial format planners used to lay out the specifics of the air campaign was that of briefings. Two days after CENTCOM planners had issued the U.S.-only Desert Storm plan, the chief CENTCOM air campaign planner, Brig. Gen. Buster Glosson, briefed his USAF wing commanders–the operators–on their role in the air campaign plan.[22] Several days later, he briefed the Secretary of Defense–a major decisionmaker–on the role of the air campaign in the theater plan. From these two briefings came the air campaign plan for Desert Storm.

As will be discussed in this and other GWAPS reports, air planners were guided by the CENTCOM concept of centers of gravity, though they modified the last one from "forces of the Republican Guard" to "military forces." They then matched these against general target sets and picked specific targets within these sets. By the time of the briefings in mid-December, 238 specific targets were selected in the following categories:

Table 2
CENTAF Target Categories (Sets) – December 1990

Target Set	Number of Targets
Strategic Air Defense	28
Strategic Chemical and Scuds	25
Leadership	32
Republican Guards and Military Support	44
Telecommunications	26
Electricity	16
Oil	7
Railroads	28
Airfields	28
Ports	4
Total	**238**

Source: (S) Brfg, "Theater Air Campaign" Briefing for Wing Commanders, 18 Dec 90, Glosson's notebook, GWAPS Box 1, Folder 4, MAP.

---

[22] Ibid.

These target sets provided General Glosson and his air campaign planners with a framework within which they constructed specific "attack plans" that were then placed within the overall construct of the four theater campaign phases.

Air planners assigned no specific objectives for Phase I, the strategic air campaign. Instead they expected to "destroy leadership's military command and control, destroy nuclear, biological, and chemical capability, disrupt and attrit Republican Guard Forces, disrupt leadership's ability to communicate with populace, destroy key electrical grids and oil storage, (and) limit military resupply capability." They estimated that the phase would last for six days, with Phase II starting on the fourth day and Phase III on the fifth day. Planners laid out a detailed "attack plan" with specific targets selected from the list of 238 for the first two days. On the succeeding four days, they planned to "reattack 20% of first and second day targets, key targets requiring additional attacks (BDA) [meaning that re-attacking would be based upon bomb damage assessment], and remainder of targets not covered during the first 48 hours." Notionally, they divided each twenty-four-hour period into four segments: "pre dawn, morning, afternoon, and night." They envisioned more than 1,000 attack sorties per day during this phase.[23]

Air planners described the objective for Phase II, KTO Air Supremacy, as "provide a threat free environment allowing unhindered air operations in the Kuwait Theater of Operations." They told Secretary Cheney that the objective was to "establish air supremacy over the Kuwaiti Theater of Operations and provide an environment conducive to the conduct of air to ground attacks." They expected 305 sorties over a two-day period to "destroy all radar controlled surface-to-air threats and establish air supremacy in the KTO." As noted earlier, this phase would commence during Phase I.

For Phase III, Shaping the Battlefield in the KTO, planners wanted to "shape the battlefield for initiation of offensive ground campaign." They further refined the definition for Secretary Cheney to "continue Phase I operations into Iraq to prevent reconstitution and resupply, SEAD

---

[23]Brfg (S), "Theater Air Campaign" Briefing for Wing Commanders, 18 Dec 1990, in Glosson's notebook in GWAPS Box 1, Folder 4, MAP.

11

Gen H. Norman Schwarzkopf in Coalition Operations center in Riyadh.

[Suppression of Enemy Air Defenses] operations as required, and battlefield preparations continue as an air operation against Iraqi ground forces in Kuwait with a focus on Republican Guards and artillery." They expected "an air operation against Iraqi focusing on the Republican Guard, approximately 600 U.S. sorties a day, with 300 sorties a day available in case of Iraqi attack into Saudi Arabia." They also saw this as a continuation of Phase II SEAD operations.

Fifty percent attrition of Iraqi ground forces by air power was expected by the planners, "arty (artillery), armor, and troops," by the fourth day of Phase III. Their projections showed ninety percent attrition by the ninth day. This phase would conclude with "Kuwaiti Theater of Operations prepared for offensive ground campaign to liberate Kuwait." They noted for Secretary Cheney that this "achieves Presidential objectives with minimal loss of life." Planners envisioned "Republican Guard Forces in the KTO . . . no longer capable of launching an attack or reinforcing Iraqi forces in Kuwait (and) should be possible for the majority of friendly forces re-occupying Kuwait to be Arab."[24]

During the four weeks between the issuance of the CENTCOM Desert Storm plan and the actual execution of the air campaign plan, air planners worked to translate the concepts into the final document–the Air Tasking Order (ATO).[25] Traditionally, they had relied upon the "five paragraph field order." However, for the Gulf War offensive planning, CENTAF planners tried a new planning tool, the so-called Master Attack Plan. It was this format and procedure that they used to translate the purpose, mission, objectives, and tasks as outlined in the Desert Storm Theater Operations Plans into the Desert Storm Air Campaign Plan on 16 January 1991.

On the eve of Desert Storm execution, planners had three Master Attack Plans, one entitled "First 24 Hours," the next "Second 24 Hours," and the last, "Third 24 Hours."[26] Each outlined several specifics: MSN# (mission number); BEN (basic encyclopedia number), TGT (target); Description; and AC (aircraft). Earlier versions of this format included a category labeled "effects" that was dropped as planning progressed. Perhaps the most significant entries on the master plan were the lists of "targets" and "description." As discussed above, air planners very early in their efforts had matched centers of gravity and military objectives against exact target categories called "target sets." They then assigned a two-digit alphabetic code with more precise target description which allowed a sense of how that mission fit into the overall air campaign plan concept.

The Master Attack Plan did not break the period into four segments as had been formulated during the earlier briefings. Rather, planners subdivided their twenty-four-hour plan into groups that focused upon a

---

[24]*Ibid.*

[25]For a detailed discussion of the ATO, both procedure and content, see GWAPS Report on Command and Control. After the war, a CENTAF planner pointed out that "the ATO was the most critical part in air campaign planning. The importance of the Master Attack Plan was the concepts embedded in the flow." Intvw, Col Sam Baptiste with A. S. Cochran, GWAPS, 10 Nov 92.

[26](S) Doc, Master Attack Plan, First 24 Hours, 1/167/91 21:21; Master Attack Plan, Second 24 Hours, 17 Jan/1600; Master Attack Plan, Third 24 Hours, 14 Jan, 2247, all found in Box 1, Master Attack Plan, GWAPS Files.

particular type target such as command and control, Scuds, or Republican Guards, as well as specific aircraft like F-117 or A-10. In some instances, these were identified as "packages"; however, more than often, air planners grouped them by a desired functional effect or target category.[27]

The first twenty-four-hour MAP was the most detailed, as planners outlined specific targets and time on target for some seven hundred combat aircraft including not only USAF aircraft but also U.S. Army helicopters, USMC aircraft and drones, and U.S. Navy aircraft and Tomahawk land attack missiles. During the first twenty-four hours, they envisioned some seventy-six individual groups of attacks, thirty-two in the first wave during darkness (H-Hour to daylight), twenty-six during daylight hours, and eighteen from dusk to midnight. The first wave featured F-117 Stealth fighters flying as individual attack aircraft, a handful of F-15Es, and some thirty U.S. Navy Tomahawk missiles. Sorties were directed against command and control and leadership facilities in Baghdad, Tallil, and south central Iraq–specifically designed to cripple Iraqi air defense. Equally important were known Scud launch areas in H-2 and H-3 that directly threatened Israel. Also scheduled were Scud storage sites as well as chemical bunkers. During daylight hours of the first day, F-16s, A-10s, B-52s, and F-111s were to strike the bulk of the targets. Sorties continued against H-2 and H-3 potential Scud launching areas, chemical weapon bunkers, and airfields. Added were more air defense installations, command and control bunkers, and Republican Guard formations. B-52s, launched from the continental United States and using conventional air-launched cruise missiles for the first time, would also strike command and control facilities. During the final phase of the first twenty-four hours, F-117s were to return against leadership and command and control targets in the Baghdad area, while other aircraft were to attack bridges and airfields.

In the second twenty-four-hour Master Attack Plan, planners scheduled fifty-four sets of strikes, again sequenced in three waves. The first wave, initially F-117s then F-111s, were to continue attacks of air defense facilities and airfields as well as biological weapons bunkers. During the daylight wave, the attacks were to be continued by A-10s, again pounding the Republican Guard just north of Kuwait, while F-16s focused on Scud production facilities and storage bunkers in the Baghdad area. Naval

---

[27](S) *Ibid.*

Tomahawk land attack missiles were to be targeted against oil and electric facilities while F-18s were to hit naval port facilities. During the final evening wave, strikes were targeted across the country. The F-117s were to return to command and control targets, while A-6s and B-52s were targeted against oil refineries. The F-111s were to strike both chemical and manufacturing facilities. Thus, in the second twenty-four-hour plan, planners shifted the air campaign from air superiority targets to war making production facilities.

The third twenty-four-hour period had always been seen by planners as the time when they would react to intelligence and bomb damage assessment which presumably would indicate targets to be reattacked. The planners laid out this scheme in the Master Attack Plan for this period, which was less definitive in targeting and overall priorities; it relied on CENTAF "to provide near real time battle damage assessments."[28] More than fifty separate sets of targets were grouped into the three wave periods. During the first midnight-to-dawn wave, F-111s, F-16s, and F-18s were to strike Republican Guard locations and military storage sites. In the daytime wave, F-14s, F-16s, and F-18s were assigned against bridges, canals, and Republican Guard, while F-16s were to strike leadership and chemical targets in Baghdad. Large numbers of A-10s were unassigned, presumably to be used against targets that needed to be hit again. RAF aircraft were to continue to pound airfields. After dusk, the F-117s were to continue to hit leadership targets, and revisit command and control facilities. A-6s were to hit highway bridges, F-111s were to strike electric transformers and chemical plants while F-15s were targeted against ammunition facilities. The final entry was for F-117s, "TBD/based on BDA"–to be determined based upon bomb damage assessment.[29] The planners thus intended to continue efforts against Iraqi war-making capabilities while awaiting intelligence on their first forty-eight-hour effort.

While planners had given some thought to what would occur after this initial seventy-two-hour period, Master Attack Plans for this period were only notional. As such, they were not part of the overall Desert Storm air campaign plan. The air campaign plan for Desert Storm that

---

[28](S) Coalition *Combined OPLAN*, p 10.

[29]*Ibid*, p 13.

launched the coalition air armada on 17 January represented the results and included these written products and the expectations they embodied. It is to the evolution of the air campaign plan that we now turn.

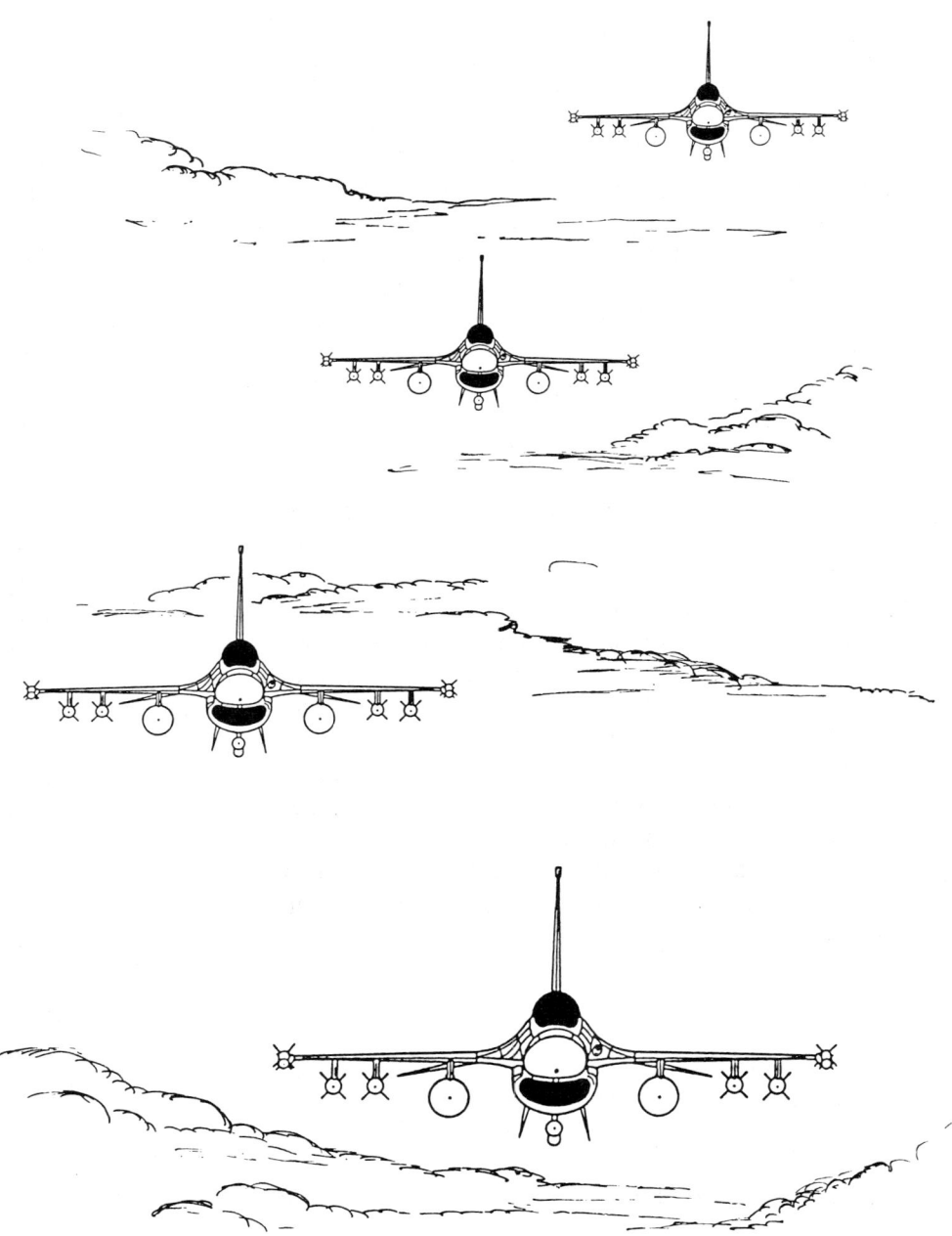

2

Pre-Crisis Air Planning for the Persian Gulf

While the essential elements of U.S. air planning for the Persian Gulf during the two decades prior to the 1990 Iraq invasion–national objectives, military strategy, and air power–were critical for the final campaign plans, the roots for each extend back sixty years.[1] An underlying aspect of U.S. national policy since 1939 had been unrestricted access to oil. What made that aspect more dominant after World War II was the decline in crude oil production in North America and the rise in production from the Persian Gulf.[2] As U.S. reliance on imported oil became more explicit in national policy, this translated into an objective of regional stability and reliance upon two conservative regimes in the region–the "Twin Pillars" of Saudi Arabia and Iran.

Designing a military strategy to support this policy proved difficult for planners who lacked a definable external threat for the region. Compared to Europe and Southeast Asia with their Soviet and Communist China threats, the possibility of active U.S. military involvement in the Persian Gulf region seemed remote. As a result, strategists relied on "containment" policy–military aid and assistance through treaty arrangements–that seemed to have worked in the preceding decades. Moreover, they viewed the Gulf within the broader context of Europe, in essence the right flank of NATO. Military planning for the past two decades relied heavily upon air power as the most appropriate response to a regional threat. U.S. military leaders supported military assistance and arms sales to Iran and Saudi Arabia and the construction of or access to airfields capable of staging large numbers of strategic and fighter bombers such as Diego Garcia and Dhahran.

---

[1] Background here is taken from Amitav Acharya, *U.S. Military Strategy in the Gulf* (New York: Routledge,1989), Michael A. Palmer, *On Course to Desert Storm: The United States Navy and the Persian Gulf* (Washington: Naval Historical Center, 1992), and works by Mr Kurt Guthe, GWAPS.

[2] United States Department of Energy figures as cited in Acharya, *op. cit*, p 7.

The overthrow of the Shah and the Soviet invasion of Afghanistan dramatically changed this. The Carter Doctrine declared as a national interest unimpeded access to Gulf oil and proclaimed that any external attempt to disrupt this flow would be repelled by necessary means, including military force. Coupled with this declaration was the swing of U.S. regional commitments from Iran to Iraq and the identification of the threat as being external–the Soviet Union. Given this direction, the first military response was the formation of a new theater command–Rapid Deployment Joint Task Force. The creation of this headquarters, separate from European-based forces, led to a subtle change in military strategy from regional stability through assistance and aid to defense and deterrence through force projection. Rapid Deployment planners quickly realized deficiencies such as lack of logistical infrastructure as well as an inadequate force structure. Still, the headquarters–which was redesignated from a temporary task force structure to a permanent unified command (Central Command) in 1983–began designing strategy and plans.

CENTCOM planners believed the dominant military force would be the ground element with its priority mission to deter aggression or defend against a Soviet thrust from Iran into Saudi Arabia. Their emphasis for the air component stressed force projection both to and within the region and highlighted the development of regional airfields, including the development of Diego Garcia as "the hub of U.S. efforts to project power into the Gulf region,"[3] and procurement of inter- and intra-theater transport and support aircraft. For direct combat application, early CENTCOM analysts envisioned air power supporting ground operations in traditional combined arms operations.

Following the Soviet invasion of Afghanistan in 1979, American contingency planning changed little throughout the 1980s despite the Iran-Iraq War. Both CENTCOM and U.S. Central Command Air Forces (USCENTAF) planners continued to address a scenario in which the Soviets would invade the region (and Saudi Arabia) through Iran. Since planners assumed that this would be part of a worldwide Soviet military strategy, CENTCOM adopted a twenty-eight day unambiguous warning time[4] as a

---

[3]Acharya, p 96.

[4]Unambiguous warning time can be defined as that period before actual hostilities during which a nation and its military forces are taking identifiable steps, such as mobilization and deployment of forces, as a prelude for military operations. Ambiguous

planning assumption and, because the command lacked prepositioned forces in the region, would use this period to deploy large numbers of ground troops and logistical support into Saudi Arabia prior to the start of hostilities. Planners therefore saw defense of Saudi ports and air fields as key initial objectives, and the importance of these potential points of entry carried forward into CINCCENT OPLAN 1002 planning prior to the 1990 Gulf crisis.

Air power planning for CENTCOM was essentially defensive in nature. Under these conditions, planners viewed tactical air power as the means to gain and maintain air superiority primarily to protect ports of entry, to serve as a force multiplier for defensive ground operations, and to participate in a ground-based counteroffensive, if needed, to reestablish preconflict international borders. Central Command planned to use any excess air power against interdiction targets. The most important aspect for air power was in the requirement for force projection into the theater by air. This led to the continued construction—even "overconstruction"—of air bases.

Senior political and military planners were surprised by the sudden collapse of the Soviet threat during the latter part of the decade. In the Gulf region this removed the major threat against which most military planning had been done. In early 1989, planners in the Office of the Secretary of Defense and Joint Chiefs of Staff (JCS) began to update plans on a worldwide basis. Under Secretary of Defense for Policy, Paul Wolfowitz undertook development of the new Defense Planning Guidance for FY 1992-97 that emphasized the importance of U.S. interests in Southwest Asia amidst regional instability that supplanted the external Soviet threat. Eventually signed by Secretary of Defense Richard Cheney on 24 January 1990, the document directed the DOD to be prepared to defend the Arabian Peninsula against regional military threats. [DELETED] Cheney highlighted his concerns by defining American goals in the following statement:

---

warning defines steps that may be related to pending operations but could also be related to non-hostile exercises or internal activities.

[DELETED] We will work with allies and friends to ensure the protection of free world oil sources. [DELETED][5]

On 16 October 1989, three months prior to the publication of the new Planning Guidance, the newly confirmed Chairman of the Joint Chiefs of Staff (CJCS), Gen. Colin L. Powell, U.S. Army, summoned Gen. H. Norman Schwarzkopf, U.S. Army, to Washington to discuss contingency planning for Southwest Asia. Powell believed that recent changes in the Soviet Union produced such dramatic changes in the world's situation that they necessitated a change of focus for the basic planning document upon which major Southwest Asia contingencies were built [DELETED] that envisioned hostilities in the Middle East as a prelude to and a secondary front in a global war in Europe.

According to a participant at the meeting, General Powell told Schwarzkopf–who became CINCCENT in November 1988–to update Central Command's existing contingency plan[6] to deter and defend the Arabian Peninsula. The focus of the revised plan, according to the Chairman, would reflect the current regional political-military situation that, by the fall of 1989, indicated how Iraq posed the greatest threat to regional stability. General Schwarzkopf's lack of response to the change of planning focus–that is, he did not indicate that Central Command was already working on this change of direction–indicated that CENTCOM had yet to undertake aggressively the updating of contingencies against potential intra-regional threats that did not involve aspects of a greater, European-based global war.[7]

---

[5](S/NF) Rpt, Rear Adm (Ret) Grant Sharp, "Sharp Study" *Planning for the Gulf War,* Draft of 3 Dec 91, prepared for Office of Principal Deputy, Under Secretary of Defense (S&R), pp 2-4. Located GWAPS holdings.

[6]USCINCCENT OPLAN 1002-88.

[7](S) Intvw, Lawrence M. Greenberg, GWAPS, with Col Clifford Krieger, USAF, Director Strategy and Operations Division, National Defense University, 21 Feb 92; (S) Notes, Col. Bryan A. Sutherland, USA, CENTCOM J-5, handwritten notes, 3 Oct 90, GWAPS and AFHRA 00881768, reel 23630.

USCINCCENT OPLAN 1002-88

General Powell wanted Schwarzkopf to update OPLAN 1002-88, "Operations To Counter Intraregional Persian Gulf Conflict Without Direct Armed Soviet Involvement," which outlined CENTCOM response, in concert with host and allied forces, to regional attacks on critical oil facilities on the Arabian Peninsula–specifically Saudi Arabia. At the time this plan was written, contingency planners considered the greatest regional threat coming from Iran. [DELETED][8] As with previous plans, they viewed force projection as critical; hence, the plan relied heavily on early deployment of USAF assets to demonstrate American resolve, protect follow-on deployment of both air and ground forces, and to assist these forces should ground combat become necessary.

In April 1988, Central Command planners forwarded OPLAN 1002-88 to the Joint Staff for review. The document received JCS approval on 31 August 1988 and was subsequently amended in February 1989. That fall, the joint command and execution community conducted a Time-Phased Force Deployment Data[9] maintenance teleconference to finalized priority deployment planning, thus essentially completing the deliberate planning process for the contingency plan.[10]

The contingency plan was primarily a deployment document that outlined only a vague notion for the use of air power along with a general concept for ground operations. Similar to other theater contingency plans, planners devoted their effort to defining forces, establishing command relationships, and developing a scheme to move forces to the theater to support CINC missions–deterrence and defense–with the possibility of some *limited* counteroffensive action. They made no mention of an offensive American operation or an independent offensive air campaign.

---

[8][DELETED]

[9]Joint planners create a Time-Phased Force and Deployment Data file during the plan development phase of deliberate planning. Information for the computerized file comes from sources throughout the Joint Planning and Execution Community and allows planners to manipulate unit deployments according to capability, manning, and lift requirements. Detailed discussions of the TPFDD and TPFDL are located in the GWAPS Logistics volume.

[10](S) Fact sheet, "USCINCCENT OPLAN 1002-90–Arabian Peninsula," Col John L. Buckley, USCENTCOM J-5-P, 1 Jun 90, GWAPS and AFHRA 00881768, reel 23630.

Central Command and Joint Staff planners allocated component force packages and deployment time phases almost identical to those in the preceding plan, OPLAN 1002-86. As a result, air forces remained virtually unchanged in type or numbers with USAF air superiority and ground attack aircraft supplemented with support aircraft and modest naval and USMC air. For ground forces planners relied on those Army and Marine units that could be moved quickly into the theater–light forces that lacked significant anti-armor capabilities. At the time, CENTCOM planners believed these forces capable of defending Saudi Arabia from the potential threat.

Table 3
USCINCCENT OPLAN 1002-88 Force Requirements

USAF	U.S. Army	USN/USMC	Special Ops
TFS[11]	Abn Corps	CVBG	
TAS	HQ	SAG	
TRS	AASLT Div (-)		
B-52	ADA Bde	MEB	
AWACS acrft	Mech Bde (on call)		
KC-135			

Source: (S) Fact sheet, Col Buckley, CENTCOM J-5-P, "USCINCCENT OPLAN 1002-90–Arabian Peninsula." MacDill AFB, 1 Jun 90, GWAPS 00881768, reel 23630, frames 598-689.

---

[11] Fighter aircraft include (in order of arrival): F-15C, F-16, F4G, F-111D, A-10A, RF-4C, F-15E, F-4E. *USCINCCENT OPLAN 1002-88.* pp xii-xiii.

Planners developed a traditional two-phase (defense and limited counterattack) concept of operations that followed a preconflict period.[12] The preconflict interval began on ambiguous warning and continued to C-Day (the beginning day of troop deployment) and reflected the necessity of some degree of international and domestic consensus before employing overt military options and the first movement of troops. During this time, planners anticipated the President employing political and economic measures against the aggressor to demonstrate U.S. resolve and, if necessary, culminating in a show-of-force. [DELETED] Finally, should a lack of warning time preempt separate preconflict actions, these steps would occur concurrently with Phase I.[13]

During Phase I, CENTCOM planners envisioned air power as an essential foundation for success. Their plan called for a defensive Phase I [DELETED] that depended heavily on early-deployed combat Air Force assets to protect deploying forces from enemy attack. Planners assumed that, due to the theater's remote location and lack of permanent U.S. military presence, the Air Force would be the first service capable of placing substantial combat resources on the Peninsula. During this defensive period air, ground, and naval forces would enter the theater and assume a defensive posture. If airfields were in friendly hands, the ground forces would arrive directly and establish local defenses for follow-on units. [DELETED] Once the critical ports of entry were secure, additional air, ground, naval, special operations forces, and amphibious forces would arrive at ports and airfields on the eastern side of the Arabian Peninsula, while naval forces ensured access to the Straits of Hormuz and the Bab El Mandeb, a strait at the southern end of the Red Sea near the spur on the southwest tip of Yemen.[14]

As part of the routine deliberate planning system used to produce OPLANs, supporting component planners produced their own contingency plans to supplement those written by the theater commander. At MacDill Air Force Base, CENTAF planners treated concepts of air power operations

---

[12](S) Fact sheet, USCENTCOM J-5-P, "USCINCCENT OPLAN 1002-88–Arabian Peninsula," 1 Jun 90.

[13](S) Background paper, HQ USAF XOXXM, "Background Paper on USCINCCENT OPLAN 1002-88 (Change 1)," 2 Jun 89, GWAPS CHC 9-2.

[14](S) Background paper, HQ USAF XOXXM, "Background Paper on USCINCCENT OPLAN 1002-88 (Change 1)," 2 Jun 89.; (S) *USCINCCENT OPLAN 1002-88, Plan Summary*, p vi.

in broad, general terms. While defining overall objectives divided into defensive and offensive phases, their overriding concern was getting forces into the theater and then, once the situation crystallized, to clarify and define specific roles for air power. They made no detailed plans for air operations, nor were they expected to do so. Instead, they called for air-to-air assets to provide defensive counterair and air-to-ground assets would arrive to support Army forces and conduct deep interdiction operations.[15]

Planners envisioned Phase II of CENTAF's OPLAN, the offensive, to begin on or after the date specified for the completion of sealift deployment. At this point, they changed the mission to offensive operations in support of and in conjunction with a ground campaign, to restore the territorial integrity of the host nation (Saudi Arabia) and terminate the conflict. As with other Cold War-era contingency plans, neither CENTAF's nor CENTCOM's OPLAN 1002-88 mentioned continuing the fight beyond [DELETED] limited offensive air strikes into the aggressor's homeland or destroy its war fighting capabilities and made no suggestions of an independent strategic air campaign.

[DELETED]

---

[15](S/NF/NC/WN) OPLAN, *COMUSCENTAF Operations Plan 1002-88*, 30 Sep 89, with Change 1, dtd 2 May 90. Located Air Force Studies and Analysis Library, AFSAA/SAKI, The Pentagon, 1D363A, document SAMI 9000283, p xi.

Table 4
USCINCCENT OPLAN 1002-88 Key Assumptions

International	Domestic	Military
	[DELETED]	

Source: (S) Fact sheet, Buckley, "USCINCCENT OPLAN 1002-90."; (S) *USCINCCENT OPLAN 1002-88*, p vii; (S/NF/NC) OPLAN, *COMUSCENTAF Operations Plan 1002-88* 30 Sep 89, with Change 1, dtd 2 May 90, pp ix-x.

Perhaps the most significant change that CENTCOM planners incorporated into the new plan were assumptions involving the size of the American response. OPLAN 1002-88 was predicated on a *limited*, though unspecified, deployment of forces to the Arabian Peninsula.

USCINCCENT OPLAN 1002-90

The month after General Schwarzkopf's meeting on the future of Southwest Asia contingency plans with General Powell in October 1989, CINCCENT directed his staff to shift its efforts from supporting a second front of a global war to updating OPLAN 1002-88 for a regional threat from Iraq against Saudi Arabia. One result of this shift was the 16 April 1990 USCINCCENT Concept of Operations that served as the basis for developing a revised, fully-coordinated OPLAN.[16]

---

[16](S/NF) AAR USCINCCENT, *Operations Desert Shield/Desert Storm, Exercise Internal Look 90 After Action Reports*, 11 Jul 91, p 2.

In November 1989, Central Command planners began the process to develop a new contingency plan. Using a routine deliberate planning schedule (Table 5), planners at MacDill Air Force Base anticipated the process to develop an approved OPLAN would take approximately twenty-two months.

Table 5
USCINCCENT OPLAN 1002-90 Milestones

2 Apr 90	Final Concept Brief to CINC
13 Apr 90	Concept to JCS for approval
28 Apr 90	Draft Plan distribution
30 Oct-9-Nov 90	*Phase I Conference*
Nov 90	*TACWAR refinement*
Dec 90	*Draft Plan with Annexes published*
Feb 91	*Phase II TPFDD Conference final draft Plan w/TPFDD*
Mar 91	*Desert Challenge Analysis*
Apr 91	*Plan to JCS*
Aug 91	*Supporting plans due*

Events precluded by the Gulf crisis

Source: (S) Fact sheet, Buckley, "USCINCCENT OPLAN 1002-90."

CINCCENT OPLAN 1002-90 Concept of Operations

Faced with new guidance that shifted the focus of a regional threat to Iraq, CENTCOM planners began to update force levels and planning assumptions for the new OPLAN. To begin with, they realized that the modest force package envisioned in OPLAN 1002-88 [DELETED] was too light to counter a potential Iraqi force [DELETED].[17]

---

[17](S/NF) USCENTCOM, *USCINCCENT OPLAN 1002-90 Concept of Operation*, 16 Apr 90, cover ltr, p 6. AFSAL, SAMI 9001253 and GWAPS CHC-13.

To respond to the increased threat level, planners significantly increased the number of U.S. ground, naval, and marine amphibious forces from those in OPLAN 1002-88. They augmented American air power with additional fighter squadrons, airlift squadrons, numbers of B-52s, and increased special operation forces dedicated to the contingency plan.[18] In addition to the increase in air power, they added armored and mechanized units to fight the armor-heavy Iraqi Army.

Schwarzkopf's concept of operation became the foundation of OPLAN 1002-90 and included expanded deployment and employment options as compared to OPLAN 1002-88. In addition to 1002-88's three operational phases–deterrent, defensive, and counteroffensive–CENTCOM planners added counterair and interdiction to the defensive phase. The revised phasing–a standard format for contingency plans–also included larger deployment to support deterrence, defensive and counterair operations, and the offensive phase to secure lost territory and end hostilities.

In Phase I, deterrence, the plan's authors envisioned rapid deployment of air, ground, naval, marine, and special operations forces to Saudi Arabia and neighboring nations with the goal of convincing Iraq that the price for further aggression would be too high for the rewards. Initially, Air Force fighter units would be deployed to Saudi Arabia along with

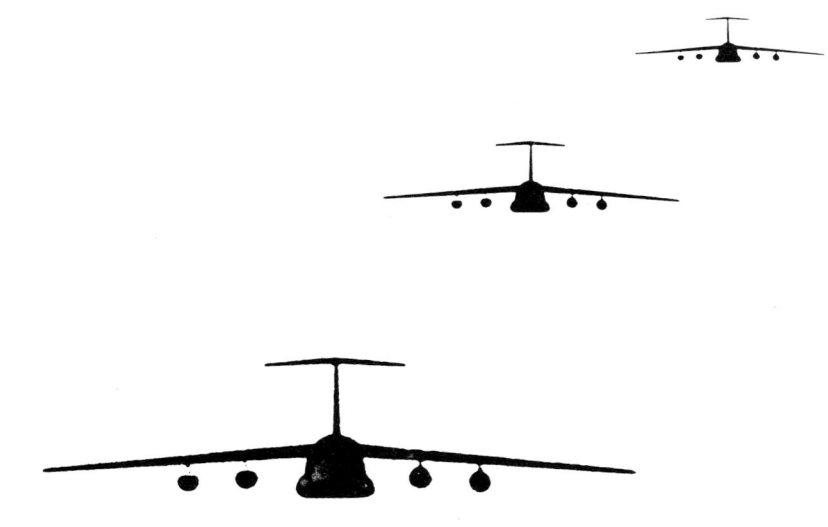

---

[18](S) Fact sheet, Buckley, "USCINCCENT OPLAN 1002-88"; (S/NF) *USCINCCENT OPLAN 1002-90 Concept of Operation*, pp 19-20.

Table 6
USCINCCENT OPLAN 1002-90 Concept of Operations Force Requirements and Deployment (Arrival) Schedule

USAF	U.S. Army	USN/USMC	Special Ops
TFS	Avn Bde TF	CVBG	
TAS	Airborne Div	MEB	
AWACS		Amphibious MEB	
	Phase II/III:		
TAS	AASLT Div(-)	BBBG	
TFS	Mech Bde(-)	CVBG	
AWACS	Mech Div (-)	MEB	
ABCCC	MTZ Bde		
EC-130	Mech Div(-)	Phase II/III:	
B-52	Mech Bde (R/O)	Amphibious MEB close	
	Mech Bde (R/O)	CVBG	
		RLT	

Note: "C" dates reflect days after Presidential deployment authority granted

Source: (S/NF) *USCINCCENT OPLAN 1002-90 Concept of Operations* 16 Apr 90, p 19-20.

carriers and special operations and Army Ranger units. They would be followed by additional fighter and support aircraft, B-52s, naval forces, and Marine forces.[19]

Planners believed that Baghdad might ignore initial American moves, and anticipated defensive and counterair/interdiction missions for Phase II. During the second phase, U.S. air forces would initiate a counterair and interdiction campaign to gain air superiority, protect U.S. forces and divert, disrupt, delay enemy forces. [DELETED][20] [DELETED]

Planners anticipated that the defensive portion of Phase II (primarily Army and Marine) would be initiated concurrently with the counterair and interdiction campaign. [DELETED]

CENTCOM planners wanted Phase III, the counteroffensive, to begin when the enemy's combat power had been sufficiently reduced to the unspecified level where the correlation of forces changed to favor the U.S. Objectives for this counteroffensive included seizing lost facilities and territory, and terminating the conflict. Despite the importance of this phase of operations, General Schwarzkopf provided his component commanders only vague guidance. [DELETED][21]

In summary, CENTCOM planners reacted to Schwarzkopf's change in intent by adding additional forces but left prior planning assumptions largely unchanged. [DELETED][22]

One of the areas in which Central Command and Joint Staff planners agreed was the time necessary to deploy significant forces. [DELETED]

---

[19][DELETED]

[20][DELETED]

[21](S/NF) *USCINCCENT OPLAN 1002-90 Concept of Operation*, pp 22-27

[22](S/NF) *USCINCCENT OPLAN 1002-90 Outline Plan*, Draft, 6 Apr 90. AFHRA in Heinrick Continuity Book. p 5

**Table 7
USCINCCENT OPLAN 1002-90 Concept of Operations Key Assumptions**

International	Domestic	Military
	[DELETED]	

Source: (S/NF) *USCINCCENT OPLAN 1002-90 Concept of Operations*, p 7.

Figure 3
Warning and Deployment Timelines

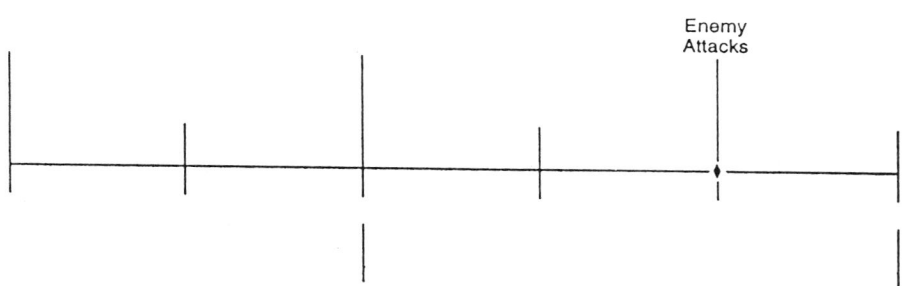

Source: OPLAN (S/NF), *USCINCCENT OPLAN 1002-90 Concept of Operations*, p16.

USCINCCENT OPLAN 1002-90 Second Draft

On 18 July 1990, CENTCOM headquarters published the second draft of *USCINCCENT OPLAN 1002-90, Operations to Counter An Intraregional Threat To The Arabian Peninsula*, that incorporated comments received from the Joint Staff and other commands after they reviewed Central Command's Concept of Operation and the May first draft of OPLAN 1002-90. By this time the new second draft included the majority of its supporting annexes, less the Time-Phased Force Deployment List. To continue the review process, CINCCENT requested additional comments on the draft by 14 September–following the scheduled Internal Look 90 command post exercise[23] (CPX)–for inclusion in the next draft OPLAN to

---

[23]Exercise Internal Look 90 (IL-90) was a USCENTCOM sponsored and conducted command post exercise conducted between 9 July and 4 August 1990 and is discussed in depth later in this chapter.

be published in early October 1990 and in preparation for the Phase I deployment conference scheduled for late October or early November. This was the OPLAN used during Internal Look 90.

While writing the draft, CENTCOM planners gave Air Force units and deployment schedules the most, albeit still minor, attention, moving up deployment dates for several [DELETED] squadrons [DELETED] and delaying slightly the departure of [DELETED] squadrons. They also increased the number of support aircraft although the draft OPLAN does not list exact numbers. [DELETED] Army, Navy, and special operation forces remained virtually identical with only minor changes. The planners did, however, increase the number of Marine forces.[24]

---

[24](S/NF) *USCINCCENT OPLAN 1002-90* Second Draft, 18 Jul 90, p iii-iv.

Table 8
Draft USCINCCENT OPLAN 1002-90 (July 90) Force Requirements and Deployment Schedule

USAF	U.S. Army	USN/USMC	Special Ops
	[DELETED]		

Source: (S/NF) *USCINCCENT OPLAN 1002-90* Second Draft, 18 Jul 90, p. iii-iv.

Table 9 compares aircraft by type and number as detailed in OPLAN 1002-90, those deployed during Operation Desert Shield, and those in theater on the eve of Operation Desert Storm. It is supplied to demonstrate the differences between planning figures and those airframes deployed. [DELETED]

Table 9
Comparison of USAF Aircraft In-Theater
OPLAN vs. Desert Shield

(Table is SECRET)

Aircraft	OPLAN 1002	In Theater 1 Nov 90	In Theater 16 Jan 91
A-10		96	132
AC-130		5	4
B-52	[DELETED]	20	21
C-21		8	8
C-130		95	132
E-3 AWACS		6	10
E-8		0	2
EC-130		13	14
EF-111		14	18
F-4G WW		36	48
F-15C		72	96
F-15E		24	48
F-16		120	210
F-111			
F-111F		32	64
F-117A		18	36
HC-130		4	4
HH-3			4
KC-10		6	22
KC-135		114	194
MC-130		4	4
MH-53J		8	8
MH-60		8	8
OA-10		0	12
RF-4C		6	18
RC-135		4	6
U-2/TR-1		5	9
Total USAF		718	1132

Table 9 (cont'd)
Comparison of USAF Aircraft In-Theater
OPLAN vs. Desert Shield

Aircraft	OPLAN 1002	In Theater 1 Nov 90	In Theater 16 Jan 91
U.S. Navy		283	552
U.S. Marine Craps		70 aircraft + 188 helo	108 aircraft + 310 helo
U.S. Army	[DELETED]	873 helo	1193 helo
JTF Proven Force		n/a	138 aircraft[b] + 7 helo
Total U.S. Aircraft		2132	3428

Notes:
(a) Number obtained by averaging carrier aircraft because specific carriers not detailed. Numbers range from 64 aircraft aboard *USS Midway* (CV-41) to 83 aboard *USS Kennedy* (CV-67).
(b) Proven Force figures include 19 C-130.

Sources: (S/NF) USCINCCENT OPLAN 1002-90 Second Draft, 18 July 1990, p iii-iv.; (S/NF) Staff Study, AFLC/XPOX; Steven B. Michael, "Operation Desert Storm: A Chronology." (Draft) OAFH, USAF, Washington, D.C., 1991; (S) "USAF Deployment Status Report as of 180505 Jan 1991," GWAPS, CHSH #68; (S) CINCCENT Sitreps, GWAPS CHST #68-1 through #68-31; (S/NF/WN/NC) GWAPS *Statistical Compendium*; (S/NF/WN) Brfg Slides, USAFE/OSC/CAT, "Desert Storm, Thursday, 17 Jan 91, D+01," 17 Jan 91, USAFE/HO, Contingency History, 14 Feb 91, Volume I, Document 2-9.

Planners retained three operational phases to deter, defend, and recapture lost territory and facilities in a mid-intensity environment, following a preconflict period during which U.S. authorities initiate intense political, diplomatic, economic and military actions to show resolve to potential enemies. Possible actions included forming regional and international coalitions, modifying foreign aid as an incentive or punishment, conducting noncombatant emergency operations, and freezing belligerent's assets in the United States.[25]

---

[25](S/NF) USCINCCENT OPLAN 1002-90 Second Draft. 18 Jul 90, pp 22-26. GWAPS NA-41.

[DELETED]

[DELETED]²⁶

[DELETED]

[DELETED]²⁷

[DELETED]

Table 10
Draft USCINCCENT OPLAN 1002-90 (July '90)
Key Assumptions

International	Domestic	Military
	[DELETED]	

Source: (S/NF) *USCINCCENT OPLAN 1002-90* Second Draft, pp viii-ix.

The planning assumptions set forth in OPLAN 1002-90 were deficient in regard to warning time, presidential willingness to authorize military

---

[26](S) Background paper, HQ USAF, XOXXM. "Background paper on USCINCCENT OPLAN 1002-90 Outline Plan." 4 Aug 90. GWAPS CHC 9-3.

[27](S) Background paper, HQ USAF, XOXXM. "Background paper on USCINCCENT OPLAN 1002-90 Outline Plan." 4 Aug 90.

actions before hostilities, cooperation among friendly regional states and the willingness of Middle East political leaders to ask for visible U.S. military assistance, and the size and complexion of the U.S. military response. However, before blame for faulty plan assumptions is placed too quickly on CENTCOM's doorstep, we should consider that similar thinking on warning and deployment times appeared in the JCS 13 July 1990 Class III Scenarios for Southwest Asia.[28]

Figure 4
Crisis Planning Assumptions vs. Actual Response

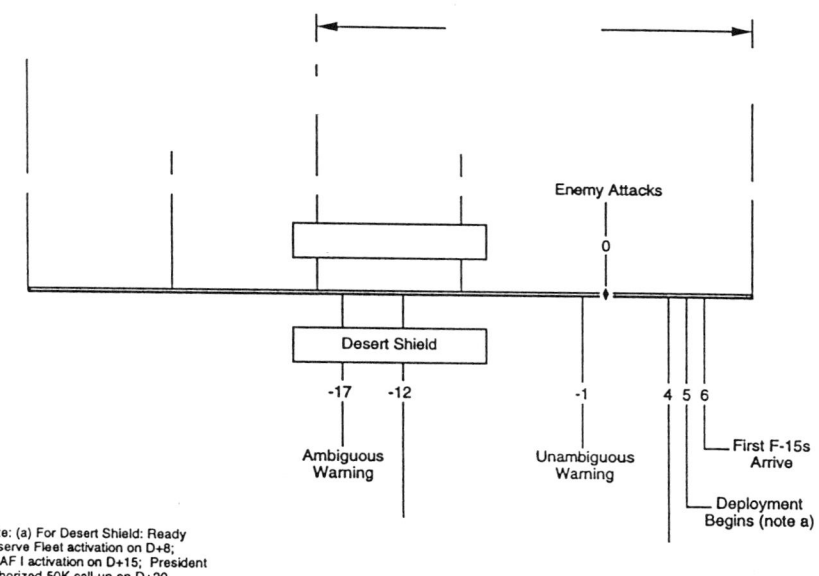

Note: (a) For Desert Shield: Ready Reserve Fleet activation on D+8; CRAF I activation on D+15; President authorized 50K call-up on D+20.

---

[28](S/NF) As part of the deliberate planning process for contingency operation plans, JCS J-8 planners developed Class III Scenarios for OPLAN 1002-90. The scenarios were based on real-world situations and intelligence estimates and, while not intended to predict the future, were developed to help guide planning and programming decisions and net assessments for all DOD agencies and commands involved in such planning. [DELETED] ((S/NF) Staff Summary, Class III Scenario Assumptions, 13 Jul 90. GWAPS Thompson files.)

Like many other "operations" plans, USCINCCENT OPLAN 1002-90 primarily was a deployment plan, geared heavily toward logistic support and troop deployment considerations with only a broad concept of combat operations. Central Command planners' thinking about precisely how forces might be employed in combat had not been committed systematically to paper.

Table 11 graphically represents the evolution of USCINCCENT OPLAN 1002 by examining key elements of each plan starting with 1002-86. Key aspects of each plan are detailed for easy comparison. An examination of key planning assumptions shows that many critical assumptions–tended to flow without much change from one edition of 1002 to the next with little concern for domestic and international politics. These assumptions also had direct effect on required force levels as shown in the breakdown for OPLAN and military service. [DELETED] Lastly, the table demonstrates relatively little change in the OPLAN's concept of execution over the years, retaining a basic three phase operation that followed traditional doctrine, flowing from deterrence to defense to counteroffensive.

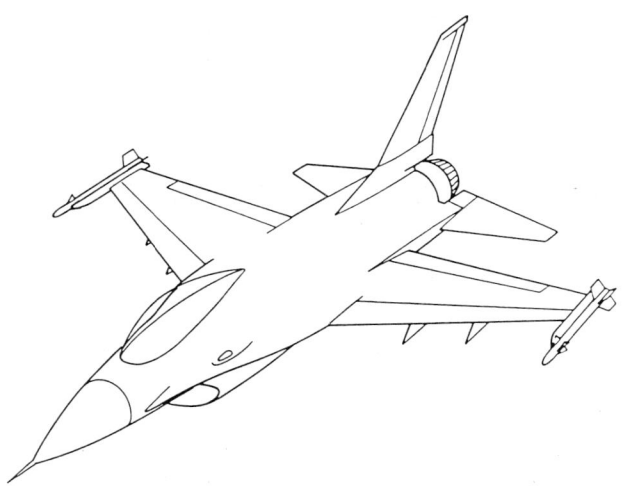

Table 11
Evolution of USCINCCENT OPLAN 1002

	OPLAN 1002-86 **December 1985**	**OPLAN 1002-88** **28 February 1989**	**OPLAN 1002-90** **April 1990**	**OPLAN 1002-90** **July 1990**
Mission	[DELETED]	[DELETED]	Counter Iraqi intraregional threat to Kuwait/Saudi Arabia.	[DELETED]
Key Assumptions	[DELETED]	[DELETED]	[DELETED]	[DELETED]
Army	[DELETED]	[DELETED]	[DELETED]	[DELETED]

Table 11 (cont'd)
Evolution of USCINCCENT OPLAN 1002

	OPLAN 1002-86 December 1985	OPLAN 1002-88 28 February 1989	OPLAN 1002-90 April 1990	OPLAN 1002-90 July 1990
Air Force	[DELETED]	[DELETED]	[DELETED]	[DELETED]
Navy	[DELETED]	[DELETED]	[DELETED]	[DELETED]
Marine Corps	[DELETED]	[DELETED]	[DELETED]	[DELETED]
Special Operations	[DELETED]	[DELETED]	[DELETED]	[DELETED]
Execution	[DELETED]	[DELETED]	[DELETED]	[DELETED]

The Role of Air Power in Deliberate Planning

Planners had very different views regarding the use of air power in peacetime and deliberate planning for regional contingencies. There were, however, some consistencies. Planners realized that the Air Force would constitute the first combat forces to reach the theater. These assets would occupy regional airfields and provide defensive protection for deploying ground forces and follow-on aircraft. If enemy forces attacked, these aircraft, along with available ground forces, would delay the enemy advance until U.S. and allied forces could initiate a counterattack to push them back. During the counteroffensive, the Air Force would support the ground campaign through traditional offensive counterair, close air support, and interdiction missions. In essence, the Air Force participated in traditional roles, providing indirect (interdiction) and direct (close air support and counterair) support for ground forces. Independent air campaigns, regardless of size or scope, simply were never mentioned.

Another important theme about air power that transcended the evolution of OPLAN 1002 was the theater commander's guidance. In contrast to that provided to other components, none of the OPLAN 1002 series of plans provided any detailed guidance about the complexion of the air campaign. This may have reflected confidence in air power's flexibility or, alternatively, a disinclination to think in terms of a distinct air campaign.

Exercise Internal Look 90

In July 1990, Central Command planners tested OPLAN 1002-90 in a regularly scheduled three-phase command post exercise at Duke and Hurlburt Fields in Florida, and at Ft. Bragg, North Carolina–Internal Look 90. In Phase I (9 to 19 July), deployment, commanders and staff moved to exercise locations and, for the first time, established command, control, and communication facilities using actual bare base equipment. Phase II (20 to 28 July), employment, consisted of three parts: (1) a two-day staff exercise to check communications and command procedures, (2) a three-day employment exercise that simulated delaying and interdiction operations for D+8 to D+10, and (3) a three-day simulation of D+18 to D+20 with emphasis on defending Saudi Arabia. Internal Look's third phase, redeployment, lasted until 4 August.[29]

To develop the scenario for the exercise, CENTCOM intelligence analysts examined national-level threat estimates[30] supported with known order of battle information and historical data from the Iraq-Iran War. [DELETED][31]

[DELETED][32]

---

[29](S) AAR, HQ USCENTCOM, *Operation Desert Shield/Operation Desert Storm*, JulY 15, 1991; (S) Brfg, USCENTAF, Internal Look 90, nd, both in GWAPS, NA-131.

[30](S) A primary source for threat assessments was the *Joint Intelligence Estimate for Planning (JIEP) Strategic Capabilities Plan FY 1992-1993*, published by the JCS in December 1989. This periodic document covers the entire world and highlights threats and capabilities of potential enemies for the Secretary of Defense, Joint Staff, Specified and Unified Commands, and Defense agencies. [DELETED] ((S/NF) Doc, JCS, *Joint Intelligence Estimate for Planning (JIEP) Strategic Capabilities Plan FY 1992-1993*, SM-991-89, 22 Dec 89, p I-6-34, GWAPS NA-335.)

[31](S/NF) Doc, *Security Environment 2000: A CENTCOM View*, US Central Command, 21 May 90, p III-2, GWAPS Glock files; (S/NF) Rpt Rear Adm (Ret) Grant Sharp, "Sharp Study" *Planning for the Gulf War*, Draft of 3 Dec 91, prepared for Office of Principal Deputy, Under Secretary of Defense (S&R), p 9, GWAPS Task Force V files.

[32]Sharp Study, p 11; and (S/NF) USCINCCENT OPLAN 1002-90 Draft Outline Plan, 6 Apr 90, AFHRA in Heinrick Continuity Book and GWAPS Greenberg files.

**Figure 5
Anticipated Iraqi Attack**

Source: Rpt (S/NF) Rear Adm (Ret) Grant Sharp, "Sharp Study" *Planning for the Gulf War*, Draft of 3 Dec 91, p 9, GWAPS Task Force V files.

All of CENTCOM's component and supporting commands sent commanders or senior staff representatives and planners to the command post exercise.³³ (Table 12) Generals Schwarzkopf and Horner attended the exercise and, with their primary staffs, participated actively throughout the simulation. For CENTAF this proved particularly helpful during Operation Desert Shield when the headquarters, all of whom had participated in exercise Internal Look, deployed to Saudi Arabia.³⁴

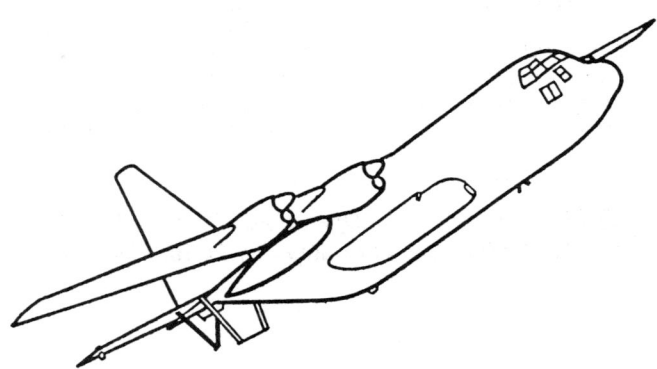

---

³³(S/NF) AAR, USCINCCENT. *Operations Desert Shield/Desert Storm, Exercise Internal Look 90 After Action Reports*, 11 Jul 91, p IL appendix, GWAPS NA-131. [The sudden emergence of the Gulf crisis in August caused delays in the publication of Exercise Internal Look after action reports.]

³⁴Personal recollections of Capt John Glock, USAF, who participated in Internal Look and served in both the CENTAF intelligence cell and the Black Hole in Riyadh.

Table 12
Exercise Internal Look 90 Participants

Atlantic Command (USLANTCOM)	National Security Agency (NSA)
Central Intelligence Agency (CIA)	Office of the Secretary of the Navy
Central Security Service (CSS)	Office of the Secretary of the Air Force
Defense Communication Agency (DCA)	Pacific Command (USPACOM)
Defense Courier Service (DCS)	Space Command (SPACECOM)
Defense Intelligence Agency (DIA)	Special Operations Command (USSOCOM)
Defense Mapping Agency (DMA)	Special Operations Component, CENTCOM
Defense Security Assistance Agency	Strategic Air Command (SAC)
Department of State	Tactical Air Command (TAC).
Federal Aviation Administration (FAA)	Transportation Command (USTRANSCOM)
Federal Bureau of Investigation (FBI)	U.S. Air Force Component, CENTCOM
Forces Command (USFORSCOM)	U.S. Army Component, Central Command
HQ, Department of the Army	U.S. Information Agency (USIA)
HQ, European Command (USEUCOM)	U.S. Marine Corps Component, CENTCOM
Joint Chiefs of Staff (JCS)	U.S. Navy Component, CENTCOM

Source: (S/NF) Doc, USCINCCENT. *Operations Desert Shield/Desert Storm, Exercise Internal Look 90 After Action Reports*, 11 July 1991, p IL appendix, GWAPS NA-131.

During the computer-driven exercise, Central Command commanders and planners examined all functional areas of joint air, ground, and naval combat with emphasis on command relationships, long-range interdiction, defensive operations, intelligence support, Patriot missile defense, freedom of sea lanes of communication, follow-on force attack, mine countermeasures, chemical operations, and special operations forces employment–all using OPLAN 1002-90 as the backdrop. While not defined in applicable documents, the use of "long-range interdiction" here can be interpreted broadly to include anything not considered offensive or defensive counterair. An examination of the associated CENTAF Target

List showed that even these non-offensive or defensive counterair categories included targets that would certainly be considered "strategic" during Desert Storm.[35] As exercise participants developed the combat situation, they used extensively the C3 computer simulations such as the Joint Exercise Support System for Ground and Air Operations, Tactical Simulation for Intelligence, and the Enhanced Naval Wargaming System for Maritime Operations.[36]

Because the plan's overall strategy was defensive, U.S. forces did not undertake large-scale offensive operations. [DELETED] However, during the final two days of the exercise (simulating D+19 and D+20), the exercise National Command Authority granted "Cross Border Authority," and planners struck a limited number of key command and control and leadership targets in Baghdad.[37] Operations players selected the targets from the Internal Look Target List prepared by CENTAF for just this contingency—presidential authority to strike important facilities in Iraq to slow their advance [DELETED]. Waiting until the final hours of the exercise to authorize actions into Iraq reflected sensitivities about offensive operations against an enemy's homeland, especially in the context of a defensive contingency plan. Its incorporation into the exercise, practically as a last minute "add on," also reveals the very limited nature of offensive air power contemplated in pre-crisis planning.

Although circumstance prevented the integration of most of the exercise recommendations into the final Desert Storm OPLAN, its timing no doubt improved the U.S. response to the Iraqi invasion.[38] Internal

---

[35] Examples of non-offensive or defensive counterair targets include: the Ministry of Defense, power plants, communication facilities, refineries, pumping and terminal stations, and NBC research, production, and storage facilities. ((S/NF/WN) Target Study, 9 TIS, "Iraqi Target Study," 15 Jun 90, GWAPS NA-168.)

[36] (S/NF) Doc USCINCCENT. *Desert Shield/Desert Storm, Internal Look 90 After Action Reports*, 15 Jul 91, p IL appendix, GWAPS NA-9. [The sudden emergence of the Gulf crisis in August caused delays in the publication of Exercise Internal Look after action reports.]

[37] (S/NF) Fact Sheet, Heidrick, "9 TIS/INT Planning Procedures," p 3.

[38] In addition to CPX Internal Look 90, CENTAF participated in a number of deployment and contingency exercises in the months preceding the Gulf Crisis. Major exercises included Quick Force 90-2 (US based CAS/ABCCC/ASOC exercise, 27-30 April), Iron Cobra 90 (US/Egyptian combined logistic field training, 19 May - 13 June), Shadow Hawk 90 (Combined US/Jordanian planning and operations exercise, 7

Look focused commanders and staffs on the theater, reviewed anticipated joint operations to include the production of an air tasking order that proved remarkably similar to that used early in Operation Desert Shield and later incorporated into Desert Storm, and highlighted Iraq's capabilities. As such, Internal Look provided the backdrop for the initial deployment of U.S. forces and was credited by the Army with "providing a solid foundation and point of departure for success on the battlefield and, more than any other single event, prepared commanders and staffs for Operation Desert Shield/Desert Storm."[39]

In addition to forcing a potential Persian Gulf crisis to the forefront of planners' thinking, Internal Look proved critical for the opening days of the Gulf War in at least three areas: (1) the development of an Iraqi target list, (2) providing initial guidance for air operations and a mission list, and (3) highlighting problems related to the incomplete nature of the OPLAN.

To produce the Internal Look target list, CENTAF intelligence officers produced a methodical "target study" based on Iraq's political, economic, and political infrastructure and capabilities. Their goal was to systematically identify those targets whose destruction would lead to achieving the objectives of OPLAN 1002-90.[40] Reflecting the shift in focus to Iraq–considered a modern, industrial society–CENTAF intelligence planners added petroleum (POL), electricity, and command, control, and communications (C3) targets to support CINCCENT objectives in gaining air superiority, protecting friendly forces, and ensuring the safety of

---

June - 1 July). For additional information on these exercises, see GWAPS Training Volume. Also, information on Shadow Hawk 90 located in USCINCCENT Joint Task Force Charlie Shadow Hawk 90 EXPLAN, 1 May 90, in Ninth Air Force History, Jan - Dec 90, Vol XV, in IRIS reel 26569, frames 868-1377. ((S) Doc, David Rosmer, *History of the Ninth Air Force/USCENTAF* Jan - Dec 90, Vol I-A, Shaw AFB, 1 Jan 92, pp 184-191, IRIS reel 26563, frames 6-349.)

[39](S/NF) Doc, USCINCCENT. *Desert Shield/Desert Storm, Internal Look 90 After Action Reports.* 15 Jul 91, p IL, GWAPS NA-131.

[40]CENTAF intelligence officers used data from OPLAN 1002-88, DIA's Automated Installation file, and various reference documents from the 9 TIS library to compile the new target list.

friendly nations' oil and transshipment facilities. In addition, known "high-value" targets such as nuclear, biological, or chemical (NBC) warfare facilities and Scuds were included. By the end of July 1990, this was the only integrated target *study* of Iraq produced by the U.S. intelligence community.[41]

Table 13
USCENTAF Internal Look 90 Target List –15 June 1990

Category	Targets	Category	Targets
Air Defense	72	POL	22
NBC	3	Military Support	22
Scuds	7	Airfields	37
Leadership	3	Ports	7
Electric	6	C3	14
Railroads and Bridges	25		
TOTAL:			218

Source: Target Study (S/NF/WN), 9 TIS, "Iraqi Target Study," 15 Jun 90.

Once Lt. Gen. Charles Horner approved their list, targeting officers searched for maps, imagery, and additional information to initiate weaponeering sheets that together made target folders for each of the 218

---

[41] Although CENTCOM produced its joint target study in late June, it was a compilation of service and component nominated targets and was not an organized study as was the CENTAF product. ((S) Intvw, Capt John R. Glock, HQ ACC/INAT, with Maj John Heidrick, 9 TIS/INT, 7 Jan 92, GWAPS Task Force V files and GWAPS NA-267.)

sites. However, many of the identified targets lacked sufficient imagery or information, particularly detailed data in DIA's Automated Installation File, to produce complete packages.[42]

In addition to the CENTAF target list, Central Command, in the spring of 1990, requested its subordinate and supporting commands submit their own nominations for the theater joint target list. This list differed from the Air Force-related CENTAF target list in that it contained target nominations from all service components–thus producing large differences in the number of targets selected for various target categories. Schwarzkopf's planners in Tampa assembled the individual lists and published the first joint target list to support OPLAN 1002-90 in late June 1990. Table 14 compares the earlier CENTAF list with the larger Central Command joint list. Considering the joint target list's multiservice nature, it is interesting to note the joint list's relatively small increase over that from CENTAF. This meager increase in targets is a result of the lack of emphasis placed on Iraq (and on the theater in general) in the years preceding the August 1990 crisis.

Lt Gen Charles A. Horner USAF, Commander 9th Air Force and U.S. Air Forces, Central Command (USCENTAF).

---

[42] Adequate imagery existed on only 128 of the 218 potential targets. For more detailed discussions on this topic, see Chapter 7, Intelligence. (Heidrick intvw.)

Table 14
Internal Look 90 (for OPLAN 1002-90) Target Lists

Target Categories		CENTAF Target List	CENTCOM Joint Target List
Leadership:	Civilian	0	0
	Military	3	4
Command, Control and Communication:			
	Military		
	AM/FM/TV	14	19
		0	2
Air Defense		72	4
Airfields		37	58
Nuclear		1	0
Biological		1	1
Chemical		1	1
Military Production and Support		22	81
Electric		6	0
POL:	Storage	9	16
	Distribution	13	3
Scuds		7	0
Republican Guard		0	0
Ground Forces		0	8
Lines of Communications		25	79
Naval Forces (Ports)		7	17
TOTALS		**218**	**293**[43]

Sources: (S/NF/WN) Target Study, 9 TIS, "Iraqi Target Study," 15 Jun 90; (S/NF/NC/WN) Doc, USCENTCOM Joint Target List, Tab A to Appx 4 to Annex B to USCINCCENT OPLAN 1002-90, 27 Jun 90.

---

[43] (S/NF) Installations listed under more than one category in the Joint Target List have only been counted once if the overall category was the same. For example, [DELETED] Naval Base was listed 11 times, however in this table it was counted twice: once as a naval installation and once as a naval headquarters.

Three months prior to Internal Look, General Horner had briefed General Schwarzkopf on a concept of air operations to support the new OPLAN 1002-90. Horner's concept recognized the contribution that air power would play in a Southwest Asia scenario and relied on deploying sizable air assets to the theater. In addition, he proposed employing Patriot missiles to defend airfields and population and religious centers[44] and integrating American forces with the Saudi Air Force and air defense system. The first aircraft to arrive would provide electronic surveillance, intelligence collection, and air defense, with follow-on units assuming counterair and ground attack roles. Horner anticipated basing his joint U.S. air forces in theater.[45]

In addition to the deployment of operational forces, General Horner discussed his concept of the Joint Forces Air Component Commander (JFACC) with CINCCENT. While expressing the need to consolidate air power under joint, noncomponent-specific control, Horner also stated his intent to generally relinquish control over Marine air forces to the Marine Air-Ground Task Force commander, but to maintain close coordination with him to ensure unity of effort.[46]

While preparing for Internal Look, in July General Horner distributed guidance to subordinate units for air aspects of Internal Look, along with information copies for CENTCOM's Joint Operations Center as well as to Marine and Naval components in the Central Command. [DELETED] The stated intent of this guidance was to assist Internal Look planners in producing an exercise air tasking order (ATO) for 26-27 July, EX D+18

---

[44]CENTCOM's command post exercise Internal Look 90 included Patriot missile play by the Army's 11th Air Defense Artillery Brigade, attached to the rapid-deployment US Army XVIII Airborne Corps. The 11th Brigade's part in the exercise involved briefings by the newly-installed brigade commander, Col Joseph G. Garrett, III, in late July to the Central Command and ARCENT commanders and staffs on the capabilities of his brigade. Garrett highlighted the deployment and operational potential of the Patriot air defense missile system. (Doc,*Whirlwind War*, Draft of Jun 92, US Army Center of Military History, Washington, DC, p 403; Bob Woodward, *The Commanders* (New York: Simon and Schuster, 1991), pp 208-209; Garrett intvw; "Desert Victory: ADA Protects Maneuver Forces During 100 Hours of DESERT STORM's Ground Campaign," *1991 Air Defense Artillery Yearbook*, p 38; *U.S. News and World Report*, 18 Mar 91, pp 34-35.)

[45](S/NF) Brfg, Lt Gen Horner to Gen Schwarzkopf, "OPLAN 1002 Air Operations," Apr 90, GWAPS NA-256.

[46]For detailed JFACC discussions see the Command and Control volume.

Table 15
Planned U.S. Aircraft Beddown – April 1990

Country	Location	Country	Location
[DELETED]		[DELETED]	

Source: (S) Briefing, "OPLAN 1002 Air Operations," Presented by Lt Gen Horner to Gen Schwarzkopf at MacDill AFB, Apr 90, in preparation for Exercise Internal Look-90. GWAPS NA-256.

(simulated exercise D+18). Important insights into General Horner's concept of air operations in Southwest Asia can be gained by examining this guidance–the first specific indications of an eventual air campaign.[47]

General Horner envisioned a much smaller force deployment than either eventually took place. [DELETED][48]

To employ his air forces, Horner developed a prioritized mission list shown in Table 16. The types of missions, along with the division of effort into the three major areas of air defense, close air support, and interdiction, reflect the defensive nature of OPLAN 1002-90 and indicate Horner's attitude, at least during the summer of 1990, to follow more traditional air power doctrine as expressed in OPLAN 1002.[49]

Table 16
Prioritized USCENTAF Mission List
Exercise Internal Look 90

1. Defend rear areas, maintain air superiority over battlefield (major effort)
2. Suppress forward deployed enemy air defenses
3. Conduct close air support for friendly troops (major effort)
4. Conduct interdiction to delay and reduce advancing enemy (major effort)
5. Conduct offensive counterair against southern airfields
6. Conduct recon of enemy rear, command and control, and lines of communication

Source: (S) Ltr, Col Richard B. Bennett, "Internal Look 90 COMUSCENTAF Air Guidance Letter," 24 Jul 90.

---

[47](S) Ltr, Col Richard B. Bennett, USAF, Dir Combat Plans to distro., Subj: "Internal Look 90 COMUSCENTAF Air Guidance Letter." 24 Jul 90. GWAPS NA-163.

[48](S) Ltr, Bennett, Subj: "Internal Look 90 COMUSCENTAF Air Guidance Letter." 24 Jul 90, GWAPS NA-163.

[49](S) Ltr, Bennett, Subj: "Internal Look 90 COMUSCENTAF Air Guidance Letter." 24 Jul 90, GWAPS NA-163.

As the exercise progressed, participants identified several areas that needed further examination or modification to meet anticipated needs. In addition to the widely accepted and CENTCOM-identified shortages of precision guided munitions and naval mine countermeasure vessels, Internal Look highlighted other problems including the need for an additional heavy corps prior to initiation of ground operations and a requirement for additional air tanker support for the carrier battle groups. Regarding deployment of units, exercise participants identified problems caused by OPLAN 1002-90's incomplete status. This problem was most acute in identifying the many separate small and generally logistic support units—more so than the large wings, divisions, or corps—needed to support a significant deployed force.[50] As many of these units required access to reserve service components, the process to acquire them required political decisions by the President on mobilization.[51]

Another proposal resulting from Internal Look that proved vital during subsequent Operation Desert Storm operations was the suggestion to change a major portion of the USMC mission in the Central Command. Rather than deploy forces ashore, Internal Look planners proposed that most of the amphibious force should be kept afloat off Kuwait City to hold thousands of Iraqi troops in place defending against a possible amphibious assault.[52]

In retrospect, while the defensive contingency plan did little to prepare the U.S. military for the offensive actions taken during Operation Desert Storm, planning and exercises that took place as part of the deliberate planning cycle formed the basis for initial defensive Desert Shield operations and highlighted difficulties that could, and did, affect actual contingency operations. The chapters that follow will trace the evolution of these pre-crisis deliberate plans and exercises as CENTCOM, CENTAF, and Air Staff planners in Saudi Arabia and Washington incorporated large portions of them into the defensive and offensive operation plans executed during Operations Desert Shield and Desert Storm.

---

[50]Doc, *Whirlwind War*, Draft of Jun 92. US Army Center of Military History, Washington, DC, p 85. GWAPS NA-304, Task Force V files.

[51](S/NF) Doc, USCINCCENT. *Desert Shield/Desert Storm, Internal Look 90 After Action Reports*. 15 Jul 91, GWAPS NA-9.

[52](S) Notes, Col Bryan A. Sutherland, USA, CENTCOM J-5, handwritten notes, 3 Oct 90, GWAPS and AFHRA 00881768, reel 23630.

3

Iraq: The Road to War

The origins of the Gulf War were rooted in Iraqi President Saddam Hussein's regional ambitions and the economic crisis which gripped his country in the wake of the Iran-Iraq War. On the military level, Iraq attempted to create a military foundation for its regional ambitions through a major build-up that began after the 1973 Arab-Israeli war. This effort gained momentum during the Iran-Iraq War and included the development of unconventional (nuclear, biological, and chemical) weapons and ballistic missiles, the creation of a massive 1.25-million-man military and the dramatic expansion and modernization of its conventional ground, air, and naval forces, and an extensive hardening program to protect the country's political and military leadership and key military assets from nuclear and conventional attacks.

Iraq's foreign policy under Saddam had been driven by an unusual combination of aggressiveness and insecurity which was largely a function of Saddam's personality.[1] While the Iran-Iraq War initially dampened his aggressive instincts and spurred him to seek rapprochement with rivals and former enemies once the war was over, Saddam, controlling the largest military in the region, soon reverted to his former pattern of aggression and paranoia. This factor, as well as Iraq's post-war economic crisis, and the tremendous power asymmetries between Iraq and its neighbors provided the background to the Gulf War.

The Iran-Iraq War ended dramatically in August 1988 after a series of successful Iraqi offensives against Iran's crumbling military. The regime–exhilarated by its successes–portrayed it as a great victory, even though Ayatollah Khomeini had not been removed, the Islamic republic had not been toppled, Iraq had not acquired an outlet to the Gulf, nor had it retained oil-rich areas in Iran. Instead, the eight-year conflict had cost

---

[1] Seth Carus, "The Genie Unleashed: Iraq's Chemical and Biological Weapons Programs," (DC: The Washington Institute for Near East Policy, 1989), Policy Paper Number 14, p 4.

Iraq 420,000 casualties (120,000 killed and 300,000 wounded), 70,000 prisoners of war held by Iran, and a generally weary and demoralized military and civilian population. It left Iraq saddled with a debt of $80 billion and a reconstruction bill estimated at $320 billion.[2] As a result, Iraq suffered from growing unemployment, inflation, and a declining standard of living which contributed to a deterioration in economic and social conditions, and growing domestic unrest.

Nonetheless, Baghdad continued post-war defense outlays at wartime levels ($12.9 billion in 1990), compounding hardships on the population. The inconclusive outcome to the war–the failure to conclude a peace treaty or a negotiated settlement–meant also that only limited demobilization could occur, since the situation at the front remained uncertain. Difficulties in integrating demobilized soldiers into the depressed civilian economy and the resultant threat of unrest kept Iraq from releasing more men from active service.

Following the Iran-Iraq War, Saddam adopted a confrontational stance towards his Arab neighbors and Israel, and abandoned his accomodationist wartime policies. While these initiatives did not appear to conform to any master plan, they highlighted a new regional role for Iraq. These steps included a brutal offensive that witnessed Baghdad's use of poison gas against Kurdish *peshmerga* guerrillas and civilians in August 1988 to crush the Kurdish opposition and punish them for disloyalty during the war. On the diplomatic front, Iraq initiated a series of inconclusive contacts with Kuwait in August and December 1988, and February 1989, concerning the demarcation of the border, with Iraq demanding, *inter alia*, the long-term lease of Bubiyan and Warba Islands; Saddam provided arms to Lebanese General Aoun to punish Syria for its support for Iran during the war. He also broadened military cooperation with Jordan to bolster the Hashemite kingdom and secure his western flank while laying the foundation for a rejuvenated eastern front against Israel. Finally, Saddam demanded from his former Arab supporters that $35 billion in war-debts be forgiven and for an additional $30 billion in aid from Saudi Arabia and other oil-producing states. If the monies were not forthcoming, Saddam warned that ". . . if they don't give it to me, I will know how to take it."[3]

---

[2]The Independent (London), 20 Jul 88.

[3]Judith Miller and Laurie Mylroie, *Saddam Hussein and the Crisis in the Gulf*, (New York: Times Books, 1990), p 12.

At the same time, Baghdad's behavior towards the U.S. and Israel revealed his deep seated insecurities. In a series of speeches in February, May, and July 1990, Saddam articulated a new vision of the international order and the region. As a result of the decline of the Soviet Union, he believed the U.S. had emerged as the preeminent superpower and would use its new freedom of action to impose its will on the Arabs and encourage Israel to embark on military adventures. Thus, he called on the Arabs to join Iraq to challenge the U.S. and create new alliances with the Soviet Union, Europe, and Japan in order to "find a new balance." This was particularly important, since the Gulf had become the "most important spot in the region and perhaps the whole world" due to the growing international demand for oil. Consequently, he demanded that the U.S. terminate its naval presence in the Gulf, called on the Arabs to transfer funds invested in the U.S. elsewhere, and threatened to use oil as a political weapon.[4]

In response, Iraq attempted to strengthen its deterrent capability against Israel and, in February 1989, U.S. intelligence detected construction of fixed ballistic missile launchers in the western part of the country.[5] His fears of Israel stemmed in part from Israel's nuclear potential as well as memories of its attack on his Osirik nuclear reactor in June 1981. In the spring of 1990, he saw international criticism of both his efforts to develop strategic weapons and Iraq's human rights record as part of a U.S.-British-Israeli conspiracy to prepare international opinion for another Israeli attack against Iraqi strategic weapon sites.[6] Within this context, Iraq announced a doctrine of deterrence based on two fundamental principles: (1) Iraq would respond to an Israeli nuclear strike with a chemical counterstrike and use appropriate means to respond to a conventional attack[7]; and (2) Iraq would assist any Arab state threatened by foreign aggression, if requested to do so.[8]

---

[4]INA, 19 Feb 90; Jordan Television, 24 Feb 90.

[5]DOD, *Conduct of the Persian Gulf War*, p 16.

[6]Radio Baghdad, 16 Apr 90. See also Radio Baghdad, 2 Apr 90.

[7]In the event of an Israeli nuclear strike, Saddam had authorized commanders of air and missile units automatically to retaliate with chemical weapons. Radio Baghdad, 16 Apr 90.

[8]Radio Baghdad, 5 Jan 90, 2 Apr 90, 16 Apr 90, and 28 May 90; INA, 7 Apr 90, 17 Apr 90, 19 Apr 90.

The conflict between Iraq and Kuwait had actually begun two decades earlier, when, in June 1961, Iraq refused to recognize the newly-independent state of Kuwait and threatened to occupy it. Subsequently, Iraq had tried to secure a foothold on Bubiyan and Warba islands and had attempted to renegotiate their common border. As part of this effort, on several occasions Baghdad created border incidents in an effort to pressure Kuwait to meet its terms. These efforts yielded no substantive changes and tensions persisted.

A second set of negotiations began after the Iran-Iraq War but, like its predecessor, was inconclusive. In April 1990, Iraq sent a confidential letter to Kuwait accusing it of territorial encroachments, and in July, tensions reached a crisis point when Iraq publicly accused Kuwait and the United Arab Emirates (UAE) of economic aggression by exceeding their OPEC quotas and driving down the price of oil. Saddam likened these policies to a "poisoned dagger" thrust into Iraq's back, claiming that his Arab brothers had cost Iraq $89 billion in income between 1981-90, and that their economic policies would cost him an additional $14 billion a year as long as they continued. He accused Kuwait and the UAE of "trying to destroy the Iraqi economy and reduce its revenues." Additionally, he charged Kuwait with "the gradual, systematic advance toward Iraqi territory" by setting up "military establishments, police posts, oil installations, and farms" on its territory, and of having "stolen" about $2.4 billion worth of oil from the Rumayla oil field which straddles the border.[9]

It was these allegations that led to the 1990 summer crisis. In mid-July, several days before Iraq leveled these accusations against Kuwait, Saddam had placed the Republican Guard on alert and ordered all eight Republican Guard divisions to deploy to the border,[10] suggesting that its campaign against Kuwait and the UAE was part of a contrived crisis intended to lay the groundwork for the invasion of Kuwait. On 24 July, Hussein met with Egyptian President Husni Mubarek and asked him to reassure the Kuwaitis that Iraq would do nothing until they had time to discuss the crisis further. But, Saddam warned, if a solution was not forthcoming, Iraq would take action rather than be economically stran-

---

[9]Speech by Saddam Hussein, Radio Baghdad, 17 Jul 90, and letter from Foreign Minister Tariq Aziz to the Arab League, Radio Baghdad, 18 Jul 90.

[10](S/NF/WN) Information Intelligence Report, hereafter cited as IIR.

gled.[11] The following day, 25 July, Saddam requested a rare meeting with the U.S. Ambassador, April Glaspie, apparently to sound out the U.S. concerning its likely response in the event of hostilities.

In the meantime, Kuwait and the UAE sought to resolve the problem and accepted a compromise at the OPEC meeting on 26 July by agreeing to higher oil prices and lower production quotas. However, these concessions failed to placate Saddam and, at a meeting in Jeddah, Saudi Arabia on 31 July, Iraqi diplomats submitted new demands: (1) that Kuwait remit $2.4 billion for oil extracted from the Rumayla field and cede the part of the oil field within its border; (2) cancel its $10 billion debt; and (3) grant Baghdad access to Bubiyan and Warba islands. These terms ultimately were rejected by Kuwait, and the talks collapsed after a few hours with Iraq accusing Kuwait of arrogance and intransigence.

It remains unclear when Saddam initiated planning for the invasion or when he decided to invade Kuwait. Fragmentary evidence suggests that his planners may have commenced their efforts as early as January 1990, and the actual preparations may have begun in May 1990.[12] The rapid deployment of eight Republican Guard divisions with 120,000 troops and 1,000 tanks to the border with Kuwait in late July is evidence of a certain amount of prior planning.

Regardless, on 2 August Iraq invaded Kuwait. It was this combination of Iraqi military power and financial need, and Kuwaiti wealth and vulnerability that Baghdad found irresistible. By invading Kuwait, Iraq intended, in a single stroke, to establish a hegemonic role in the Gulf and secure the means to fulfill its regional ambitions and its self-proclaimed historical mission as the leader of the Arab world. Conquest of Kuwait would put it in control of $208 billion in Kuwaiti financial assets, twenty percent of the world's proven oil reserves and permit unimpeded access to the Gulf. Most Iraqis–who looked upon Kuwaitis with contempt and envy–supported the invasion.[13] Three days later, Baghdad announced the

---

[11]*New York Times*, 23 Sep 90.

[12][DELETED]

[13]Most senior military officers supported the invasion. Nonetheless, there was some opposition within the military to this move. According to press reports, approximately 120 officers, including six generals, were executed after expressing opposition to the invasion. *Al-Majallah*, 9 Jan 91, pp 14-15, 18.

mobilization of nearly 25 divisions and the Popular Army to reinforce its forces in Kuwait and strengthen its deterrent posture.[14]

It appears that Saddam intended to rule Kuwait through a puppet government installed after the invasion. However, in response to the harsh international reaction to the invasion, on 8 August he announced the "eternal" and "irreversible" annexation of Kuwait and its incorporation as Iraq's "19th Province."[15] Baghdad commenced the "Iraqization" of Kuwait's state institutions and population, while systematically plundering the country. Iraqi civilian and military intelligence organizations and Popular Army personnel were introduced to fulfill internal security duties, Iraqis and Palestinians were resettled in Kuwait, Kuwaitis were encouraged to leave, Kuwait's administration was reorganized and cities and streets renamed to eliminate all vestiges of an independent identity. Likewise, Baghdad ordered foreign embassies closed, Iraqi currency substituted for Kuwaiti currency, and Iraqi identity cards, licenses, and personal papers issued to all residents. In addition, a great deal of equipment belonging to the Kuwaiti armed forces was removed to Iraq, as was about $4 billion in gold bars and foreign currency reserves from the central bank, 50,000 cars, the country's eighteen-month supply of foodstuffs, consumer goods, and valuables from shops and private homes.[16]

While Iraq had the means to invade Saudi Arabia, Saddam apparently did not intend to do so. While Saddam had prepared the Iraqi people for the invasion of Kuwait with a media campaign calculated to inflame passions against the country and its people, he conducted no such campaign against Saudi Arabia. While his planners may have drawn up plans for such an operation, there is no evidence to indicate that Iraqi forces had rehearsed them or were prepared for such a contingency.[17]

Early in the crisis, Saddam announced that "if (a) war breaks out between the United States and Iraq . . . I think that the United States will no longer be superpower number one. And the harm that will be inflicted

---

[14]INA, 2 Aug 90; Radio Baghdad, 5 Aug 90.

[15]Radio Baghdad, 8 Aug 90.

[16]Bengio, *Iraq*, p 26.

[17]Gen H. Norman Schwarzkopf, *It Doesn't Take a Hero*, (New York: Bantam Books, 1992), pp 313-314, 331.

on the invaders will be even more severe than what they experienced in Vietnam, and Iraq will come out on top."[18] Within this context, Saddam fashioned a political-diplomatic strategy calculated to fracture and undermine the U.S.-led coalition, to deter the coalition from going to war, and undermine or circumvent the sanctions which had been imposed after the invasion of Kuwait. His military strategy complemented his political-diplomatic strategy focusing on concentrating sufficient forces in the theater to deter the coalition from going to war, or producing sufficient casualties in the event of war to fracture the coalition.

He was confident that Iraq's relative strengths and the coalition's relative weaknesses preordained a favorable outcome for Iraq. Central was his assumption that the U.S. and the coalition possessed only two options–a long and costly war, or sanctions–and that the coalition would not hold together long enough for either to have a significant impact on Iraq. In a newspaper interview published shortly after the invasion, Saddam stated that if the U.S. attacked Iraq expecting a rapid victory, it would be proven wrong, since a war would continue "for some time." Iraq had fought for eight years against Iran, and "if need be," Saddam stated, it could fight for "three, four, or five or six more years." In a protracted war, the U.S. would be unable to maintain "its level of supremacy," since its "international position" would decline as the war dragged on while Iraq "will not remain alone in such a war" due to the mobilization of popular opinion in the Arab world. Conversely, if the U.S. chose to continue sanctions, Iraq was "prepared . . . to stand this for years."[19] Thus, Saddam believed that whether the U.S. chooses "war or boycott," it "will lose."[20]

Saddam believed that the possibility of death and destruction on a massive scale would deter the U.S. from going to the brink as he and his senior government spokesmen, and the Iraqi media repeatedly warned that the coming war would be long, world-wide in scope, and bloody.[21] If attacked by nuclear weapons, he promised that Iraq would retaliate with

---

[18]Radio Baghdad, 30 Aug 90.

[19]*Milliyet*, 19 Sep 90.

[20]From Saddam's 21 August open letter to President Bush. Radio Baghdad, 21 Aug 91.

[21]Radio Baghdad, 7 Jan 91; *Der Spiegel*, 8 Oct 90.

chemical weapons. In the event of war, he would attack Israel, launch terrorist attacks against U.S. interests around the world, use foreign detainees as human shields at strategic installations, and destroy oil installations in Saudi Arabia and elsewhere in the region leading to economic chaos and environmental disaster.[22]

Baghdad had clearly underestimated the depth of the change in Soviet foreign policy and the amount of support he could expect from this quarter. Saddam also may have reasoned that the Soviet Union would play its traditional role of counterbalance to the U.S., persuading Washington not to attack Iraq and, if necessary, intervene to save it from defeat. He apparently hoped that Moscow would ignore the sanctions and continue to provide military assistance. In the end, the Soviet Union supported the UN efforts to expel Iraq from Kuwait and abided by the sanctions.[23]

Concurrently Saddam attempted to gain the support of the ArabIslamic world by portraying Iraq as the defender of the Arabs and Islam, the Palestinian cause, and the guardian of Arab dignity and honor. Iraqi propaganda idealized Iraqi motivations, wrapped Iraqi policies in a cloak of virtue, and employed appeals for Arab and Islamic solidarity (emphasizing themes such as *jihad* and anti-imperialism) while impugning the motives of the U.S. and its allies. Saddam expected the Arab world to support Iraq against what he perceived as illegitimate and weak governments.[24] He also expected that Arab troops in the coalition would not fight against their Iraqi brethren, but would either join the Iraqis or break and run. The Iraqi ambassador to Washington, Muhammad Sadiq al-Mashat, stated in a December interview that "It is an illusion if anyone thinks that an Egyptian or a Syrian or a Moroccan will fight the Iraqis.

---

[22]INA, 18 Aug 90; In a television interview in late December, Saddam warned that "if aggression were to take place, we should assume that Israel has taken part in it. Therefore, without asking any questions we will strike at Israel. If the first strike is dealt to Baghdad or the front, the second strike will target Tel Aviv." INA, 27 Dec 90. See also Radio Baghdad, 23 Sep 90; Jordan Television, 9 Jan 91; Radio Baghdad, 23 Sep 90.

[23]Norman Cigar, "Iraq's Strategic Mindset and the Gulf War: Blueprint for Defeat," *Journal of Strategic Studies*, Mar 92, p 20.

[24]*Ibid*, p 17.

If they are forced by military orders to fight, then there will be mutinies and revolts against their leaders."[25]

Finally, Saddam fostered divisions between the U.S., Western Europe, Japan, and other members of the coalition through diplomatic initiatives, bilateral dialogues, and the selective release of detainees. With the failure of Iraq's efforts to forestall the emergence of a U.S.-led coalition, Saddam tried to destabilize Egypt, Saudi Arabia, and other hostile Arab governments, by issuing appeals to "the Arab masses and all Muslims" to revolt against the "oil amirs [sic]."[26] Moreover, he accused the Saudis of placing the holy places under "foreign protection" and allowing "infidel" troops to defile them with "alcohol, whores, and all kinds of heroin and narcotics," of permitting Israeli aircraft and troops into Saudi Arabia, and of permitting coalition troops with AIDS to introduce the virus into the region.[27]

As part of an effort to establish a diplomatic fall-back position and project an image of flexibility, Iraqi officials floated a number of private proposals for a diplomatic solution involving a partial withdraw from Kuwait that would still leave Iraq in control of the Rumayla oil fields and Bubiyan and Warba Islands. According to Jordan's King Hussein, Saddam told him after the invasion that he had decided to seize all of Kuwait, instead of the part of territory long in dispute, because he expected the United States to defend the sheikhdom with force and believed he would be in a stronger position militarily and politically if he could eventually withdraw to a point that left Iraq with the disputed territory only.[28] These efforts may have also been intended to delay military action and split the coalition.

In the event war came, Saddam believed he could defeat or inflict heavy losses on the U.S. and the coalition and emerge from the war with most of his military capabilities intact. This would ensure the survival of his regime and he would be in a strong position to dominate the re-

---

[25]*Jordan Times*, 31 Dec 90.

[26]Radio Baghdad, 10 Aug 90.

[27]Radio Baghdad, 20 and 25 Aug 90; INA, 25 Aug 90.

[28]*The Jordan Times*, 17 Oct 90. For additional details concerning Iraqi hints of flexibility, see FBIS Trends, 31 Oct 90, pp 2-3; FBIS Trends, 28 Nov 90, pp 5-6.

gion. Thus, his military strategy hinged on ensuring his own survival while creating a credible defense that would deter the U.S. or, if deterrence failed, lead to a protracted ground war. Saddam claimed that as such a war dragged on, U.S. resolve would wane as their casualties mounted and that the coalition would fracture as more countries (particularly the Arab and Islamic countries) rallied to his side. These factors, Saddam believed, would increase the likelihood of a diplomatic settlement on his terms.[29]

In a February 1990 speech to the Arab Cooperation Council, Hussein stated that "all strong men have their Achilles' heel" and that "the United States has been defeated in some combat arenas" despite "all the forces it possesses" and has shown signs of "fatigue, frustration, and hesitation when committing aggression." Thus, the United States "departed Lebanon immediately when some Marines were killed" while the "whole U.S. administration would have been called into question" had the forces that took Panama "continued to be engaged" by the Panamanian armed forces.[30] And, in a subsequent interview with German television, Saddam stated that "We are sure that if President Bush pushes things toward war . . . once 5,000 of his troops die, he will not be able to continue the war."[31]

This was particularly important, since the Iraqis believed that their experience during the Iran-Iraq War demonstrated the importance of national will and morale on the outcome of wars.[32] In assessing U.S. and Iraqi military capabilities, Saddam believed that Iraq's experience in its war with Iran and his own reading of history, proved that ground forces comprised the branch of decision in warfare. It followed that the air force was not decisive. On the other hand, Iraq–with 1.2 million men under arms, 66 divisions, 5,800 tanks, 5,100 infantry fighting vehicles, and 3,800 artillery pieces–had one of the largest armies in the world, one that was experienced and battle-tested. Saddam believed that the army would be able to expand to meet any new coalition deployments and, as

---

[29]See the interview with Saddam in the Turkish paper, *Milliyet*, 20 Sep 90, cited previously.

[30]Jordan Television, 24 Feb 90.

[31]INA, 22 Dec 90.

[32]*Al-Jumhuriyya*, 2 Nov 90, p 3, in Cigar, p 15.

a result, the coalition would not be able to bring to bear sufficient ground combat power to achieve its objectives.³³ For example, in an interview in the early phase of the crisis, he explained that:

> The United States depends on the air force. The air force has never decided a war in the history of wars. In the early days of the war between us and Iran, the Iranians had an edge in the air. They had approximately 600 aircraft, all U.S.-made and whose pilots received training in the United States. They flew to Baghdad like black clouds, but they did not determine the outcome of the battle. In later years, our air force gained supremacy, and yet it was not our air force that settled the war. The United States may be able to destroy cities, factories and to kill, but it will not be able to decide the war with the air force.³⁴

Saddam and his generals did expect that a short (several days) air campaign would precede the ground campaign. They expected that Iraqi air defenses and passive defensive measures (hardening high value targets, dispersed and dug-in forces, and hiding mobile assets) would protect his ground and air forces and missiles from coalition air power.³⁵ Previously he had expressed great confidence in the survivability of his mobile missile force, asserting in April that "if (Israel) strike(s) one missile base, what will that mean? Is it the only base we have built? Our missiles are mobile. Today you see them in Baghdad, tomorrow in Mosul, and the next day you launch them from Basra al-Sulaymaniyah, or al-Qadisiyah governorate. We can launch missiles every hour and from different places. For each base they hit or destroy on the ground, we will manufacture and build another one."³⁶ They believed that coalition air power and high technology weaponry would be adversely affected by the harsh desert climate, and that clouds, smoke, and dust would obscure observation of the battlefield, hindering the location and identification of targets, and degrading the performance of complex weapons systems.³⁷ This added

---

³³Radio Baghdad, 19 Nov 90.

³⁴Radio Baghdad, 30 Aug 90.

³⁵Lt Col Sergey Bezlyudnyy, "I Taught Saddam's Aces to Fly," *Komsomolskaya Pravda*, 23 Feb 91, p 3. *Sawt al-Sha'b*, 12 Jan 91, p 15, quoted in Cigar, p 18; INA, 19 Apr 90.

³⁶INA, 19 Apr 90.

³⁷*Sawt al-Sha'b*, 12 Jan 91, quoted in Cigar, p 19.

to his belief that the coalition would not be able to bring to bear its technological advantages (particularly with regard to fire support and electronic warfare) during a ground campaign, while Iraqi "experience, readiness to sacrifice, and morale" would prove the decisive factor in determining the outcome of a war with the U.S.-led coalition.[38]

The Iraqi build-up and mobilization that preceded the war was intended as an all-out effort to field the largest possible force in the Kuwaiti theater while retaining the smallest force necessary to maintain security at home. Prior to the invasion of Kuwait, Iraq's ground forces consisted of eight corps with forty-six standing divisions. Following the invasion, Saddam's generals fielded an additional twenty-five divisions, including four new Republican Guard infantry divisions, two new regular armored divisions, and more than twenty new and reserve regular infantry divisions.[39] In addition, they reactivated the Popular Army, with nearly five million people (mainly teenagers and men over forty) volunteering to serve to fulfill occupation duties in Kuwait and provide rear area security at home. In addition, the military command distributed arms to Ba'ath Party members.[40] Even the pro-regime Kurdish militias (originally formed during the war with Iran) were reactivated to help secure the home front.[41]

Baghdad took other steps to increase its readiness. In August, Iraq dispersed its inventory of Al-Hussein missiles from the central missile support facility at Taji to deployment areas in western and southern Iraq as a defensive measure and to ready them for possible retaliatory strikes. [DELETED][42] In addition, the army transferred chemical munitions to air bases and storage bunkers in southern Iraq, and established several decontamination facilities. The chemical munitions were subsequently withdrawn shortly before the war, possibly in response to retaliatory

---

[38]*Al-Jumhuriyya*, 2 Nov 90, cited in Cigar, p 15.

[39]INA, 2 Aug 90; Voice of the Masses, 2 Aug 90; Radio Baghdad, 5 Aug 90; INA, 23 Aug 90.

[40]Baghdad Television, 23 Aug 90; Radio Belgrade, 6 Aug 90.

[41]Radio Amman, 28 Dec 90.

[42][DELETED]

threats by western political and military leaders.[43] The regime also used the prolonged build-up period prior to the war to evacuate critical equipment from its unconventional weapon production facilities, as well as missiles, chemical, and biological weapons from storage facilities which it anticipated would be hit by coalition bombing.[44] In October, Saddam replaced Chief of Staff Lt. Gen. Nizar 'Abd al-Karim al-Khazraji (a political appointment) with Lt. Gen. Hussein Rashid Muhammad al-Tikriti, one of Iraq's most outstanding soldiers. In December he replaced Defense Minister General 'Abd al-Jabber Shanshal, another political officer, with Lt. Gen. Sa'di Tu'ma 'Abbas al-Jabburi, an experienced and capable commander.

President Bush's decision on 8 November to deploy the VII U.S. Corps and additional air and naval forces proved a turning point in the Iraqi mobilization, causing Saddam to alter his assessment of the likelihood of war. In his view, deployment of the VII Corps to the region "will make it easier [for the U.S.] to push things toward war, not peace" and raised the chances of war to "50-50."[45] As a result, on 19 November, Baghdad announced that it would send another 250,000 troops (including 150,000 draftees and reservists, 60,000 farmers previously exempted from service to participate in the winter harvest—especially important considering international sanctions) and seven divisions to the theater. The Armed Forces General Command concluded that as a result of these mobilizations, the U.S. would need three million men to attain the necessary three to one force ratio to achieve its objectives. The Iraqis saw the new U.S. deployment as proof of the success of their previous mobilization efforts. An Iraqi general, writing in mid-November, stated that the U.S. "would have started shooting" already if not for the Iraqi "countermeasures" which have "rendered the chances of (U.S.) success . . . less likely." Moreover, he continued, the "fresh (U.S.) reinforcements rushed to the area will fail to be of any significant effect" since Iraq enjoys a

---

[43]Remarks of Maj Karen Jensen (USA), UN Special Commission Chemical and Biological Weapons Inspector, Non-Proliferation Breakfast Group Press Luncheon, 19 Aug 92.

[44]Statement of the Director of Central Intelligence before the U.S. House of Representatives Armed Services Committee Defense Policy Panel, 27 Mar 92; Statement of the Director of Central Intelligence before the U.S. House of Representatives Committee on Banking, Finance, and Urban Affairs, 8 May 92.

[45]Intvws with Saddam carried by INA, 17 Nov 90, and Paris TV, 2 Dec 90.

number of advantages, including "the element of surprise . . . the edge in land forces in terms of numbers, equipment . . . field experience . . . (and the) ability to transfer the field of battle beyond the immediate theater of operations."[46] Saddam was confident that the 250,000 troops to be added to those already in the theater as well as a large number of troops with "more than a decade of fighting experience" would more than counterbalance the additional 100,000 U.S. troops to be deployed in the region.[47]

The actual number of troops added by these mobilizations probably fell far short of this number, however, as many reservists and conscripts failed to report for duty. Moreover, nearly all of the divisions organized during this period were low-grade formations that lacked personnel, equipment, and spares. For instance, the 27th Infantry Division, deployed to the theater in late November with about seventy-five percent of its authorized strength. The armed forces subsequently called up an additional 37,000 men to bring the 27th and other infantry units like it up to ninety percent of their authorized strength. However, only 5,000 men reported for duty in response to this call-up. The 27th, which had requested augmentees, received none.[48]

To protect his ability to direct his military, Saddam relied on an elaborate system devised to protect him against coups. Saddam used a variety of sites as work-places and residences, including underground bunkers in the Baghdad area, various government buildings, palaces, private residences, two dozen mobile command vehicles (modified civilian recreation vehicles) and even mosques in order to complicate efforts to locate him.[49] His whereabouts and movements were routinely shrouded in secrecy, and he moved frequently, rarely remaining in one place for more than a few hours, relying on false convoys and look-alikes to confuse potential coup-makers or assassins. Moreover, he exercised

---

[46]Baghdad Radio, 19 Nov 90. Staff Maj Gen Mundhir 'Abd-al-Rahman Ibrahim, "The American Decision and the Crisis of War or No War," *Al-Qadisiyah*, 17 Nov 90, p 3.

[47]INA, 22 Nov 90.

[48][DELETED]

[49]For instance, Soviet envoy Y. A. Primakov related in a post-war interview that a wartime meeting he had with Saddam and the Ba'ath leadership in Baghdad was, to his surprise, held in a private residence, and not a government facility. *Literaturnaya Gazeta*, 27 Feb 91, p 4.

command and control of the military through a sophisticated, redundant, and secure system of communication that had proved its reliability and efficiency during the Iran-Iraq War when Saddam came to rely heavily on face-to-face meetings [DELETED] and also used messengers to communicate with his generals.[50] Saddam's preference for face-to-face meetings probably also stemmed from a desire to more directly influence the conduct of the war and to control and intimidate his generals through his personal presence.

By December, and probably several months earlier, Iraq ceased operations at facilities involved in unconventional weapon and ballistic missile production and development. The regime removed and dispersed critical equipment and materials, as well as stocks of chemical and biological weapons, to ensure that damage to its weapon production capabilities would be minimized and it could emerge from the war with at least some of its unconventional military capabilities intact.[51] Finally, in December, Iraq stepped up civil defense preparations and exercises in Baghdad and elsewhere, including an evacuation exercise involving 1.5 of the 4 million residents of the capital and published instructions on nuclear and chemical defense in order to shore up popular support for the regime and prepare the people for war.[52]

Saddam took measures to ensure the survival of the air force, which he viewed as Iraq's strategic deterrent arm. He apparently believed that if necessary, his air force could ride out the war in their hardened shelters, which Soviet advisors had told him were invulnerable to conventional weapons, "even superaccurate ones."[53] In addition, Iraq dispersed a number of military transport and civilian aircraft to several neighboring countries prior to the onset of hostilities.[54] According to an article that appeared after the war in the armed forces daily newspaper, *Al-Qadisiyah*, Iraq struck an agreement with Iran in early January 1991

---

[50][DELETED]

[51]Radio Cairo, 25 Oct 90.

[52]Radio Baghdad, 19 Dec 90; *Al-'Iraq*, 20 Dec 90, p 10; Radio Baghdad, 22 Dec 90; Radio Monte Carlo, 22 Dec 90; Radio Baghdad, 24 Dec 90; *Al-'Iraq*, 31 Dec 90, p 10.

[53]Sergey Bezlyudnyy, "I Taught Saddam's Aces to Fly," *Komsomolskaya Pravda*, 23 Feb 91, p 3.

[54][DELETED]

to allow Baghdad to send military and civilian transport aircraft there, for safekeeping, during the war. [DELETED][55]

Iraqi air and air defense planners operated on the assumption that while its air force could not contest coalition control of the skies, its ground-based air defenses could neutralize or degrade the coalition's effectiveness. While ground-based air defenses would provide point defense of vital civilian and military targets, the air force would conduct hit and run or suicide operations against high value targets such as AWACS aircraft and large naval vessels in the Gulf, and attempt to pick off straggling coalition aircraft.[56]

Finally, Saddam's planners took great pains to ensure the Republican Guard and heavy regular army divisions which formed the backbone of the army would survive a coalition attack. Vehicles were deeply dug-in and camouflaged, while formations were widely dispersed to reduce their vulnerability to air attack.[57] Vehicle and weapon crews constructed personnel bunkers nearby where they could sleep and spend their free time. It was expected that these measures would significantly degrade the effectiveness of coalition air attacks.

Units were expected to observe strict operations security. Saddam, in a meeting with his commanders in early January, exhorted them to establish both primary and alternate headquarters, to camouflage vehicles, change vehicle bumper numbers from time to time, and remove all signs indicating unit locations,[58] and to move their units frequently to complicate detection by reconnaissance satellites. In addition, the military command enforced strict communication security procedures, to include severe punishment (death or imprisonment) for violations of radio discipline.[59]

Saddam played a major role in the formulation of war plans and held several meetings with members of the general staff, as well as corps and

---

[55][DELETED]

[56][DELETED]

[57][DELETED]

[58][DELETED]

[59][DELETED]

division commanders in the theater, to discuss his concept of the war plan.[60] Many of his commanders did not seriously believe that Saddam would lead Iraq to war and felt that he would withdraw from Kuwait at the last moment. One saw the systematic looting of Kuwait as evidence that the invasion of Kuwait was just a raid and an indication that Iraq would eventually withdraw.[61] Regardless, commanders were hampered by a lack of detailed planning guidance. Corps commanders provided division commanders with only general mission-type orders (such as "defend in sector") and very little additional guidance.[62] Most detailed planning occurred at the division level and below, with very little coordination between echelons or adjacent units.[63]

A problem for Saddam and his commanders was the lack of detailed information about coalition intentions and capabilities necessary for detailed planning. Although Iraq had archival SPOT satellite imagery, it was probably unable to acquire much current imagery due to sanctions. Iraq's prewar collection effort included a small number of aerial electronic intelligence and photographic reconnaissance platforms, ground reconnaissance patrols, and the use of bedouin as human intelligence sources, although these efforts failed to yield significant information to assist planning. Moreover, whatever information was available to the General Staff was not shared with tactical commanders. Each corps disseminated a general daily situation report but provided little else in the way of detailed intelligence, and division commanders likewise rarely shared information with their subordinates.[64] Many commanders complained that they were forced to rely on the BBC, Voice Of America, or Radio Monte Carlo for coalition order of battle information and situation updates.[65] They were unable to test their assumptions concerning coalition intentions and capabilities before the war or develop a realistic

---

[60]Caryle Murphy, "Papers Left in Kuwait Offer Glimpse of Iraqi Occupiers," *The Washington Post*, 6 Oct 91, p A30.

[61]Patrick Cockburn, "Lower Death Toll Helped Saddam," The Independent (UK), 5 Feb 92, p 11. Vern Liebl, "The View from the Other Side of the Hill," Command Magazine, Nov-Dec 1991, p 33.

[62][DELETED]

[63][DELETED]

[64][DELETED]

[65][DELETED]

defensive plan based on a correct assessment of coalition capabilities and the range of options available to them.

Finally, Saddam suffered from an inadequate appreciation of the capabilities of his own forces. Commanders frequently misreported the condition of their units–particularly readiness and maintenance problems, low morale, and widespread desertion–for fear of retribution.[66] This problem was compounded by the considerable resources, time, and effort absorbed by defensive military construction projects in the theater. The construction of defenses absorbed considerable resources, time, and effort. Iraqi defenses in theater consisted of defensive belts along the border with Saudi Arabia, as well as reinforced and camouflaged fighting positions, and dispersal revetments and personnel bunkers located in depth throughout the theater.

The quality of the engineer effort varied dramatically within the theater. Defensive works built for the Republican Guard and some of the better regular armored and mechanized divisions were well executed and offered good cover and concealment in deep, and well laid-out, equipped bunkers.[67] Conversely, many constructed for the lower grade armored and mechanized units and front-line infantry units lacked adequate resources or time to prepare, and consequently their defensive works were not constructed in accordance with doctrinal standards.[68]

Since many units lacked adequate engineer support, defensive preparations consumed a great deal of time, and prevented many units from either conducting training and other activities necessary to maintain combat readiness prior to the war or from digging-in properly.[69] As a result, many of the units lacked adequate cover and concealment when the air campaign began.[70] When the air campaign began, two battalions of one Iraqi brigade were completely exposed, while one battalion was dug-in to a depth of less than one meter. In a humorous aside, the men

---

[66] [DELETED]

[67] Hammick, "Iraqi Obstacles," p 989.

[68] *Ibid*, pp 989, 991.

[69] [DELETED]

[70] [DELETED]

in one unit hoped for a B-52 strike in their proximity so that they could shelter their exposed vehicles in the resulting bomb craters.[71]

Along the border with Saudi Arabia, the Iraqi front-line defenses consisted of two linear belts of brigade-size fighting positions with positions for tanks, artillery, and infantry, reinforced by mine fields and obstacles, including fire trenches, tank ditches and berms, and barbed wire.[72] While the plan was well conceived, it was poorly implemented.[73] Many positions were poorly designed and constructed and lacked mutual support, with gaps along sector boundaries, and obstacles were often not covered by fire.[74] Defenses in some areas, moreover, had been neglected–alternate fighting positions and trenches filled up with sand while some mine fields had been exposed by the wind and the mines could be seen by air and ground forces.[75] Units defending the coast were deployed in lightly reinforced buildings and trenches which overlooked obstacles, including mine fields, hedgehogs, stakes, concertina, and booby-traps, arrayed on the beach and beyond the water line, as well as offshore mine fields. Shore based defenses were reinforced by Silkworm missiles, tanks, artillery, and naval commando forces.[76]

The Iraqis made extensive logistical preparations before the war to support the defense of Kuwait, creating an impressive logistical infrastructure in the theater. In addition to several major permanent GHQ (theater) level supply depots in southern Iraq, numerous corps and division level supply depots were established in central Kuwait that contained sufficient ammunition, food, water, POL, and spares to support sustained combat.[77] In addition, Iraqi engineers built more than 2,000 kilometers of roads in Kuwait, a 150-kilometer railroad spur-line to connect Kuwait city with the Iraqi national railroad, and installed a 100-kilometer water

---

[71][DELETED]

[72][DELETED]

[73]Murray Hammick, "Iraqi Obstacles and Defensive Positions," *International Defense Review*, Sep 91, pp 989-991.

[74]Hammick, "Iraqi Obstacles," p 989.

[75]DOD, *Conduct of the War*, p 113.

[76]Hammick, "Iraqi Obstacles," p 991.

[77][DELETED]

pipeline connecting southern Iraq with Kuwait.[78] These theater-level stocks were supplemented by unit-level stocks (down to company level) of food, water, and ammunition, which in most units were sufficient for between 10-30 days of combat.[79]

The Republican Guard enjoyed priority logistic support, followed by the regular heavy armored and mechanized divisions, and finally the regular infantry divisions at the front.[80] The fact that Iraqi planners organized their theater logistical structure around major theater depots located in southern Iraq, that they did not establish larger depots in Kuwait, and that they did not protect the main supply route in the theater with air defense assets indicated that the military command did not anticipate that coalition aerial interdiction would significantly degrade their logistical effort. Despite these preparations, the long distance between deployed divisions and their respective depots resulted in the attrition of wheeled transports even before the war began.[81]

By January 1991, Iraq had eleven corps or corps-level headquarters and sixty-six divisions, eight corps or corps-level headquarters and elements of fifty-one divisions (including Republican Guard units),[82] all of its regular armored and mechanized divisions, and a large number of infantry divisions, in the Kuwaiti theater. The build-up occurred in two major surges. From August to September, with the arrival of lead elements of the U.S. XVIII Airborne Corps in Saudi Arabia, Iraq committed a large number of active units to the Kuwaiti theater, including the Republican Guard divisions, nearly all of its heavy armored and mechanized divisions, and its best infantry divisions, which were later joined by a number of newly mobilized reserve divisions. They also ordered two major call-ups of military retirees and reservists during this period. In addition, a number of foreign Arab workers and students were impressed into military service (a practice from the war with Iran), while the regime

---

[78] Jordan TV, 7 Nov 90; INA, 4 Sep 90.

[79] Many units also installed underground water storage tanks. INA, 8 Jan 91; [DELETED].

[80] [DELETED]

[81] [DELETED]

[82] (S) Four [DELETED] Republican Guard units [DELETED] stayed at home to maintain internal security. [DELETED].

announced a general amnesty in August for prisoners and detainees in an effort to increase available manpower and to consolidate domestic support for the regime. These Iraqi forces deployed primarily in the southeastern corner of Kuwait–the expected focus of a possibly coalition attack. From November to December, following the U.S. decision to deploy the VII Corps, Iraq conducted four additional call-ups and newly mobilized and formed infantry divisions were deployed to fill gaps along the border with Saudi Arabia and to extend the western flank of its defenses.

Knowing that a stated coalition objective was the liberation of Kuwait City, Iraqi strategists focused on its defense. They assumed that the main effort would likely consist of an assault through Khafji along the coastal road in the east, with supporting efforts, including a thrust from the west up the Wadi al-Batin towards Kuwait City, and an amphibious assault near Kuwait city in the east.[83] Iraqi forces were deployed to support an attrition strategy intended to maximize coalition casualties. The first line of defense consisted of two obstacle belts behind which were deployed a large number of infantry divisions, backed by heavy armored and mechanized units deployed in depth, organized into corps (tactical), theater (operational), and GHQ (strategic) reserves. Ground forces were organized into geographic corps (the III, IV, VI, and VII Corps, and the Gulf Operations Forces) with defined areas of responsibility, or maneuver corps (the Republican Guard, the Jihad Corps, and the II Armored Corps) with specific functions. During the course of the build-up, Iraqi forces in the theater underwent several reorganizations in order to rationalize command and control and better meet the perceived threat–additional corps were committed to the theater or created in response to operational requirements, areas of responsibility were adjusted, and units were realigned.[84]

---

[83]Hammick, "Iraqi Obstacles," p 991.

[84]For instance, in November, III Corps units withdrew to behind the Wafra oil fields in order to simplify the defense of their sector.

Figure 6
Iraqi Ground Force Deployment in the KTO – 16 January 1991

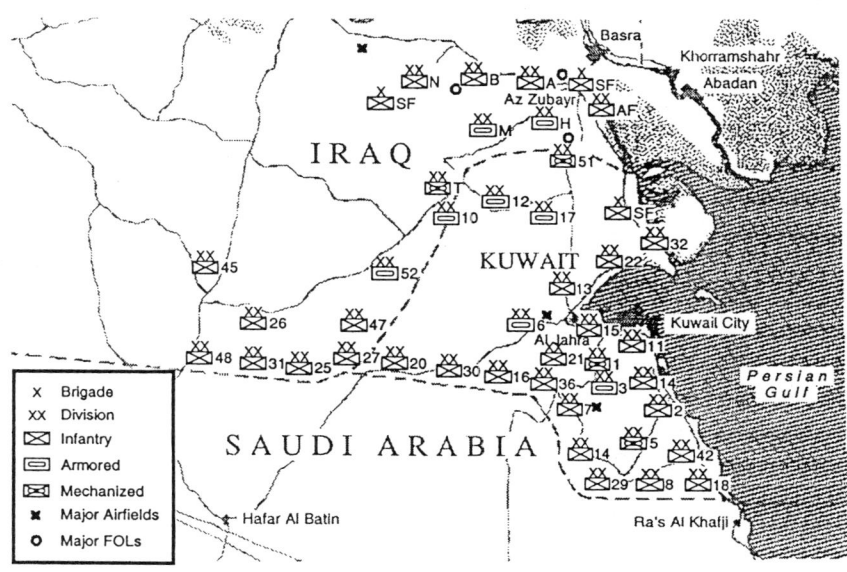

Legend of Iraqi Republican Guard Divisions:			
T = Tawakalna	H = Hammurabi	B = Baghdad	AF = Al Faw
M = Madinah	N = Nebuchadnezzar	A = Adnan	SF = Special Forces

Sources: Multiple sources including Rpt (S/NF/WN) *Conduct of the Persian Gulf Conflict: An Interim Report to Congress*, Pursuant to Title V Persian Gulf Conflict Supplemental Authorization and Personnel Benefits Act of 1991 (Public Law 102-25), July 1991.

In accordance with Iraqi defensive doctrine, planners ordered front line infantry divisions to defend in sector from prepared positions, reducing coalition forces and forcing them to reveal their main effort. At the appropriate time, tactical reserves would counterattack coalition penetrations in their respective sectors. The operational reserve would then either block or counterattack coalition penetrations, further attriting coalition forces in the process. After the coalition main effort had been reduced by the tactical and operational reserves, the Republican Guard–the strategic reserve–would conduct a corps-level counterattack against the flanks of the surviving coalition force to destroy it. However, the Iraqi plan oriented towards the defense of Kuwait City had not anticipated other contingencies, such as a wide flanking attack from the west.[85] Nor did most Iraqi units have the ability to rapidly redeploy for an attack from this direction, due to the lack of prepared defenses in this area and a shortage of organic transport.

In addition to a narrowly-focused defensive plan, none of the Iraqi units deployed in theater were at full personnel or equipment strength. While nearly all the Republican Guard units deployed at about ninety-five percent authorized strength, most of the regular army units deployed at about seventy-five to eighty-five percent of their authorized strength, and many lost an additional twenty to twenty-five percent through desertion even before the onset of hostilities, bringing many units down to fifty to sixty percent strength on the eve of the war.[86] The low level of readiness of many units was manifested by equipment and personnel shortages, and low in-service equipment rates due to inadequate maintenance and a lack of spares. These factors, in concert with the general phenomena of war weariness, the harsh conditions at the front, and the negative impact of Iraqi propaganda on its own troops, served to undermine morale even before the eruption of hostilities. Finally, none of the infantry divisions deployed with their assigned reconnaissance regiments or commando battalions–the former had been consolidated at corps level while divisional commando battalions had been disbanded as part of an effort to reduce manpower requirements prior to the war. [DELETED][87]

Shortages of qualified personnel in key positions affected many units. In some, tanks and crew-served weapons were not fully manned, a problem that was exacerbated by desertions prior to the commencement of hostilities. Moreover, personnel replacements often were not available. In addition, due to the expansion of the army, many units were commanded by personnel with insufficient rank and experience, resulting in

---

[85][DELETED]

[86][DELETED]

[87][DELETED]

brigades being commanded by lieutenant colonels, battalions by majors, companies by lieutenants, and platoons by non-commissioned officers.[88]

Personnel problems extended beyond the theater and adversely affected Saddam's military operations. Officers suspected of disloyalty were often executed or retired from the military. Prior to the Gulf War Saddam relieved his defense minister, chief of staff, and at least two corps commanders, and executed a number of senior officers who had opposed the invasion of Kuwait. While these moves ensured that the military remained compliant, it also ensured that on the eve of the war several key slots were filled by inexperienced officers, and that command relationships had not been routinized when the war began.

Finally, thousands of Iraqi soldiers deserted and hundreds defected to coalition forces prior to the war. Reports of desertions among Iraqi soldiers serving in Kuwait surfaced as early as August 1990, and the problem was apparently serious enough by October 1990 for the General Staff to order the formation of execution squads in each unit to deter desertion.[89] In one extreme case, 52d Armored Brigade air defense [DELETED] platoon of the 52d Armored Division [DELETED] deserted *en masse*.[90] In addition, the fact that Iraq was facing a thirty-one nation coalition that included the U.S., Britain, France, as well as a number of Arab and Islamic states caused some Iraqi soldiers to question the justice of their cause, as well as their odds of survival.[91] In other units, ethnic cleavages compounded the desertion problem. [DELETED][92]

Sanctions had an expected effect on Iraqi readiness and sustainability. On the operational and tactical level, they resulted in lower maintenance standards and spares shortages that had a significant impact on readiness rates. By the time the war began, about twenty percent of Iraqi combat aircraft were grounded due to maintenance problems, as Iraq had depended on Soviet and other foreign technicians–who had left the

---

[88][DELETED]

[89]AFP, 12 Aug 90 ; [DELETED].

[90][DELETED]

[91](S) *Ibid.*

[92][DELETED]

country—to maintain its air force.⁹³ Likewise, the army was unable to conduct depot-level maintenance due to the loss of foreign personnel. Much of the equipment was in poor condition to begin with, due to Iraqi maintenance practices and the shortage of spares, which was exacerbated by sanctions. All this prevented the repair of deadlined vehicles and equipment deployed in theater.⁹⁴

By January, Baghdad had deployed elements of several fighter squadrons to 'Ali al-Salem and Ahmed al-Jaber air bases in Kuwait and to forward and dispersal airfields in southern Iraq, supplemented by fixed (SA-2/3) and mobile (SA-6) surface-to-air missiles and anti-aircraft artillery units.⁹⁵ In addition, the Iraqi air force logged abnormally high rates of air activity in the months prior to the war, indicating intensified preparations and efforts to enhance readiness.⁹⁶ Air force activities including heavy transport and resupply operations (largely in support of the logistical build-up in the Kuwaiti theater), defensive fighter patrols over southeast Iraq and Kuwait, reconnaissance flights (including photo reconnaissance and ELINT and SIGINT collection missions), electronic jamming missions directed at coalition communications, Adnan I/Baghdad airborne early warning aircraft operations, training, and test/evaluation flights, day and night ground-controlled and independent intercept training, air-to-air and air-to-ground training (including deep strike as well as battlefield support missions), airfield and area familiarization training, and limited probes of Saudi airspace to test coalition alert and response procedures. As the 15 January deadline for the withdrawal of Iraqi forces from Kuwait approached, the prewar surge in air activity was followed by a lull (starting in early January).⁹⁷

In spite of this, by mid-January, Saddam seemed confident that the United States would not initiate hostilities but, if it did, that he had ordered all necessary preparations.⁹⁸ The armed forces had completed

---

⁹³"A Soviet Operational Analysis," p 59.

⁹⁴[DELETED]

⁹⁵(S/NF/WN) Steven B. Michael, *The Persian Gulf War: An Air Staff Chronology of Desert Storm/Desert Shield*, (DC: Center for Air Force History: 1992).

⁹⁶(S/NF/WN) *Ibid*, p 85.

⁹⁷[DELETED]

⁹⁸Radio Moscow, 16 Jan 91.

most of their defensive preparations, which were intended to deter U.S. and coalition forces, or engage them in a costly ground campaign if deterrence failed. [DELETED][99]

In the end, Saddam believed that the balance of power favored Iraq and that the U.S. would not attack his dug-in military. He had opted for confrontation rather than compromise. At the same time, his constant public repetition of Iraq's claims to Kuwait and his repeated refusal to countenance withdrawal made him a prisoner of his own rhetoric and limited his political freedom of maneuver. In this context, Saddam may have interpreted the offer by President Bush on 30 November for a meeting of foreign ministers as a sign of U.S. weakness. This meeting was portrayed by First Deputy Prime Minister Taha Yasin Ramadan as a U.S. "retreat" in the face of "world and Arab public opinion."[100] At the 9 January meeting between Secretary of State James Baker and Foreign Minister Tariq 'Aziz in Geneva, Iraq reiterated its adherence to its 12 August initiative as the sole acceptable basis for the settlement of the crisis. This was rejected by the U.S., sealing the fate of this last-minute effort to avert war.

Saddam's strategy proved to be flawed by misjudging the coalition's cohesion and resolve, and he ceded the initiative to dictate the time, place, and terms of battle to his enemies. He had overrated both his appeal among Arab nations and the fragility of the coalition. His efforts to undermine the coalition were contingent on others acting in an anticipated fashion, and when they did not, his military-diplomatic strategy collapsed. Nonetheless, several Arab coalition members felt constrained to adopt a number of self-imposed limitations on their participation in the war in order to limit their vulnerability to Iraqi propaganda and to appease domestic opinion. In the end, a combination of adroit U.S. diplomacy, the caution of Arab coalition members in not exceeding the limits imposed by popular sensibilities, and Israeli restraint enabled the coalition to preserve its cohesion.

The Iraqi army that U.S. and coalition forces faced on the eve of the war suffered from numerous self-inflicted wounds which put them at a significant disadvantage. The dramatic expansion of the army before the

---

[99][DELETED]

[100]Radio Baghdad, 4 Dec 90.

war had weakened Saddam's army rather than strengthen it. Although the Republican Guard was at nearly full strength, the regular army divisions were not. This situation adversely affected the confidence of his troops. In addition, the regular army–recently bolstered with large numbers of untrained recruits–was weary from a decade of combat against Iran and the Kurds and demoralized by the prospect of a war against the coalition.

Finally, Iraqi arrogance–which afflicted both Saddam and his generals–and which manifest itself in a predisposition to inflate Iraqi capabilities and underestimate those of their enemies, had a significant impact on his assessment of the balance of forces. These important, yet difficult to quantify, factors influenced nearly every decision made prior to the war and precluded Saddam or his advisors from accurately identifying coalition strengths and weaknesses, and recognizing Iraq's own significant shortcomings.

4

Policy Objectives, Restraints, and Constraints[1]

Policy Objectives

Throughout the entire planning effort for the Gulf War, leaders such as Generals Schwarzkopf and Horner and their military planners such as Gen. Buster Glosson and Col. John A. Warden, consistently worked from and to achieve national objectives that were laid out early in the crisis. The President and his Secretary of Defense themselves prescribed this guidance, and those charged with writing the Gulf War plan worked to ensure that these defined the strategic aims of their campaign plans.

The President himself outlined the objectives. From the outset, he clearly had more in mind than just to deter or repel an Iraqi invasion of Saudi Arabia, a point not lost in either Washington or Riyadh. Within a week of the Iraqi invasion of Kuwait, he announced "[f]our simple principles" that would guide U.S. actions in the crisis. These policy objectives were: (1) securing the immediate, unconditional, and complete withdrawal of Iraqi forces from Kuwait; (2) restoring the legitimate government of Kuwait; (3) assuring the security and stability of the Persian Gulf region; and (4) protecting American lives.[2] The President deliberately made a clear statement of objectives to ensure that U.S. diplomatic and military responses to Iraqi aggression were aligned with the central aims of U.S. policy. Repeated recitations of these ends by ranking Bush Administration officials guaranteed that they would remain at the forefront of U.S. strategies for resolving the crisis. Between the outbreak of the crisis and the start of the war, the "four simple principles" were unchanged and gave strategic guidance for its conduct.

---

[1] This chapter is drawn from a more extensive treatment of the subject, Kurt Guthe, etc, GWAPS files.

[2] Address to the Nation Announcing the Deployment of United States Armed Forces to Saudi Arabia, 8 Aug, in *Public Papers of the Presidents of the United States: George Bush, 1990 (Book II)* (Office of the Federal Register, National Archives and Record Administration, 1991), p 1108.

The degree to which military leaders and their planners were sensitive to these objectives throughout their planning was evident in the slides that they used in the various key briefings of their efforts as well as the numerous versions of the plans produced from August 1990 through January 1991. In all cases, they explicitly cited these strategic goals. From being listed at the beginning of the 2 September OPORD for Phase I to the 16 December OPLAN and 17 January coalition plan where they were characterized as the "National Objectives," these objectives formed the boundaries for operational planners.[3]

For them, the meaning of the first two objectives was clear-cut as they recognized that, with the failure of diplomatic efforts and economic sanctions, it would be necessary for military operations to dislodge the Iraqi army from Kuwait. The meaning of the third objective was not as clear. The liberation of Kuwait and the defense of Saudi Arabia and other nations in the region obviously would contribute to the "security and stability of the Persian Gulf." In addition, however, the objective could be interpreted as requiring military operations to reduce the long-term as well as the immediate threat from Hussein's armed forces. The vice president had suggested such a view only a month before the start of the war, when he warned that even if the first two objectives were realized, the U.S. would still have to ensure security and stability in the region. "[W]e will still have to work to see that the President's final objective–maintaining security and stability in the region–is achieved. We cannot allow a situation in which an aggressive dictator has a million-man army, thousands of tanks and artillery pieces, hundreds of jets, and access to billions of petro-dollars."[4] The Secretary of Defense also voiced similar concern, saying that "[i]f Iraq's ambitions are not curbed they will just grow stronger . . . . its military power will be greater. It will come armed not just with 5,600 tanks, a million-man army, chemical weapons and ballistic missiles [but also could] possess nuclear weapons and long-range-missiles to deliver them."[5]

---

[3](S/NF) COMUSCENTAF OPORD, Offensive Campaign–Phase I, 2 Sep 90, p 1, GWAPS; and (S/NF) USCINCCENT OPLAN Desert Storm, 16 Dec 90, p 4, AFHRA 0269602.

[4]Remarks at the Foreign Policy Research Institute, 18 Dec 90, in *US Department of State Dispatch*, 24 Dec 90, p 350.

[5]Hearings before the Committee on Armed Services, Senate, *Crisis in the Persian Gulf Region: U.S. Policy Options and Implications*, 101st Congress, 2d sess (Washington, 1990), p 657. After the war, Cheney said publicly that U.S. military objectives in the

The planners could thus use this objective to justify operations aimed at not just ejecting Iraqi forces in Kuwait but also eliminating Baghdad's offensive capabilities for committing future acts of aggression. Likewise, they could have interpreted this to suggest as a military objective the elimination of Saddam Hussein; for with him out of the way, many planners were convinced that the Iraqi army would withdraw from Kuwait, a move that would fulfill the first U.S. policy aim in the Gulf conflict. Conceivably, the goal of improving the long-term security and stability of the region also would have been furthered by the presence of a less bellicose government in Baghdad. The case for a link between eliminating the Iraqi dictator and promoting the third objective of assuring the security and stability of the Gulf was plausible; however, little documentary evidence in the planning exists to date. Indeed, as will be discussed later, civilian authorities were unwilling to make Hussein's political or physical demise an explicit U.S. objective.[6]

Planners had most difficulty with the fourth objective, which referred to the U.S. citizens Saddam Hussein held hostage. In their eyes, this implied that any planned military action against Iraq had to take their safety into account. As will be discussed later, this was a consideration, until December, when they hostages were released. As the final plan as executed came after this objective was achieved, a clear understanding of its influence remains difficult to assess.

Restraints

Having set the policy objectives for which the Desert Storm campaign would be waged, the top civilian authorities implicitly placed some restraints on military leaders and thus military planners. Notionally, the President and his Secretary of Defense sought an oversight role with regard to the evolving war plans. On the surface, they appeared to want to avoid "micromanaging" their military commanders and planner. Generals Horner and Glosson were adamant in their desire to avoid the problems of Rolling Thunder air campaign against North Vietnam, when President Johnson and his chief civilian advisers selected targets and

---

Gulf War "were two-fold: to liberate Kuwait, and secondly, to strip Saddam Hussein of his offensive military capability, of his capacity to threaten his neighbors." (Transcript, Remarks to the Detroit Economic Club, 14 Sep 92, p 7).

[6](S) Intvw, Gen Glosson with GWAPS Staff, 12 Dec 91, Cochran notes.

made other tactical decisions during their "Tuesday luncheons" at the White House.[7] The President referred to this when announcing the start of the air campaign, ". . . this will not be another Vietnam . . . . Our troops will have the best possible support in the entire world, and they will not be asked to fight with one hand tied behind their backs."[8] Cheney, too, saw strategy as his province, and operational planning as that of the military.[9] According to one of his deputies, ". . . what distinguished the President's . . . and also Secretary Cheney's management of this was not to try to micro-manage the details. Secretary Cheney said at one point . . . it's their plan, they have to make it, but before this is finished, I'm going to own it. And to be sure he knew and had confidence in everything about it."[10]

The Gulf War introduced a new dimension in oversight, primarily through the use of secure STU-III telephones.[11] During the Vietnam war and subsequent conflicts, senior military leaders had communicated on a regular basis outside established direct channels through a process called "back channel," a privileged "eyes only" telecommunications link that facilitated direct message traffic among senior officers without fear of compromise. In theory, no one but the addressee read these personal messages. The STU-III allowed this form of private communications to continue, but this time by secure and instantaneous telephone. Though

---

[7]Maj Gen Buster C. Glosson, quoted in John D. Morrocco, "From Vietnam to Desert Storm," *Air Force Magazine*, Jan 92, p 73; (S) intvw, Glosson, 6 Mar 91, p 11; (S) intvw, Center for Air Force History with Maj Gen Buster C. Glosson, 12 Dec 91, p 26, GWAPS, Historical Advisor's files; Richard Mackenzie, "A Conversation with Chuck Horner," *Air Force Magazine*, Jun 91, p 63; (S) intvw, GWAPS staff with Lt Col David A. Deptula, 20 and 21 Dec 91, p 3, GWAPS.

[8]Address to the Nation Announcing Allied Military Action in the Persian Gulf, 16 Jan 91, in *Weekly Compilation of Presidential Documents* (Office of the Federal Register, National Archives and Records Administration, 21 Jan 91), Vol 27, p 51.

[9]Videotaped talk, Col Garry R. Trexler, "The OSD [Office of the Secretary of Defense] Perspective," to Air War College Course 6328: Desert Shield and Desert Storm–Lessons for the Future, 9 Mar 92; (S) intvw, Kurt Guthe, GWAPS, with Trexler, 26 Mar 92. During Desert Shield/Desert Storm, Trexler was Military Assistant in the Office of the Deputy Secretary of Defense.

[10]Transcript, American Enterprise Institute for Public Policy Research, "The Gulf War Conference," 7 Dec 91, pp 239-240.

[11]For more information on the impact of the STU-III telephone on the Gulf War, see GWAPS report on Command and Control.

General Schwarzkopf was adamant that no one in theater talk to Washington without going through channels, his directive was disregarded virtually from the onset. General Horner talked on a regular basis with the Air Force Chief of Staff, General McPeak, while his Army counterpart did so with the Army Chief of Staff. General Glosson talked frequently with a wide variety of official contacts both inside and outside of military channels during the planning phase.[12] The so-called "Black Hole" institutionalized daily contact between air planners and the Air Staff that widened within the Washington community.[13] General Glosson's deputy planner, Lt. Col. Deptula, remained assigned to Secretary Rice's office throughout the war, maintained constant contact with individuals there, returned several times to Washington to conduct direct briefings on the planning effort for both the Secretary and General McPeak.[14]

Though participants on this Gulf War "back channel" communications have been open to discussions since the war, precise documentation on what was actually discussed, confirmation with whom it was discussed, and evidence as what the actual outcome was remains sketchy at best. One can, however, assume that this practice introduced a new and much more subtler form of micro-management. The STU-III telephone allowed quick and secure discussion about extremely sensitive planning information on a scale never before in warfare. Though "off line" and out-of-channel briefings to individuals outside of the planning community facilitated bureaucratic procedures and assisted in solving logistical problems, larger number of individuals in the Washington area, both military and otherwise, were aware of the planning situation.

On a formal basis, there were several key briefings by General Glosson, the chief air planner, during which the President, the Secretary of Defense, and the Chairman of the Joint Chiefs of staff (their chief military adviser) exercised oversight such as the 13 September briefing

---

[12](S) Intvw, Horner with GWAPS Senior Staff, Shaw AFB, SC, 9 Mar 92, Cochran notes; (S) Intvw, ARCENT Historian with Cochran, Ft. Leavenworth KS, 24 Mar 92: (S) Intvw, CENTCOM Historian with GWAPS, MacDill AFB, FL, 20 Apr 92, Cochran notes; (S) Glosson intvw, *op cit*, Cochran notes.

[13]For more on the Black Hole, see GWAPS report on Command and Control.

[14](S) Intvw, Secretary Rice with GWAPS Senior Staff, Washington DC, n.d. Cochran notes.

for General Powell, the 10 and 11 October briefing for the President, Secretary of Defense, and the Chairman, and the 20 December discussions with Secretary of Defense and the Chairman in Riyadh (and reported to the President after leaving the theater and returning to Washington). The substance of these briefings will be developed in greater detail in Chapter 6. During these meetings, the chief air planner reviewed national and military objectives, concept of operations, forces available, planned targets (in some detail), execution sequence, and expected results. In November, as the possibility of the offensive operation became more evident, members of the Joint and Air Staff began at the secretary's own request a series of briefings intended to familiarize him with various aspects of war planning and air operations. The subjects included air power missions (e.g., interdiction, close air support), target categories, strike package planning, sortie deconfliction, munitions effects, and collateral damage.[15]

One explicit way in which civilian authorities exercised restraint during the planning for the air campaign was in review of target lists. Listed below is a version of the target list that was current at the outset of the war and was given to the CINCCENT, the Chairman of Joint Chiefs, and the Secretary of Defense. This list, or one like it, was used in the target review sessions involving Powell, Cheney, Baker, and Bush.

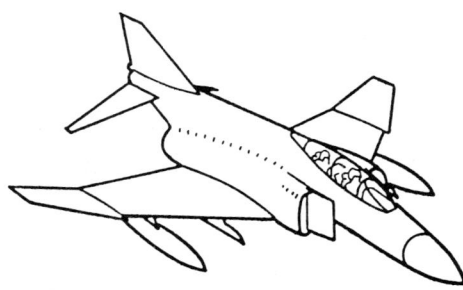

---

[15](S) Memo, Lt Col Paul Dordal to DJS, subj: Proposed SECDEF Briefings, 3 Nov 90, GWAPS; Trexler intvw, 26 Mar 92; and Bob Woodward, *The Commanders* (New York, 1991), p 330.

Figure 7
Extract from "THE" Target List
Provided to CINC, CJCS, SECDEF

FIGURE DELETED

The list is broken down into a dozen categories, with the objective for each category summarized, individual targets identified, target locations indicated by geographic coordinates and region, strike aircraft matched against targets, strike times recorded, and the area around each target characterized as "isolated," "sparsely populated," "residential," "industrial," containing chemical weapons facilities, or having hospitals or mosques. [DELETED][16]

General Powell took steps to ensure that the staffs in the White House and the Pentagon would not get involved in the details of target selection. General Glosson confirmed that the Chairman of the Joint Chiefs "did not permit anybody . . . in Washington to have a copy of the

---

[16]Target list, with the following handwritten note by Deptula: "This was the target list, by category (target set), with objectives for that target set and weapon system fragged on which day with comments concerning population density–'THE' target list we started the war with–copy to CINC, CJCS, and SECDEF."

(authoritative) target list," and said that Powell was very effective in keeping second guessers away during the war.[17]

In December, planners for the Desert Storm air campaign plan had finalized their target list, and various versions were circulated at the highest level in Washington.[18] Several days before the offensive began, for example, Cheney reportedly showed the President the targets to be struck in the imminent air offensive.[19] The next day, Secretary of State James Baker and Under Secretary of State for Political Affairs Robert Kimmitt went to the Pentagon to examine the target list with Cheney and Powell. After the war, the Chairman recalled that he "personally took them through the target list and the nature of the targets and [explained] in general why they were selected, what we were hoping to achieve."[20] According to Kimmitt, "it was very clear to both Secretary Baker and me . . . . that those political considerations that had been expressed, both at the Cabinet level and [in the Deputies Committee of the National Security Council], had been well taken into account, and we both left the meeting very comfortable from a political perspective."[21] Planners made very few changes. [DELETED][22]

Though formal restraints by civilian authorities on the military planners were never articulated, in retrospect five can be identified. First, casualties among Iraqi noncombatants would be held to a minimum. Second, harm to structures of cultural and religious significance to the Iraqi people would be avoided. Third, damage to the Iraqi economy and its capacity for postwar recovery would be limited. Fourth, the lives of the hostages held by Iraq would be protected *to the extent possible*. Fifth, nuclear weapons would not be used.

---

[17]"did not permit . . . list": Glosson quoted in Casey Anderson, "War Planner: Civilians Didn't Change Target List," *Air Force Times*, 8 July 91, p 27; "effective in keeping . . . if they did": (S) intvw, Glosson, 12 Dec 91, p 25.

[18](S) Intvw, Gen Scowcroft with GWAPS staff, 23 Sep 92, Cochran notes.

[19]*The Commanders*, p 364.

[20]Transcript, "The Gulf Crisis: The Road to War," Part 3 of a three-part television series conceived and arranged by the American Enterprise Institute for Public Policy Research and produced by Brian Lapping Associates for the Discovery Channel, p 4.

[21]"The Gulf War Conference," p 236.

[22][DELETED]

One of the most interesting restraints concerned targeting Saddam Hussein himself. While key policy-makers expressed reservations about targeting him, they did nothing to discourage such action and sanctioned efforts to weaken his government. As noted earlier, General Glosson pushed for a commitment from the President for Hussein as a target at the early October briefing. Secretary of State Baker managed to deflect this initiative to the extent that the question was never really addressed. After the war, General Schwarzkopf opined that Hussein never could be considered a legitimate target for the simple reason that he was too difficult to track down–as had General Noriega in Just Cause.[23] General Scowcroft confirmed this rationale in postwar discussions.[24]

With respect to the first implicit restraint, limiting civilian casualties, the President set the tone from the outset. Many times throughout the crisis, the President publicly declared that "the United States has no quarrel with the Iraqi people."[25] In discussions with Generals Horner and Glosson, he made clear that it was imperative to limit civilian losses.[26] The president formalized this requirement in his war directive for Desert Storm.

While presidential stress on limiting harm to innocent Iraqis undoubtedly arose from deep-rooted moral beliefs, it also reflected political realities. Both civilian and military leaders recognized that domestic and international support for military action against Saddam Hussein would disappear rapidly if large numbers of noncombatants were killed or maimed in coalition attacks. Glosson, remembering Vietnam, believed that sustained popular support was essential if the air campaign was to

---

[23] H. Norman Schwarzkopf, *It Doesn't Take a Hero* (New York, 1992), pp 499-500.

[24] (S) Scowcroft intvw, Cochran notes.

[25] Address Before a Joint Session of the Congress on the Persian Gulf Crisis and the Federal Budget Deficit, 11 Sep 90, in *Public Papers of the Presidents of the United States*, p 1221. See also Address to the People of Iraq on the Persian Gulf Crisis, 16 Sep 90, in *ibid.*, p 1239; Address Before the 45th Session of the United Nations General Assembly, 1 Oct 90, in *ibid.*, p 1331; Remarks to United States Army Troops Near Dhahran, Saudi Arabia, 22 Nov 90, in *ibid.*, p 1669; Address to the Nation Announcing Allied Military Action in the Persian Gulf, p 52.

[26] (S) Intvw Horner, 4 Mar 92, p 1; Horner, speech at Dadaelian Dinner, 11 Sep 91, p 1; Horner, quoted in Barry Shlachter, "A U.S. General Assesses the War After One Year," *Ft. Worth Star-Telegram*, 17 Feb 92, p 15; (S) intvw, Glosson, 6 Mar 91, pp 11-12; Glosson, cited in "From Vietnam to Desert Storm," p 73.

achieve its objectives.[27] He also remembered World War II, feeling that the public would not tolerate "another Dresden."[28] With regard to the Iraqi populace, both he and many of his planners believed that focused air strikes that enervated Hussein's regime while sparing his subjects would help separate ruler from ruled, promoting conditions for the Iraqi leader's overthrow.

Such Presidential instruction for planners of the air campaign also meant limited collateral damage. All were conscious that the Law of Armed Conflict prohibited direct attacks on civilian populations. The overall tone here was set by Colonel Warden and his initial plan, Instant Thunder, showed both perception and sensitivity to civilian causalities and collateral damage. What the President's concerns did, in Glosson's view, was to make the Black Hole err on the side of caution in planning strikes that might cause collateral damage.[29] These same concerns may also have indicated that his unwillingness to micromanage war planning was conditional. As the civilian casualties incurred in Al Firdos bunker incident was to demonstrate, Iraqi civilian losses under certain circumstances could prompt the higher authorities–in this case, General Powell, to set aside their objections to micromanagement. In retrospect, both civilian authorities and military planners may have been overzealous on this point.

Following the example set by Colonel Warden and Instant Thunder planners, air campaign planners incorporated the civilian casualty/collateral damage restraints underscored by President Bush in the planning for the air campaign. In Phase I, the strategic air campaign of the operations order specified that "Civilian casualties and collateral damages will be kept to a minimum. The target is Saddam Hussein's regime, not the Iraqi populace . . . . Anything which could be considered as terror attacks or attacks on the Iraqi people will be avoided."[30] In the 16 December OPLAN, planners likewise required that planned strikes accord with the guidance issued by the National Command Authorities (the

---

[27](S) Intvw, Glosson, 12 Dec 91, p 9.

[28](S) Intvw, Glosson, 9 Apr 92.

[29](S) Intvw, Glosson, 6 Mar 91, p 11.

[30](S) OPORD, "Offensive Campaign–Phase I," 2 Sep 90, p 3.

President and the Secretary of Defense).³¹ Estimates of the number of civilian casualties incidental to F-117A/GBU-27, F-111F/GBU-24, and sea-launched cruise missile attacks on Baghdad were sent to the Black Hole by Checkmate in the fall of 1990.³² To limit noncombatant injuries and deaths, planners avoided hitting certain targets, checked all targets in the Baghdad area for collateral damage conflicts, timed strikes to maximize their effectiveness and minimize civilian casualties, employed weapon systems with the best delivery accuracy (F-117s and F-111Fs with laser-guided bombs) against targets in densely populated areas, reduced the likelihood of target misidentification through thorough aircrew familiarization with flight routes and targets and used attack axes that lessened the chance of weapons landing outside targeted areas.³³

While planners took pains to hold down civilian casualties, they also hoped that some of the effects of attacks on military-related targets would fuel popular opposition to Hussein and the war effort. Indeed they expected an overthrow of the Iraqi regime. One of the purposes behind targeting the telecommunications network, according to General Glosson, was "to put every [Iraqi] household in an autonomous mode and make them feel they were isolated. I didn't want them to listen to radio stations and know what was happening. I wanted to play with their psyche[s]."³⁴ General Horner believed the strikes would disrupt the electrical system, bring the war home to the people of Baghdad, and show that Saddam Hussein was powerless to counter the U.S. air offensive.³⁵ One of the air campaign planners thought that one of the messages of the shutdown of electrical power was, "Hey, your lights will come back on as soon as you get rid of Saddam."³⁶ The planners expected that the bombing campaign would produce bonus *psychological* effects on the will

---

³¹(S) OPLAN Desert Storm, 16 Dec 90, p B-4-2.

³²(TS/S) Memo, Col John A. Warden III to Brig Gen Buster C. Glosson, 14 Nov 90, GWAPS,; and (S/NF/WN) Rpt, BDM International, Inc., *Threat Related Attrition (Threat) Model Application*, BDM/MCL-91-0036-TR (McLean, Va., 1991), GWAPS.

³³(TS/LIMDIS/SAR) Talking Paper, "Limiting Collateral Damage," [no author; no date], GWAPS; Horner, quoted in "A Conversation with Chuck Horner," p 61.

³⁴(S) Intvw, Glosson, 12 Dec 91, p 15.

³⁵Horner, cited in Julie Bird, "Horner: Further AF Role in Gulf Not Needed," *Air Force Times*, 18 Mar 91, p 8.

³⁶(S) Intvw, Center for Air Force History with Lt Col David A. Deptula, 8 Jan 92, p 43, GWAPS, Historical Advisor's files.

of the Iraqi people on conjunction with the role of the enemy population in Colonel Warden's "five rings" conceptual framework and Checkmate's Instant Thunder plan.

The second restraint that planners worked under was to limit damage against structures of cultural and religious significance to the Iraqi people. Reasons here were similar to those defining the first restraint. During General Glosson's 11 October briefing at the White House, the President asked the Chairman of the Joint Chiefs to make certain that no religious or historically valuable structures were on any target list for the air campaign. Powell assured the president that planners had taken this limitation into account from the very start, and Glosson noted some of the measures taken to spare religious buildings.[37] As a result, planners constructed a Joint No-Fire Target List for the air campaign, drawn up with the aid of the State Department and the intelligence agencies, that included a significant number of religious and historical structures.

The third implicit restraint placed upon planners by civilian authorities limited damage to the Iraqi economy and its capacity for postwar recovery. Of most interest to planners here was its energy-producing sector. Their aim here was to deny support for military operations without prolonging postwar recovery. Thus, for example, they selected transformers as aim points for strikes against electric power plants, which would take months to repair, rather than generator halls, which would take years.[38] [DELETED] Campaign planners themselves were concerned about from the outset. In recounting the briefing he received from Colonel Warden and the Checkmate team on 17 Aug, Schwarzkopf recalled that, "Though no one had told us, 'We don't want you to destroy Iraq as a nation,' my assumption in directing the planners had been that the United States would continue to need Iraq as a regional counterbalance to Iran. Warden had come up with a strategy designed to cripple Iraq's military without laying waste to the country."[39]

---

[37](S) Glosson, Memorandum for the Record, Subj: Q&A During Presidential Briefing, 11 Oct 90.

[38]Memo, Brig Gen Buster C. Glosson to All Plans Offices, subj: Target Guidance, 12 Jan 91. This memo actually was issued in February, but dated 12 Jan to reflect the fact that the instructions it contained had been expressed verbally before the start of the war.

[39]H. Norman Schwarzkopf, *It Doesn't Take a Hero* (New York, 1992), p 318.

[DELETED]⁴⁰ Glosson, prior to the war, foresaw a U.S. role in helping to rebuild the Iraqi economy, particularly the electrical power system, and thus wanted to make that task no more difficult than necessary.⁴¹

Colonels Warden and Deptula likewise had Iraq's postwar reconstruction in mind, and thought the ability to supply or deny assistance in restoring the oil and electrical power industries would give the United States leverage over Baghdad.⁴² While these positions were not derived from strategic guidance coming from the White House or the Pentagon, they were consistent with the general U.S. policy of fostering a balance of power in the Persian Gulf region. After the war had begun, the President confirmed this, arguing that the objective of assuring security and stability in the Gulf required that Iraq not be destroyed or "so destabilized that [it] could become a target for aggression."⁴³ Of most significance here, planners, commanders, and decisionmakers presupposed that in the postwar reconstruction of Iraq Saddam Hussein would be toppled as a consequence of Desert Storm.

The third restraint concerned targeting facilities at which hostages were located, one that became irrelevant in the final stages of planning when the hostages were released. However, as noted earlier, protecting American lives was one of the "four simple principles" that the president outlined as defining U.S. policy in the Gulf crisis. When Hussein took hostages and employed them as "human shields" to ward off air strikes on Iraqi military and industrial installations, a tension was created for planners between the need to safeguard American lives and the other three objectives of U.S. policy. The President sought to undercut Saddam

---

⁴⁰[DELETED]

⁴¹(S) Intvw, Glosson, 12 Dec 91, p 17; (S) intvw, Glosson, 9 Apr 92.

⁴²(S) Deptula intvw, 8 Jan 92, pp 39, 41, 42 and 43; GWAPS Task Force VI draft, "Attacking the 'Strategic' Core of Iraq's Military Power," 30 Apr 92, p 7.

⁴³Remarks at the Annual Convention of Religious Broadcasters, 28 Jan 91, in *Weekly Compilation of Presidential Documents* (Office of the Federal Register, National Archives and Records Administration, 4 Feb 91), Vol 27, p 88. See also Address Before a Joint Session of the Congress on the State of the Union, 29 Jan 91, in *ibid.*, p 94; and The President's News Conference, 5 Feb 91, in *Weekly Compilation of Presidential Documents*, 11 Feb, Vol 27, p 127.

Hussein's tactic by declaring on a broadcast carried on Iraqi TV that, "Hostage-taking . . . will not work . . . it will not affect my ability to make tough decisions."[44]

Yet all involved with planning had to take into consideration the fate of the hostages in any decision involving the crisis. As one State Department official later admitted, "It would have been . . . double tough to start bombing a place when you have three thousand Americans in there."[45] Those planning the air campaign recognized the importance of the hostages as they kept track of targeted installations where hostages were held. General Glosson had a backup slide for his 11 October briefing at the White House that contained a list of targets with hostages.[46] Whether the President or his top advisers privately told Generals Schwarzkopf, Horner, or Glosson not to hit those targets is unclear from available evidence. According to Wolfowitz, "the President made it clear that we were not going to have our war plans constrained by [Saddam's] use of people as human shields."[47] Horner, when asked in a postwar interview whether the use of hostages would have "affected the employment of air power," replied, "Not one iota. We knew where the hostages were being kept, but even so, you cannot be blackmailed in war."[48] His deputy, however, has said that Glosson ordered that targeting installations with hostages be avoided. Consequently, very few (some elements of the electrical power system protected by "human shields") were targeted with Tomahawk cruise missiles.[49]

Any problems associated with the hostages disappeared when Hussein released his prisoners in early December. This move, in the words of one of Baker's deputies, made "the lives of a lot of people a lot easier, from

---

[44] Address to the People of Iraq on the Persian Gulf Crisis, p 1239.

[45] Quoted in U.S. News & World Report, *Triumph Without Victory: The Unreported History of the Persian Gulf War* (New York, 1992), p 189.

[46] Briefing, 11 Oct 90. See also (S) briefing, "Offensive Campaign: Phase I," 3 Sep 90, GWAPS, CHP Folder 3 (A notation by Deptula on the cover of this briefing reads, "3 Sept Draft for CINC.")

[47] "The Gulf War Conference," p 194.

[48] (S) Intvw, Burton with Lt Gen Charles A. Horner, Mar 91, p 27, GWAPS.

[49] Deptula intvw, 8 Jan 92, p 50. See also "Limiting Collateral Damage" and John M. Broder, "With Its Hostages Out, U.S. Revises List of Iraqi Targets, *Los Angeles Times*, 13 Dec 90, p 1].

military planners through the President, who was very concerned about people getting caught in harm's way."[50] In retrospect, it seems clear that, had they not been released, the air campaign plan would have been influenced. Put another way, the release of the hostages also released planners from what could have been a major restraint.

The final restraint faced by planners concerned nuclear weapons, which were not part of the plan for the Desert Storm offensive air campaign, as White House officials never seriously considered their employment.[51] [DELETED][52] [DELETED].

Political authorities and their chief military commanders were influenced by numerous factors here. First were their expectations that the large and capable conventional forces assembled in the Gulf were sufficient to achieve the objectives of the planned campaign. Likewise, they felt that there simply were no targets warranting the use of nuclear weapons. They also realized that any revelation of plans to use nuclear weapons would have severely eroded support both at home and abroad for U.S. military actions against Iraq. Lastly, they recognized the tradition of nonuse and the likely long-term political costs of nuclear use.[53] Nuclear threats may have been conveyed to the Iraqi leader to deter him from employing weapons of mass destruction, but operational plans emphasized nonnuclear strikes against high-value targets in retaliation for chemical or biological attacks. The primary option that planners and senior officials maintained was retaliation with chemical weapons, as will be discussed in greater detail in Chapter 6.

Though senior officials and planners both hoped for the demise of Saddam Hussein, all were wary of making that an express aim of Desert Storm. Soon after the air campaign began, Bush said publicly that, "We

---

[50] Robert Kimmitt, in "The Gulf War Conference," p 193.

[51] R. Jeffrey Smith and Rick Atkinson, "U.S. Rules Out Gulf Use of Nuclear, Chemical Arms," *Washington Post*, 7 Jan 91, p A1. (S) Intvw, Horner with GWAPS Staff; (S) Intvw, Glosson with GWAPS Staff, Cochran notes.

[52] (S) OPLAN Desert Storm, 16 Dec 90, p C-1-1.

[53] "U.S. Rules Out Gulf Use of Nuclear, Chemical Arms"; John M. Broder, "U.S. Forces Have No Nuclear Arms in Gulf States, No Plans to Use Them," *Los Angeles Times*, 2 Oct 90, p 6.

are not targeting any individual."[54] Powell and Schwarzkopf also announced publicly that Saddam Hussein was not specifically targeted.[55] There seem to have been at least three reasons for this reluctance. First, prior to the war, some were concerned that targeting Hussein might be contrary to Executive Order 12333, which prohibits U.S. Government involvement in "assassination."[56] This was a major reason cited by Secretary Cheney in his relief of Air Force Chief of Staff General Michael Dugan, and it sent a clear message to the chief air campaign planner on this point.[57] Second, planners were aware that the United Nations (UN) resolutions around which the coalition coalesced said nothing about eliminating Saddam Hussein. They appeared to realize that setting goals that went beyond those of the UN would necessitate complex and possibly counterproductive negotiations with the allies.[58] Third, and perhaps most important, they were conscious that they could not guarantee strikes aimed at killing Hussein would have their intended effect, remembering the difficulties in tracking Manuel Noriega during Operation Just Cause the previous year.[59] Adopting the physical demise of Hussein as a stated objective, and then failing to meet that objective would mar the military

---

[54] "The President's News Conference on the Persian Gulf Conflict," 18 Jan 91, in *Weekly Compilation of Presidential Documents*, 21 Jan 91, p 56.

[55] Transcript, Gen Colin L. Powell, news briefing (with Secretary of Defense Cheney), The Pentagon, 16 Jan 91, p 5; transcript, Gen H. Norman Schwarzkopf, new briefing, Riyadh, 18 Jan 91, p 4.

[56] Executive Order 12333–United States Intelligence Activities, 4 Dec 81, in Office of the Federal Register, National Archives and Records Administration, *Codification of Presidential Proclamations and Executive Orders* (Washington, 1989), p 647.

[57] (S) Intvw, Glosson with GWAPS, dated, Cochran notes. Transcript, Secretary of Defense Dick Cheney, news briefing, The Pentagon, 17 Sep 90, p 1.

[58] President Bush, Remarks on the Nomination of Edward R. Madigan as Secretary of Agriculture and a Question-and-Answer Session with Reporters, 25 Jan 91, in *Weekly Compilation of Presidential Documents*, 28 Jan 91, Vol 27, p 80; Vice President Quayle, cited in "Quayle on Hussein: 'He is totally irrational'," *U.S. News & World Report*, 18 Feb 91, p 27; Robert Kimmitt, in "The Gulf War Conference," p 293.

[59] (S) Intvw, Gen Scowcroft with GWAPS, Cochran notes; *Triumph Without Victory*, p 142; Robert Gates, "The Gulf Crisis: The Road to War," Part 3, p 19; transcript, Gen Colin L. Powell, news briefing (with Secretary of Defense Cheney), The Pentagon, 17 Jan 91, p 6; Schwarzkopf, in *Department of Defense Appropriations for 1992*, p 277.

as well as political success of Desert Storm. After the war, both General Schwarzkopf and his chief air planners confirmed this view.[60]

The President and his advisers were less hesitant about authorizing actions intended to bring about Saddam Hussein's political demise, which, Iraqi politics being what it was, would have brought about his physical demise as well. The President had approved operations designed to weaken popular support for the Hussein government and directed that if Iraq used nuclear biological and chemical weapons, supported terrorist acts, or destroyed Kuwaiti oil fields. [DELETED] It is worth noting that the President, in his 5 January letter to Saddam Hussein (which Baker showed to Foreign Minister Tariq 'Aziz at their 9 January meeting in Geneva) cited these same three "unconscionable acts" as requiring the "strongest possible response" from the United States, one that would make the Iraqi leader and his country "pay a terrible price."[61]

Despite somewhat ambiguous policy guidance, the chief architects of the air campaign targeted Saddam Hussein and planned air operations meant to create conditions conducive to his overthrow. [DELETED][62] Planners believed that Hussein, as a military commander, was a legitimate target during the war.[63] As noted above and more to the point, they clearly expected that Saddam Hussein's demise would result in the Army's withdrawal from Kuwait, thus achieving one of the major national objectives.

Planners not only wanted to incapacitate the Hussein government [DELETED] but to try to change it.[64] [DELETED][65] [66] [DELETED] [67]

---

[60]H. Norman Schwarzkopf, *It Doesn't Take a Hero* (New York, 1992), pp 499-500; (S) Intvw, Glosson with GWAPS staff, Cochran notes.

[61]Statement by Press Secretary Fitzwater on President Bush's Letter to President Saddam Hussein of Iraq, 12 Jan 91, in *Weekly Compilation of Presidential Documents*, 21 Jan 91, Vol 27, pp 43-44.

[62](S) Glosson intvw, 12 Dec 91, pp 29 and 31; Deptula intvw, 8 Jan 92, p 30.

[63](S) Intvw, Glosson, 12 Dec 91, p 29; Deptula intvw, 8 Jan 92, p 36.

[64](TS) Doc, USCINCCENT CC J3 to JCS Joint Staff, subj: Follow-Up Execute Order–USCINCCENT OPORD 001 for Desert Storm, 1700IZ Jan 91, GWAPS, CHC 8-1.

[65]*Observations on the Air Campaign Against Iraq*, p 17.

Brig Gen Buster Glosson confers with his chief planner, Lt Col David Deptula, in Riyadh.

[66](S) Draft Working Paper, Augmentation Cell, Central Command J-5 War Plans Division, Offensive Campaign Concept–Ground Campaign Concept of Operations, 14 Oct 90, Appendix E, *Central Command J-5 Plans War Division Augmentation Cell After Action Report*, GWAPS.

[67]"Air ops summary of air war." The copy of summary in GWAPS D-19H bears a notation by Deptula that reads, "As provided by L/C Deptula and BG Glosson during 1½ hour discussion with Gen Horner."

Constraints

While higher authorities prescribed restraints essentially as the "don'ts" for the planners of the air campaign, they also laid out some "dos" or constraints. There were two key constraints: (1) planners had to insure that any offensive was both quick and decisive; and (2) they had to neutralize Iraqi Scud (or Scud-derived) short-range ballistic missiles in early in offensive air operations. General Glosson and his planners were in total agreement with the first, and it served from the very beginning as a guiding principle in the planning of the air campaign. The second proved more difficult for all, as it concerned civilians more than military planners.

Top civilian officials left little doubt in their statement that they expected rapid victory to avoid high casualties and military stalemate, both of which would undermine support for the campaign against Iraq.[68] The President "instructed [his] military commanders to take every necessary step to prevail as quickly as possible and with the greatest degree of protection possible" for U.S. and allied forces.[69] This guidance was consistent not only with the principles of war but with senior military leaders' belief in the costs of gradualism in Vietnam. As Horner recalled (after mentioning the Vietnam experience), "We were absolutely going to be the most violent and intensive campaign possible, the reason being it seemed like the only way to shorten the war, limit the suffering, and get this thing over as quickly as possible."[70]

---

[68]President Bush, The President's News Conference, 30 Nov 90, in *Public Papers of the Presidents of the United States*, p 1720; Secretary of State Baker, in Hearings before the Committee on Foreign Relations, Senate, *U.S. Policy in the Persian Gulf*, 101st Cong, 2d sess (Washington, 1991), pt 1, p 107; Secretary of Defense Cheney, in Hearings before the Committee on Armed Services, House of Representatives, *Crisis in the Persian Gulf: Sanctions, Diplomacy and War*, 101st Cong, 2d sess (Washington, 1991), p 570; Vice President Quayle, Address to the Los Angeles World Affairs Council, 8 Jan 91, *US Department of State Dispatch*, 14 Jan 91, p 28.

[69]"Address to the Nation Announcing Allied Military Action in the Persian Gulf, p 51.

[70]Speech at Dadaelian Dinner, 11 Sep 91, p 4.

To ensure a swift and sure victory, the President and his advisers were prepared to send to the theater whatever forces were necessary.[71] As a general principle, Bush, along with Cheney, Powell, Baker, and Brent Scowcroft believed that in conflicts calling for the employment of military power, the United States should assemble and apply "overwhelming force" capable of crushing the enemy in short order and with minimal loss of life.[72] In November, after the President and his advisers had decided to increase substantially the U.S. forces deployed in the Gulf so as to give the coalition "an adequate offensive military option," planners were informed that CENTCOM would have all the forces needed for a successful campaign should the decision be made for offensive action.[73] The President, in Glosson's words, "decided to give [us] all the forces that we wanted or could use."[74] As will be developed in Chapter 6, some air planners believed that the USAF already had sufficient forces to execute at least Phase I of the campaign. Indeed by the start of the war, General Glosson's deputy characterized the situation as "an overabundance of air assets."[75] Thus air planners never had to face a question of priorities in achieving the "quick victory" constraint; rather they had the luxury of doing essentially whatever they chose.

The constraint requiring prompt destruction of enemy Scuds proved to be more significant for planners. From early in the crisis, officials at the White House, State Department, and Defense Department were preoccupied with the Scuds.[76] With these missiles maintained under tight centralized control, Saddam Hussein had the capability to attack Israel

---

[71](S) Intvw, Gen Scowcroft with GWAPS Senior Staff, Cochran notes.

[72]Rick Atkinson and Bob Woodward, "Gulf Turning Points: Strategy, Diplomacy," *Washington Post*, 2 Dec 90, p A1. See also, Powell, cited in *Triumph Without Victory*, p 71.

[73]The President's News Conference on the Persian Gulf Crisis, in *Public Papers of the Presidents of the United States*, p 1581; "all the forces . . . would be the U.S. strategy": (S/NF) Rpt, Rear Adm Grant Sharp, *Planning for the Gulf War* (draft), 3 Dec 91, p 43, GWAPS.

[74](S) Intvw, Glosson, 12 Dec 91, p 9.

[75](S) Intvw, Center for Air Force History with Lt Col David A. Deptula, 29 Nov 91, p 52, GWAPS, Historical Advisor's files.

[76]Wolfowitz, Kimmitt, Dennis B. Ross, and John H. Kelly, in "The Gulf War Conference," pp 258, 259, 262 and 267; and Cheney, in "The Gulf Crisis: The Road to War," Program 3, p 7.

and threaten the basis for the coalition. To avert this danger, the United States launched a number of diplomatic efforts to persuade Israel to show restraint in the face of Iraqi provocations. Several days before Desert Storm began, the President sent Deputy Secretary of State Lawrence Eagleburger and Paul Wolfowitz to Jerusalem to discourage the Israelis from launching either preemptive or retaliatory strikes against Iraq. Eagleburger told Prime Minister Yitzhak Shamir that the United States would treat any attack by Hussein as a *casus belli* and take immediate military action. Significantly, Eagleburger assured Shamir that U.S. air operations rapidly would neutralize the Scuds that threatened Israel from sites in western Iraq.[77]

The degree to which civilians in Washington worried about the Scuds more than military planners in Saudi Arabia became evident in October when JCS planners, at the instigation of Secretary Cheney and with input from one of his primary civilian deputies, seriously considered moving ground forces into the suspected Scud launching areas. CENTCOM planners as well as their commander regarded such efforts as unrealistic, not considering either the terrain or the possibility that the Iraqis might well counterattack into the void left by the US troop movement.[78] In December, this option again surfaced in Washington. Although the option was twice rejected by CENTCOM planners, it did alert them and their commanders to the degree of policy-makers' concern about the Scuds and suggested some civilian doubt about the ability of air power alone to deal with the problem posed by the Scuds.

After the war, senior leaders, including the President's national security adviser, admitted that they had underestimated the threat posed by Saddam Hussein's missiles.[79] Military leaders viewed the Scuds as

---

[77] *Triumph Without Victory*, pp 208-211.

[78] (S/NF) Rpt, U.S. Central Command/Joint Forces and Theater Operations, *J-5 Plans After Action Report*, Vol VI: *Miscellaneous Documents* (MacDill AFB, Fla., 1991), Tab X (Combat Analysis Group After Action Report), GWAPS; *J-5 Plans After Action Report*, Vol I: *After Action Report (Basic Report with Tabs)*, Tab P (SAMS [School of Advanced Military Studies]); *Planning for the Gulf War*, pp 40-41. On Defense Department involvement, see "Operation Scorpion" attached to ltr from Harry Rowen to Alexander Cochran, Apr 92, GWAPS, NA 271; (S) intvw, Lawrence Greenberg, GWAPS, with Col Paul Dordal, J-3, 20 Feb 92, GWAPS; *Triumph Without Victory*, pp 167-168; and (S) intvw, Glosson, 9 Apr 92, p 12.

[79] (S) Intvw Scowcroft with GWAPS, Cochran notes.

"militarily irrelevant" (Schwarzkopf), "not militarily significant" (Glosson), and "lousy weapon[s]" (Horner).[80] At the time of war, some planners recognized that the military unimportance of the missiles did not make them politically inconsequential. However, Horner and Glosson, by their own admissions, failed at the time to recognize was just how critical the neutralization of the Scud threat was to the civilian leadership and the diplomatic conduct of the war.[81] Neither were they precise in communicating their own view of this constraint to civilians. During the 20 December briefing in which General Horner reviewed the air campaign plan with Cheney, Wolfowitz, and Powell, the Secretary of Defense asked for the details of how the Scuds would be eliminated. He explained that all the fixed launch sites would be hit, but that some Scuds would be fired because, "[y]ou can't get them all."[82]

It does seem clear that commanders and planners in the theater neglected to prepare for any aggressive Scud-hunting because they considered the missile threat of little *military* consequence. They proposed a plan to silence the fixed launchers, destroy a limited number of suspected launch-and-hide locations for mobile launchers (to do what could be done, short of a major armed-reconnaissance effort). Through this, they hoped to alleviate the pressure from Israel and Washington while maintaining the integrity of the strategic air campaign. Perhaps it might also deny Iraq the capability to produce ballistic missiles in the future. The alternative was to a search-and-destroy operation that promised a costly and unproductive diversion of strike sorties from the main objectives of the strategic air campaign.[83]

In retrospect, planners entered this war with policy objectives that defined the strategic aims of their campaign. Likewise, they operated within the context of restraints that told them what not to do and constraints that gave them a sense of what needed to be done. In combination, these ends and conditions created the parameters within which the air campaign plan for the Gulf War was built.

---

[80] Schwarzkopf, "Talking with David Frost" (transcript of TV interview), 27 Mar 91, p 4; (S) Intvw, Glosson 6 Mar 91, p 7; Horner, Speech at Dadaelian Dinner, 11 Sept 91, p 5.

[81] (S) Intvw, Horner, 4 Mar 92, p 10; Horner, Speech at Dadaelian Dinner, 11 Sept 91, p 5; and (S) intvw, Glosson, 6 Mar 91, p 7.

[82] (S) Intvw, Horner, 4 Mar 92, p 10.

[83] For additional discussion and analysis on the effectiveness of the Scud campaign, see GWAPS *Effectiveness* Report.

5

Instant Thunder and Desert Shield

Planners of the Gulf War air campaign used two other planning efforts–one a concept plan for an independent air offensive devised in the early days of the crisis by Air Staff planners in Washington and the other an on-going series of plans written by the CENTAF staff in Riyadh to defend Saudi Arabia. Both of these planning efforts contributed to the Desert Storm air campaign.

Interestingly, the first plan that was executed was one that surprised both CENTCOM and CENTAF planners. Within hours of the outbreak of the crisis, General Powell directed the immediate execution of USCENTAF Rapid Response Plan (RRP) 1307-88, a CENTAF-only contingency plan for a demonstration-sized combat Air Force package into the region. [DELETED] Planners anticipated the arrival of the first aircraft in theater within 48 hours of notification and become operational on C+4 (four days after the beginning of deployment). They also included unspecified options for including carrier battle group assets and shipborne Tomahawk Land Attack Missiles to increase strike capabilities.[1] The plan mentioned no specific threat and was never intended to be used to counter a force as large and potentially capable as the Iraqi war machine.[2]

At the same time, General Powell issued a warning order informing the American military community of the crisis on the Arabian Peninsula. To assist commanders in preparing their forces for possible employment, Joint Chief of Staff (JCS) warning orders contain references to appropriate OPLANs. In this case, General Powell referenced RRP 1307-88, not the

---

[1]David L. Rosmer (S) *Ninth Air Force/USCENTAF in Desert Shield: The Initial Phase, August 1990.* Shaw AFB, SC: Headquarters, Ninth Air Force/USCENTAF. [10 Jan 92], p 52, GWAPS NA-188; Rosmer, (S) *History of the Ninth Air Force/USCENTAF Jan-Dec 90,* Vol. I-A, 1 Jan 92. AFHRA, p 82.; (S) Background paper, HQ USAF, XOXXM. "COMUS-CENTAF Rapid Reaction Plan 1307-88." 3 Aug 90, GWAPS CHC 9-1

[2](S) Brfg Slides, USCENTCOM, "Preliminary Planning." 2-6 Aug 90, GWAPS NA-117 and AFHRA, Desert Shield file; folder USCENTCOM Preliminary Planning, 2-6 Aug 90.

1002 plan.³ This no doubt reflected 1002-90's incompleteness as well as the capability to incorporate 1307's forces into larger follow-on deployment. But, most importantly, it reflected his uncertainty on the nature of the U.S. political response, a decision to be made by the President. In this context, the initial responses by affected commands–Military Airlift Command, Strategic Airlift Command, and Ninth Air Force in particular–was for a limited, exclusively USAF response.

Commanders and planners at CENTCOM's supporting commands and agencies worked under these assumptions for the first three days of the crisis. At Tactical Air Command, commanders reviewed 1307 objectives and, lacking further JCS guidance, assumed a relaxed posture. From the outset, it was clear that the Chairman's choice of contingency options was inadequate to meet the potential threat. Yet, it demonstrated his concern about rushing to deploy light ground forces specified in the 1002-series of plans to Saudi Arabia at a time when the host nation had yet to request such assistance and when the massed Iraqi army stood within easy striking distance.

Matters changed on 4 August when President Bush convened a National Security Council (NSC) meeting at Camp David to discuss possible options and military preparations that would alter the complexion of the American response to Baghdad's aggression.⁴ After CIA representatives presented an assessment of Iraqi strength in Kuwait, Schwarzkopf briefed the President on OPLAN 1002 and indicated that he would need one month to position minimum defensive forces and [DELETED] to reach the full OPLAN 1002 force levels [DELETED]. In addition, he stated a target date upon which it would be practical to pursue offensive operations.⁵

---

³(S) Rpt, *Project AIR FORCE Desert Shield Assessment*, Vol II Draft WD-5270/1-AF. Santa Monica: The RAND Corp, Mar 91, GWAPS NA-26; (S/NF) Doc, USCINCCENT, *Desert Shield/Desert Storm, Internal Look 90 After Action Reports*, 15 Jul 91.

⁴Present at the morning meeting were President Bush, Vice President Quayle, White House Chief of Staff John Sununu, National Security Advisor Adm Brent Scowcroft, Mid-East Security Advisor Richard Haass, White House Press Secretary Marlin Fitzwater, Secretaries Baker and Cheney, Under Secretary of Defense Paul Wolfowitz, Generals Powell and Schwarzkopf, CENTAF Commander Lt Gen Horner and his Chief of Staff Maj Gen Robert Johnston, JCS J-3 Lt Gen Thomas W. Kelly, CIA Director William Webster, and JCS J-2 VAdm J. "Mike" McConnell. (Rosmer, *9th AF History*).

⁵Rosmer, (S) *9th AF History*; (S) Intvw, AFCHO with Lt Gen Charles Horner, 28 Jan 91.

During the meeting, General Horner raised the possible use of air power to thwart an Iraqi invasion of Saudi Arabia. First he outlined a conceptual plan for a limited strategic air campaign against high value targets that the President could use to retaliate against Baghdad if they used chemical weapons against allied troops. Then, he maintained that American aircraft operating from Saudi bases and from aircraft carriers in the Persian Gulf and Red Sea could fly several hundred combat sorties a day and establish air superiority within a period of days.[6] General Horner thus provided capabilities immediately available to the President in lieu of the acknowledged problems of distance and deployment schedules for large numbers of heavy ground forces.

Others at the meeting–Secretary of Defense Richard Cheney and NSC Advisor Brent Scowcroft–emphasized that significant numbers of ground forces would be necessary to protect Saudi Arabia and cautioned the President on the limits of air power to achieve national objectives without the ground element. General Powell felt that, while air power was important, the defense of Saudi Arabia would require the deployment of substantial numbers of ground forces. He cautioned: "If you want to deter, don't put up a phoney deterrence. . . .If you do it, do it real and do it right." The meeting concluded with no firm decision. President Bush chose rather to see whether Saudi King Fahd Ibn Abdel-Aziz would ask for assistance. While the President contacted King Fahd to offer military assistance, Schwarzkopf, Horner, and CENTCOM Chief of Staff Maj. Gen. Robert Johnston returned to Florida.[7]

The following day, 5 August, President Bush again met with his close advisors, this time in Washington and agreed to alert the 82d Airborne Division. He directed Secretary Cheney to lead a special team to Riyadh and meet with King Fahd and his senior military and political advisors to secure a request for U.S. assistance. The team, composed of Cheney, Gates, Horner, Schwarzkopf, Wolfowitz, Williams, Ambassador Charles W. Freeman, Jr., and representatives from State and the CIA, met with

---

[6] Rosmer, (S) *9th AF History*, p 2.

[7] (S/NF) USCENTCOM, *Operations Desert Shield/Desert Storm, Exercise Internal Look 90 After Action Report*, 15 Jul 91, GWAPS NA-117.

King Fahd on 6 August and succeeded in convincing the monarch of U.S. resolve to act swiftly and decisively to defeat Iraq's invasion. The King requested U.S. military assistance.[8]

Between the 4 August Camp David meeting and the departure of Cheney's special negotiation team to Riyadh, General Powell informed the military community to forget RRP 1307 and use USCINCCENT OPLAN 1002-90 for planning. As commands received the new guidance, planning resumed at an accelerated pace.[9]

For decisionmakers and their military planners alike, the opening days of the Gulf crisis were filled with uncertainty and general anxiety over both the nature of the anticipated U.S. response and Baghdad's intentions. Military commanders were all too conscious of the inadequacy of existing contingency plans to deal with the emerging situation. It was clear to them that, whatever the eventual U.S. response, U.S. air forces would comprise the preponderance of the initial available force.

This fact was not lost on General Schwarzkopf either. Recent experiences in Internal Look had demonstrated the need for an additional offensive option–not only to dislodge Iraq from Kuwait but more immediately to retaliate should Saddam Hussein use chemical weapons or harm hostages. Within this context, he turned to the US Air Force. As Gen. Michael J. Dugan, Air Force Chief of Staff, was away from Washington, on 8 August, Schwarzkopf spoke to the Vice Chief, Gen. John M. Loh, and requested help in finding ways to retaliate against some new hostile act by Iraq–seizure of the American embassy in Kuwait, for example, or a chemical attack.[10]

Members of the Air Staff already were thinking about an air campaign that might, by itself, eject Iraqi forces from Kuwait. On the day before Schwarzkopf's call to Loh, Col. John M. Warden III, deputy director of plans for warfighting concepts, had sent members of his staff

---

[8] (S/NF) *Ibid.*

[9] (S) *Project AIR FORCE Assessment of Operation Desert Shield* Working Draft. WD-5270-1-AF. Santa Monica: The RAND Corp, Jan 91, GWAPS NA-25.

[10] (S) Intvw, Diane T. Putney, Center for Air Force History, with Gen H. Norman Schwarzkopf (USA, ret), 5 May 92, GWAPS, NA 268; (S) memo, Wayne Thompson, GWAPS, subj: Visit to TAC HQ, 30 Oct 91, GWAPS, Historical Advisor's Files.

to begin work on the idea in the Checkmate briefing room in the basement of the Pentagon.[11]

Within a few days, this planning group had written a briefing for General Loh which contained the essentials of what became known as Instant Thunder. They took the President's objectives from his speech of 8 August: (1) Iraqi withdrawal from Kuwait; (2) restoration of Kuwaiti sovereignty; (3) security and stability of the Persian Gulf; (4) protection of American lives. Initially they expressed the President's third objective as securing the free flow of oil, but soon recognized the President's broader interest in stability. The Checkmate planners used the President's objectives to fashion military objectives: (1) force Iraqi withdrawal from Kuwait; (2) degrade Iraq's offensive capability; (3) secure oil facilities; (4) render Saddam ineffective as a leader.[12]

The centerpiece of Instant Thunder in Colonel Warden's view was his fourth military objective. His book, *The Air Campaign*, had suggested that command was a center of gravity to be attacked, but had cautioned that a commander would be difficult to target and that his staff might be able to carry on without him. Warden viewed the decision element of command, while more important, as usually less vulnerable to attack than other elements. Rather it was the information gathering and communication elements that should be targeted. The commander could be rendered ineffective by isolating him from his forces and his sources of information through attacks on his communications and his intelligence gatherers

---

[11] Although not used previously for war planning, the Checkmate facility had been the setting for prominent undertakings involving the other services and the intelligence agencies. For most of the years following its establishment in 1976 by Gen David C. Jones (USAF Chief of Staff), Checkmate used red and blue teams to examine possible wartime interaction between Soviet and NATO forces in Europe and the Middle East. Checkmate had also hosted a joint effort to further interservice cooperation in projects like the Joint Surveillance and Target Attack Radar System (JSTARS). In response to CENTCOM's spring 1990 draft of Operations Plan 1002-90, Col Warden had sent a Checkmate team to visit CENTAF and CENTCOM headquarters where his team argued for an air offensive which he called "the air option." On the eve of the Gulf crisis in July 1990, a Checkmate team participated in the Naval War College's Global War Game, where the scenario that caught the most attention was an Iraqi invasion of Kuwait and Saudi Arabia.

[12] (S) Brfg, Col John A. Warden III for Gen John A. Loh, VCSAF, "Iraqi Air Campaign," 8 Aug 90, GWAPS, CHSH 7-11; (S) notes, Lt Col Bernard E. Harvey, Checkmate, 7-8 Aug 90, GWAPS, CHP 9-1.

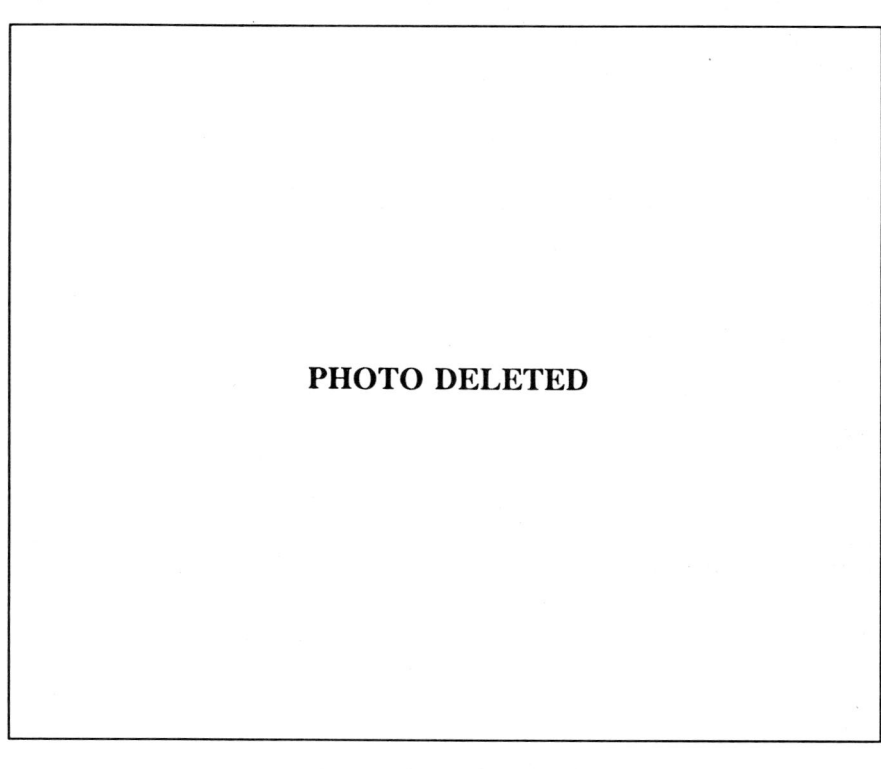

Devising the Instant Thunder plan in the Air Staff's Checkmate office in the Pentagon.

(for example, his radars).[13] As to the relatively slight possibility of killing the enemy leader, while Warden was writing his book in 1986, the Air Force and the Navy came close enough to killing Libya's dictator to cause a sharp reduction in his international activity.

---

[13]John A. Warden III, *The Air Campaign* (Washington: National Defense University, 1988), pp 51-58. Warden sought to meet a need for a book about the theory and practice of air warfare at the operational level (rather than the strategic or tactical level). His advice on how to conduct an air campaign is bolstered by historical examples, especially from World War II. He borrowed Clausewitz's emphasis on the enemy center of gravity: "Perhaps the most important responsibility of a commander is to identify and strike appropriate enemy centers of gravity" (p 10).

During the four years between the Libyan raid and the Gulf crisis, Warden developed his thoughts on attacking enemy command into a targeting concept illustrated by five concentric rings. The central ring in his theory of target importance was leadership. He planned attacks on the other four rings (key production, infrastructure, population, and fielded forces on the outer rim) in terms of their potential effect on leadership. Many viewed his notion of concentric rings as a dangerous oversimplification. Yet Warden believed that the simplicity of his model was a great strength both for planning under pressure and for selling the resulting plan to decisionmakers.[14] Indeed this very simplicity would shape the Gulf War air campaign plan.

At the heart of Warden's plan was the targeting of leadership. The Iraqi situation seemed tailor-made for the theory. Saddam was not merely the Iraqi commander. As Iraq's dictator, he seemed to be the source of most of America's problems with Iraq. An Iraq without Saddam promised to be an Iraq with which the United States would have much better relations. Since killing Saddam from the air would require luck, Warden hoped to isolate Saddam not only from his forces but also from his people. Even if Saddam survived, he might lose his capability to govern and he might be overthrown. Television and radio stations would be attacked so that they could be taken off the air and replaced by coalition broadcasts delivering the message that the Saddam regime was the objective of the attack and not the Iraqi people.[15]

By trying to avoid civilian casualties, Warden clearly anticipated the President's preferences. But Warden was not being cautious. Rather he thought he was making a positive contribution to his own strategy by designing a campaign which would divide Saddam from the Iraqi people–not bolster Saddam's control through hostility to a common American enemy. In Warden's view, the Iraqi people should be the target of psychological operations, not bombs; damage to the Iraqi economy should be quickly repairable at the end of the war with American help.[16]

---

[14]The fullest exposition of Warden's five rings theory is his unpublished 1990 essay "Centers of Gravity: The Keys to Success in War," GWAPS, Historical Advisor's Files.

[15]Col Warden's views may be traced in his series of (S/NF/WN/NC) Instant Thunder briefings, 8-17 Aug 90, GWAPS, CHSH 5 and 7.

[16](TS/LIMDIS) Instant Thunder Campaign Plan, 17 Aug 90, GWAPS. CHSH 9, p 3.

Warden was also conscious that twenty-five years earlier President Lyndon Johnson's worries about civilian casualties had resulted in an air campaign against North Vietnam that took a mounting toll because it lasted years—years that were also costly for American aircrew and aircraft and left many in the Air Force bitterly determined to avoid a repetition. An OV-10 pilot in Vietnam, he was determined to avoid such gradualism and named his plan Instant Thunder to emphasize the rapidity with which he planned to defeat Iraq from the air.[17]

Instant Thunder was an air campaign designed to last some six to nine days against eighty-four strategic targets, all of which were in Iraq not Kuwait. With the exception of attacks on Iraq's air defenses and its deployed chemical weapons, Warden's campaign would leave Iraq's fielded forces intact. He expected Iraq to withdraw from Kuwait without much of a fight.

Two days after General Schwarzkopf requested input from the Air Staff, Warden briefed him on his concept in Florida. The next day, as requested by the CENTCOM commander, Warden briefed General Powell in Washington. Given the lack of attention to attacking enemy ground forces, Warden might have encountered considerable skepticism, but he was offering Schwarzkopf and Powell the only offensive option they would have for months. Schwarzkopf said that the briefing restored his confidence in the Air Force. Powell's major objection was that he wanted Iraqi tanks destroyed so that Saddam could not again threaten Iraq's neighbors.[18] Warden had a green light to continue his planning.

For several weeks, Warden would devote little thought to attacking ground forces. Rather his immediate concern about Iraqi ground forces was to deal with the argument that Instant Thunder might trigger an Iraqi invasion of Saudi Arabia. He argued that Iraqi ground forces would not

---

[17][DELETED](S) rpt, Maj (Robert M.) "Sky" King, Checkmate, Trip to CENTAF and CENTCOM, 6 Jul 90, with Warden's note to Alexander, HQ USAF/XOX, 9 Jul 90, GWAPS Historical Advisor's Files.

[18]Harvey Notes, 10-11 Aug 90, GWAPS, CHP 9-1; (S) memos, Lt Col Harvey, subj: Brfgs to CINCCENT and Chairman JCS, 10-11 Aug 90, GWAPS, CHP 7-1 through 7-4; (S) intvw, Lt Cols Richard Reynolds, Suzanne Gehri and Edward Mann, Air University CADRE, with Dr Donald B. Rice, Secretary of the Air Force, 11 Dec 91, GWAPS, NA 234. After telling his Checkmate briefers on 10 Aug that they had restored his confidence in the Air Force, Schwarzkopf repeated that view to Secretary Rice on 15 Aug.

want to expose themselves by moving south beyond their ability to supply themselves effectively, but if they did, ninety-six A-10s, forty AV-8Bs, thirty-six F/A-18s, thirty AH-1Ws and seventy-five AH-64s would have no trouble stopping them before they could reach Dhahran or Riyadh. There would be no need to divert other aircraft from the strategic air campaign. Whatever might happen, Warden insisted that the strategic air campaign should go forward, for it was the strategic air campaign that would win the war. He frequently referred to Germany's Schlieffen Plan to invade France early in the First World War, a plan which Warden thought had been gutted of the necessary force to make its great enveloping sweep to the right effective.[19]

Once the Instant Thunder concept had gained approval, the Checkmate planning group was enlarged and began converting Warden's concepts into an executable plan. Staff officers from other parts of the Air Staff, from the Air Force Intelligence Agency, from the major commands, from Central Air Forces and from the other services joined the effort in the Pentagon basement. As many of these people as possible were jammed into Checkmate's offices. Lt. Col. Ronnie Stanfill, a Libyan raid planner, recruited two pilots (Maj. Michael B. Hoyes and Maj. Allen E. Wickman) who had flown on the raid. Stanfill was one of four lieutenant colonels Warden relied on most heavily for Instant Thunder. The others were Lt. Col. David A. Deptula (from the Secretary of the Air Force's staff support group), Lt. Col. Bernard E. Harvey, and Lt. Col. Richard Stimer.[20] Stimer was responsible for deception: Harvey served as Warden's special assistant; Stanfill and Deptula organized most of the rest of the growing Checkmate staff to prepare an operations plan.

Stanfill and Deptula as lieutenant colonels were in awkward positions. They could not take charge of the full colonels who came from Tactical Air Command (TAC) and Strategic Air Command (SAC). Warden asked the three TAC colonels (Richard E. Bigelow, Richard D. Bristow and Douglas S. Hawkins) to help his deputy, Col. Emery M. Kiraly, develop plans for attacking Iraqi ground forces. Because the TAC commander,

---

[19] Brfg, Warden to Lt Gen Adams, HQ USAF/XO, Instant Thunder, 13 Aug 90, 1330, GWAPS, CHSH 5-17. Gen Schwarzkopf did not like the Schlieffen Plan analogy and told Warden not to use it. See (S) notes, Lt Col Bernard E. Harvey, Checkmate, 17 Aug 90, GWAPS, CHP 9-4.

[20] Stanfill, Harvey and Stimer all belonged to Warden's directorate; Deptula had worked there before joining the Secretary's support group.

Gen. Robert D. Russ, objected to any Air Staff role in campaign planning, his emissaries were viewed with suspicion by some Air Staff planners. TAC had already sent to General Horner in Riyadh the text of Warden's first briefing with TAC's proposed alternative. TAC planners envisioned a more gradual air campaign with much more emphasis on interdiction and close air support of ground force movement.[21] As for SAC, its participation in the Checkmate planning group was enthusiastic and substantial, ultimately with ten personnel under Col. Mike Mankin.[22]

General Powell had told the Air Staff to bring the other Services into the Checkmate planning group. The Navy sent a half dozen officers under Capt. William Switzer, and the Marines sent a similar group under Lieutenant Colonel Slade Brewer. In addition to briefing the Chief of Naval Operations and the Commandant of the Marine Corps, Colonel Warden also prepared a briefing for the Chairman to give the President. When Warden returned to Central Command in Florida with a draft plan on 17 August, the Instant Thunder briefing bore the logo of the Joint Chiefs of Staff, and he was accompanied by Major General James W. Meier (USAF) from the Joint Staff.[23]

---

[21] Msg, Brig Gen Griffith, HQ TAC, to Lt Gen Horner, subj: Air Campaign Briefing, 100145Z Aug 90, GWAPS CHP 13A. Horner also had a CENTAF officer in Checkmate.

[22] (S) Rpt, J. Parsons, HQ SAC/XPA, "Air Staff Desert Shield Planning," GWAPS, NA 27.

[23] (S) Rpt, Capt Johnson (USN), J-3/JOD, subj: CINCCENT Trip, 17 Aug 90, GWAPS, NA 203; (S) briefing slides, Checkmate to Chairman JCS, 14 Aug 90, for briefing to President, 15 Aug 90, GWAPS, CHSH 5-16.

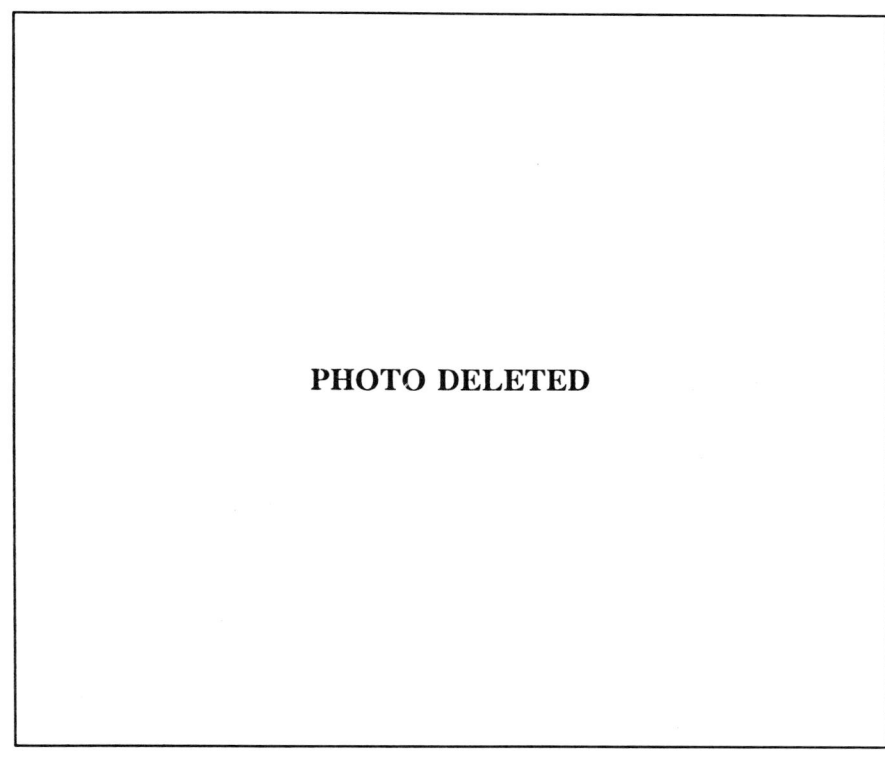

Air Force, Navy, and Marines representatives select and allocate targets for Instant Thunder at Checkmate in the Pentagon.

The foundation for Instant Thunder's target selection scheme was Colonel Warden's five rings theory. Planners divided the central leadership ring into two target categories: (1) the Saddam Hussein regime; (2) command and control and telecommunications. Considering the importance of the regime in Warden's thinking, this target category was slim indeed, with only five targets. [DELETED] By January the regime category alone would swell to more than thirty targets.[24]

Checkmate planners divided telecommunications targets between a command and control category of nineteen targets within the leadership ring and a strategic air defense category of ten targets (of which two were

---

[24] (TS/LIMDIS) Instant Thunder Campaign Plan, 17 Aug 90, Annex C, Operations, GWAPS, CHSH 9, p 15.

telecommunications sites not collocated with air defense control centers) within the fielded forces ring. The original telecommunications targets were radio and television sites. [DELETED][25]

From the outset, however, Iraq's electrical grid offered Warden planners an indirect way of getting at Iraqi telecommunications as well as industry and lighting. Colonel Warden believed that "putting out the lights" in Baghdad would have a psychological impact, and he thought that backup generators would quickly prove inadequate once the national grid had ceased to function. His electrical target category within the key production ring consisted of seven power plants and three transformer stations. Although more electrical targets would be added, the initial list may well have been sufficient to take down the grid. Planners hoped at least to reduce Baghdad's power supply by sixty percent and Iraq's as a whole by thirty-five percent. An interesting aspect of Warden's thinking on electrical targets was his desire to do as little long-term damage as possible by avoiding generators and bombing switching yards. Just as he wanted to avoid civilian casualties for his own reasons, Warden was not reacting to a cautious Bush administration in seeking to limit damage to electrical production. Rather, Warden's own strategy envisioned a prosperous postwar Iraq.[26]

Warden expected that the United States would help Iraq get back on its feet after the war, partly to underscore that the enemy had been the Iraqi regime rather than the Iraqi people, partly to build a prosperous Iraq which would neither attack its neighbors nor be attacked by them, and partly to get Iraq's oil flowing again to America's allies. His planners sought to reduce oil products available for Iraqi consumption by seventy percent. Oil targets totaled three refineries and three military fuel depots. Planners would eventually add more than a dozen oil targets to the list. Like the electrical targets, most of the key oil targets were obvious from the beginning.[27]

---

[25](TS/LIMDIS) *Ibid*, pp 13 and 16-17.

[26](TS/LIMDIS) *Ibid*, p 18; (S) brfg, Col Warden to Gen Schwarzkopf, "Iraqi Air Campaign Instant Thunder," 17 Aug 90, GWAPS, CHSH 7-11.

[27](TS/LIMDIS) Instant Thunder Campaign Plan, Annex C, p 19; 17 Aug 90 briefing.

Warden's views on oil and electricity were a variation on traditional targeting. He knew that World War II U.S. Army Air Forces plans to focus on electricity had not been executed and that the U.S. Strategic Bombing Survey had concluded that electricity should have been a focus. He also knew that in the debate between those who favored oil targets and those who favored railroads, a critical function of the railroads had turned out to be the transport of coal fundamental to German industry. In Iraq, oil was clearly fundamental, but was it a good target? The American experience bombing oil storage in North Vietnam had not been successful, because the North Vietnamese had been able to disperse their oil in barrels adequate to meet their relatively light needs. Similarly, North Vietnamese portable generators had sufficed in a country which had never used much electricity. For Warden, however, the Iraqi economy and military more closely resembled the Germany of 1940 than the North Vietnam of 1965.[28]

What was new about Warden's targeting of electricity and oil was his intention to avoid long-term damage. Not only did this reflect his certainty that the war would be short, but also his equal certainty that American bombing could be so accurate that parts of a facility could be bombed while purposely leaving specific parts unscathed. His confidence in the precision of American bombing would prove largely warranted, but his philosophy of bombing did not travel as far as he hoped. Wing operations and intelligence officers were accustomed to seeking maximum damage, and generator halls were the obvious electrical target. When left to choose their own aim points, they would choose generator halls.[29]

Warden expected that shutting down the electrical power grid would have a pervasive effect on military and civilian activities, but he did not consider specifically the impact on water pumping. Since his war would last little more than a week at most and the United States would quickly turn on the electricity again, the civilian water supply may not have caused him much concern even had he thought of it.

---

[28]See *U.S. Strategic Bombing Survey, Summary Report, European War* (Washington, 1945), pp 12-14. Warden's *Air Campaign* argues that "power and transportation are particularly critical: Interviews and studies after World War II indicated that power and transportation were the weakest points in German and Japanese war production"(p 43).

[29]See the GWAPS report on Effectiveness.

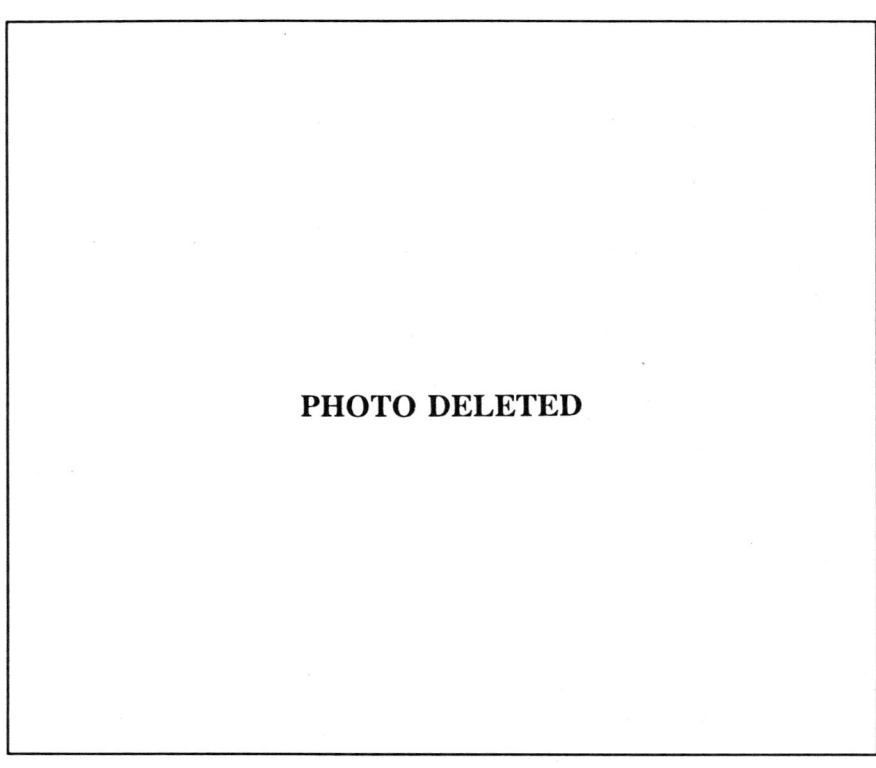

Ajaji Electrical Power Plant.

Within the key production ring, electricity and oil were Warden's war winners, but for the long-term stability of the Middle East, he knew that it was essential to destroy Iraq's capability to produce nuclear, biological and chemical weapons. No aspect of Checkmate intelligence was weaker than its knowledge of this target category. Since before Israel's F-16 raid on the nuclear research facility at Al Tuwaitha near Baghdad in 1981, that site had been well known. But the newer and more important facility at Al-Atheer only began to attract the attention of American intelligence near the end of the Gulf War. Although the major biological weapons center at Salman Pak was on Central Command's July 1990 target list, Warden's intelligence analysts did not acquire imagery for it during his initial search and it was not on the Checkmate list which went to Schwarzkopf. Indeed Checkmate did not become aware of a significant near-term biological threat for several weeks. As for nuclear weapons, the American intelligence community estimated that Iraq could produce a crude nuclear weapon by the end of 1992.[30]

In contrast to their fairly relaxed view about the immediacy of Iraq's nuclear and biological capabilities, Warden and his planners took the chemical threat more seriously. Iraq had used chemical artillery shells during the Iran-Iraq War. There was a possibility that Iraq's long range delivery systems, its Scud missiles and its aircraft, could attack Riyadh, Dhahran, or Israel with chemical warheads. An attack on Israel might provoke a retaliation which could threaten Arab loyalty to the coalition. Prospects for stopping such an attack were not bright. Checkmate targeted the Scud storage facility at Taji together with Tallil Airfield and chemical storage bunkers, but some Scud launchers were known to be mobile, and in the months to come more chemical bunkers would be discovered. There was a good possibility of eliminating the production of chemical weapons at Samarra and Habbaniya, but Warden had to admit that Checkmate could not solve the Scud problem.[31]

The remainder of Warden's key production ring and his infrastructure ring were treated rather perfunctorily by his plan. Instant Thunder listed fifteen military supply depots, factories, and repair shops, including the ammunition dumps north of Baghdad at Taji and Tikrit (Saddam's home town). Two ammunition dumps south of Baghdad near An Nasiriyah were also targeted, but ammunition storage sites closer to the new front in Kuwait were not yet identified. Since Warden's war was projected to last only a few days, Checkmate did not give much attention to interdiction, and the infrastructure ring contained only three targets: the Baghdad

---

[30] For the evolution of U.S. intelligence estimates of Iraqi nuclear capabilities, see the Joint Atomic Energy Intelligence Committee's (S/NF/RD) rpt 90-0094, Nov 90, GWAPS, CHSH 114-4. On Checkmate's later involvement in biological targets, see GWAPS, CHSH 100. Salman Pak was on Checkmate's 12 Aug 90 list (CHSH 18-18) of 90 targets but was subsequently cut. SECDEF: Final Report to Congress Conduct of the Persian Gulf War Apr, 1992, p 97

[31] 17 Aug 90 (TS/LIMDIS) brfg; Instant Thunder Campaign Plan, Annex C, p 14. The problem of locating mobile Scuds in time to attack them on the ground remained unsolved throughout the Gulf War.

rail yard, the Az Zubayr rail yard near Basra, and the As Samahwah railroad and highway bridge over the Euphrates between Baghdad and Basra.[32]

Colonel Warden took a keen interest in his population ring, but since he wished to minimize civilian casualties, no bombing targets were listed there. Nevertheless, destruction of targets in other rings was intended to produce psychological effects. [DELETED] This was the aspect of Instant Thunder which would receive the least attention in Desert Storm, when troops in Kuwait would be bombarded by leaflets but Baghdad would be more bombed than propagandized.[33]

Although fielded forces constituted Warden's outermost ring, their priority in his bombing scheme was not necessarily last. True, Warden largely ignored the big Iraqi army deployed in Kuwait and southern Iraq–for him those forces were most dangerous as a distraction from the principal business of bombing. Iraq's air defenses, on the other hand, and Iraq's ability to project air power provided targets at the top of Warden's list. On this priority no airman was apt to disagree. Nevertheless, in the light of later knowledge, Checkmate's list of air defense targets was far from complete. Iraq's air defense headquarters in Baghdad led the list, but Checkmate targeted only two of the four sector operations centers in Iraq. [DELETED]. Of the subordinate intercept operations centers, Checkmate targeted only three, all in the southern sector. In the months preceding Desert Storm, planners would learn much more about Iraq's air defense system, and the remaining operations centers would be targeted along with dozens of radar and surface-to-air (SAM) missile sites.[34]

Instant Thunder sought to suppress rather than destroy Iraqi SAMs and aircraft. SAM and early warning radars would be jammed and threatened by radar-seeking missiles. Iraqi runways would be cratered and mined. American aircraft would attack Iraqi aircraft on the ground and in the air, where they would be deprived of their accustomed control from operations centers on the ground. In these ways coalition aircraft would

---

[32] (TS/LIMDIS) Instant Thunder Campaign Plan, Annex C, p 20.

[33] (TS/LIMDIS) *Ibid*, Annex J; 17 Aug 90 (S/NF/WN/NC) brfg. See the GWAPS report on Effectiveness.

[34] (TS/LIMDIS) Instant Thunder Campaign Plan, Annex C, p 13. Iraq set up a fifth sector operations center in Kuwait.

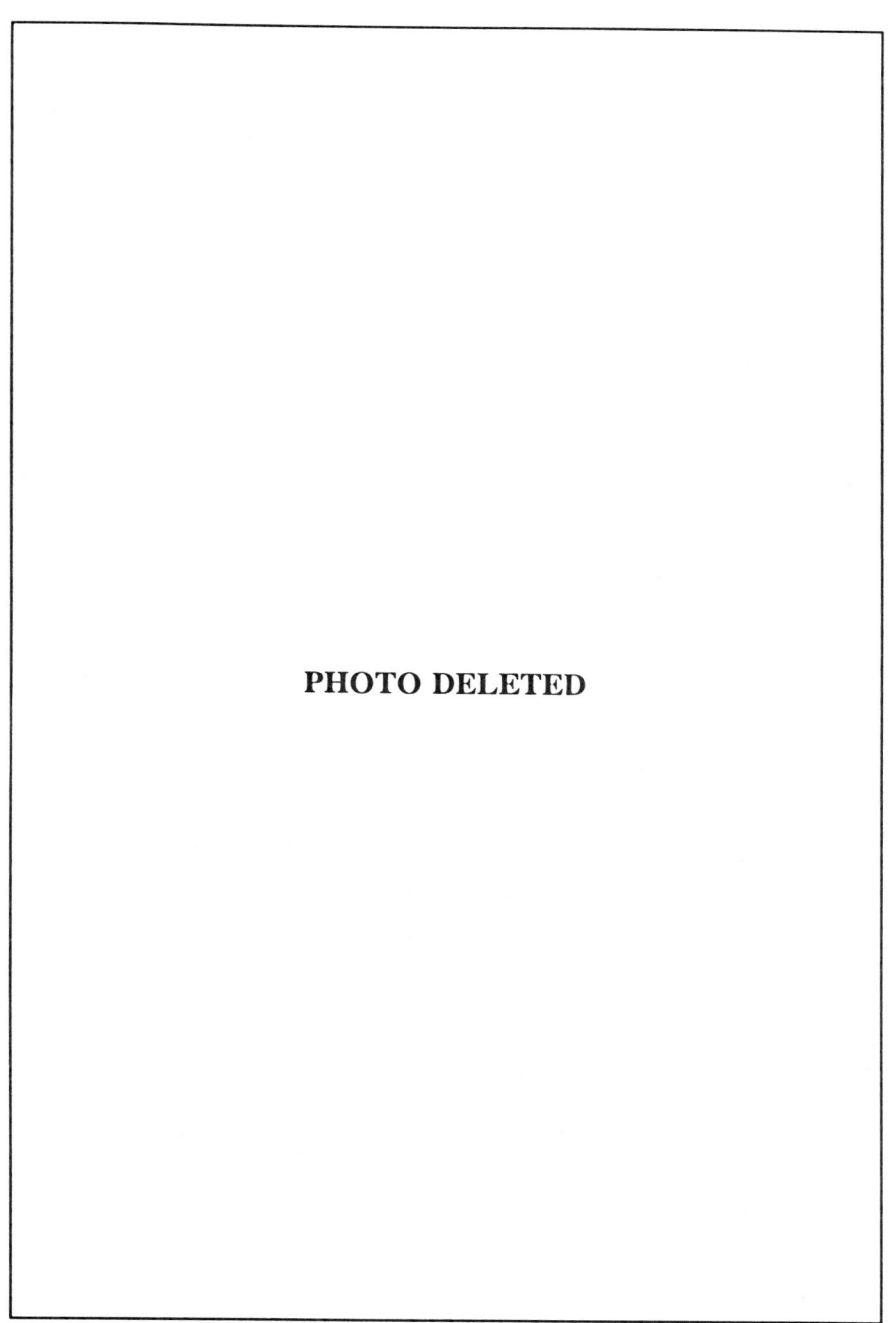

**Baghdad Air Defense Headquarters, Rashid Airfield.
Command bunkers and support facilities.**

gain quick control of the medium altitude airspace–safely above most anti-aircraft artillery. But Checkmate targeted only eight of Iraq's principal airfields, and Desert Storm's airfield target list would ultimately be ten times as long.[35]

As will be discussed in greater detail in Chapter Seven of this report, intelligence played a vital role in air campaign planning. The rudimentary state of intelligence on Iraq was a major problem. When the Air Force's director of targets, Col. James R. Blackburn, Jr., began to support Colonel Warden's effort on 8 August, he first obtained a computer listing of all known targets in Iraq from the Defense Intelligence Agency and a much shorter list from Central Command of 48 targets in which Central Air Forces was most interested. Blackburn brought a staff of thirteen targeteers to Checkmate, where they began to work with planners in selecting targets and desired mean points of impact.[36]

Blackburn's targeteers found that while they were supporting a planning effort authorized by General Schwarzkopf, Central Command was continuing to develop its own target list with priority for assistance from the Defense Intelligence Agency. Blackburn ameliorated the low priority of his effort by sending his people to visit Defense Intelligence Agency analysts in their offices. Imagery was taken from Air Force Intelligence Agency archives and reproduced; requesting the collection of new imagery at this point seemed out of the question. Through these ad hoc methods, Blackburn's team was able to come up with 84 targets which fit the planners' target categories and for which enough imagery was available to select impact points and pin-prick the photographs accordingly. During this week of work, Central Command prepared its own list of 109 targets, 76 of which were on the 84-target Checkmate list. On 16 August, Central Command authorized Checkmate to select impact points for all 109 targets, and for the first time Blackburn had sufficient priority to task the Defense Intelligence Agency for assistance. By 23 August, the pin-pricked photographs were in St. Louis at the Defense Mapping Agency, which converted the pin pricks into exactly mensurated coordinates for each desired mean point of impact.[37]

---

[35](TS/LIMDIS) *Ibid*, p 21.

[36](S/NF) Memo, Col James R. Blackburn Jr, Dir of Targets, HQ USAF, subj: USAF/INT Targeting/MC&G Support to Desert Shield, 17 Oct 90, GWAPS, NA 269.

[37](S/NF) *Ibid*.

While coping with intelligence problems, Warden's planners tried to use computer analysis to fine tune their plan. As they developed Instant Thunder, they fed aircraft data into their Theater Warfare Model together with Colonel Warden's estimate of the importance of each target category and subcategory.[38] Computer runs helped planners to estimate munitions requirements: for [DELETED] laser-guided bombs; Tomahawk sea-launched cruise missiles; air-launched cruise missiles; Maverick television-guided missiles; anti-radar missiles; cluster bombs; unguided high-explosive bombs. [DELETED]. If Instant Thunder had been flown as modeled, it would have achieved an intensity comparable to actual Desert Storm operations flown in January 1991, despite the fact that Desert Storm would use twice as many aircraft. Instant Thunder's intensity was to be attained by sending attack aircraft on two sorties per day, twice the rate of Desert Storm.[39]

Checkmate planners believed that the timing and sequence of strikes could have a major impact on the success of an air campaign. Their campaign would attempt initial strikes on all major targets within the first two days–beginning at night by attacking Iraq's air defenses. To get the maximum number of strike sorties on the first night, they wanted to send a wave soon after dusk and return many of the same aircraft on a second wave just before dawn. Subsequently there would be one wave each morning, afternoon, and night. Colonel Deptula introduced a strike sortie flow list, a planning device which would be renamed "master attack plan." Targets for each wave were listed in the sequence they would be struck and the type and number of aircraft to attack each target was specified. For example, the initial F-117 strikes on opening night were then planned against the air defense sector operations centers. Eight F-117s were scheduled against each target. The sortie flow list broke the attack on each sector operations center into two cells of four F-117s each. [DELETED] Before turning the flow list into an air tasking order,

---

[38] The Theater Warfare Model and the computer analysts who ran it had been in Checkmate only a few months when the Gulf crisis broke. The model had not been designed to support campaign planning but to support the budget process through the old mission area analysis division, which Warden had recently merged with Checkmate.

[39] (TS/LIMDIS) Instant Thunder Campaign Plan, Annex D, pp 3-4; intvw, Wayne Thompson, GWAPS, with Joseph T. McNeer, Synergy Inc, 23 Jan 92; (S) intvw, Thompson with Maj Roy "Mack" Sikes, HQ USAF/XOXWF, 7 May 92. See also Col Warden's (S) estimates of target category importance, 8 and 11 Aug 90; Theater Warfare Model printouts, 11-13 Aug 90; both in GWAPS Historical Advisor's Files.

planners would have to add a time on target for each strike. A flow list permitted planners to grasp quickly when each strike was supposed to occur in the context of other strikes.[40]

Checkmate held meetings of pilots with expertise in the available aircraft types to determine which aircraft should attack each target. Navy and Marine pilots attended these meetings. Although Checkmate planners hoped for coalition participation, they could only assign American aircraft to targets at this point. The resulting flow list for the first two days would be changed again and again in the coming months as available forces and knowledge of targets and air defenses increased.[41]

At the Checkmate meetings, Navy representatives were confident that A-6s and F-18s could attack Baghdad targets. Similarly, Air Force pilots thought that F-15Es, F-111s, and F-16s could go downtown. Consequently, F-117s and cruise missiles did not have the exclusive role in Baghdad strikes they would later assume when Central Air Forces decided not to risk their more vulnerable aircraft in the highest threat areas. Instant Thunder scheduled as many as eight F-117s to attack a single target like the Tallil sector operations center. Not only would the number of F-117s available increase, but most targets would be assigned a single F-117 and consequently F-117s could hit a high percentage of the well-defended targets.[42]

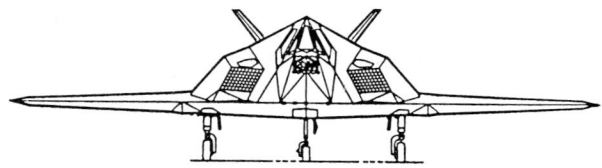

---

[40](TS/LIMDIS) Instant Thunder Campaign Plan, Annex C, p 39.

[41](S) Notes, Wayne Thompson, Checkmate historian, Final Attack Flow Meeting, 16 Aug 90, 1130, GWAPS Historical Advisor's Files.

[42]Lt Col Deptula began to put each F-117 on a different target in late Aug 90. (S) Intvw, Wayne Thompson, GWAPS, with Deptula, Pentagon, 26 Aug 91.

PHOTO DELETED

Above, Navy pilots participate in target planning in Checkmate for Instant Thunder. Below, Marine pilots participate in target planning in Checkmate.

PHOTO DELETED

Planners envisioned that cruise missiles would play a prominent role. [DELETED]. The Air Force's air-launched cruise missiles were scheduled to join the first night's attack. The very existence of these air-launched conventional cruise missiles was so closely held that Checkmate planners used the term "LRB" (for "long range bomb") in planning documents so that their security classification could be held to a reasonable level. [DELETED][43]

When Colonel Warden delivered the Instant Thunder plan to General Schwarzkopf in Florida on 17 August, the plan ran to about 200 pages with more than a dozen annexes. Warden believed that this effort had given Central Command a two-week head start on a plan that might have to be executed in less than two weeks. But execution was in fact five months away, and Checkmate's role in planning an air campaign would continue throughout those months and beyond. That role would necessarily change from leading to supporting the offensive air planning effort. Schwarzkopf told Warden to take his plan to Saudi Arabia where General Horner had already been given a preliminary overview of the concept. Horner was less than delighted with Air Staff involvement, and he sent Warden back to Washington. But Horner kept three of Warden's planners (Deptula, Harvey, and Stanfill) and inadvertently created a context for the evolution of Warden's remaining planners in Washington as a support office for Horner's planners in Riyadh.[44]

---

[43](TS/LIMDIS) Instant Thunder Campaign Plan, Annex C, pp 39-45.

[44](S) Intvw, GWAPS with Lt Gen Horner, 9 Mar 92; (S) Harvey notes, Warden's briefing of Horner, 20 Aug 90, GWAPS, CHP 9-4; (S) transcript, Lt Gen Horner's taped responses to written questions of CMSgt John Burton, CENTAF historian, Mar 91, GWAPS, CHP 13A; (S) Thompson notes, Warden's debriefing to Checkmate staff on trip to Saudi Arabia, 22 Aug 90, 0815, GWAPS Historical Advisor's Files. See also GWAPS rpt on command and control.

Checkmate planners present Instant Thunder plan to LtGen Horner in Riyadh. L to R: LtCol Bernard E. Harvey; Col John A. Warden III; LtCol David A. Deptula; LtCol Ronnie A. Stanfill.

The Instant Thunder plan that General Horner received on 20 August used new technologies to refurbish ideas about strategic bombing that could be traced at least to the Army Air Forces in World War II. These technologies permitted a much different air campaign than any which had ever been waged. The old American preference to strike at urban targets without destroying the surrounding neighborhoods could now be implemented. But did Americans or their allies know enough about Iraq to pick the right targets? General Horner's coolness to Instant Thunder was a reaction not only to its source but also to its disregard for what he considered the most important target, the Iraqi army which threatened to move into Saudi Arabia. If Instant Thunder triggered such an invasion, would there be enough air power to stop it by bombing either those forces or their supply lines or Baghdad? Horner could not build up much enthusiasm for an offensive air campaign until a large coalition ground force lay between him and the Iraqi army.[45]

Since General Horner's arrival in Saudi Arabia (he had been a member of Secretary Cheney's party in early August and had remained as the Acting CENTCOM commander until General Schwarzkopf arrived in late August), all planning had been defensive. Since the outbreak of the crisis, General Schwarzkopf and his CENTCOM planners understood their mission as being to deploy forces to the Arabian Peninsula and to undertake actions with host nation forces to deter and, if necessary, counter Iraqi attacks on the Arabian Peninsula to protect key oil facilities and maintain U.S. and allied access to the region's vital resources—oil.[46] To accomplish this, he now anticipated deployments of U.S. forces in numbers smaller than outlined in the draft version of OPLAN 1002-90, probably due to concerns about getting enough credible combat force to Saudi Arabia to deter further Iraqi moves southward. Since he lacked completed, coordinated deployment plans for the forces specified in OPLAN 1002, [DELETED] he began to select forces that were combat ready and could be moved with a minimum of delay.

In the days immediately following the start of the crisis, CENTCOM planners anticipated an initial deployment of eleven tactical fighter squadrons,[47] one B-52 squadron, along with two carrier battle groups, the 82d Airborne Division, a Marine Expeditionary Brigade, one Ranger Regiment, and a Special Forces Group. A scheduled second major deployment would begin three and four weeks later and include five fighter squadrons [DELETED], a third and fourth carrier group, and the *Missouri* and *Wisconsin* battleship groups. The initial ground forces would likewise be bolstered by an Army aviation brigade, the 101st Air Assault Division, a mechanized infantry brigade, and two more Marine expeditionary brigades. From the end of this phase until week 17, the last deployments mentioned, Central Command planners called for a second B-52 squadron, a fifth carrier battle group, and another mechanized infantry division and armor brigade. While these figures differed from

---

[45](S) *Ibid.*

[46](S) Brfg, "USCENTCOM Preliminary Planning. 2-6 Aug 90," GWAPS NA-117.

[47](S) Aircraft arriving in theater by C+11 (listed in order of first arrival) included F-15, AWACS, RC-135, KC-135, C-130, F-16, F-15E, F-4E, EF-111, EC-130, F-111, F-117, and B-52. (Brfg (S), "USCENTCOM Preliminary Planning, 2-6 August 1990.")

those eventually deployed (see comparison of air assets in Chapter 2, Table 9), they provide an insight into Schwarzkopf's thinking at the beginning of the crisis when his priorities were to get forces into theater, protect these troops from a numerically superior enemy, and defend vital ports and installations in Saudi Arabia.

Lacking early strategic warning, and as a result, nearly a month's time for an orderly and balanced deployment of forces, General Schwarzkopf was first concerned about getting a sizable number of air superiority and ground attack aircraft into the theater. Once these "shooters" were on hand, he could concentrate on deploying enough ground forces to Saudi Arabia to deter Baghdad from moving south. If this failed, or if Iraq decided to move during the early phases of ground troop deployment, Schwarzkopf had to rely on his air power to both reduce and delay the enemy while simultaneously providing air cover for American ground forces. Although this concept of air operations was never called a defensive air campaign plan, in fact it was just that and provided the foundation upon which defensive planning for Operation Desert Shield would be based.

As shown in the following table, after two weeks of deployment Schwarzkopf anticipated having an airborne division at his disposal, in addition to a dozen fighter squadrons supplemented with a B-52 squadron and two carrier battle groups patrolling the skies and poised to blunt any Iraqi move into the Saudi Kingdom.[48] [DELETED]. By the end of the first month, however, the deployed combat forces Schwarzkopf envisioned during his preliminary planning in August exceeded those in the pre-crisis operations plan.

---

[48](S) Brfg, USCENTCOM "Preliminary Planning," 2-6 Aug 90.

Table 17
Force Requirements and Deployment Schedule
U.S. Central Command Preliminary Planning

	Week 1		Week 2		Weeks 3-4	Weeks 5-17
USAF	2 F-15 Sqn	C+1	1 F-111 Sqn	C+11	5 TFS	1 B-52 Sqn
	5 AWACS	C+1	1 F-117 Sqn	C+11		
	3 RC-135	C+1	2 F-16 Sqn	C+11		
	12 KC-135	C+1	1 B-52 Sqn	C+11		
	48 C-130	C+1				
	3 F-16 Sqn	C+3				
	1 F-15 Sqn	C+3				
	1 F-15E Sqn	C+3				
	1 F-4E Sqn	C+3				
	1 EF-111 Sqn	C+3				
	1 EC-130 Sqn	C+3				
	15 KC-135	C+3				
U.S. Army	1 Airborne Bde		2 Airborne Bde		1 Mech Infantry Bde 1 Air Assault Div 1 Aviation Bde	1 Armor Bde 1 Mech Div
USN/USMC	2 Carrier Battle Groups		1 Marine Expeditionary Bde		2 Carrier Battle Groups 2 Battleship Battle Grp 2 Marine Exped Bde	1 Carrier Battle Group 1 Regimental Landing Team
SOF			1 Special Forces Grp 1 Ranger Regt			

Source: (S) Brfg, USCENTCOM "Preliminary Planning," 2-6 August 1990.

Schwarzkopf's early planning assumptions showed the difference between writing a deployment plan, where weak or unfounded assumptions had been used to make the contingency effective, and implementing an actual combat deployment against a real and potentially powerful foe. The long-planned scenario of deploying credible deterrent forces to Saudi Arabia prior to Iraqi military actions disappeared on the morning of 2 August when Baghdad attacked Kuwait. Instead of basing time-phased deployment on early warning and presidential authority to commence operations before hostilities, Central Command's preliminary planning used assumptions based on the facts at the time, i.e., current, real political and military constraints, and Iraqi armed forces within striking distance.

Table 18
USCINCCENT Preliminary Planning Assumptions

International	Domestic	Military
	[DELETED]	

Source: (S) Brfg, USCENTCOM, "Preliminary Planning," 2-6 August 1990.

CENTCOM planners facing other problems identified through proposed target sets had already begun to affect early plans for a war with Iraq. In addition to thirteen economic and ten military command, control, and communication and air defense targets identified in precrisis exercises, a new "political" category appeared on a proposed CENTCOM targets list. Heretofore unmentioned in contingency planning, the political category (incorporated by CENTCOM planners after discussions with the Air Staff Checkmate office on the Instant Thunder plan) included the presidential palace in Baghdad. It appears clear that traditional military, economic, and infrastructure targets would be supplemented with others, whose purpose would be to weaken the Iraqi leadership by destroying visible symbols of Saddam's power and invulnerability.[49]

---

[49](S) *Ibid*; (S) Lt Col Fischer, HQ USCENTCOM, CAC, faxed these slides to Lt Col Guilette, USCENTAF, Battle Staff, on 4 Aug 90.

An essential element in planning for the Gulf War was integrating Saudi forces and support efforts into the U.S.-developed plans. On 14 August, just eight days after King Fahd requested U.S. military assistance, Central Command took a significant step to increase planning coordination with the Saudis with the formation of the U.S./Saudi Joint Directorate of Planning (JDOP) at the Saudi Ministry of Defense headquarters in Riyadh. The organization, first discussed by the CENTCOM J-5 and the Saudi J-3 on 8 August, was chartered by U.S. and Saudi military leaders to help develop combined operation plans and consisted of the CENTCOM J-3, J-5, several Saudi general officers, and a working group of U.S. and Saudi field grade planners (Saudi J-3/5). The group set up operations in a large, common office area and shared two conference rooms. This proximity proved vital in promoting interaction and cooperation among the planners and, despite initial problems with language and Saudi attitudes toward staff work, enhanced overall theater combined planning.[50]

Their first *combined* plan, OPORD 003, directed the deployment and possible employment of U.S. forces to defend Saudi Arabia. Published on 20 August 1990 as an interim combined defense plan, OPORD 003–built on USCINCCENT OPORD 001[51] (published 10 August)–was updated periodically and was intended to help American commanders understand Saudi capabilities, intentions, tasks, authorized liaison, and coordination with coalition forces to establish an integrated defense. In the order, planners assigned CENTCOM forces the mission to act in concert with Saudi and coalition regional forces in defense of Saudi Arabia and to be prepared to conduct other operations as required. The concept of operations outlined by the joint planners was to delay and reduce attacking forces as far forward as possible. U.S. forces shielded Jubayl and Ad Dammam/Dhahran to protect deploying U.S. forces at major airfields and sea ports of debarkation. In the event of an Iraqi attack, General Horner, as joint forces air commander, would coordinate an interdiction campaign

---

[50](S/NF) Doc, USCENTCOM *Desert Shield/Desert Storm, Internal Look 90 After Action Reports*, 15 July 1991; (S/NF) Doc USCENTCOM *J5 Plans After Action Report*, pp 5-6, GWAPS NA-259; (S/NF) Rpt, Rear Adm (Ret) Grant Sharp, "Sharp Study" *Planning for the Gulf War*, Draft of 3 Dec 91, prepared for Office of Principal Deputy, Under Secretary of Defense (S&R), p 26, GWAPS Task Force V files.

[51](S) Msg, USCINCCENT OPORD 001, 101100Z Aug 90.

to gain air superiority, delay and interdict enemy forces, and isolate the battlefield.[52]

Although the plan's distribution was limited to U.S. commands, it was developed by the joint planning group and contained Saudi input. Combined OPORD 004[53] (based on OPORD 003 and published 17 September) continued its predecessor's objectives and intent and became the basis for the final defensive plan published by the Joint Directorate of Planning, *Combined OPLAN for Defense of Saudi Arabia*, on November 29, 1990. [DELETED].[54]

Signed by Rear Adm. Grant Sharp, USN, and Maj. Gen. Yousef Mohammed Al Madan, representing Central Command and the Saudi Ministry of Defense and Aviation respectively, the *Combined OPLAN for Defense of Saudi Arabia* dealt mainly with administrative command and control procedures that provided valuable coordination and employment information during the period before the arrival of additional U.S. forces and subsequent redeployment in anticipation of offensive operations. Joint Directorate planners retained the broad scope and generally defensive guidance from previous plans in their *Combined OPLAN*, and relied heavily on forward defense using ground and air interdiction to slow an enemy advance.[55] [DELETED]

---

[52]There was also a USCINCCENT OPORD 002 for maritime interdiction. (OPORD (S), USCINCCENT Desert Shield OPORD 002, Defense of Saudi Arabia, GWAPS IRIS 23993, frames 616-653); Information on Combined OPORD 003 contained in (S) Msg, USCINCCENT OPORD 003, Desert Shield Operations, 201230Z Aug 90, GWAPS IRIS 10261, frames 1075-1140.

[53](S) Msg, USCINCCENT OPORD 004 for Operation Desert Shield, 171345Z Sep 90, GWAPS IRIS 23981, frames 106-147.

[54](S/NF) Rpt Rear Adm (Ret) Grant Sharp, "Sharp Study" *Planning for the Gulf War*, Draft of 3 Dec 91, prepared for Office of Principal Deputy, Under Secretary of Defense (S&R), p 17. GWAPS holdings; (S/NF) Doc, USCENTCOM *Desert Shield/Desert Storm, Internal Look 90 After Action Reports*, 15 Jul 91.

[55](S) OPLAN HQ US Central Command and Joint Forces and Theater of Operations, *Combined OPLAN for Defense of Saudi Arabia*, 29 Nov 90, GWAPS CHC 18-4 and IRIS 10261 frame 1181.

In a major deviation from normal procedure, CINCCENT waived the normal requirement for subordinate commands to submit supporting plans for the *Combined* OPLAN of 29 November. [DELETED].[56] [DELETED].[57]

[DELETED]. Instead, they focused on defending and repelling Iraqi forces from the Kingdom of Saudi Arabia. To accomplish this, planners relied on traditional forward defense doctrine that traded time for space while allied ground, air, and naval forces reduced advancing Iraqi forces through a series of defensive meeting engagements and air interdiction attacks without becoming decisively engaged. [DELETED]. The role of U.S. and allied air forces envisioned in the OPLAN likewise followed traditional doctrine to:

> ... support the land campaign. [DELETED] Air forces provide counterair, interdiction, and close air support to land forces throughout the area of operation.[58]

Although the U.S./Saudi Joint Directorate of Planning got off to a good start—early on briefing Saudi planners on OPLAN 1002-90—the special group soon was overwhelmed trying to deal with wartime coordination. While the Joint Planning Group remained active throughout the operation and produced a total of four combined operation plans,[59] the primary focus for its members became a forum to identify and resolve coalition problems, to institutionalize a plan development process for the Saudis and, perhaps most importantly, to provide a conduit for rapid access to Saudi policy makers. Planning for Operation Desert Shield and Desert

---

[56](S) *Ibid.*

[57](S) OPLAN originally TS/NF/SPECAT, USCINCCENT, *U.S. OPLAN Desert Storm*, 16 Dec 90, p 6, GWAPS, CHC 18-2.

[58](S) OPLAN, HQ US Central Command and Joint Forces and Theater of Operations, *Combined OPLAN for Defense of Saudi Arabia*, 29 Nov 90, p 6, GWAPS CHC 18-4 and IRIS 0268606.

[59]The four major plans were: 1. (S) Combined OPLAN for Defense of Saudi Arabia, 29 Nov 1990 (GWAPS IRIS 10261 frame 1181 and CHC-18-4); 2. (S) Combined OPLAN for Defense and Restoration of Kuwait, 13 Jan 1991 (GWAPS IRIS 10261 frame 1438 and CHC-18-5); 3. (S) Combined OPLAN to Eject Iraqi Forces from Kuwait, 17 Jan 1991 (GWAPS IRIS 10261 frame 1615); and 4. (S) Combined OPLAN for Defense of Kuwait and Saudi Arabia, 22 Feb 1991 (GWAPS IRIS 23981 frame 208 and CHC-18-3).

Storm remained with CENTCOM planners supported by the Air Staff's Checkmate special planning office in Washington.⁶⁰

CENTAF planners, who only ten days before had been involved in wargaming at Internal Look in Florida, also were preparing for battle in Riyadh with the knowledge that at that time the United States lacked sufficient forces in theater to stop an anticipated Iraqi armored attack on Saudi Arabia. They knew that the threat was real, that enemy intent was vague, and that their first priority was defense. To accomplish this, they first had to deal with two major problems encountered during the early phases of Operation Desert Shield–bedding down arriving aircraft and integrating and coordinating this infant force with arriving ground troop units and with host nation air forces.⁶¹ Although the GWAPS Logistics report deals with these problems in much greater depth, these two areas are directly related to CINCCENT OPLAN 1002-90 or, more precisely, to their lack of detailed precrisis planning.

This does not imply that the writers of OPLAN 1002 were negligent in identifying either the importance or the difficulty involved in these related issues, but only that the plan was immature and incomplete. In addition, there was not a great deal of history in dealing with this problem for the Arabian Peninsula. Previous contingency plans identified air-related deployment difficulties but, due to sensitivities about American presence in the region and a lack of diplomatic agreements between Washington and regional governments, the plan provided little more than outlines for basing American air power. [DELETED].⁶² Fortunately, despite a small number of miscues between American planners and local sheiks–such as when a 4th TFW flight of twenty-two F-15Es was denied landing rights at Seeb, Oman on 8 August 1990, and had to be diverted in-flight to Thumrait, Oman–events tended to follow this wishful scenario

---

⁶⁰(S/NF) Doc, USCENTCOM *Desert Shield/Desert Storm, Internal Look 90 After Action Reports*, 15 July 1991; (S/NF) Doc USCENTCOM *J5 Plans After Action Report*, pp 5-6.

⁶¹(S/NF) Intvw, Dr Perry Jamison and Mr Rick Davis from AFHO and Dr Barry Barlow, CENTAF/HO with Lt Gen Charles Horner, COMCENTAF/9th AF, 4 Mar 92. Tapes at AFCHO.

⁶²(S/NF) Ltr, Maj Gen R. B. Johnston, USMC, CENTCOM Chief of Staff, to USCINCLANT et al., subj: Review of USCINCCENT OPLAN 1002-90 (Second Draft), 13 Jul 90, cited in (S/NF) Study, William Y'Blood, Center for Air Force History, *The Eagle and The Scorpion*, Washington DC, 1992, p 23.

in the fall of 1990.⁶³ Top commanders firmly placed blame for initial deployment problems on the draft and incomplete OPLAN which Schwarzkopf was forced to execute. [DELETED]. The beddown problem was not addressed at Internal Look, but should have been.⁶⁴

Between 8 and 18 August, CENTAF operation and intelligence officers developed two defensive plans. In the first, known as both the "D-Day Plan" or "ATO Bravo," they countered the possibility of a large-scale Iraqi attack on Saudi Arabia with an integrated, two-day Air Force and naval air campaign against enemy forces in Kuwait and Iraq, and a transition to full-scale American offensive operations. To meet General Schwarzkopf's stated objectives–that remained basically unchanged since the July version of OPLAN 1002-90⁶⁵–CENTAF planners developed an air concept of operation that relied heavily on planning at Internal Look in July and included a detailed air tasking order for the first day and rough planning for the second. Planners intended the two-phase D-Day Plan to disrupt and reduce an Iraqi ground thrust as quickly as possible and thus allow arriving U.S. ground forces time to deploy to defensive positions under friendly air cover.

In the plan's first stage, planners envisioned concentrating counterair, interdiction, and close air support on a series of "kill boxes" placed astride probable Iraqi avenues of approaches. In the event of an Iraqi attack, they saw U.S. E-3 AWACS directing Air Force and Navy aircraft⁶⁶ against enemy ground formations as they entered these designated, although arbitrarily placed, kill boxes.⁶⁷ To ensure 24-hour coverage,

---

⁶³(S/NF) Chronology "Desert Shield Contingency Historical Chronology," USCENTAF 02 Aug - 17 Nov 90. AFHRA in Vol XIX of 9th AF 1990 Command History, p 1.

⁶⁴(S/NF) Intvw, TSgt Turner, CENTAF/HO with Maj Gen Thomas R. Olsen, 30 Sep 90. GWAPS and AFHRA, 23978, frames 6-174.

⁶⁵[DELETED] ((S/NF) Document, *Draft OPLAN 1002-90*, USCENTCOM, 18 Jul 90, p C-15-2, GWAPS NA-41.)

⁶⁶(S/NF) Brfg, Cmdr D. W. McSwain, USN. "Riyadh Perspective," 27 Aug 91. GWAPS NA-254.

⁶⁷The ATO Bravo kill boxes differed significantly from those used later during Desert Storm. Unlike the Desert Storm areas that covered the entire KTO, ATO Bravo planners drew arbitrary boxes only along Iraqi lines of supply and suspected routes of advance (primarily roads) through Kuwait and into Saudi Arabia. As such, there were many fewer than used for Desert Storm. (Glock intvw)

planners developed separate tasking orders and alert packages for day or night initiation to attack command, control, and communication targets in Iraq as well as the Iraqi Corps headquarters. The difference in the two alert packages involved calling for more capable night attack precision-guided munition-capable aircraft (F-111F and A-6E) to be used in darkness instead of F-16s and F/A-18s specified for daytime retaliation.

After these initial air attacks, CENTAF planners wanted to transition to limited counterattacks in phase II with constant close air support and attacks on other targets taken from their Iraqi Target Study, supplemented with targets identified since they arrived in the theater. The CENTAF targets included southern airfields, air defense sites, ammunition storage areas, troop concentrations and critical command, control, and communication nodes in the south. As the situation stabilized and the United States established air superiority, additional command, control and communication targets, electrical power production facilities, refineries, the petroleum distribution system, and the nuclear facility on the June CENTAF Target Study moved up the priority target list.[68]

(S) On August 14, General Horner accepted the D-Day Plan that lacked only designated fire support coordination lines from Army Forces Central Command (ARCENT). By that time–thanks to newly arrived strike aircraft that included twenty-two F-15E, forty-six F-15C, forty-four F-16, and fourteen B-52Gs, with an additional seventy-two A-10, eighteen F-117A, twenty-four F-4G, and six B-52G due within the week–the CENTAF targeting cell was able to apportion most of its effort for offensive counterair operations with the remaining designated for battlefield and limited deep interdiction.[69] As with nearly all airpower planning, early emphasis on obtaining air superiority was the first step toward freedom of mobility and action, especially against a ground-based enemy.

---

[68](S/NF) Study, William Y'Blood, Center for Air Force History, *The Eagle and The Scorpion*, Washington DC, 1992, p 78; also Olsen and Glock interviews.

[69](S/NF) *Ibid.*

Figure 8
D-Day Plan (ATO-Bravo) Proposed Targets

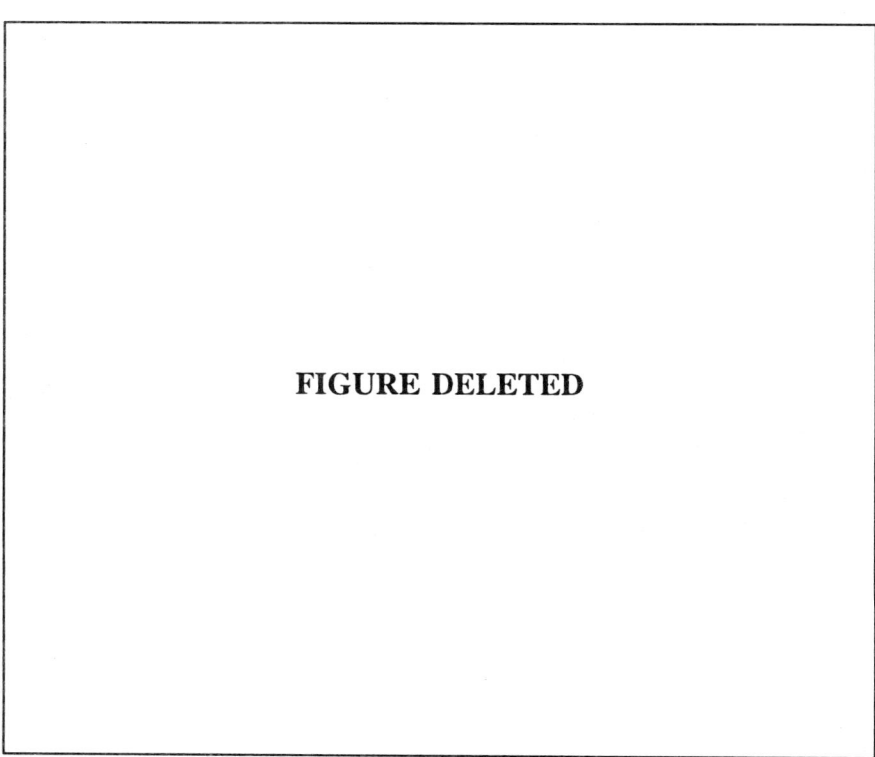

Following the execution of the D-Day Plan, CENTAF planners intended to revert to a normal air tasking order cycle using the full range of non-alert U.S. and coalition aircraft. By the end of August, CENTAF planners expanded the D-Day plan to include known Scud targets in western Iraq as well as other new targets. Once initiated, and after the hand-off to the full tasking order, they anticipated that the combination of the D-Day Plan with the transition to full offensive air operations would destroy significant

Iraqi armor, artillery, and ground forces.[70] Unlike most tasking orders produced to meet a specific requirement and then be superseded, the D-Day Plan evolved continuously, changing to reflect new aircraft (and capabilities) as they arrived in theater and incorporating new targets as they were identified by the intelligence community. Most, if not all, of the targets identified in the D-Day plan eventually found their way into offensive tasking for Operation Desert Storm.[71]

Even when it became obvious to senior U.S. commanders in late September that Baghdad was not going to attack Saudi Arabia,[72] the D-Day plan retained its importance. Unlike other special, security-classified offensive plans being developed in the Black Hole and known only to a few planners and commanders, the D-Day plan retained its less restrictive collateral classification and was widely distributed to U.S. and coalition planners. Thus, although it was never implemented, the D-Day plan focused planning efforts on retaliatory and air-to-ground strikes, as well as allied attacks on a limited number of strategic targets included in its transition to the full-scale offensive campaign. By doing this, it demonstrated the intent for coalition air forces to eventually conduct offensive operations against Iraqi forces in both Kuwait and Iraq while serving as a facade for, and effectively masking the full scope of offensive operations being planned in the still highly compartmented Desert Storm plan.[73]

The second defensive plan produced by CENTAF targeteers was known as the "Punishment ATO (Air Tasking Order)." The purpose of this plan was a single retaliatory response to a preemptive Iraqi chemical Scud attack on U.S. or allied forces. Unlike the D-Day plan, the Punishment ATO did not include provisions for transitioning to large-scale, continuous

---

[70](S) Brfg, Cmdr Purser, NAVCENT-Riyadh, "Follow-On D-Day 'ATO BRAVO'." 21 Nov 90. GWAPS CHC-14; (S/NF) Fact Sheet, Heidrick, "9 TIS/INT Planning Procedures," p 5, GWAPS NA-267; (S/NF) Brfg, Cmdr D. W. McSwain, USN. "Riyadh Perspective," 27 Aug 91, GWAPS NA-302.

[71](S/NF) Fact Sheet, Heidrick, "9 TIS/INT Planning Procedures," p 4.

[72]Evidence obtained from interviews between GWAPS personnel and Generals Horner and Glosson, and Commander C. W. McSwain, USN, strongly suggest that after mid-September 1990, neither Gen Schwarzkopf, Horner nor Glosson expected a preemptive Iraqi attack against US and allied forces in Saudi Arabia. ((S/NF) Intvw, Dr Alexander Cochran, GWAPS, with Lt Gen Horner, Brig Gen Glosson, and Cmdr McSwain, GWAPS Task Force V Cochran files.)

[73](S/NF) Fact Sheet, Heidrick, "9 TIS/INT Planning Procedures," p 5.

offensive operations. Work on the Punishment ATO began on the evening of 8 August after General Horner directed General Olsen to develop a list of strategic targets in Iraq. Produced in only 48-hours under the tutelage of Col. James Crigger, then CENTAF Forward DCS/Operations, the short-fuzed plan contained a tasking order for retaliatory strikes against seventeen installations specifically chosen to punish Baghdad and hinder its war-making capability. Like the D-Day plan, CENTAF planners relied heavily on work done for General Horner's April discussions with General Schwarzkopf.[74]

If implemented, the Punishment ATO would have directed U.S. aircraft to hit political, petroleum, and power grid targets that included the known nuclear and biological facilities, the Presidential Palace. [DELETED]. One of the major problems faced by Horner's planners in developing this response was the lack of complete targeting packages on the seventeen potential targets.[75] Despite these problems, Punishment ATO provided CINCCENT a strong retaliatory strike without depleting his overall capability to adequately defend U.S. forces in Saudi Arabia. Unlike the D-Day plan that received continuous attention and revision, work on the Punishment ATO stopped in mid-August and, by mid-September, the one-shot retaliatory plan quickly lost its relative importance as planners shifted from defensive to offensive operations.[76]

---

[74]Rosmer, *9th AF History*; (S) Intvw, AFCHO with Lt Gen Charles Horner, 28 Jan 91, p 2.

[75](S/NF/WN) Target study. 9 TIS, "Iraqi Target Study," GWAPS NA-168.; Rosmer, *Ninth Air Force/USCENTAF In Desert Shield: The Initial Phase*, p 63.; (S) Olsen intvw.

[76](S/NF) Intvw, Dr Alexander Cochran, GWAPS, with Lt Gen Horner, Brig Gen Glosson, and Cmdr McSwain, GWAPS Task Force V Cochran files.

Figure 9
Punishment ATO Attack Plan

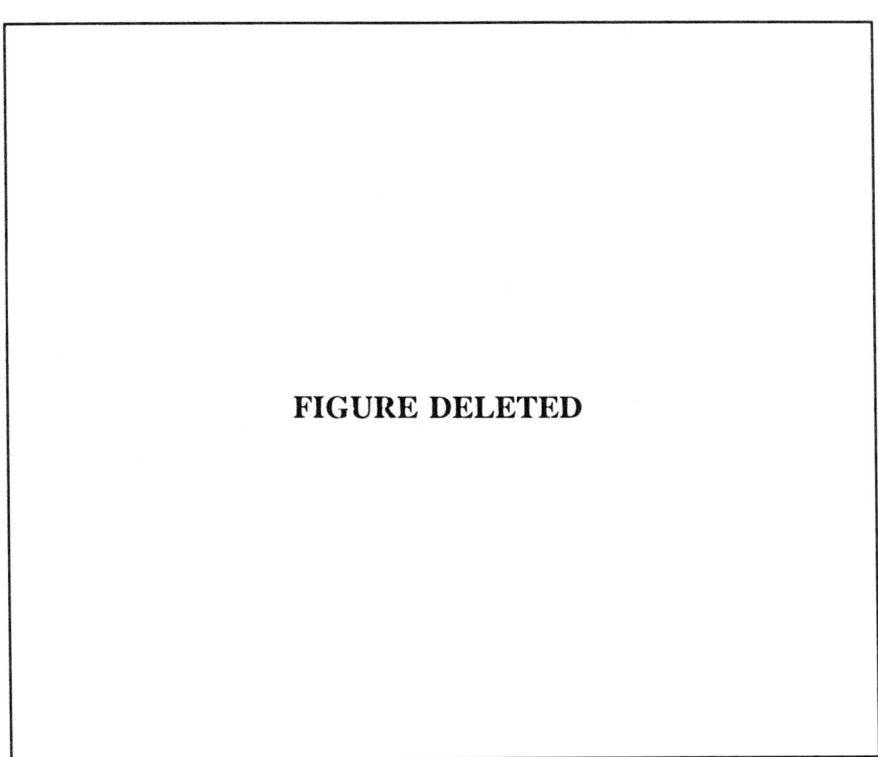

In mid-August, General Horner learned that General Powell had authorized detailed work on an offensive air campaign against Iraq and that initial work was being done by the Checkmate office in Washington.[77] Then, after Colonel Warden and his planners briefed General Horner on Checkmate's Instant Thunder plan on 20 August, some CENTAF

---

[77]Doc, Air War College lesson, "Planning the Air Campaign," Air War College, Maxwell AFB, AL.

planners[78] were given access to the proposed offensive campaign and realized for the first time that their mission had expanded from defending Saudi Arabia to preparing a large-scale offensive air campaign.[79]

For several weeks only a few CENTAF planners and intelligence analysts were assigned to the development of Instant Thunder. But, as the second phase of air tasking declined in importance, General Horner shifted more of his resources to offensive planning. By late December, the defensive phase was no longer being maintained and all CENTAF's planners and targeteers were supporting offensive planning.[80]

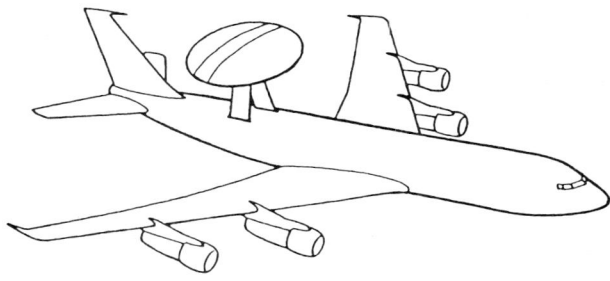

---

[78]This initial group of CENTAF planners included: Col Hubbard and Captains Heidrick and Glock (CENTAF Intelligence) and Majors Rhoeler and Null (CENTAF Operations).

[79](S/NF) Fact Sheet, Heidrick, "9 TIS/INT Planning Procedures," p 5.

[80]For detailed discussions of the CENTAF reorganization that created the Guidance, Allocation, and Targeting Division (GAT) refer to Chapter 6, GWAPS Command and Control report.

6

Evolution of the Offensive Air Campaign Plan

During the five months between the formulation of the Instant Thunder air campaign plan and the execution of the offensive air campaign plan as part of Operation Desert Storm, air planners sought to translate the national objectives as articulated by the President and his political advisers and the military strategy outlined by General Schwarzkopf and his theater planners into a design that exploited air power to its maximum.

The Bush administration very early in the Gulf crisis had provided General Schwarzkopf with four specific national objectives: 1) secure the immediate, unconditional, and complete withdrawal of Iraqi forces from Kuwait, 2) restore the legitimate government of Kuwait, 3) assure the security and stability of the Persian Gulf region, and 4) protect American lives. These provided the initial boundaries within which the air campaign planners operated.

Airpower resources were the first available in adequate numbers to General Schwarzkopf for possible offensive uses. Thus while both CENTCOM and its Army planners were faced with the daunting task of planning an offensive for which they had scant resources and in which they had little confidence (at least until the October decision to commit VII Corps from Europe), planners in the Black Hole or the Special Planning Group moved out ahead in their offensive planning, using conceptual notions from Instant Thunder.

CENTCOM planners adopted the conventional "estimate of the situation" and "five paragraph order" approach, no doubt reflecting the Army orientation of their commander. Command guidance was given to planners against which they evaluated various courses of action. They recommended one for the commander, and after approval, constructed a plan along a simplified format that moved from a summary of the situation and a statement of overall purpose to a detailed assignment of tasks for subordinate commands and a discussion of logistics and command and control arrangements. This format was also used by the Joint Staff.

General Glosson's planners adopted another approach, one that proved logical and familiar to Air Force officers. Yet it was distinctly different from that used by both CENTCOM and the Joint Staff. Though the precise origins of this format are still not clear, in general the process looked as listed below in Figure 10:

Figure 10
Concept To Execution Planning

FIGURE DELETED

It provided General Glosson and his planners with a clear and logical construct.[1] Similarly, General Glosson used it to assure senior decision makers that the air plan was linked directly to national objectives. He continually used the same set of briefing slides outlining objectives, centers of gravity, and target categories to brief President Bush, General Powell, Secretary Cheney, and General Schwarzkopf.[2]

---

[1](U) For further discussion of this format and background, see chapter 7, (S) GWAPS report on Effects and Effectiveness.

[2](S) General Glosson Briefs, GWAPS BH 3-60.

General Glosson and his planners started from the presidential objectives, confirming these with General Horner as soon as he began work. Glosson then addressed "centers of gravity." Colonel Warden and his planners had outlined four in their Instant Thunder plan: "(1) Saddam Hussein's political and military leadership and internal control network; (2) his strategic chemical warfare capability; (3) the telecommunications, industrial, and transportation systems that support his rule; and (4) critical military systems such as the Iraqi air defense network."[3] In their initial Operations Order, Offensive Campaign, Phase I, issued on 2 September 1990, Glosson's planners used these verbatim.[4] Eleven days later, when General Glosson briefed General Powell, these had been consolidated into three: (1) leadership, (2) military forces, and (3) infrastructure.[5] By December, the "infrastructure" center of gravity would be replaced by "nuclear-chemical-biological capability."

(U) Warden had used ten target categories:

- Strategic Air Defense
- Strategic Chemical, including one Scud storage facility, one nuclear research facility, and one biological warfare facility
- National Leadership
- Telecommunications (civil and military)
- Electricity
- Oil–Internal Consumption (Refineries and storage, not oil fields)
- Railroads (one bridge and two rail marshalling yards)
- Airfields
- Port (only one target)
- Military Production and Storage.[6]

Warden's planners had then selected 84 targets from within these categories (See Table 19, Target Growth by Category).

---

[3](S/NF/WN/NC) Instant Thunder Campaign Plan presented to CINCCENT 17 Aug 90 by Col John Warden, GWAPS CHSH 9.

[4](S) COMUSCENTAF Operations Order (U), Offensive Campaign, Phase I, 2 Sep 90.

[5](S) Brfg for CJCS, 13 Sep 90, in Glosson's Briefs, Folder 60, Box 3, GWAPS.

[6](S/NF/WN/NC) Instant Thunder Campaign Plan, C-12, *op cit.*

Table 19
Target Growth by Category

	Instant Thunder	13 Sep 90	11 Oct 90	1 Dec 90	18 Dec 90	15 Jan 91
Strategic Air Defense	10	21	40	28	27	58
Chemical/NBC	8	20	20	25	20	23
Scuds	n/a	n/a	note a	note a	16	43
Leadership	5	15	15	32	31	33
C3 (Telecom)	19	26	27	26	30	59
Electricity	10	14	18	16	16	17
Oil	6	8	10	7	12	12
Railroads and Bridges	3	12	12	28	28	33
Airfields	7	13	27	28	28	31
Naval and Ports	1	4	6	4	4	19
Military Support	15	41	43	44	38	62
Republican Guard	n/a	note b	note b	note b	12	37
Breaching	0	0	n/a	n/a	0	6
SAMs	0	0	n/a	n/a	0	43
Totals	**84**	**174**	**218**	**238**	**262**	**476**

Snapshot Dates:
- 13 Sep 90   CJCS Briefing
- 11 Oct 90   Presidential Briefing
- 1 Dec 90   Theater Campaign Briefing
- 18 Dec 90   Secretary of Defense Briefing
- 15 Jan 91   Day before Desert Storm

Notes:
(a) Scuds included in Chemical category
(b) Republican Guards included in Military Support category

Source: (S) Brfg slides for snapshot dates located in "General Glosson Briefs," GWAPS Box 3, Folder 60.

Gen Glosson (Right Center) goes over offensive air planning with his Black Hole planners in Riyadh.

Instant Thunder planners had specified an attack priority for these targets as part of the attack flow plan that they felt would be dictated by intelligence "and with emphasis on preventing retaliatory chemical attacks and securing air superiority." They laid out the priority as chemical delivery systems, air defense systems, command and control nodes, leadership, telecommunications, industrial infrastructure, and military support facilities.[7] In subsequent plans, Glosson's planners dropped such explicit listings of priorities but continued to develop the Instant Thunder flow list that became known as the master attack plan. Though only two target categories (Scuds and Republican Guard) were added, the numbers of targets within each category grew rapidly (See Table 19).

---

[7] (S/NF/WN/NC) *Ibid*, p C-2.

In deciding which targets to attack, planners were influenced by the overall theater campaign and how air power fit into General Schwarzkopf's overall concept. Generals Horner and Glosson translated this concept into specific applications of air power against specific targets.

Just how General Schwarzkopf envisioned air power and CENTAF as part of his concept was fairly clear. From the outset he thought an offensive would probably be necessary to eject Iraqi forces from Kuwait. In his postwar memoirs, he credited Colonel Warden's Instant Thunder briefing as crystallizing his own thoughts on a four–phased plan to do so, designating it Desert Storm.[8] At that time, the only offensive option he had entailed air power. His planners, as well as their boss, were convinced that the plan did not allocate sufficient ground forces to CENTCOM for any scheme of maneuver other than a frontal attack into the teeth of the entrenched Iraqi army in the Kuwait Theater of Operation (KTO).[9] Thus he turned to air power initially, should he be directed to go on the offensive.

This limitation disappeared in October when President Bush decided to double U. S. forces allocated to CENTCOM, most notably the addition of the VII Corps from Germany. CENTCOM and its Army planners were now able to envision ground phase of an offensive option that offered a promised degree of success through a flanking maneuver west of the Iraqi forces in the theater. Now General Schwarzkopf had sufficient forces to plan for a combined arms offensive operation.

By December, CENTCOM planners envisioned Desert Storm in four phases as follows:

       Phase I - Strategic Air Campaign
       Phase II - Air Supremacy in the KTO
       Phase III - Battlefield Preparation
       Phase IV - Ground Offensive Campaign

---

[8](U) Gen H. Norman Schwarzkopf, *It Doesn't Take a Hero*, Bantam Books, NY, Oct 92, pp 319-320.

[9](S) Intvw, Col Richard Swain, ARCENT Historian, Ft. Leavenworth, KS, Apr 92, Cochran notes.

At that time, they assigned the following tasks to General Horner and CENTAF. Phase I was to

> ... be conducted against targets in Iraq focusing on enemy centers of gravity. The air campaign will progressively shift into the KTO to inflict maximum enemy casualties and reduce the effectiveness of Iraqi defenses and isolate the KTO. ... A multi-axis ground, naval, and air attack will be launched ... to create the perception of a main attack in the east.

Among other tasks, General Schwarzkopf instructed General Horner to

> ... conduct the strategic air campaign phase to destroy Iraq's strategic air defense, aircraft/airfields; chemical, biological and nuclear capability; leadership targets; command and control systems; RGFC forces; telecommunications facilities; and key elements of the national infrastructure such as critical LOCs, electric grids, petroleum storage, and military facilities, cut key bridges, roads and rail lines to block withdrawal of RGFC forces, cut bridges, roads and rail lines to block reinforcement and/or resupply of Iraqi forces from the west and isolate Iraqi forces in the KTO, and to provide air support (CAS) throughout all phases.[10]

By December, CENTAF planners had completed their own plan, as will be discussed shortly. Thus CENTCOM planning specifics here did not influence them. However, from the earliest planning stages, Generals Horner and Glosson were aware of General Schwarzkopf's concept of operations. Their planner used this along with the centers of gravity to develop target categories. From this effort came an air concept of operations that would carry out the tasks assigned by General Schwarzkopf.

For air planners there was one mission that had to be accomplished prior to attacking centers of gravity–the achievement of air superiority. Air superiority, the ability to use the enemy's airspace, was their first and foremost concern for airpower planners. Defined in joint doctrine as "the degree of dominance in the air battle of one force over another which permits the conduct of operations by the former and its related land, sea and air forces at a given time and place without prohibitive interference by the opposing force," the air planners looked at "gaining and maintain-

---

[10](S) CENTCOM Operation Plan, *op cit.*

ing the freedom of action to conduct operations against the enemy."[11] For reasons not entirely clear, both CENTCOM and CENTAF planners substituted the goal of air *supremacy* for air *superiority* in writing their plans (though it was changed back to the latter when the actual operation order was issued on 16 January 1991). Air supremacy, while defined in joint doctrine at the time as "that degree of air superiority wherein the opposing air force is incapable of effective interference," was only mentioned in air force doctrinal manuals. Interestingly, it was General Schwarzkopf rather than General Horner who insisted a separate Phase II be devoted to air superiority in the Kuwait theater campaign plan.[12] CENTAF planners had intended to pursue air superiority in both Iraq and the Kuwait theater from the beginning of Phase I.

Air campaign planners needed air superiority for several reasons. First, air operations to eliminate the Iraqi integrated air defense system and render its Air Force ineffective were essential before most coalition aircraft could attack the centers of gravity with low losses.[13] (Planners intended to use F-117s against centers of gravity without air superiority). Second, planners needed to insure that Iraq would not execute air strikes against the coalition. Prior to the war, there were fears that once the allied campaign began, Saddam would react with punitive air attacks, perhaps involving chemical weapons, on coalition forces or economic facilities.[14] Third—and most important to General Schwarzkopf—air superiority was required to disguise the movement of large ground forces in eastern Saudi Arabia to forward positions farther to the west. From there coalition ground force could deliver a sweeping "left hook" into the Iraqi right flank "under the cover of the air campaign,"[15] but they could not start moving until the air campaign was underway. If coalition air power controlled the skies, planners assumed that Saddam and his commanders could not acquire intelligence on coalition movements through aerial

---

[11](U) JCS Pub 1-02, 1 Dec 89. Also see (U) AFM 1-1, 1984, 2-11.

[12](S) Intvw, Gen Horner with GWAPS, Feb 92, Cochran notes.

[13](S) MR, Lt Col David A. Deptula, subj: Observations on the Air Campaign Against Iraq, Aug 90 - Mar 91, 29 Mar 91, p 3, GWAPS, Safe #12, D-01.

[14][DELETED] (S/NF/WN/NC) Navy SPEAR; and (S) CENTCOM, Operation Desert Storm OPLAN, p B-22.

[15](S) CENTCOM, Operation Desert Storm OPLAN, pp 5, 11 and 12.

reconnaissance. And if they did realize what was taking place, coalition air power could be used to thwart attempts to redeploy Iraqi forces.[16]

Air planners also intended to conduct their overall campaign without suffering unacceptable losses, a presidential objective. While civilian decision makers and military commanders never explicitly defined what would constitute "unacceptable losses," they received estimates of likely aircraft attrition at various points in the planning of the campaign. For example, at the end of August, CENTCOM analysts projected that during the six-day Phase I strategic air campaign, Iraqi ground defenses and fighter interceptors would inflict a loss of 56 aircraft. In the two-day Phase II air battle over the Kuwait theater, they predicted that antiaircraft and surface-to-air missiles deployed in Kuwait would down 10 to 15 aircraft. In the 6-day Phase III air operations against the Iraqi army, they forecast the loss of 48 to 78 aircraft [DELETED]. This early estimate put losses at 114 to 141 aircraft for the first three phases of the campaign.[17] These predictions made it even more essential that air superiority be achieved quickly.

To achieve this, planners designated two specific target categories—strategic air defense and airfields. Under the first category, they listed a variety of targets: Iraqi command-and-control centers, communications nodes, and radars to "induce the maximum amount of shock and violence" against enemy air defenses.[18] To counter this threat, the initial Instant Thunder plan identified ten targets, 12% of the total targets. As the Desert Storm air campaign plan matured through January 1991, this number of targets grew to 58; however, the percentage of total targets (12%) remained constant.[19]

Early in the crisis, the Special Planning Group had identified the centralized command-and-control system managing Iraqi air defenses as

---

[16](U) Iraqi use of remotely piloted vehicles for aerial reconnaissance never matured into an a significant issue.

[17](S) U.S. Central Command, Offensive Campaign: Desert Storm, Briefing, 24 Aug 90 [CINC briefed to CJCS 24 Aug; CJCS briefed to President 25 or 26 Aug].

[18](U) Horner, Speech at Dadaelian Dinner, 11 Sept 91, p 4.

[19](S) Instant Thunder Campaign Plan, C-12, *op cit.*

a key vulnerability.[20] This system, called "Kari," was a web of reporting posts, interceptor operations centers (IOCs), sector operations centers (SOCs), and the national air defense operation center (ADOC). The intercept centers received information from the reporting posts, provided data to the SOCs, and controlled intercepts by fighter aircraft or surface-to-air missiles. Sector centers correlated the data from the intercept centers, monitored the large sectors into which Iraqi airspace was divided and determined how fighters and surface-to-air missiles would be allocated against hostile aircraft. The air defense centers, located in the capital, coordinated activities among the sectors and reportedly was under the direct control of Saddam. Using early warning radars, the reporting posts gathered air surveillance information.[21]

They intended to attack elements of the air defense command-and-control system in the first 48 hours of the air campaign, the air defense center in Baghdad as well as the sector and intercept centers located at sites throughout Iraq and in occupied Kuwait. Ground-based early warning radars (as well as two rudimentary early warning aircraft) also were slated for attack.[22] They felt that the air defense command centers did not need to be destroyed, but simply rendered inoperative.[23] Planners expected that command and control of the Iraqi air defense network also could be degraded through tactics not involving direct attacks on critical nodes. [DELETED].[24] In addition, some thought that damage to Baghdad electric power facilities caused by cruise missile strikes shortly after

---

[20](S) Deptula intvw, 8 Jan 92, p 48.

[21](S) Defense Intelligence Agency, Iraqi Ground and Air Forces Doctrine, Tactics and Operations, p 115; (S/WN/NF/NC) Navy SPEAR, P 3-11.

[22](S) Master Attack Plans for the first and second 24 hours of the air campaign, CHST Folder #57–CENTAF Master Attack Plans, Items 57-4 and 57-5.

[23](S) Deptula intvw with GWAPS staff, 20 and 21 Dec 91, p 7; (S) Deptula intvw, 20 Nov 91, p 11; (S) Deptula intvw, 29 Nov 91, p 45; (S) Deptula intvw, 8 Jan 92, pp 21-22; and (S) Deptula, "Lessons Learned," p 11.

[24](S/NF/WN/NC) SPEAR messages, 10 Aug 90 and 23 Aug 90, in Black Hole Box 8, Folder 9; (S) Iraq Gnd and Air Forces, Doctrine, Tactics and Ops; [DELETED] (S/NF/WN/NC) Navy SPEAR; (S) Glosson intvw, 12 Dec 91, p 29; and (S) Deptula intvw, 8 Jan 92, p 15.

H-Hour might impair air defense operations by shutting down equipment or at least forcing units to switch to emergency generators.[25]

Planners intended to strike all main operating bases and active dispersal airfields of the Iraqi Air Defense Force and Air Force. Runways, support facilities, and hangars at the airfields were to be attacked.[26] Their objective here was to deny enemy aircraft the use of airfield runways and shoot down any Iraqi aircraft that managed to take off.[27] Colonel Warden's planners initially had identified 7 airfields. By October, Black Hole planners had tripled that number. In the final effort, they selected 31 targets in this category, 6% of the planned overall effort. [DELETED].[28]

Part of the air superiority mission included the suppression of surface-to-air missiles batteries through the use of electronic countermeasures or high-speed antiradiation missiles. Planners anticipated destroying a number of surface-to-air missile sites, most in Kuwait, through bombing sorties. While conventional (non-stealthy) and low-observable F-117 strike aircraft were neutralizing enemy air defenses, planners scheduled other F-117s and cruise missiles for strikes on select leadership, command-and-control, and electric power targets before actual air superiority or supremacy was achieved.[29] This reflected the planners' beliefs that there was

---

[25](S) Master Attack Plan for the first 24 hours of the air campaign, CHST Folder #57–CENTAF Master Attack Plans, Item 57-4; and (S) Deptula intvw, 8 Jan 92, pp 17 and 40-41.

[26](S) Target list; Offensive Campaign, Briefing, 20 Dec 90 in CHP Folder 3, Lt Col Deptula, Air Campaign Briefings #1–Copy (3-ring notebook) ["Gen Horner Brief to SECDEF"]; and (S) Master Attack Plans for the first and second 24 hours of the air campaign, CHST Folder #57–CENTAF Master Attack Plans, Items 57-4 and 57-5.

[27](S) Master Attack Plans for the first and second 24 hours of the air campaign, CHST Folder #57–CENTAF Master Attack Plans, Items 57-4 and 57-5.

[28][DELETED]

[29](S) Master Attack Plans for the first and second 24 hours of the air campaign, CHST Folder #57–CENTAF Master Attack Plans, Items 57-4 and 57-5.

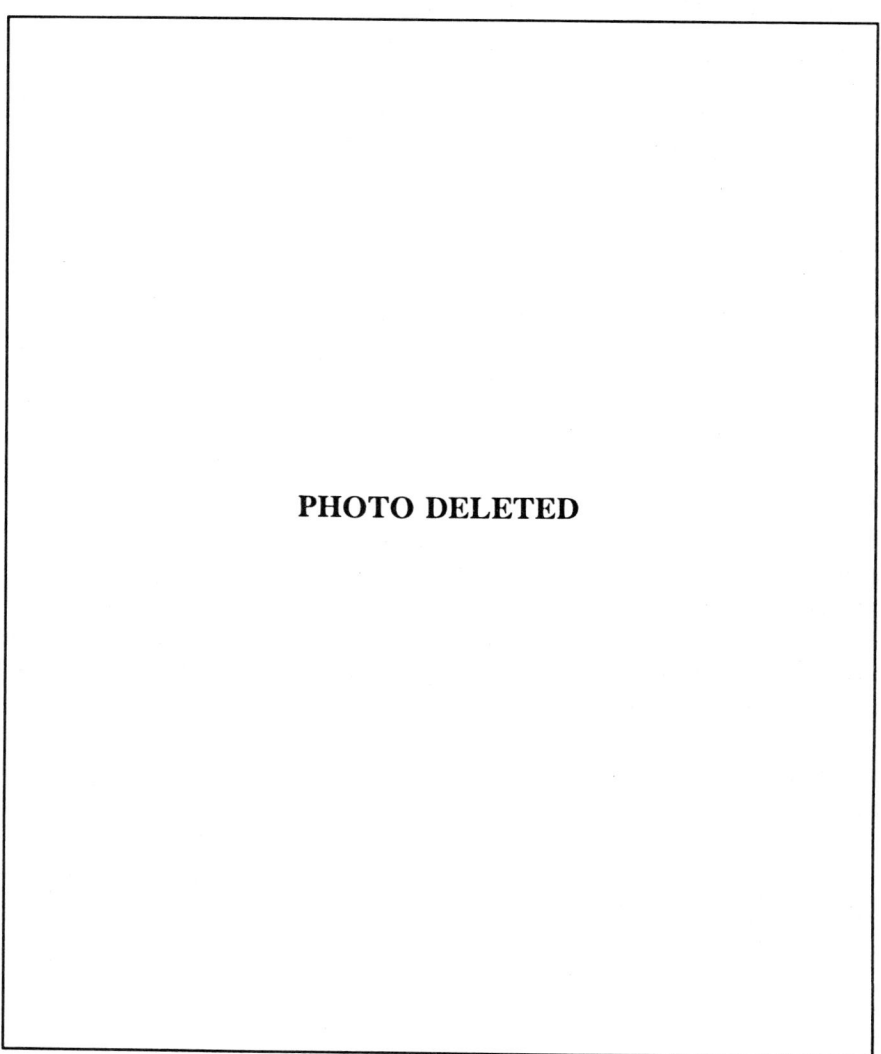
Al Taqaddum Airfield.

"an inherent degree of air superiority built into any stealth platform."[30] With stealth aircraft, there was no need to "roll back" opposing defenses, progressively destroying them from the periphery inward, before other campaign objectives could be pursued.[31] Moreover, F-117 missions did not require other aircraft for suppression of enemy air defenses and force protection routinely included in strike packages built around non-stealthy aircraft. Finally, F-117s could be employed against targets in Baghdad, where it would have been difficult to silence all of the antiaircraft artillery without causing inordinate collateral damage.[32]

The first center of gravity to be attacked was "leadership." The Instant Thunder plan had focused heavily upon the "leadership ring," and the CENTCOM list had placed it first among its centers of gravity. Just how to attack this targets category proved a matter of considerable debate among both planners and senior decision makers. [DELETED].[33] [DELETED]. During the first 48 hours of the campaign, they included attacks on the Baghdad presidential residence and bunker, among other government facilities. [DELETED][34]

Planners selected leadership targets they believed could weaken Saddam's power to govern with attacks against Iraqi's internal security organs, political elite, and armed forces (special attention devoted to shattering the Republican Guard).[35] They even selected an otherwise insignificant pilot training base near Tikrit to be struck by two B-52s in the first hours of Phase I operations because Saddam and many of his

---

[30](S) Deptula intvw, 20 Nov 91, p 13. See also (S) Deptula intvw with GWAPS staff, 20 and 21 Dec 91, p 6.

[31](S) Deptula, "Lessons Learned," p 24; (S) Deptula intvw, 20 Nov 91, pp 13-14; (S) Glosson intvw, 12 Dec 91, p 32; and (S) Glosson intvw, 9 Apr 92.

[32](S) Deptula, "Lessons Learned," p 25.

[33](S) Intvw, Gen Scowcroft with GWAPS staff, *op cit*, Cochran's notes.

[34](S) Master Attack Plans for the first and second 24 hours of the air campaign, CHST Folder #57–CENTAF Master Attack Plans, Items 57-4 and 57-5; and Msg (TS/SPECAT), USCINCCENT CC J2 to JCS, Subj: USCENTCOM Target List for Operation Desert Shield, Change 4 (U), 091200Z Dec 90.

[35](TS) Target list Msg, USCINCCENT CC J2 to JCS, Subj: USCENTCOM Target List for Operation Desert Shield, Change 4 (U), 091200Z Dec 90; and (S) Master Attack Plans for the first and second 24 hours of the air campaign, CHST Folder #57–CENTAF Master Attack Plans, Items 57-4 and 57-5.

inner circle and senior commanders came from the Tikrit area, and since "there were no really lucrative targets in downtown Tikrit," planners wanted to "make sure that people in Tikrit knew that war had come to their [hometown, that it] wasn't just located down . . . in the KTO."[36] They also slated elements of the Iraqi military command for attack during the first and second days of the war, such as the Ministry of Defense building, the Ministry of Defense computer center, air force headquarters, and the headquarters of military intelligence.[37] They targeted the Republican Guard not only because of its military importance in the Kuwait theater but more because they considered it a "critical node of [the] Hussein regime."[38]

The Black Hole planners also sought to isolate and "incapacitate" Saddam Hussein's regime by targeting the leadership's military command and control and disrupting the leadership's ability to communicate with the Iraqi people.[39] Wanting to separate the regime from the army and people, the Back Hole expected that severing Hussein's communication links with forces in the field would impair coordination of operations while striking command-and-control system for employing Scud missiles and weapons of mass destruction.[40] Such strikes would inhibit communi-

---

[36] (S) Master Attack Plan for the first 24 hours of the air campaign, CHST Folder #57–CENTAF Master Attack Plans, Items 57-4; Quote is from Deptula (S) intvw, 8 Jan 92; and MFR (S), K. M. Beck, Historian, Talk by Maj D. Karns, SAC/DOOI, [Reflections on STRATFOR Role in Persian Gulf War (U)], to SAC Bomb-Nav Conference, 23 Apr 91, in (S) History of the Strategic Air Command, 1 Jan - 31 Dec 1990, Volume XI–Supporting Documents, 9 Mar 92, p 2.

[37] (S) Master Attack Plans for the first and second 24 hours of the air campaign, CHST Folder #57–CENTAF Master Attack Plans, Items 57-4 and 57-5; and Msg (TS/SPECAT), USCINCCENT CC J2 to JCS, Subj: USCENTCOM Target List for Operation Desert Shield, Change 4, 091200Z Dec 90.

[38] (S) Target list.

[39] (S) MR, Lt Col David A. Deptula, subj: Observations on the Air Campaign Against Iraq, Aug 90 - Mar 91, 29 Mar 91, p 3, GWAPS, Safe #12, D-01; Congressional hearing (U), Lt Gen Charles A. Horner, Hearings before the Committee on Armed Services, Senate, *Operation Desert Shield/Desert Storm*, 102d Cong, 1st sess (Washington, 1991), p 237; brfg (S/LIMDIS), Theater Campaign, 1 Dec 90, GWAPS, CHP Folder 3.

[40] (S) CENTCOM, Operation Desert Storm OPLAN, pp B-11, B-45, B-63, and B-68; (TS) US Central Command, Offensive Campaign: Desert Storm, Briefing, 24 Aug 90 (S) [CINC briefed to CJCS 24 Aug; CJCS briefed to President 25 or 26 Aug); (S) COMUSCENTAF Operations Order, "Offensive Campaign–Phase I," pp 2, 5, B-4 and C-1; (S) "Air ops

cations from Saddam to the Iraqi people, reducing his own propaganda efforts both within and beyond Iraqi borders.[41] To do this, they targeted radio transmitters, receivers and relays; television transmitters; communications centers; public telephone and telegraph facilities; fiber-optic cable repeaters; and command posts.[42] By creating a sort of communications vacuum, planners believed that they would help "incapacitate" the regime. Initially planners identified this category as telecommunications but eventually it was called command, control and communications (C3).

At both CENTCOM and CENTAF, planners seemed to believe that not only could they incapacitate Saddam's government (or, in the words of the Desert Storm execute order, "neutralize [the] Iraqi National Command Authority"), but they might even change it, though they remained vague on just how this might happen.[43] With Saddam out of the way, air planners hoped that the Iraqi army would withdraw from Kuwait, a move that would fulfill the first U.S. policy aim in the Gulf conflict. This expectation of air power was most prevalent between late August and the middle of September when the strategic air campaign was the principal

---

summary of air war written by Lt Gen Horner after 8 ½ days of combat 261100Z91," in TACC CC/DO Current Ops Log (NA-215), and (S) D-19H–Gen Horner Air War Summary Meeting with Deptula, 26 Jan 91; (S) Glosson intvw, 12 Dec 91, p 29; Lt Col Bernard C. Harvey, quoted in James P. Coyne, *Airpower in the Gulf* (Arlington, VA, 1992), p 44; and Intelligence message, Subj: Possible C3 Node, 13 Jan 91, S/NF/NC/OC.

[41](S) Target list; (S) Deptula intvw, 20 Nov 91, p 1; (S) Deptula intvw, 8 Jan 92, p 38; and Harvey, quoted in *Airpower in the Gulf*, p 44.

[42](S) Target list; (S/NF/NC/OC) Intelligence message, Subj: Possible C3 Node, 13 Jan 91; (S) Deptula intvw, 8 Jan 92, pp 23 and 40; and (S) Master Attack Plans for the first and second 24 hours of the air campaign, CHST Folder #57–CENTAF Master Attack Plans, Items 57-4 and 57-5.

[43](TS) Msg USCINCCENT//CCJ3 to RUEKJCS/Joint Staff, Subj: Follow-Up Execute order–USCINCCENT OPORD 001 for Desert Storm (U), 170001Z Jan 91 CHC Folder #8, CENTCOM - OPORD, CHC Document #8-1.

PHOTO DELETED

Kirkuk Radio Transmssion Relay Site.

military option available to the United States; however, it remained present throughout the development of the plan.[44]

Instant Thunder planners had identified five targets in the leadership category and 19 in telecommunications, respectively 5% and 23% of the total effort, or 28% overall. While Black Hole planners added considerably to both categories - leadership growing to 33 and C3 to 59 - the final proportion of this larger effort devoted to leadership and C3 was reduced to 19% in the final plan.

The second center of gravity addressed by the air planners was called "infrastructure" by Instant Thunder planners and initially by CENTCOM. Before the 11 October briefing for the President, CENTCOM had redesignated the category as "Nuclear-Chemical-Biological Capability." This center of gravity would give planners and decision makers their biggest challenge; in retrospect, it gave them their biggest disappointment. By January 1991, most considered destruction of Iraq's nuclear, biological, and chemical (NBC) warfare capability to be on par with smashing Saddam's regime and dominating enemy airspace as main objectives of the initial operations planned for the air campaign.[45]

Planners were not overly concerned with the nuclear threat, though they were aware that Iraq was working to build a nuclear weapon. An intelligence report in November estimated that with a "crash program," Iraq might fabricate one or two "crude nuclear explosive devices" in, at best, six months to a year. The utility of these devices would have been limited, however, by their dubious reliability, low yield, and lack of

---

[44](S/LIMDIS) See Offensive Campaign: Phase I, Briefing, 27 Aug 90, in CHP Folder 3, Lt Col Deptula, Air Campaign Briefings #1–Copy (3-ring notebook) ["Version to accommodate Gen Horner inputs on 26 Aug brief–Built by Glosson & Deptula"]; COMUSCENTAF Operations Order, "Offensive Campaign–Phase I," pp 2-5; Offensive Campaign: Phase I, Briefings (Draft), 2 Sep 90 (S/LIMDIS), in CHP Folder 3, LT COL Deptula, Air Campaign Briefings #1–Copy (3-ring notebook) ["3 Sept Draft for CINC]; and Offensive Campaign: Phase I, Briefing, 13 Sep 90 (S/LIMDIS), in CHP Folder 3, Lt Col Deptula, Air Campaign Briefings #1–Copy (3-ring notebook) ["Brief to CJCS in Riyadh–Built by Glosson & Deptula. Briefed by Glosson"]

[45](S) Intvw, Rich Davis, Center for Air Force History, with Lt Col David A. Deptula, 20 Nov 91, p 14, GWAPS, (S) intvw, Center for Air Force History, with Deptula, 8 Jan 92.

delivery vehicles. [DELETED].⁴⁶ Given the state of the Iraqi nuclear program and the expected time line for the conflict, planners assumed that "[n]uclear weapons will not be used."⁴⁷

They had different feelings about chemical and biological threats. Intelligence analysts were aware that Iraq had stockpiled several tons of mustard and nerve agents, integrated chemical weapons into its military planning, and had employed these weapons against the Iranians and the Kurds. They also knew that Iraq had the potential for using two biological agents, anthrax and botulinum toxin.⁴⁸

Understandably, CENTCOM and its component commands assumed throughout that Saddam would use his chemical weapons in the event of hostilities. The President and his Secretary of defense were told in mid-October that "Iraqi forces will use chemical weapons."⁴⁹ This was reiterated to Secretary Cheney and General Powell in December.⁵⁰ Analysts were less certain about Baghdad's use of biological agents, primarily because of its lack of operational experience with these weapons.⁵¹ They could only speculate that Saddam might resort to biological weapons to

---

⁴⁶[DELETED] See also (S) OPLAN Desert Storm, 16 Dec 90, pp B-44 - B-45.

⁴⁷(S) OPLAN Desert Storm, 16 Dec 90, p 8. See also 20 and 21 Dec 90 CENTCOM briefing to SECDEF and CJCS.

⁴⁸[DELETED] msg (TS/SPECAT), DIA, to USCENTCOM Rear, USCINCCENT, Info USCENTAF Fwd, subj: Salman Pak CBW Research, Production, and Storage Facility, 011335Z Oct 90, GWAPS, CC-61-8/CC Folder 68; paper [DELETED] with memo (TS/SPECAT/LIMDIS), Maj Gen Burton Moore, CENTCOM J-3 to COMUSCENTAF/DO, [classified title], 20 Dec 90, GWAPS, BH, Box 12, Folder 2; CENTCOM OPLAN (S/NF) Desert Storm, 16 Dec 90, pp B-45 - B-49, AFHRA 0269602.

⁴⁹(S) Brfg, Maj Gen Robert Johnston, CENTCOM Chief of Staff, for Joint Staff and National Command Authorities, "CENTCOM Offensive Campaign," 10 and 11 Oct 90, in rpt (S), CENTCOM J-5 Plans, Augmentation Cell, *After Action Report* [Vol IX SAMS], Tab C, 28 Feb 91, GWAPS, NA 259.

⁵⁰(S) OPLAN Desert Storm, 16 Dec 90, pp 6, 7-8 and B-60; Briefing, CENTCOM for Secretary of Defense Richard B. Cheney and Gen Colin L. Powell, CJCS, 20 and 21 Dec 90, in rpt (S), CENTCOM J-5 Plans, Augmentation Cell, *After Action Report* [Vol IX SAMS], Tab T, 28 Feb 91, GWAPS, NA 259.

⁵¹(S) OPLAN Desert Storm, 16 Dec 90, pp 7-8 (emphasis added). [DELETED]

preempt a coalition offensive, achieve certain battlefield objectives, or save himself and his regime from destruction.[52]

CENTCOM told CENTAF "to destroy Iraqi capability to produce and weapons of mass destruction," and to achieve this end "as early as possible."[53] Because planners considered chemical weapons to be the most probable threat in August, they had created a chemical target category. Later on, they added nuclear and biological targets to this chemical category. Instant Thunder planners had picked seven suspected chemical weapons facilities and the nuclear research facility at Tuwaitha near Baghdad. By November, the list had grown to 25 targets with the addition of suspected manufacturing plants and additional bunkers. In terms of overall effort, the percentage of total targets (10%) remained constant throughout plan development.

This target category surfaced a new series of problems for planners. Given the presidential desires to minimize civilian casualties, they pondered possible widespread dispersal of radioactive contaminants, chemical agents, or virulent microorganisms and toxins that might result from bombing. They feared high-explosive bombs striking these buildings might produce clouds of aerosolized agents that could travel long distances, contaminate large areas, and poison thousands or even millions of people within and outside Iraq.[54]

CENTCOM planners realized that destroying Iraq's nuclear-biological-chemical capabilities was a coalition war aim in case Saddam launched chemical or biological attacks. [DELETED][55]

---

[52](S) OPLAN Desert Storm, 16 Dec 90, pp 5-6; [DELETED]

[53](S) OPLAN Desert Storm, 16 Dec 90, pp 4 and 9.

[54](U) Horner Dadaelian speech, p 4; (U) Lt Gen Charles A. Horner, cited in David A. Brown, "Iraqi Nuclear Weapons Still Intact," *Aviation Week & Space Technology*, 1 July 91, p 23; (S) Deptula intvw, 20 and 21 Dec 91, p 8; (S) intvw, Rich Davis, Diane T. Putney, and Perry Jamieson, Center for Air Force History, with Lt Col David A. Deptula, 29 Nov 91, p 41, GWAPS, Historical Advisor's File; (S) Deptula intvw, 8 Jan 92, p 24.

[55][DELETED]

[DELETED].⁵⁶ [DELETED].⁵⁷

The final center of gravity to be attacked was military forces and aligned with the CENTCOM assigned mission to "destroy Iraqi offensive military capability."⁵⁸ Black Hole planners used two target categories here: "Republican Guards and military support" and "Ports". Instant Thunder planners had picked 15 targets under the category of "Military Support": primarily the infrastructure for Iraq's armed forces. This comprised 18% of the overall effort. At the urging of Generals Schwarzkopf and Powell, this category was expanded to include strikes on the Republican Guard (hence the new category designation). By early December, the number of targets had grown to 44; however the overall percentage of total targets remained at 18%. Warden's planners had picked only one naval port. By December, General Glosson's planners had added three more naval facilities.

Air planners intended to attack the key elements of the military as well as their supporting industries. They included military aircraft, ballistic missiles, and Republican Guard units as military targets while including defense research and development centers, armaments plants, POL (petroleum, oils, and lubricants) and electric power facilities in the industrial grouping.⁵⁹ They intended to gut the foundations of Iraqi

---

⁵⁶[DELETED]

⁵⁷[DELETED]

⁵⁸(S) Desert Storm, 16 Dec 90, p 4.

⁵⁹(S) Lt Col David A. Deptula, USAF, subj: Observations on the Air Campaign Against Iraq, Aug 90 - Mar 91, 29 Mar 91, p 2, GWAPS, D-01; (U) Lt Gen Charles A. Horner, in Hearings before the Committee on Armed Services, Senate, *Operation Desert Shield/Desert Storm*, 102d Cong, 1st sess (Washington, 1991), p 237; (S) Deptula intvw, 20 and 21 Dec 91, p 10.

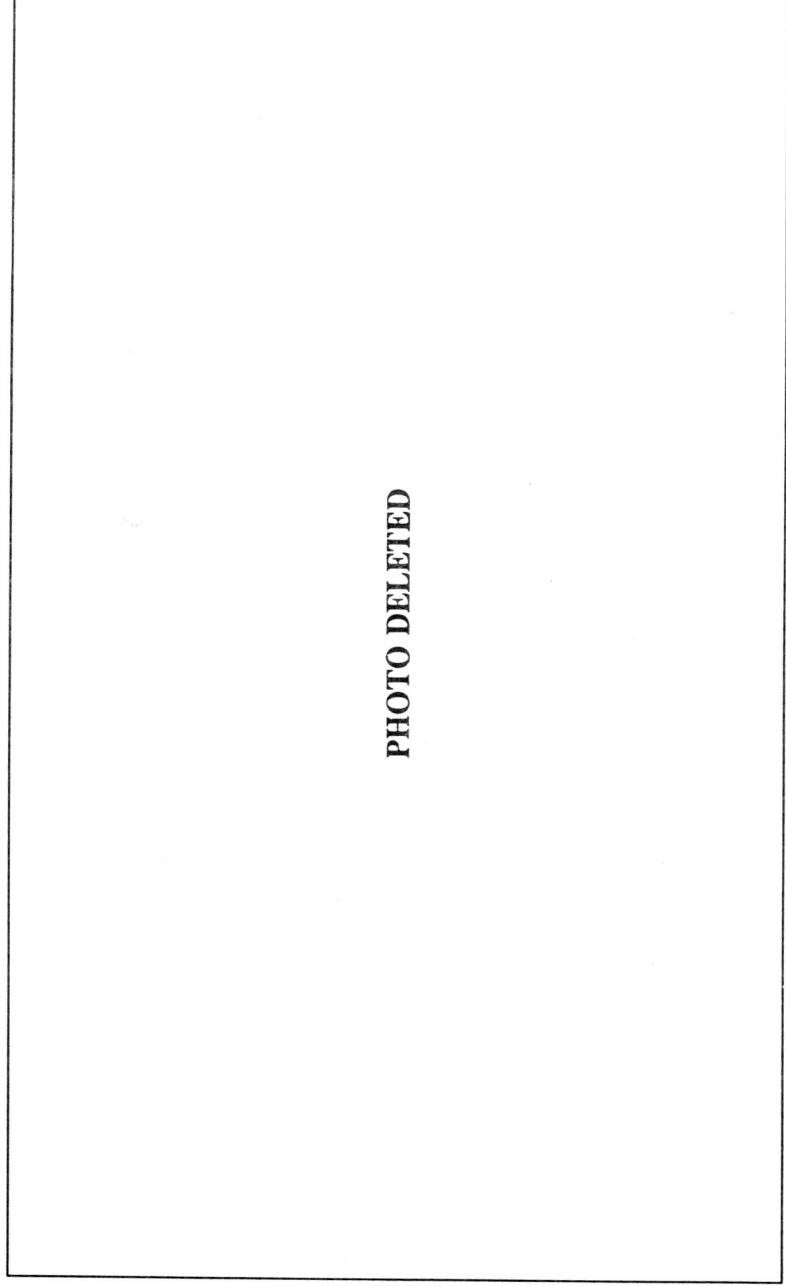
Baghdad Aircraft Repair Depot.

military strength and thus not only compel a withdrawal from Kuwait, but also prevent additional Iraqi aggression, a rationale consistent with the strategic goal of assuring the security and stability of the Persian Gulf region.

Development of this part of the air campaign plan revealed a philosophical difference between short-range military and long-range political objectives. A quick and decisive air offensive might destroy enough of Iraq's military strength to free Kuwait and bring hostilities to a close, yet end before depriving Iraq of its ability to commit future acts of aggression. These potential conflicts did not go unnoticed. Generals Powell and Schwarzkopf, motivated by concerns about postwar regional stability, intended from the start to eliminate the offensive ground power of the Iraqi army before it withdrew from Kuwait. During the 11 August briefing in which he was shown the conceptual plan for Instant Thunder, the Chairman of the Joint Chiefs maintained that the strategic air campaign should not simply pressure Saddam to pull out of Kuwait. Rather, it should continue until the Iraq army was destroyed. [DELETED][60] Schwarzkopf, too, wanted the army de-fanged, and was "obsessed" (Glosson's word) about trapping and annihilating the Republican Guard before it could retreat.[61] For the theater commander and the President's principal military advisor, assuring the stability of the Gulf (Bush's third policy objective) evidently was at least as important as freeing Kuwait (the first policy objective).

Air planners worried that the conflict could end before the bombing campaign could cause major damage to the Iraqi military establishment. Glosson feared that the campaign might last no more than a few days, that "all of a sudden the war was going to stop and . . . we [would] have a hell of a lot more stuff to do."[62] At the time, he believed that offensive air operations might be shut down prematurely by an Iraqi surrender, an offer by Saddam to negotiate a political settlement, or a unilateral

---

[60](S) Lt Col Ben Harvey, HQ USAF/XOXWS, subj: "Instant Thunder" Briefing to CJCS, 11 Aug 90. GWAPS, CHP 7-4; *Airpower in the Gulf*, p 45; Capt Ed O'Connell, "Desert Storm: A Look Into Air Campaign Planning," unpublished manuscript, n.d., p 6. See also (S) Deptula intvw, 1 Nov 90, p 18; (S) Deptula intvw, 20 Nov 91, p 12; (S) Deptula intvw, 29 Nov 91, pp 42-43.

[61](S) Deptula intvw, 12 Dec 91, pp 24 and 25.

[62](S) *Ibid*, p 51.

bombing halt by the coalition.[63] Thus as the plan execution date grew closer and additional aircraft arrived in country, Black Hole planners sought to spread sorties across as many of the target categories as possible, rather than concentrate on the neutralization of all or most targets in one category before the next became the focus of attacks.[64]

Another problem arose as top civilian decision makers paid increasing attention to destruction of Scuds. Instant Thunder planners limited Scud targets to a storage facility in the chemical target category and a warhead plan in the military production category. However, as the perceived importance grew of wiping out Saddam's ballistic missile force in order to prevent attacks against Israel that could provoke retaliation, draw the Jewish state into the war, and thus lead Arab countries to abandon the carefully built coalition, the Black Hole planners created a separate Scud target category. By late December, they had identified and targeted 16 weapons complexes and fixed launch sites, 6% of the target base at that time. By mid-January, that percentage of total targets had grown to 9% as planners now listed 43 targets.

The President, in prewar guidance, said that efforts should be made to "preclude" missile strikes on Israel, Saudi Arabia, and other countries in the region, as well as attacks on coalition military forces. Thus planners selected targets to "[r]educe [the] offensive threat to regional states and friendly forces" by attacking fixed launchers, support bases, surveyed launch sites for mobile launchers, aircraft shelters in which

---

[63](S) Deptula intvw, 20 Nov 91 pp 22-23; (S) Deptula intvw, 8 Jan 92, p 10; (S) Deptula intvw, 20 and 21 Dec 91, p 11.

[64](S) Deptula intvw, 20 and 21 Dec 91, p 11.

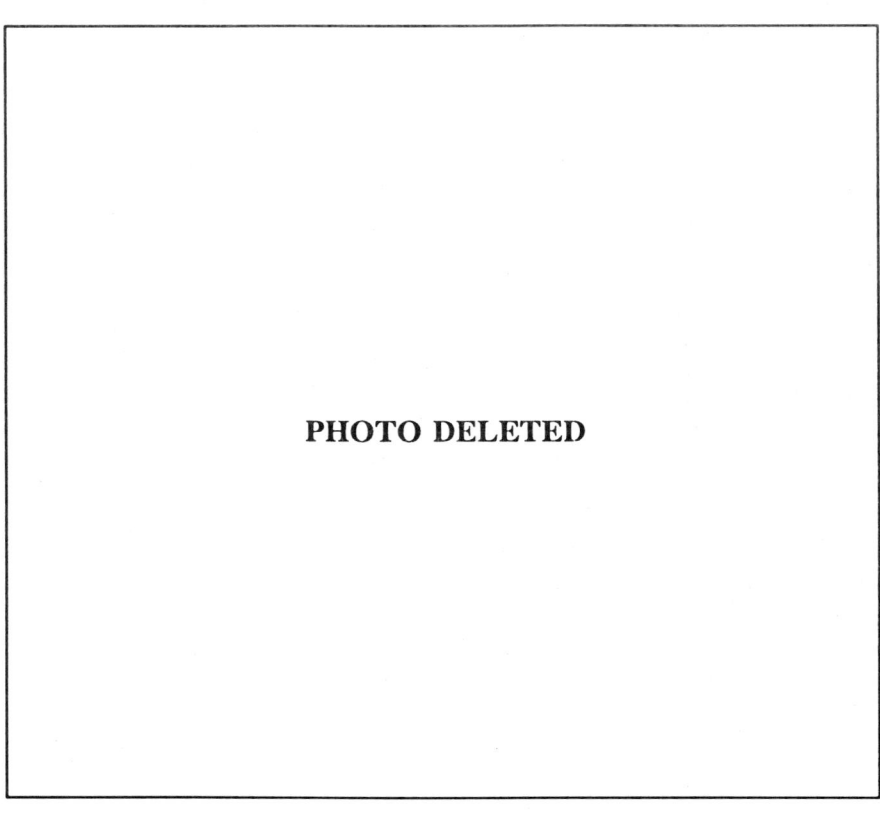

Jalibah SRBM Launch Complex. Four surveyed positions (B1 - B4).

mobile launchers might be hidden, and–in keeping with the need to diminish Iraq's long-term military potential–missile research and production facilities.[65] Very early on, General Horner had informed Secretary Cheney that some number of mobile launchers would escape destruction and fire their missiles.[66] However, no one seemed attuned to the magnitude of the problem that would be posed by mobile launchers.

---

[65] (S) Target list (with objectives for each target category, including Scuds), GWAPS, BH, Other Documents, Folder 8.

[66] (S) Horner intvw, 4 Mar 92, p 42.

Complicating this was incomplete nature of U. S. knowledge about the size, character, and operation of the Iraqi Scud force. Intelligence analysts thought Iraq to have some mix of several hundred Scud B, Hussein, and Abbas missiles.[67] [DELETED].[68] They had located complexes for fixed launchers in the western part of the country oriented toward Israel. [DELETED].[69] In contrast, they had "[n]o accurate accounting of numbers of mobile launchers or where they were based [or] hiding."[70]

The CENTCOM and CENTAF commanders and their staffs viewed these missiles as ineffective weapons against the military facilities and forces of the coalition. Given the limited accuracy and small high-explosive payload of the Scuds (the Soviet-produced Scud B and its longer-range, Iraqi-built variants, the Hussein, and Abbes), they were more of a terrorist weapon against cities than a serious threat to military forces.[71]

The problem for the air planners was tracking and attacking Iraqi mobile missiles. [DELETED][72] The infrastructure for the Scud force was targeted, the mobile launchers were not. For planners, mobile Scuds represented an intractable problem. [DELETED].[73] [DELETED].[74]

---

[67](S/NF/WN), subj: SRBM Fact Sheet (U), 14 Jan 91, GWAPS, CIS 32; (S) OPLAN Desert Storm, 16 Dec 90, p B-14; (S) Brfg, "Offensive Air Campaign," 20 Dec 90.

[68](S/NF) Fact/Information Sheet; (S) Brfg, "Offensive Air Campaign," 20 Dec 90.

[69](S) Desert Storm Scud Missile Working Group III, Desert Storm Scud Missile Lessons Learned Conference, 28-30 May 91, p 9, GWAPS, NA 108.

[70](S) How to Kill Scud Missiles. See also intvw (S/NF/WN), Diane T. Putney, Center for Air Force History and Ronald H. Cole, JCS Historical Division, with Rear Adm J. "Mike" McConnell, 14 Feb 92, GWAPS, NA 261.

[71](S) Intvw, Senior GWAPS staff with Lt Gen Charles Horner, Shaw AFBSC, 9 Mar 91; also intvw (S) Capt Edward P. O'Connell, GWAPS, with DIA, DB-6, 19 Aug 92, GWAPS, notes in Kurt Guthe's files; intvw (secure telecom) (S), Capt Edward P. O'Connell and Kurt Guthe, GWAPS, with DIA, DX-7, 1 Sept 92, GWAPS, notes in Kurt Guthe's files.

[72](S) Intvw, 8 Jan 92, p 47.

[73](S/NF/WN) Memo, JIC [Joint Intelligence Center]/Iraqi Scud Targeting Support Cell (TSC) to JIC, subj: Lessons Learned From Operation DESERT STORM (U), 6 Mar 91, Capt Edward P. O'Connell's files; intvw (S), Kurt Guthe, GWAPS, with Capt John R. Glock, 8 Sep 92.

To belay Israeli anxiety about Saddam's ballistic missiles, planners did assign aircraft missions in the vicinity of the H-2 and H-3 airfields in western Iraq, an area where Scuds were located. [DELETED].[75] [DELETED].[76]

General Horner still recognized that Scuds might compel Israel to retaliate against Iraq, and he made preliminary plans to deal with that situation. General Schwarzkopf believed that an Israeli decision to strike back could have had grave political, as well as military, consequences and might destroy the coalition.[77] [DELETED]. Israeli violations of Jordan's airspace could draw that country into the war.[78]

[DELETED].[79] [DELETED].

---

[74](S) Background paper (S), Maj Russ Thompson, Capt Tom Clemmons, Capt Philip Sauer, Lt Ed Zellen, How to Kill Scud Missiles: Lessons Learned from Desert Storm (S), n.d., attached to memo (S), Capt Tom Clemmons to 9TIS/CC/IN/INT/INA, subj: Scud Lessons Learned Conference Trip Report (S), 5 June 91, in Capt John Heidrick's Desert Storm Continuity Book (S/NF), available from AFHRA.

[75](S) Memo, to RADM [Conrad] Lautenbacher [NAVCENT Riyadh] from Brig Gen Buster C. Glosson, subj: H-2/H-3 Area Coverage Day 1, n.d., GWAPS, BH, Box 11C, Folder 21.

[76](S) Attack Plan for first 24 hours. See also briefing (S/NF), Cmdr Donald W. "Duck" McSwain for Vice Adm R.M. Dunleavy, "Riyadh Perspective (USN)," n.d., GWAPS, NA 254.

[77](S/NF) TV intvw with Frost, 27 Mar 91, p 3.

[78](S/NF) Intvw, 4 Mar 92, p 40.

[79](S) Doc, "Third Party Attack on Iraq," n.d., GWAPS, BH, Box 13, Folder 5, BH 13-5-3.

[DELETED].⁸⁰ [DELETED].⁸¹ [DELETED].

[DELETED].⁸²

By aligning the three centers of gravity plus air superiority against target categories and following the construct laid in the Instant Thunder plan, General Glosson's planners laid the foundation for the Desert Storm air campaign plan. The three target categories not specifically aligned–Electricity, Oil, and Railroads and Bridges–were cast in the larger missions for air power such as interdiction and attacking the morale of the people. Together these targets constituted 19% of the Instant Thunder and September CENTAF Target List. In the final Desert Storm plan, this percentage of total targets dropped to 13% primarily because of the static nature of these target categories while the others were growing.

From the outset of the Gulf crisis, General Schwarzkopf thought in terms of a phased offensive operation.⁸³ So did his air component commander and principal air planner.⁸⁴ Only Colonel Warden's Instant Thunder plan sought to win the war in only six days of bombing. In August, air power was all that was available to planners for an offensive operation. Thus Instant Thunder seemed a viable plan without phasing to other offensive operations. However, by early September, planners in the Black Hole had incorporated this concept into the larger CENTAF plan in which the air campaign outlined in Instant Thunder was specified as Phase I.

---

⁸⁰(TS) "Response to Enemy Preemptive First Strike," briefing, n.d.; and intvw, Lt Col Mark B. "Buck" Rogers, by A. Howey (GWAPS), 19 Feb 92, p 8. (TS) Master Attack Plan, 12 Dec 90, p 1 [Black Hole Files, Box 4, Folder 7]; and (TS) Rogers, "Desert Shield/Storm After Action Report," p 2.

⁸¹(TS) "Response to Enemy Preemptive First Strike."

⁸²(TS) Master Attack Plan, 10 Jan 91, p 1 [Black Hole Files, Box 4, Folder 7]; and "Reflex: Response to Enemy Preemptive First Strike."

⁸³(U) Schwarzkopf memoirs, pp 319-320.

⁸⁴(S) Intvw Gen Horner with GWAPS staff, Feb 92, and (S) intvw Gen Glosson with GWAPS Apr 92, Cochran notes.

For CENTCOM theater planners of Desert Storm, the first two phases remained the air-only campaign against Iraqi targets (Phase I) and the achievement of air superiority over the Kuwait theater (Phase II). What changed after mid-October were Phases III and IV. Significantly though, the entire concept of operations rested on the success of air power in Phases I and II, which were essential to permit Phase III's 50% attrition of ground forces in the Kuwait theater and cover the movement of ground forces into attack positions for Phase IV.

The question for planners became the CENTAF transition from a total air war (Phases I, II, and III) to the conduct of the combined arms war (Phase IV). From early in their planning effort, CENTCOM planners envisioned that this transition would be a fifty percent attrition of Iraqi forces in the KTO prior to the launching of Phase IV, the ground offensive. As early as 14 August, General Schwarzkopf's combat analysis group concluded that for a coalition offensive to be successful with a single corps, the air campaign would have to achieve fifty percent attrition of enemy ground forces first.[85]

General Glosson first discussed the fifty percent goal in September with Lt. Col. Joe Purvis, chief of a special group of Army ground planners which Schwarzkopf had recruited from graduates of the Army's School of Advanced Military Studies at Fort Leavenworth. Just exactly what was meant by fifty percent attrition remained unclear, not to mention who would determine when that the goal had been reached. At that time, army planners seemed most interested in bombing armor, artillery, and troops.[86]

One reason that General Glosson may not have pushed the point at that time was his hope that air power might prevail alone. As he

---

[85] (S) Rpt, Combat Analysis Group, 21 Mar 91, in Vol VI of CENTCOM J-5 After Action Rpt, GWAPS NA-259. (U) The Bush administration's November decision to double the forces for a two-corps ground offensive did not change the computer calculations because intelligence reported that Saddam had also deployed more forces to the KTO.

[86] (S) Intvw, GWAPS staff with Maj Gen Glosson, Pentagon, 4 Apr 92; Chronology (S), SAMs Team, Tab P in Vol I of Centcom J-5 After Action Rpt, 5 Mar 91, GWAPS NA-259. Speech, Gen Glosson, Air War College, 27 Oct 92.

confided to an Air Force historian at the time,

> I think it's accurate to portray the history of the Air Force as one in which it has always been in support of either the ground forces, the sea forces, or the Marines. With the exception of Libya, there have not been many instances that one can refer to and say this was an air operation. In that context, this was and is an entirely different situation. We're being asked to meet Presidential established objectives solely with the use of air power. Now there are a lot of critics that say that can't be done. I don't happen to be one of those individuals. I believe, with the objectives that the President has laid down, if we execute this air campaign and the leadership has the patience, he will realize all the objectives that he's established to include the country of Kuwait being returned to the proper people and the removal of Iraqis from Kuwait. I say that because I'm firmly convinced that the intensity and the freedom the President has laid out in guidelines for us in executing this air campaign, permits us to go to the trunk of the tree, or the heart, and we're not snipping on limbs. We are absolutely decimating the leadership of Iraq and we are making his capacity to command and control both the military and getting information to his civilian populace almost impossible. We are making it for all practical purposes impossible for him to resupply the troops that he has in Kuwait. So once you've done that, the only thing you have to do is have the **patience to wait out the effect of what you've already accomplished.**[87]

He predicted that about ten days after "we complete" Desert Storm's first phase (the strategic air offensive in Iraq), the Iraqi army in the Kuwait theater would begin to run out of food and water. By then they would be enduring the full force of the third phase of Desert Storm, the direct attack on their positions, their supplies, their tanks, their artillery and their morale.

The key question for planners was just how long it would take for air power to achieve the fifty percent figure. First to tackle this were analysts with Air Staff's Checkmate planning group. In mid-October, the RAND Corporation had briefed the Air Staff on the results of their Gulf wargame, suggesting that Iraqi ground forces be bombed by B-52s for at

---

[87](U) Words in boldface indicate General Glosson's emphasis. (S) Intvw, MSgt Theodore J. Turner, CENTAF history office, with Brig Gen Glosson, Riyadh, 18 Oct 90.

least a month before a coalition ground offensive. Donald Rice, the Secretary of the Air Force (and former head of RAND), took an interest in the RAND briefing and directed that Warden make his own examination of Phase III. Warden believed that the Bush administration had to be persuaded that air power in Phase III could destroy the Iraqi army, and he told his staff that their Phase III study was "the most important work in Washington now."[88]

Checkmate analysts assumed that precision-guided munitions would be used for destruction of armor and artillery while cluster bombs would be used against troops in the open. They concluded that nine days were required to achieve fifty percent destruction of Iraqi armor, artillery and troops in Kuwait only. Informed of these results on 23 October, Glosson noted that Schwarzkopf's emphasis was on the Republican Guards in southern Iraq, not the front line troops in Kuwait.[89]

Checkmate analysts ran the model again, this time against both the Republican Guards and the Iraqi forces in Kuwait. Comments from the Air Force's Center for Studies and Analysis and from RAND caused them to adopt a more conservative estimate of the percentage of sorties which would find a target to bomb (the Joint Munitions Effectiveness Manual's standard of seventy-five percent, rather than the ninety-five percent they first used with the justification that targets were easy to spot in the desert). Checkmate concluded in early November that twenty-three days would be required to reach fifty percent attrition.[90]

---

[88](S) Notes, Wayne Thompson, Checkmate historian, 16 Oct 90, GWAPS Historical Advisor's Files.

[89](S) Notes, Wayne Thompson, Checkmate historian, 23 Oct 90, GWAPS Historical Advisor's Files.

[90](S) The series of Checkmate briefings reporting its findings are in GWAPS CHSH 6 and 8; see especially the briefings of 19 Oct (8-10) and 31 Dec (6-2). (U) The same model was rerun at the end of December increasing the estimate of the number of Iraqi forces in the KTO. Now analysts predicted that twenty-two days and 24,000 strike sorties would be required to reach a fifty percent attrition.

Since this estimate did not take into account the increase in U.S. forces being deployed, General Glosson reduced it to seventeen days in a briefing for General Schwarzkopf.[91] CENTCOM cut it further. The Desert Storm Operations Plan of 16 December allotted only eight days for Phase III. General Schwarzkopf remained adamant not to launch the ground offensive until his intelligence staff could tell him that the opposing force had been degraded fifty percent by air. His planners left the duration of Phase III in the Operation Order of 16 January "to be determined."[92]

For CENTAF planners, the integration of the emerging ground campaign plan with the fully mature air campaign plan in mid-December solidified their overall concept of operation. The realization that the air campaign would probably be executed led to a reorganization and series of briefings for wing commanders. General Horner established a unified planning organization under General Glosson with Colonel Deptula's Iraq cell and Lt. Col. Samuel J. Baptiste's KTO cell. Before this merger, the Iraq cell had been totally involved with the offensive planning for Desert Storm while the KTO cell had handled the Desert Shield defensive planning as well as the daily air tasking orders for daily training flights. Now the KTO planners focused on offensive planning for Phases II, III, and IV while the Iraq group continued to work on Phase I plans. In addition to putting General Glosson in charge of all planners, General Horner made him an air division commander over the fighter wings. After Glosson briefed his fighter wing commanders on the impending campaign, General Horner used essentially the same briefing for Secretary Cheney and General Powell when they visited Riyadh in mid-December.[93]

---

[91](S) Brfg, Theater Campaign, Glosson to CINC, 1 Dec 90, GWAPS CHP 3-1.

[92](S) USCINCCENT OPORD 91-001, Desert Storm, 161735Z Jan 91, GWAPS NA-357; USCENTCOM OPLAN (S), Desert Storm, 16 Dec 90, AFHRA 269602.

[93](S) Brfg, 18 Dec 90 Theater Campaign Brief to Wing Commanders, Tab 4, Gen Glosson Briefs, Box 3, Folder 60, GWAPS Files.

Above, on way to Riyadh briefing. L to R: Lt Col Ben Harvey, Lt Col John Warden, Lt Col Dave Deptula, Lt Col Ron Stanfield. Below left, Gen Powell in Saudi Arabia. Below right, Secretary of Defense Richard Cheney in Saudi Arabia.

Glosson's briefing for his wing commanders outlined the campaign's four phases: Phase I - Strategic Air Campaign; Phase II - KTO Air Supremacy; Phase III - Destroy Enemy Ground Forces in KTO; and Phase IV - Ground Attack. He also laid out the three centers of gravity, Leadership, Nuclear-Chemical-Biological Capability, and Military Forces. He specified the results for each phase: for Phase I, to destroy leadership's military command and control, destroy nuclear-biological-chemical capability, disrupt and attrit Republican Guard Forces, disrupt leadership's ability to communicate with populace, destroy key electrical grids and oil storage, and limit military resupply; for Phase II, destroy all radar-controlled surface-to-air threats and establish total air supremacy in the Kuwait Theater of Operations; for Phase III, make certain that Iraqi forces in the Kuwait Theater of Operations were no longer capable of resisting attack, let along launching an attack; and for Phase IV, complete the destruction of the Republican Guard Forces, remove Iraqi forces from Kuwait, and restore the legitimate government of Kuwait.

Glosson covered each phase briefly, outlining essentially how air power would be used in each and for how long (Phase I-6 days; Phase II-2 days; Phase III-14 days, and Phase IV-18 days). The phases overlapped (e.g., Phase II started during Phase I) and the total campaign was projected to last 32 days.[94]

Glosson's briefings used maps with targets by target categories (airfields, air defense, SAM/AAA threat, Scud threat, Scud storage, Scud production, chemical, biological and nuclear production, and storage facilities). The details of the first 48 hours of the air campaign were summarized as listed in the charts below. On the first day, attacks would start after midnight (Figure 11) against 7 groups of targets, leadership in the Baghdad area, air defense operation centers near Baghdad and Tallil,

---

[94](S) Brfg, 20 Dec 90 CENTAF/CC Brief to the SecDef, Tab 5, *ibid*.

Figure 11
Attack Plan First Day, AM - Night

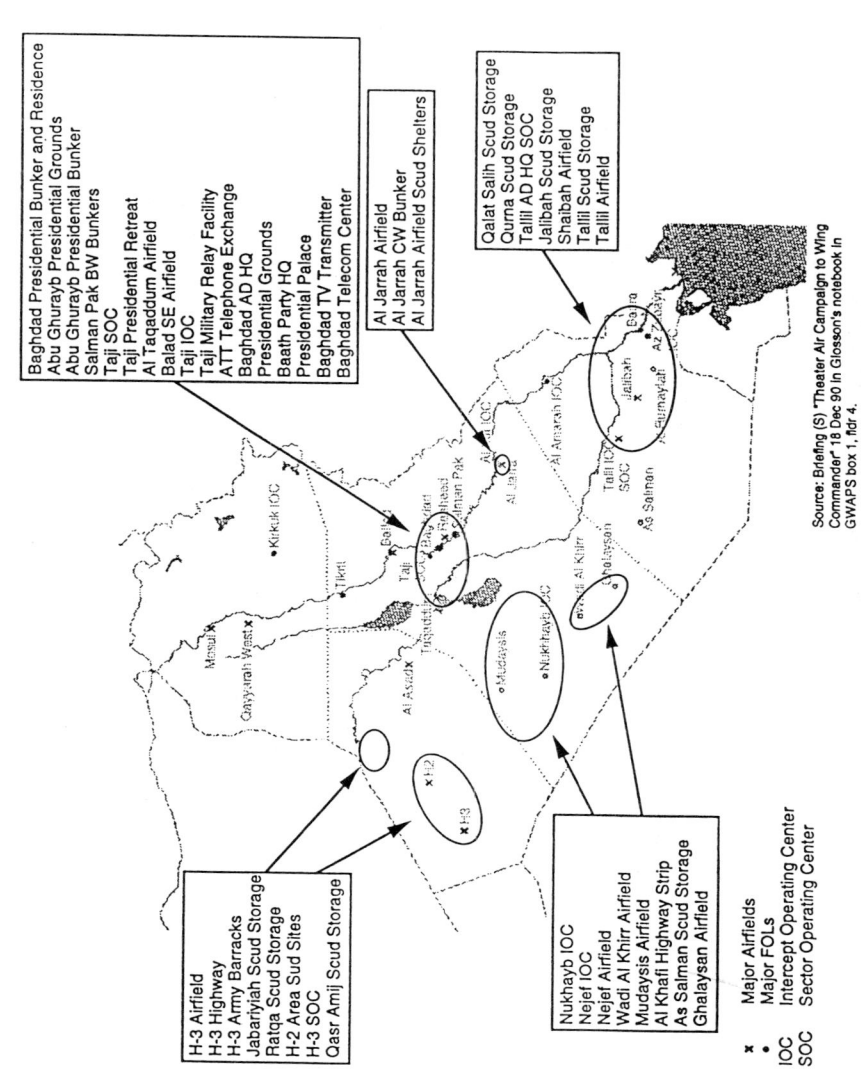

Figure 12
Attack Plan First Day, AM - Day

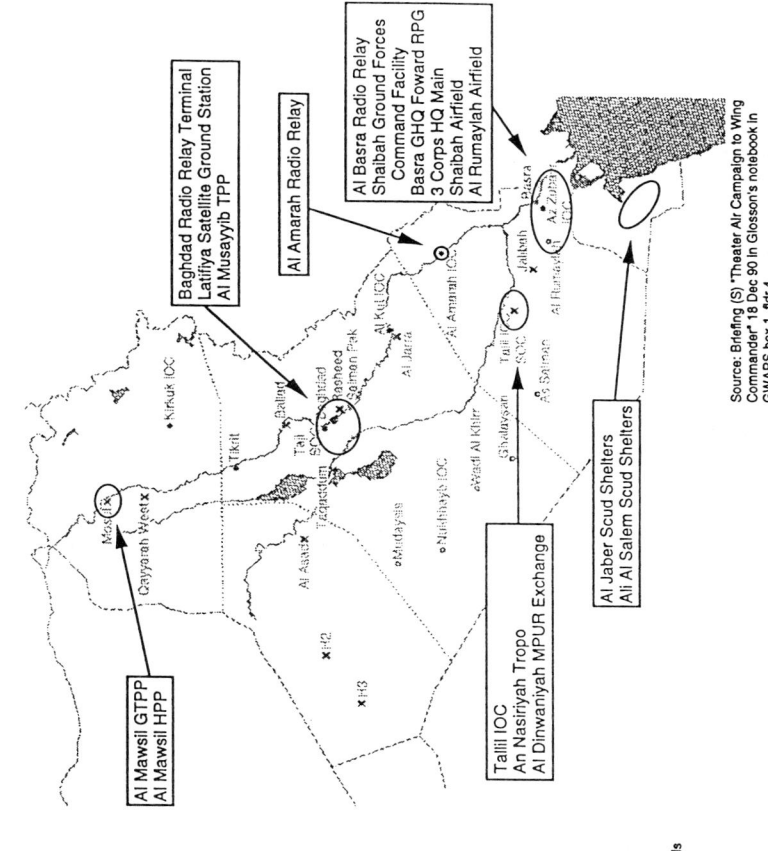

Figure 13
Attack Plan First Day, PM - Day

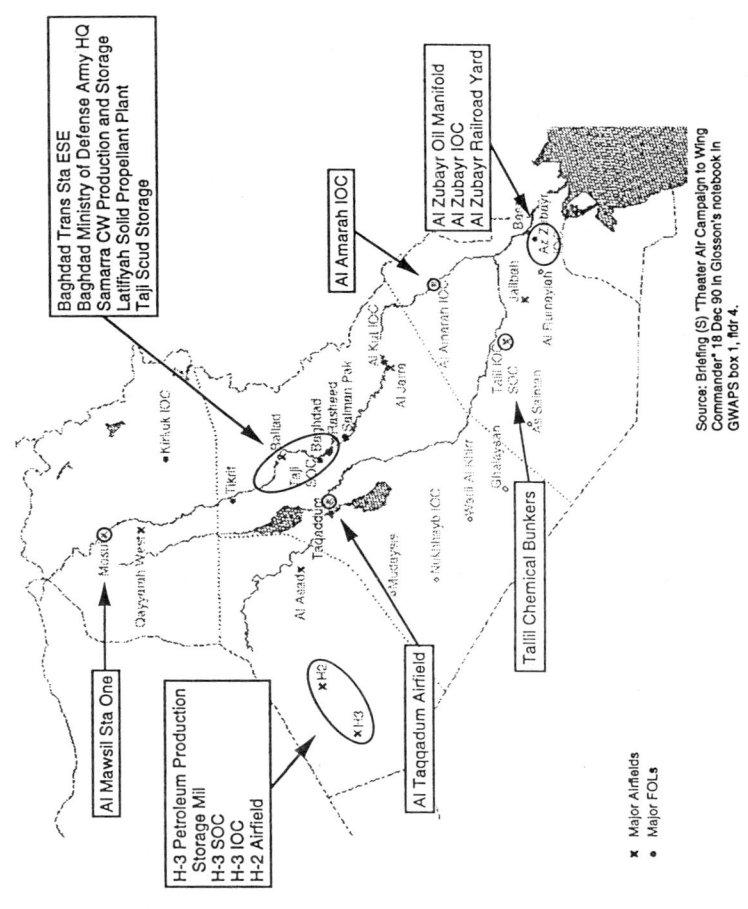

Figure 14
Attack Plan First Day, PM - Night

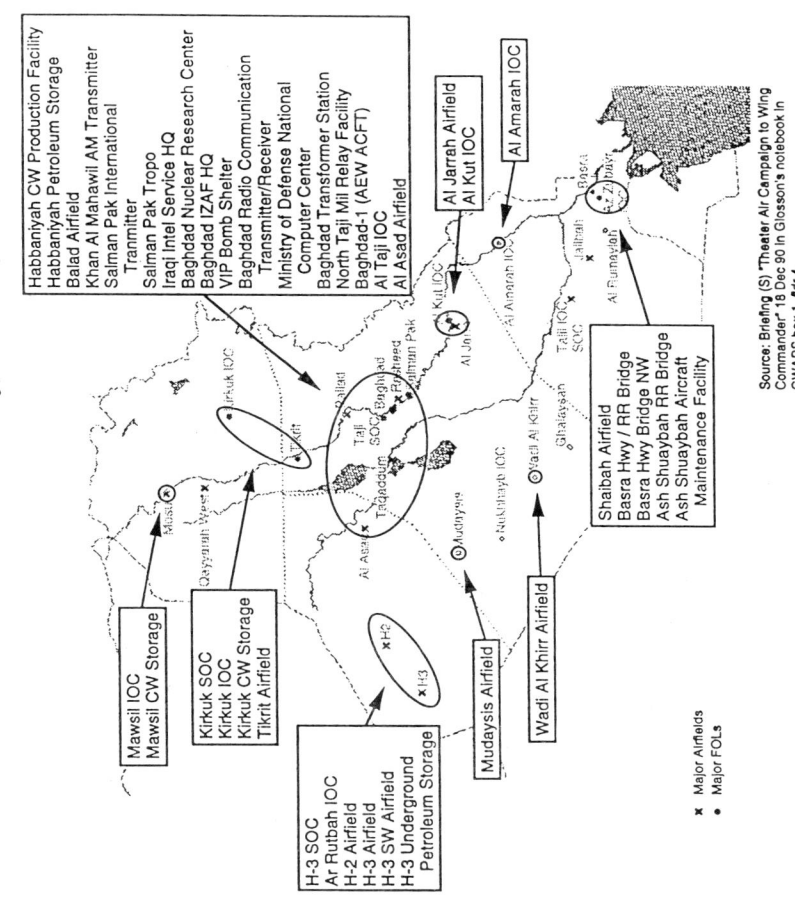

Figure 15
Attack Plan Second Day, AM - Night

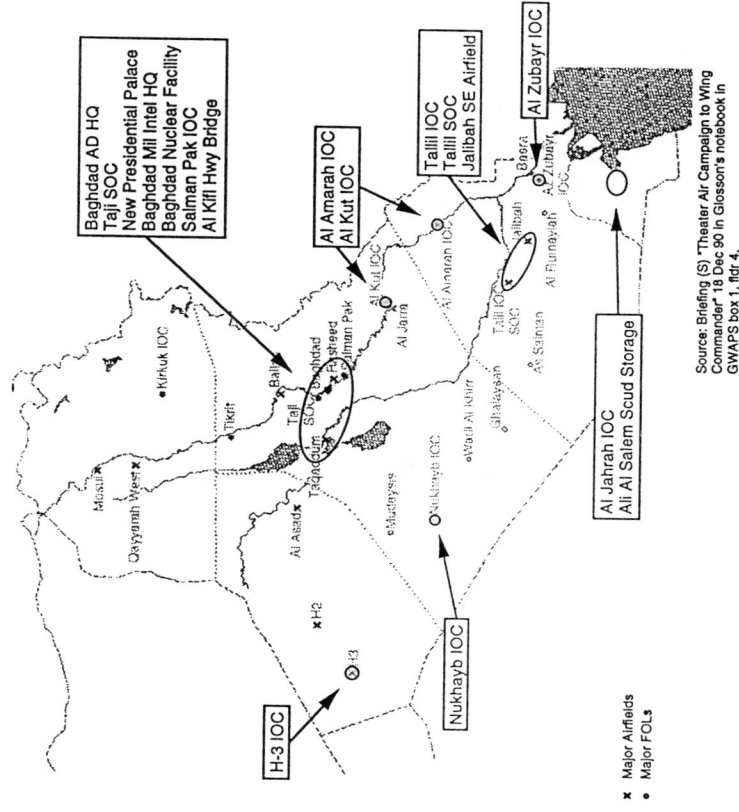

**Figure 16
Attack Plan Second Day, AM - Day**

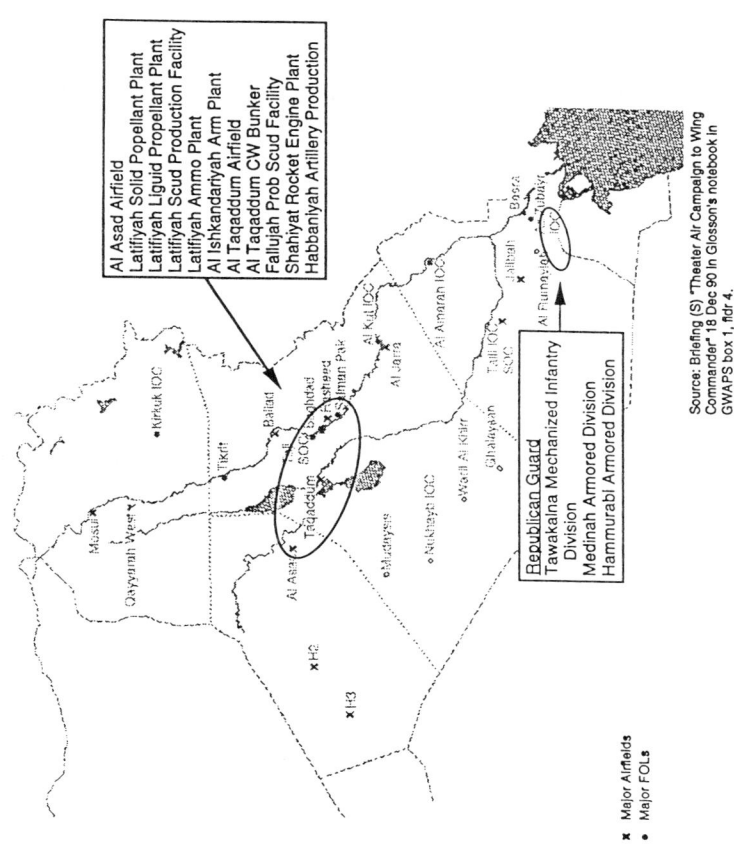

**Figure 17
Attack Plan Second Day, PM - Day**

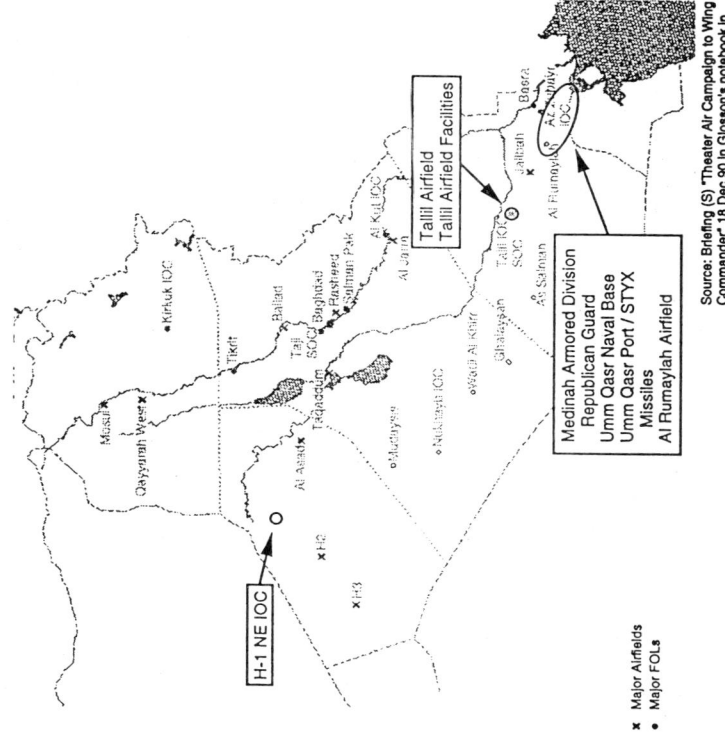

Figure 18
Attack Plan Second Day, PM - Night

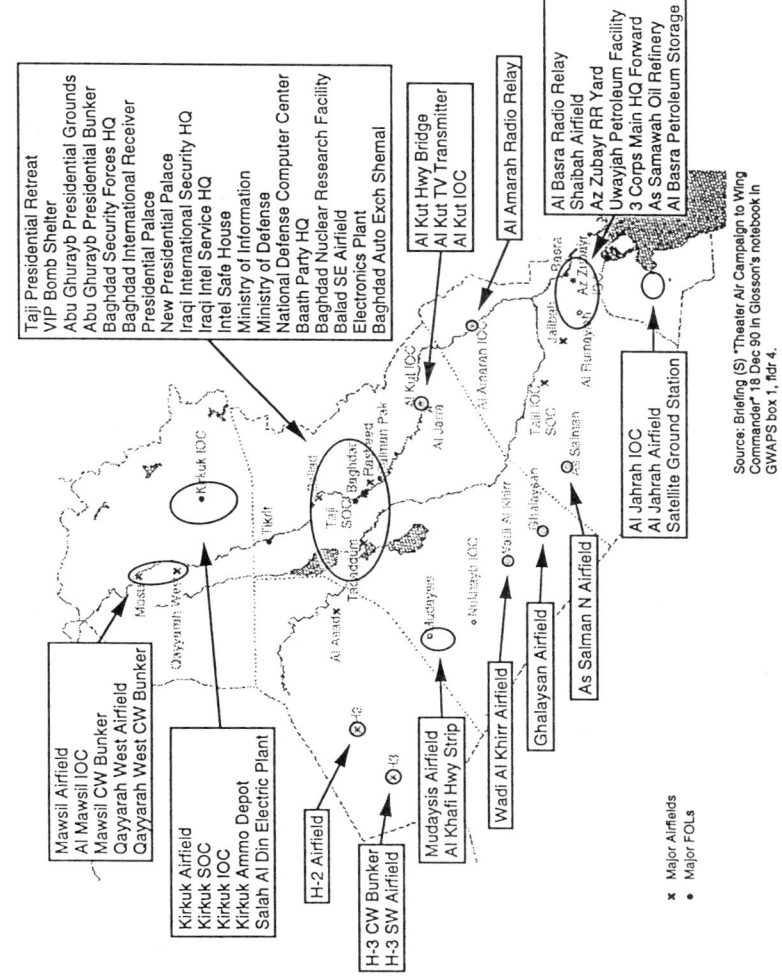

183

airfields and Scud storage sites in Al Jarrah area, Scud storage and airfield just north of Kuwait, airfields and strategic air defense targets along the southwestern Iraq border, and Scud sites in the H-2 and H-3 area. The second wave would start at first light (Figure 12) with attacks against command and control and electrical targets in northern Iraq, the Baghdad area, along the northern Kuwait border and in the Tallil area, while Scud sites were to be struck in Kuwait itself. The third wave of the first 24 hours would be in the afternoon (Figure 13) again against Baghdad, chemical bunkers and air defense sites in southern Iraq, oil facilities and railroad on the Iraq-Kuwait border, and again against Scud targets in the H-2 and H-3 area. The final strikes of the first 24 hours (Figure 14) after dark featured once again leadership, command and control, and other targets in the Baghdad area, airfields in central and eastern Iraq, strategic air defenses and chemical storage bunkers in the north, and another strike against targets in the H-2 and H-3 area.

The second 24 hour period began after midnight (Figure 15) with strikes planned primarily against strategic air defense targets in western, central, and eastern Iraqi, more attacks against leadership targets in Baghdad along with the nuclear research facility at Tuwaitha, and Scud storage facilities in Kuwait. In the early daylight of the second day (Figure 16), strikes were to be flown against Scud, chemical, and biological production facilities in the Baghdad area while the Republican Guard Forces located just north of Kuwait were to be hit. The second afternoon strikes were scheduled (Figure 17) against Iraqi military forces to include a navy port just north of Kuwait, the Tallil Airfield, and H-1 air defense headquarters. The final wave of airstrikes would be launched after dark hitting all over Iraq (Figure 18) including massive strikes against leadership targets in the Baghdad area, air fields and air defense installations along the Iraqi-Saudi Arabia border, airfields, air defense installations in northern Iraq, H-2 airfields, airfields in Kuwait, and major production facilities just north of the Kuwait border.

Day Three through Six would consist of reattack of 20% of first and second day targets, key targets requiring additional attacks (obtained from BDA), and the remainder of targets not covered during the first 48 hours. Thus in the first six days (Phase I) of the air campaign, planners intended to strike all 262 target listed on the 18 December target list. (See Table 20)

Table 20
Target Growth by Category

	Instant Thunder	13 Sep 90	11 Oct 90	1 Dec 90	18 Dec 90	15 Jan 91
Strategic Air Defense	10	21	40	28	27	58
Chemical/NBC	8	20	20	25	20	23
Scuds	n/a	n/a	note a	note a	16	43
Leadership	5	15	15	32	31	33
C3 (Telecom)	19	26	27	26	30	59
Electricity	10	14	18	16	16	17
Oil	6	8	10	7	12	12
Railroads&Bridges	3	12	12	28	28	33
Airfields	7	13	27	28	28	31
Naval & Ports	1	4	6	4	4	19
Military Support	15	41	43	44	38	62
Republican Guard	n/a	note b	note b	note b	12	37
Breaching	0	0	n/a	n/a	0	6
SAMs	0	0	n/a	n/a	0	43
Totals	84	174	218	238	262	476

Snapshot Dates:
    13 Sep 90   CJCS Briefing
    11 Oct 90   Presidential Briefing
    1 Dec 90   Theater Campaign Briefing
    18 Dec 90   Secretary of Defense Briefing
    15 Jan 91   Day before Desert Storm

Notes:
    (a) Scuds included in Chemical category
    (b) Republican Guards included in Military Support category

Source: (S) Brfg slides for snapshot dates located in "General Glosson Briefs," GWAPS Box 3, Folder 60.

The plan for Phase II was not as precise but did list a number of sorties. All attacks would take place in or just north of Kuwait. [DELETED].

For Phase III, Defining the Battlefield in the Kuwait theater, planners projected 600 aircraft per 24-hour period. They expected to destroy 50% of the Republican Guard armor, artillery, and personnel by the end of the fourth day. Then shifting to the regular ground forces while continuing Phase operations into Iraq to prevent reconstitution and resupply and Phase III operations to suppress enemy air defenses as required, they projected 50% attrition of armor on the tenth day, artillery on the eleventh day, and personnel on the twelfth day.

For the final phase, Ground Campaign, the briefing only mentioned missions for the ground units: "secure coast and seal battlefield" for the Marines, "liberate Kuwait City and seal battlefield" for the Saudi forces, "destroy Republican Guard" for VII U.S. Corps and "control access to KTO and seal battlefield" for XVIII U.S. Corps. This phase was anticipated to last fourteen days.

During the four weeks between these briefings and execution of the plan, only two major changes were made. First, new aircraft arrived and planners adjusted the master attack plans and air tasking orders. The number of F-117s in theater had doubled from 18 to 36 in early December (and would increase again to 42 during the campaign); F-111Fs increased from 32 to 64 by mid December; F-15Es from 24 to 48 by early January. Most of these precision-bomb droppers were allocated into Phase I targets before being shifted to Phase III targets; the F-117s would focus on Phase I targets throughout the campaign. Newly deployed F-16s (90 for a total of 210) and A-10s (42 for a total of 144) could be dedicated to Phase III from the beginning of the campaign.[95]

Second and most significant, planners almost doubled the size of their overall target list adding 214 targets (See Table 20). They added two new categories - breaching with 6 targets and surface-to-air missile sites with 43. Other categories almost doubled with strategic air defense adding 31, chemical adding 27, military support adding 24, and C3

---

[95](U) For more deployment data, see the (S/WN/NF/NC) GWAPS *Statistical Compendium*.

adding 29. Scuds (which had been separated from chemical in December) almost tripled its number with 43, while naval and ports went from 4 to 19.

The remainder of the planning effort for Desert Storm was spent refining master attack plans for the first seventy two hours. General Horner decided not to prepare air tasking orders before the campaign for more than the first two days–the situation after that he judged too unpredictable. There was a sense that the beginning of the campaign was critical to everything that followed, and there was a need to adjust to better intelligence and more aircraft.[96] Planners did fashion what they called master attack plan "shells" for the third and fourth day; however, they essentially listed the aircraft available for these days.[97]

By early January, CENTAF planners had settled on 477 individual targets (See Table 21). They now labored to determine which were to be hit first, during either the first, second, or third twenty four hours, or held until latter. They also tried to determine which targets would require restrikes. They chose 60% of the targets on the list to hit in the first seventy two hours. (See Figure 19) Their priority for the first twenty four hours–as had been since the Instant Thunder days–went towards the achievement of air superiority with 34% of the targets in the strategic air defense and airfield categories. Second, were strikes against communications (14%) followed by equal number of strikes against Scuds, leadership, and chemical weapons, all categories designated as centers of gravity. During the second twenty four hours, they again assigned air superiority as the top priority (43%) and moved leadership into second (19%). Significantly, they programmed almost 70% of the restrike missions against these target categories (strategic air defense, airfields, and leadership). In the third twenty four hours, they scheduled 20% of the strikes against airfields, 22% against leadership, and 19% against railroads and bridges. During this series of strikes, planners began a shift to military support (15%) and Republican Guards (8%).

After the first seventy two hours, planners presumably would direct strikes against the remaining targets not struck (the breaching and

---

[96](S) Intvw, Dr Perry Jamieson, Center for Air Force History, with Lt Col Baptiste, Shaw AFB, SC, 5 Mar 92.

[97](S) Intvw, Lt Col Robert Eskridge with A. S. Cochran, 16 Dec 92.

surface-to-air missile target categories were clearly to be struck after Phase I). Many of these targets to be struck were military support (22%) and Scuds (13%).

In the remaining days before the air campaign, planners continually reviewed target selection, making last minute adjustments. Most of these had to do with assignment of aircraft. There were also minor changes in targets scheduled for strikes. In essence, the plan remained unchanged.[98]

On 16 January, the Desert Storm air campaign plan was ready. Rather than a formal operation order like that issued by CENTCOM, CENTAF issued an air tasking order for each twenty-four-hour period. Day One would begin at 0300 Saudi time on 17 January and end at 0300 on 18 January. Little had changed from the plan outlined in the previous month to the wing commanders. For each package, planners specified time on target, mission number, target category and target number, a brief description of the target, and the number and type of aircraft assigned to hit that target. Planners also listed missions for aircraft without specific targets such as combat air patrol for F-15Cs, suppression of enemy air defenses for F-4Gs and EF-111s, Scud alert for F-15Es, deception for drones, and reconnaissance for RF-4Gs.

Planners had air tasking order ready for the first two days, but, in keeping with General Horner's wishes, had only rather sketchy master attack plans for third day and nothing for the subsequent days. Planners left sorties open on the third day (including F-117s) to restrike whatever would be indicated, presumably by bomb damage assessment. They would develop plans for the third and successive days as the air campaign unfolded. While planners may have had in mind what targets would be hit in the remaining three days of Phase I, they did not commit this to paper until after the first day's plan had been executed.

---

[98](S) Target Attacks by Day/Aircraft, 15 JAN/2000, Dough Hill data base, etc.

Table 21
ATO Targets Planned for Attack by Day

	8 January 1991						15 January 1991				
	Total	1st 24 hrs	2d 24 hrs	3d 24 hrs	Re-strikes	Not Hit	Total	1st 24 hrs	2d 24 hrs	3d 24 hrs	Re-strikes	Not Hit
Strategic Air Defense	54	22	14	2	13 1-3x[a]	27	58	26	21	7	15 7-3x	9
Chemical	19	12	6	6	5 1-3x	2	23	10	8	10	8 1-3x	3
Scuds	44	13	2	0	2	30	44	13	3	0	4	28
Leadership	33	12	14	20	13 1-3x	2	33	13	13	16	13 6-3x	4
C3 (Telecom)	59	17	7	8	2	29	59	17	14	3	3	32
Electricity	17	11	2	3	0	1	17	13	11	2	9 1-3x	0
Oil	12	4	2	6	0	0	12	6	4	2	3	2
Railroads & Bridges	33	8	4	17	7	8	33	7	2	16	2	10
Airfields	31	20	18	18	19 7-3x	0	31	28	17	13	19 16-3/4x	3
Naval/Ports	17	0	2	2	0	13	19	2	7	3	2	10
Military Spt	71	4	2	16	1	51	62	5	14	17	4	39
Republican Guard	38	3	4	9	4	25	37	4	4	4	4 2-3x, 1-4x	31
Breaching	6	0	0	0	0	6	6	0	0	0	0	6
SAMs	43	0	0	0	0	43	43	0	0	0	0	43
Totals	477	126	77	107	66	237	477	144	118	93	86	220

Note:
(a) Notation indicates a number of targets to be restruck and the times it will will be restruck; ie, 1-3x indicates one target will be restruck 3 times; 16-3/4x indicates 16 targets will be restruck 3 or 4 times.

Sources: (S) Attack Database compiled by Maj. Hill, GWAPS; (S) Doc, 15 January 1991 Target Attack by Day and Aircraft, in GWAPS MAP file.

**Figure 19
ATO Targets by Category**

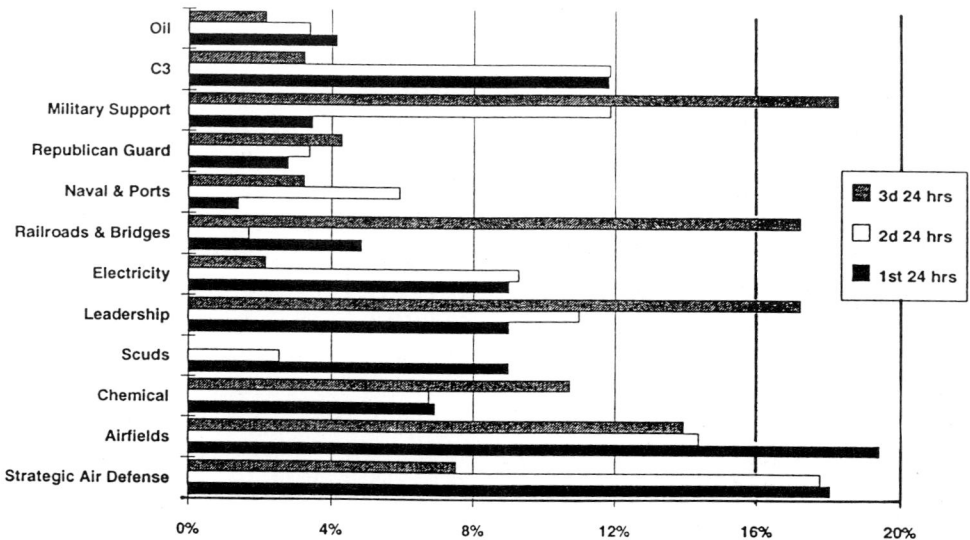

As General Horner was keenly aware, no plan could be expected to survive in detail after the first moment of execution. Consequently, CENTAF air campaign planners devoted an extraordinary amount of work to the first 48 hours of a campaign projected to last thirty two days. Whatever happened in the first two days, planners would be under great pressure to prepare air tasking orders for the following days in no more time than it took to execute them.

7

Intelligence For Air Campaign Planning

As in past conflicts, intelligence enabled the planning for Desert Shield and Desert Storm—it did not formulate it. In the case of defensive planning for USCINCCENT OPLAN 1002-90, intelligence analysts were caught in the post-Cold War transition from Soviet-European emphasis to smaller, but more numerous regional threats. As a result of the region's relatively low priority before Desert Storm, their information on Iraq was less than comprehensive and woefully out of date. Even when those analysts who were watching the Arabian Peninsula detected early signs that Baghdad might be preparing for military operations, they were unable at first to capture the attention of senior policy makers who, up until the summer of 1990, had been advised that Iraq had been exhausted by its war with Iran and would limit its bellicosity to the diplomatic arena.[1]

In February 1990, Gen. H. Norman Schwarzkopf tasked the commander of his air component, Lt. Gen. Charles Horner of Ninth Air Force (CENTAF) to develop a concept of air campaigns for OPLAN 1002-90, the new contingency plan for the defense of the Arabian Peninsula (particularly Saudi Arabia) against an attack from Iraq. As part of this effort, CENTAF intelligence planners began to select potential targets in Iraq and Kuwait to support Horner's objectives to gain air superiority, protect friendly nations, their oil fields and transshipment facilities, and delay and attrit Iraqi forces. In addition to these general objectives, Horner added the requirement to counter the potential Iraqi chemical threat with a series of retaliatory strikes against high value facilities in Iraq.[2]

---

[1] [DELETED] (S/NF) Doc, *Security Environment 2000: A CENTCOM View*, US. Central Command, 21 May 90, p III-3; [DELETED] GWAPS Glock files.

[2] (S/NF) Intvw, Perry Jamison, Rich Davis, and Barry Barlow with Lt Gen Horner, 4 Mar 92, p 12, GWAPS NA-303.

The intelligence officers first developed seven traditional target sets to meet Horner's objectives. (Table 22) Unlike their later plans, this first look at Iraq limited potential leadership targets to those facilities directly involved in military command and control. Likewise, they planned strikes against the Iraqi infrastructure with the intent to deny direct support to the military and therefore limit Baghdad's offensive capability. They selected "high value" targets solely to dissuade Baghdad's use of chemical or biological weapons against U.S. and friendly forces.

From this baseline, intelligence planners developed specific target lists for each of their major categories using the Joint Target List from CINCCENT OPLAN 1002-88, the Automated Installation File (AIF),[3] and other documents in their reference. Within each category, they selected only those targets or facilities they believed directly supported the stated objectives of OPLAN 1002-90.(See Table 7-2) Air bases across Iraq housing fighters and fighter-bombers were selected to meet the offensive counterair objective. To delay and reduce attacking forces, they selected interdiction targets such as bridges and supply depots.[4] Close air support would be directed as required to blunt the expected Iraqi attack. Finally, in response to Iraq's chemical threat, the targeteers chose sites including chemical weapons production and storage and "high value" targets that targeteers believed the Hussein regime would not want to place in jeopardy.[5]

---

[3] The Defense Intelligence Agency maintains a computerized database known as the Automated Installation File. The AIF served as a baseline for all target databases and is the single most authoritative source for U.S. targeting. With its Basic Encyclopedia (BE) numbering system, it stores, manipulates, and allows retrieval of a wide variety of target information. The AIF does not prioritize targets, but rather serves as a menu from which planners can select, or exclude, targets to achieve the objectives of any contingency or operation plan.

[4] (S) Brfg, "OPLAN 1002 Air Operations," by Lt Gen Horner to Gen Schwarzkopf at MacDill AFB, Apr 90, in preparation for Exercise Internal Look-90. GWAPS NA-256.

[5] (S) Horner briefing.

Table 22
CENTAF Target Sets by OPLAN 1002-90 Objectives

Objective	Target Sets	Components
Gain and maintain air superiority	Air Defense System	Air defense command, control and communication (C3) network EW/GCI Radars Surface-to-air missile sites Airfields
Protect friendly nations, oil fields, and transshipment facilities	Offensive Air System	Airfields Air Force C3
	Offensive Missile System	Ballistic Missile sites Offensive Missile C3 Missile Support Facilities
	Weapons of Mass Destruction System	Nuclear, Biological, and Chemical storage facilities NBC production facilities
Delay and attrition of ground forces	Ground Force System	Ground Forces Ground Force C3 Lines of Communications Logistics/support facilities
Counter chemical	NBC System	NBC storage NBC production
	High value target System	Targets of high value to enemy

Source: Brfg (S), "OPLAN 1002 Air Operations," by Lt. Gen. Horner to Gen. Schwarzkopf at MacDill AFB, April 1990. GWAPS NA-256.

Table 23
CENTAF Target List – 15 June 1990

GAT Category	Known Targets	GAT Category	Known Targets
Airfields	37	Leadership (military)	3
Chemical	1	Military Support	22
Nuclear	1	POL Storage	9
Biological	1	POL Distribution	13
C3 (military)	14	Naval	7
Electrical	6	Air Defense	72
Lines of Communication	25	Scuds	7
Total Targets:			**218**

Source: Target Study (S/NF/WN), 9 TIS, "Iraqi Target Study," 15 Jun 90.

As the lists took shape, CENTAF targeting officers began to build target folders. These target-specific portfolios contained an annotated 1:250,000 map, existing imagery, available miscellaneous data on the target, and a weaponeering sheet. At this stage, the intelligence analysts discovered that many of the installation file records (the primary source of targeting information) were incomplete and lacked information on construction, function, or military significance. In many cases, no supporting information was available. In addition, there was a significant lack of imagery on 128 of the 218 potential targets they had identified. To complicate this important issue further, imagery that did exist generally was outdated (some dated back to 1973) and therefore of limited use. In April, the CENTAF Intelligence staff (the 9th Tactical Intelligence Squadron) submitted its target recommendations to General Horner and informed him of existing intelligence shortfalls.[6] CENTAF targeteers completed their Iraqi Target Study on 15 June 1990, and used it both during Exercise Internal Look 90 and as the foundation for initial defensive and retaliatory planning during Operation Desert Shield.

At the same time CENTAF intelligence planners were assembling their target list for General Horner, the Central Command staff queried its component commands (Army, Navy, Marines and Special Operations) for additional target nominations for the Joint Target List that would accompany OPLAN 1002-90. The CENTCOM joint target list was completed on 27 June 1990 and is shown below in Table 24 alongside the CENTAF target list. It is interesting to note the different numbers of targets in several of the categories in each target list. For example, the CENTAF list detailed seventy-two air defense facilities while the CENTCOM list contained only four. Also, CENTAF showed twenty-two military production and twenty-five communication targets while CENTCOM specified eighty-one and seventy-nine respectively. The reason for these discrepancies depended on each command's particular focus. CENTAF planners naturally concentrated on air-related targets, while planners at CENTCOM had a joint outlook and thus incorporated facilities important to ground, naval, and marine forces and eliminated some air-related facilities that they felt were of a lesser value.

---

[6](S) Intvw, Capt John Glock with Maj John Heidrick, 9 TIS/INT, 7 Jan 92, GWAPS NA-267.

Figure 20
CENTAF Iraqi Target Study – Kuwait

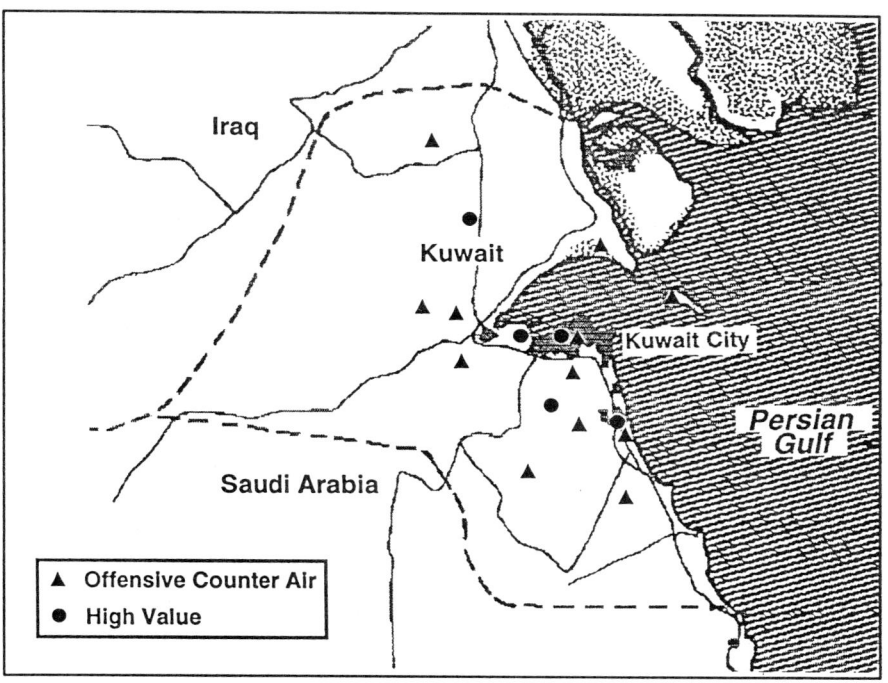

Source: Doc (S/NF/WN), 9 TIS/INT, Iraqi Target Study, 15 Jun 90, GWAPS NA-168.

**Figure 21a and 21b
CENTAF Iraqi Target Study Attack Plan – Iraq
All Positions Approximate**

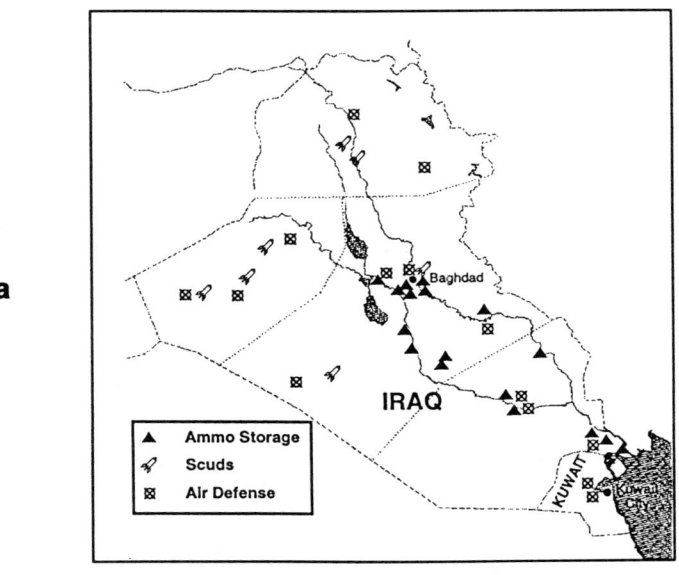

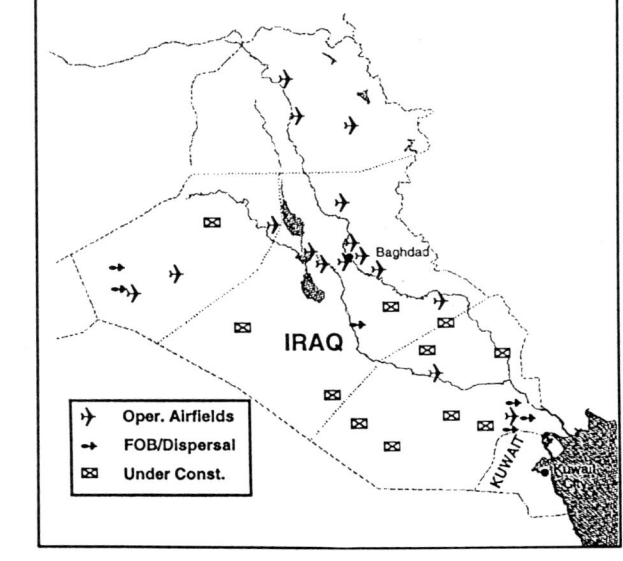

**Figure 21c and 21d
CENTAF Iraqi Target Study Attack Plan – Iraq
All Positions Approximate**

c
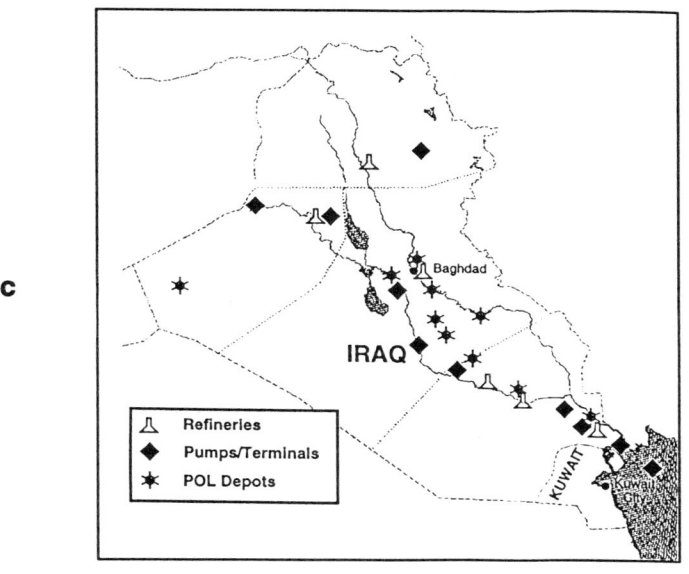

d
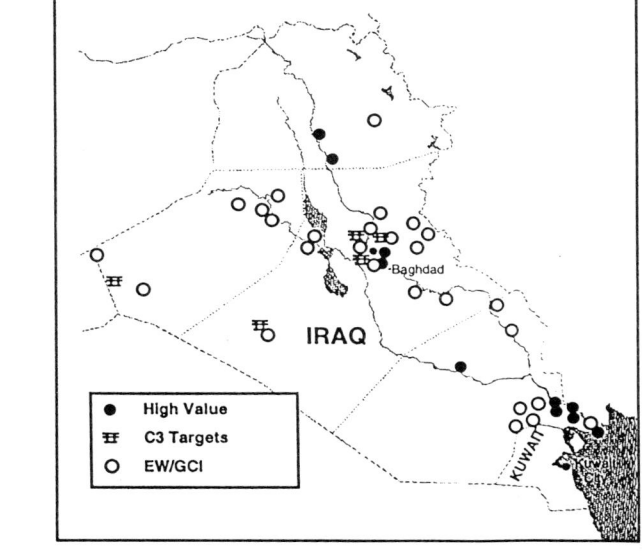

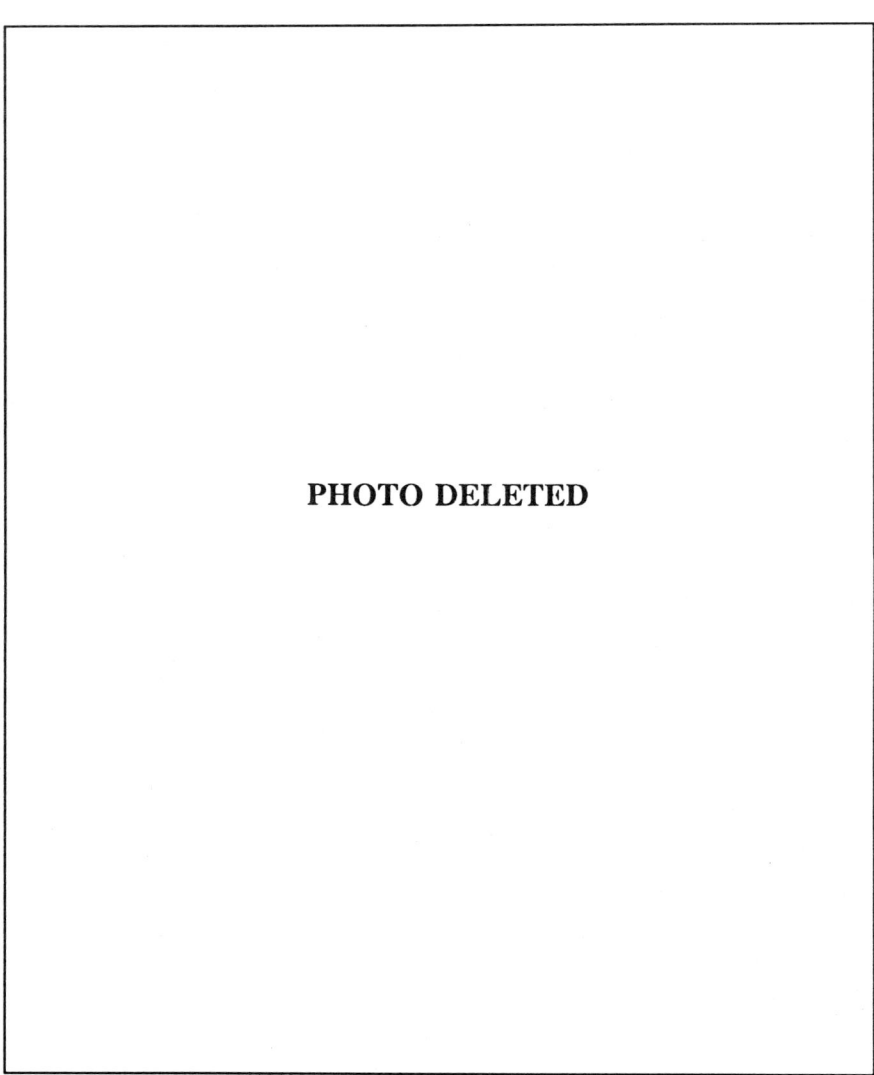

Rumaylah Ammunition Storage Area.

Table 24
CENTAF and CENTCOM Target Lists

Target Categories	CENTAF 15 Jun 90	CENTCOM 27 Jun 90
Leadership: Civilian	0	0
Military	3	4
Command, Control and Communication:		
Military	14	19
AM/FM/TV	0	2
Air Defense	72	4
Airfields	37	58
Nuclear	1	0
Biological	1	1
Chemical	1	1
Military Production and Support	22	81
Electric	6	0
POL: Storage	9	16
Distribution	13	3
Scuds	7	0
Republican Guard	0	0
Ground Forces	0	8
Lines of Communications	25	79
Naval Forces	7	17
Total Targets	**218**	**293**

Sources: Target Study (S/NF/WN), 9 TIS, "Iraqi Target Study," 15 Jun 90; Doc (S/NF/NC/WN), USCENTCOM Joint Target List (JTL), *USCINCCENT OPLAN 1002-90*, Annex B, Appx 4, Tab A, 27 Jun 90.

These two lists reflected target development accomplished through the deliberate planning system by 2 August 1990. Despite the fact that these lists were produced before Iraq invaded Kuwait and became the focus of increased U.S. intelligence gathering, they provided a sound foundation for Desert Shield and Desert Storm. Yet, both target lists clearly lacked adequate information on nuclear, biological and chemical target sets while, by the nature of precrisis plan objectives and policies, ignored civilian leadership completely in favor of military headquarters. Mobile Scuds were ignored, and only seven fixed launchers were identified on the CENTAF target list. Despite these oversights, CENTAF planners identified forty-six percent of the targets eventually planned for the first day of the air campaign and listed on the 16 January 1991 Master Attack Plan. Likewise, the CENTCOM target list detailed forty-four percent of the first-day targets. Combined, the two list identified sixty-three percent of the targets on Desert Storm's D-Day air tasking order.[7]

The target lists maintained by the intelligence staffs did not, nor were they intended to, contain *all* identified potential targets in Iraq. To the contrary, target lists detailed only those installations listed in the installation files that intelligence and operations planners thought necessary to achieve the objectives of a specific plan. Thus, separate contingency plans developed for different scenarios–for example, removal of citizens from an embassy under hostile conditions as opposed to large scale military operations–would by nature require quite divergent target lists. The following graphic (Table 25) supports this important notion and summarizes, according to target categories developed and used by Brig. Gen. Buster Glosson's Guidance, Apportionment, and Targeting division (the Black Hole) for air tasking order development throughout the war, all Iraqi installation file records that existed at the outbreak of the crisis, as well as the much smaller number that planners believed were required to achieve for the defensive objectives in OPLAN 1002-90.[8]

---

[7](S/NF/WN) Target Study, 9 TIS, "Iraqi Target Study," 15 Jun 90; (S/NF/NC/WN) Doc, USCENTCOM Joint Target List (JTL).

[8](S/NF/NC/WN) GAT (Black Hole) categories and AIF (Automated Installation Files) records are used throughout this chapter to analyze and compare target growth.

Table 25
Known Iraqi Targets by GAT Category – 2 August 1990

GAT Category	TGTS	GAT Category	TGTS
Airfields	122	Leadership/Military Support	126
NBC	40		
C3	201	Oil	211
Electrical	230	Naval	46
		Railroads and Bridges	532
		Strategic Air Defense	493
		SAMs	214
		Scuds	24
Known Target Related Records:		2,239	
Total AIF Records:		3,302	

Source: Target database (S/NF), compiled by Capt John Glock, GWAPS. Information extracted from DIA AIF reports for the dates shown.

Table 25 demonstrates the selective nature of target list development as well as the broad coverage of diverse installations provided by the Automated Installation File. Taking the second area first, one notices a difference of 1,063 entries between the number of the file entries on 2 August 1990 and the total number of potential targets. This resulted from the encompassing nature of the file that contained records for all types of installation [DELETED]. A comparison of this table with Table 24 also highlights a significant difference between the number of potential targets on the CENTAF and CENTCOM target lists (218 and 293) and those identified in the AIF.

This raises the question of what the U.S. intelligence community knew of Iraq's and Saddam Hussein's intent and physical capabilities. [DELETED].[9] However, Iraq had emerged from the Iran-Iraq War with

---

[9][DELETED]

the most formidable military in the Gulf:

[DELETED].[10]

In May 1990, CENTCOM's intelligence staff estimate of Baghdad's military ambitions was that "Iraq is not expected to use military force to attack Kuwait or Saudi Arabia to seize disputed territory or resolve a dispute over oil policy."[11] Gen. Schwarzkopf's analysts also chose to reinforce the [DELETED] warning about Iraqi military strength:

> Iraq's army significantly outnumbers all others on the Arabian Peninsula. Additionally, it possesses bombers and fighters with sufficient range to strike oil fields and other strategic targets. . . .It currently has the capability to conduct a *limited* ground offensive as well.[12]

Amidst heightened tensions between Iraq and Kuwait in the summer of 1990 and the resulting increased level of U.S. intelligence gathering and analysis, on 25 July 1990, an intelligence analyst, attempted to warn senior administration and military decision makers about potential Iraqi aggression.[13] [DELETED].[14] [DELETED].

Yet, the U.S. intelligence community saw the Iraqi Army as the largest, most experienced, and best-equipped regional force. Moreover, Baghdad possessed and had demonstrated the unique capability in the region to conduct multicorps offensive operations.[15] By January 1991, both DIA and CIA had fair estimates of the number of Iraqi troops and equipment deployed in the KTO. (Table 26 and Figure 22) The Washington-based intelligence analysts did have, however, an excellent picture of how the Iraqi Army and Republican Guard divisions were deployed into three stages: (1) front lines to meet, slow, and reduce an initial allied

---

[10][DELETED]

[11](S/NF) Doc, *Security Environment 2000: A CENTCOM View*, U.S. Central Command, 21 May 90, p III-3.

[12]Emphasis added. (S/NF) *Security Environment 2000: A CENTCOM View*, p III-2.

[13][DELETED]

[14](S/NF) Intvw, Capt John R. Glock, GWAPS, with [DELETED], 10 Jul 92.

[15](S/NF) Doc, DIA, *Iraqi Ground and Air Forces Doctrine, Tactics and Operations* (C/NF), DDB-2600-6123-90, Defense Research Reference Series, Feb 90, GWAPS Glock file, pp 134-135.

attack; (2) tactical and operational reserves of armor and mechanized divisions throughout central Kuwait and southern Iraq to reinforce and block coalition penetrations; and (3) Republican Guard divisions north and west of Kuwait as strategic reserve to counterattack the main coalition attack.[16]

Table 26
Estimates of Iraqi Ground Forces – 16 January 1991

Major Item	Total	In KTO
Personnel	1 Million	336,000[17]
Tanks: including T-72	5,000+	3,475
Armored Personnel Carriers	10,000+	3,080
Artillery	3,000+	2,475

Source: Report (S/NF/NC/WN), DIA, *Military Intelligence Summary, Vol III, Part II, Middle East and North Africa (Persian Gulf)*, Jul 90; [DELETED]

On the eve of the Gulf War, the Iraqi army consisted of eleven corps or corps-level headquarters with seventy-one divisions, including twelve Republican Guard divisions, six armored divisions, three mechanized infantry divisions, and fifty-one infantry divisions. Fifty-one of these divisions were deployed in the KTO, with another four Republican Guard brigades in Baghdad, eighteen infantry divisions along the Turkish border, two infantry divisions along the Syrian border, and three divisions on the Iranian border.[18]

---

[16](S/NF/NC) Memo, Director CIA, subj: Iraq as a Military Adversary, SNIE Memorandum to Holders of SNIE 36.2-5-90 (C/NF), 2 Jan 91.

[17]Personnel figure contains adjustments to 540,000 total for actual unit manning (-120,000) and troops on leave (-84,000) for 43 divisions and independent brigades in KTO on 17 January 1991, [DELETED] US House of Rep. Comm. on Armed Services, Defense for a New Era, Lessons of the Persian Gulf War (Wash, DC. 1992)

[18](S/NF) Brfg, at GWAPS; DOD, *Conduct of the War*, p 111.

Table 27
Iraqi Pre-War Ground Order of Battle

Republican Guards (12 Divisions)

Hammurabi Armored Division	**Medina Armored Division**
Tawakalna Mechanized Division	Baghdad Mechanized Division
Al-Faw Infantry Division	Nebuchadnezzar Infantry Division
Adnan Infantry Division	Special Forces Division
Al-Nida' Infantry Division	Al-'Abed Infantry Division
Al-Mustafa Infantry Division	Al-Quds Infantry Division

Armored and Mechanized Infantry Divisions (6 AD/3 Mech)

3d AD	**12th AD**	1st Mech
6th AD	**17th AD**	5th Mech
10th AD	**52d AD**	51st Mech

Infantry Divisions (51)

2d ID	**18th ID**	**25th ID**	32d ID	39th ID	**47th ID**
4th ID	**19th ID**	**26th ID**	33d ID	40th ID	**48th ID**
7th ID	**20th ID**	**27th ID**	34th ID	41st ID	**49th ID**
8th ID	**21st ID**	**28th ID**	35th ID	42d ID	50th ID
11th ID	22d ID	**29th ID**	**36th ID**	44th ID	53d ID
14th ID	23d ID	**30th ID**	37th ID	**45th ID**	54th ID
15th ID	24th ID	**31st ID**	38th ID	46th ID	56th ID
16th ID					

Boldface entries indicate units located in the KTO during the war

Notes:
(a) The Hammurabi, Medina, and Tawakalna Divisions spearheaded the invasion of Kuwait while the remaining Republican Guard divisions served as follow-on and reserve forces. The Al-Nida', Al-'Abed, Al-Mustafa, and Al-Quds Divisions were formed after the invasion of Kuwait and performed internal security roles during the war.

(b) Eight infantry divisions remain unidentified.

Sources: Multiple.

Figure 22
Iraqi Ground Force Deployment in the KTO – 16 January 1991

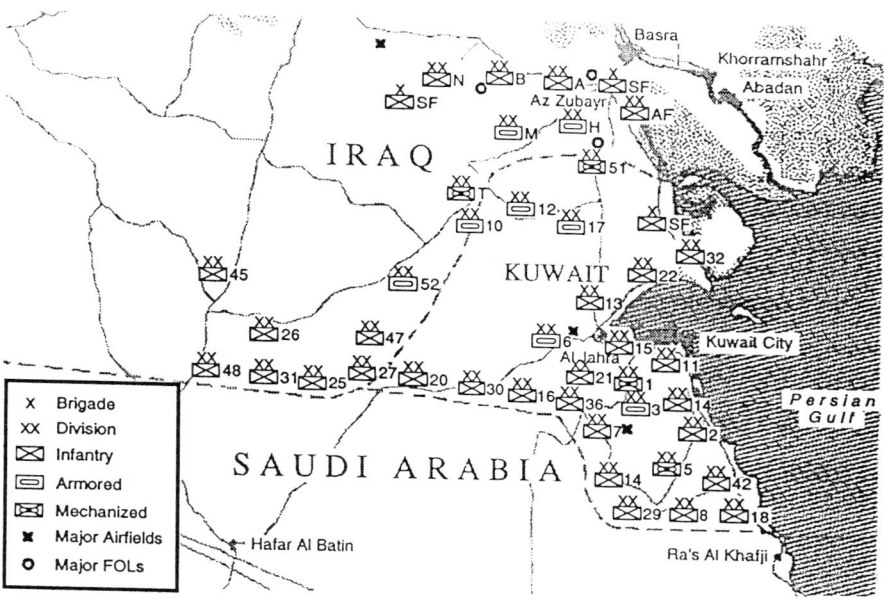

Legend of Iraqi Republican Guard Division:			
T = Tawakalna	H = Hammurabi	B = Baghdad	AF = Al Faw
M = Madinah	N = Nebuchadnezzar	A = Adnan	SF = Special Forces

Sources: Multiple sources including Rpt (S/NF/WN) *Conduct of the Persian Gulf Conflict: An Interim Report to Congress*, Pursuant to Title V Persian Gulf Conflict Supplemental Authorization and Personnel Benefits Act of 1991 (Public Law 102-25), Jul 91.

Regarding air forces, the national intelligence community saw the Iraqi Air Force as capable of threatening its neighbors but hindered by highly centralized planning, a lack of fully trained pilots, and a defensive doctrine.[19] In a paper prepared for General Powell during the early weeks of the crisis, DIA emphasized that despite its large size and capable aircraft (Table 28) the Iraqi Air Force was unable to defend its airspace during the Iran-Iraq War and had preferred to protect its aircraft and pilots than risk them to accomplish difficult missions.[20] [DELETED] Iraq would be unable to defend its airspace from a coalition attack and would either be neutralized quickly in the air or would choose to withhold its aircraft from action in hardened shelters. After only a few days of combat [DELETED] the only real threat to coalition pilots would come at low level [DELETED] from antiaircraft artillery and portable surface-to-air missiles.[21]

As mentioned previously, American intelligence recognized the highly centralized nature of the Iraqi military and political systems. And this leadership resided in the person of Saddam Hussein. The CIA, DIA, and State Department devoted a great deal of effort examining him and concluded that he would remain in power for the foreseeable future despite the presence of numerous, ineffective, and demoralized opposition groups.[22] Intelligence analysts saw that Saddam Hussein based his power structure on three interrelated pillars–the Ba'ath Party, intelligence and security services, and the military. Saddam and the Ba'ath Party maintained their power through a pervasive, effective and harsh intelligence and security apparatus that periodically infiltrated and decimated internal opposition groups.[23] Thus, both CENTCOM and CENTAF staffs targeted leadership before the crisis erupted, but only the military portion of this

---

[19](S) Doc, "Air ops summary of air war written by Lt Gen Horner after 8 ½ days of combat 261100Z91," in TACC CC/DO Current Ops Log, GWAPS NA-215; and (S) D-19H–Gen Horner Air War Summary Meeting with Deptula, 26 Jan 91 ("As provided by L/C Deptula & BG Glosson during 1 ½ hour discussion with Gen Horner"); [DELETED] (S/NF) Doc, DIA, *Iraqi Ground and Air Forces Doctrine, Tactics and Operations* (C/NF), DDB-2600-6123-90, DIA, Feb 90, p 110.

[20]Paper, "Iraqi Air Defense Capabilities," DIA/DB-8C3, for CJCS, n.d. (cover letter dated 24 Aug 90, stated the paper was prepared during the past two weeks.)

[21][DELETED]

[22](S/NF/WN/NC/PR) Docs, *MIS, Volume III, Part II, Middle East and North Africa (Persian Gulf)*(C/NF), DIA, Jul 90, Iraqi section p 1; [DELETED] State Department, Memorandum for Brent Scowcroft, Subject: "Options Paper on Iraq," May 16, 1990 p 2.

[23](S/NF/WN/NC/PR) *Ibid.*

foundation that supported the Baghdad regime.[24] The inclusion of additional political targets into air campaigning occurred only after the United States was committed to Operation Desert Shield.

Table 28
Iraqi Air Force as of 2 August 1990

Major Items	Estimated Number
Personnel	18,000
All-Weather Fighter	326
VFR Fighter	140
Fighter Bomber	292
Ground Attack	46
Bomber	15

Source: Doc, (S/NF) DIA, *Iraqi Ground and Air Forces Doctrine, Tactics and Operations*, DDB-2600-6123-90, Feb 90; Report (S/NF/NC/WN), DIA, *MIS, Vol III, Part II, Middle East and North Africa (Persian Gulf)*, Jul 90.

U.S. intelligence analysts also had a long-standing interest in Iraq's preoccupation with developing weapons of mass destruction. [DELETED].[25]

[DELETED].[26] [DELETED].[27]

---

[24] The CENTCOM Joint Target List did not include government control centers or ministries. The CENTAF (9 TIS) Iraqi Target Study did not have a leadership category. Both lists included military headquarters as Command and Control targets.

[25] [DELETED]

[26] (S/NF) Intvw, Capt John R. Glock, GWAPS, with [DELETED] CIA, 10 Jul 92.

[27] CENTAF may not have known of Al Qaim because it did not [DELETED] carry a nuclear related category code in the AIF.

PHOTO DELETED

Al Qaim Superphosphate Plant. Uranium Enrichment Facility.

A second aspect of Baghdad's weapons program that attracted U.S. attention was chemical. Before the war, the intelligence community agreed that Iraq had embarked on a long-term chemical weapons program with the goal of becoming self-sufficient in the production of precursor chemicals, chemical agents, and chemical munitions.[28] While not yet self-sufficient, Iraq already had produced and weaponized large quantities of blister and nerve agents and adapted them for delivery by standard and cluster bombs, air-to-surface rockets, artillery and mortar, and possibly for surface-to-surface missiles, including Scuds.[29]

As important as knowledge of Iraq's chemical capabilities was to U.S. theater campaign planners on 2 August 1990, information on Baghdad's intentions was even more sought after. Everyone knew they had chemical weapons and that they had used them in the past, but would Saddam Hussein order their use against U.S. forces if we became embroiled in the region? [DELETED].[30] American military planners assumed this throughout their planning.

The final leg of the Iraqi weapons triad was biological warfare. Based on prewar information and analysis, Iraq possessed the most advanced and aggressive biological warfare program in the third world. This arsenal contained anthrax and botulin toxin; and their scientists continued research into several other agents, while their military intended to use them if Iraqi territory was threatened.[31] Iraq was also thought to be able to produce the munitions to deliver the toxins, although there was no hard evidence at the time to prove it.[32] This, however, did not lessen the potential threat, since many existing Iraqi chemical weapons could be used to deliver biological toxins.[33]

---

[28] [DELETED] Also (S/NF/WN) *Offensive Chemical Warfare Programs in the Middle East* (C), DIA, 15 Mar 90, p 6.

[29] (S/NF/WN) [DELETED] NTIC-DA31.

[30] (S/NF) *Iraqi Ground and Air Forces Doctrine, Tactics and Operations* (C/NF), DIA, Feb 90, pp 74-75.

[31] (S/NF/WN) Paper, [DELETED], unknown author, n.d. The paper was included in a package of DIA reports produced for the Secretary of Defense, CJCS, *et al* Cover letter dated 24 Aug 90.

[32] (S/NF/WN) Paper, [DELETED], NTIC-DA31, 7 Aug 90.

[33] (S/NF/WN) Paper, [DELETED].

Warned of this serious potential threat, U.S. theater air campaign planners naturally sought information on all known biological production and storage facilities. [DELETED] As a result, the sole biological warfare facility known by theater planners was Salman Pak with its four suspected storage bunkers.[34]

Disagreements among military and civilian intelligence analysts on Iraqi equipment and capabilities went beyond Baghdad's weapons of mass destruction to include different views on its short-range ballistic missile program. Key within this area was knowledge about Iraqi Scud missiles where, once again, information available before the crisis was sketchy and limited. DIA believed that Baghdad had purchased approximately 600 missiles from the Soviet Union between 1976 and 1979 along with twenty-two mobile Scud-B MAZ-[DELETED] transporter-erector-launchers capable of launching Iraq's standard and modified Scuds.

Figure 23
Intelligence Estimates of Iraqi Scud Missiles

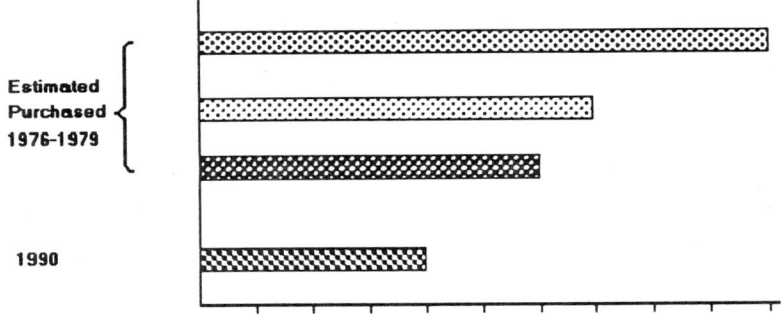

In addition, DIA estimated that Baghdad built as many as 12-15 more launchers domestically, bringing the potential number to 34-37. [DELETED]. Discounting the missiles expended during the eight-year Iraq-

---

[34][DELETED]

Iran War, U.S. intelligence estimated that Iraq had approximately 400 missiles and between 22 and 37 mobile launchers when they invaded Kuwait.[35]

With the Iraqi invasion of Kuwait and the launching of Operation Desert Shield came an associated surge of intelligence-gathering and analysis to support yet undetermined U.S. military and political response options. CENTCOM and DIA, [DELETED][36] activated Crisis Situation Rooms and Crisis Action Teams, as did Ninth Air Force/CENTAF, MAC, SAC, and TAC following the Warning Order issued by the Chairman, Joint Chiefs of Staff, at 0759Z 2 August.[37] From that moment until the initiation of the air campaign in January 1991, Iraq supplanted all other areas as the primary focus for the intelligence community.

Iraq's increased priority caused significant growth in its Automated Installation File entries. Intelligence collection resoureces were redirected to scour Iraq and Kuwait for targets that presented direct or potential threats to Saudi Arabia, Israel, and coalition forces as they deployed to the Arabian Peninsula. As new threats or political or economic facilities were identified, intelligence analysts added them to the file. Existing installation file entries also received new attention, with emphasis placed on updating and expanding available information in the national database. As a result (see Table 29), the overall Iraqi Automated Installation File grew some thirty-eight percent (potential targets grew by forty-three percent) between August 1990 and January 1991. This marked the greatest period of quantitative growth in intelligence information on Iraq and far exceeded that which occurred during or after the war.

---

[35](S/NF/WN) Brfg, [DELETED] DIA (Technical Intelligence) to GWAPS, 30 Sep 92; (S/NF/NC/WN/PR) Doc, *MIS, Vol III, Part II, Middle East and North Africa (Persian Gulf)*, [DELETED] Jul 90, p 15; (S/NF) Brfg, *USCENTCOM Preliminary Planning 2-6 August 90*, USAF HRA Desert Shield Files, n.d.

[36][DELETED]

[37][DELETED]

Table 29
Known Iraqi Targets by Category – 16 January 1991

GAT Category	Records	Number Increase	Percent Increase
Airfields	128	6	5
NBC-Associated	60	20	33
C3	604	403	200
Electrical	242	12	5
Military Leadership & Support	213	87	69
Oil	218	7	3
Naval	53	7	15
Railroads and Bridges	596	64	12
Strategic Air Defense	674	181	37
SAM-Associated	285	71	33
Scud-Associated	121	97	404
Target-related records:	3,194 (+955 entries or 43% growth)		
Total records:	4,543 (+1,241 entries or 38% growth)		

Source: Target database (S/NF).

The target growth reflected in the above table occurred more as a result of an expanding collection rather than assigning relative importance by senior political and military policy makers to individual target categories. [DELETED].[38]

Others facilities, such as airfields, electrical, oil, and naval bases, while important, generally were well known and documented before the crisis–although not always fully annotated or supported with timely imagery. Even the most important categories–nuclear-biological-chemical, command-control and communications, air defense, and Scuds–experienced uneven growth due to a combination of excellent Iraqi security measures to prevent disclosure (nuclear-biological-chemical grew by twenty targets). The sudden increase of targets could also be attributed to post-invasion dispersion of fielded Iraqi forces (command-control-communications and air defense grew by 584 sites), and even to changes in accounting methods.

Significant additions to the categories of weapons of mass destruction during Desert Shield included the Al Qaim nuclear facility (added to both the Joint Target List and the Master Target List by 15 August 1990) and the biological warfare-related Salman Pak installation and its associated bunkers. [DELETED].[39] [DELETED].

Meanwhile, planners at Checkmate passed DIA information about three additional biological production facilities and seventeen storage bunkers to theater planners.[40] This increase in potential targets caused the biological storage category to achieve the greatest percentage of growth during Desert Shield, moving from only two known facilities on 2 August to nineteen identified sites by the time the air campaign began.

---

[38](S) Brfg, "USCENTCOM Preliminary Planning 2-6 Aug 90," USAF HRA Desert Shield Files, n.d.; CENTAF list is the "Prioritized Political Target List," n.d.; (S) MSG, From CCJ2-P, subj: USCENTCOM Joint Target List for Operation Desert Shield, dtg 162005Z Aug 90.

[39](S/NF/RD) Rpt, Joint Atomic Intelligence Committee, Nuclear Proliferation Working Group, JAEIC 90-009X Nov 90, GWAPS, CHSH 114-4. See also (S/NF) OPLAN Desert Storm, 16 Dec 90, pp B-44 - B-45.

[40][DELETED]

Of all the Black Hole target categories, Scuds had the second most dramatic growth during Desert Shield, rising from twenty-four installation file entries on 2 August to some 121 records by 16 January 1991. The increase in targets did not equate to increased knowledge but rather reflected a change in DIA's accounting methodology. Beginning in December, DIA issued individual basic encyclopedia target numbers to each launch site and associated facility rather than using a single entry for an entire facility. Thus, a facility with several fixed launch sites that, prior to the end of 1990 had a single target number, suddenly grew to multiple entries without an associated substantive growth in knowledge about the facility. Some new sites were also located and added to the file, but their numbers were insignificant, when compared to military and political problems caused by Baghdad's surface-to-surface missiles during Desert Storm.

This was what CENTCOM and CENTAF air campaign planners knew about Iraq on the eve of war in January 1991. The air campaign plan for Desert Storm, so carefully massaged for five months, likewise was based on this body of knowledge. Senior military and political leaders also used it as the blueprint with which to judge the effectiveness and success of the air campaign. Unknown targets, or those with outdated or incorrect information, would cause oversights or misdirected effort that could have been used more profitably against other threats. As will be highlighted in the following section that compares pre- and postwar knowledge, outdated or inaccurate information further complicated air planning as was made abundantly evident in the two areas of nuclear production and mobile Scuds.

Intelligence enabled the plan–it did not formulate the plan. As such, it functioned in a manner consistent with its traditional role of supporting combat operations, although in this case, it was late to join the planning process. There is no evidence to suggest that Air Staff Checkmate operational planners who developed the Instant Thunder plan used intelligence information to sculpt their concept of operations. Rather, they used intelligence to locate and define targets within the series of large, objective-oriented target categories upon which their plan, and eventually the Desert Storm air campaign, was built.

When aerial campaign planning shifted from the Air Staff to CENTAF in Riyadh, its basic tenet of striking a broad range of targets whose destruction would influence Baghdad to cede to U.S. political objectives was already well-established, and planners went with it. Intelligence still played an important role supplying operational planners with details of specific targets and constantly adding new ones, but it did not cause significant modification to the concept or execution of air campaign plans.

By the time the air campaign commenced in January 1991, the intelligence community had identified the majority of potential enemy facilities. Of the sixteen Black Hole target categories that have been examined in this study, four (nuclear, biological production, leadership, and strategic air defense) experienced more than forty-five percent growth during and after the war. In fact, there was almost no growth in the target base during Desert Storm. CENTCOM operations and intelligence planners froze the database just prior to initiating Desert Storm, both to avoid confusion during the anticipated period of accelerated combat activity and to provide intelligence analysts the opportunity to purge the existing database of duplicate or inaccurate entries made during Desert Shield.[41] One of the few additions to the target database during the war was the Al Atheer nuclear facility. Air planners became aware of this site during Desert Storm and added it to the Master Target List after the air campaign was underway.[42] Therefore, most of the growth detailed in Table 30 actually occurred after the ground war from information obtained both during the campaign and from postwar surveys and inspections.

---

[41]Intvw, Mr Lawrence M. Greenberg, GWAPS with Maj Lewis Hill, USAF, GWAPS based on his first-hand experience during Desert Shield/Desert Storm and the GWAPS Target Strike Database.

[42](S/NF/WN/NC) MTL (originally TS/LIMDIS), dated 1/16/91, BH, Master Target Folder, Box 2, Folder 23.

Table 30
Growth of Known Iraqi Targets by GAT (CENTAF) Category
Before and After Operation Desert Storm

GAT Categories	Known 16 Jan 91	Known July 92	# Change 16 Jan 91 - Jul 92	% Change 16 Jan 91 - Jul 92
Airfields	128	122	-6[a]	-5
NBC-Associated	60	86	26	43
C3	604	692	88	15
Electrical	242	266	24	10
Military Leadership & Support	213	270	59	62
Oil	218	224	6	3
Naval	53	53	0	0
Railroads and Bridges	596	620	24	4
Strategic Air Defense	674	988	314	47
SAM-Associated	285	328	43	15
Scud-Associated	121	154	33	36
Total identified targets	3,194	3,813	619	19
Total Records	4,543	5,153	610[b]	13

Notes:
(a) Six sites identified as airfields were removed from the AIF after the war.
(b) New targets outnumber new records due to movement of some known untargeted sites to targeted categories.

Sources: Target database (S/NF)

While the Automated Installation File contained the information mentioned above, operation planners in General Glosson's Guidance, Apportioning, and Targeting (Black Hole) cell selected targets and planned for strikes on only those specific facilities that supported the campaign's objectives. Table 31 examines the growth in the target sets maintained by the Black Hole and demonstrates an expansion that far exceeded that of the larger Installation File.

Table 31
Growth of GAT Target Sets
Before and After Operation Desert Storm

GAT Categories	16 Jan 1991	17 Feb 1991	26 Feb 1991	# Change	% Change
Airfields	31	38	46	15	48
Chemical (NBC)	23	23	34	11	48
C3	56	84	146	90	161
Electrical	17	22	29	12	71
Leadership	33	37	44	11	33
Military Support	73	77	102	29	40
Oil	12	12	28	16	133
Naval	17	20	20	3	18
Railroads and Bridges	33	46	95	62	188
Republican Guards	37	38	39	2	5
Strategic Air Defense	56	73	85	29	52
SAMs	45	45	45	0	0
Scuds	48	52	59	11	23
Total GAT targets	**481**	**567**	**772**	**291**	**60**

Sources: Doc (S), Master Target Lists for indicated days located in Master Attack Plan "Day Folders" at GWAPS.

[DELETED].[43] In fact, most of the additional nuclear facilities came to light only after the war and as a result of defectors, United Nations inspections, and continued efforts by the U.S. intelligence community.

The thirty-six-percent increase in Scud-related targets resulted primarily from counting individual launch and support sites rather than

---

[43](S/NF) [DELETED] interview.

Ash Shargat Missile Facility. Scud support facility.

PHOTO DELETED

Table 32
Overall Growth of Known Iraqi Targets by GAT Category

GAT Categories	Known 2 Aug 90	Known 16 Jan 91	Known July 92	# Change Aug 90 Aug 90 - Jul 92	% Change 2 Aug 90 - Jul 92
Airfields	122	128	122	0	0
NBC-Associated	40	60	80	46	107
C3	201	604	692	491	244
Electrical	230	242	266	36	16
Military Leadership & Support	126	213	270	144	106
Oil	211	218	224	13	6
Naval	46	53	53	7	15
Railroads and Bridges	532	596	620	88	17
Strategic Air Defense	493	674	988	495	100
SAM-Associated	214	285	328	114[c]	53
Scud-Associated	24	121	154	130[d]	583
Total identified targets	**2,239**	**3,194**	**3,813**	**1,574**	**70**
Total Records	3,302	4,543	5,153	1,851	56

Notes:
(a) Increase resulted from defector reports and postwar UN inspections.
(b) Growth resulted from counting dispersal sites to which munitions were moved after original facilities were struck.
(c) 86% of this growth resulted from counting tactical SAM sites.
(d) 64% of growth resulted from assigning each surveyed launch site and fixed launcher an individual record. Others came from sites nominated as targets by Israeli intelligence during the war.

Sources: Target database compiled [DELETED]. Information extracted from DIA AIF reports for the dates shown.; also Brfg (S/NF/WN),[DELETED] DIA, presented to GWAPS 30 Sep 92.

grouping several into a single Scud launch complex as had been calculated prior to the war. [DELETED].[44] [DELETED].[45]

The confusion regarding Baghdad's Scud program persists to this day. [DELETED][46]

Another way to examine how intelligence influenced the planning and execution of Desert Storm's air campaign is to look at target growth in each of the Black Hole-defined categories. Figure 24 graphically illustrates the evolution of these target categories. The chart highlights the growth of individual Installation File entries correlated to specific categories for three snapshot periods–what was known before the invasion of Kuwait on 2 August, on the eve of the air campaign on 16 January, and a baseline of what was known in the summer of 1992. This last snapshot includes those targets discovered while the war was in progress as well as others found by U.S. and United Nation forces and inspectors after the conflict.

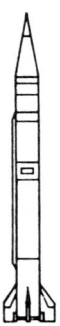

---

[44]Article, Reuven Pedatzur, "The Gulf War, A First Critical View," *Maarahot* 321, May-June 1991, pp 6-1, cited in unpublished paper by Dr Aron Pinker, "Israel and the Gulf War," n.d., Greenberg files. Mr Pedatzur is a lecturer in political science at the Tel-Aviv University and a military reporter for *Haaretz*.

[45](S/NF/WN) Brfg, [DELETED] DIA Target Intelligence, to GWAPS, 30 Sept 92.

[46][DELETED]

**Figure 24
Growth of Iraqi AIF Targets by Category
July 1990 - July 1992**

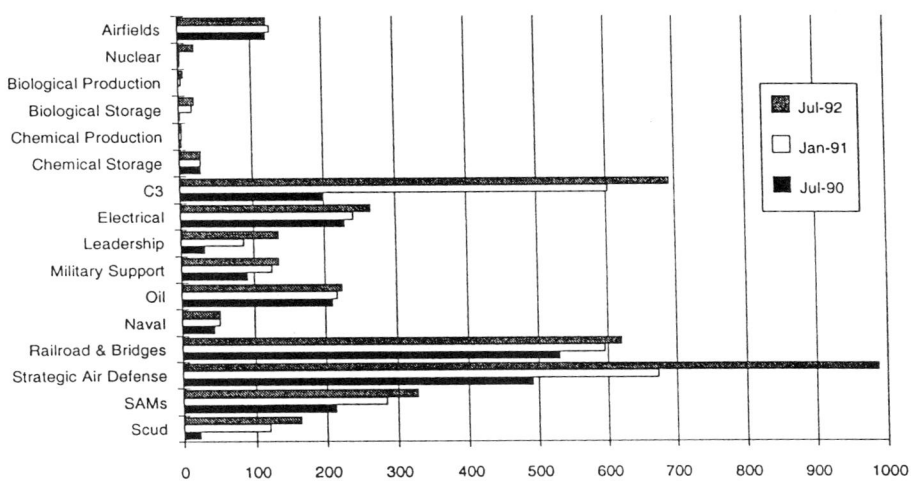

Source: Targets Database (S/NF), compiled by Capt John Glock, GWAPS.

The initial decision to assigned responsibility for producing an air campaign in a highly compartmented special planning cell within the Air Staff rather than relying on established theater organizations in effect segregated the theater intelligence apparatus from the planners. This should not imply that there was no intelligence input to the Instant Thunder plan, only that it was done beyond the realm in which CENTAF intelligence operated. In fact, the CENTAF intelligence staff was not given access to the air campaign until 18 August, a week after it received JCS blessing and had become the *de facto* CENTCOM air campaign plan.[47] By entering at such a late date, the established intelligence community had

---

[47](S) Intvw, Capt John R. Glock, HQ ACC/INAT, with Maj John Heidrick, 9 TIS/INT, 7 Jan 92, GWAPS Task Force V files and GWAPS NA-267.

little opportunity to influence plan development and had no choice but to assume a supporting role. The concept was set, intentions were preformed, and all intelligence was asked to do was supply the targets.

The largest single external force affecting the role of intelligence in war planning was the sudden collapse of the Soviet Union and the apparent end of the Cold War. Caught in this transition, the community had not yet reallocated its considerable intelligence-gathering apparatus or its human analytical resources from Western Europe and nuclear conflagration to the broader, and often more difficult arena of conventional regional conflict. Space and air breathing platforms positioned and well suited for monitoring Soviet missile fields and troop movements were both mis-positioned and mal-equipped for watching the Arabian Peninsula. A satellite designed to observe individual silos or detect activity in the limited area of a missile field, for example, was ill-equipped to scan the Iraqi desert searching for mobile Scud launchers. In addition, and of equal importance, was the division of labor throughout the intelligence analysis community where the Soviet threat had received unchallenged resource priority for nearly five decades. There, the relaxation of tensions with the East Block had not yet resulted in a redistribution of assets to bring other areas of interest out of their relative and routine obscurity. This fledgling redirection of effort directly resulted in the inadequate and outdated condition of the Iraqi Automated Installation File on 2 August 1990.

8

Planning the Gulf War Air Campaign: Retrospective

What then was the Gulf War air campaign plan on the eve of its execution in mid-January 1991? On paper, it consisted of three master attacks plans that outlined the details of the upcoming air war—minute-by-minute, hour-by-hour, aircraft-by-aircraft, target-by-target—of the first seventy-two hours. It was also a vision of air power in the minds of its planners who had spend the five months since the invasion of Kuwait crafting one of the most complex air campaign plans in history. Yet, its roots came from pre-Gulf War crisis planning, modified to reflect the expectations of planners as they faced new military and political factors in the late summer of 1990.

With respect to precrisis contingency plans for the Gulf region, several points deserve repeating. Planners had very different views on how to employ air power. Air forces in general and the U.S. Air Force in particular were assigned the traditional role to protect deploying ground troops and eventually providing direct support for a ground campaign that would reestablish preconflict territorial boundaries. At the time that regional contingencies plans were developed, the focus was on Europe, where the employment of air power was carefully confined to support ground forces due to political considerations and fears of escalation. Planners gave no serious consideration of operations that required a long-term independent, or even semi-autonomous, air campaign to precede the ground battle. Indeed, the entire series of plans assumed that the central element of a conflict in Southwest Asia would be ground warfare, with air forces providing them protection.

Perhaps because of this, the plans devoted little time and space to the CENTAF mission. By contrast to sometimes specific guidance provided by CINCCENT to his other component commanders concerning the concept of operation and employment of ground forces, none of the OPLAN 1002 series of plans provided any detailed guidance about the complexion of the air campaign. What little guidance appeared was general in nature and limited to broad objectives such as deterrence, defense, and supporting ground forces. Perhaps CENTAF planners believed in the flexibility of air power and chose to rely on this inherent capability to "play it by ear" according to the circumstances at the time. In the few instances when planners abandoned their ambiguous stance on air power, such as the introduction of the Joint Forces Air Component Command concept in 1002-88, they dwelt on administrative matters and command relationships without venturing into a discussion of combat operations. Even then, however, one is hard pressed to find clear, definitive guidelines for the Joint Forces Air Component Command.

On the eve of the Gulf crisis, OPLAN 1002-90 contained overly optimistic and unrealistic assumptions with respect to requests for assistance, deployment authorizations before hostilities, and warning times. A key was the assumption that thirty days would be available for deployment of significant forces. Planning appears to have been built around this deployment "truth" regardless of actual warning times. Just as importantly, the need for thirty days to get U.S. forces into position seems to have driven the more important assumption on presidential deployment authorization; that it, that the President would authorize combat deployment before hostilities—in essence "launch on warning." This is a prime example of "reverse planning" where less than precise assumptions are given unwarranted veracity in order to support a plan that depends on moving significant forces a great distance into generally unprepared positions.

Exercise Internal Look surfaced a number of problems for planners with respect to the use of air power in a Gulf contingency. One of these was the lack of any planning for the defense of Kuwait. At the time, CENTCOM lacked the forward based troops or even access agreements with regional governments that would be necessary to defend the Emirate. Also noted were difficult strategic lift considerations and Kuwait's small size and shared border with Iraq. Thus faced with these serious handicaps that made defense of Kuwait militarily untenable, CENTCOM planners decided to sidestep the entire issue and concentrate on defending Saudi Arabia.

The exercise also alerted intelligence analysts to their lack of adequate information on targets in Kuwait and Iraq. They began a more aggressive effort here and developed the first Iraqi target list in June 1990. The majority of the targets that they selected subsequently showed up on the Instant Thunder target list and later served as the foundation of Desert Storm targeting. They also attempted to bring to the attention of operational planners the inadequacies in the bomb damage assessment process as it existed in mid-1990. Here they were less than successful both during the exercise and only days later when the invasion of Kuwait precluded any further steps. Perhaps the most significant aspect of Internal Look was the degree to which it focused planners on the problem ahead.

In retrospect, precrisis planning had not yet matured to an acceptable level when the Iraqi invasion took place. But even in its incomplete form, the 1002 plan provided a deployment scheme that pushed air power to the front as the most readily available combat resource, even if it lacked any substantive employment scheme to cope with the invasion. Not surprisingly, given this planning vacuum, General Schwarzkopf turned initially to air power to provide both an immediate defensive capability and then his first offensive option.

During the five-month period between the invasion of Kuwait and Desert Storm, air campaign planners developed and refined the air campaign plan that was the centerpiece of the CENTCOM offensive campaign launched in mid-January 1991. They were significantly influenced by several factors.

The first factor was the list of national objectives laid out by President Bush early in the crisis and the constraints and restraints that were developed around those goals during subsequent months. From the outset, air planners kept these foremost in their efforts, selecting centers of gravity to achieve them. Two of these goals, the withdrawal of Iraqi forces from Kuwait and the restoration of Kuwait government proved relatively easy to translate into achievable military objectives and thus to measure when achieved. The third, protection of American lives became a moot point when hostages were released in December. However, the remaining objective, the security and stability of the Persian Gulf, proved to be both difficult to define and impossible to achieve. Targets chosen to achieve this vague goal included not only the destruction of nuclear, chemical, and biological weapons and the Iraqi army but also leadership in general and Hussein in particular. In retrospect, the problem here became finding the military means–such as air power–to achieve a political goal: political stability.

While national objectives gave planners their initial direction, the Instant Thunder plan produced by the Air Staff in Washington during the initial days of the crisis not only provided CENTCOM planners with the needed offensive option which 1002-90 sorely lacked; it provided the conceptual base and overall blueprint from which the Special Planning Group and eventually CENTAF worked initially to fashion the concept of operations. Conceived as a one component and single-phased air campaign, the target categories that were selected by Colonel Warden's planners remained throughout the five months of planning. While many of the actual targets selected had already been identified by CENTAF during Internal Look, the more important fact was the percentage of total targets in each category remained fairly consistent as noted in Table 33.

Table 33
Percentage of Total Targets by Category

	Instant Thunder	Desert Storm Phase I
Strategic Air Defense	12	13
Chemical/NBC & Scuds	10	15
Leadership	6	8
C3 (Telecom)	23	14
Electricity	12	4
Oil	7	3
Railroads&Bridges	4	8
Airfields	8	7
Naval & Ports	1	4
Military Support & Republican Guard	18	23

Note:
"Chemical/NBC and Scuds" and "Military Support and Republican Guards" categories are shown combined as in the Instant Thunder plan.

Sources: (S) Instant Thunder plan presented to CINCCENT 17 Aug 90 by Col John Warden, GWAPS CHSH 9; (S) Brfg slides in "General Glosson Briefs," GWAPS Box 3, Folder 60.

PHOTO DELETED

Tuwaitha Nuclear Research Center. Markings designate potential targets highlighted by Checkmate planners.

PHOTO DELETED

Hardened Aircraft Shelters and Bunkers at Tallil Airfield.

The significant growth in percentages (chemical, nuclear-biological-chemical, Scuds, military support, and Republican Guard) and comparable drop in other categories (C3, electricity, and railroads and bridges) reflect the planners' reaction to specific guidance from Washington as the plan developed.

Conceptually, Instant Thunder represented a radical revision in the way both air and theater planners viewed the application of air power. The offensive use of air power at the same time that the coalition was espousing a defensive strategy resulted in this concept being "tightly held" within both CENTCOM and the coalition planning community. These two factors resulted in Instant Thunder planners and their successors in the Black Hole working under extreme "close-hold" circumstances. In retrospect, these conditions may have aggravated the operator-intelligence split that will be discussed below.

The third factor that determined the development of the final air campaign plan were those efforts made by the CENTAF planners concerned with both the defensive and offensive planning in support of Desert Shield, the defense of Saudi Arabia. A goal of this planning was to deter Iraqi aggression against Saudi Arabia, and this never occurred. Though there is good reason to believe that the Iraqis never intended to attack past Kuwait, one must assume that planners were successful here. More to the point were target development and selection that occurred during this planning as well as the exercising of the Air Tasking Order (ATO) system in the daily tasking for both training and air defense. While Instant Thunder provided the blueprint, efforts such as ATO Bravo and the Punishment ATO fleshed out the detail for the final Desert Storm plan.

General Glosson's decision to assign planners in the Special Planning Group to develop offensive planning while others in the KTO Cell worked on defensive planning in essential isolation from each other was dictated by security reasons mentioned above. However, it did lead to an elitist "we" on the part of the Black Hole planners versus "they" for the KTO planners that prevailed even after the two cells merged in December.

Planners were also influenced by the CENTCOM theater campaign. Contingency plans for the region had always envisioned a phased operation, and planners continued this approach after the crisis erupted. Initial CENTCOM thinking followed the phases outlined in the 1002 family of plan. In September, while planners contemplated the one corps attack into the teeth of the Iraqi army in Kuwait, they still envisioned the campaign in four phases. Even when the plan was significantly modified in substance after the November decision to increase the force level, the four phases remained. Within this context, air planners had consistently regarded the initial phase as an air-only option against targets deep in Iraq. The remaining phases were to achieve air superiority over the area of ground operations, shape the battlefield, and then operate in conjunction with ground forces. The four phased concept of theater operations shaped the approach for air planners and guided their own concept of operations.

Theater campaign plans featured air power as the essential element in all but the final phase. Planners were clear here–without air power, their plans simply would not work. There never was any doubt to CENTAF planners as to the centrality of their efforts to the overall theater plan. In retrospect however, air planners stayed focused upon the initial phase at the expense of planning for the latter phases. This raised concerns by other component commanders and their planners as to just how well-prepared CENTAF was for entire campaign.

The final factor that influenced air planners was the process which they chose to translate objectives into plans, one that focused upon designated centers of gravity. Instant Thunder planners had aligned these against specific target categories. General Glosson's planners continued this approach, refining categories and selecting additional targets. What emerged from this was an air concept of operations that allowed the development of a master attack plan. From this scheme, air planners then fashioned detailed twenty four hour attack plans. The logic of system was well understood by select Black Hole planners as well as by some in the Washington Checkmate cell.

A problem with the process was that, while it was understood by the offensive air campaign planners in the Black Hole, it was not so clearly grasped by those outside of that tightly controlled group. This tended to aggravate the "we" versus "they" condition already cited. Likewise, the process assumed that bomb damage assessment would be readily available and form the basis for most planning after the initial two days of strikes. In retrospect, this proved to be erroneous assumption, even though Exercise Internal Look experiences had alerted planners to these problems. (Likewise, the process allowed planners to focus all their efforts upon the first two days of the plan, a factor already cited.)

Within the U. S. Air Force traditionally has existed an invisible but finite wall between the operations and intelligence staffs. It existed prior to the crisis as evidenced in the problems surfaced during Exercise Internal Look with regard to bomb damage assessment, and it continued throughout the planning efforts in both Washington and Saudi Arabia. The situation was aggravated by the fact that Cold War priorities had resulted in the paucity of background information on Iraq among intelligence analysts, as evidenced by deficiencies in the Automated Installation File. Intelligence was behind operations from the outset.

Intelligence analysts never really caught up with operational analysts in Gulf War planning; thus they did not play a full role in planning the air campaign. Intelligence functioned in a manner consistent with its traditional role of supporting combat operations, although in this case, it was late to join the planning process. There is no evidence to suggest that Air Staff Checkmate operational planners who developed the Instant Thunder plan used intelligence information to sculpt their concept of operations. Rather, they used intelligence to locate and define targets within the series of large, objective-oriented target categories upon which their plan, and eventually the Desert Storm air campaign, was built.

Perhaps because intelligence analysts lacked detailed or up-to-date targeting information on Iraq at the start of the crisis, operators initially bypassed established intelligence channels and later were reluctant to return to it. This was most evident in targeting the Scuds where operations planners ignored both mobile launcher and Baghdad's Scud employment strategy. Intelligence analysts realized they had been circumvented and did not seem to volunteer information, remaining in a "reactive" rather than assume an "anticipatory" mode. Most obvious here was the lack of appreciation of Iraqi intention in Kuwait after September as well as the tendency to "worse" case the Iraqi army as being a formidable foe rather than the "hollow force" that it now appears to have been.

In retrospect, intelligence support for planning of the air campaign was simply not adequate. Perhaps because planners had all the resources that they required from September to execute their plan, no one sought to correct the problem. When operational planners needed intelligence, they worked around the problem through direct contacts to Washington. The real solution, however, was neither at the operator nor intelligence level. Rather it was at the next higher.

As a result of these roots and influences, the air campaign plan on the eve of its execution was several things. First it was a series of twenty-four hour master attack plans in which the planners clearly laid out by aircraft, target, target category, and phasing the first seventy-two hours of the theater campaign. What they expected after the first three days in what was projected to be a month long campaign remained notional. They had constructed several more days of master attack plans that were really "strawmen" upon which further detailed planning could be done. Of course while they had four weeks to fashion two days, now they would only have one day to work on one day.

The first days of the air campaign plan were remarkably similar to those proposed five months before by Instant Thunder planners. Desert Storm priority of attack and percentage of overall sorties went towards the same keys for success–strategic air defense and leadership. What CENTAF planners had added was at the direction of Washington–Scuds and chemical weapons. They demonstrated faith in new technology specifically, sending stealth aircraft against targets without suppression of enemy air defenses; and confidence in air power in general by sending strength against strength, aircraft against air defenses.

What was most central to the Desert Storm air campaign plan was the planners' own vision of success, their own vision of victory. By concentrating all their efforts toward the first phase of the overall theater campaign plan, they implicitly stated their vision that air power alone would prevail and victory would come within the first week. Just how realistic that conviction was to be tested in the hostile and dark skies over Iraq on January 17, 1991.

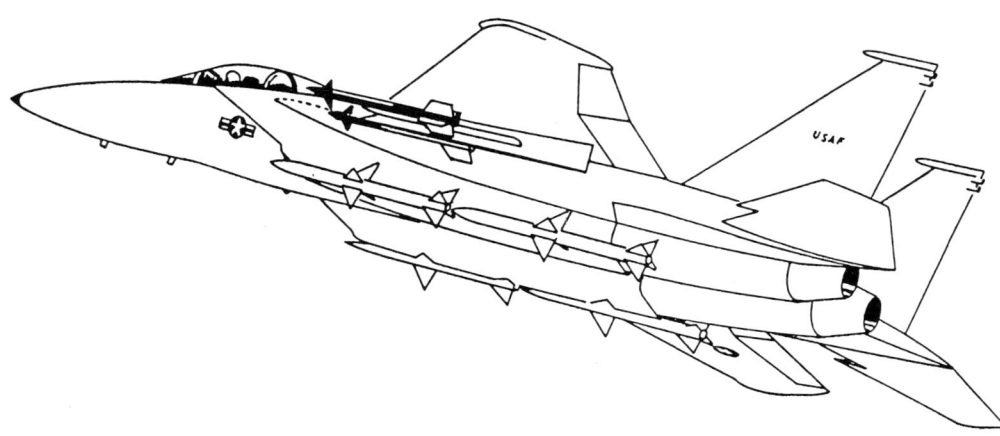

Appendix A

Table 34
Military Organization Glossary

Abbreviation	Definition	Personnel	Typical Major Components
US Army			
AASLT Div	Air Assault Division	16,100	9 Infantry Battalions
Abn Corps HQ	Airborne Corps Headquarters	250-350	Administrative staff & support for Corps
Abn Div	Airborne Division	13,600	9 Infantry Battalions
ADA Bde [a]	Air Defense Artillery Brigade	1,500-2,500	3-5 Air Defense Artillery Battalions
Airborne Bde	Airborne Brigade	4,800	3 Infantry Battalions
Armor Div	Armor Division	17,250	6 Armor Battalions + 4 Infantry Battalions
Armor Bde	Armor Brigade	5,300-5,500	2-3 Armor Battalions + 1-2 Infantry Battalions
Avn Bde [a]	Aviation Brigade	600-1,800	1-3 Aviation Battalions + Support
Mech Div	Mechanized Infantry Division	17,500	5 Armor Battalions + 5 Infantry Battalions
Mech Bde	Mechanized Infantry Brigade	5,500	1-2 Armor Battalions + 2 Infantry Battalions
MTZ Bde	Motorized Brigade	equivalent to Armor Brigade	
Ranger Regt	Ranger Regiment	1,750	3 Ranger Battalions
SFG [b]	Special Forces Group	450-675	2-3 Special Forces Battalions + Support

Table 34 (cont'd)
Military Organization Glossary

Abbreviation	Definition	Personnel	Typical Major Components
US Navy & US Marine Corps			
BBBG [c]	Battleship Battle Group	3,500-4,000	1 Battleship, 1 Cruiser, 1 Destroyer, 2 Frigates, 1 Support ship (oil or ammo)
CVBG [c]	Carrier Battle Group	6,300-7,500	1 Carrier with 8-10 air squadrons, 2-3 Cruisers, 1-2 Destroyers, 1-2 Frigates, 2 Support ships (oil and ammo)
MAGTF [c]	Marine Air-Ground Task Force	Highly tailored	Combined air, ground, logistic team of combat, aviation and support elements under single commander
MARDIV [c]	Marine Division (USMC)	20,000-25,000	3 Infantry Regiments of 3 Infantry Battalions, 1 Artillery Regiment, and 1 Tank Company each
MEB [c]	Marine Expeditionary Brigade (USMC)	15,000-18,000	Mix of Infantry, Artillery, Armor, and organic fixed-wing and helicopter support and attack aircraft
RLT [c]	Regimental Landing Team (USMC)	8,000-9,000	Same as MEB but smaller
BLT [c]	Battalion Landing Team (USMC)	1,000-1,500	Marine Infantry Battalion + support
SAG [c]	Surface Action Group	equivalent to Battleship Battle Group	

Notes:
(a) Organization highly flexible and tailored to fit individual task
(b) Organization tailored to geographic area of responsibility
(c) Organization varies according to task and area of responsibility

Sources: Intvws (U), Mr. John Wilson, Reference Division, US Army Center of Military History, Washington, D.C.; Capt (Ret) Paul Bloch, USN, GWAPS; Mr. Robert Aquilina, Reference Branch, US Marine Corps History Office, Washington, D.C.

Index

A

A-10 14, 15, 34, 113, 137, 186
A-6s 15, 124
ABCCC 28, 46
AC-130 34
ad hoc 121
ADA 22, 51, 233
Adnan 77, 80, 204, 205
ADOC 152
AFHRA 20, 21, 29, 42, 54, 84, 105, 136, 160, 168, 173
AFLC 35
AIF 192, 200, 201, 207, 216, 220, 222
air assault division 128, 235
air campaign 1, 3-5, 9-11, 13, 15-17, 21, 24, 41, 53, 65, 72, 85, 86, 88, 90-94, 96, 97, 98-101, 105, 107-114, 116, 117, 121, 123, 126-129, 136, 141, 142, 143, 148-153, 155-157, 159, 162, 164, 167, 169, 170, 171, 173, 175, 184, 188, 190, 191, 200, 210, 211, 213, 214, 215, 221-226, 229, 230, 231, 232
air defense 5, 6, 10, 14, 48, 50, 51, 53, 70, 75, 79, 115, 116, 120, 122, 123, 131, 137, 145-147, 149-153, 175, 184-187, 193, 194, 199, 201, 206, 212, 213, 215-217, 220, 226, 231, 234, 235
air defense artillery 51, 233
air division 173
air interdiction 133, 134
air power 9, 12, 17-19, 21, 23, 24, 27, 40, 41, 46, 51, 53, 65, 88, 96, 104, 107, 120, 127, 129, 135, 143, 148, 150, 151, 157, 169, 170-172, 175, 223-226, 229, 230, 232
Air Staff 3, 54, 80, 87, 88, 105, 108, 110, 112-114, 126, 131, 135, 171, 214, 221, 226, 231
air superiority 15, 19, 22, 29, 47, 53, 107, 129, 133, 137, 147, 149-151, 153, 155, 169, 170, 187, 191, 193, 230
air supremacy 2, 5, 7, 11, 148, 150, 175
air tasking order 13, 47, 51, 124, 136, 138, 139, 188, 200, 230
airborne early warning 80
airfields 5, 10, 14, 15, 17, 18, 23, 41, 48, 50, 51, 53, 80, 121, 132, 137, 145, 146, 149, 151, 153, 168, 175, 184, 185, 187, 189, 193, 199, 201, 212, 213, 216, 217, 220, 226
Al Faw 77, 205
Al Firdos 92
Al Jarrah 184
Al Madan 133
Al Qaim 207, 208, 213
Al Taqaddum 154
Al Tuwaitha 118
Al-Atheer 118
Al-Hussein 66
al-Jabber Shanshal 67
An Nasiriyah 119
anthrax 160, 209
antiaircraft artillery 80, 121, 155, 206
antiradiation missiles 153
Aoun, General 56
Arab Cooperation Council 64
ARCENT 51, 87, 137, 148
area of operation 134
area of responsibility 236
ARM 69
Army Air Forces 117, 127
artillery 6, 12, 51, 64, 74, 80, 84, 119, 121, 139, 155, 170-172, 186, 203, 206, 209, 233, 234
assumptions 4, 19, 25, 26, 29, 30, 36-39, 61, 70, 72, 94, 106, 130, 131, 224, 232
Atlantic Command 44
ATO (see also air tasking order) 13, 51, 136, 138-141, 189, 190, 229
ATO bravo 136, 139, 231
automated installation file 47, 49, 192, 201, 211, 216, 223, 230

235

AV-8Bs 113
AWACS 22, 28, 34, 70, 128, 130, 136
Az Zubayr 120
Aziz, Tariq 58, 81, 99, 107

B

B-52s 5, 6, 14, 15, 22, 27, 28, 29, 34, 74, 128-130, 155, 171
Baker, James 80, 88, 90, 91, 96, 99, 102, 106
Baptiste, Samuel 13, 173, 187
basic encyclopedia 192
Basra 6, 9, 65, 120
battalion landing team 236
battle damage 15
battleship 130
battleship battle group 236
BBBG 28, 234
BDA (see also bambdamage assessment) 11, 15, 184
BDE 22, 28, 130, 233
beddown 52, 136
BEN 13, 164, 174
Bigelow, Richard E. 113
biological warfare 145, 209, 210, 213
biological weapons 14, 55, 67, 69, 118, 160, 192, 226
Black Hole 44, 87, 92, 93, 139, 143, 147, 152, 153, 156, 159, 162, 165, 169, 200, 214-216, 221, 229, 230,
Blackburn, James R. 122
BLT 236
bomb damage assessment 15, 188, 225, 230
botulin 209
botulinum 160
breaching 146, 185-187, 189
Brewer, Slade 114
bridges 6, 9, 14, 15, 48, 146, 149, 169, 185, 187, 189, 192, 201, 212, 216, 217, 220, 226, 229
briefings 10, 11, 13, 51, 52, 84, 87, 88, 91, 94, 96, 98, 104, 109, 111, 112, 114, 116, 126, 134, 144, 146, 148, 151, 153, 156, 159, 160, 164, 168, 169, 172-175, 185, 186, 192
Bristow, Richard 113

Bubiyan 56, 58, 59, 63
Bush, George 61, 64, 67, 81, 83, 88, 92, 97-99, 102, 106, 107, 116, 143, 144, 148, 164, 170, 172, 225

C

C-12 145, 151
C-130 34, 35, 128, 130
C-21 34
C-Day 23
C3 (see also command, control, and communications) 46-48, 146, 157, 159, 185, 186, 189, 193, 201, 212, 216, 217, 220, 226, 229
Camp David, MD 106, 108
carrier battle group 54, 105, 128-130, 236
carriers 29, 35, 54, 105, 107, 128-130, 203, 236
CAS (see also close air support) 46, 149
casualties 4, 56, 61, 64, 76, 90-93, 101, 111, 112, 116, 120, 149, 161
CAT 35
CBW 160
CENTAF 9, 10, 13, 15, 23, 24, 44-50, 54, 105, 106, 109, 112, 114, 126, 135-142, 148-150, 152, 153, 155-157, 161, 167, 169-171, 173, 175, 187, 188, 190, 191, 193-197, 199-201, 206, 207, 211, 213, 214, 216, 222, 223, 224, 226, 229-231 234
CENTAF intelligence 44, 47, 142, 191, 194, 222
CENTAF target study 137
CENTCOM (see also Central Command) 1, 10, 13, 18-27, 29, 31, 32, 37, 42-44, 48, 50, 51, 54, 87, 102, 104-107, 109, 112, 128, 131, 132, 135, 143, 144, 148, 149-151, 155-157, 159-162, 167, 170, 173, 188, 191, 194, 199-202, 206, 207, 211, 214, 215, 222, 224-226, 229, 230
CENTCOM target list 200
centers of gravity 2, 4, 10, 13, 109, 110, 111, 144, 145, 149, 150, 155,

159, 162, 169, 175, 187, 225, 232
Central Command 2, 9, 18-22, 26,
    29, 31, 38, 41, 42, 44, 49, 51, 54,
    100, 104, 114, 118, 121, 126, 128,
    130, 131, 132-134, 137, 151, 156,
    191, 194, 202
Central Intelligence Agency 44
Central Security Service 44
Chairman of the Joint Chiefs of Staff
    20, 87, 211
Checkmate 93, 94, 109, 110,
    112-115, 118-121, 123-127, 131,
    135, 141, 171, 172, 213, 214, 228,
    230, 231
chemical 1, 2, 5-7, 10, 11, 14, 15, 44,
    48, 50, 55, 57, 62, 66, 67, 69, 84,
    89, 97, 99, 107, 108, 112, 118, 119,
    139, 145, 146, 147, 149, 150, 159,
    160, 161, 165, 175, 184-187, 189,
    191-193, 199, 200, 209, 213, 217,
    226, 229, 232
chemical warfare 1, 145, 209
chemical weapons 57, 62, 84, 89, 97,
    99, 107, 108, 112, 118, 119, 150,
    160, 161, 187, 192, 209, 232
Cheney, Richard 11, 12, 19, 84, 86,
    88, 90, 98, 102-108, 128, 144, 160,
    166, 173, 174
Chief of Naval Operations 114
Chief of Staff 67, 79, 87, 98,
    105-109, 135, 160
China 17
CIA (see also Central Intelligence
    Agency) 44, 106, 107, 202, 203,
    206, 207
CINCCENT 19, 20, 25, 26, 31, 35,
    47, 51, 88, 112, 114, 134, 135, 140,
    145, 192, 223, 227
CJCS (see also Chairman, Joint Chiefs
    of Staff) 20, 89, 145, 146, 151,
    156, 159, 160, 164, 185, 206, 209
close air support 41, 53, 88, 114,
    134, 136, 137, 192
cluster bombs 123, 172, 209
Coalition 1, 2, 4-7, 9, 12, 15, 17,
    61-67, 70-72, 75-82, 84, 91, 98,
    102, 103, 111, 119, 120, 124, 128,
    132, 134, 138, 139, 150, 151, 161,
    165, 167, 168, 170, 172, 203, 206,

211, 229
Cold War 24, 191, 223, 232
combat air patrol 188
combined OPLAN 1, 2, 4-7, 9, 15,
    133, 134
COMCENTAF 135
command and control 2, 5, 11, 13-15,
    46, 51, 53, 69, 76, 86, 87, 115, 126,
    133, 142, 144, 147, 149, 152, 156,
    171, 175, 184, 192, 207
command post exercise 31, 41, 43, 51
command, control and communication
    50, 137, 193, 199
Congress 77, 84, 91, 95, 119, 205
continental United States 14
contingency plans 20, 21, 23-25, 26,
    27, 46, 54, 105, 108, 135, 191, 200,
    223, 230
Corps:
    VII Corps 67, 76, 143, 148, 186
    XVIII Airborne Corps 51, 75
    XVIII U.S. Corps 186
counterair 24, 27, 29, 41, 45, 46, 51,
    53, 134, 136, 137, 192
CPX 31, 46
Crigger, James 140
CSS 44
CVBG 22, 28, 234

D

D-Day 8, 136-140, 200
D-Day plan 136-140
DCA 44
deception 113, 188
Defense Courier Service 44, 140
Defense Department 103, 104
Defense Intelligence Agency 44, 121,
    152, 192
Defense Mapping Agency 44, 121
Defense Planning Guidance 19
Defense Security Assistance Agency
    44
Department of Defense 98
Department of Energy 17
Department of State 44, 84, 101, 102
deployment planning 21
Deptula, David 86, 87, 89, 93, 95,
    96, 99, 100, 103, 113, 123, 124,

237

126, 127, 150, 152, 153, 155-157, 159, 161, 162, 164, 165, 173, 174, 206
Deputies Committee 90
Desert Shield 25, 33-35, 42-44, 46, 47, 54, 80, 86, 105-108, 114, 121, 129, 132-136, 140, 155, 156, 162, 169, 173, 191, 194, 200, 207, 211, 213-215, 230
Desert Shield/Storm 169
Desert Storm 1, 2, 4-7, 9, 10, 13, 16, 17, 25, 33, 35, 42-44, 46, 47, 51, 54, 80, 84, 85, 86, 90, 91, 93, 95, 97, 99, 100, 103, 105-107, 120, 121, 123, 132-136, 139, 143, 146, 148, 150, 151, 156, 157, 160, 161, 162, 164, 167-171, 173, 185, 187, 188, 191, 200, 213, 214, 215-217, 221, 225, 226, 229, 230, 231, 232
desired mean point of impact 121
Dhahran 17, 91, 113, 119, 132
DIA (see also Defense Intelligence Agency) 44, 47, 49, 160, 167, 201-203, 206, 207, 209, 210, 211, 213, 214, 220, 221
Diego Garcia 17, 18
Divisions:
  AASLT DIV 22, 28, 235
  101st Air Assault 128
  24th ID 204
  82d Airborne 107, 128
DMA 44
DOC 13, 42, 44, 46, 47, 50, 51, 54, 100, 106, 132, 133, 135, 141, 168, 189, 191, 195, 199, 200, 202, 206, 207, 211, 217
doctrine 18, 38, 53, 57, 77, 134, 149, 150, 152, 202, 206, 207, 209
DOD (see also Department of Defense) 19, 37, 57, 74, 203
drones 14, 188
Dugan, Michael 98, 108

E

E-3 34, 136
E-8 34
Eagleburger, Lawrence 103
EC-130 28, 34, 128, 130

EF-111s 34, 128, 130, 188
Egypt 46, 58, 62, 63
electric 5, 15, 48, 50, 94, 149, 152, 153, 162, 199
electrical power 93, 95, 96, 118, 117, 137
electricity 10, 47, 117, 118, 145, 146, 169, 185, 189, 226, 229
electronic warfare 66
ELINT 80
engineer 72
Europe 17, 20, 57, 63, 109, 143, 223
European Command 44
exercises 19, 46, 47, 54, 69, 131

F

F-4G 34, 137, 188
F-15 15, 128, 130
F-15E 14, 22, 34, 124, 135, 128, 130, 137, 186, 188
F-16 14, 15, 22, 34, 118, 124, 128, 130, 137, 186
F-111s 14, 15, 34, 124, 128, 130
F-117 14, 15, 93, 123, 124, 128, 130, 150, 153, 155, 186, 188
F-117A 34, 93, 137
FAA 44
FAHD 107, 108, 132
FBI 44
Federal Aviation Administration 44
Federal Bureau of Investigation 44
Fitzwater, Marlin 99, 106
France 79, 113
Freeman, Charles W. 107

G

G-Day 8
GAT 142, 193, 200, 201, 212, 216, 217, 220
GBU-24 93
GBU-27 93
GCI 193
generator halls 94, 117
Germany 113, 117, 148
global war 20, 25, 109
Glock, John 42, 44, 48, 136, 137, 142, 167, 191, 194, 201, 202, 207,

Glosson, Buster 10, 11, 83, 85-87, 89-101, 103, 104, 139, 140, 144-149, 152, 155, 157, 159, 162, 164, 168, 169-173, 175, 185, 200, 206, 216, 227, 230, 231
government of Kuwait 1, 2, 83, 143, 175
Griffith, Brig. Gen. 114
ground forces 5, 12, 21-23, 41, 50, 64, 66, 74, 76, 104, 106, 107, 112, 113, 128, 129, 136, 139, 148, 150, 170, 171, 175, 186, 193, 199, 203, 223, 224, 230
ground order of battle 204

H

H-1 184
H-2 14, 168, 184
H-3 14, 168, 184
Haass, Richard 106
HARM 60, 90, 91, 97, 108
Harvey, Bernard 109, 112, 113, 126, 127, 157, 164, 174
HAS 62, 64, 65, 84, 91, 96, 171, 202, 232
Hawk 46, 47
Hawkins, Douglas 113
HC-130 34
helicopters 5, 6, 14, 236
HH-3 34
Horner, Charles A. 44, 48, 49, 51-53, 83, 85-87, 91, 93, 96, 97, 100, 102, 104-107, 114, 126, 127, 128, 132, 135, 137, 139, 140, 141, 142, 145, 148-151, 153, 156, 157, 159, 161, 162, 166, 167-169, 173, 187, 188, 190, 191-194, 206
hostages 85, 90, 95-97, 108, 225
Hoyes, Michael 113
human intelligence 71
human shields 62, 95, 96
Hussein, Sadam 2, 55, 56, 58, 63, 64, 66, 67, 84, 85, 91, 92, 93, 95-100, 103, 104, 108, 115, 145, 156, 167, 192, 201, 206, 209, 226

I

infantry 64, 66, 68, 72, 74-78, 128, 130, 203, 204, 235, 236
infrastructure 5, 18, 47, 74, 111, 119, 131, 145, 147, 149, 159, 162, 167, 192
Instant Thunder 92, 94, 105, 109, 110, 109, 111, 112, 113-116, 119, 120, 123-127, 131, 141-143, 145-148, 151, 155, 159, 161, 162, 164, 165, 169, 185, 187, 214, 222, 225-227, 229-232
integrated air defense system 150
intelligence staff 173, 194, 202, 222
interdiction 19, 24, 27, 29, 41, 42, 44, 45, 53, 75, 88, 114, 119, 132-134, 136, 137, 169, 192
Internal Look 25, 31, 32, 41-44, 46-48, 50-54, 106-108, 132, 133, 135, 136, 192, 194, 224-226, 232
Iran 17, 18, 21, 42, 55, 56, 58, 61, 64-66, 69, 70, 75, 82, 94, 119, 191, 202, 206, 211
Iran-Iraq War 18, 55, 56, 58, 64, 69, 119, 202, 206
Iraq cell 173
Iraqi air force 80, 205-207
Iraqi army 27, 81, 84, 85, 106, 120, 127, 128, 148, 151, 157, 164, 171, 172, 202, 203, 226, 229, 231
Iraqi target study 46, 48, 50, 137, 140, 193-197, 199, 200, 207
Israel 14, 56, 57, 62, 65, 103, 105, 118, 119, 165, 167, 168, 211, 221

J

J-2 106
J-3 104, 106, 114, 132, 160
J-5 20-23, 54, 100, 104, 132, 160, 170
J-8 37
Japan 57, 63
JCS (see also Joint Chiefs of Staff) 19, 21, 26, 37, 42, 44, 100, 104-106, 112, 114, 150, 155, 156, 167, 222
JIC 167

Johnston, Robert 106, 107, 135, 160
Joint Atomic Intelligence Committee 213
Joint Chiefs 19, 20, 44, 87-89, 94, 114, 164, 211
Joint Chiefs of Staff 19, 20, 44, 87, 114, 211
Joint Directorate of Planning 132-134
Joint Force Air Component Commander 9, 51
Joint Munitions Effectiveness Manual 172
Joint no-fire target list 94
Joint Staff 21, 22, 29, 31, 42, 100, 114, 144, 157, 160
Joint target list 49, 50, 192, 194, 199, 200, 207, 213
Joint Task Force 18, 35, 47
Joint Task Force Charlie 47
Jordan 56, 57, 62-64, 75, 168
JSTARS 109
Just Cause 91, 98

K

Kari 152
Karns, D. 156
KC-10 34
KC-135 22, 34, 128, 130
Kelly, Thomas 103, 106
Kennedy, USS 35
Khafji 76
kill boxes 136
Kimmitt, Robert 90, 97, 98, 103
Kiraly, Emery 113
Kirkuk 158
KTO (see also Kuwait theater of operations) 4-6, 9, 11, 13, 77, 136, 148, 149, 156, 170, 172, 173, 175, 186, 202-205, 230
KTO cell 173, 231
Kuwait 1, 2, 4-7, 9, 11-13, 15, 39, 54, 56, 58-63, 66, 71, 74-76, 78-81, 83-85, 99, 106, 108, 109, 112, 119, 120, 130, 134, 136, 139, 143, 148, 150-153, 156, 157, 164, 170-172, 175, 184, 186, 191, 195, 200, 202-204, 211, 221, 223-225, 230, 231

Kuwait theater of operations 4, 11, 175
Kuwaiti 11, 12, 59, 60, 66, 75, 80, 99, 109

L

leadership 2, 5, 10, 11, 14, 15, 46, 48, 50, 55, 68, 104, 111, 115, 131, 145-147, 149, 153, 155, 156, 159, 171, 175, 184, 185, 187, 189, 192, 193, 199-201, 206, 207, 212, 215-217, 220, 226, 232
leaflets 120
Leavenworth 87, 148, 170
Lebanon 64
Libya 110, 171
lines of communication 6, 53, 193
logistics 9, 21, 135, 144, 193
Loh, John 108, 109
Los Angeles Times 96, 97

M

MAC (see also Military Airlift Command) 211
Madinah 77, 205
MAGTF 236
major commands 113
Mankin, Mike 114
MAP (see also master attack plan) 10, 11, 14, 189, 194
MARDIV 236
Marine Corps 40, 44, 114, 234
marine division 236
Marine Expeditionary Brigade 128, 234
marines 64, 114, 115, 171, 186, 194
MASS 97, 156, 161, 193, 207, 210, 213
master attack plan 13-15, 123, 147, 153, 156, 169, 187, 200, 217, 230
master target list 213, 215
Maverick 123
MC-130 34
McConnell, Mike 106, 167
McPeak, Gen. 87
McSwain, D.W. 136, 139, 140, 168
MEB 22, 28, 236

mech div 28, 130, 233
mechanized infantry division 128, 233
Meier, James 114
MH-60 34
Midway 35
Military Airlift Command 106
military construction 72
military production 5, 50, 145, 165, 194, 199
military support 10, 48, 146, 147, 162, 185-188, 193, 201, 217, 226, 229
mine countermeasures 44
Ministry of Defense 46, 132, 133, 156
missiles 1, 6, 14, 15, 44, 51, 55, 57, 65-67, 69, 74, 80, 84, 93, 96, 101, 103-105, 119, 120, 123, 124, 126, 151-153, 156, 162, 165-168, 186, 188, 193, 206, 209, 210, 211, 214, 219, 223
Missouri 128
mobility 137
mobilization 18, 54, 60, 61, 66, 67
Moore, Burton 160
MTL 215
Muhammad al-Tikriti 67
munitions 54, 66, 88, 123, 137, 172, 209, 220
mustard 160

N

national command authorities 92, 160
National Security Agency 44
National Security Council 106, 107
NATO 17, 109
naval 4-6, 15, 17, 22, 23, 27, 29, 44, 46, 50, 51, 54, 55, 57, 67, 70, 74, 109, 114, 134, 136, 146, 149, 162, 185, 187, 189, 193, 194, 199, 201, 212, 213, 216, 217, 220, 226
NAVCENT 139
Navy 14, 17, 32, 35, 40, 44, 110, 114, 115, 124, 125, 136, 150, 152, 184, 194, 234
NBC (see also nuclear, biological, and chemical) 46, 48, 146, 159, 185, 193, 201, 212, 216, 217, 220, 226
Nebuchadnezzar 77, 204, 205
nerve 160, 209
network 93, 145, 152, 193
New York Times 59
Ninth Air Force 47, 105, 106, 140, 191, 211
Nizar 'Abd al-Karim al-Khazraji 67
Noriega, Manuel 91, 98
North Vietnam 85, 112, 117
North Vietnamese 117
nuclear 1, 2, 5-7, 11, 48, 50, 55, 57, 61, 69, 84, 90, 97, 99, 118, 119, 137, 140, 145, 149, 159, 160, 161, 175, 184, 193, 199, 200, 207, 213-215, 217, 223, 226, 228, 229
nuclear program 160
nuclear reactor 57
nuclear weapons 61, 84, 90, 97, 119, 159, 161
nuclear, biological, and chemical 11, 55, 159, 193

O

OA-10 34
offensive 1-4, 6, 9, 11-13, 21, 24, 27, 41, 45, 46, 53, 54, 56, 84, 85, 88, 90, 92, 93, 96, 97, 100-103, 105, 106, 108, 109, 112, 126, 128, 133, 136, 137, 138-143, 145, 147, 148, 151, 153, 156, 159-162, 164, 165, 167, 169-173, 192, 193, 202, 209, 225, 226, 229-231
Office of the Secretary of Defense 19
Office of the Secretary of the Air Force 44
Office of the Secretary of the Navy 44
oil 4, 10, 11, 15, 17, 18, 20, 21, 48, 55-59, 62, 63, 76, 95, 99, 109, 116-118, 128, 145, 146, 169, 175, 184, 185, 189, 191, 193, 201, 202, 212, 213, 216, 217, 220, 226, 234
oil production 17
Olsen, Thomas 136, 137, 140
Oman 135
OPEC 58, 59
operation order 150, 173, 188

operation plan 1, 9, 149, 192
operational level 110
operations order 92, 145, 156, 159
OPLAN 1, 2, 4-7, 9, 15, 19-39, 41,
    42, 44, 46, 47, 49-54, 84, 92, 93,
    97, 106, 108, 128, 133-136, 150,
    156, 160, 161, 167, 173, 191-194,
    199, 200, 213, 224, 235, 236
OPLAN 1002-88 20-27, 39, 47, 192
OPLAN 1002-90 21, 22, 25-33,
    35-39, 41, 42, 44, 47, 49-51, 53,
    54, 108, 128, 134, 135, 136,
    191-194, 199, 200, 224
OPLAN Desert Storm 1, 2, 4-7, 9,
    84, 93, 97, 134, 160, 161, 167, 213
OPORD 9, 84, 92, 100, 132, 133,
    157, 173
OPORD 001 100, 132, 157
OPORD 002 133
OPORD 003 132, 133
OPORD 004 133
opposing air 150
order of battle 42, 71, 204
OSD 86
Osirik 57
OV-10 112

P

Pacific Command 44
Panama 64
Patriot 44, 51
Persian Gulf 17, 21, 47, 57, 77, 80,
    83, 84, 86, 91, 95, 96, 98, 102, 103,
    107, 109, 119, 143, 156, 164, 203,
    205-207, 211, 225
phase I 4, 9, 11, 23, 26, 27, 32, 41,
    84, 92, 96, 103, 145, 148-151, 155,
    156, 159, 169, 170, 173, 175, 184,
    186, 188, 226
phase II 5, 6, 11, 12, 24, 26, 28, 29,
    41, 137, 148, 150, 151, 170, 175,
    186
phase III 6, 11, 12, 29, 148, 151,
    170, 172, 173, 175, 186
phase IV 6, 7, 148, 170, 175
planners 1, 2, 4-7, 9-19, 21-27, 29,
    32, 35, 37, 38, 40, 41, 43, 44, 46,
    47, 49, 51, 54, 59, 60, 70, 75, 77,

83-85, 87, 90, 92-95, 97, 98,
    99-106, 108, 109, 114-116,
    119-121, 123, 124, 126, 127, 128,
    131-145, 147-153, 155, 156, 157,
    159-162, 164, 165, 167, 168-171,
    173, 184, 186-188, 190-192, 194,
    200, 209, 210, 213-216, 222-226,
    228, 230, 231, 230-232
planning 2, 3, 13, 17-21, 23, 26, 29,
    33, 36-38, 40, 42, 43, 46, 54, 59,
    71, 83-88, 92, 95, 96, 101, 103-105,
    108, 109, 111-114, 121, 123, 125,
    126, 128, 129-137, 139, 141-144,
    147, 149, 151, 160, 164, 170, 171,
    173, 187, 191, 194, 200, 205, 209,
    211, 213, 214, 221-226, 229-231
POL 47, 48, 50, 74, 162, 193, 199
POL distribution 193
POL storage 193
population 51, 56, 60, 89, 94, 111,
    120
Post 31, 41, 43, 51, 55, 56, 68, 71,
    97, 102, 191, 213
Powell, Colin 20, 21, 25, 88-90, 92,
    94, 98, 102, 105-108, 112, 114,
    141, 144, 145, 160, 162, 164, 173,
    174, 206
precision guided munitions 54
president 23, 54, 55, 58, 61, 64, 67,
    81, 83-88, 90-99, 102-104, 106,
    107, 109, 111, 112, 114, 143, 144,
    148, 151, 156, 159, 160, 164, 165,
    171, 224, 225
presidential palace 131, 140
presidential residence 155
propaganda 62, 78, 81, 157
Proven Force 35
psychological operations 111
Punishment ATO 139-141, 230
Purvis, Joe 170

Q

Quayle, Dan 98, 102, 106

R

RAF 15
RAND 106, 108, 171, 172

Ranger 29, 128, 130, 235
RC-135 34, 128, 130
readiness 66, 72, 78-80
reconnaissance 70, 71, 78, 80, 105, 151, 188
reconstitution 11, 186
recovery 90, 94
Red Sea 23, 107
Reflex 169
regimental landing team 130, 236
regular army 70, 78, 82
reliability 69, 159
reorganization 142, 173
Republican Guard 1, 2, 5, 6, 10-15, 50, 58, 59, 66, 70, 72, 75-78, 82, 146, 147, 155, 156, 162, 164, 175, 184, 185, 186, 199, 203-205, 226, 229
research and development 162
reserves 59, 60, 76-78, 203
resupply 9, 11, 80, 149, 171, 175, 186
RF-4C 22, 34
Rice, Donald 87, 112, 172
RLT 28, 236
Rogers, "Buck" 169
Rolling Thunder 85
Ross, Dennis B. 102
Royal Saudi Air Force 9
RRP 1307 105, 108
Rumayla 58, 59, 63
Russ, Robert 114, 168

S

SA-2 80
SA-2/3 80
SA-6 80
SAC (see also Strategic Air Command) 44, 113, 114, 156, 211
Saddam Hussein 2, 55-72, 79-82, 85, 91-93, 95-99, 103, 104, 108, 109, 111, 112, 115, 119, 131, 145, 150, 152, 155-157, 159-161, 164, 165, 168, 170, 201, 206, 209
SAG 22, 236
Salman Pak 118, 119, 160, 210, 213
SAM 13, 104, 120, 146, 170, 175, 185, 189, 201, 212, 216 217, 220

SAR 93
Saudi Air Force 9, 51
Saudi Arabia 12, 17-19, 21, 22, 24, 25, 27, 39, 42, 44, 54, 56, 59, 60, 62, 63, 72, 74-76, 83, 84, 91, 104-107, 109, 112, 126-130, 132-136, 139, 140, 142, 150, 165, 174, 184, 191, 202, 211, 224, 229, 230
Schwarzkopf, Norman 12, 20, 21, 25, 27, 29, 43, 49, 51, 52, 60, 83, 87, 91, 94, 96, 98, 99, 104, 106-108, 112, 113, 116, 119, 121, 126, 128-130, 136, 139, 140, 143, 144, 148-150, 162, 164, 168-170, 172, 173, 191-193, 202, 225
Scowcroft, Brent 90, 91, 98, 102, 104, 106, 107, 155, 206
Scud 14, 15, 101, 104, 105, 119, 138, 139, 145, 156, 165, 167, 168, 175, 184, 188, 210, 212, 216, 218-221, 223, 221
Scud alert 188
Scud-B 167, 210
Scuds 10, 14, 48, 50, 103-105, 119, 146, 147, 165-168, 185, 187-189, 193, 199-201, 209, 210, 213, 214, 217, 226, 229, 231, 232
SEAD 11, 12
SEAL 186
sealift 24
SECDEF (see also Secretary of Defense) 88, 89, 119, 153, 160, 175
Secretary of Defense 10, 19, 20, 42, 83-88, 93, 98, 102, 105-107, 132, 133, 146, 160, 174, 185, 209
Secretary of State 81, 90, 91, 102, 103
Secretary of the Navy 44
sector operations center 120, 123, 124
security 2, 4, 42, 44, 60, 66, 70, 75, 83-85, 90, 95, 104, 106, 109, 126, 139, 143, 155, 164, 191, 202, 204, 206, 213, 225, 230
SFG 235
Shadow Hawk 46, 47
Shamir, Yitzhak 103

Sharp, Grant 20, 42, 43, 103, 132, 133
Shaw AFB 47, 87, 105, 187
short-range ballistic missile 210
SIGINT 80
SILKWORM 74
situation report 71

smoke 65
SNIE 203
SOF (see also special operations forces) 130
Southeast Asia 17
SPEAR 150, 152
special forces 77, 128, 130, 204, 205, 233
Special Forces Group 128, 235
special operations 23, 27, 29, 40, 44, 194
Special Operations Command 44
special operations forces 23, 27, 44
Special Planning Group 143, 151, 226, 230
SPOT 57, 71, 172
SRBM (see also short range ballistic missile) 166, 167
Stanfill 113, 126, 127
Star 91
State Department 94, 96, 103, 206
stealth 14, 155, 234
stealthy 153, 155
Stimer, Richard 113
strategic air campaign 3-5, 11, 24, 92, 105, 107, 113, 148, 149, 151, 157, 164, 175
Strategic Air Command 44, 113, 156
strategic air defense 10, 115, 145, 146, 149, 151, 184, 185-187, 201, 212, 215-217, 220, 226, 232
Strategic Bombing Survey 117
strategy 17, 18, 20, 46, 61, 64, 76, 81, 86, 94, 102, 103, 111, 116, 143, 229, 231
STRATFOR 156
STU 86, 87
suppression of enemy air defenses 155, 188, 234

surface-to-air missile 153, 186, 188, 193
surge 80, 211
Switzer, William 114
Syria 56
Syrian 62, 203

T

TAC (see also Tactical Air Command) 44, 108, 113, 114, 211
TACAIR 6
TACC 157, 206
Tactical Air Command 44, 106, 113
Tactical Intelligence Squadron 194
tactical level 79, 110
Taji 66, 119
Tallil 14, 119, 124, 175, 184, 230
tanks 59, 64, 74, 75, 78, 84, 112, 171, 203
target list 46-50, 88-90, 94, 118, 121, 137, 153, 155-157, 166, 169, 184, 186, 192-194, 199-201, 207, 213, 215, 225
target lists 50, 88, 192, 199-201, 217
Tawakalna 77, 204, 205
TEL 62, 221
TFS 22, 28, 130
TFW 135
The Times 189
Thumrait 135
Tikrit 119, 155, 156
time-phased force deployment data 21
time-phased force deployment list 31
TIS (see also Tactical Intelligence Squadron) 46-48, 50, 139, 140, 142, 193-195, 199, 200, 207, 222
Title V 77, 205
Tomahawk 14, 15, 96, 105, 123
TPFDD 21, 26
TPFDL 21
TR 34, 93
TR-1 34
Tu'ma 'Abbas al-Jabburi 67
Turkish 64, 203
Tuwaitha 118, 161, 184, 228

U

U.S. Air Force 44, 223
U.S. Army 6, 14, 20, 22, 28, 33, 35, 44, 117, 130
U.S. Central Command (see also Central Command) 9, 18, 104, 130, 133, 134, 151, 156, 202
U.S. Information Agency 44
U.S. Navy 14, 35, 44
U-2 34
UK 71
UN 62, 67, 98, 220
United Arab Emirates 58
United Nations 91, 98, 217
United States 64
US Air Force 108
US Army 51, 54, 233, 234
US Marine Corps 236
US Navy 236
USAFE 35
USCENTAF 18, 42, 47-49, 53, 105, 131, 136, 140, 160
USCENTCOM (see also Central Command) 1, 9, 21, 23, 26, 31, 42, 50, 105, 107, 128-133, 135, 136, 155, 156, 160, 173, 199, 200, 211, 213
USCINCCENT 1, 2, 4-7, 9, 20-23, 25-33, 35, 36, 38, 39, 42-44, 46, 47, 50, 54, 84, 100, 106, 108, 131-135, 155, 156, 157, 160, 173, 191, 199, 235, 236
USEUCOM 44
USIA 44
USLANTCOM 44
USMC (see also Marine corps) 14, 22, 28, 33, 54, 130, 135, 234
USN (see also U.S. Navy) 22, 28, 33, 114, 130, 133, 136, 139, 168, 234
USNR 206
USPACOM 44
USS Midway 35
USSOCOM 44
USTRANSCOM 44

V

Vietnam 61, 85, 86, 91, 102, 112, 117
Voice of America 71

W

Warden, John A. 83, 92-95, 108-121, 123, 126, 127, 141, 145, 148, 153, 162, 169, 172, 174, 226, 227
wargame 171
wargaming 46, 135
Washington 3, 17, 20, 35, 51, 54, 55, 62, 71, 83, 84, 87-90, 97, 98, 102, 104, 105, 107, 108, 110, 112, 117, 126, 135, 137, 141, 156, 162, 172, 203, 226, 229, 230-232, 234
Washington Post 71, 97, 102
weaponeering 48, 194
weapons of mass destruction 97, 156, 161, 193, 207, 210, 213
weather 207
Webster, William 106
Wickman, Allen 113
Williams 107
WIN 113, 169
Wisconsin 128
Wolfowitz, Paul 19, 96, 103, 105-107
World War II 17, 92, 110, 117, 127

Y

Y'Blood, William 135, 137
Yemen 23

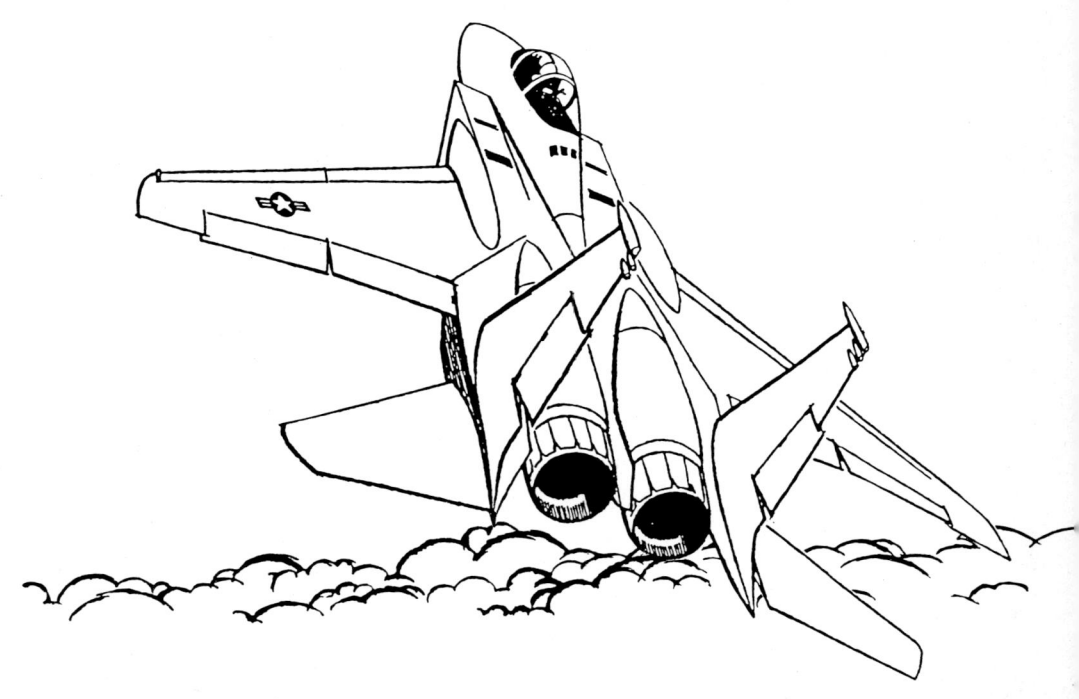

Part II

Command and Control

Part II

Command and Control

Task Force Chief

Dr. Thomas C. Hone

Principal Authors

Dr. Thomas C. Hone
Dr. Mark D. Mandeles
Lt. Col. Sanford S. Terry

Principal Contributors

Dr. Eliot A. Cohen
Maj. Robert J. Heston
Lt. Col. Frank D. Kistler
Maj. Anne D. Leary
Ms. Georganne Thibault

Contents

Report Acknowledgements ix

Introduction xi

1 Command and Control: Methodology and Concepts 1

2 Case Studies in Command and Control 7

3 Lt. Gen. Charles Horner as the First Joint Force
   Air Component Commander 41

4 Building the Tactical Air Control System 77

5 The CENTAF TACC 131

6 The Black Hole and Its Impact 157

7 The TACC and GAT in Desert Storm 205

8 BDA and the Command and Control
   of the Air Campaign 265

9 The Airborne TACS at War 305

10 Conclusion 329

Index 395

Appendixes

1 Definition of Terms 339

2 The Origins of the JFACC 351

3 Use of C3 Modeling Aids to Prepare for and Predict War . . . 369

4 Gulf War Command Arrangements 381

Tables

#	Title	Page
1	AA Package of F-111s Attacking H3 and H2 Airfields	25
2	Support Package of Table 1	25
3	Tasking Draft of Master Attack Plan	28
4	F-15E as Tasked on Targeting Worksheet	36
5	D+23, Air Tasking Order Y, 9 Feb 1991 - F-15E (4th Tactical Fighter Wing based at Al Kharj)	40
6	Gulf War Communications Planned versus Actual	110
7	Planned Activities: Day 2 of the Air Campaign in Directorates for Campaign Plans and Combat Operations	209
8	Planned Sorties versus ATO Changes (Days 1, 2 and 3)	213
9	ATO Changes, Day 1-Day 43	216
10	Sorties Planned, Sorties Changed, Target and Timing Changes Day 1 through Day 43	233
11	Anti-Scud Sorties	244
12	Total Reconnaissance Sorties, 17 Jan - 28 Feb 1991	257
13	Imagery Exploitation and Production In-theater (October 1990)	285
14	Areas of Sensor Commitment	285
15	Total Air Force Munitions Expenditure versus B-52 Munitions Expenditure	292

Figures

1. The Planning Cycle 9
2. First Draft of Master Attack Plan 11
3. Completed, Approved Master Attack Plan 12
4. Target Planning Worksheet 16
5. Air Tasking Order 18
6. Air Tasking Order Change Logbook 20
7. Air Tasking Order Change Sheet 22
8. Mission Report (MISREP) 23
9. Targets and Bases From Which F-111Fs Launched the Mission 26
10. Map of Area Flown 33
11. Tactical Air Control System (TACS) 78
12. Saudi Eastern Sector Control Center at Dhahran 93
13. AWACS Orbits over Saudi Arabia 98
14. Organization of Saudi Air Defense Sectors 122
15. Tactical Air Control Center Divisions 133
16. CENTAF Organizational Structure 134
17. Four Major Functional Divisions of the Combat Plans Division 136
18. Combat Planning Staff Works With Others To Develop Air Tasking Orders 138
19. Combat Operations Division In Riyadh 140

20	Combat Operations	141
21	Prewar Plan of Intelligence Organization to Support TACC	143
22	Page From Air Tasking Order	146
23	Proposed Sorties Apportionment	151
24	CENTAF Forward Organization	161
25	"Black Hole" Strategic Air Command Planners	165
26	Relationship of Saudi Air Force Building to SCIF	178
27	Relationship Among Planners Before Reorganization	188
28	Relationship Among Planners After Reorganization	189
29	Anticipated Planning Cycle	194
30	Reality: Timeline	211
31	Planned Sorties (ATO) versus Sorties Changed (TACC Change Log)	220
32	Sorties Changed as a Percentage of Sorties Planned	222
33	Sum Weather-related Changes	226
34	Map Showing Assigned Targets	238
35	Theater Intelligence Organizational Relationships	273
36	Collection Management Flow of Requests to CENTCOM, National and Tactical Theater Assets	276
37	U.S. and Saudi AWACS Orbits Near the Border with Iraq	306
38	The Service Chain of Command	383
39	The Unified Combatant Command Organization	386

Report Acknowledgements

This study of command and control in Desert Shield and Desert Storm led the individuals of the Task Force throughout the United States as well as to Europe. Members journeyed, among other sites, to the office of Lt. Gen. Charles A. Horner at Shaw AFB, South Carolina, to Space Command Headquarters, Colorado, to the Office of the Secretary of the Air Force in the Pentagon, to the Tactical Air Command at Langley AFB, Virginia, and to Rome Laboratory at Griffiss AFB, New York. On all travels, numbers of talented and cooperative officers, enlisted personnel, and civilians extended their welcome and rendered their assistance. We hope our effort justifies the help they gave us.

Piecing the story of command and control in Desert Shield and Desert Storm presented a formidable challenge. It was impossible to read all the relevant documents or interview the multitude of command and control personnel active in the Middle East during the conflict. Nevertheless, the Task Force uncovered an impressive mass of documentation. In our efforts to do so, we were ably supported by the following individuals: Capt. Guy Cafiero, who provided materials on AWACS and ABCCC, Capt. Linwood N. Gray, our expert in air traffic control; Maj. Lewis D. Hill, who pulled the GWAPS sortie database into shape; retired Col. Donald A. Kellum, who uncovered the full story of close air support from records at Shaw AFB; Capt. Edward L. Simpkins, who worked to untangle the story of bomb damage assessments; and Lt. Col. B. John Wampler, for his advice on our Chapter 6. All made essential contributions to the Task Force's understanding of command and control in the Gulf War.

The Task Force is also indebted to our reviewers: Dr. Thomas Keaney, Lt. Gen. Anthony J. Burshnick, USAF (Ret.), Lt. Col. Robert D. Eskridge, Prof. Richard H. Kohn, Lt. Col. Daniel Kuehl, Prof. James Q. Wilson, Lt. Gen. Robert E. Kelley, USAF (Ret.), Mr. Barry Watts, Dr. Wayne Thompson, Col. Emery M. Kiraly, Mr. Larry Lausten, Gen. Michael J. Dugan, USAF (Ret.), and Lt. Col. David A. Deptula. We particularly want to thank General Kelley for his efforts to help us master the finer points of controlling air operations at the theater level.

Dr. Mark Mandeles, the Deputy Task Force Leader, and Lt. Col. Sanford Terry, the Task Force's Chief Military Advisor, carried the burden of the day-to-day research and administration. Along with Dr. Thomas Hone, they wrote the bulk of the report. Finally, the Task Force owes a debt it cannot repay to Ms. Cecelia A. French, our administrative assistant, resident optimist, and manager. We could not have completed this report without her hard work and her professionalism. Thanks are due also to Mr. Chris Pankow, who had the thankless job of editing our manuscript.

Command and Control is a controversial subject. There are as many types of command and control experts as there are expert economists, and, like economists, they often disagree among themselves about what they do, what they should study, and about what really matters in their field. Dr. Eliot A. Cohen, Director of GWAPS, gave us freedom to decide what we meant by command and control. Though there are three principal authors of the study, all errors of fact and of judgment are the responsibility of the head of the Task Force, Dr. Thomas C. Hone.

Introduction

The *Command and Control* report is not a detailed history of command and control of air operations during Desert Shield and Desert Storm. Instead, the report considers those command and control issues that are inherent to the use of air power and crucial to its effective use. The first chapter outlines the problems facing the task force and the approach used in analyzing the command and control process. Chapter 2 illustrates the complexity of modern air operations as revealed in specific air operations conducted during Desert Storm. The examples used in the chapter were chosen at random from among thousands, but they show how important it was for different types of aircraft to work closely together on a routine basis. Such close coordination required a tight linkage among different parts of a large air operations plan. It placed a heavy burden on planners. If they decided to change one element of their plan, they had to be sensitive of its effects on other elements. As the examples show, changes to operations plans tended to cascade through the theater-wide Air Tasking Order.

Chapter 3 analyzes the performance of Lt. Gen. Charles A. Horner, the first Joint Force Air Component Commander (JFACC). Horner's formal responsibility was to plan and direct a theater-wide air campaign against Iraq and its forces. The chapter discusses the authority he was given as JFACC and how he used it, his relationship to the theater commander (General Schwarzkopf) and to his fellow component commanders, his leadership style, and his approach to Coalition warfare. As the first JFACC, Horner stepped into a new and controversial position. Chapter 3 discusses his actions and what they may portend for future Joint Force Air Component Commanders.

Horner directed the theater Tactical Air Control System (TACS) through the Tactical Air Control Center (TACC). Chapter 4 describes the TACS and explains how its components were assembled during Desert Shield. The center of the Tactical Air Control System is the Tactical Air Control Center, a ground-based complex of command and control and communications personnel and their equipment. Chapter 5 describes how the TACC was set up in Riyadh and how it was organized. Chapter 6 describes the "Black Hole"–the secret ad hoc organization put together during Desert Shield by Brig. Gen. Buster Glosson to plan the air offensive against Iraq. It also discusses what happened when, in December

1990, the Black Hole became the Guidance, Apportionment, and Targeting (GAT) cell (and officially replaced CENTAF Combat Plans) at the heart of the TACC in Riyadh.

Chapter 7 continues the analysis of the Tactical Air Control Center by examining how it operated during Desert Storm. The interaction between the Black Hole and the other organizational elements of the TACC was awkward. The Black Hole's planners found it difficult to work smoothly with their colleagues in intelligence and operations, and the resulting friction affected the process of compiling the Air Tasking Order, which in turn influenced the conduct of the air campaign. Chapter 7 also shows that what senior air commanders in the Tactical Air Control Center thought was happening in the air campaign was sometimes not what was happening at all. That senior commanders had problems keeping track of the "real" air war should come as no surprise; their counterparts in earlier air wars had the same problem. Finally, Chapter 7 covers the command and control problems of detecting Scud missile launches and then of hunting mobile Scud launchers. The latter, not surprisingly, turned out to be much harder than the former.

Chapter 8 examines the valuative side to command and control during the air campaign by explaining and then analyzing the process of bomb damage assessment. A number of organizations participated in this process, including intelligence agencies located outside the theater (and beyond the control of the theater commander). Bomb damage assessment also was conducted within the Tactical Air Control Center, in ways not planned for before Desert Storm began. The result was a very complicated and often confused process.

Chapter 9 considers airborne command and control, especially that exercised by the personnel in the Airborne Warning and Control System (AWACS), the Joint Surveillance, Targeting and Reconnaissance System (JSTARS), and the Airborne Battlefield Command and Control Center (ABCCC) aircraft. In managing airspace defense, aerial refueling, and air-to-ground operations, these systems revealed the maturing capability of airborne, decentralized command and control.

Chapter 10 pulls all the chapters together around the distinction introduced earlier in this section: the difference between organizational outputs and outcomes and the likelihood that the two will be confused during wartime. The original *United States Strategic Bombing Survey* noted that the air campaigns conducted against Germany and Japan were handicapped by large gaps in intelligence (both prewar and during the war) and by a lack of integrated military command at the theater level and above. The *Strategic Bombing Survey* prompted action to remedy these defects. Such action, designed to connect organizational outputs systematically to the outcomes produced by those outputs, was still being taken as late as 1986, when the Goldwater-Nichols act was passed, and through the late 1980s, when the Services were discussing the proper role and authority for the Joint Force Air Component Commander. The chapters in this report will show the progress in solving these two major problems.

Security Review

The Gulf War Air Power Survey reports were submitted to the Department of Defense for policy and security review. In accordance with this review, certain information has been removed from the original text. These areas have been annotated as [DELETED].

1

Command and Control: Methodology and Concepts

> The command and control process is made up of a series of actions. . . . The process begins with assessing the battlefield situation from available information. Following this assessment, the commander decides on a course of action. The commander then implements this decision by directing and controlling available forces. The final step. . .is evaluating the impact of the action on both friendly and opposing forces. This evaluation then serves as an input into an updated assessment of the situation, and the process continues.[1]

This concept of the command and control process is straightforward; its practice in war, however, is difficult. Appendix 2 to this report ("The Origins of the JFACC"), which reviews the history of command and control of air forces at the theater level, shows just how difficult it has often been to implement "the command and control process" in past air conflicts. In the case of the coalition war against Iraq, multinational air forces were wielded successfully against complex air defenses to achieve an overwhelming battlefield victory. We will explain how U.S. air forces were organized and led to that victory, working from the definition of "the command and control process" given by Tactical Air Command Manual 2-1 quoted above. We will focus on the challenges of implementing "the command and control process" during Desert Shield and Desert Storm, how those challenges were dealt with–sometimes successfully and sometimes not–and the consequences of specific actions taken for theater-level command and control during the conflict.[2]

---

[1] Tactical Air Command, TAC Manual 2-1, *Tactical Air Operations*, Aug 1991, pp 5-1 and 5-2.

[2] At the end of 1991, Air Force Chief of Staff General Merrill A. McPeak stated publicly that the command and control process for the air war against Iraq might have collapsed altogether if it had been subjected to "really difficult combat conditions." Tony Capaccio, "USAF Chief Pans War's Command Chain," *Defense Week*, 2 Dec 1991, p 1.

The Task Force's Perspective

During Desert Shield and Desert Storm air operations, command and control was exercised by individuals working in specific offices within larger organizations, as often visualized in line and box organizational diagrams. Yet organizations are not just line diagrams. A set of boxes and lines on a chart does not do justice to the complexity, flexibility, and power of the kinds of organizations through which air commanders exercise the control of air units.

The Tactical Air Control System–the focus of this report–is, for example, a collection of organizations, including (to name just a few) the Tactical Air Control Center (TACC), one or more Air Support Operations Centers (for Army-Air Force coordination), and the small but critical groups of personnel who man systems such as AWACS (Airborne Warning and Control System) and ABCCC (Airborne Battlefield Command and Control Center) aircraft. Each of these parts of the overall organization (the Tactical Air Control System) is itself a structured but flexible collection of trained personnel and the coordinated activities in which they engage.

The purpose of these organizations (and many others) is to implement or support the directives of a theater-level commander. Put another way, what these organizations do (communicate, analyze, decide, etc.) and how they do it is the command and control process. It is that process that this Gulf War Air Power Survey Task Force has studied.

We approached the process from two perspectives: outputs and outcomes. An organization's outputs are what it does. Wings and squadrons, for example, fly missions. Organizational outcomes are the results that its outputs produce. Ideally, outputs, such as sorties, produce the right outcomes, such as degraded enemy defenses.

Generally, senior commanders find it difficult during combat to distinguish outputs from outcomes and to discover outcomes. In fact, the inability to discern outcomes (damage to specific enemy capabilities) is usually the reason why senior commanders focus strongly on outputs, such as sortie rates. Professional soldiers understand this. Gen. Norman Schwarzkopf, for example, wanted measures of how air attacks against Iraqi army targets in Kuwait were reducing the combat capability of Iraqi divisions opposed to coalition forces. He was outcome-oriented, and properly so. He also understood that his desire for outcome indicators could easily be interpreted by his and his component commanders' staffs as a need for numbers of outputs. To avoid what he regarded as a potentially dangerous focus on outputs, Schwarzkopf actually discouraged staffs in the theater from gathering and reporting certain kinds of output data.

General Schwarzkopf and his component commanders understood that they had to stay focused on **outcomes**. They also understood, however, that doing so would not be easy. Poor weather, the uncertainties of reconnaissance, and deliberate deception and defense on the part of the Iraqis would all combine to obscure outcomes. At the same time, as U.S. and allied forces struggled to plan and then mount missions from unfamiliar bases during the inevitable confusion caused by a rapid build-up, even **outputs** would be uncertain and obscure. As Lt. Gen. Charles A. Horner, the Joint Force Air Component Commander later observed, command in war is a matter of "managing chaos."[3] Put another way, senior commanders found that staying focused on outcomes was always a serious challenge. It required constant attention to all the elements of the command and control process.

The Task Force has focused on how that attention was given, by whom, under what circumstances, and on the results produced. As a result, the chapters which follow pay much more attention to people and to their interactions (with one another and with the machines they operated) than to "hardware" (such as communications equipment). The study assumes that successful command and control–the balancing of outputs to achieve desired outcomes–is not a given but instead requires careful planning and deliberate, continuous management–to say nothing of the exercise of sound military judgment–by personnel at all levels.

The paradox of modern military command at the theater level is that, though the responsibility of one officer, it must be exercised within a set of complex organizations. Commanders such as General Schwarzkopf and Lieutenant General Horner understood that they had to do more than find their enemy's weak points and direct forces against those points. They also had to make sure that what they wanted done (the "outputs" to achieve the desired "outcomes") was in fact done and done in the right way. Obviously, they had to work through their staffs and through their subordinates' staffs. They had practiced doing just that. Yet they also knew, even before August 1990, that planning could not anticipate all the

---

[3](S) Intvw, Barry Barlow, Richard G. Davis, and Perry Jamieson with Lt Gen Charles A. Horner, Commander 9th AF, 4 Mar 1992.

factors that would affect their ability to command and control the forces assigned to them. No matter how much they and their staffs practiced, they would have to deal with unanticipated problems–to adapt–once a crisis unfolded.

The story of that adaptation and its consequences for command and control of the air campaign is one of the most interesting to come out of the war with Iraq. It is important because military command and control rests on the assumption that there will almost always be a difference between peacetime exercises and wartime action. Military command and control is, consequently, flexible and adaptable. Peacetime exercises are less a form of drill than learning experiences. The most fruitful peacetime simulations add to the skill, confidence, and sophistication of personnel in command and control organizations.

What a commander wants to take with him into war is a set of organizations that can learn while they execute their missions. What those organizations can learn in peacetime is not so much precisely what to do in war but how to learn, and learn quickly, what to do. If they learn how to learn, then they give the commander (and every member of his force) an advantage. They give him added skill in assessing a situation, choosing among alternative courses of action, implementing the course he directs, and then studying its effects. Supported by such adaptable, quick-to-learn organizations, a commander can seize the military initiative and keep it until victory is achieved.

However, there always will be a tension between organizational adaptability and organizational procedures in military command and control. If, facing the uncertainty and stresses of war, the personnel in military command and control organizations abandon their practiced and codified procedures and create informal and ad hoc organizations and procedures, they run two risks. The first is that they will get bogged down in efforts to put together a new structure to support the theater commander. That is, they will spend too much time just explaining what they're doing and why to the other elements of command and control with which they must work. The second risk is that their new procedures will actually not work as efficiently as they anticipate, leaving them with ineffective command and control at the theater level.

Command and control personnel must, therefore, balance the need to respond to the situation against the equally important need to maintain a structure within which information can be organized and analyzed and decisions made and quickly communicated. As Lieutenant General Horner observed, there will be chaos in war, but that chaos must be managed. Just how that was done during Desert Shield and Desert Storm is the concern of this report.

The Problems of Studying Command and Control

It is difficult to describe accurately wartime command and control for several reasons. First, it is not easy to obtain accurate information on the behavior of the personnel and equipment that together comprise command and control systems. After all, the people who directed the air campaign against Iraq and all the supporting air activity were primarily interested in winning the war. Available records make that point clear. Not everything which might now throw light on the workings of command and control in the Gulf War was written down—or saved.

Consequently, great use has been made of the testimony of participants and witnesses, despite the obvious risks that their memories may have faded or that they may have reinterpreted their experiences with hindsight. People also tend to see different things depending on their organizational positions. In this study, the testimony of some witnesses and participants may differ from or even contradict that given by others. The study has tried to canvass all perspectives and all points of view in order to cover all the detail of the command and control process, but there was simply not enough time to gather and consider carefully all the important perspectives on command and control of air operations in the war against Iraqi control.

A second problem is that operations Desert Shield and Desert Storm generated huge amounts of data. Researchers were like crash investigators trying to discover what had caused an airplane to go down: there was so much evidence, and so much of that evidence was in the form of fragments, that it was difficult sometimes to know where to begin and when to stop collecting. Even worse, the substantial volume of information made available to researchers did not guarantee that the really crucial records had been preserved. As General Schwarzkopf himself noted in his memoirs, for example, "there was no official record of many" of the communications between him and Gen. Colin Powell, Chairman of the Joint Chiefs of Staff.[4]

This problem of not being sure of having enough of the right information was to some degree a function of the extensive use of secure telephones (for both conversations and facsimiles) during Desert Shield and Desert Storm. In addition, many command and control organizations and relationships affecting the air campaign were ad hoc–invented and then disbanded once their tasks were completed. Several of these organizations left few records of their activities; others left many records. The Task Force tried to avoid becoming "captured" by those records kept in the greatest quantity. However, we cannot be sure that the records kept and then given to it reflect a full and accurate record of command and control at all levels.

The final problem which hindered effective research was the unreliability of records retained by some command and control organizations, especially once the air war began in earnest in mid-January 1991. For example, the accuracy of the entries in the Air Tasking Order Change Log kept by personnel manning the Tactical Air Control Center in Riyadh during Desert Storm is questionable. It is likely that the GWAPS Composite Sorties Database also contains errors. Yet these documents had to be used by the Task Force; they held the best data available.

These three general problems–not always having the right information, being overwhelmed by all the information that was preserved, and being forced to use some unreliable information because nothing better was available–forced the Task Force to spend a great deal of time just reviewing its sources and cross-checking its data. Thus, inferences drawn from our data reflect the limitations of those data.

---

[4]H. Norman Schwarzkopf with Peter Petre, *It Doesn't Take a Hero* (New York, 1992), p 325.

2

Case Studies in Command and Control

The air campaign in the Gulf War required the planning, tasking, and execution of more than 2,000 sorties a day.[1] The planning and execution of this daily operation was an effort of immense complexity, involving such tasks, among many others, as coordinating times over target into time blocks of 15 minutes or less. Sorties frequently were planned and flown in "packages," groups of aircraft supporting one another in an attack against a particular target or target area. A package normally consisted of ground attack aircraft accompanied by fighter aircraft (providing escort or cover against enemy aircraft), and electronic combat and defense suppression aircraft (jamming or destroying enemy air defenses). Attack and fighter aircraft frequently had to refuel in order to reach their targets or to loiter in the target area. Their flights, therefore, had to be coordinated with those of tanker aircraft. In addition, while enroute to and from the target area, they might receive command guidance, threat updates and warnings, or targeting updates from airborne command and control or intelligence gathering aircraft.

The process of planning for the launch of only a few sorties is not necessarily difficult; planning to launch more than 2,000 sorties a day from many locations is extremely complex. The following two case studies will give the reader a sense for how this vast enterprise was orchestrated by illustrating the planning and tasking process and the challenges confronted. The cases were chosen at random; our purpose is to portray difficulties encountered in controlling an air campaign and in documenting its conduct. We begin with a general description of how attacks were planned and coordinated.

---

[1] A sortie is defined in JCS Pub 1-02 as "an operational flight by one aircraft" (*Department of Defense Dictionary of Military and Associated Terms*, 1 Dec 1989, p 337). During Operation Desert Storm, coalition aircraft flew an average of 2,847 sorties per day. On 23 Feb 1991, 3,279 sorties were flown, the greatest daily total of the war. On 20 Jan 1991, 2,311 sorties were flown–the fewest number of the war. (GWAPS Composite Sorties Database; see GWAPS *Statistical Compendium*.

The Planning Cycle

The cycle of selecting, developing, tasking, executing, and evaluating a mission is less complicated when these individual tasks for a single day are considered in isolation.[2] Figure 1 depicts the planning cycle.[3] An appreciation of the complexity of this planning cycle is essential to understanding the case studies.

The planning cycle started when the Guidance, Apportionment and Targeting (GAT) cell[4] arrived at work.[5] For the purposes of this description, we call this Day 1 of the planning cycle. The officers in this cell began planning by translating General Horner's guidance (who, in turn, received guidance from General Schwarzkopf), into a coherent,

---

[2] The normal planning cycle required three days, although that cycle could be circumvented at a number of points in order to take advantage of fresh information or in order to cope with unexpected changes (e.g., bad weather or maintenance problems). On any single day, the planners worked on planning, coordination, and orchestration tasks for "today," "tomorrow," and the "day after tomorrow." See Chapter 5 for a more detailed discussion of the three day planning cycle.

[3] (S) USCENTAF Combat Plans Handout, Jan 1991, pp 1-6. See also Briefing, Lt Col David A. Deptula, SAF/OSX, "The Air Campaign: Planning and Execution, 26 Nov 91"; see also Briefing, Lt Col Sam Baptiste, 9th AF, "ATO Preparation," 4 Dec 1991.

[4] The GAT, also known as the "Black Hole," came into existence after the reorganization of the CENTAF staff in Dec 1990. This reorganization incorporated the Special Planning Group–the original Black Hole–into the CENTAF Tactical Air Control Center (TACC) staff (see GWAPS Chapter 5). During Desert Storm, the GAT operated out of a room in the basement of the Royal Saudi Air Force Headquarters building in Riyadh. This room, measuring approximately 30 feet by 50 feet, was divided by plywood walls into eight office spaces: (a) the Iraqi and Kuwaiti theater planning cells, (b) the Integrated Air Defense System (IADS) cell, (c) the Battlefield Coordination Element (BCE), (d) the Nuclear, Biological, Chemical, (e) Scud cell, (f) Administration, (g) Studies and Analyses, and (h) an office for Gen Glosson.

[5] There was no "official" starting time for the beginning of the planning cycle. Lt Col Deptula briefed that the planning cycle began at 0800 local time. Lt Col Deptula was chief planner in the CENTAF Special Planning Group during Desert Shield, and director, Strategic Planning Cell during Desert Storm. (Briefing, Lt Col David Deptula, SAF/OSX, "The Air Campaign: Planning and Execution," 26 Nov 1991.) The Jan 1991 USCENTAF Combat Plans Handout showed the ATO cycle starting with a 1000 CC (Gen Horner) discussion with the GAT (pp 1-6). Lt Col Sam Baptiste, Chief of Weapons and Tactics at 9th AF HQ, did not give any specific timeframe for this start of the planning process. (Briefing, Lt Col Baptiste, "ATO Preparation," 4 Dec 1991.)

Figure 1
The Planning Cycle

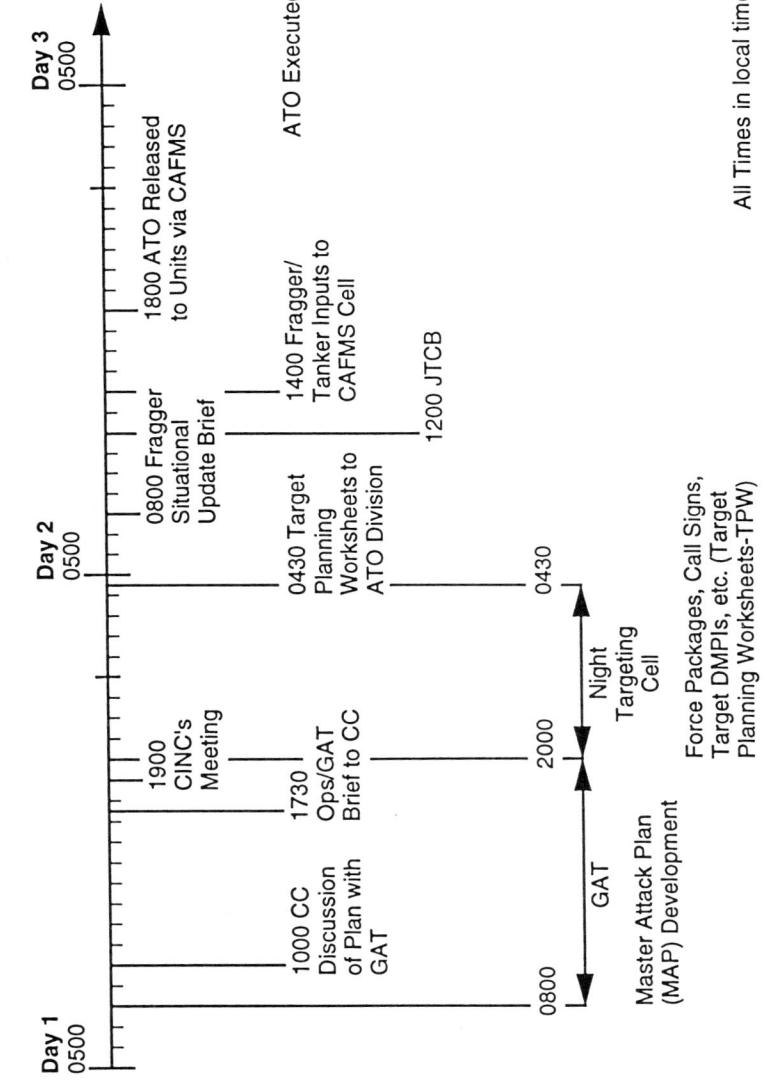

All Times in local time.

coordinated plan–the Master Attack Plan (MAP). In addition to the Commander in Chief's guidance, the attack plan also included intelligence information received overnight and bomb damage assessment from various sources. For example, at least one member of the GAT would attend the morning meeting in the Tactical Air Control Center's combat operations area, during which the night shift gave way to the day shift. This meeting relayed information on the previous day's missions and updated the next day's planned missions for officers working the oncoming shift. It also provided opportunity for General Horner to issue guidance and instruction to the Central Command Air Forces staff as a whole. Later, around 1000L, General Horner also would speak informally with GAT officers and receive updates on the course of planning.

The GAT worked on the attack plan for Day 1 from approximately 0800 in the morning until 1800 at night. As the sample page at Figure 2[6] indicates, the first draft of the Master Attack Plan consisted of handwritten worksheets, which contained six kinds of information: (a) the time on target (TOT) for the attack, (b) a mission number (often left blank in the first iteration), (c) the basic encyclopedia number (BEN–a standard reference to the Defense Intelligence Agency's automated installation file identifier), (d) a target code (based on the Guidance, Apportionment, and Targeting cell's own categories, which consisted of a two-digit number and a one- to three-letter identifier, such as "L" for leadership and "SC" for Scud-related), (e) a target description (normally the name and short description such as "ammunition storage"), and (f) the number and type of aircraft conducting the attack. The Master Attack Plan would be keyed into a personal computer file as it was built. Gen. Buster C. Glosson, Director, Campaign Plans, signed completed attack plans. Figure 3 shows the first page of a completed, approved Master Attack Plan for 21 January 1991.[7]

---

[6](S) Master Attack Plan Draft, 21 Jan 1991, D+4, 5th 24 Hours, GWAPS BH, box 1, folder 9.

[7](S) Master Attack Plan, 21 Jan 1991, D+4, 5th 24 Hours, GWAPS BH, box 1, folder 9.

Figure 2
First Draft of Master Attack Plan

\[colspan\]	MASTER ATTACK PLAN				
N	DAY + 4			APPROVED	
TOT*	MSN#	BEN	TGT	DESCRIPTION	AC
1800-15		[DELETED]	SC43	QASR AMIJ SCUD STOR	4 F-15E
1800-15		[DELETED]	SC44	WADI AMIJ SCUD STOR	4 F-15E
1815-30		[DELETED]	SC46	WADI AL JABARIYAH STOR	4 F-15E
1815-30		[DELETED]	SC45	WADI AR RATQA STOR	4 F-15E
0030-0045		[DELETED]	A31	AN NUMANIYAH AFLD FAC	8 F-15E
0040-0055		[DELETED]	MS01	RUMAYLAH AMMO STOR	8 F-1J

11

Figure 3
Completed, Approved Master Attack Plan

6:48 PM
20 JAN/1600

MASTER ATTACK PLAN
FIFTH 24 HOURS

1/20/91
APPROVED

TOT*	MSN#	BEN	TGT	DESCRIPTION	AC
0115 -0130	4401A(U)	[DELETED]	A30	H-3 AFLD SW SEAD (RED SEA GROUP)	10 GR-1
0200	3321A 3322A 3323A 3324A 3325A 3326A	[DELETED]	SAD68 SAD67 L06 L08 L16 L15	I-HAWK NW BAG I-HAWK TNG SITE INTERNAL SECURITY HQ MINISTRY OF DEFENSE PRESIDENTIAL PALACE TAJI PRESIDENTIAL RETREAT	1 F-117 1 F-117 1 F-117 1 F-117 1 F-117 1 F-117
0200 TO 0215 *388TFW		[DELETED]	RG03 RG04	MEDINAH CP HAMURABI CP	4 F-16L 4 F-16L
0210 TO 0230		[DELETED]	SC42 SAD06 SAD05 SAD25 SC31 SC32	3004N 04742E/FROG BATT SCUD C2 BKR - KANMALL 314019N 0471434E AL AMARAH IOC & GCI SITE 292345N 0473739E AL JAHRAH IOC/CP 292105N 0473830E 5TG AD SEC OPS CTR AL SALEM 292105N 0473830E AL JAHRAH MISSILE FAC 291902N 0473752E AL JAHRAH AMMO STOR (SCUD) SEAD SEAD SWEEP/FORCE PROTECT	4 F-111 4 F-111 4 F-111 4 F-111 4 F-111 4 F-111 4 F-4G 4 F-4G 8 F-15C
0215	3327A 333?A 3331A 3335A 3335A 336?7 0?4? 334?A *DUAL DOOR GBU-10	[DELETED]	L04 L19 C21 C22 CCC28 L34 Q.11 SAD28 C23	N TAJI C3 FAC #2 INTEL SERVICE HQ ABU GHURAYB BW PT ABU GHURAYB VACCINE PT BAG TELECOM CTR NAT C3 BKR NUC RESRCH FAC AL TAJI IOC TAJI BW FAC	1 F-117 2 F-117 1 F-117 2 F-117 1 F-117 1 F-117
0215 TO 0230	4411A(U) 4421A(U) *COORD EF-111 W/MSN 0471X	[DELETED]	A08 A31	AR RUMAYLAH SEAD AN NUMANIYAH SEAD	8 GA-1* 8 GR-1 2EF-111

A draft Master Attack Plan would be largely completed when the night targeting cell (NTC)[8] arrived at 1800 in the evening. The night targeting cell officers would adjust and "massage" the draft attack plan by weaponeering the targets,[9] building and coordinating force packages, assigning call signs, and performing the other tasks required to translate the concept embodied in the plan into an executable plan. This process was very informal; the night targeting cell did not follow a "checklist procedure." For example, the B-52 representative would examine the nominated B-52 targets and missions on the draft attack plan. First, in conjunction with intelligence planners, he would do a quick "sanity check" on the targets to identify any glaring inconsistencies or errors. Second, he would coordinate support from defense suppression or escort aircraft, if so required by the target area threat or planned tactics. He would then complete the target planning worksheet with the applicable weapon and aimpoint selection data. Finally, he would contact all the applicable units via secure telephone to give them a "heads up" on the forthcoming Air Tasking Order.[10]

---

[8]The GAT night shift became the nucleus for the CENTAF NTC once Desert Storm began and the tempo of the planning process increased. The NTC was identified as an organization under the Combat Planning Division of the CENTAF Combat Plans Organization (S) (USCENTAF *Combat Plans Handout*, Oct 1990, p ii). After the CENTAF reorganization in Dec 1990, the NTC does not appear on the Jan 1991 (S) USCENTAF *Combat Plans Handout* organizational chart as a distinct division or organization within the Campaign Plans organization (p ii). Rather, the term, "night targeting cell" referred to the night shift in the GAT and ATO Divisions, which collectively built the packages, filled in the target planning worksheets, etc. People assigned to many functional divisions throughout the CENTAF staff were involved in this process.

[9]Weaponeering "is the process of determining the quantity of a specific type weapon required to achieve a specified level of damage to a given target, considering target vulnerability, weapon effects, munitions delivery errors, damage criteria, probability of kill, weapon reliability, etc. When the objective of force employment is to employ lethal force against a target, targeteers use a variety of weaponeering methodologies to determine expected damage levels. These weaponeering methodologies include both nonnuclear and nuclear weaponeering techniques. Common to both methodologies is aimpoint selection and weapons effects analysis." Department of the Air Force, *An Introduction to Air Force Targeting*, AF Pamphlet 200-17, 23 Jun 1989, p 21.

[10]Based on personal experience of a Task Force IV member. Lt Col Sanford S. Terry, then Major, was assigned to the SAC Strategic Forces Advisors (STRATFOR) at USCENTAF Headquarters, Riyadh, Saudi Arabia from 26 Jan 1991 to 25 Apr 1991. While in this position, Lt Col Terry worked in the night shift in the GAT and performed the functions normally performed by the NTC.

As planners assembled packages, they coordinated the package support (for example, mission times on target and numbers of aircraft) to make scarce resources, such as F-4Gs, available to support as many strike packages as possible. Changes made to a particular sortie had to be coordinated with the other night targeting officers and the officers in the daytime Iraq and Kuwaiti theater cells. In this way the initial pencil draft of the Master Attack Plan was updated throughout the night until it was completely coordinated. The 1900 Commander in Chief's meeting each evening provided another source of changes to the draft plan.[11] Changes from the 1900 meeting also were coordinated through the night targeting cell.

Targets and missions of B-52s (above) were supported by as many as possible F-4Gs (below).

---

[11](S) Intvw, Office of Air Force History with Lt Col Deptula, SAF/OSX, 20 Nov 1991.

The night targeting cell coordination process resulted in the entries on the target planning worksheet (TPW). Every sortie that released a weapon on a target had a worksheet completed for that particular mission. In addition, the worksheet for each attack package included support sorties such as suppression of enemy air defenses and combat air patrol missions. The target planning worksheet, when filled in properly, included all the information necessary for Central Command Air Force officers to build an Air Tasking Order, from which unit officers would plan their assigned missions and fly a particular sortie.[12] Figure 4 shows a target worksheet filled in for six B-52s attacking a target on 9 February 1991.[13] This worksheet gave all the target and mission information necessary for officers from the 1708th (Provisional) Bomb Wing to plan and execute the particular mission. Such information included the following: (a) recommended ordnance, (b) the package designator, (c) supporting aircraft and their mission numbers, (d) air refueling instructions, (e) specific target objectives and aimpoints, and (f) probability of destruction derived from the Joint Munitions Effects Manual, or JMEM.[14]

By 0430L of Day 2, the target planning worksheets were completed and given to the Air Tasking Order (ATO) Division,[15] who completed the coordination (among tankers, air space controllers, and units)[16] and entered the tasking data into the Computer Assisted Force Management System (CAFMS), the computer-based system used to disseminate the

---

[12] The individual weapon system representatives filled out TPWs to varying degrees of completeness; the purpose of this exercise was to ensure that the fundamental tasks involved in successfully flying the particular aircraft mission or package had been completed.

[13] (S) USCENTAF Target Planning Worksheet, D+23, 9 Feb 1991, GWAPS, BH Box 9.

[14] Intelligence officers train to determine a particular level of target destruction. Formulae and weapons data found in the JMEMs and data on specific aircraft capability and weapons loads form the basis of targeteering–determining the number and type of weapon needed to achieve a desired probability of kill. JMEMs are discussed at length in GWAPS Volume II.

[15] (S) USCENTAF *Combat Plans Handout*, Jan 1991, pp 1-6. See also briefing, Lt Col Sam Baptiste, "ATO Preparation," 4 Dec 91.

[16] Air refueling tasking was not included in the MAP. This coordination was very difficult because of the high density of planned air traffic and the requirements for aerial refueling support.

Figure 4
Target Planning Worksheet

SECRET (WHEN FILLED IN)

CC: ", CORPS, FIGHTERS, FT, COMPASS CALL
RC: 4, AWACS, TANKERS, FTR DIV CM

TARGET PLANNING WORKSHEET

FOR ATO D+23   NAME: AL HADITHAH PET REF/STORAGE   MSN#: 26xx-Y   PKG: VB
DATE: 9 Feb 91   BE: [DELETED]   TOT: 04/2403-13   PH:
Page 1 of 1   REQN: 014   COORD: 34-04.217N 042-21.667E   MSN TYPE: INT   TGT ID: 1708 PBW

	ACFT	ORDNANCE	SCL	CC	SSPD	PD	D#	AIMPOINT/OBJECTIVES/REMARKS
WEAPONEER	6 x B-52	46 x MK82	4517L		.07		333	POL STORAGE TANKS

MISSION	AIRCRAFT	CC	ORDNANCE	MSN	OPERATIONS COMMENTS
TARGET ATTACK	6 x B52(E)	X	4517L	2641B	
FORCE PROTECTION	2 x F-15(E)		47493	2641C	
EC					
RECCE					

AWACS: W C M
ABCCC: W M
JSTARS:
PRE:
POST:

TGT INTEL COMMENTS

OPR: 9AF/INA
DATE: 1 JAN 91

SECRET (WHEN FILLED IN)

CLASSIFIED BY: COMUSCENTAF
DECLASSIFY ON: OADR

'completed Air Tasking Order to the tasked Air Force units.[17] This remaining airspace and air refueling information was due to the CAFMS operators no later than 1400L on Day 2 of the planning cycle,[18] so that the tasking order could be transmitted by 1800L.[19]

After receipt of the tasking order, sometime around 1800L, each unit would begin its own mission planning. The order's effective period began at 0500L.[20] If the process was flowing smoothly the minimum amount of planning time a unit had between Air Tasking Order receipt and time on targets was eleven hours. Delays at any part of the cycle could delay the unit's receipt of the tasking order, thus reducing its time for planning. Figure 5 provides one page of a Central Command Air Forces-published Air Tasking Order.[21]

Guidance, Apportionment, and Targeting Cell officers could change the Master Attack Plan, and the subsequent Air Tasking Order, before the air order was transmitted to the units. For example, officers working at night could change the pencil draft of the attack plan based upon the 1900 Commander in Chief's meeting, late intelligence information, or Mission Reports. It is possible to follow the development of the Master Attack Plan[22] from its initial draft to the final form approved by General Buster C. Glosson, Director, CENTAF Campaign Plans, because most of the printed plans have two clock times or dates/times printed on them.

---

[17]At times, the completed daily ATO was approximately 1,000 pages long (this was not an everyday occurrence). It contained all the information a unit needed to plan and fly each particular mission. The CENTAF ATO was based upon the ATO message format found in the U.S. Joint Message Text Format Handbook published by the Joint Chiefs of Staff. (Joint Chiefs of Staff Publication 6-4, *U.S. Message Text Formatting Program*, OPR: AF/XOFI, Oct 1992, Chapter 3.)

[18]Briefing, Lt Col Sam Baptiste, "ATO Preparation," 4 Dec 91.

[19]*Ibid.*

[20]*Ibid.*

[21](S) Air Tasking Orders, GWAPS, CSS Safe 6, Desert Shield - 20 Jan 1991. For a definition of each individual field and nomenclature in a CENTAF ATO see GWAPS Volume II, Chapter 3.

[22]For example, changes to missions, targets, and TOTs can be tracked by arraying successive iterations of a MAP for a particular day.

Figure 5
Air Tasking Order

PENTAGON
OPERATIONS DIRECTORATE

```
       COMMENTS:
MSNDAT
TGTLOC
REFUEL                                          [DELETED]
REFUEL
AMPN/
       COMMENTS: TAW MECH ARTY//
MSNDAT/
TGTLOC/                                         [DELETED]
AMPN/
       COMMENTS: MINISTRY OF INFO//
MSNDAT
TGTLOC
AMPN/                                           [DELETED]
       COMMENTS: MINISTRY OF INFO//
MSNDAT
TGTLOC
REFUEL                                          [DELETED]
REFUEL
AMPN/
       COMMENTS: BAGHDAD NUC FAC//
MSNDAT
TGTLOC
REFUEL                                          [DELETED]
REFUEL
AMPN/
       COMMENTS: BAGHDAD NUC FAC FAC//
MSNDAT/
TGTLOC/
REFUEL/                                         [DELETED]
REFUEL/
AMPN/ REMARK IDENTIFIER(S): A E J K T
       COMMENTS: MED ARTY CP//
MSNDAT/
TGTLOC/
REFUEL/                                         [DELETED]
REFUEL/
AMPN/ REMARK IDENTIFIER(S): A C E F K T
       COMMENTS: NAJEF IOC/RDR//
MSNDAT/
TGTLOC/
REFUEL                                          [DELETED]
REFUEL
AMPN/
       COMMENTS: NEJEF NEW AFLD//
MSNDAT/
TGTLOC/
REFUEL/                                         [DELETED]
REFUEL/
AMPN/ REMARK IDENTIFIER(S): A E K T
       COMMENTS: AL JAHRAH MSL FAC//
NARR/ UNIT REMARKS:   35TFW
UNIT REMARKS A
SEE TANKER SPINS FOR AAR INFORMATION.
UNIT REMARKS C
CONTACT CENTRAL AWACS FOR DIRECT CONTROL, USE CENTRAL COMM PLAN.
UNIT REMARKS E
CONTACT EAST AWACS FOR DIRECT CONTROL, USE EAST COMM PLAN.
UNIT REMARKS F
THIS PACKAGE IS TASKED FOR MULTIPLE TARGETS.  SEE MISSION
COMMANDER OPORD IN CAFMS.
UNIT REMARKS H BT
```

AIR FORCE MESSAGE MCN=91020/20676 TOR=91020/1723Z TAD=91020/1739Z CDSN=MAP374
PAGE 2 OF 2
201555Z JAN 91
SECT 14 OF 94

The first clock time, given by date and time, was entered into the document by the keyboard operator. In the Master Attack Plan in Figure 3, this date/time identifier is 20 Jan/1600. The second time, given just as a clock time, was generated by the computer as it printed the copy of the plan. On Figure 3, this clock time identifier is 6:48 pm.

Changes made to a Master Attack Plan had to be coordinated, regardless of whether the night targeting cell was compiling the target planning worksheets or the ATO Division was assembling the Air Tasking Order–otherwise, the order would be released with obsolete data. While attack plan changes did not pose a large coordination problem to the night targeting staff, they were a larger problem for the ATO Division, a Central Command Air Forces staff component. The ATO Division was not collocated with Guidance, Apportionment, and Targeting; it was manned by officers who were unfamiliar with their people and procedures. In most cases the ATO Division never saw a Master Attack Plan; the plan was used by the targeting team and senior staff and was not distributed widely. Conscious coordination between the GAT and the ATO Division was necessary whenever changes were made after the target planning worksheets had been completed. In the absence of this coordination, conflicts and errors regarding times on targets, targets, and mission support cascaded to the units below. In addition, since targeting planners could be less certain that their plans were even executed, there would be more uncertainty that planned outcomes had been achieved.

New or different tasks were assigned to units even after the ATO was published. Initially, the change logbook in the Tactical Air Control Center (TACC) Combat Operations Division (also known as the "Bubble") was the only means to track the changes and ensure that they were coordinated among the units effected.[23] Figure 6 displays a page from this log covering 19 January 1991 (D+02, ATO D).[24] Combat Operations officers executed each Air Tasking Order and managed the change process once an order had been published. A tasking order change sheet was

---

[23] Assuming GAT officers informed Combat Operations Division officers of MAP changes made after the ATO was published.

[24] (S) USCENTAF TACC change logbook, GWAPS, NA #370.

Figure 6
Air Tasking Order Change Logbook

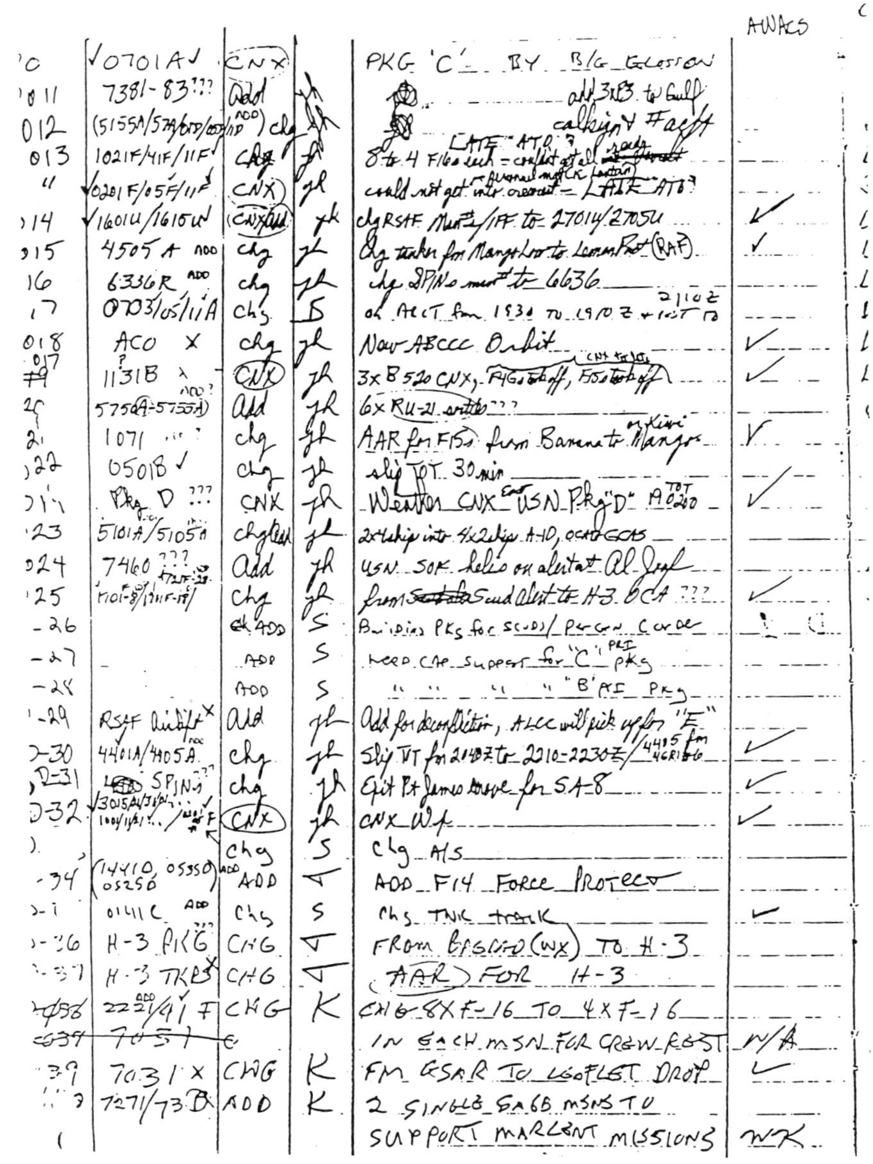

developed during the first week of the war (illustrated in Figure 7)[25] to cope with the number and complexity of the changes that occurred in early Air Tasking Orders. This sheet was used to change, add, or cancel missions and to ensure that all the applicable coordination had been done by Combat Operations. While the change logbook and sheets do not cover every change that occurred, they provide a generally accurate picture of the process and execution of changes to a tasking order.

Unit-level officers would complete a Mission Report (MISREP) after each sortie containing information critical to the targeting team planners, such as the pilot's perception of his weapon accuracy, information on threats encountered, and takeoff and landing times. Figure 8 shows a unit MISREP.[26] Mission Reports varied greatly in quality. In some cases, pilots viewed completion of them as formality; in others, pilots gave detailed accounts of what they had seen. Even the most accurate of observers, however, could err in recalling events from attacks launched at several hundred miles per hour and 10,000 to 20,000 feet above the target. While completion of a Mission Report culminated a particular Air Tasking Order planning cycle, the reports were not systematically forwarded to Guidance, Apportionment, and Targeting. Certain kinds of mission-related products were forwarded to the targeting cell, notably videotapes of bomb drops. Unfortunately, videotape recorders (capable of recording weapon impact on the target) were only available on a few systems: F-117A, the F-15E, and the F-111F.[27] Furthermore, the quality of imagery from these systems varied, with the F-117A probably providing the best infrared imagery for use in bomb damage assessment.

The process of planning, tasking, executing, and evaluating aircraft sorties as flown under the command of General Horner, the Joint Force Air Component Commander, during Desert Storm was complex. In

---

[25](S) Master Attack Plan, D+22, 8 Feb 1991, 23rd 24 Hours, GWAPS, BH Box 1, Folder 27. (U) The ATO change sheet illustrated is a later version of the form used to make changes. An earlier version existed. It had a slightly different format but ordered essentially the same information.

[26](S) Mission Report, 211700Z Jan 1991, 363d TFW, Mission #0401F, 21 Jan 91, 363d TFW OSS/OSIO.

[27]All fighter aircraft have airborne video tape recorders; most of these systems film the heads-up display only at weapons release.

Figure 7
Air Tasking Order Change Sheet

UNIT: 37 TFW		CHANGE#:		TANKER:	
BASE ID:		SODO:		AIRSPACE:	
INPUT TIME:		CCO:		AWACS:	
REQUESTED BY:		VAN ENTRY #/BY:	/	ABCCC	
ATO ID: X		TARGET REQUESTOR: OLD	NEW		
CIRCLE:	ADD ON	CHANGE	CANCEL	PACKAGE COORD:	
REASON FOR CHANGE:				TYPE	FDO

ITEM:	ONE	TWO	THREE	FOUR	FIVE
MISSION:	3304 A	3316 B - 3355 B			
PACKAGE:					
CALLSIGN:					
TTL # A/C / ADDED	/	/	/	/	/
ACFT TYPE	1 F-117	12 F-117			
AMSN					
ALERT					
SCL1					
SCL2					
SIF (MODE 2)					
SIF (MODE 3)					
SUPPORT MSN 1:					
SUPPORT MSN 2					
SUPPORT MSN 3					
SUPPORT MSN 4					
REMARK ID					
MSN TGT LOC	*	**			
TOT/OS					
TFT					
MSN LENGTH					
TANKER PRE	MSN #	ARCT	TRACK	ALTITUDE	OFFLOAD
POST					

* CHANGE 1st TGT FROM C40 TO [DELETED] A02 AL TAQADDUM AFLD HARDENED SHELTER (GBU-27)

COMMENTS ** FOR ALL SECOND GO MISSIONS CHANGE BRIDGE TGTS TO [DELETED] A02 AL TAQADDUM AFLD HAS (GBU-27)

Figure 8
Mission Report (MISREP)

SECRET

02   211700Z   JAN   91   00   SSSS   IN

       363 TFW PROVISIONAL//IN//
       USCENTAF//IN//

SECRET

OPER/DESERT SHIELD//

MSGID/MISREP/363TFW/2101004//

MSN NO:0401F/BXF-16//

A. TARGET IDENTIFIER/LOCATION:HABBANIYAH POSS CW PROD FACILITY 2/ [DELETED] 332850N0433900E//

B. DTG/TOT: 211312Z//

C. RESULTS: SUCCESSFUL/16 X MK 84 EXPENDED/REVIEW OF VTR SHOWS HITS ON 4 EASTERN STORAGE AREAS AND PROB HITS ON PRODUCTION AREA AND WESTERN STORAGE AREA//

D1. TARGET OBSERVATION: MODERATE 37 MM AAA IN TGT AREA/RCVD U RWR IN TGT AREA PROB FROM AL TAQADDUM AND NORTH OF TGT AREA//

D2. ENROUTE OBSERVATION: GHALAYSAN AFLD APPEARED TO HAVE ONE CRATER ON NORTH SIDE OF RNWY, ONE ON TAXIWAY, AND ONE NEAR BUNKERS/RCVD SA-2 RWR PROB FROM SA-2 VIC 3300N04340E//

D3. TARWI: 0081X//

REMARKS: AWACS REPORTED U/I ACFT 20NM SE OF AL ASAD HDG SOUTH/POSS AAM FIRED BY UNK ACFT//

SAME AS RELEASER

  MARK A. COOTER, CAPT, INO, 2435
CRC:
                     SECRET   211700ZJAN91

In addition, as the preceding discussion illustrates, it was a labor-intensive system based upon written products communicated through several different groups of planners, each with a specific function. The following two case studies illustrate how the process worked, problems encountered with the process, and how problems were overcome.

AARDVARKS BUSTING BUNKERS, D+16, 2 FEB 1991, ATO R

This case study examines use of precision munitions to attack hardened aircraft shelters (HASs). It follows F-111Fs from the 48th Tactical Fighter Wing (TFW) tasked to attack these targets on D+16, 2 February 1991; this was ATO "R." The mission involved a group of these aircraft (known unofficially as "Aardvarks") to attack the airfields at H-2 and H-3, in western Iraq. The ATO day, D+16, began at 020200Z and ended at 030200Z and covered taskings in the period 020001Z to 030300Z.[28]

F-111Fs (above) were known unofficially as "Aardvarks."

The first pencil draft of the Master Attack Plan for D+16 lists a large package of F-111Fs attacking the H3 and H2 airfields, between 0200Z -

---

[28](S) Air Tasking Orders, GWAPS, CSS safe 6, Desert Shield - 1 Feb 1991.

0220Z.[29] Tables 1 and 2 present this package, identified as "AA," and its support package. Figure 9 shows the targets and bases from which the F-111Fs launched the mission.

Table 1
AA Package of F-111s Attacking H3 and H2 Airfields

Mission Number	GAT Target Number	Target	Number of Aircraft
0111A	C05	H3 Afld CW Bunker BE# A	Four F-111F
0121A/0131A	A03	H3 Afld HAS/RWY/FAC BE# A	Twelve F-111F
0141A	A11	H2 Afld HAS/RWY/FAC BE# B	Four F-111F

Table 2
Support Package of Table 1

Mission Number	Mission	Number of Aircraft
0151X	SEAD	Two EF-111
0161W	SEAD	Two F-4G
0171C	Sweep/Force protection	Two F-15C

[SEAD: suppression of enemy air defenses.]

---

[29] (S) Master Attack Plan, D+16, 2 Feb 1991, 17th 24 Hours, GWAPS, BH Box 1, Folder 21.

**Figure 9
Targets and Bases From Which
F-111Fs Launched The Mission**

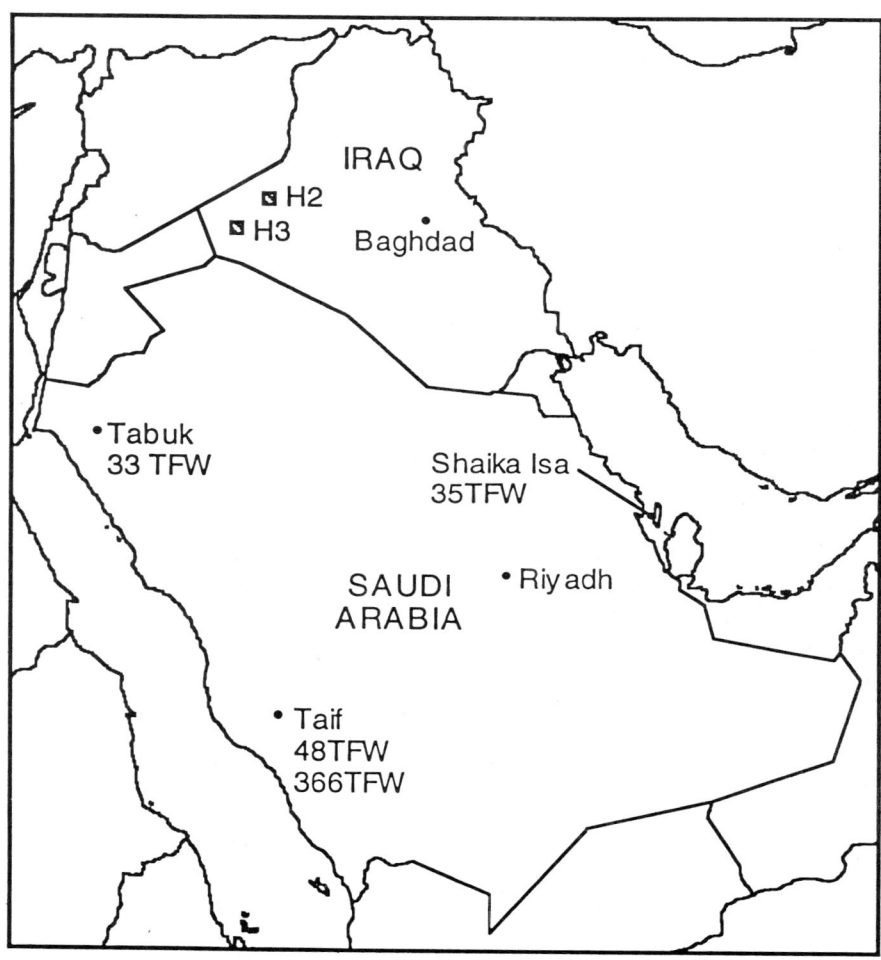

The first source of error in this attack plan is in the designation of the targets. Targets were identified on this draft plan in two ways: (a) by the Black Hole's nomenclature (C05, A03, and A11), which had been devised as an attempt to simplify the targeting process, and (b) by the basic encyclopedia (BE) numbers. The draft attack plan BE number given for the chemical warfare bunker at H-3 was incorrect. The target for mission number 0111A, C05/H-3 AFLD CW bunker, was listed with BE number A. Yet, this BE number is inconsistent with the Master Target List (MTL) description of target C05 as the H-3 AFLD (munitions storage facility chemical bunker), with BE number C.[30] The H-3 airfield facilities, A03 in the target list, had a BE number A.[31] The attack plan draft, while listing the desired target as the chemical warfare bunkers at H-3, C05, listed the BE number for the airfield facilities at H-3, A03, instead.

A second pencil copy of the Master Attack Plan draft had small changes to the planned package, and missions and numbers of aircraft for the package were laid out in greater detail.[32] Table 3 shows the tasking as it appeared in this draft. The suppression of enemy air defenses support, sweep/force protection, and the times on targets had not changed from the original pencil draft. However, confusion over the specific tasking at the H3 airfield remained. Mission number 0111A was still targeted against the H3 AFLD CW bunker (GAT target number C05), but the BE number remained the BE A—which corresponded to the GAT target number A03 for the H3 airfield facilities.

With two minor exceptions, the target planning worksheets completed for this package were the same as the two drafts of the Master Attack Plan.[33] The first exception was an increase from two to four in mission 0161W's F-4Gs, and second, the error in the listing of the BE number for the chemical warfare bunker was corrected. Each mission, except 0111A, was given the task of attacking hardened aircraft shelters. Mission 0111A was tasked to attack the chemical warfare bunker at the H3 airfield (C05 on the target list). Remaining ordnance was to be expended on the airfield facilities as detailed in the worksheets. Coordinates were given for specific structures to be attacked, and all the missions were tasked to use precision-guided weapons (GBU-24 or GBU-10) against the targets.

---

[30](S) Master Target List, GWAPS, BH Box 8.

[31]*Ibid.*

[32](S) Master Attack Plan, D+16, 2 Feb 1991, 17th 24 Hours, GWAPS, BH Box 1, Folder 21.

[33](S) Target Planning Worksheets, ATO D+16, 2 Feb 1991, HQ 9th AF/OSX, Shaw AFB, NC, Lt Col Jeffrey Feinstein.

Table 3
Tasking Draft of Master Attack Plan

Mission Number	GAT Target Number	Target	Number of Aircraft
0111A	C05	H3 Afld CW Bunker BE #A	Four F-111
0115A	A03	H3 Afld HAS/RWY/FAC BE #A	Four F-111
0121A	A03	H3 Afld HAS/RWY/FAC BE #A	Four F-111
0125A	A03	H3 Afld HAS/RWY/FAC BE #A	Four F-111
0141A	A11	H2 Afld HAS/RWY/FAC BE #B	Four F-111

There were three printed draft attack plans for this particular day. The dates and times on these plans show they were constructed after the target planning worksheets were turned into the ATO Division. The first draft attack plan had a computer-printed date/time of "2/1/91 9:32 am" (operator-entered date/time is 1 Feb/1700).[34] The second plan was dated "2/2/91 12:28 pm" (operator-entered date/time is 1 Feb 1200).[35] The final plan, which was signed by General Glosson, was dated "2/1/91 3:41 pm" (operator-entered date remained 1 Feb 1200).[36] These three versions of

---

[34] (S) Master Attack Plan, D+16, 2 Feb 1991, 17th 24 Hours, GWAPS, BH Box 1, Folder 21.

[35] (S) *Ibid.*

[36] (S) *Ibid.*

the Master Attack Plan had identical tasking for package AA–the times on targets, support and fighter escort aircraft remained as planned in the earliest draft attack plans.[37] However, the target focus shifted as successive draft plans were printed. The tasking on the three printed versions of the Master Attack Plan called for all the missions to H3 to focus on the chemical warfare bunkers (GAT target number C05), instead of the hardened aircraft shelters.[38] But, the target BE number on these printed attack plans remained the BE number for the H3 airfield–not the BE number for the CW bunkers.

The Air Tasking Order printed for D+16 contained the tasking for the 48th Tactical Fighter Wing package AA as detailed on the target planning worksheets, with the exception that the time on target was changed to 0100Z–0130Z. This tasking order assigned mission 0111A to attack the H3 airfield CW bunker.[39] The specific BE number for that H3 airfield CW bunker, number C, was placed in the unit remarks section under item Z. The other missions to H3, 0115A, 0121A, and 0125A were assigned to attack H3 airfield. The BE number for these missions in remark Z, number A, was the correct BE number for the H3 Airfield facilities. The tasking order stated the first priority for attack was the remaining hardened aircraft shelters at the H3 airfield. Remaining ordnance was to be expended on the airfield facilities, exactly as detailed in the targeting worksheets. Unit remark V detailed the sorties' desired mean points of impact (DMPIs) as the remaining hardened aircraft shelters followed by the airfield facilities. Mission 0141A was tasked against the H2 airfield (with the correct BE number for that airfield) and had similar instructions in the remark V.[40] However, these air tasking instructions did not correspond to the targets assigned the 48th Tactical Fighter Wing in the attack plans printed after the targeting worksheets had been submitted to the ATO Division.

---

[37] The number of F-4Gs tasked to SEAD in the draft MAPs increased from two to four on the TPWs.

[38] As noted above, these three MAPs were printed after the TPWs were turned into the ATO Division.

[39] (S) Air Tasking Orders, GWAPS, CSS Safe 6, Desert Shield - 1 Feb 1991.

[40] The tasks assigned in the published ATO for SEAD and fighter sweep/force protection were as detailed in the TPWs and the MAPs. The ATO tasking for the F-15 escort mission (mission 0171C from the 33d TFW at Tabuk), the Wild Weasel support (mission 0161W from the 35th TFW at Shaika Isa), and the EF-111 support (mission 0151X from the 366th TFW at Taif), also matched the F-111 package ATO tasking exactly.

Apparently, no one in the ATO Division was alerted to the discrepancy between instructions for this mission contained in the Air Tasking Order and the Master Attack Plan (as signed by General Glosson). The tasking order change logbook for 2 February 1991 (ATO R) showed only one change to any of the aircraft in this package; change "R-58" denoted a change to the air refueling for the EF-111 suppression of enemy air defense support mission, 0151X.[41]

The attacks prosecuted by the F-111s may be followed from the Mission Reports.[42] For mission 0111A, two of the four aircraft assigned to attack the chemical warfare bunkers at H-3 dropped bombs successfully, destroying CW bunkers 2 and 4 at the H3 airfield. The other two aircraft had laser and radar problems and did not release any bombs. The Mission Report noted that two other chemical warfare bunkers and several hardened aircraft shelters were targeted but not attacked.[43] The unit also identified the target attacked with the BE number for the airfield, and not with the BE number for the chemical warfare bunker–the target assigned the unit by the Air Tasking Order.

The Mission Report is sketchy for mission 0115A.[44] The unit reported that two aircraft successfully dropped two GBU-10s each, the third aircraft dropped one of two GBU-10s successfully, and the fourth aircraft was unsuccessful. The report did not specify which targets were attacked. The target description and the BE number reported for this attack were for the H3 airfield and facilities. Most of the Mission Reports describe anti-aircraft fire.[45]

Mission 0121A reported limited success.[46] One aircraft did not release its weapons, two aircraft had no guidance on their weapons, and a fourth

---

[41] (S) USCENTAF TACC change logbook, GWAPS, NA #370

[42] The 48th TFW assigned individual mission numbers to its aircraft. For example, mission 0111A in the MAP became missions 0111A, 0112A, 0113A, and 0114A. Other units did not follow this practice.

[43] (S) 48th TFW Mission Report, 030530Z Feb 1991, GWAPS Missions Database.

[44] This mission was identified by the 48th TFW as missions 0115A-0118A.

[45] (S) 48th TFW Mission Report, 030341Z Feb 1991, GWAPS Missions Database.

[46] The MAP mission 0121A consisted of four aircraft; the unit separated that mission into four separate missions, 0121A-0124A.

reported a successful hit on a hardened aircraft shelter. The Mission Report identified the mission target as "H-3 AFLD HAS/CW BUNKER."[47]

Only one aircraft from the fourth package against H-3, Mission 0125A,[48] successfully hit H-3. No specific target information was provided.[49] The fifth and final package, Mission 0141A,[50] directed against H-2 was unsuccessful. Only three of the four aircraft were mentioned in the Mission Reports, and they aborted the mission because of cloud cover over the target.[51] All of the support missions, 0151X, 0161W, and 0171C, flew as tasked.[52]

What was achieved in this attack? Was information about these missions fed into plans for future attacks? There are no unambiguous answers to these questions. Aircraft from four separate bases were coordinated and arrived at their targets. However, only four bombs from two aircraft landed on the chemical warfare bunkers initially targeted in the Master Attack Plan. Five other aircraft reported hitting their targets. But, given the inconsistency between the Air Tasking Order and the final attack plan, it is not clear whether the targets attacked were those specified in the former or the latter. Given the organizational obstacles to receiving appropriate information, it also is not known whether targeting cell planners or Central Command Air Forces staff received information about this mission, or whether adjustments were made in future plans and orders.

---

[47](S) 48th TFW Mission Report, 030445Z Feb 1991, GWAPS Missions Database.

[48]The Mission Report separated this mission into four missions, numbered 0125A-0128A.

[49](S) 48th TFW Mission Report, 030405Z Feb 11991, GWAPS Missions Database.

[50]The Mission Report separated this mission into four missions, numbered 0141A-0144A.

[51](S) Mission 0143A was not reported. 48th TFW Mission Report, 030440Z Feb 1991, GWAPS Missions Database.

[52](S) 48th TFW Mission Report, mission number 0151X, 030415Z Feb 1991, GWAPS Missions Database. See also CAFMS-derived data, GWAPS Missions Database.

STRIKE EAGLES ON CALL, D+23, 9 Feb 91, ATO Y

This case study examines how F-15E aircraft from the 4th Tactical Fighter Wing (based at Al Kharj) were targeted by the Joint Surveillance and Target Attack Radar System (JSTARS). The missions were tasked and flown on D+23, 9 February 1991, ATO Y. Figure 10 provides a map of the area flown.

By 9 February, F-15Es had been largely diverted from the strategic targets campaign to Scud hunting, road reconnaissance, and JSTARS targeting. The concept of JSTARS targeting was very similar to an intercept type of mission. The aircraft would launch, contact an airborne controller, and attack a target assigned by that airborne controller. In this case, instead of the controller being on AWACS or Airborne Command, Control and Communication (ABCCC) aircraft, it was on the JSTARS aircraft. The tasking order provided back-up targets if the JSTARS did not have targets for the F-15Es. The intent of JSTARS targeting was to provide F-15Es with near-real-time targets.

The earliest drafts of the Master Attack Plan for D+23 assigned F-15E aircraft to perform road reconnaissance or to fly along convoy routes rather than to JSTARS targeting. The final printed and approved plan containing the tasking for the JSTARS targeted F-15Es was prepared at 1300 on 8 February–the day before the mission was to be flown and several hours after the target planning worksheets would have been submitted to the ATO Division.[53]

---

[53](S) Master Attack Plan, D+23, 9 Feb 1991, 24th 24 Hours, GWAPS, BH Box 1, folder 28.

**Figure 10
Map of Area Flown**

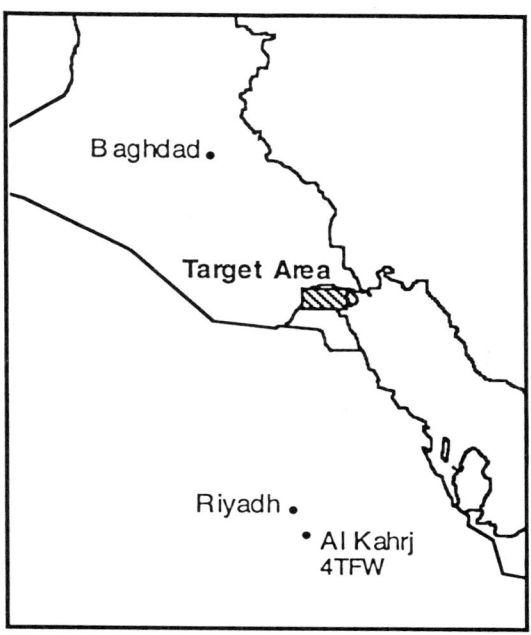

The targeting worksheet turned in to the ATO Division matched the tasking later included in the Master Attack Plan. This worksheet listed eight separate F-15E missions allotted to JSTARS targeting for D+23.[54] Each mission, two aircraft, was assigned a fifteen-minute time on target block. Every fifteen minutes, two F-15Es would be available for JSTARS-directed targeting. The blocks started at 1515Z-1530Z and continued

---

[54](S) Target Planning Worksheets, ATO D+23, 9 Feb 1991, HQ 9th AF/OSX, Shaw AFB, NC, Lt Col Jeffrey Feinstein.

F-15E aircraft (above) were targeted by the Joint Surveillance and Target Attack Radar System (JSTARS) (below)

until 2045Z-2100Z. Table 4 displays the F-15E missions, as tasked on the targeting worksheet and the attack plan printed subsequently.[55]

The target planning worksheets and the approved version of the Master Attack Plan for Air Tasking Order Y (D+23, 9 February 1991) contained identical taskings.[56] Unit remarks J provided information on how the mission would be controlled and who would be responsible for passing targets to the aircraft. Unit remarks K listed the backup targets for each flight should JSTARS targeting not be available.

No tasking order change sheets for ATO Y affected any of these JSTARS targeted F-15E missions. However, an entry in the Tactical Air Control Center Air Tasking Order change log (for D+23, ATO Y) changed two missions. Change Y-38 cancelled missions 3507 and 3511A "due to Aircrew/ A/C."[57] No reasons for this unavailability were given in the change log. The unit reported, through CAFMS, that those two mission were cancelled because of "aircrew/aircraft availability."[58] The other missions appear to have flown as tasked.

The targets struck by the F-15E missions, and whether they struck a JSTARS-assigned target or their tasked backup target, can be tracked in two ways. The first method is to review the JSTARS mission log and the JSTARS End of Mission Report. The JSTARS mission log recorded the significant events of each mission. The End of Mission Report, submitted by the mission commander, detailed the aircraft tasked and the targets struck. The second method of tracking targets struck by each mission is through the unit Mission Report.

---

[55] The Jan 1991 USCENTAF *Combat Plans Handout* specified that the utilization rate for the F-15E would be 2.00 sorties per day. The mission numbers 3501A, 3503A, and 3505A appearing later as 3501B, 3503B, and 3505B show where aircraft planned to fly in the earlier TOT blocks were replanned to fly in later TOT blocks as well. In actual practice, the unit might have not always used the same specific aircraft due to maintenance, battle damage, etc. However, the missions would have been flown.

[56] (S) GWAPS, CATO folder 17, Day 24, D+23, 9 Feb 1991.

[57] This remark means that the aircrew or aircraft were unavailable. USCENTAF TACC change log book.

[58] (S) CAFMS-derived data, GWAPS Missions Database.

Table 4
F-15E as Tasked on Targeting Worksheet

Mission Number	Time Over Target
3501A	1515Z-1530Z
3503A	1545Z-1600Z
3505A	1615Z-1630Z
3507A	1645Z-1700Z
3511A	1715Z-1730Z
3501B	1945Z-2000Z
3503B	2015Z-2030Z
3505B	2045Z-2100Z

JSTARS missions were assigned the task to "locate and pass to assigned fighter aircraft targets for immediate attack in the Kuwait Theater of Operations (KTO) with emphasis on Republican Guard Ground Order of Battle and mechanized/armor units in the first echelon tactical reserve."[59] The JSTARS mission 027 was assigned this duty for 9 February 1991.[60]

According to the JSTARS mission log, mission 3501A, using call sign Edsel 01, contacted JSTARS at 1503Z, twelve minutes before the planned time on target.[61] The two F-15Es were directed to an "assembly area of 70 plus" vehicles, which were then successfully struck with twenty-four Mark 82 five hundred pound bombs.[62] Edsel 01's Mission Report indicated that the F-15E's saw the vehicles in the aircraft's forward-looking infrared vision system.[63] The attacks were actually conducted at 1536Z, or six minutes after the planned time on target.[64]

---

[59] (S) USCINCCENT Msg 131700Z Jan 1991, subj: Joint STARS Utilization.

[60] This Joint STARS mission number was not a CENTAF ATO-assigned mission number.

[61] (S) Joint STARS Mission Log, D+23, 9 Feb 1991, GWAPS NA 340; (S) microfiche, Joint STARS Mission and Log Reports, Desert Storm, Jan - Mar 1991.

[62] Edsel 01 reported to Joint STARS that the attack was successful.

[63] (S) 4th TFW Mission Report, 091910Z Feb 1991, GWAPS Missions Database.

[64] (S) *Ibid.*

The F-15E mission 3503A (call sign Buick 03) checked in with the JSTARS at 1527Z.⁶⁵ The aircraft were directed to "AAA site 294937N 472842E,"⁶⁶ and at 1615Z reported inflight bomb damage assessment of "successful–four gun emplacements hit, no secondaries but concentration of troops to north."⁶⁷ The Mission Report reported the bomb damage assessment as "unknown" and included the following target description: Buick 03 designated probable small RDR return that may have been AAA–not really sure. Aircrew reported numerous vehicles in laager (circle) approx 1/2NM from tgt. JSTARS directed Buick 04 to tgt vehicles nearby. Buick 04 tgted cluster of vehicles in area also in laager, 1/2 - 3/4NM from tgt. No secondaries reported following weapons release.⁶⁸

The F-15E mission 3505A (call sign Stingray 05) checked in with the JSTARS at 1605Z⁶⁹ and was assigned a target consisting of an "assembly area of 70 plus veh 295347N 470323E (vicinity of Edsel 01 target)."⁷⁰ At 1620Z Stingray 05 reported inflight bomb damage assessment of "successful–vehicles located."⁷¹ However, the unit reported bomb damage assessment as "unknown" in its Mission Report for mission 3505A. The target observation stated "Stingray flight reported numerous vehicles in circular formation–both jets tgted vehicles in area. Stingray Flight reported good radar designation from both jets. Aircrew noted possibly one secondary–but not sure if it was a long bomb–following weapons release."⁷²

---

⁶⁵(S) Joint STARS Mission Log, D+23, 9 Feb 1991, GWAPS NA 340; (S) microfiche, Joint Stars Mission and Log Reports, Desert Storm, Jan - Mar 1991.

⁶⁶Note: the 4th TFW and the Joint STARS controllers used different conventions to express geographic coordinates. The 4th TFW expressed coordinates in terms of degrees, minutes, and seconds. The Joint STARS controllers expressed coordinates in terms of degrees, minutes, and tenths of minutes. At a minimum, the use of these different conventions added a translation task to the many activities performed by pilots and controllers. If such calculations were not performed, the pilot and airborne controller communicated about distinctly different sites.

⁶⁷(S) Joint STARS End of Mission Report, D+23, 9 Feb 1991; (S) microfiche, Joint STARS Mission and Log Reports, Desert Storm, Jan - Mar 1991.

⁶⁸(S) 4th TFW Mission Report, 091900Z Feb 1991, GWAPS Missions Database.

⁶⁹(S) Joint STARS Mission Log, D+23, 9 Feb 1991, GWAPS NA 340; (S) microfiche, Joint STARS Mission and Log Reports, Desert Storm, Jan - Mar 1991.

⁷⁰(S) Joint STARS End of Mission Report, D+23, 9 Feb 1991; (S) microfiche, Joint STARS Mission and Log Reports, Desert Storm, Jan - Mar 1991.

⁷¹(S) Ibid.

⁷²(S) 4th TFW Mission Report, 091915Z Feb 1991, GWAPS Missions Database.

The inconsistency between the inflight bomb damage assessment reported to JSTARS and the postattack Mission Report was not resolved.

Missions 3507A and 3511A were cancelled. There is no JSTARS mission log or End of Mission Report record of mission 3501B checking in with JSTARS. Mission 3501B, according to the Unit Mission Report, attacked the alternate target. The Unit Mission Report contained the following remarks: Edsel flight reported could not comm with JSTARS or ABCCC, pressed with alt tgt. Edsel flight was 2 minutes from alt tgt and AWACS called and said they had a priority tgt. Edsel flight proceeded and dropped on alt tgt (Edsel commented too late–gas was also a factor).[73] The alternate target attacked, listed in the Air Tasking Order for JSTARS aircraft and as reported in the Mission Report, was a revetted logistics site at 3001.1N 04747.5E.[74]

At 2000Z, according to the JSTARS mission log, the second Buick 03, mission 3503B "checked in" and was "Sent to Alleycat + Bulldog for SAR."[75] The JSTARS End of Mission Report also reported that Buick 03 was "diverted to SAR."[76] However, the F-15E's, stated "Buick flight reported never able to contact JSTARS. ABCCC finally came on and gave tgt. Buick flight had to hold for 20 minutes before getting tasking." The unit reported that the F-15Es attacked an artillery battery at 2914.34N 04713.22E with unknown damage assessment. The report also included a target observation and declared that twenty-four MK-84 weapons were released on the target.[77]

The final F-15E mission in this case study, mission 3505B, never appeared on the JSTARS mission log or End of Mission Report. The Unit Mission Report stated that "Stingray flight reported could not contact ABCCC and JSTARS could not get a tgt passed. After numerous attempts on all freqs Stingray flight pressed on with back-up tgt." The pilots reported "unknown" bomb damage assessment against a fuel storage area

---

[73](S) 4th TFW Mission Report, 100125Z Feb 1991, GWAPS Missions Database.

[74](S) GWAPS, CATO folder #17, Day 24, D+23, 9 Feb 1991.

[75]The acronym SAR stands for Search and Rescue. See Joint STARS Mission Log, D+23, 9 Feb 1991; (S) microfiche, Joint STARS Mission and Log Reports, Desert Storm, Jan -Mar 1991.

[76](S) Joint STARS End of Mission Report, D+23, 9 Feb 1991; (S) microfiche, Joint STARS Mission and Log Reports, Desert Storm, Jan - Mar 1991.

[77](S) 4th TFW Mission Report, 100112Z Feb 1991, GWAPS Missions Database.

at 3001N 04739E, which was one of the backup targets included in the Air Tasking Order.[78]

This relatively simple account has three features of interest. First, the discrepancies between inflight bomb damage assessment—the comments of pilots relayed to JSTARS—and the postattack Mission Reports generated by the unit intelligence based upon postmission pilot interviews suggest some of the difficulty in reliably assessing damage, particularly as a result of attacks prosecuted at night. Second, the persistent problems in communication are noteworthy, even though the aircraft showed up pretty much as scheduled, and on time. It is striking that of eight missions planned two were cancelled, and three were unable to link up with JSTARS. Only three missions went as planned (see Table 5). Finally, the organizational complexity of scheduling many different aircraft placed great analytical, computational, communication, and bargaining demands on planners. The size, difficulty, and tempo of the planning effort—as the Guidance, Apportionment, and Target planners constructed daily plans for more than 2,000 sorties—affected how the centralized control of air power would be controlled.

---

[78](S) 4th TFW Mission Report, 100046Z Feb 91, GWAPS Missions Database.

Table 5
D+23, Air Tasking Order Y, 9 February 1991
F-15E (4th Tactical Fighter Wing based at Al Kharj)

Mission Number	Launch	Contacted ABCCC or AWACS	Contacted JSTARS	JSTARS Target	Alt ATO Target	Inflight BDA Reported as	MISREP BDA Reported as
3501A	yes	yes	yes	yes	--	"successful"	"BDA unknown"
3503A	yes	yes	yes	yes	--	"successful"	"BDA unknown"
3505A	yes	yes	yes	yes	--	"successful–vehicles located"	"BDA unknown"
3507A	no						
3511A	no						
3501B	yes	yes	no	no	yes	--	--
3503B	yes	yes	no	--	--	--	"BDA unknown"
3505B	yes	no	no	--	yes	--	"BDA unknown"

3

Lt. Gen. Charles Horner as the First Joint Force Air Component Commander

Lt. Gen. Charles A. Horner, USAF, the first wartime Joint Force Air Component Commander (JFACC), was also Commander, Ninth Air Force/CENTAF.[1] His authority as Joint Force Air Component Commander was assigned by Gen. H. Norman Schwarzkopf, the theater commander, but his authority as Commanding General of the Ninth Air Force was independent of his Joint Force command. How General Horner balanced these two interrelated positions, each with its own set of responsibilities, will be the primary focus of this chapter.

General Horner's primary concerns in early August 1990, when he was the acting Commander in Chief in Riyadh,[2] was to "beddown" the arriving forces in the theater and to prepare those forces for the defense of Saudi Arabia against an attack by Iraqi forces. Gen. Schwarzkopf returned to the United States after briefing King Fahd on the threat to the Saudi Kingdom and on plans to orchestrate the movement of forces into the CENTCOM Area of Responsibility. General Horner stayed in Riyadh to put together a basic command organization and to work out command relations with the Saudis. He regarded the latter task as one of the most important he would carry out during what became Desert Shield and Desert Storm.[3]

Horner's actions and decisions can be understood only in the context of an initially confused and constantly changing military situation. With hindsight, it is tempting to forget that, in August and September, Horner had to focus on organizing the air assets present in Saudi Arabia into a force that could deter the Iraqis from moving their ground forces south

---

[1] Ninth Air Force is a peacetime command, under the Tactical Air Command. In the Gulf, Lt Gen Horner was commander of CENTCOM's air component (CENTAF).

[2] On 6 Aug 1990, after a briefing for Saudi King Fahd, Gen H. Norman Schwarzkopf named Lt Gen Horner CINCCENT Forward. H. Norman Schwarzkopf with Peter Petre, *It Doesn't Take a Hero* (New York, 1992), p 306.

[3] (S) Intvw, CMSgt John Burton with Lt Gen Charles A. Horner, Mar 1991.

or from sending their air force against American and Saudi forces operating from Saudi airbases. Given the great aerial victory of Desert Storm, it is also understandable why observers might forget that the command and control infrastructure (for example, communications, meteorological forecasting, intelligence analysis, photo reconnaissance) available to Horner and his staff was extremely limited in August 1990 and then changed constantly in the months of Desert Shield. Finally, it would be a mistake to ignore the fact that the position of Joint Force Air Component Commander was not only new[4] but somewhat controversial (see Appendix 2 for historical background to this controversy). Some Marines, for example, referred to the Joint Force Air Component Commander as a "coordinator" but not a "commander" even after the war was over.[5]

Given this setting, it should come as no surprise that General Horner, in his public statements and confidential interviews, identified four issues which required most of his attention and time as the first Joint Force Air Component Commander. The first issue came from the need to adapt the

---

[4]The USCINCCENT operations order for Desert Shield, issued 10 Aug, which had made him the JFACC and had given him responsibility for recommending to General Schwarzkopf "apportionment of theater air sorties" and for "coordinating interdiction planning." (S) Msg, 101100Z Aug 90, OPORD/USCINCCENT, "Task Organization," Sections 3E26D2 and 3E26M.

[5](S) Intvw, Thomas C. Hone, Lt Col Frank D. Kistler, Mark D. Mandeles, Maj Sanford S. Terry with Brig Gen Richard I. Neal, USMC, 13 Jan 1992. (Hereafter referred to as Neal Intvw, 13 Jan 1992); (U) an even stronger position was taken by Lt Gen Royal N. Moore, Jr, USMC (Marine air commander in Desert Storm) in the U.S. Naval Institute *Proceedings*, Nov 1991, pp 63-70. On the other hand, Maj William R. Cronin, USMC, refers to the JFACC is referred to as a "commander." See Cronin, "C³I During the Air War in South Kuwait," *Marine Corps Gazette*, Mar 1992, pp 34-37.

Gen Schwarzkopf's 10 Aug operations order contained a clause which stated, as the Omnibus Agreement required, that the "Marine Air-Ground Task Force (MAGTF) Commander will retain operational control of his organic air assets." (S) Msg, 101100Z Aug 90, OPORD/USCINCCENT, "Task Organization," Section 3E26G. The order also gave Horner, as JFACC and CENTAF Commander, the authority to require the air units in the theater to consult in their planning and execution of interdiction operations, but it did not give him the authority to "compel agreement" if they differed over the proper conduct of those operations. As the order noted, when and if air units under different component commanders could not agree on the conduct of interdiction missions, "the matter shall be referred to USCINCCENT." (S) Msg, 101100Z Aug 90, OPORD/USCINCCENT, "Task Organization," Section 3E26M.)

Tactical Air Control System (TACS) to coalition warfare.[6] The second issue had its roots in the other Services' concerns about the JFACC. The third issue grew out of the relationship between General Schwarzkopf, as the theater commander, and General Horner, as his chief air deputy. The final issue concerned General Horner's methods of directing the air campaign against Iraq through the Tactical Air Control System. This chapter will consider General Horner's approach to each of these issues.

The JFACC and the Coalition

On 4 March 1992, Gen Horner told Air Force historians that his first priority was to set up an effective working relationship with the leaders of the armed forces of Saudi Arabia.[7] Prior to the deployment, there had been no combined Saudi-U.S. command organization. Horner, however, had worked with Lt. Gen. Ahmad Ibrahim Behery, commander of the Royal Saudi Air Force (RSAF) for several years, and the two got along well.[8] Yet when Secretary of Defense Richard Cheney offered U.S. forces to the Saudi government on 6 August, there was no combined operations plan. Both an organization and a combined (or coalition) operations plan had to be created as U.S. and allied forces moved into the theater.[9]

---

[6]See Chapters 4 and 5 for a discussion of the Tactical Air Control System and Tactical Air Control Center established in the theater.

[7](S) Intvw, Barry Barlow, Richard G. Davis, and Perry Jamieson with Lt Gen Charles A. Horner, Commander, 9th Air Force, 4 Mar 1992. (Hereafter referred to as Horner Intvw, 4 Mar 1992.) (U) Horner had done the same in his Mar 1991 interview, cited earlier. Dealing successfully with the other members of the coalition is a theme that runs consistently through all the interviews of Lt Gen Horner, including that conducted by GWAPS investigators on 9 Mar 1992.

[8](S) Intvw, Wayne W. Thompson with Lt Gen Ahmad Ibrahim Behery, 11 Jul 1992.

[9]On 20 Aug, the third version of CINCCENT's basic operations order charged Horner, as COMUSCENTAF, with furnishing "counterair, interdiction, and close air support to U.S. and Saudi forces. . . ." [(S) Msg, Desert Shield OPORD, 201230Z Aug 90, Section 3C10.] The operations order specified that his command would do so through a Tactical Air Control Center (TACC) manned jointly by U.S. and Saudi personnel. [Msg (S), Desert Shield OPORD, 201230Z Aug 90, Section 3E2.]

General H. Norman Schwarzkopf with Lt Gen Khalid bin Sultan bin Abdul Aziz, the Saudi theater commander (above); Lt Gen Charles A. Horner, USAF (left); Secretary of Defense Richard Cheney confers with Generals Calvin Waller, Colin Powell, and Norman Schwarzkopf (below).

As the Department of Defense later reported to Congress, the Saudi government agreed separately with each allied nation that sent forces. In the case of the United States, "initial agreement allowing the entry of U.S. forces into Saudi Arabia provided for 'strategic direction' of U.S. forces by the Saudi Military Command," through CENTCOM "assumed the phrase to mean general guidance at a strategic level with no actual command authority. . . ."[10] Initiative in the production of allied guidance lay with General Schwarzkopf. His staff–CENTCOM–had the only detailed plan (OPlan 1002-90) for the defense of Saudi Arabia, and they briefed it soon after their arrival in the theater to a combined planning group composed of CENTCOM Plans and Policy personnel, Saudi Ministry of Defense and Aviation operations officers, and various other Saudi and American officers.[11] The CENTCOM and Saudi personnel then worked together to produce, on 20 August, Operations Order 003 as a working plan for the defense of Saudi Arabia.[12]

The two nations did not create a tightly knit combined command, despite close cooperation by U.S. and Saudi staff officers in planning the defense of Saudi Arabia. Instead, they kept their existing command structures separate, but parallel. At first, General Horner, acting in Schwarzkopf's place as CINCCENT Forward, dealt directly with Gen. Mohammed al-Hammad, the Saudi Chief of Staff, while General Olsen worked with General Behery (Commander, Royal Saudi Air Force). Likewise, Rear Adm. Grant Sharp, CENTCOM's Plan and Policy officer, and Schwarzkopf's Navy deputy talked directly with Vice Adm. Salim al-Mofadi Talal, head of the Royal Saudi Navy, and Lt. Gen. John Yeosock, CENTCOM Army component commander, cooperated with Saudi Lt. Gen. Yusif Abdul Rahman al-Rasheed. Rather quickly, it became apparent to Horner that the key Saudi military commander was in fact Lt. Gen. Khalid bin Sultan bin Abdul Aziz, a prince of the royal family.[13] As General Khalid gradually gained more official authority (he was eventual-

---

[10] Department of Defense, *Conduct of the Persian Gulf War*, Apr 1992, p I-7.

[11] *Ibid.*

[12] (S/NF) Rpt, *Headquarters, U.S. Central Command, After Action Report, Operation Desert Shield, Operation Desert Storm*, 15 Jul 1991, p 6.

[13] (S) Horner Intvw, 4 Mar 1992; (U) Horner communicated with Lt Gen Khalid by copying the Saudi practice of speaking with "innuendo and notion."

ly appointed the Saudi theater commander, General Schwarzkopf's counterpart, in October), Horner's dealings with him grew more direct.[14]

According to the Central Command *After Action Report*, the continuation of parallel U.S. and Arab (the Saudis spoke for all the Gulf Cooperation Council forces) commands "required close coordination between USCINCCENT and General Khalid in all planning, operational and logistics matters."[15] This was accomplished through the coalition Coordination, Communication and Integration Center (known as the "C³IC") in Riyadh, which had been formed from a rudimentary combined headquarters set up in early August by Army Maj. Gen. Paul Schwartz, who had been serving as General John Yeosock's deputy when Iraq invaded Kuwait.[16] In Schwartz's combined headquarters, a Saudi officer translated CENTCOM operations instructions and regulations into Arabic, General Khalid signed them, and then they became the guidelines for the C³IC.[17]

The C³IC was a "bridge" between CENTCOM and the Saudi command.[18] From the Joint Force Air Component Commander's perspective, however, the C³IC was not the appropriate tool for coordinating all coalition air units across the theater. The proper tool was the Air Tasking Order, or ATO. One of the JFACC's tasks was to bring the Saudis into the ATO process–without at the same time making them feel captives of U.S. procedures or subordinate to U.S. officers. As it happened, the Saudis seemed to welcome the ATO process. As General Horner noted, the Saudis "were faced with this monster coming into their midst. They had no idea how to control it, and the training ATO gave them a way to control it."[19] The existence of a Saudi air defense system based on U.S.-

---

[14](S/NF) Rpt, *U.S. Central Command, After Action Report*, 15 Jul 1991, pp 6-7; (S) Horner Intvw, 4 Mar 1992.

[15](S/NF) Rpt, *HQ, U.S. Central Command, After Action Report*, 15 Jul 1991, p 7.

[16](S) Horner Intvw, 4 Mar 1992.

[17](S) *Ibid*.

[18]Department of Defense, *Conduct of the Persian Gulf War*, Apr 1992, p 494.

[19](S) Horner Intvw, 4 Mar 1992; Lt Gen Ahmad Ibrahim Behery, RSAF Commander, made the same point to Wayne W. Thompson in an interview on 11 Jul 1992.

made equipment (such as AWACS) also helped U.S. and Saudi air commanders and their staffs to work together, as did the fact that "airmen have English as their language."[20]

Though CENTCOM's planning staff was the "focal point for combined planning and integration of U.S. and coalition planning efforts,"[21] CENTAF personnel worked with their Saudi counterparts to develop daily air tasking orders.[22] This was in fact a cooperative effort. As, first, CINCCENT Forward and, later, as Joint Force Air Component Commander, General Horner did not, for example, unilaterally dictate the scope of U.S. and coalition theater air operations. On 18 August, for instance, Horner, at the request of the Saudi government, removed all low-altitude jet aircraft flights, all practice air-ground attacks, and all supersonic aircraft runs from the ATO.[23] By the end of September, however, these restrictions were hampering the training of deployed U.S. air units, and Horner, again in his role as JFACC, pressed Lt. Gen. Ahmad Ibrahim Behery to open Saudi air ranges to U.S. aircraft. It took a month for Horner to win his point.[24]

The cooperative relationship with the Saudis continued throughout Desert Storm. The Current Operations Log of the Tactical Air Control Center, for instance, contains several examples of direct communications from General Khalid and Brig. Gen. (Prince) Ahmad bin Musaid As-Sudayri, the Royal Saudi Air Force's Chief of Operations, to the duty officer at the Tactical Air Control Center through Horner's operations deputy, Maj. Gen. John Corder.[25] General As-Sudayri also recalled that he often dealt directly with Generals Horner and Glosson during Desert

---

[20](S) *Ibid*; Speech, Lt Gen Charles Horner, Dadaelian Dinner, 11 Sep 1991, p 9.

[21](S/NF) Rpt, *Headquarters, U.S. Central Command, After Action Report*, 15 Jul 1991, p 10.

[22](S) Horner Intvw, 4 Mar 1992.

[23](S/NF/WN) William T. Y'Blood, *The Eagle and the Scorpion* (Washington, DC, 1992), p 93.

[24](S/NF/WN) *Ibid*, p 132.

[25](S) TACC/CC/DO Current Ops Log, entries for 29 Jan 1991 (no time given) and 30 Jan 1991 (1310Z). Microfilm No. 0882616, Checo Team, GWAPS New Acquisition File No. 215.

Storm.²⁶ The American officers did not abandon cordial and close relations with the Saudis once the air war began.²⁷

In addition to the Saudis, the JFACC had to deal diplomatically with senior military officers from other nations. During Desert Storm, Horner grew concerned about British Royal Air Force losses suffered during low-level attacks on Iraqi airfields. As he later recalled, "I wanted to tell the British not to fly low level, but I wouldn't . . . . I just suggested we have a multi-national tactics board."²⁸ The suggestion had, apparently, the desired effect. Horner believed that the British understood his signal and realized that it had freed them from adherence to an accepted tactic. If so, then he had achieved his goal as JFACC without resorting to a direct assertion of his formal authority as Schwarzkopf's air deputy. Horner could also, like any seasoned diplomat, ignore a potential *cause celebre*. When the French army ground commander insisted that only French aircraft fly over his forces, Horner remembered saying, "Yes, you are absolutely right," but he also noted that French planes nevertheless "flew where it was best for them to fly."²⁹

These instances suggest that the JFACC's influence extended beyond what was considered to be his formal authority (directing the theater-wide air effort), but his formal authority (exercised through the Tactical Air Control Center) was real enough.³⁰ It included not only the responsibility

---

²⁶(S) Intvw, Wayne W. Thompson with Brig Gen (Prince) Ahmad bin Musaid As-Sudayri, RASF Chief of Operations, Jul 1992.

²⁷On 28 Jan 1991, for example, Maj Gen Corder wrote to Brig Gen Glosson suggesting that the authors of the Master Attack Plan organize packages of Gulf Cooperation Council aircraft for strikes in order to "build a network of military cooperation." See the (S) TACC/CC/DO Current Ops Log.

²⁸(S) Horner Intvw, 4 Mar 1992.

²⁹(S) Horner Intvw, 4 Mar 1992; (U) Brig Gen Claude Solanet, commander of French air units just before and during Desert Storm, said Horner deserved a lot of credit for the success of the air campaign, and that Horner was like a "big brother." [(S) Intvw, Wayne W. Thompson with Brig Gen Claude Solanet, 30 Apr 1992.] Brig Gen Solanet obviously accepted Horner's judgment about where French aircraft should fly.

³⁰The authority of COMUSCENTAF was spelled out in the CINCCENT OP Order for Operations Desert Shield (1100Z, 10 Aug 1990, in GWAPS Files). As the Order noted, "JFACC responsibilities include: . . . Planning, coordinating, allocating, and tasking based on USCINCCENT apportionment decisions. . . . Direct Coordination with COMUSARCENT, COMUSMARCENT, COMSOCCENT, COMUSNAVCENT, COMJTFME and supporting forces to ensure integration of air operations within USCINCCENT's Concept of Operations. . . .

for producing the daily Air Tasking Orders, but also the air-to-air and air-to-ground Rules of Engagement. In October 1989, CENTCOM Regulation 525-11 had established these rules for emergency deployment of U.S. aircraft to the Middle East. On 9 August 1990, the President had approved supplements to those existing rules to cover the likelihood that Iraqi and U.S. aircraft might engage in the skies over the Kuwait/Saudi border. The Chairman of the Joint Chiefs had informed CENTCOM of the President's decision immediately, and Schwarzkopf's operations order, issued the next day (10 August), put the Rules of Engagement of Regulation 525-11–supplemented by the additions from the President–into effect.[31]

One week later, the CENTAF staff issued specific "transition rules of engagement" for U.S. aircraft, and the Joint Force Air Component Commander was allowed by the Chairman of the Joint Chiefs of Staff to reveal "certain portions of both the peacetime and transition [rules] ROEs" to the Saudis and other members of the coalition.[32] This was a delicate issue. Rules of Engagement were ultimately the President's responsibility as commander-in-chief; he could not delegate that responsibility to a coalition command. Yet, the United States could not impose its rules on the coalition without consultation. In consequence, the Commander in Chief and the Joint Force Air Component Commander had to persuade the other coalition members to adopt the American rules. Doing so took a lot of time.[33] An important consequence, however, was that the JFACC's authority to coordinate the employment of coalition air forces was sustained.

Integrate supporting Maritime air resources through COMJTFME. . . . Serve as the Area Air Defense Commander (AADC) with the authority to establish and operate a combined, integrated air defense and Airspace Control System in coordination with component and other supporting and friendly forces. . . . Serve as coordinating authority for USCENTCOM interdiction operations with the responsibility of coordinating interdiction planning and operations involving forces of two or more services or two or more forces of the same service. . . . Conduct Counterair, Close Air Support, and Interdiction operations. . . . Support Airdrop, Airland, and Aerial Resupply operations for U.S. and friendly forces, as directed. . . . Assume responsibility for Combat Search and Rescue Operations. . . ." (Section 3E26)

[31](S) Msg, "Task Organization," Operation Desert Shield, USCINCCENT, MacDill AFB, FL, 101100Z Aug 90, Section 3F8.

[32](S/NF/WN) *The Eagle and the Scorpion* (Washington, DC, 1992), p 71.

[33](S/NF/WN) *Ibid*, p 71.

The JFACC and the Other Services

As Joint Force Air Component Commander, General Horner also attempted to reduce potential friction between his Tactical Air Control System and the other Services, who would have to work within it.[34] The interaction between Horner and Lt. Gen. Walter Boomer, U.S. Marine Corps, Central Command, was important. The Marine Corps had never been comfortable with the idea that an overall theater air commander would be able to shift Marine Corps aircraft away from the direct support of their ground forces.[35] The language of the 1986 "Omnibus Agreement" among the Services (that the "Marine Air-Ground Task Force [MAGTF] Commander will retain operational control of his organic air assets") was Section 3E26G of CINCCENT's 10 August operations order.[36] That section also noted that "Sorties in excess of MAGTF direct support requirements will be provided to the Joint Force Commander for tasking through the air component commander . . . ," and "Nothing herein shall infringe on the authority of the . . . Joint Force Commander, in the exercise of operational control, to assign missions . . . to insure unity of effort . . . ."[37] The 10 August operations order, like the Omnibus Agreement, did not reconcile the two very different views of the Marine Corps and the Air Force regarding the JFACC's authority.

It did not take long for these different views to conflict. On 19 September 1990, the Marine Corps liaison officer attached to CENTAF prepared a classified memo for CENTAF's Director of Operations in which he called the latter's attention to what seemed to be inadequate planning for "actions on D+1 and D+2 . . . where ground and air strategy will

---

[34] See James P. Coyne, *Airpower in the Gulf* (Arlington, VA, 1992), p 155; (S) Horner Intvw, 4 Mar 1992; Speech, Lt Gen Charles A. Horner, Dadaelian Dinner, 11 Sep 1991, p 8. Lt Gen Boomer, the leader of the Marine Corps component, confirmed Horner's view that, as JFACC, he had dealt judiciously with his fellow component commanders. According to Boomer, Horner's initial comment to him when they met face-to-face for the first time in the theater was, "I don't want your airplanes. I just want to win the war." (S) Intvw, GWAPS with Lt Gen Walter Boomer, USMC, 17 Feb 1992.

[35] See Appendices 2 and 4.

[36] 1986 "Omnibus Agreement," p III-5.

[37] *Ibid*, pp III-5 and III-6.

intertwine in a joint effort to influence the battlefield."³⁸ The Marine officer was concerned about developing means for managing "air power over a fluid battlefield."³⁹ The Marine Corps had a technique for managing close air support which placed control over such sorties in the hands of specially trained personnel in Division Air Support Centers (DASCs). Strikes farther away from front line positions were managed by a Tactical Air Operations Center (TAOC), which monitored and directed aircraft in separate High Density Airspace Control Zones (HIDACZs).⁴⁰ The Marine liaison was trying to move his Air Force counterparts in CENTAF toward an organization that looked familiar.

Lt. Gen. Royal N. Moore, Jr., the commander of Marine air units in the theater, may have felt that the efforts of his liaison officer had failed. After the war, Moore acknowledged that he had "kind of gamed the ATO process" because it did "not respond well to a quick-action battlefield."⁴¹ Moore openly referred to the ATO process as one of "coordination," and he described his method of dealing with it:

> What I did . . . was write an ATO that would give me enough flexibility . . . . So I might write an enormous amount of sorties, and every seven minutes I'd have airplanes up doing various things–and I might cancel an awful lot of those. This way I didn't have to play around with the process while I was waiting to hit a target.⁴²

By contrast, a *Marine Corps Gazette* article argued that Marine commanders questioned the effectiveness of the Joint Force Air Component Commander concept during Desert Storm because they did not understand why it took as long as it did for Marine air assets to shift their focus from

---

³⁸(S) Memo, "ATO Planning Beyond D-Day," from Marine Liaison, CENTAF, to Director of Operations, CENTAF, 19 Sep 1990, GWAPS Microfilm Files.

³⁹(S) *Ibid.*

⁴⁰(S/NF) Briefing, Desert Storm MARCENT Command Brief, 28 Mar 1991, GWAPS Task Force 4 File.

⁴¹Lt Gen Royal N. Moore, Jr., USMC, "Marine Air: There When Needed," U.S. Naval Institute *Proceedings*, Nov 1991, p 63. See also (S/NF) Briefing, Desert Storm MARCENT Command Brief, Mar 28, 1991, GWAPS Task Force 4 Files.

⁴²Lt Gen Royal N. Moore, Jr., USMC, "Marine Air: There When Needed," U.S. Naval Institute *Proceedings*, Nov 1991, p 63.

targets in rear areas to targets in southern Kuwait opposite Marine ground units.[43]

However, to prevent further division of the airspace and air defense system among the various components, Horner adopted the existing Saudi air defense system.[44] To work safely, the Saudi system had to have a daily Air Tasking Order; Tactical Air Control Center personnel, working with RSAF officers, produced the ATOs. So the need for a daily ATO, according to Horner, "established the Joint Force Air Component Commander. . . . Without the ATO, you don't have the JFACC. With the ATO, you don't have anything but a JFACC."[45]

Adopting the Saudi air defense system also helped General Horner justify turning down a suggestion in early August by the Commander, Middle East Force, Vice Adm. Henry Mauz, that the Navy and Air Force each take responsibility for separate "Route Packages" like those used in the air war against North Vietnam.[46] Horner remembered being adamantly opposed to this proposal.[47] He was just as strongly opposed to creating a buffer zone along Iraq's border with Iran; it was too much like what had been done in the air campaign against North Vietnam.[48] Horner may have misinterpreted Admiral Mauz's suggestion. The Air Force liaison officer attached to Mauz's command (NAVCENT) noted in his end of tour report that NAVCENT had recommended to the Joint Force Air Component Commander that the latter create an "omnibus ATO as a fallback," just in

---

[43] Maj W. R. Cronin, USMC, "C³I During the Air War in South Kuwait," *Marine Corps Gazette*, Mar 1992, p 35.

[44] (S) Horner Intvw, 4 Mar 1992.

[45] (S) Horner Intvw, 4 Mar 1992.

[46] (S) Intvw, GWAPS with Lt Gen Charles A. Horner, 9 Mar 1992.

[47] (S) Horner Intvw, 4 Mar 1992; (U) the 10 Aug 1990 Operations Order had specifically told the Navy's Commander, Joint Task Force Middle East to "Be prepared to conduct counterair, close air support, and interdiction operations; provide aircraft sorties to the JFACC. . . . " (Section 3E28E.) However, it is important to remember that Lt Gen Horner accepted something very much like Route Packages when he divided Iraq between the forces responding directly to him from Riyadh and those operating as part of Joint Task Force Proven Force in Turkey (see Chapter 7, footnote 42). Horner was concerned about the symbolism of a geographic separation of Navy and Air Force responsibilities.

[48] (S) Horner GWAPS Intvw, 9 Mar 1992.

case a terrorist or Scud attack put the Tactical Air Control Center in Riyadh out of action.[49]

If the JFACC had misinterpreted a Navy proposal, it would not have been an isolated incident. A Navy captain (sent by the Director of the Navy's Historical Center to NAVCENT [at sea on command ship *Blue Ridge*] and to the Navy's carriers operating as part of Desert Storm) wrote a critical trip report on his return from the theater. He observed that "several senior officers expressed reservations about the Navy's involvement in an air campaign centrally directed" by a Joint Force Air Component Commander. They apparently feared the consequences of flying missions in accordance with the instructions given by an Air Tasking Order which their staffs did not create. As the captain noted, however, "the Navy has no alternative to the ATO system."[50]

The Air Force liaison officer to the Navy also commented on the Navy's concerns with the Joint Force Air Component Commander's role. He felt that the Navy officers' doubts about this role were expressed as "an attitude of resentment towards the Air Force and distrust of the CENTAF staff, reflected by such measures as the close scrutiny of every document establishing procedural guidance for the conduct of the air war in a search for the hidden agendas they were believed to contain."[51] CENTAF officers did not help matters by using stationery with the Ninth Air Force letterhead to issue JFACC directives.[52] CENTAF officers manning the Tactical Air Control Center also left the wrong impression with their Navy liaison colleagues, two of whom noted that

> Early on, the USAF committed fully to the forward deployment and utilization of every possible facet of their force structure. This

---

[49](FOUO) Memo, "End of Tour Report as Air Force Liaison Officer to Commander, U.S. Naval Forces, Central Command (COMUSNAVCENT/AFLO), for Operations Desert Shield/Desert Storm, from 12AF/SE to COMUSNAVCENT/01, 5 Mar 1991, p 3.

[50]Memo, "Trip Report," from Capt S. U. Ramsdell, USN, to Director, Naval Historical Center, 14 May 1991, p 3.

[51](FOUO) Rpt, "End of Tour Report as Air Force Liaison Officer to Commander, U.S. Naval Forces, Central Command," 5 Mar 1991, p 2.

[52]Intvw, Thomas C. Hone, Maj Anne D. Leary, Mark D. Mandeles with Col Peter F. Herrly, USA, Joint Staff, 19 Feb 1992. Note, no JFACC stationery was printed for use in Desert Shield and Desert Storm.

positioning was only thinly veiled . . . as positioning and preparation for the upcoming 'Battles with Congress.' The JFACC planning cell had a member of the Secretary of the Air Force's personal staff–he was the second senior member in the planning cell. There never was any question that the senior leadership in the Air Force was a constant factor in the direction of the 'war plan.'[53]

Inadvertent indiscretions aside, Navy and Joint Force Air Component Commander relations were complicated by several avoidable problems. The first was having Vice Adm. Stanley Arthur, CENTCOM Navy Component Commander, at sea, on *Blue Ridge*. Indeed, as the Navy captain cited earlier discovered, Admiral Arthur himself was "frustrated with his location." He "was not in a position to influence the unified commander directly nor to participate effectively in the JFACC process . . . ," and he knew it, but he decided not to try to change his location because, when he took command during Desert Shield, *Blue Ridge* was already acting as the command ship, and a move ashore would have complicated planning for Desert Storm.[54] Related to this problem was another: the fact that he also had responsibilities as Commander, Seventh Fleet that kept him from spending time dealing directly with the Joint Force Air Component Commander.[55] Finally, there was the inconvenience caused by the fact that Air Tasking Orders had to be flown out to the carriers daily because the Navy had not installed (and, as it happened, could not take) terminals for the Air Force's Computer Assisted Force Management System.[56]

---

[53](S) Background Paper, Desert Shield and USN Strike Planning, Cdr Donald W. McSwain and Cdr Maurice Smith, Dec 1990, Task Force 4 Files, GWAPS.

[54]Rpt, "Trip Report," Capt S. U. Ramsdell, USN, 14 May 1991, p 5.

[55](FOUO) Rpt, "End of Tour Report as Air Force Liaison Officer to Commander, U.S. Naval Forces, Central Command," 5 Mar 1991, p 7.

[56]One reason the Navy did not install CAFMS terminals was the absence of a worldwide CAFMS system. The software for European terminals was incompatible with terminals used in the Pacific. Navy carriers could be deployed in any theater or in several theaters in quick succession. They needed a universal system. As it happened, the only such "system" was hand delivery.

Relations between the Navy at Riyadh and the Joint Force Air Component Commander's staff were professional.[57] However, the fact that Navy personnel afloat (on *Blue Ridge* and on the carriers) had not worked with the CENTAF staff before Desert Shield and could not do so in person during the months before Desert Storm meant that they did not develop an understanding of the Air Tasking Order process and how best to participate in it.[58] An Air Force liaison officer to CENTCOM's Navy Component Commander's staff argued that this lack of experience and understanding led the Navy staff to create a "Fleet Defense" sortie category "to give NAVCENT the flexibility to strike targets felt to be important to the Navy but ignored by the" regular ATO process.[59] Avoiding ATO tasking did not fully solve the Navy's problem, which was rooted in carrier aviation's lack of a command and control system effective in sustaining an extended air campaign.[60]

Horner did not let tension between CENTAF and NAVCENT staff afloat shape his approach to NAVCENT. Admiral Mauz, for example, sent a group of Navy intelligence officers to Horner in August to augment the still-arriving Ninth Air Force command staff, and, in Horner's own words, "we formed a joint Air Force/Navy intelligence operation right off the start to do air intelligence. That was a big step in faith on the part of the Navy."[61] After Mauz had been replaced as the Navy component commander by Admiral Arthur, Arthur and Horner had occasion to disagree about who should issue the Rules of Engagement governing Navy combat air patrol fighters flying above the Persian Gulf. Arthur wanted Schwarzkopf to promulgate the rules; Horner asserted that it was a Joint Force Air Component Commander responsibility. Horner told Arthur to appeal his case to General Schwarzkopf. Arthur did, Horner

---

[57]As noted by the Air Force NAVCENT liaison officer and the Navy captain cited above. See (FOUO) Rpt, "End of Tour Report as Air Force Liaison Officer to Commander, U.S. Naval Forces, Central Command," 5 Mar 1991; Memo, "Trip Report," from Capt. S. U. Ramsdell, USN, to Director, Naval Historical Center, 14 May 1991.

[58](FOUO) Rpt, "End of Tour Report as Air Force Liaison Officer to Commander, U.S. Naval Forces, Central Command," 5 Mar 1991, pp 5-6.

[59](FOUO) *Ibid*, p 5.

[60]Memo, "Trip Report," from Capt S. U. Ramsdell, USN, to Director, Naval Historical Center, 14 May 1991, p 4.

[61](S) Horner Intvw, 4 Mar 1992.

offered his rejoinder, and Schwarzkopf decided in Horner's favor.[62] As Horner later noted, he did not feel that Arthur had unfairly challenged his authority, or that Schwarzkopf, in making his decision, had shown any lack of confidence in Horner's ability to work successfully as JFACC.[63]

Fortunately, Admiral Arthur and General Horner kept the tone of their communications professional, even when the issue at hand was serious for them both. On 23 January 1991, for example, Arthur complained to Horner directly about the lateness of the Air Tasking Order: "Since Day Three, the ATO time late has been driving all of us to distraction."[64] Given the delay in completing the ATO, Arthur believed that there was too much pressure to maintain a high rate of sorties. He also told Horner that "None of the aircraft that are a threat to me have been targeted even though they are in the open."[65] In ending his message, however, Arthur noted that "the coordination there in Riyadh is super," and he closed with "Keep 'em flying. Very respectfully, Stan."[66] Horner responded by describing his staff's efforts to "have the ATO available to the units 12 hours prior to the effective time of the ATO," and by sharing Arthur's concern about untargeted aircraft.[67] As Horner observed, "Fighter pilots who pass up aircraft in open when striking an airfield don't have the big picture."[68] But Horner also reminded Arthur that the air campaign was based on the guidance of the Commander in Chief, which placed less priority on strikes against Iraqi forces in Kuwait than on attacks against Iraq's leadership, its nuclear, chemical and biological installations, and its command and control facilities.[69] Horner finished by thanking Arthur for

---

[62](S) Ibid; also, Msg (S/NF), from COMUSNAVCENT, to USCENTAF, "Personal for Lt Gen Horner from Arthur," subj: "Rules of Engagement," 0 112120Z Jan 91 ZYB, 27-22 GWAPS File.

[63](S) Horner Intvw, 4 Mar 1992; also, (S/NF) Msg, from COMUSNAVCENT, to USCENTAF, "Personal for Lt Gen Horner from Arthur," subj: "Rules of Engagement," 0 112120Z Jan 91 ZYB, 27-22 GWAPS File.

[64](S) Msg, from COMUSNAVCENT, to USCENTAF, subj: Air Campaign, 23 Jan, 0727Z, in GWAPS Deptula File, No. 36D.

[65](S) *Ibid.*

[66](S) *Ibid.*

[67](S) Msg to COMUSNAVCENT, from USCENTAF, CC, subj "Air Campaign," 26 Jan 1991, 2130Z, in Deptula File, GWAPS.

[68](S) *Ibid.*

[69](S) *Ibid.*

"your candidness" and by saying, "Jointly, we will successfully meet all ... objectives. ..."[70] This exchange seems typical of the Horner-Arthur message traffic, and it confirms Horner's postwar assertions that his relationships with the other component commanders were professional and mutually respectful.

As Joint Force Air Component Commander, Horner was willing to make tradeoffs with senior officers in the other Services in order to avoid, apparently, open conflicts over the JFACC's status and authority. Marine General Royal Moore wrote that Horner approached him during Desert Storm to offer trading Air Force sorties for Marine air sorties and making "tradeoffs back and forth as we worked through the air war."[71] General Horner did not appear to regard incidents of such horse trading as diminishing his authority as JFACC. However, he also admitted that the U.S. air effort was never really pressured by Iraq: "We never had to make a decision as to whether the French brigade died or the Marine brigade died or the Saudi brigade died. If we had had to make those kinds of decisions, it would have been a lot more difficult."[72]

In fact, Horner's relationship with the Marine Corps also was shaped by instructions from Schwarzkopf, once the air campaign was well under way, for Horner to consult regularly and carefully with the ground commanders. On 31 January, Schwarzkopf told Horner that

> Target development and nomination during the early phases of the campaign were clearly led by the ... (JFACC). As we move into battlefield preparation, maneuver commander input into the target selection process becomes even more important. Therefore, the opportunity for corps and other subordinate commanders to plan for and

---

[70](S) *Ibid.*

[71]"Interview: Lt Gen Royal N. Moore, Jr.," U.S. Naval Institute *Proceedings*, Nov 1991, p 64.

[72](S) Horner Intvw, 4 Mar 1992.

receive air sorties to fly against targets of their choosing must increase.[73]

To provide for that opportunity, Schwarzkopf had Horner meet daily with Lt. Gen. Calvin Waller (Schwarzkopf's deputy). Schwarzkopf instructed the two officers to allocate sorties among the ground commanders at the beginning of each Air Tasking Order cycle. The ground commanders could review that allocation and, if necessary, request changes. Horner and Waller would evaluate any change requests in time to submit a final allocation recommendation to Schwarzkopf by forty-eight hours prior to the execution of the ATO.[74] Implementing this process left Horner and Waller with two agenda items daily. The first was to develop a recommended initial allocation of sorties (seventy-two hours prior to the execution of the ATO). The second was to take the comments of the ground commanders on yesterday's recommended allocation, review them, and then make a final proposal to Schwarzkopf (forty-eight hours prior to ATO execution).

On 1 February, Schwarzkopf told Lt. Gen. Boomer:

> I want you and Chuck Horner to work together to ensure that we strike key Iraqi targets in Southeastern Kuwait. We must continue to utilize the JFACC concept to integrate all available air assets while giving you maximum flexibility to shape the battlefield . . . continue to work closely with CENTAF and keep them informed of your intent and the focus of your efforts. . . .[75]

This was not unambiguous support for the position that the JFACC was solely responsible for planning the air campaign. It explains Horner's decision to negotiate with General Boomer (and Marine General Moore), and it also shows how the decision by the Joint Chiefs to affirm both the

---

[73](S) Msg, from USCINCCENT, to COMUSCENTAF, subj: "Air Apportionment Planning," 31 Jan 1991, 1650Z, in TACC/CC/DO Current Ops Log, Microfilm No. 0882616, GWAPS New Acquisition File No. 215. (U) Written on this message is a note from Maj Gen Corder: "This msg is an important piece of the Air/Land Battle puzzle. . . ."

[74](S) *Ibid.*

[75](S) Msg, to CG I MEFMAIN, from CINCCENT, info to CENTAF, subj: "Marine Aviation," 1 Feb 1991, 1330Z, in (S) TACC/CC/DO Current Ops Log, Microfilm Roll Number 0882616, CHECO.

Joint Force Air Component Commander concept and the Omnibus Agreement created a context for disagreement between the Joint Force Air Component Commander and the Marine Corps component commander.

In postwar interviews, though, Horner recalled being less concerned about the Marines, who came equipped with their own close air support, or the Navy than about the Army.[76] He wanted as many aircraft as possible engaging the enemy at any given time once Desert Storm began. "Push CAS" promised to give the JFACC the sorties required by the Commander in Chief and, once the ground war started, those needed by the Army as well. During Desert Shield, Horner also decided that Army division and corps commanders probably would ask for more sorties than they would really need because they would not want to risk running short.[77] He was trying, as JFACC, to anticipate their true needs and plan accordingly.

Horner's concern that the theater ground commanders would press General Schwarzkopf for control over air support sorties dated from at least 11 November 1990. On that day, General Glosson, responsible to Horner for planning the offensive air campaign against Iraq, briefed the ground commanders, and they objected to what they felt was their inability to control the air attacks planned against Iraqi forces dug-in in Kuwait.[78] The ground commanders' concerns did not go away, even as the bombing launched during Desert Storm progressed. During a Desert Storm conference in February 1991 among Schwarzkopf and his component commanders, Army corps commanders and the Army Component Commander's staff "bitterly complained that the Air Force

---

[76]For example, Horner had developed the "Push CAS" concept (in April 1990) because he did not want aircraft sitting on runways waiting for a call from attacking Army divisions.

[77](S) *Ibid*, p 12.

[78]Rpt, Excerpts from HQ CENTCOM/Joint Forces and Theater Operations, J-5 Plans After Action Report, Vol. I - After Action Report, Chronology. Wayne W. Thompson also interviewed Maj Gen Rhame, commander of the 1st Infantry Division (VII Corps) during Desert Shield and Desert Storm, and Maj Gen Rhame noted that he and his fellow division commanders in the VII Corps had been quite irritated by Brig Gen Glosson's brief to them because it gave them no control over what they regarded as their own airspace. Intvw (S), Wayne W. Thompson with Maj Gen Rhame, Jul 1992.

was not hitting the targets they had chosen."⁷⁹ As Horner later recalled, "I knew that was going to happen." As he also had expected, the Marines, "out of self-protection," followed the Army's lead.⁸⁰ Horner believed that they acted on a misunderstanding of the best use of airpower and the tendency of Army corps to "fight in isolation."⁸¹ In response to the ground commanders' demands that sorties be allocated to their fronts, Horner apparently dug in his heels and said "No." Recalling this incident later, Horner said, "Schwarzkopf laughed when I fell on my sword. He didn't give any support at all. But then he summarized it by saying, 'Guys, it's all mine, and I will put it where it needs to be put." The CINC never raised the issue again.⁸²

Yet Schwarzkopf took a very active role in determining targets once the initial objectives of the strategic campaign against Iraq were met and air units shifted their efforts to isolating and weakening Iraq's army in Kuwait. For example, in the three weeks before the ground war began, the Army and Marine component commanders submitted ranked lists of targets to Schwarzkopf's operations staff. With the help of the intelligence officers in CENTCOM who were in touch with Washington, the operations staff led by Maj. Gen. Burton R. Moore would then brief Lt. Gen. Calvin Waller, Schwarzkopf's deputy, and Waller would consult with Horner (per Schwarzkopf's 31 January message). Horner would then brief the Commander in Chief.⁸³

As Horner discovered through experience, however, Schwarzkopf apportioned air assets across the front of the ground formations. In the evening briefings where targeting choices were presented to the Commander in Chief, Schwarzkopf–as Horner remembered–would say things like, "Why are you hitting them? I want THEM [emphasis in the transcript] hit! Do you understand? THEM!" Horner and Glosson would "just sit there and take notes."⁸⁴

---

⁷⁹Frank N. Schubert and Theresa L. Kraus, eds, *The Whirlwind War: the United States Army in Operations Desert Shield and Desert Storm*, Draft, (Washington, DC, 1992), p 276.

⁸⁰(S) Horner Intvw, 4 Mar 1992.

⁸¹(S) *Ibid.*

⁸²(S) *Ibid.*

⁸³(S) Neal Intvw, 13 Jan 1992.

⁸⁴(S) Horner Intvw, 4 Mar 1992.

The Joint Force Air Component Commander and the Commander in Chief

General Horner believed that he had a very good professional relationship with General Schwarzkopf. That is, the Commander in Chief had, in Horner's view, a clear idea how to use his JFACC and what the Joint Force Air Component Commander's authority should be, and that approach was one which Horner himself accepted. However, Horner also made a strong effort to develop a close personal relationship with his commander. Horner believed that his endeavor to complement his professional relationship to the Commander in Chief with his effort to win Schwarzkopf's personal trust paid off. In Horner's view, the benefit was that Schwarzkopf became "very trusting with the Air Force."[85] Horner also understood that Schwarzkopf was under pressure from Washington, and he acted to help him by having the personnel in the Tactical Air Control Center, during Desert Storm, quickly send reports of the air action to Schwarzkopf's staff. As Horner told the center, the CENTCOM staff would "get Mucho Heato from D.C." when they could not "feed the Info Monster every 3-4 hours."[86]

Horner recalled only one problem: his relationship with Schwarzkopf's Operations staff, headed by Maj. Gen. Burton Moore. Horner did not want CENTCOM Operations to control his access to Schwarzkopf; he believed that, as a commander, he should report directly to the Commander in Chief, his superior.[87] CENTCOM Operations already had many duties, for example, the responsibility to support the Commander in Chief in all warfare areas, not simply aviation. The Operations staff was, consequently, flooded with information from all component commanders and spent most of their time organizing that information for the Commander in Chief.[88] Ideally, Schwarzkopf's Operations staff should have played a strong role in organizing and supporting a theater command-level joint targeting board. The board,

---

[85] (S) Horner Intvw, 4 Mar 1992; (U) and, in his memoirs, Schwarzkopf praised the way Horner managed the process of putting together the air campaign: "Horner had done an extraordinary job." See H. Norman Schwarzkopf with Peter Petre, *It Doesn't Take a Hero* (New York, 1992), p 420.

[86] (S) TACC/CC/DO, Current Ops Log, Microfilm No. 0882616, CHECO, 30 Jan 1991, 1701Z, GWAPS New Acquisition File No. 215.

[87] (S) Horner GWAPS Intvw, 9 Mar 1992.

[88] (S) Neal Intvw, 13 Jan 1992.

composed of the component commanders, could have advised Schwarzkopf regarding the proper allocation of air sorties across the theater. It also could have served as a forum in which the Commander in Chief would make the reasons for his choices regarding the allocation of airpower clear to his component commanders. The concept of a board was packaged with the concept of the Joint Force Air Component Commander; the idea was that board would advise the Commander in Chief, and the Joint Force Air Component Commander would then implement the Commander in Chief's guidance across the theater, using all available aviation resources.

Schwarzkopf did not organize such a board. He vested responsibility for planning the air campaign in Horner's organization (specifically the Tactical Air Control Center), which had the expertise and personnel required to put such a plan together, and he continued to rely on Horner and on Horner's subordinates (such as General Buster C. Glosson) to implement the overall air campaign plan once the war actually began. In off-the-record postwar interviews, representatives of the Marine Corps and the Joint Staff argued that Schwarzkopf probably made a mistake in not creating such a board.[89] The Deputy for Operations, however, was not convinced that "CENTCOM's operations staff" could have done the required work or that General Schwarzkopf even believed that it needed to be done.[90]

---

[89]There was a Joint Target Coordination Board, but its members were not general officers or even full colonels. (S) See USCENTAF Combat Plans records and schedules, GWAPS Microfilm No. 23654, Frames 773 (S) (USCENTAF Combat Plans Handout, 1 Jan 1991) and 852 (S) (USCENTAF Combat Plans Handout, 1 Oct 1990). See also Chapter 6.

[90](S) Neal Intvw, 13 Jan 1992; (U) note, an officer in CENTCOM J-3(Air) stated that his chief, Maj Gen Moore, vetoed a suggestion by several officers of the J-3 staff in October 1990 that Moore recommend to Schwarzkopf creation of a high-level joint targeting board. Intvw, Maj Anne D. Leary with Lt Col Royce Crane, CENTCOM J-3/Air, Apr 14, 1992.

Regardless of the reasons for not establishing a theater command-level target advisory board, the absence of such a board meant that a formal communications channel did not exist for Army corps commanders to express their concerns to the Commander in Chief and the Joint Force Air Component Commander about targeting. From their perspectives, the coalition air attacks were not doing a lot of apparent damage to enemy forces facing Army units. Instead, the ground commanders approached Schwarzkopf's deputy, Gen. Calvin Waller.[91] Schwarzkopf, however, followed the progress of the air campaign against Iraqi ground units using information made available to him by Horner. The latter described the process this way:

> I would never give Schwarzkopf BDA [battle damage assessment] because I didn't want to get into the 'what have you done for me lately' type thing. He understood that, but every night . . . Buster [BGen Glosson] would give me that data [tank plinkings, etc.], and then I would always have it open on my notebook right there. Schwarzkopf would always look at it . . . .[92]

Army and Marine representatives were always present at the 1900L target selection briefings given by Horner and Glosson to Schwarzkopf and his complete staff, but these briefings focused on gaining Schwarzkopf's approval of a list of targets.[93]

Horner did not have the authority to create a forum to discuss targeting on his own. Only Schwarzkopf could have created a joint targeting board, just as it was Schwarzkopf's responsibility to use the CENTCOM staff to keep the ground commanders aware of the progress of the air campaign against the Iraqi units arrayed opposite them. But there was no effective joint campaign oversight on the part of CENTCOM's staff. The fact that CENTCOM operations officers served as shift workers in CENTCOM's operations room, instead of matching reports from the JFACC against an overall theater combined arms campaign plan, tends to

---

[91] (S) Intvw, 13 Jan 1992.

[92] (S) Horner Intvws, 4 Mar 1992 and with GWAPS, 9 Mar 1992.

[93] (S) Neal Intvw, 13 Jan 1992.

substantiate this point.[94] Schwarzkopf had delegated management of the air campaign to Horner, but Horner's staff lacked the resources required to explain the theater-wide and corps-specific consequences of the air war to Army and Marine ground commanders.

The uncertainty shifted once the ground war began. Then, it was the Joint Force Air Component Commander who was concerned, especially about fratricide.[95] How fast were the ground units moving? Where were the ground units? Or, were the fire support coordination lines too far out so that coalition strike aircraft could not attack vulnerable enemy targets?[96]

Horner's philosophy regarding close air support was straightforward: " . . . if it's inside the Fire Support Coordination Line, don't bother to tell me. If it's [not], put it in the ATO. Get the air cover; get the ECM support; get the TOT; get the coordination; get all the benefits from being in the ATO."[97]

To support the ground commanders, the JFACC had developed time-phased fire support coordination lines, activated by code words, so that ground units could move into areas that had been under his control

---

[94]Intvw, Maj Anne D. Leary with Lt Col Royce Crane, CENTCOM J-3/Air, 14 Apr 1992.

[95](S) Horner Intvw, 4 Mar 1992. (U) The (S) TACC/CC/DO Current Ops Log has an entry from 17 Feb 1991 where Horner writes, "NO MORE Fratricide . . . NO MORE!" On 18 Feb, Horner wrote, "NO FRATRICIDE." On 24 Feb (1352Z), the DCO sent a message to all wing operations centers, telling them to caution the squadrons. The Current Ops Log is Microfilm Roll Number 0882616.

[96]An air-ground coordination problem sometimes effected the FSCL when ground commanders (who established the FSCLs) moved the FSCL with insufficient warning to the JFACC/TACC. For example, on 17 Feb (1503Z), the Army's Battlefield Coordination Element notified the TACC that the XVIII Airborne Corps had moved its FSCL "3 minutes ago" without warning TACC personnel. (S) (TACC/CC/DO Current Ops Log, 1503Z, 17 Feb 1991, Microfilm Roll Number 0882616, CHECO.) That same day, the Marine Corps liaison officer in the TACC had informed the 9th Air Force colonel heading the staff there that a Marine FSCL would change in five minutes. There had been "no prior coordination" with the TACC. (S) (TACC/CC/DO Current Ops Log, 1454Z, 17 Feb 1991.)

[97](S) Horner Intvw, 4 Mar 1992.

without risking attack by friendly air forces.[98] The problem, according to a CENTAF staff officer questioned a year after the ground war took place, was that the Army's Battlefield Coordination Element in the Tactical Air Control Center could not speak for both corps, so that the JFACC (and the staff of the Tactical Air Control Center) did not always know just where the advancing Army units were.[99] By contrast, the Army's draft version of its official history of Desert Storm says that the Army worked directly with Air Force wings to avoid fratricide.[100] Despite such differences, all accounts of close air support and battlefield air interdiction during the ground war note that it was almost impossible in many cases for the JFACC's staff to track the ground advance, despite Horner's efforts to guarantee effective air-ground staff coordination.[101]

The Joint Force Air Component Commander and the Tactical Air Control Center

The last issue concerns General Horner's methods of directing the air campaign through the Tactical Air Control System's (TACS) Tactical Air Control Center (TACC). The center worked for Horner, turning his guidance (which supposedly reflected the theater commander's overall plan) into a Master Attack Plan (MAP), and then into a daily air tasking order (ATO). The center also evaluated reports from the wings to determine the effectiveness of missions already flown so that Control Center mission planners could base their plans on an accurate assessment of what had already been achieved across the whole theater. Details of the tasking process during Desert Storm will be presented in Chapter 7, but it is important here to discuss General Horner's approach to managing the Tactical Air Control Center (which in turn managed the air campaign).

In 1992, Horner said that he deliberately rejected the option of having the Tactical Air Control Center prepare Desert Storm ATOs beyond the

---

[98](S) Briefing, Lt Col Perozzi, CENTAF Staff, 9 Mar 1992, Shaw AFB, SC.

[99](S) Conversation with Lt Col Perozzi, 9 Mar 1992, Shaw AFB, SC.

[100]*The Whirlwind War: the United States Army in Operations Desert Shield and Desert Storm*, p 277.

[101]This made Horner very angry because he believed it was an Army problem. (S) Horner GWAPS Intvw, 9 Mar 1992.

first two days.[102] He wanted the Guidance, Apportionment, and Targeting planners to learn "how to do chaos war."[103] Yet, he did not want chaos in the Control Center. There was some risk of that because, first, the workload (in terms of numbers of sorties) on center personnel was beyond what they had trained for. Second, in order to give it the strength required to handle that heavy load of sorties, the addition of large numbers of personnel to CENTAF's Tactical Air Control Center meant that there were a lot of strangers in the organization.[104] For example, the peacetime strength of CENTAF's Control Center was about 300 personnel; during Desert Storm, the number was close to 2,000, counting intelligence specialists.[105] This added strength was required for the center to put together Air Tasking Orders with large numbers of sorties. As General Glosson observed, "We had a system established that should have supported about 1,500 to 2,000 sorties a day, 2,400 max. . . . [O]n about day ten I was asking them to produce an ATO in excess of 3,000 sorties a day. They had never experienced anything like that."[106] Maj Gen John A. Corder, Horner's operations deputy at CENTAF, later confirmed Glosson's portrait of the Command Center personnel initially struggling during Desert Storm to produce daily tasking orders on time.[107]

Horner employed at least four tactics during Desert Storm to ensure that the CENTAF Control Center operated as well as it could under the circumstances. One was to bring in General Corder,[108] who arrived in Riyadh on 22 November 1990 in order to add the authority of his rank to match the Army's rapidly growing theater force (and rank) structure. As a major general, Corder could (and did) deal more easily with senior CENTCOM staff officers than did Col. James Crigger, who was Corder's

---

[102](S) Horner Intvw, 4 Mar 1992.

[103](S) Horner Intvw, 4 Mar 1992. (U) Horner rejected preparation of more scripted ATOs because he believed that type of planning was inappropriate for the action-reaction of conventional warfare. See (S) Chapter 7.

[104]See (S) Chapter 6 for a more detailed discussion of the make-up of the Black Hole and TACC.

[105](S) Briefing, Lt Col Pfiefer, USAF, CENTAF Staff, 9 Mar 1992, Shaw AFB, SC.

[106]Notes from "Planning and Execution of the Offensive Air Campaign Against Iraq," (S) intvw, Brig Gen Buster Glosson, 6 Mar 1991, RSAF HQ, Riyadh, SA, p 23.

[107](S) Intvw, GWAPS with Maj Gen John A. Corder, May 18, 1992.

[108]Gen Corder led the Tactical Air Warfare Center at Eglin AFB, FL.

predecessor as operations deputy.[109] Another was to make General Glosson, Schwarzkopf's behind-the-scenes offensive air campaign planner during Desert Shield, the leader of the organization which produced the Master Attack Plan during Desert Storm.[110] A third was to make sure that either he or Glosson was available to visit the Control Center at any time once the air war began.[111] A fourth was to give Glosson responsibility for releasing videotapes or photographs to the media during Desert Storm.[112] In these cases, Horner used his authority as Air Force component commander to place Air Force officers whom he knew in positions where he believed that, as JFACC, he needed subordinates in whom he could place special trust.

His concern was to put together quickly a working, effective organization that included significant allied participation. He naturally turned to those officers whom he knew and with whom he had worked. As he noted at the time,

> I got people together based on personalities (not organizational and management skills). American lives are very disorganized and chaotic. They wait until one o'clock to decide to go to the ball game. But they go. I got these particular people together to fight the war. We'll fight and win and then the organization will disappear.[113]

This comment reveals Horner's approach to organizing for theater air war: people mattered more than structure, or organization. Winning mattered more than running an efficient operation. The legitimacy of his command organization was less a function of the way it worked than of the character of the people who staffed it. The paragraphs which follow will explore this philosophy of command in more detail. Chapters 6 and 7 will discuss the organizational consequences which this philosophy created within the Tactical Air Control Center.

---

[109](S) Neal Intvw, 13 Jan 1992; see also (S) Chapter 6.

[110](S) See Chapter 6.

[111](S) Intvw, GWAPS with Maj Gen Buster C. Glosson, 14 Apr 1992.

[112](S) *Ibid.*

[113](S) Intvw, Lt Gen Charles A. Horner, USAF, GWAPS Microfilm Files No. 269523, p 609.

During Desert Storm, Horner usually would visit the Control Center early, at 0530, to talk with Glosson in the Guidance, Apportionment, Targeting group about the Master Attack Plan. Horner would then make a brief presentation to as many as 400 personnel gathered in the Control Center.[114] These brief, informal talks show Horner as coach, as when he exhorted center personnel to "Ask questions,"[115] or to speak up if they had any "good ideas about tactics or target selection."[116] On 31 January, he told these personnel that "we've got to be prepared to manage chaos; we've got to keep the units informed; and we've got to be able to react without jerking the units around too much."[117] Since wing representatives worked in the Control Center, these short speeches were also a means Horner used to communicate indirectly with the wings. Through the center, informally, he sent the wings messages regarding target priorities (for example, Scuds were high priority on 20 January but not by the 24th)[118] and his campaign priorities ("We just can't have casualties" on 30 January, but "No excuses" regarding close air support on 24 February).[119] He also reassured his team, as when he told them, after he and they learned that there had been civilians in the Al Firdos bunker, "war is groping in the dark,"[120] or when he said that "we can expect to go through a learning curve again as ground operations start."[121] Horner usually made these kinds of comments in the company of General Behery, the Saudi Air Force Commander. Horner often went out of his

---

[114] Before 11 Feb, Horner would talk to the TACC staff at 0730. After that date, the talks were scheduled for 0900. (S) TACC/CC/DO Current Ops Log, 11 Feb 1991, 1010Z, Microfilm No. 0882616, CHECO, GWAPS New Acquisitions File No. 215.

[115] "Daily Comments of Lt Gen Charles A. Horner, 17 Jan through 28 Feb 1991," HQ USCENTAF Office of History, 20 Mar 1991, p 1 (comment from 17 Jan 1700 talk).

[116] Ibid, p 3 (0730 talk on 18 Jan 1991).

[117] Ibid, p 22 (31 Jan talk at 1700).

[118] Ibid, p 5 (0730 talk on 20 Jan), and pp 11-12 (1700 talk on 24 Jan).

[119] Ibid, p 18 (0730 talk on 30 January), and p 63 (0900 talk on 24 Feb).

[120] Ibid, p 41 (1700 talk on 14 Feb).

[121] Ibid, p 56 (1700 talk on 21 Feb).

way to promote and praise coalition cooperation, and he was careful not to ridicule Iraq or its common soldiers.[122]

Once he had made his morning presentation within the Control Center, Horner examined the Air Tasking Order. Then he often met again with General Glosson until noon, when–during Desert Storm–he would present the Air Tasking Order for the next day's operations to Army, Marine Corps, and Navy officers representing the other component commanders. Horner was then "free" (officially) until later in the afternoon, when he would visit the center again, make another short speech at 1700, and then, at 1800 (or so), meet again with General Glosson. Both would visit General Schwarzkopf at 1900 to brief the Commander in Chief about the progress of the air campaign and the JFACC's plans for future operations.

The Tactical Air Control Center was not just a sounding board or instrument Horner used to control the direction and scope of the air campaign. It also was also a source for targets and the missions flown against the enemy. It was the organization that turned guidance into specific plans and mission directives for the air units. As such, it was not a passive organization. Its members were expected to turn a concept of operations into specific missions. This is why Horner chose Glosson to be his chief campaign planner. Glosson understood what the air campaign was supposed to achieve. As Horner told center personnel during Desert Storm, "Bean counters are concerned about holes in runways. They are missing the point."[123] Glosson was made chief planner to make sure the point was emphasized. At the same time, the planners and the Air Tasking Order "fraggers" had to work together smoothly if the tasking were to emerge from the center on time. As Horner stressed, "We're servants, we're not masters."[124] Time and again during Desert Storm, he emphasized the need

---

[122] *Ibid*, p 33; on 8 Feb, for example, Horner expressed the hope that Hussein would be overthrown by his own military before the land campaign began, thereby saving many Iraqi lives. 0730 talk.

[123] *Ibid*, p 10 (0730 remarks, 23 Jan).

[124] *Ibid*, p 15 (1700 talk, 26 Jan).

of the Control Center to stick to a routine that put out the Air Tasking Order on time and kept the number of late changes down.[125]

But some of the problems Horner perceived in his Control Center were the consequences of decisions which he himself had made as the Air Force component commander. If, as JFACC, Horner needed an effective Tactical Air Control Center, then, as Air Force component commander, he had to apportion operational authority over his many air units among his subordinates. On 5 December 1990, he organized CENTAF for war by creating two provisional air divisions, the 14th and the 15th, each headed by a brigadier general, to serve alongside the two (the 17th and the 1610th Airlift Division) already in place. The 14th Air Division(P) was established to "provide operational control of assigned tactical fighter wings," while the 15th folded together electronic warfare, reconnaissance, command and control, and other units.[126] With his appointment as commander, 14th Air Division(P), Glosson became a major operational authority as well as the commander of the planners scoping out the offensive air war against Iraq. Glosson's deputy planner, Brig. Gen. Glenn A. Profitt, became head of the 15th Air Division(P). Brig. Gen. Patrick P. Caruana, Strategic Force commander since 8 August, had led the 17th Air Division(P) since 24 August. In one stroke, General Horner gave his two "Black Hole" senior planning leaders top positions in CENTAF's combat organization.[127]

This decision had several consequences. First, once the air campaign began, it drastically increased the workload of Generals Glosson and Profitt. In retrospect, Glosson, for example, said his hands were full–probably too full–as the chief planner and as 14th Air Division(P) commander.[128] Yet Horner's decision reduced his span of control. His

---

[125] On 16 Feb, at his 1700 talk, Horner said, "A lot of business is done over the telephone, and we need to keep a record of it." (p. 47) The (S) TACC/CC/DO Current Ops Log for 13 Feb 1991 (1733Z) noted, "World event: ATO Out on time . . . . Of course it . . . required 231 changes but it got out on time."

[126] Msg, CCWGORG, from Lt Gen Horner, 120600 Z, GWAPS File.

[127] (S) See Chapter 6.

[128] (S) Intvw, GWAPS with Maj Gen Buster C. Glosson, 14 Apr 1992. (U) In the (S) TACC/CC/DO Current Ops Log for 28 Jan 1991, Horner observed that "I came to work RESTED only to find Profitt and Glosson looking like ____. They don't know enough to go to bed." Horner was teasing them. He knew very well that they were overworked. But that was their job.

primary operational deputy, General Glosson, was also his senior planner. Meetings between the two, which took place at least twice every day during Desert Storm, covered both plans and operations.¹²⁹ As Joint Force Air Component Commander, Horner had to devote a great deal of time and thought to resolving issues with the Saudis and other allies, dealing with the other Service component commanders, and supporting General Schwarzkopf. As commander, CENTAF, Horner had also to carry operational responsibilities. By combining his plans and operations deputies, Horner reduced the number of subordinates he had to deal with and guaranteed that the operational concept basic to the air campaign was translated directly into the Air Tasking Order, the JFACC's primary control tool. However, offsetting these advantages was one disadvantage: Glosson could–and did–bypass the Air Tasking Order process and issue orders directly to his wing commanders.¹³⁰

When Iraq invaded Kuwait, Glosson was serving as the Deputy Commander, Middle East Joint Task Force. When CENTCOM was ordered to implement OPlan 1002-90, Glosson's position was superseded by the movement of CENTCOM and CENTAF into Saudi Arabia, and he approached General Horner. What matters here is that he had personal contacts at very high levels in the National Security Agency, the Central Intelligence Agency, and the White House.¹³¹ Glosson also had a "personal relationship" with the Secretary of Defense. During Desert Shield, the Secretary, according to the general, called him in Riyadh to ask what role air power would play if the coalition attacked Iraq.¹³² Finally, Glosson had had a direct relationship with General Schwarzkopf since becoming the Commander in Chief's chief air campaign planner.

---

¹²⁹(S) Horner GWAPS Intvw, 9 Mar 1992; (S) GWAPS with Maj Gen Buster C. Glosson, 14 Apr 1992.

¹³⁰(S) Intvw, GWAPS with Maj Gen Buster C. Glosson, 14 Apr 1992. (U) Glosson said that he had very strong support from his wing commanders, six of whom had worked for him before in one capacity or another. See also Chapter 7.

¹³¹(S) Intvw, GWAPS with Maj Gen Buster C. Glosson, 9 Apr 1992. See also (S) Chapter 6.

¹³²(S) *Ibid.*

There was some potential for Glosson to run the air war on his own. He and his Black Hole staff were convinced, when Desert Storm began, that they—better than anyone else in the Control Center—understood the concept of operations on which the air campaign was based.[133] As his deputy, Lt. Col. David A. Deptula, wrote at the end of March 1991, "There was no misunderstanding or dilution of intent of the plan between the planner and those executing the plan because the same individual was in charge of both."[134] Guidance, Apportionment, and Targeting was a special kind of battle staff, and Glosson was its leader. As Deptula later said, he and his colleagues did not just match air assets against a list of targeting priorities.[135] Instead, they applied a concept of operations to a campaign.[136] What matters in this chapter is whether General Horner, as JFACC, was in fact the actual leader of the Tactical Air Control Center, despite whatever views the Guidance, Apportionment, Targeting staff might have held.

The evidence indicates that he was. There are, for example, many cases in the Tactical Air Control Center's Operations Log where Horner issues instructions to the Tactical Air Control Center (those on fratricide have already been mentioned), or where he approves actions taken by his subordinates. In mid-February, he ordered a strong bombing effort against an Iraqi division that had mistreated coalition POWs.[137] He also directed the Control Center to check up on requests for air support by units of the Special Operations Command near the border with Iraq.[138] There are other examples. Taken together, they indicate that Horner was tracking the course of the air campaign and directing that course when he believed he had to do so.[139]

---

[133](S) See Chapter 7.

[134](S) Background Paper, Lt Col David Deptula, 29 Mar 1991, GWAPS Files.

[135](S) Briefing, Lt Col David A. Deptula, SAF/OSX to GWAPS, 20 Nov 1991, p 21.

[136](S) *Ibid*, p 43.

[137](S) TACC/CC/DO Current Ops Log, 0000Z, 12 or 13 Feb 1991.

[138](S) *Ibid*, 1300Z, 16 Feb 1991.

[139]Glosson often referred to Horner as "Boss" in the (S) TACC/CC/DO Current Ops Log. See, for example, the entry for 0300Z, 26 Feb 1991.

Summary and Review

The idea that there should be a theater-level air commander reaches back to World War II, when, on a temporary basis, it was implemented in the European Theater, though the commander, General Eisenhower, was not himself an aviation officer.[140] As an issue among the Services, the idea carries through the Korean War and the conflict in Southeast Asia. In these cases, senior Air Force officers argued persistently for a "single manager for air" across the theater.

With what results? It is difficult to say because it is impossible to take that one factor–the existence of a Joint Force Air Component Commander–and separate its influence on the conduct and outcome of the air war from so many others. The overwhelming allied air superiority reduced the amount and degree of conflict over resources among allies and among Services. Fewer resources, or a more effective opponent, might have increased competition within the coalition for aviation. Experience and the personality of key leaders mattered, too. The fact that Horner had worked for three years as CENTAF commander before Desert Shield was, in his mind, crucial. He knew the area and key people in friendly governments; he was on friendly terms with other component commanders, such as generals Yeosock and Boomer; he was able to work well with his chief, General Schwarzkopf, because he already understood his command's problems and potential. He had, both as JFACC and as CENTAF commander, trained and energetic and talented counterparts and subordinates.

Even the enemy helped. As CENTCOM Forward in August 1990, Horner was concerned that his command and his force might be forced to withdraw in the face of a concerted Iraqi assault, much as U.S. forces withdrew when pressed by North Korean forces in the summer of 1950. Instead, theater air forces had time to prepare for an offensive campaign, one which Horner, Schwarzkopf and other senior officers–supported by the President–vowed would not be a repeat of the 1960's Rolling Thunder effort against North Vietnam.[141]

---

[140] See Appendix 2.

[141] See Lt Gen Horner's comments in Larry Grossman, "Beyond Rivalry," *Government Executive*, Vol. 23, No. 6, (Jun 1991), p 13.

Perhaps a better question to ask is "Did the JFACC act in ways which supported the legitimacy of his position?" The answer seems to be "yes." If Horner made any mistake in this capacity, it was to fail to have ready a truly joint Tactical Air Control Center when Iraq invaded Kuwait. But he was not alone in this error. The Navy and Army, component commanders did not insist that Horner accept as deputies in the Control Center general officers from their staffs. The Navy, Army and Marine component commanders did send teams of liaison officers to support the JFACC, but that was not the same thing. Horner recalled that he preferred officers from other Services to act as liaisons rather than to work for him (as JFACC).[142]

Horner's experience also suggests a close relationship between technology and the effectiveness of command and control. The Tactical Air Control Center Operations Log for 20 February contains this observation: "An amazing event has just occurred: we were able to talk secure, direct to all four AWACS, simultaneously . . . we also had an air picture from coast to coast at the same time. Unheard of.[143]" One minute later, the Tactical Air Control Center lost the air picture from the Navy. As the Log noted, "Perfection didn't last quite as long as hoped for." Nevertheless, this—and similar—incidents may be glimpses of a future, perhaps not very distant, when a theater air commander will be able to follow the course of an air campaign in real time, intervening selectively to take advantage of the flexibility of air power. As it was, using essentially paper and pencils supplemented by personal computers and systems such as Computer Assisted Force Management System, the Joint Commander and his Control Center organized and coordinated an overwhelmingly successful joint and coalition air campaign of unprecedented magnitude. Nothing like it had ever been done before.

General Horner could not and did not plan on using this technology. The Control Center which supported him did not use very sophisticated management support systems. No part of the center, for example, used interactive software, even though such a system might have proved its worth to the planners who sketched out their alternatives with paper and pencil and tracked the course of the air campaign with charts drawn by

---

[142](S) Horner GWAPS Intvw, 9 Mar 1992.

[143](S) TACC/CC/DO Current Ops Log, 1030Z, 20 Feb 1991.

hand, mission videotapes taken directly from returning aircraft, and Cable News Network broadcasts.[144] Center personnel did try the MSS-II system, where data from the reports of returning aircraft were fed into an automated display system. Unfortunately, as Deptula pointed out, " . . . it's just like a computer, garbage in and garbage out."[145] That is, there was more to the automation of command and control than the development of interesting electronic displays. Having more—especially more immediate—information on what was happening in the air campaign was useful, yet it was not sufficient to give the Control Center a significantly improved ability to control the course of the campaign. To have improved control, the center needed an interactive, automated Air Tasking Order planning and development process, as well as a system equally rapid and reliable to feed damage assessments back into that process.

Finally, General Horner's perception of which issues mattered to him as JFACC is a list that future Joint Force Air Component Commanders might want to consider. As noted in the beginning of this chapter, there were four types of such issues: (a) those concerning allies, (b) those among the Service component commanders, (c) those affecting the JFACC's standing with the theater commander, and (d) those related to the JFACC's management of the organizations—mainly the Tactical Air Control Center—through which he maintained control over theater air. The importance of these issues will change from case to case. However, failure to give any one set of issues due attention is likely to rob the Joint Force Air Component Commander of the legitimacy he needs to gain and hold the confidence of the theater commander, allies, or other component commanders.

---

[144](S) Draft Transcript of a Briefing to GWAPS by Lt Col David Deptula, 20 Nov 1991, p 24. See also Notes from "Planning and Execution of the Offensive Air Campaign Against Iraq," (S) intvw with Brig Gen Buster Glosson, 6 Mar 1991, pp 17-18.

[145](S) *Ibid*, pp 17-18.

4

Building the Tactical Air Control System

Lt. Gen. Charles A. Horner, the Joint Force Air Component Commander, exercised his authority through his Tactical Air Control System, or TACS. As Tactical Air Command Regulation 55-45 notes, the TACS is "the organization, personnel, procedures, and equipment necessary to plan, direct, and control tactical air operations and to coordinate air operations with other Services and Allied Forces."[1] This chapter has two tasks. First, it will provide a basic understanding of how a TACS and its major components function. Second, it will describe how selected major components of the Central Command Air Forces TACS were assembled during Desert Shield. Our primary focus will be on the deployment and initial operation of the basic airborne elements of the TACS–the Airborne Warning and Control (AWACS) and Airborne Battlefield Command and Control Center (ABCCC) aircraft, crews, and planning staffs. We also will examine the communications which linked these aircraft to one another and to command positions on the ground. These airborne and ground components of the TACS were tools used by General Horner to control the air campaign.

Major Components of a TACS

Each theater or contingency where air forces are employed, whether in conjunction with ground forces or by themselves, requires some form of tactical control of planning and operations. The major components of the TACS provide the air component commander with the tools necessary to adapt his specific command and control system to his unique requirements. This first section will describe the major components of the TACS used in support of both air-to-ground and air-to-air operations. Figure 11 illustrates these components.

---

[1]Tactical Air Command Regulation 55-45, *Tactical Air Force Headquarters and the TACC*, 8 Apr 1988, p 5-1. See also Joint Pub 1-02 (formerly JCS Pub 1), *Department of Defense Dictionary of Military and Associated Terms*, 1 Dec 1989.

Figure 11
Tactical Air Control System (TACS)

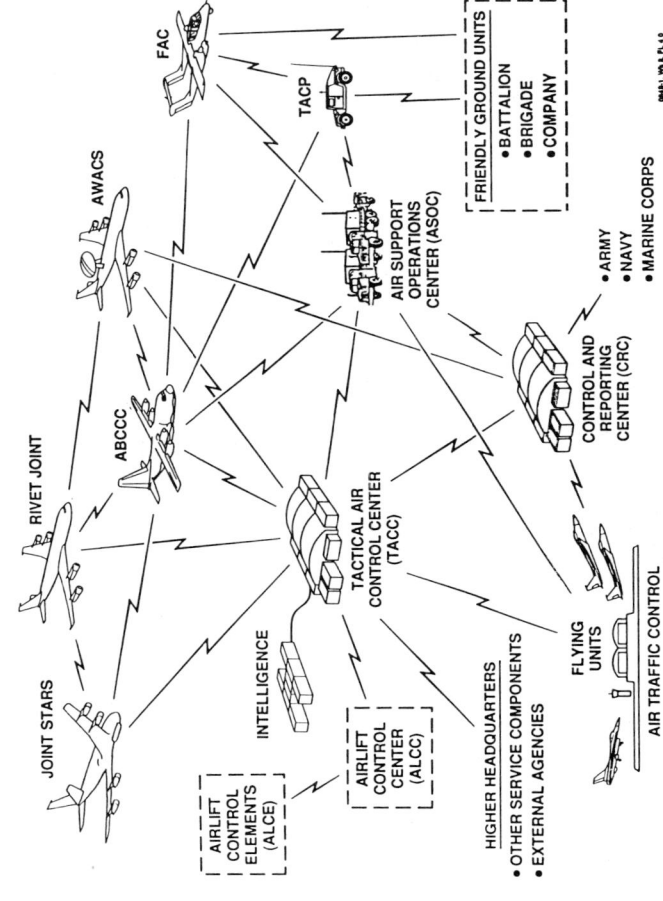

Tactical Air Control Party

The Tactical Air Control Party (TACP) consists of experienced tactical aircrews, tactical air command and control specialists, communications personnel, and technicians collocated with each appropriate command echelon of the supported ground forces. TACPs are subordinate to the Air Support Operations Center (ASOC), deploy with Army divisions, brigades, and battalions,[2] and "advise and assist the ground commander, request and coordinate preplanned and immediate tactical air support, and meet other requirements of the individual ground force echelon supported."[3] The Tactical Air Control Party passes requests for air support from the ground commander to the Air Support Operations Center. TACPs provide a "picture" of the ground situation to air forces to direct air attack against enemy units and help prevent fratricide. Intermediate echelon TACPs may coordinate requests for air support as they travel up the chain of command.

Forward Air Controller

The Forward Air Controller (FAC), either ground or airborne, functions as an extension of the TACP and performs terminal attack control for close air support (CAS) missions or acts as a tactical air coordinator. The forward air controller operates close to enemy forces and helps the attacking pilot identify friendly and enemy positions. He can also direct the pilot providing close air support to the specific target.

Air Support Operations Center

Air Support Operations Centers (ASOCs) are specialized Air Force operation centers responsible for detailed execution planning, direction, and control of the tactical air effort in close air support[4] of land forces.[5] They

---

[2] TAC Manual 2-1, p 5-21.

[3] TAC Regulation 55-45, *Tactical Air Force Headquarters and the TACC.*

[4] "Close air support is the application of aerospace forces in support of the land component commander's objectives." (Air Force Manual 1-1, *Basic Aerospace Doctrine of the United States Air Force,* Mar 1992).

[5] The Marine corollary to the ASOC is the Division Air Support Center (DASC). The DASC has corresponding responsibilities (to the ASOC) and similar subordinate groups (such as TACPs and FACs).

are located at the senior Army tactical headquarters levels (normally corps) and collocated with the corps-level Tactical Operations Center (TOC). In a multicorps environment, there is normally one Air Support Operations Center for each corps, and each of these Air Support Operation Centers reports individually to the Tactical Air Control Center (TACC).[6] Air Support Operations Center personnel are under the control of the TACC, and they pass immediate Army requests for air support to the TACC. In turn, the Tactical Air Control Center usually grants Air Support Operations Center personnel authority to schedule forward air controller missions flown in support of Army maneuver units (such as battalions).[7] In addition to passing Army requests for air support to the TACC, the Air Support Operations Center provides Air Force expertise to senior Army tactical elements, assisting and advising on the capabilities and limitations of airpower, coordinating on Joint Air Attack Team (JAAT) missions in support of air-land operations, and establishing and operating the Air Force air request net to control close air support and reconnaissance sorties distributed to the corps by the TACC in the air allocation process.[8]

Control and Reporting Center

Three elements of the Tactical Air Control System are each capable of directing airborne aircraft to the target area. The first of these, the Control and Reporting Center (CRC), is a ground station which normally uses ground- or AWACS-based radar to control air traffic. Once it receives a request for air support from the Air Support Operations Center, the Control and Reporting Center directs available aircraft from within its area of control to where they are needed or passes control of aircraft to another portion of the TACS (Airborne Battlefield Command and Control Center or Forward Air Controller). If the Control and Reporting Center does not have resources available to fill the request, it will request assistance from either AWACS (which can divert airborne assets) or from the Tactical Air Control Center (which can launch ground alert aircraft).

---

[6] The TACC is the senior air element of the TACS. It is described in detail in Chapter 5 of this report.

[7] TAC Manual 2-1, *Tactical Air Operations*, Aug 1991, p 5-20.

[8] *Ibid*, p 5-3.

Tactical Air Command Regulation 55-45 states that inherent in Control and Reporting Center functions

> are the requirements to supervise subordinate radar elements, provide threat warning for friendly aircraft, implement procedures to ensure that air defense assets of all services are employed in mutually supporting roles, establish coordination procedures based on friendly artillery plans, establish the means for air traffic regulation/identification, and support air rescue operations . . . . The CRC detects and identifies hostile airborne objects, recommends changes in air defense warning conditions and, when authorized, assigns weapons (aircraft and ADA [air defense artillery]), plus scrambles/diverts air defense capable aircraft.[9]

AWACS and the Control and Reporting Center can be used in combination or separately, depending upon how the airspace is organized. For example, the AWACS, because of its large radar and radio coverage, may be assigned to control the airspace over an entire sector of the theater including enemy territory. The ground-based Control and Reporting Center may be assigned a small subsector on the friendly side of the line between friendly and enemy airspace. In this case the AWACS would identify and track hostile aircraft as they approach friendly lines and warn the CRC of the potential threat. As enemy aircraft enter the CRC's subsector, the CRC could direct air or ground forces to shoot them down.[10]

Airborne Battlefield Command and Control Center

The Airborne Battlefield Command and Control Center (ABCCC) is a containerized command and control center designed for EC-130E aircraft. It contains communications equipment rather than radars or other sensors. Its main role is to coordinate strike aircraft carrying out air-to-ground missions. Like the Control and Reporting Center, the ABCCC can direct airborne aircraft to support requests from the Air Support Operations Center. ABCCC crews, headed by a Director, Airborne Battlestaff, serve as flying tactical air control centers or air support operations centers. Weapons and aircraft controllers on the ABCCC direct forward air control

---

[9] TAC Regulation 55-45, *Tactical Air Force Headquarters and The Tactical Air Control Center*, 8 Apr 1988.

[10] The AWACS could direct friendly air defenders to engage the hostile aircraft while still over enemy territory.

aircraft, airlift flights into their area, and air strikes against ground targets. ABCCC personnel control flights in their area by monitoring and maintaining communications among all the various aircraft (strike, reconnaissance, and transport) "working" their area. However, the ABCCC is not limited to coordinating ground attack missions and can be used to complement almost any battlefield command and control agency. ABCCC communicators also talk with their counterparts on AWACS and RIVET JOINT (discussed later in this chapter) and pass along situational and threat data from these systems to the aircraft focused on air-to-ground operations.

This combination of the Tactical Air Control Parties, Air Support Operations Centers, and Airborne Battlefield Command and Control Centers is designed to facilitate Army-Air Force communication and coordination from the battalion level all the way up to the joint force level at theater air command headquarters. Army Battlefield Coordination Element (BCE) personnel (described in detail later in this chapter), after consulting with the Army's component commander, help shape the Air Tasking Order. The BCE, in turn, advises ABCCC crews what sorties to expect in their areas of operation. Forward air controllers, Tactical Air Control Parties, and Air Support Operations Centers sense the ground situation, call for air support, and then direct that air support when it arrives overhead. The ABCCC backs up both the Tactical Air Control Center and the Air Support Operations Center; its crew can work both functions in case communications with these ground command elements are disrupted or lost. Finally, by talking to all aircraft flying in its area, the ABCCC can respond to immediate changes in the air or ground situation, exercising control over air-to-ground operations when necessary.

The mobility and communications advantage inherent in the Airborne Battlefield Command and Control Center platform enable it to stay abreast of the current ground and air situation within its assigned area of responsibility. And because the ABCCC is airborne, it normally can manage tactical forces operating beyond the normal communication coverage of ground TACS elements such as the Air Support Operations Center and Control and Reporting Center.

Airborne Warning and Control System

The Airborne Warning and Control System (AWACS) is both an airborne radar surveillance and control platform and the working location of the Airborne Command Element (ACE)–the direct link to the Joint Force Air Component Commander. The AWACS, like the Control and Reporting Center and ABCCC, can direct aircraft to fulfill Air Support Operation Center requests.

The E-3 AWACS provides highly mobile, survivable airborne surveillance and command and control functions for tactical and air defense forces. The AWACS

> has the ability to provide detection and control of aircraft below or beyond the coverage of ground-based radar, or when ground-based radar elements are not available. The AWACS radar and radio coverage permits air defense warnings, aircraft control, navigational assistance, coordination of air rescue efforts and changes to tactical missions.[11]

The E-3, operating in conjunction with U.S. Marine Corps, Navy, Army, Air Force, and allied units, provides a radar picture spanning the entire theater of operations[12] that can be data-linked with other TACS facilities. During Desert Shield/Desert Storm, it provided real-time information to most coalition command centers. The E-3 is capable of establishing a data sharing network with the RC-135V RIVET JOINT, ABCCC, TACC, and Navy E-2 Hawkeyes.

The AWACS also provides support to all aircraft requiring pre- and poststrike air refueling. Normally, the air combat plan contains a detailed plan to match tanker aircraft with aircraft requiring aerial refueling; however, last minute changes in targets or takeoff times may require en route modification to the refueling plan. AWACS, using its radar picture and radio contact with aircraft, can direct refuelings at any time.

---

[11]TAC Regulation 55-45, *Tactical Air Force Headquarters and The Tactical Air Control Center.*

[12]While an individual AWACS has a limited radar coverage, multiple aircraft "pictures" can be linked together to cover a vary large geographic area.

Additional Airborne Platforms

Two additional airborne platforms, while not officially part of the Tactical Air Control System, were critical elements of the command and control system during the Gulf War. RIVET JOINT (RC-135V) is an electronic intelligence collection platform that works with AWACS and selected ground sites to provide enhanced awareness of enemy air and ground activity. [DELETED][13] RIVET JOINT flies a standoff profile as close to the target airspace as the threats permit.[14]

The second platform, the Joint Surveillance and Target Attack Radar System (JSTARS),[15] provides near-real-time wide-area surveillance and deep targeting capability to ground and air commanders.[16] The system is able to detect, locate, and track high-value targets, such as mobile missile launchers, vehicle convoys, logistics depots, and assembly areas, and pass this information to air and ground commanders.[17] The intelligence information from RIVET JOINT and JSTARS is relayed to ground and air commanders to assist them in assessing the combat situation and allocating air assets.

---

[13](S) Department of Defense, *Conduct of the Persian Gulf War: Final Report to Congress*, Apr 1992, Appendix T, "Performance of Selected Weapon Systems."

[14][DELETED] (S/NF) USAF TAWC, *Tactical Air Forces Guide for Integrated Electronic Combat*, Oct 1987, pp A-18, A-19; see also Jeffrey T. Richelson, *The U.S. Intelligence Community*, Second Edition (Cambridge, Massachusetts, 1989), p 177; William E. Burrows, *Deep Black: Space Espionage and National Security* (New York, 1986), pp 169-71.

[15]The Joint STARS platform designation is the EC-135.

[16](S) DOD, *Conduct of the Persian Gulf War: Final Report to Congress*, Apr 1992, Appendix T, "Performance of Selected Weapon Systems."

[17]Intvw, Thomas C. Hone, Maj Anne D. Leary, Mark D. Mandeles with Brig Gen George K. Muellner, DCS/Requirements, TAC, 16 Apr 1992. See also, for example, Peter Grier, "Joint STARS Does Its Stuff," *Air Force Magazine*, Jun 1991, pp 38-42; Edward H. Kolcum, "Joint STARS E-8s Return to U.S.; 20-Aircraft Fleet Believed Assured," *Aviation Week and Space Technology*, 11 Mar 1991, p 20.

Basic airborne elements of the TACS are the Airborne Warning and Control System (AWACS) (above), and Airborne Battlefield Command and Control Center (ABCCC), interior view (right); Rivet Joint (below) works with AWACS to provide enhanced awareness of enemy activity.

Air Traffic Control and Air Defense Systems

During combat, the control of the airspace over the theater frequently is relinquished by the civil air traffic control authorities and turned over to the military, which divides the airspace into sectors and subsectors depending upon the size of the theater. Each sector or subsector is then placed under the control of an element of the TACS, such as AWACS or a Control and Reporting Center. Control of airspace is turned over to the military because of (a) the high volume of air traffic, (b) the necessity to provide specialized control of military aircraft, and (c) the requirement to defend against possible attack by enemy air forces. Most of the procedures for airspace control and defense are theater specific. We will discuss the particular procedures used in the Gulf later in this chapter.

TACS in Support of Land Forces

Air attacks conducted to support ground forces are controlled in four ways: through (a) the Air Tasking Order (which assigns specific aircraft to ground-attack missions, often against specific targets), (b) the actions of Air Support Operations Centers (which schedule and coordinate the flights of forward air controllers), (c) Tactical Air Control Parties (which accompany ground units), and (d) ABCCC, a specially modified C-130 aircraft (which is an extension of the Combat Operations Division of the Tactical Air Control Center). Air Force missions in support of Army ground operations are under Air Force control. At the same time, such missions must respond to Army needs, and those needs will depend on the tactical situation in which Army maneuver units (battalions, brigades and divisions) find themselves.

When the Rapid Deployment Joint Task Force (RDJTF), the forerunner of USCENTCOM (U.S. Central Command), was formed in early 1980, the Air Force's Tactical Air Command (TAC) and the Army's Training and Doctrine Command (TRADOC) were completing new air-land battle procedures that placed less emphasis on the central region of Europe, had worldwide applicability for unilateral Army and Air Force operations, and focused on contingencies that were more likely to occur, such as defense of critical facilities in the Persian Gulf region. The new procedures also increased emphasis on defeating second echelon forces by extending the battlefield to include enemy forces that would have a near-term effect on air-land operations and require more detailed coordination between the air component commander (ACC)[18] and the land component commander (LCC) in the Air Tasking Order (ATO) development process.

The Army and Air Force components (later USARCENT and USCENTAF) of the Rapid Deployment Joint Task Force adopted the Tactical Air Command-Training and Doctrine Command procedures for use during exercises and contingency plans. The RDJTF evolved into the Unified Command for Southwest Asia, U.S. Central Command, which was activated on 1 January 1983. Although the new doctrine grew out of the "31 Initiatives"[19] Army-Air Force Agreement of 1982 and had its beginning as the first TAC-TRADOC "Camouflage Manual" addressing joint attack of the second echelon, (J-SAK) it had far-reaching implications beyond second echelon attack. The new doctrine recognized, for the first time, the concept of a single air component commander and land component commander and increased the amount of joint coordination required between land and air units in conducting tactical air support for land forces. To accomplish this increased coordination, the Army formed the Battlefield Coordination Element (BCE),[20] an organization of approximately twenty-five Army personnel to be collocated with the Tactical Air Control Center[21] during wartime with a mission to process land force requests for tactical air support, monitor and interpret the land battle situation for the Tactical Air Control Center, and provide the necessary coordination between air and land elements through face-to-face coordination with the air component headquarters and the Tactical Air Control Center.[22]

---

[18]Later referred to as the Joint Force Air Component Commander during joint or combined operations.

[19]Richard G. Davis, *The 31 Initiatives: A Study in Air Force - Army Cooperation* (Washington, DC, 1987).

[20]The Battlefield Coordination Element (BCE) " . . . is COMUSARCENT's [Commander, US Army Central Command] coordination agency which exchanges detailed operational and intelligence information with the . . . " Air Force's command and control organizations. "The BCE processes USARCENT's requests for tactical air support, monitors and interprets the USARCENT battle situation for the TACC, and provides the necessary interface for the exchange of current operational and intelligence data." (USCENTAF Regulation 55-45, *United States Central Command Air Force Air Employment Planning Process*, 27 Jun 1990, p 3-12).

[21]The TACC is described in detail in Chapter 5 of this report.

[22]TACP 50-29 and TRADOC Pam 525-45, *General Operating Procedures for Joint Attack of the Second Echelon*, 31 Dec 1984, p 3-1.

The new air-land battle procedures did not change organization or command, control, and communications in Air Force TACS units designed to support various land echelons; the overall tactical command and control system remained the Air Ground Operations System. The system still consisted of two parts, Air Force elements of the TACS dedicated to supporting the land component commander in conducting air-land operations, and Army Air Ground System elements which interact with TACS units to ensure that tactical air support is responsive and meets Army requirements.

The Tactical Air Control System and Army Air Ground System perform two functions in providing air support to land operations. First, they provide a conduit through which land force commanders at all levels can request air support. This conduit transfers requests (a) for immediate air support by troops engaging the enemy and (b) to strike targets which could affect future land operations. Second, the two systems' interaction is designed to prevent fratricide; they help pilots distinguish enemy from friendly forces and keep friendly ground forces from shooting down friendly aircraft.

How Command and Control for Close Air Support Works

The preceding paragraphs described the concept and historical context of tasking and control of air power in support of land operations. The remainder of this section will put the pieces together by describing how requests for air support, specifically close air support, flow from the requester to bombs or bullets on target. We must begin by explaining the two different types of requests for close air support, each with its own coordination or control channels: "immediate" requests, wherein air support is needed at once by the troops on the front lines, and "preplanned close air support," which comprises requests for support of future operations.

Requests for immediate close air support usually originate at the lowest levels of the land force's command structure–the individual platoon or company. These requests are made to a Tactical Air Control Party, where they are validated and then passed to the Air Support Operations Center.[23] The Air Support Operations Center, normally collocated with the Army Corps Tactical Operations Center, ranks the requests with

---

[23] TACPs at the intermediate echelons between the requester and ASOC can intervene if necessary. Silence by the intermediate TACPs usually means concurrence with the request.

those from other air control parties based upon urgency and the commander's operational plans.

From this point a description of the process becomes more complicated, because there are several routes a request could follow depending upon how the airspace is organized. It is feasible, depending upon available resources and the allocation of these resources, to have the airspace over the battlefield under the control of a Control and Reporting Center, Airborne Battlefield Command and Control Center, Airborne Warning and Control System, the Air Support Operations Center, or a combination. For example, if the Air Support Operations Center is controlling the close air support aircraft, the Air Support Operations Center simply calls on the radio to the available aircraft in their sector and direct them to the area where support is needed. If the Air Support Operations Center is controlling the airspace but does not have any aircraft available to support the request, it could call the Tactical Air Control Center and request support. The TACC will direct aircraft on airborne alert to the Air Support Operations Center's area of responsibility or, if necessary, launch aircraft from ground alert.[24]

In a more complicated example, we'll suppose that the Air Support Operations Center is not the controlling agency—assume that the subsector over the battlefield is controlled by Airborne Command, Control, and Communications, and that Airborne Warning and Control is controlling the entire sector. In this case, the ASOC would forward the request to ABCCC. If aircraft were available, ABCCC would direct them to the appropriate area. If aircraft were not available, ABCCC would contact the AWACS, which would direct aircraft from its resources into the subsector for ABCCC's control. If the AWACS was also short of resources, it, like the Air Support Operations Center in the case above, would contact the Tactical Air Control Center to divert or launch fixed-wing alert aircraft.

In our notional example, once the ASOC, ABCCC, AWACS, or CRC (which also could be controlling the airspace) directs the flight to the appropriate area, the flight is told to contact the forward air controller (FAC) (either airborne or on ground). The FAC helps the strike aircraft identify the target and friendly forces and directs the attack.

---

[24](S/NF) Multi-Command Manual (MCM) 3-1, *Tactical Employment*, Volume I, *General Planning and Employment Considerations*, 19 Dec 1986.

Preplanned close air support[25] is handled in a slightly different way. Requests for close air support of planned operations originate throughout the command and control system, from both staff agencies and field units–anyone who anticipates a need for air support. These requests are " . . . collected by the Battlefield Coordination Element of the TACC and prioritized to support ground force objectives."[26] From here the targets go through the planning process, are tasked in the Air Tasking Order,[27] and flown by the tasked unit.

TACS in Support of Air Operations

A major task of the Tactical Air Control System is to control friendly aircraft in flight. This is a multifaceted task with a number of objectives in mind. For example, the TACS:

(1) allows the Joint Force Air Component Commander the flexibility to retask aircraft en route to ensure effective and efficient application of air power within a very dynamic combat environment;

(2) ensures airborne control of where strike aircraft and tanker aircraft meet for pre- and poststrike aerial refueling;

(3) controls friendly airspace to deconflict air traffic and avoid midair collisions, much like a civilian air traffic control system; and

(4) identifies and tracks enemy aircraft to direct interceptions.

The system components described earlier are used by the JFACC to build a TACS to meet the specific needs of his operation. Since the procedures and rules of engagement that govern the operation of the airborne portion of the TACS are situationally dependent, we will not attempt to describe the many options available to the commander. The specific procedures used in the Gulf are discussed later in this chapter and in following chapters.

---

[25](S/NF) *Ibid.*

[26](S/NF) *Ibid*, p 4-3.

[27]The planning process and the Air Tasking Order are described in (S) Chapter 5.

Establishment of the Central Command Air Forces
TACS in the Theater

The immensity of the task of deploying, assembling, manning, and operating the TACS cannot be emphasized enough.[28] In the Gulf War, the U.S. Central Command Commander in Chief's initial mission was to "deploy to the area of operations and take actions in concert with host nation forces, friendly regional forces, and other allies to defend against an Iraqi attack into Saudi Arabia and be prepared to conduct other operations as directed."[29] This mission was enormously complex[30] and extremely risky.[31] The complexity of the task and the rapidly changing requirements of the mission simply could not be supported by the limited host nation command and control systems. Host Nation Command and

---

[28] Military leaders of both allies and former adversaries expressed great admiration for this phase of the operation. See, for example, "More Than an Operation, Less Than a War: Interview with Brig Gen 'Y,' *Beit'On Chel Ha'Avir*, January 1992 (translated by Aron Pinker).

[29] (S/NF) Msg, 101100Z Aug 90, USCINCCENT to Supporting Commands, subj: USCINCCENT Order for Operation Desert Shield. The military objectives for maritime interdiction were transmitted separately.

[30] For example, in the issue of transportation communications, Air Force Logistics Command (AFLC) declared that the Joint Operations Planning and Execution System, a component of WWMCCS, was not designed to accommodate the type of rapid changes as occurred in Desert Shield. In addition, no arrangements were made to ensure the proper flow of communications. See AFLC JULLS Number 01048-44637 DS90 Database. See also (S) *Logistics* report.

[31] (S) On 12 Aug 1990, Schwarzkopf's Combat Analysis Group argued that as of C+7, American and Saudi forces were insufficient to defend Al Jubayl against an attack by only three Iraqi divisions. (S/NF) AAR, CENTCOM J-5, Combat Analysis Group, 21 Mar 1991, p 7.

Lt Gen Horner described his thoughts about this situation in a public speech:

The idea was that we were to deter an Iraqi invasion of Saudi Arabia, and if an invasion did come we had to be prepared to defend .... Those were some of the worst nights of my life, because I had good information as to what the Iraqi threat was, and, quite frankly, we could not have issued speeding tickets to the tanks as they would have come rolling down the interstate highway on the east coast. It was an opportunity the Iraqis did not take, but every night we'd get some more forces, and we'd sit down and get a game plan of what we'd do if we came under attack. (Lt Gen Charles A. Horner, Speech to Business Executives for National Security, 8 May 1991.)

Control capabilities had to be augmented by Air Force equipment and personnel to accommodate the needs of the combined command.

Saudi AWACS

U.S./Saudi cooperation in the use of AWACS began in 1979, when the government of the United States permitted U.S. manufacturers to sell E-3 AWACS aircraft to Saudi Arabia. Under the Elf One program, the Air Force sent four of its own AWACS aircraft to supplement and exercise with the new Saudi AWACS force. The combined U.S./Saudi AWACS focused mainly on the threat of Iranian air action against Saudi Arabia during the war between Iraq and Iran. The nine-year effort familiarized numbers of U.S. AWACS aircrew and maintenance personnel with their Saudi 6th Flying Wing counterparts and with the facilities in Riyadh. Though the formal Elf One program ended in April 1990, the U.S. AWACS aircraft sent to Saudi Arabia as part of Desert Shield returned to the same facilities and quarters they had used during Elf One.[32]

Saudi AWACS aircraft were controlled from the Saudi Eastern Sector Control Center at Dhahran (as shown in Figure 12). This facility had ultra-high-frequency, line-of-sight radios to communicate with orbiting Saudi AWACS, and the AWACS themselves had the ability to communicate their airborne radar "picture" to escorting Saudi fighters flying combat air patrols. However, what the Saudis had in place in August 1990 was much different from the tactical air control system to which U.S. aircrews were accustomed. The Saudis, for example, had neither a Tactical Air Control Center nor an Air Support Operations Center. Their Eastern Sector Control Center was simply designed to keep Iranian aircraft from making surprise attacks on Saudi airfields and destroying Saudi aircraft on the ground.[33]

---

[32](S) Memo, "Notification and Employment," from Capt Guy Cafiero, to Task Force 4, Aug 1992, in GWAPS Task Force 4 AWACS File.

[33](S) Briefing, "Saudi Command and Control Structure," Surveillance Procedures Brief, Desert Shield, Captains J. Larson, E. McNamara, and K. Warburton, GWAPS Task Force 4 AWACS File.

Figure 12
Saudi Eastern Sector Control Center at Dhahran

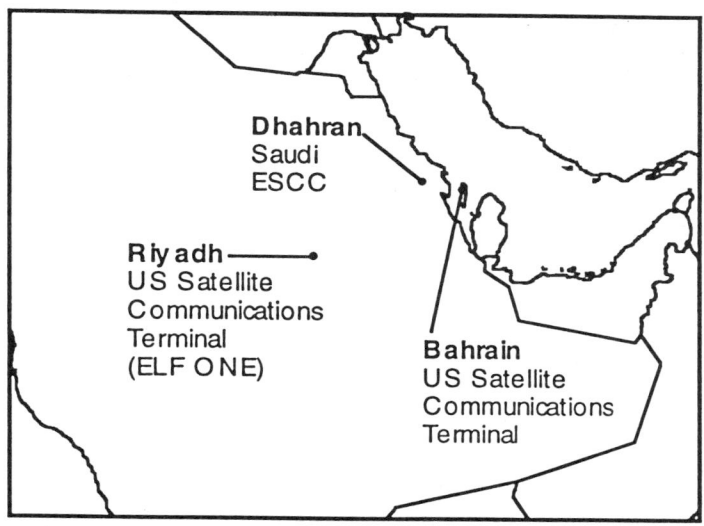

Existing Communications Facilities in Saudi Arabia

When Iraq invaded Kuwait, the United States had three small communications centers in the theater: one satellite communications terminal each in Bahrain and in Riyadh (which was being dismantled after being used to support Elf One operations[34]) and a terrestrial communications link between Bahrain and Dhahran.[35] There also were commercial satellite links at Riyadh and Dhahran (see Figure 12). However, the authors of Operations Plan 1002-90 had no illusions about the status of communications in place in Saudi Arabia. In April 1990, they noted that, if U.S. forces were committed to the defense of Saudi Arabia, "communications support will be austere with heavy reliance on early airlift and satellite systems."[36] Saudi Arabia had a digital commercial phone system, but it was not well developed throughout the country and did not extend to all

---

[34] (S) Intvw, Col Charles M. Pettijohn, Commander, 4409th OSW, 29 Dec 29 1990.

[35] James P. Coyne, *Airpower in the Gulf* (Arlington, VA, 1992), p 157.

[36] (S) USCINCCENT OPLAN 1002-90, "Outline Plan," 16 Apr 1990, p 32.

of the members of the Gulf Coordination Council.[37] Senior Saudi military leaders did not have secure high-frequency radio links to their own ground forces.[38] Finally, Saudi air defenses were so oriented toward the threat of an Iranian sneak attack that the Saudi government could not guarantee Central Command that the latter's command and communications equipment, once deployed, would be shielded from air attack by the larger and more capable Iraqi air force.[39]

Initial Deployment of AWACS

On 2 August, the 552d Airborne Control Wing at Tinker Air Force Base was notified to prepare to deploy five E-3 AWACS aircraft to Riyadh. The aircraft and their crews were ready to leave within a day. On 7 August, the aircraft were ordered to Saudi Arabia, and they reached Riyadh after a 17-hour nonstop flight. On 8 August, eight C-141s and three C-5s left Tinker with support equipment and over 400 operations, maintenance, and support personnel.[40] The first U.S. E-3 flew an orbit over Saudi Arabia on 10 August, escorted by F-15s of the 1st Tactical Fighter Wing.[41]

Though the 507th Tactical Air Control Wing, which manned the Ninth Air Force Tactical Air Control Center and its associated Message Processing Center in Riyadh, did not arrive in the theater from Shaw Air Force Base until 14 August, U.S. AWACS functioned effectively from the moment they flew. AWACS aircraft normally functioned as an element of the TACS–as an airborne extension of the Tactical Air Control Center and its associated ground-based radars.[42] However, if the TACC were attacked and damaged, or if its communications were disrupted, AWACS aircrew

---

[37] DOD, *Conduct of the Persian Gulf War*, p K-28.

[38] *Ibid*, p K-30.

[39] (FOUO) "AF/PRIS RSAF Transition Air Defense System Proposed," Version 2.0, 25 Jul 1990, pp 3-5.

[40] (S) Memo, "Notification and Employment," from Capt Guy Cafiero, to Task Force 4, Aug 1992, in GWAPS Task Force 4 AWACS File.

[41] (S) "Operations History," 552d Airborne Warning and Control Wing, History Office, Chap. II, p 19, Task Force 4 AWACS File, GWAPS.

[42] Brief, "AETACS," Tactical Air Command, 28th Air Division, 552d AWACS Wing, nd, Task Force 4 AWACS File, GWAPS.

could monitor and direct the fighters and electronic warfare aircraft that engaged in air-to-air combat and strikes against enemy targets.

U.S. AWACS aircraft had an advantage over their Saudi counterparts in this regard because one of the U.S. AWACS always carried an "Airborne Command Element," or "ACE team."[43] Headed by a colonel, the ACE team could, when necessary, assume the command authority of a Tactical Air Control Center over aircraft flying combat air patrol with an AWACS or over airborne strike formations preparing for an attack mission.[44] As Mission Director, the colonel heading the ACE team was responsible for seeing to it that COMUSCENTAF guidance, as set forth in the Air Tasking Order and Rules of Engagement, was followed. Usually, he was supported by five other officers: a deputy and specialists in fighter operations, intelligence, airborne refueling, and electronic warfare.[45] The presence of this trained team of combat planners and leaders gave U.S. AWACS the ability to direct air operations.

Because of the rapid deployment of AWACS aircraft and their support personnel, U.S. and Saudi E-3s could fly one, 'round-the-clock radar surveillance orbit by 17 August. This gave Central Command Air Forces a rudimentary defensive counterair capability. The obstacle to flying more orbits was numbers. Though an E-3 could fly, with midair refueling, a maximum of twenty-two hours, aircrew fatigue could limit flights to half that, or a bit more.[46] It also took about an hour for a fresh E-3 to fully relieve one which had been at its post, and an alert, back-up E-3 was always kept on the ground or in the air, in case the E-3 flying its orbit had a major equipment malfunction. [DELETED] Because of these considerations, E-3s initially flew shorter flights than they would have in, say, Europe, but they flew more flights to maintain the necessary coverage.

---

[43] USAF AWACS are E-3C variants and have significant upgrades over the E-3As sold to Saudi Arabia. The E-3C variants had a greater sensor and communications capability as well as provisions for HAVE QUICK antijamming equipment. Mark Lambert, ed, *Jane's All the Worlds Aircraft 1991-92* (Alexandria, VA, 1991), pp 364-5.

[44] Memo, "Airborne Command Element," from Capt Guy Cafiero, to Task Force 4, GWAPS, Aug 1992, in Task Force 4 AWACS File.

[45] Brief, "AWACS-ACE Integration," Maj Kevin Dunlevy, Jul 1992, Task Force 4 Special AWACS File, GWAPS.

[46] (S/NF) Multi-Command Manual (MCM) 3-1, *AWACS*, Vol. XV, see especially "E-3 Capabilities and Limitations."

This rotating schedule forced the E-3 crews and the AWACS personnel to work long hours. [DELETED]⁴⁷ The demands of the theater were already placing significant stress on the entire AWACS force.

It was crucial that the U.S. and Saudi AWACS fly, however, because the Tactical Air Control Center, its associated Message Processing Center in Riyadh, and the Control and Reporting Center in Dhahran were not operational by the 17th. The AWACS aircraft, supported by RC-135 RIVET JOINT aircraft (from the Strategic Air Command's 55th Strategic Reconnaissance Wing), were the first line of detection and control in the air defense of the coalition build-up in Saudi Arabia.⁴⁸

[DELETED]⁴⁹

By September, the basic elements of a mature Tactical Air Control System (including airborne and ground elements) were operational or in the process of becoming operational. The question was whether the TACS could shift from a defensive posture to an offensive one. In September, AWACS crews had begun preparing for offensive operations by developing a "Tactics Certification Program," which gave them practice in offensive counterair operations, search and rescue procedures, protecting certain "high value" assets (such as EF-111 electronic warfare aircraft), and controlling tanking operations.⁵⁰

---

⁴⁷[DELETED] (S) Brief, Lt Col Mark Benda, subj: "AWACS Availability and Proposed Changes," AF/XOOTC, 1 Nov 1990.

⁴⁸(S) Briefing, "AWACS & GND TACS," as of 17 Aug 1990, 0550, XO Brief, 17-18 Aug 1990, CSS Folder No. 166, CSS Safe No. 3, GWAPS. RIVET JOINT operations are described in R. S. Hopkins, III, "Ears of the Storm," *Air Force Magazine*, Vol. 75, No. 2 (Feb 1992).

⁴⁹(S) Strategic Reconnaissance Center, HQ Strategic Air Command, *RC-135 RIVET JOINT Integration Guide*, 30 Nov 1990.

⁵⁰Memo, "Desert Shield Tactics Certification Program," from 552d AWACW/DO, to All Crewmembers, nd, Task Force 4 AWACS File, GWAPS.

In September, the 552d AWACS Wing also set up a formal Tactics Planning Cell in the Tactical Air Control Center. The Cell planned daily AWACS missions, briefed AWACS crews, and compiled a set of "lessons learned." Members of the Cell also monitored the performance of AWACS personnel to see if the "Tactics Certification Program" training was in fact working. Within the Cell, a Mission Planning Team took the daily Air Tasking Order and provided those parts of it (especially the communications instructions) necessary to effective AWACS coordination of airborne operations to the AWACS crews. (S) "Deployed Tactics Cell Responsibilities (for Large Force E-3 Deployments)," 552d

Central Command Air Force communications personnel also worked to improve the communications between the Tactical Air Control Center in Riyadh and the AWACS aircraft in their orbits in northern Saudi Arabia. [DELETED][51,52,53] [DELETED][54,55]

AWACS E-3s flew four orbits: one over the eastern part of the border area, a second over the central portion, a third over the western part, and a fourth–working as a back-up–near King Khalid Military City.[56] [DELETED][57] Figure 13 displays these orbits.

By the end of October, CENTAF was ready to test its maturing AWACS system. Beginning 0600Z on 25 October, E-3s from the 552d AWACS Wing and the Saudi 6th Flying Wing flew four continuous orbits for the next 36 hours. According to an official account, "The operation was tasked through the CENTAF daily ATO and involved nearly every flying unit in-theater."[58] Combined, the Saudi and U.S. units flew almost 200 hours;

AWACS Wing Tactics Planning Cell Continuity Book, Sep 1990, Task Force 4 Special AWACS File, GWAPS.

[51]Figure 13 depicts the general orbit areas that the AWACS aircraft flew during Desert Storm. The distance from the Central AWACS Orbit over Rahfa was approximately 400 miles from the TACC in Riyadh. An AWACS orbiting around 35,000 feet, given near perfect atmospheric conditions, would have a line-of-sight UHF range of about 250 miles to ground-based UHF receivers. Increasing the altitude of the AWACS to increase the line-of-sight range does not necessarily increase the range of the UHF radio. In general, the effective range of an UHF radio depends on the power output of the transmitter and the gain of the receiver. Letter, HQ 552d AWACW Provisional/DOW to MCCs and ASOs, Capt Kirk R. Warburton, 25 Feb 1991.

[52][DELETED]

[53][DELETED]

[54](S) "552D Airborne Warning and Control Wing," Operations History, p 24.

[55]Col Randy Witt, ed (DCS, Communication and Computer Systems, HQ USCENTAF and 9th AF, Headquarters United States Central Command Air Forces, Riyadh, Saudi Arabia, Mar 1991), *Air Force Tactical Communications in War, the Desert Shield/Desert Storm Comm Story*, pp 2-10 and 2-11.

[56](S) Chart, 552d AWAC Wing, Capt E. McNamara, Sep 1990, in Task Force 4 AWACS File, GWAPS.

[57](S) "Surveillance Procedures Briefing," Tactics Planning Cell, Training Program, Capts J. Larson, E. McNamara, and R. Wolarer, in Task Force 4 AWACS File, GWAPS.

[58](S) "Surge Operations Procedures, 24-26 Oct 1990," Capt S. Chewning, 552d AWACS Wing, in Task Force 4 AWACS File, GWAPS.

about three-fourths of that time was spent on station. E-3s refueled 17 times and controlled 96 fighters, 350 strike aircraft, and 110 tankings.[59]

Figure 13
AWACS Orbits over Saudi Arabia

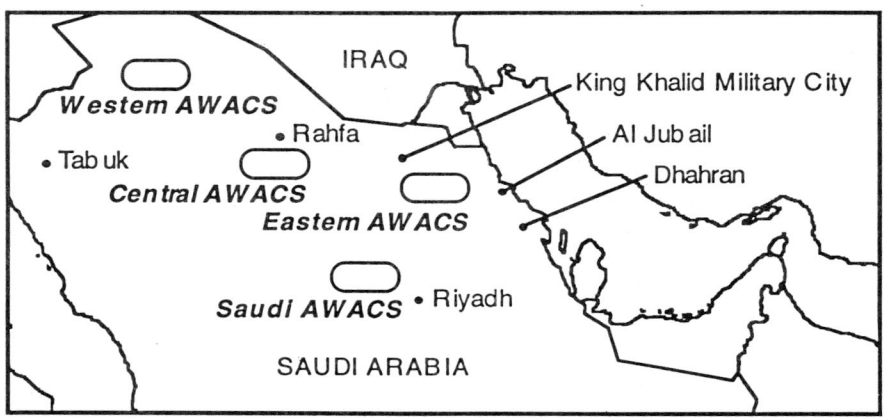

The exercise was a success. It demonstrated that both U.S. and Saudi control centers could be linked simultaneously with the orbiting AWACS. It also showed that adjacent E-3s could "cover" for one another while one refueled and that adjacent AWACS aircraft could avoid interfering with one another's radar transmissions. The exercise also substantiated the value of having a back-up or "goalie" AWACS. It also proved that a voice and digital net could link all the major air control centers in the theater. As the 552nd Wing's report noted, the AWACS aircraft maintained "a massive JTIDS and Link 11 [for the Navy] picture that spanned comm connectivity throughout the theater, as well as mutual strike and CAP [combat air patrol] responsibilities."[60] With the completion of this exercise, U.S. and coalition AWACS units had shown that the airborne coordination of a massive air campaign against Iraq was possible; the AWACS component of the Tactical Air Control System was ready for war.

---

[59] (S) "Surge Operations Procedures, 24-26 Oct 1990."

[60] (S) "Surge Operations Procedures, 24-26 Oct 1990," para 8.

Airborne Battlefield Command and Control Center

On 26 August, the aircraft and personnel of the 7th Airborne Command and Control Squadron deployed to Sharjah airfield in the United Arab Emirates. Within a day of its deployment, the Squadron had one ABCCC aircraft on alert; within three days, the Squadron was prepared for 'round-the-clock wartime operations.[61] Ninth Air Force had already deployed its Battlefield Coordination Element on 14 August, as part of the movement of the elements of the TACC.[62] Similarly, the 682d Air Support Operations Center deployed with the elements of the XVIIIth Airborne Corps.[63] Central Command Air Forces judged its Tactical Air Control System, the overall architecture necessary to execute full-scale operations, operational by 9 September.[64]

The 7th Airborne Command and Control Squadron deployed even though it was short five of its authorized twelve Director, Airborne Battlestaff positions. One Director was left behind at Keesler AFB to conduct acceptance testing of the new ABCCC "capsules."[65] CENTAF staff rounded up another two officers who could serve as Directors. The other positions went unfilled. Despite this handicap, the Squadron organized enough battlestaffs to support initially deployed Army units.[66] To com-

---

[61](S) "7th Airborne Command and Control Squadron (7 ACCS)," Lessons Learned, Para: "Unit Introduction," nd, Task Force 4 ABCCC File, GWAPS.

[62]"Observations on Joint Combat Operations at Echelons Above Corps," Lt Col W. G. Welch, US Army, *Air Land Bulletin*, TAC-TRADOC Alfa, No. 92-1 (31 Mar 1992), p 14.

[63]Rpt, "Northern Area Command," Lt Col M. Simek, US Army, in "Desert Storm Conference–Lessons Learned," 712 ASOC, Bergstrom AFB, TX, nd, Task Force 4 ABCCC File, GWAPS.

[64](S) "Concept of Operations, Tactical Air Request Net, CAS, Interdiction and ABCCC," 9 Sep 1990, GWAPS Microfilm Roll Number 23603, Frames 1054-1066.

[65]The "capsule" is a module containing communications equipment and battlestaff consoles, each with high-resolution cathode ray tube multicolor displays. The capsule III replaces capsule II, which was an upgraded version of a system developed in 1964 and used in Vietnam. See Peter Rackham, ed, *Jane's C^3I Systems 1991-92* (Alexandria, VA, 1991), p 78.

[66]"7th Airborne Command and Control Squadron (7 ACCS)," Lessons Learned, No. 11, "Undermanning of Critical Crewmember Positions," nd, Task Force 4 ABCCC File, GWAPS. Each ABCCC squadron normally flew six aircraft and twelve crews, allowing the squadron to keep one aircraft in the air at all times. In September, the 7th ACCS could only field ten crews and eight Directors.

municate with the deployed Marine Corps Direct Air Support Center, ABCCC aircraft began carrying Marine officers on 11 September. By 20 September, the Marine liaison officers could maintain reliable and constant contact with their Direct Air Support Center colleagues.[67]

A month after arriving in the theater, the 7th Airborne Command and Control Squadron and its six aircraft were moved to Riyadh. That put the ABCCC crews in close contact with the Battlefield Coordination Element personnel in the Tactical Air Control Center. This was essential if the two groups were to work out a concept of operations for the ABCCC, sell it to Lieutenant General Horner, and then train for it.[68] At about the same time, a Marine liaison officer flying on an ABCCC aircraft first directed CENTAF attack aircraft in coordination with the Marine Direct Air Support Center.[69] Joint Service coordination of air-ground operations was a reality.

The crew of the orbiting ABCCC could talk to aircraft in its area, as well as to the Tactical Air Control Center and the Air Support Operations Centers. It would do the same for forward air controllers and the Marine Direct Air Support Center. [DELETED] For these reasons, the ABCCC battlestaff was very dependent on having the Air Tasking Order as a guide to the types and numbers of aircraft it would have to control during a mission cycle.

ABCCC battlestaffs successfully controlled air-ground action during the major exercise of 25-26 October 1990. The exercise was the first large one which covered all the coalition and allied forces. Central Command Air Forces flew approximately 600 close air support sorties each day of the exercise to test its concept of operations, with apparent success.[70] From it, CENTAF drew four lessons. First, the multinational character[71]

---

[67](S) "ABCCC Marine Liaison Team Det Chronology," 5 Mar 1991, USMC Liaison Team, 7th ACC Squadron, in Task Force 4 ABCCC File, GWAPS.

[68] "7th Airborne Command and Control Squadron (7 ACCS)," Lessons Learned, "Unit Introduction."

[69](S) "ABCCC Marine Liaison Team Det Chronology," 5 Mar 1991.

[70](S) Memo, "Desert Shield Training and Exercises," USCENTAF, 20 Mar 1991.

[71] One officer described the situation as a "federation of tribes." (This description is attributed to LtC M. Simek, U.S. Army, in the Northern Area Command's "After Action Report." Desert Storm Conference, "Lessons Learned," 712 ASOC, Bergstrom AFB, TX.) Each "tribe" had its own communications equipment acquired from a variety of sources. Some of the equipment was incompatible with that of other "tribes."

of the Northern Area Command meant that its tactical air control parties could not contact the Combined Air Support Operations Center directly via the U.S. HF Tactical Air Request Net. Instead, their requests for air support had to be radioed (via UHF) to a senior air control party selected by the Joint Force Air Component Commander. The latter would review their requests, set priorities among them, and then pass the ranked requests to the Combined Air Support Operations Center, where they would be reviewed again, this time by Saudi or American army officers. The need for this two-stage review process was the second lesson drawn from the major exercise. The third lesson was that ABCCC battlestaff could indeed serve as the Joint Force Air Component Commander's on-scene, air-ground battle managers, allocating "push CAS" to "the most lucrative targets."[72] The fourth lesson was that British air liaison officers, trained to NATO air support standards, could work as an integral part of the U.S. Tactical Air Control System.[73]

In December, CENTAF attack aircraft flew night exercise attacks against U.S. Army formations to practice identifying targets and to refine the command and control of air-ground operations. The lessons learned in these (and other) practice sessions were codified in CENTAF's "Concept of Operations for Command and Control of TACAIR in Support of Land Forces," issued 1 January 1991. This directive made specific the guidance later implemented during Desert Storm. Specifically,

a. close air support took place only short of the Fire Support Coordination Line and required "the supported ground commander's clearance . . . ";

b. air interdiction sorties tasked in the Air Tasking Order but without a "preplanned target" were to be directed to kill zones by ABCCC;

---

[72](S) "Concept of Operations, CAS, Interdiction and the TACS," 22 Nov, Change 1, CENTAF, GWAPS Microfilm No. 23654, Frames 413-421.

[73]Intvw, Col Donald Kellum, USAF (Ret), with Lt Col R. E. Duncan, Chief USCENTAF TACS Division, 1 Jul 1992, Shaw AFB, SC.

c. kill zones beyond the Fire Support Coordination Line were "assumed to be open unless closed by the TACC DCO [display console operator]" those short of the Line could only be opened by "the applicable land component force commander";

d. Air Support Operations Centers and the Marine Corps Direct Air Support Center were to give attacking aircraft "a Forward Air Controller (FAC) call sign, contact frequency, and contact point";

e. preplanned close air support sorties whose targets were already struck were open to ABCCC direction into a kill zone; and

f. untargeted air interdiction sorties would be directed into a kill zone by ABCCC.[74]

This concept of operations made the ABCCC "an airborne extension" of the Combined Tactical Air Control Center.[75] By January 1991, Central Command Air Forces possessed *all* of the Air Force's ABCCC aircraft, and their crews and communications were tested in a three-day exercise conducted at the end of the first week of that month.[76]

Joint Surveillance Target Attack Radar System

The Joint Surveillance Target Attack Radar System (JSTARS) was the product of a joint Air Force/Army project to develop a sensor and controller that would do for the ground battle what AWACS had done for the air battle. JSTARS was still in full-scale engineering development in 1990; no operational tests had been conducted by the Air Force and Army on the whole system when it was deployed to Saudi Arabia in 1991.

JSTARS was developed to aid air-ground coordination in attacks against second echelon forces of the Warsaw Pact on the NATO front.

---

[74](S) "Concept of Operations for Command and Control of TACAIR in Support of Land Forces," (hereafter "Concept of Operations," 1 Jan 1991), 1 Jan 1991, USCENTAF/DO, Combat Plans, Task Force 4 ABCCC File, GWAPS, Section 3 and Section 5.

[75](S) "Concept of Operations," 1 Jan 1991, Section 6.

[76](S) Msg, 2244Z, 15 Jan 1991, from Joint Staff, Washington, to USCINCCENT, CC-J3, subj: "Airborne Relay Command and Control Units."

JSTARS itself is basically a combination of five subsystems: (a) a modified Boeing 707, which serves as the airborne platform; (b) an advanced radar which can focus on moving targets or on terrain features; (c) an operations and control display and software integration package which processes radar returns and generates target graphics; (d) a secure voice and data link which ties the JSTARS aircraft to other aircraft and to ground terminals; and (e) an Army-developed Ground Station Module which allows Army personnel attached to corps commands to analyze radar data sent from the plane via a special Surveillance and Control Data Link.[77]

JSTARS was not supposed to become operational until the mid-1990s, but it was deployed in the Gulf War because of a set of successful developmental exercises staged in Europe in September and October 1990. One witness to these controlled tests was Lt. Gen. Frederick Franks, commander of the Army's VII Corps. Franks and his superior, NATO commander Gen. John Galvin, recommended JSTARS to General Schwarzkopf, and the latter asked for a briefing on the system.[78] The briefing, given by a team of officers from the Tactical Air Command, the Army's Training and Doctrine Command, and the military agencies developing the system, warned General Schwarzkopf that JSTARS was by no means a completed system. What it could do was search for moving targets across the likely front, conduct a detailed real-time radar search of a much smaller ground area, and provide the data needed to build maps of areas swept by its radars. [DELETED][79]

Even with these limitations, Schwarzkopf asked for JSTARS soon after being briefed; the Joint Chiefs ordered the Air Force and Army to deploy the system on 21 December. General Schwarzkopf had been told that using JSTARS would cost a lot of money (about a million dollars per day), but, as he told Col. George K. Muellner of the Tactical Air Command, who briefed him on the system, he didn't care if deployment cost a

---

[77]"Concept of Operations for the Joint Surveillance Target Attack Radar System (Joint STARS)," Section I, HQ Tactical Air Command/XPJB, GWAPS Microfilm No. 10238, Frames 382-442.

[78]Intvw, Thomas C. Hone, Maj Anne D. Leary, and Mark D. Mandeles, with Brig Gen George K. Muellner, Deputy Chief of Staff for Requirements, HQ TAC/DR, Langley AFB, 16 Apr 1992.

[79](S/NF/WN) Briefing, "Joint STARS, Support of Desert Shield," GWAPS Microfilm Roll No. 10238, Frames 443-475, nd (the actual presentation was 17 Dec; see brief, "Joint STARS, Desert Storm," by Brig Gen G. Muellner, TAC, and Col M. Kleiner, TRADOC, in Task Force 4 Joint STARS File, GWAPS).

billion dollars a day–he meant to have JSTARS.[80] Muellner, his associates at Tactical Air Command and the Army's Training and Doctrine Command, contractor employees, and personnel from the Air Force Systems Command began preparing for the move to the Middle East. One of their tasks was to prepare a detailed "concept of operations" that would inform the users of the system of its capabilities and limitations. As Muellner recalled later, "there was nobody on the execution side that really understood the system."[81] They also had to get two aircraft ready (remember that these aircraft were test platforms) and assemble as many working Ground Station Modules (each of which was built on an Army five-ton truck) as possible.

At the beginning of January 1991, the Tactical Air Command's Deputy Chief of Staff, Requirements formally warned the Air Force Chief of Staff of the risk in sending JSTARS to the Middle East. The software was "only two-thirds complete," communications on the aircraft were being altered to fit those in use in the theater, system operators were not prepared for combat, and maintenance and logistics were primitive.[82] To make JSTARS work, the Air Force would have to deploy civilian industry and government technical personnel who had never served in combat positions.[83]

On 9 January 1991, the Tactical Air Command and the Air Force Systems Command agreed on a concept of operations for JSTARS.[84] On 11 January, the two E-8A aircraft flew nonstop to Saudi Arabia. Colonel Muellner had convinced General Horner to base the aircraft with the AWACS and RIVET JOINT aircraft at Riyadh. Muellner believed that the three airborne systems would work together better if they were based together. Muellner also recalled that Central Command Air Forces head-

---

[80] Intvw, Hone, Leary, and Mandeles with Brig Gen G. K. Muellner, 16 Apr 1992. According to the TAC Historian's account, CENTCOM first requested Joint STARS in *August* 1990. See Chap. 3, "Requirements," *1990 TAC History*, HQ TAC/HO.

[81] Intvw, Hone, Leary, and Mandeles with Brig Gen G. K. Muellner, 16 Apr 1992.

[82] (S) Ltr, proposed, from HQ TAC, Office of the Commander, to Chief of Staff of the Air Force, 4 Jan 1991, CC-010706, in Task Force 4 Joint STARS File, GWAPS.

[83] TAC's *1990 History* (Chapter III, p 16) noted that the newly created 4411th Joint STARS Squadron had sixty Air Force personnel, five from the Army, and sixty-eight from private industry. The Ground Station Module detachment had forty-two Army personnel and seven from industry.

[84] (S) Draft, "Desert Shield Concept of Operations," 9 Jan 1991, GWAPS Microfilm Roll Number 10238, Frames 476-522.

quarters was ten minutes away, while Central Command was twelve minutes off, and "Gen Yeosock's ARCENT [Army Central Command] was right there in the city."[85] The six Ground Support Modules (one came from the United Kingdom) were sent to the headquarters of the XVIII and VII corps, Marines Central Command, ARCENT Forward, ARCENT (for use by CENTCOM J-2), and CENTAF's Tactical Air Control Center.

JSTARS (above) was the product of a joint Air Force/Army project.

The JSTARS "Employment Concept" stated that "USCENTAF will use JSTARS as an aid to destroy and disrupt enemy forces through real time targeting."[86] This was in line with Army expectations, especially those of Lt. Gen. Franks.[87] However, formal operational control of JSTARS was in the hands of the Commander in Chief, U.S. Central Command, who was to "provide guidance and direction for JSTARS employment."[88] This established the potential for conflict between the Joint Force Air

---

[85]Intvw, Hone, Leary, and Mandeles with Brig Gen G. K. Muellner, 16 Apr 1992.

[86](S) "USCENTAF Joint Surveillance and Target Attack Radar System (Joint STARS) Employment Concept," GWAPS Microfilm Roll Number 10238, Frames 523-532.

[87]Intvw, Hone, Leary, and Mandeles with Brig Gen G. K. Muellner, USAF, 16 Apr 1992.

[88](S) USCENTAF, "Joint STARS Employment Concept," Section II–"Command and Control," Microfilm Roll No. 10238, Frames 523-532.

Component Commander and CENTCOM J-2 over JSTARS tasking. The "Employment Concept," for example, noted that "The JFACC exercises operational command and control over JSTARS through the CENTAF Deputy Commander for Operations. Requirements for JSTARS . . . support from ground component commands will be consolidated by USCENTCOM/J2 and will then be passed to the JFACC/TACC."[89] Put another way, JSTARS was given two missions: real-time targeting and intelligence.

The "Employment Concept" laid out a pattern of operations for real-time JSTARS applications. The JSTARS crew would update the locations of interdiction targets as attack aircraft entered kill zones; AWACS controllers would "hand off" attacking aircraft to JSTARS for "refined target coordinates."[90] For close air support, JSTARS, with the permission of the appropriate Air Support Operations Center or of the Marine Corps Direct Air Support Center, would pass target coordinates to close air support flights.[91] This policy gave the weapons controllers on JSTARS an important role in both interdiction and close air support.

Developing a Communications Infrastructure

Before continuing with a description of the developing Tactical Air Control System, it is important to discuss the creation of the communications infrastructure which tied together the system's ground elements (such as the Tactical Air Control Center) and those in the air (AWACS and ABCCC, for example). The construction of this infrastructure—this complex network of communications—proceeded along with the deployment of the elements of the TACS. The infrastructure itself also served many users besides those who formed the TACS. Satellite communications, for example, were used to send intelligence data to the theater and route requests for spare parts from the theater to bases in the United States. Most of the communications network built in the theater was not involved with the operations of the TACS. However, the evolution of the network affected the strength of the TACS; that is, as the former grew more sophisticated, the elements of the latter became more integrated.

---

[89](S) USCENTAF, "Joint STARS Employment Concept," Section III–"Concept of Employment," para D, Microfilm Roll No. 10238, Frames 523-532.

[90](S) USCENTAF, "Joint STARS Employment Concept," Section III–"Concept of Employment," para F.2.b., Microfilm Roll No. 10238, Frames 523-532.

[91]*Ibid*, para F.3.

No matter what the Saudi government could offer in the way of communications support, Central Command planned to deploy its own communications equipment and personnel. On 8 August 1990 the initial communications package for CENTCOM arrived in the theater (without support from the Joint Operational Planning Execution System[92]). This package, the Joint Communications Support Element (JCSE), included a "super high frequency (SHF) multichannel satellite terminal, several ultra high frequency (UHF) single-channel tactical satellite (TACSAT) terminals, and associated terminal equipment, to provide secure voice, facsimile and Defense Switched Network (DSN), Automatic Digital Network (AUTODIN), and Worldwide Military Command and Control System connectivity."[93] The Joint Communications Support Element[94] linked Riyadh to Washington through the Worldwide Military Command and Control System (WWMCCS). It also allowed Central Command Forward to establish UHF tactical satellite links to U.S. forces deploying to the theater.[95]

Central Command Air Forces communications were slower to arrive. The CENTAF Advanced Echelon of twenty-two people arrived in the theater on 8 August. Their initial contact with the CENTAF and CENTCOM rear elements was not accomplished until 10 August, using the ultra-high-frequency tactical satellite system that they had installed in the basement of the Royal Saudi Air Force Headquarters building in Riyadh.[96] Contact between CENTAF and its deploying units was established by telephone and through the tactical satellite communications equipment at Elf One, which, though then manned by "liaison personnel only," was alongside

---

[92] The Joint Operational Planning Execution System (JOPES) is a manual and software system used by TRANSCOM to assemble transportation requirements, such as TPFDDs. JOPES was not flexible enough to be used for initial crisis planning, and was not usable until after C+12. (S/NF/NC/ORCON) Briefing, HQ TAC, "Desert Storm Lessons Learned," in USAF Desert Shield/Desert Storm Hot Wash, Maxwell AFB, AL, 12-13 Jul 1991.

[93] *Conduct of the Persian Gulf War*, p K-27.

[94] The JCSE is organized under the Chairman, Joint Chiefs of Staff. Its purpose is to provide tactical command, control, and communication support for operations by the unified and specified commands. The JSCE deployed to the Riyadh included both UHF and SHF SATCOM radios, line-of-sight radios, HF radios, and circuit and message switching equipment (*Conduct of the Persian Gulf War*, p 27).

[95] *Conduct of the Persian Gulf War*, pp K-27, K-28.

[96] *Air Force Tactical Communications in War, the Desert Shield/Desert Storm Comm Story,* Colonel Randy Witt, ed, DCS, Communication and Computer Systems, HQ USCENTAF and 9th AF, Headquarters United States Central Command Air Forces, Riyadh, Saudi Arabia, Mar 1991.

the Saudi AWACS control center.[97] As the *Plans* report of the Survey shows, the Commander in Chief, Central Command had chosen to change the priority for the shipment of forces into the theater to favor combat units.[98] One result was that communications units arrived slower than planned.[99] Without the planned communications support, Tactical Air Control Center personnel were forced to find alternative means of communicating with their deployed units. For example, the TACC sent out initial Air Tasking Orders to U.S. wings through the Airlift Control Center tactical satellite computer interface and via high-frequency, "quick-reaction package" equipment in airlifted vans.[100]

Deploying fighter aircraft wings also lacked communications support. On 8 August 1990, for example, F-15s flying from Langley AFB, Virginia, landed at Dhahran without their dedicated combat communications unit. Until the latter arrived from Warner Robbins AFB, Georgia, three days later, the deploying unit relied on Secure Telephone Units (STU-IIIs) and a small Rapid Initial Communications Kit (which linked with UHF tactical satellites) to talk to CENTAF. The wing initially received the Air Tasking Order in hard copy form from Military Airlift Command C-21s, which flew nightly circuits among the airfields where U.S. aircraft deployed.[101]

This delay was typical. In early August 1990, combat communication equipment from three stateside locations in Georgia, Florida, and Oklahoma arrived in theater 3 to 14 days after the aviation package it supported. By the eighth day of deployment, only four C-141 equivalent loads of communications equipment had been moved.[102] The discrepancy

---

[97] "Air Force Tactical Communications in War," p 1-7; (S) Intvw, Col. Charles M. Pettijohn, Commander, 4409th OSW, 29 Dec 1990.

[98] See also H. Norman Schwarzkopf with Peter Petre, *It Doesn't Take a Hero* (New York, 1992), pp 306, 310-12.

[99] (S/NF/NC/ORCON) Briefing, HQ TAC, "Desert Storm Lessons Learned," in USAF Desert Shield/Desert Storm Hot Wash, Maxwell AFB, AL, 12-13 Jul 1991. See (S) Table 5-1, below, for comparison of projected and actual dates for receipt of selected key communications equipment.

[100] "Air Force Tactical Communications in War," pp 1-7 and 1-8. This "fix" was possible because the first Air Tasking Orders were relatively short.

[101] (S) Ltr, Col James Crigger, Jr., DCS/O, USCENTAF FWD/DO to COMALF ALCC, subj: C-21 Taskings, 21 Aug 1990.

[102] (S) Briefing, TAC Desert Shield Lessons Learned, Jun 1991.

between the planned and actual movement of communications support meant there were only 135 USAF communications technicians in the Gulf, instead of the planned 1,128. Moreover, it was difficult to locate and activate much of the communications manpower destined for deployment.[103] More than two-thirds of Air Force combat communications personnel deployed to the Gulf were part of the Air National Guard and Reserves, and these specialists could not be called up for extended service without a Presidential order.[104] Table 6 illustrates the difference between the planned and actual numbers of communications systems and personnel in-theater.

On 12 August the Saudi Government agreed to merge its commercial phone system with the tactical phone networks of CENTCOM's components.[105] This move opened the way for the construction of an in-theater telephone network based upon the Secure Telephone Unit (STU-III). STU-IIIs were used extensively to provide secure voice and fax communication capabilities as CENTCOM and CENTAF forces deployed to the theater. Maj. Dave Schultz, one of the initial communications Advanced Echelon personnel who arrived in the theater on 8 August 1990, noted

> Host nation commercial telephone service was the most readily available source of communications, but we had to follow a bureaucratic process, tightly controlled by the Saudis to obtain these lines, which ultimately required a formal request from the USCENTAF/CC to the RSAF [Royal Saudi Air Force] commander. Once this was accomplished, we were able to acquire the remaining seven internal lines available in the RSAF building and use STU-IIIs brought over with the ADVON [Advanced

---

[103] Difficulties in locating manpower were partly a result of not initiating an immediate reserves call-up, and the rotation policy of Guard volunteers.

[104] Intvw, Maj Anne D. Leary and Mark D. Mandeles with Brig Gen Bruce J. Bohn, 23 Mar 1992. The shortage of personnel *stayed* critical. On 26 Nov 1990, for example, the Air Force Chief of Staff informed CENTAF Rear at Langley AFB that "The combat communications units have deployed all available assets and personnel." That is, the Air Force could not support CENTAF's request for additional equipment and personnel by drawing on regular or Air National Guard units. (S) Msg, from NGB Andrews AFB, MD, to USCENTAF Rear, Langley AFB, VA, subj: "Selected reserve Call-Up of TTC-39A UTC for Operation Desert Shield."

[105] *Ibid*, p 1-8.

Echelons] package for secure voice communications to the rest of the world.[106]

Table 6

Gulf War Communications
Planned versus Actual[107]

[DELETED]

The STU-III hooks quickly into any digital telephone system and, when in secure mode, automatically encodes voice or digital messages sent over it. As noted in the Title V Report, use of the STU-IIIs, especially for transmitting data from personal computers, was "unprecedented" during the first month of Desert Shield.[108] However, the extensive use of STU-IIIs was an undesirable alternative; using the STU-IIIs to link computers "degraded secure voice service and restricted computers to low data-interchange rates."[109] Given the state of Saudi Arabia's communications infrastructure and the inability to get other forms of communications to the theater, there were no other options. Deployed wings needed information—especially the daily Air Tasking Orders.

The widespread use of the STU-IIIs caused some headaches for Central Command and Central Command Air Forces, however. As one senior officer noted, "a lot of people picked up their STU-IIIs and took them with

---

[106]*Air Force Tactical Communications in War, The Desert Shield/Desert Storm Comm Story,* ed by Colonel Randy Witt, DCS, Communications and Computer Systems, HQ USCENTAF and HQ 9th AF, Headquarters United States Central Command Air Forces, Riyadh, Saudi Arabia, Mar 1991.

[107](S/NF/NC/ORCON) Briefing, HQ TAC, "Desert Storm Lessons Learned," in USAF Desert Shield/Desert Storm Hot Wash, Maxwell AFB, AL, 12-13 Jul 1991.

[108](S) Department of Defense, *Conduct of the Gulf War* (Washington, DC, 1992), p K-41. (There also is an unclassified version of this report.)

[109](S) *Ibid,* p K-41.

them."[110] This had not been anticipated, and, in consequence, the ground radios sent with the deploying wings were not compatible with the unexpected STU-IIIs.[111] This was a technical problem, eventually fixed. Harder to solve was the diplomatic problem caused by the Saudis' desire to possess the STU-IIIs, which were based on a sensitive technology; the Saudis had never before been given access to it. To satisfy the coalition, the National Security Agency, which set policy for the use of cryptographic equipment, modified a commercial version of the STU-III (the SVX-2400) and distributed sets to Arab forces in September.[112] An SVX-2400, however, could only communicate with another of its type; it could not link with a STU-III. Neither could the SVX-2400s work with the STU-IIs used by NATO forces. As a result, U.S. commanders had to use multiple phones and lines to talk to all the members of the coalition.[113] Finally, the Saudis demanded a lot more SVX-2400s than Central Command or the National Security Agency had anticipated, and the need to service all the additional phone sets placed a major burden on deployed Agency personnel.[114]

The need for so many phone lines threatened to swamp the tactical satellites being used in the theater as well as the Saudi phone system. The advantage of the Defense Department's voice switched phone network was (and is) its priority levels, so that urgent calls can take precedence over routine communications. Even so, users state their own priority level, and the system is open to abuse–normally not a problem because of the large capacity of the network. During Desert Shield, however, so-called "priority" input quickly overwhelmed the network's capacity; in late September, only sixty-five percent of users were gaining access to the system on the first try. Central Command Air Forces got access to the network under control by the beginning of Desert Storm, but only by sharply limiting the number of "morale" calls from Air Force units in the theater to the United States "Official" calls were given strict

---

[110]Intvw, Maj Anne Leary and Mark Mandeles, with Brig Gen Bruce J. Bohn, 23 Mar 1992.

[111]*Ibid.*

[112]"Air Force Tactical Communications in War," p 2-38.

[113]*Ibid*, pp 2-38 and 2-39.

[114]*Ibid*, pp 2-40 through 2-43.

precedence.[115] Central Command also helped by constructing a network of microwave transmission towers which handled calls among bases in the United Arab Emirates, Qatar, Bahrain, and Saudi Arabia.[116]

While the lack of infrastructure for rapid, reliable, and secure data communications within the theater forced CENTCOM and CENTAF, as more personnel deployed, to rely on voice messages passed over the STU-IIIs, other equipment–satellite terminals and dishes, and high- frequency transmitters and receivers–was pressed into service as soon as it reached the theater. CENTCOM's command and control problem was to take this equipment as it came and organize it into an effective network. Brig. Gen. Roscoe M. Cougill, USAF, Central Command's director of communications and computers, later observed, "We were building our communications . . . as the forces deployed. We built, modified and remodified on a daily basis."[117] CENTCOM and CENTAF forces deployed, communications personnel responded, and CENTAF's super high-frequency network was largely in place by the end of August.[118]

Early in August, however, Central Command Air Forces and Central Command communicators differed over the kind of satellite links they thought the theater should have. CENTAF communications planners wanted to link Air Force units deploying to Riyadh and Dhahran directly to the Defense Satellite Communications System through Ground Mobile Forces "gateways."[119] CENTCOM J-6 feared that allowing CENTAF to put such a system in place would lead to multiple direct links (through multiple "gateways") to satellites from major units of the other Services. That,

---

[115]"Air Force Tactical Communications in War," pp 1-16 and 1-17. According to (S) HQ, US Central Command *After Action Report*, 15 Jul 1991 (p 20), the voice switched network handled a maximum of 700,000 telephone calls a day.

[116]"Air Force Tactical Communications in War," pp 4-6 and 4-7. The microwave towers began as a back-up to the tactical satellites but eventually became the primary communications system within much of the theater. However, it took three months just to gain Saudi approval to build the microwave towers.

[117]Coyne, *Airpower in the Gulf*, p 158.

[118]Intvw, Thomas C. Hone with Maj John Murray, CENTCOM J-6, 10 Mar 1992. See daily AF/XO briefing for the locations of SHF network.

[119]Defense Communications Systems Ground Mobile Forces Gateways are the entry for satellite communications into the defense-wide communications network. Signals are fed to the these gateways from tactical satellite terminals. "Air Force Tactical Communications in War," footnote 8, p 8.

in turn, would likely undercut CENTCOM's intent (set forth in the second draft of Operations Plan 1002-90) to control access to satellite band width.[120] Bandwidth was the scarce resource, and the commander of CENTCOM J-6, Brigadier General Cougill, did not want to let it out of his control.[121] He believed that satellite bandwidth would be quickly saturated if he did.

The compromise struck between CENTAF and CENTCOM was the "hub" concept, in which the satellite gateways would be shielded from saturation by shunting all CENTAF communications into a hub before they were relayed to an orbiting satellite.[122] The amount of access through the hub was dictated by CENTCOM. CENTAF, however, was permitted to build its own system of "spokes" into the hub, thereby allowing CENTAF communicators to control the rate at which digital communications flowed through their whole theater system. The compromise gave both CENTCOM and CENTAF the kind of control over communications flow that each believed it needed.[123]

The first theater hub was established at Thumrait Air Base, Oman, because it was beyond Scud range and, given the fluid situation in August, it was likely to remain in place no matter how units were moved around within Saudi Arabia.[124] Al Dhafra, in the United Arab Emirates, was the second hub; in late November 1990, Riyadh became the third.[125] To accommodate the data flow through these three hubs, Space

---

[120] See (S) GWAPS, *Space Operations in the Gulf War*, Chapter 3.

[121] Coyne, *Airpower in the Gulf*, p 158.

[122] "Air Force Tactical Communications in War," p 1-13.

[123] (S) HQ, US Central Command, *After Action Report*, 15 Jul 1991, noted that the decision to adopt the "hub" concept made the theater communications system "truly *joint*"(p 20). The reason was that CENTCOM J-6 stood astride the hubs, and J-6 was in fact a joint staff, working under the CINC's theater guidance. If each component had a separate gateway to the Defense Satellite Communications System, then the components would have had to negotiate with one another and with the CINC for bandwidth. Given the "inordinate number of unplanned requirements for radios and phones," (p 1-6 of "Air Force Tactical Communications in War"), such negotiations would have been chaotic. The compromise focused both CENTCOM and CENTAF on their proper responsibilities: CENTCOM as "traffic cop" and CENTAF as communicator to and among the deployed units and elements of the TACS.

[124] "Air Force Tactical Communications in War," p 1-14.

[125] *Ibid*, pp 1-14, 1-15.

Command, with the permission of the Joint Chiefs, reoriented a "spare" Defense Satellite Communications System satellite.[126] The Defense Communications Agency was also authorized to use the United Kingdom's SKYNET satellite and to lease bandwidth on commercial satellites.[127] CENTCOM J-6's concern in August 1990 that the data flow through uncoordinated satellite "gateways" might overwhelm the Defense Satellite Communications System seems to have been justified.[128]

Types of Tactical Communications

Within the Tactical Air Control System there are basically two forms of communication–voice and digital. The latter links two display terminals; that is, they share the same radar picture, or the second gets a filtered piece of the picture displayed on the first. [DELETED][129] With digital links, two platforms need not talk to communicate; they share displays.

Voice communication is carried by radio, usually ultra-high frequency or high frequency. During Desert Shield and Desert Storm, U.S. aircraft "talked" to one another and to the ground by using HAVE QUICK, a frequency-hopping antijam system. HAVE QUICK radios change their frequencies many times each second in order to keep enemy signals intelligence personnel from eavesdropping on or jamming friendly communications. The key to the successful application of this technology is the ability to synchronize all the HAVE QUICK radios in a given area to the

---

[126](S) Leland Joe and Dan Gonzales, *Command and Control, Communications, and Intelligence in Desert Storm Air Operations*, draft report, WD(L)-5750-AF, Chap. VII, "ADP and Long-Haul Communication Systems," (Santa Monica, 1991). Also, (S) Briefing, Lt Gen T. S. Moorman, Jr., USAF, Commander, Air Force Space Command, at Space Command HQ, Peterson AFB, CO, 16 Dec 1991.

[127](S) Briefing, Lt Gen T. S. Moorman, Jr., USAF, Commander, USAF Space Command, at Space Command HQ, Peterson AFB, CO, 16 Dec 1991. The commercial satellites used were those of the INTELSAT and INMARSAT systems. The Navy also used UHF MILSATCOM satellites. See also (S) Msg, from USCENTAF, to RUEJDCA/Defense Communications Agency, Washington, DC, subj: "Defense Comm System Satellite Rqmt-Desert Shield," 15 Nov 1990.

[128](S) For example, HQ US Central Command *After Action Report*, 15 Jul 1991 (pp 20-1) [DELETED].." Lt Gen T. S. Moorman, Jr., Commander, Air Force Space Command, in a 16 Dec 1991 briefing to GWAPS staff, characterized the war against Iraq as the "first satellite communications war–both inside and outside the theater."

[129][DELETED] See (S) "JTIDS Operations in the Persian Gulf," no author, nd, JTIDS Folder in Task Force 4 AWACS File, GWAPS.

same pattern of frequency-hopping. [DELETED] However, since the Saudis lacked HAVE QUICK, talking to the Saudis meant taking a much greater risk of being overheard or of being jammed. So there was the danger, during the early days of Desert Shield, that Iraqi forces would jam U.S.-Saudi voice radio links.

The challenge facing Central Command Air Forces controllers and communicators during Desert Shield was to link the elements of a multinational Tactical Air Control System *without* at the same time revealing more than absolutely necessary about sensitive U.S. equipment, procedures, and tactics. The Tactical Air Control Center, for example, needed secure communications with the following U.S. elements of the Tactical Air Control System: the Airlift Control Center, the Control and Reporting Center, the Air Support Operations Center, the Marine Corps Tactical Air Operations Center, the Navy, and the Army's air defense command post (controlling Hawk and Patriot surface-to-air missile batteries). The Tactical Air Control Center also needed secure communications with *Saudi* air operations and air defense centers. Finally, the Tactical Air Control Center needed the *right* kinds of links (digital or voice) with each element of the overall Tactical Air Control System.

Though the architecture of linkages that evolved was complex (and not easily described), it worked, as the AWACS exercise of late October showed. Digital data links tied together elements of the Tactical Air Control System that needed to share data. AWACS radar displays also were transmitted to the Tactical Air Control Center and the Saudi Air Command Operations Center in Riyadh. The Tactical Air Control Center took the AWACS picture sent to it and transmitted it to the Control and Reporting Center, which then retransmitted it to the Marine Corps Tactical Air Operations Center. The latter sent it to Navy ships.[130]

---

[130](S/NF) *Tactical Analysis Bulletin*, Vol. 91-2 (Jul 1991), USAF Tactical Fighter Weapons Center, 57th Fighter Weapons Wing, Nellis AFB, Nevada, Chapter 11. (S) Also "E-3 Ops in Desert Shield," from HQ, Tactical Air Command, to Air Staff, XOORC, 19 Dec 1990, plus various untitled connectivity charts and diagrams. The various linkages changed over time, making it difficult to describe *the* TACS network. In several cases, for example, TADIL A links were replaced by TADIL J. Units tried to open the best links they could, and, with theater communications literally changing from day to day, the records of communications links are either spotty or difficult to trace.

A more effective system would have linked the U.S. AWACS *directly* with all U.S. air defense assets in its vicinity. Such multi-Service, multiplatform direct data links did not exist. [DELETED]

[DELETED][131,132]

[DELETED][133]

Deployment of Communication and Control Systems–The Air Tasking Order Problem

Arguably the most important task facing the quickly developing communications system in the theater was its ability to support the Tactical Air Control Center in transmitting an Air Tasking Order to the deployed units. The first Air Tasking Order was transmitted through a combination of a Saudi-only military fax system, the use of the Airlift Control Center UHF tactical satellite, and the message terminals in the Quick Reaction Package vans with the deployed wings.[134] Eventually, the Computer Assisted Force Management System (CAFMS) was used to transmit the Air Tasking Order throughout the theater.

CAFMS used dedicated computer terminals and specially formatted software to organize and print the Air Tasking Order. The CAFMS central processor, located at the Tactical Air Control Center in Riyadh, was eventually linked directly to Wing Operations Centers, and additional terminals to receive the Air Tasking Order via CAFMS were set up at Control and Reporting Centers, Air Support Operations Centers, and the Marine Corps Tactical Air Operations Center.[135] By December, Central

---

[131](C) Memo, untitled, 552d AWAC Wing, Capt E. McNamara, 23 Jan 1991, in Task Force 4 AWACS File, GWAPS.

[132](S/NF) *Tactical Analysis Bulletin*, Vol. 91-2, Jul 1991, p 11-5.

[133](S) Memo, "E-3 Ops in Desert Shield," from HQ. TAC, to Air Staff, XOORC, 19 Dec 1990.

[134]*Air Force Tactical Communications in War, The Desert Shield/Desert Storm Comm Story*, ed, Col Randy Witt, DCS, HQ USCENTAF and 9th AF, Headquarters USCENTAF, Riyadh, Saudi Arabia, Mar 1991.

[135](S) Briefing, "Computer Assisted Force Management System," SAT/Pre-GOSC Review, 21 Dec 1990, Maj Rick Jensen, Desert Shield RRP, Case No. 023. Each CAFMS van took input from 20 terminals in the Tactical Air Control Center and sent it to 11 remote terminals via AUTODIN (the Defense Department's Automatic Digital Network).

Command Air Forces had three CAFMS central processors in place, each of which communicated directly with eleven remote terminals. But there was a need for five more central processors and their associated terminals. On 24 December, U.S. Air Force Headquarters directed the Tactical Air Command to procure the additional equipment.[136]

This action did not enable CENTAF and Navy communicators to get Air Tasking Orders to Navy carriers electronically by the beginning of Desert Storm, despite what appear to have been their best efforts. When CAFMS first became operational during Desert Shield, its operators in the Tactical Air Control Center made paper tape copies of daily Air Tasking Orders and then sent them to a Navy UHF communications van in Riyadh. The van beamed the contents of the daily Orders via satellite to the Navy's Automatic Digital Network (AUTODIN) switching center on Guam. There, the Air Tasking Order was fed into the Navy's Computer Processing and Routing System, which then sent it back to Navy carriers via a Defense Communication System satellite.[137] The ATOs took this circuitous route during the first weeks of Desert Shield because the carriers did not have CAFMS terminals and because, initially, the paper tapes did not fit the Navy's communications formats.[138]

Other forms of transmission to the aircraft carriers were tried, but none bettered the means developed during Desert Shield: voice radio communications by Navy liaison officers serving in the Tactical Air Control Center supplemented by hand-delivered, hard-copy Air Tasking Orders flown directly to the carriers themselves.[139] Because the carriers lacked super high-frequency terminals, the Tactical Air Control Center could not send the ATOs to them.[140] [DELETED][141] Using hand-

---

[136]Msg, from HQ, USAF, to HQ, TAC (Langley AFB), subj: "Combat Mission Need Statement for the Computer Assisted Force Management System (CAFMS)," 24 Dec 1990, 1200Z, SCMC/71718.

[137]"Air Force Tactical Communications in War," pp 2-26 and 2-27.

[138]"Air Force Tactical Communications in War," p 2-27.

[139]"Air Force Tactical Communications in War," pp 2-27 through 2-32 list all the measures tried. The Task Force found no reliable evidence that Air Force communications personnel deliberately ignored Navy concerns or that Navy communicators did not try hard to tie up to the ATOs produced by the TACC.

[140]"Air Force Tactical Communications in War," p 2-30.

delivered copies of the Air Tasking Orders proved a hardship for Navy air sortie planners, especially for Navy airspace controllers on its AEGIS missile cruisers stationed in the Persian Gulf, but the problem could not be overcome either before or during Desert Storm.[142]

Communications Architecture for Desert Storm

In October 1990, one U.S. Air Force communications officer, after returning from an inspection trip to Riyadh, argued that communications in the theater had grown like a cancer.[143] There was some truth to this claim. During Desert Shield, Central Command established more "connectivity" in Saudi Arabia than had been assembled in Europe since the end of World War II. [DELETED][144] The communications established by Central Command Air Forces alone were staggering.

In effect, the components, under Central Command's guidance, established and maintained a huge data flow–a veritable torrent within the theater and between the theater and other commands (especially Washington). CENTAF's problem was to ensure that this tremendous flow did not undermine the communications which held together the various parts of the Tactical Air Control System. To solve this problem, CENTAF staff set up an Airborne Communications Planning Cell in the Tactical Air Control Center in Riyadh to manage the allocation of all radio frequencies among all the elements of the Tactical Air Control System.[145] By January 1991, the daily Air Tasking Orders contained over 900 frequencies–the TACC's Airborne Communications Planning Cell was allocating "virtually the

---

[141] C. Kenneth Allard, in *Command, Control, and the Common Defense* (New Haven, 1990), explains how this happened (pp 189-237). Norman Friedman, in *World Naval Weapons Systems 1991/92* (Annapolis, 1991), describes the Navy systems and their functions.

[142] "Exocets, Air Traffic, and the Air Tasking Order," by LCdr L. Di Rita, USN, in *Proceedings* of the U.S. Naval Institute (Aug 1992, pp 59-63), places the blame for this problem of coordination on CENTAF in particular and on the Air Force in general. However, his analysis of the causes of the problem is much less secure than his statement of how the late arrival of the ATO affected the operations of the airspace managers on the AEGIS cruisers.

[143] (S) Briefing, "After Action Report," Maj James Hale, Air Force SPACECOM, 5 Oct 1990, to XOO, USAF HQ, Washington.

[144] (S) Defense Science Board, *Lessons Learned During Operations Desert Shield & Desert Storm*, (Washington, DC, May 1992), p 5.

[145] "Air Force Tactical Communications in War," p 2-8.

entire spectrum."[146] Inevitably, this caused some problems. The Saudis, for example, did not have a frequency assignment policy, so their communications sometimes interfered with those of CENTCOM and CENTAF. Similarly, U.S. Army units located under AWACS and ABCCC orbits also broadcast in ways which blocked transmissions from and to the aircraft.[147] Finally, there were so many frequencies in use that the Airborne Communications Planning Cell in the Tactical Air Control Center stopped changing them daily, and that posed a communications security risk.[148] Yet the only major communications problem within the Tactical Air Control System not overcome by the beginning of Desert Storm was the delivery of daily Air Tasking Orders to Navy carrier task forces.

Other Support for the TACS

Air Space Control

Air defense and combat air traffic control are two key, *related* functions of the Tactical Air Control System.[149] The TACS, when it works effectively, allows an air commander and his forces to keep enemy aircraft away from high-value friendly targets while admitting into friendly airspace combat and transport aircraft. During Desert Shield and Desert Storm, the normally complex problem of monitoring, controlling, and defending a large airspace was compounded by the need to support the Saudi civil air traffic control process without supplanting it. In addition, Lt. Gen. Horner, as theater Airspace Control Authority, was responsible for seeing to it that aircraft from a multinational coalition flew freely above their own ground forces and those of their allies. This was no simple task. Even more than in the cases of communications and intelligence, the creation of effective airspace monitoring and control required the development of sensible, workable policy, as well as the installation of equipment and the deployment of trained personnel.

The Saudis insisted on deliberate airspace control of all coalition aircraft, and they required that a training range schedule be published

---

[146] *Ibid*, p 2-13.

[147] *Ibid*.

[148] *Ibid*, p 2-16.

[149] Although the air traffic control function is part of the TACS, it is not pictured in Figure 11.

(and strictly followed) for each of the thirty-six air training ranges two weeks in advance.[150] For that to happen, daily Air Tasking Orders issued jointly by the Royal Saudi Air Force and Central Command Air Forces had to cover all training flights in theater. The Saudi government, however, did not have an integrated airspace monitoring and control system (radars supported by effective communications and displays).

In the mid-1980s, the United States and Saudi Arabia had agreed to have the Boeing Company develop and field an integrated airspace monitoring and control system called "Peace Shield," which would tie together ground-based radars and control facilities with AWACS aircraft. The system was not in place in August 1990,[151] so coalition air forces, especially U.S. air forces, would not be able to track the many training flights they wanted to schedule—one reason why it took Lieutenant General Horner a month to persuade the Saudis to allow training flights on a large scale.

As it was, the Saudis had British Ground Air Navigation Aids (GENA) radars of 1960s vintage at Tabuk, Dhahran, Salbuk, Taif, and Khamis Mushayt, and three of the newer Peace Shield radars at Rafha, Nairyah, and Qaysumah, along the Persian Gulf.[152] None of the air defense operations centers slated to serve as command posts for Peace Shield were complete. As a result, U.S. forces had to bring their own airspace control systems and personnel, and equipment brought by CENTAF often was electronically incompatible with what the Saudis already had deployed. As one memo noted, there was "limited exchange of real time situation information between the Saudi and US" systems.[153] Saudi AWACS aircraft, for example, could not send their air radar picture directly to their U.S. AWACS counterparts. Instead, it went first to the Saudi Sector Operations Center in Riyadh; then, only part of it was transferred to the adjacent U.S. Tactical Air Control Center. Similarly, though the TACC could provide the Saudi AWACS Information System in the Sector Operations Center with the full U.S. AWACS picture, that picture could not

---

[150] Trip Report, Capt Robert L. Humbertson, HQ AFSOC/SCF, nd (after 7 Feb 1991).

[151] Rpt (S), "Talking Paper on Saudi C3," Maj Anne Leary, for AF/XO, nd.

[152] Rpt (S), "Talking Paper on Saudi C3," Maj Leary. Also, (S) "Background Paper on Desert Shield C2," Maj Leary, XOOTC, 7 Aug 1990.

[153] (S) Rpt, "Background Paper on Desert Shield C2," Maj Leary, XOOTC, 7 Aug 1990.

be transmitted to airborne Saudi AWACS aircraft.¹⁵⁴ In practice, this meant that Saudi F-15s accompanied Saudi AWACS during the early days of Desert Shield (on daytime patrols), while U.S. AWACS worked with U.S. interceptors during their nighttime circuits.¹⁵⁵

Air Defense

Air defense is really more than just defense. It is also a matter of *not* shooting down friendly aircraft. In the case of the Gulf War, moreover, U.S. forces had to be integrated into "the existing Saudi/Gulf Cooperation Council (GCC) air defense system. . . . " Under this system, allied airspace was "divided into seven air defense/airspace control sectors to allocate air defense and airspace management resources."¹⁵⁶ Figure 14 illustrates the organization of Saudi air defense sectors.

[DELETED]¹⁵⁷,¹⁵⁸

[DELETED]¹⁵⁹,¹⁶⁰

[DELETED]¹⁶¹

---

¹⁵⁴(S) Rpt, "Background Paper on Desert Shield C2," Maj Leary.

¹⁵⁵(S) Rpt, "AWACS Orbits," Maj John Adams/CSS Tac Clt, 14 Aug 1990.

¹⁵⁶(S) *Ibid*, p 1, para 2b.

¹⁵⁷(S) CENTAF, Report, Air Defense Information Gathering Visit, 9-12 Oct 1990.

¹⁵⁸(S) *Ibid*, p 2-2.

¹⁵⁹(S) *Air Defense and Airspace Control Procedures for Operation Desert Shield* and interviews with USCENTAF staff.

¹⁶⁰(S) *Air Defense and Airspace Control Procedures*, p 2-3.

¹⁶¹(S) *Ibid*.

Figure 14
Organization of Saudi Air Defense Sectors

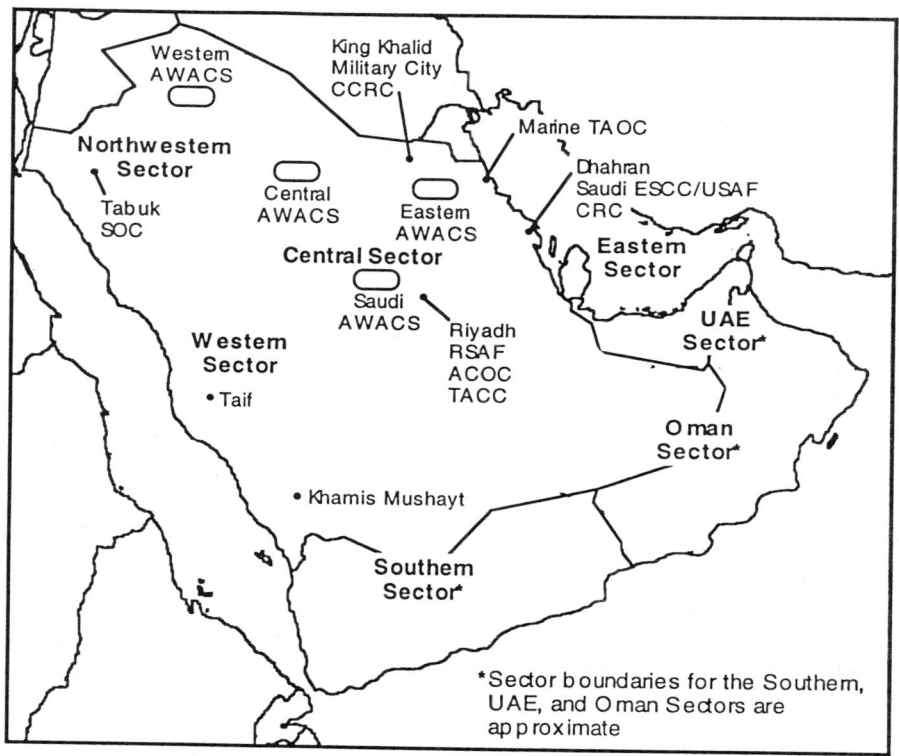

The traditional organization for a U.S. air defense system is based upon three lines of defense. The first line is composed of surface-to-air missiles (SAMs) deployed in a line parallel to the front: the "SAM belt." This line of defense is backed up by air-to-air fighters tasked to destroy any enemy aircraft which penetrate the SAM belt. The final defense against enemy air attacks are point air defense short-range, surface-to-air missiles and antiaircraft guns defending high-value assets such as airfields, command and control centers, and supply depots.

The air defense system was modified to meet local conditions. [DELETED][162] The first line of air defense became the airborne and ground alert air defense aircraft. In addition, there was no U.S. point air defense; the U.S. Army did not deploy point defense missiles and guns that were not already part of the ground units being sent to the Gulf.

The purpose of this–or any–air defense system is to defend friendly forces from attack by fixed wing aircraft, helicopters, or ballistic missiles. To accomplish this task, a basic air defense system consists of some means (for example, radar) to detect enemy target, and then to destroy them (by surface-to-air missiles or antiaircraft artillery). Because the first line of defense against enemy fighters and bombers consisted of valuable and scarce AWACS E-3 aircraft, it was important to keep Iraqi aircraft from getting in among the AWACS and shooting them down. That placed a premium on knowing the identity of radar contacts *as early as possible*. But this was not easy given the many different types of coalition aircraft that were flying in the theater. To distinguish friend from foe, coalition forces employed a combination of electronic and procedural means.

The primary electronic means of identifying aircraft was IFF (Identification Friend or Foe) equipment–transponders on aircraft which responded automatically to special cueing signals broadcast by friendly radars. U.S. aircraft carried IFF transponders which could respond to coded signals from radars in four modes. [DELETED] However, IFF *alone* could not discriminate between friendly and enemy aircraft. Procedural measures had to be established which would apply equally to all allied aircraft and yet not allow Iraqi aircraft to penetrate allied airspace safely.[163]

There are many different procedural methods for identifying friendly and enemy aircraft. Some are used by friendly aircraft to ensure their safe passage from their bases to the target and back. Other procedures identify certain flight characteristics, that (when unknowingly used by enemy aircraft) identify those aircraft as hostile. Both approaches were used during the Gulf War. The Air Tasking Order, for example, specified takeoff times, flight routes, and the times when coalition aircraft would appear over their designated targets. With this information, air defense

---

[162][DELETED] (S) Msg, USCINCCENT to JCS, et al., 191200Z Jan 1991, subj: COMUSCENTAF Wartime Rules of Engagement, para 4C.

[163](S) Information Paper, "Identification Friend or Foe (IFF) Procedures," DAMO-FDE, 14 Sep 1990.

units would know when to anticipate the appearance of friendly aircraft. The Special Instructions attached to the Air Tasking Order and the Airspace Control Order identified Minimum Risk Routes, or air corridors, through which friendly aircraft were expected to fly when entering or leaving coalition airspace. The Commander in Chief Central Command also promulgated Rules of Engagement which defined hostile acts. For example, any unidentified aircraft flying an "attack profile" against friendly forces could be assumed "hostile."[164]

Airspace Management

Airspace management is the complement to air defense. The latter aims to keep out intruders. The former aims to keep friendlies from interfering with one another, especially over friendly territory. In short, airspace managers are the traffic cops of the sky, regulating the movement of aircraft along air corridors, within air refueling tracks, and around friendly fields.

During Desert Shield and Desert Storm, the Central Command Air Forces combat airspace management branch used a unique computer tool, the Combat Airspace Deconfliction System (CADS), to build the Airspace Control Order. No other Air Force Major Command or numbered air force had the system. In April 1990 Lieutenant General Horner warned General Schwarzkopf that the skies over Saudi Arabia and Kuwait would be congested with aircraft if the United States had to deploy sizeable forces to the region.[165] Horner told Schwarzkopf that the boundary between Kuwait and Iraq was roughly the distance between Tampa and Miami. Refueling operations in this area for a high number of sorties would saturate the available airspace, endangering both tankers and the aircraft they were refueling.[166] The lack of airspace might severely limit the ability of air forces to generate numbers of sorties *safely*.[167]

---

[164](S) Msg, USCINCCENT to JCS, et al., 191200Z Jan 1991, subj: COMUSCENTAF Wartime Rules of Engagement, para 4A(6).

[165](S) Briefing, Lt Gen Charles A. Horner, CENTAF, "OPLAN 1002, Air Operations," to Gen Schwarzkopf.

[166](S/NF) Study, "Desert Shield/ Desert Storm Tanker Assessment," HQ Strategic Air Command, Plans and Resources (XP), 23 Sep 1991.

[167](S) T. A. Marshall, *Strategic Air Command Bomber and Tanker Operations in Desert Storm*, draft report, Rand Corporation, 1991 (WD[L]-56608-AF), p 28.

The expectation of crowding led Central Command Air Forces staff to plan on introducing U.S. air traffic controllers and their equipment if and when a crisis began. Pre-Desert Shield plans, however, did not accurately forecast the tremendous volume of air traffic, which threatened to overwhelm the ability of the existing route structure to handle it.[168] For example, the Jeddah Air Control Center handled the air routes that connected Saudi Arabia with Europe and Africa. Prior to 2 August 1990, the Jeddah Air Control Center handled approximately 36,000 operations per month. By 15 September 1990, the traffic flow at Jeddah Air Control Center had increased to an average of 54,000 operations per month, and it remained at that level until 15 January 1991.[169]

Because of large gaps in radar and radio coverage in Saudi airspace, serious flight safety problems quickly emerged as the volume of air traffic increased during Desert Shield. To regain control over the situation, Central Command Air Forces brought more air traffic control equipment and personnel into the theater. Eventually, there were 7 deployed Radar Approach Control Facilities, augmentation to 17 airbase towers, and liaison elements in 3 host nation air control centers. Staffing numbered 161 controllers at U.S. facilities, 85 U.S. controllers augmenting host nation controllers, 60 controllers in the liaison function, and 14 controllers on the CENTAF staff to help manage combat airspace.[170] The Army, Navy, and Marines also deployed their organic combat air traffic control equipment and controllers to support helicopter, marine, and carrier air operations.

By Desert Storm, combat airspace managers separated multi-Service, multinational air forces flying 3,000 sorties per day in a complex airspace structure. The numbers of areas, zones, routes, and orbits which had to be monitored and controlled are impressive:

- o   160 restricted operation zones
- o   122 airborne refueling orbits
- o   32 combat air patrol areas

---

[168]Ltr, from Maj J. H. Steeves, Chief, Air Traffic Control Operations & Procedures, DCS/Operations, USAFE, to HQ, AFCC/ATCO, subj: Gulf War Study.

[169]Ltr Capt Morris J. Spence, Chief, Combat Airspace Plans/Programs to GWAPS, TF-IV, subj: Terminal ATC, Theater ATC, Role of Liaison, 24 Apr 1992.

[170]Fax, Maj Howdeshell, AFCC Air Traffic Svc to Maj Leary, SAF/OSG, subj: Air Traffic in Support of Desert Storm, 27 May 1992.

- 10 air transit routes
- 36 training areas
- 76 strike routes
- 60 Patriot engagement zones
- 312 missile engagement zones
- 11 high-density aircraft control zones
- 195 Army aviation flight routes
- 14 air corridors
- 46 minimum risk routes
- 60 restricted fire areas
- 17 air base defense zones
- numerous Aegis engagement zones.[171]

Outside the theater, some portions of the world's civilian air traffic control network were initially swamped by the rapid increase in military air movement through their regions.[172] One reason for this was that many areas lacked the radio and radar coverage required to give ground controllers positive control of flights. To overcome this lack of coverage, an aircraft flying outside positive radar coverage usually is given an Altitude Reservation for a specific period of time, allowing the spacing between aircraft to be maintained by time intervals and altitude separation. During Desert Shield, this worldwide system was disrupted by the large increase in the number of flights crossing the oceans and going into theater. Stateside air flow planners did not always anticipate the effect increased military air movements would have on the world's civil air traffic control system. Initially, the planned and scheduled deploying aircraft flights could not get approved flight plans due to congestion in the altitude reservation portion of the worldwide civil air traffic control system. In the Pacific, for example, it took the U.S. defense attaches' involvement with certain host nation governments to get the regional Air Traffic Control Centers to issue timely altitude reservations for transiting U.S. military aircraft.[173]

---

[171] (S) Defense Science Board, *Lessons Learned During Operations Desert Shield & Desert Storm*, (DDRE, May 1992), pp 20-1.

[172] Ltr Capt Todd G. Baker, Chief, PACMARF, 633d Operations Support Squadron to Maj Christianson, HQ PACAF/DOF, subj: Gulf War Study Tasking [Air Control Centers], 28 Apr 1992.

[173] *Ibid.*

A typical air traffic control tower during Desert Storm.

At the start of the air campaign on 16 January 1991, the military took wartime control of the airspace over Saudi Arabia. At 0300L on 16 January 1991, the Jeddah Air Control Center had 315 civilian aircraft under its control. With only 10 minutes of notification, the center began transferring aircraft from civilian to military control. In 48 minutes all civilian air traffic either landed or departed the flight information region. In the neighboring Egyptian flight information region, numerous missions were bound for Saudi Arabia. U.S. air traffic control liaisons assisted the Egyptians in coordinating landing permission at Cairo East International for some of the missions and assisted in arranging with the Jeddah Air Traffic Control Center for critical military missions to continue.[174] The ease and safety in transitioning the airspace from national peacetime control to wartime coalition military control reflected exceptional planning and cooperation.

---

[174] Ltr Maj Steeves, Chief, ATC Operations & Procedures, DCS/Operations, USAFE to HQ AFCC/ATCO (Capt Gray), subj: Gulf War Study. [Input to letter was provided by Capt Ray A. Mandery, who deployed as air traffic control liaison to Cairo, Egypt during Desert Shield and Desert Storm.]

Meteorology

Meteorological support for CENTAF and CENTCOM was, like many communications units, deployed late to the theater. According to a Joint Chiefs Memorandum of Policy, the Air Force was supposed to provide staff meteorological support to Commander in Chief Central Command *and* to the component commanders under him.[175] This requirement was not met by the small meteorological staff deployed. As planned, Central Command's Staff Weather Officer flew to Saudi Arabia in August with the rest of the CENTCOM staff, but he and his personnel depended on the 5th Weather Wing at Langley Air Force Base, Virginia, to supply them with data from the Defense Meteorological Satellite Program. In mid-September, a special van for receiving the satellite data was flown to Riyadh.[176] Moreover, the rest of the meteorological support for CENTCOM and its components flowed piecemeal into the theater, and the number of personnel who did deploy did not match the standard called for by accepted doctrine.

Summary and Review

This chapter has surveyed the development of the Tactical Air Control System in the theater. It has not been a detailed survey. We tried to show how elements of the TACS function, and how complicated developing the TACS was. The TACS is the working manifestation of what Air Force personnel refer to as "centralized control and decentralized execution." As such, its conceptual architecture is straightforward. AWACS aircraft, for example, monitor the movement of friendly and hostile aircraft, pass their pictures of the air situation to fighters and ground command centers, and then direct other aircraft to carry out the orders which commanders on the ground give to that portion of the Tactical Air Control System.

Yet, the actual communications links which supported this part of the Tactical Air Control System were quite complex, involving equipment and personnel from multiple Services and nations. Moreover, the actual links were less than ideal, and they were modified, over time, to fit the peculiarities of the situation in the Gulf. So the straightforward conceptual architecture described in official manuals was modified–sometimes literally "on the fly."

---

[175](S) Intvw, Maj Thomas R. MacPhail, USAF, Arlington, VA, 9 Dec 91.

[176]*Ibid.*

The growth of the Tactical Air Control System was delayed by the Commander in Chief's decision to put a higher priority on the movement of combat units into the theater. However, in a month, Central Command Air Forces had put together a working Tactical Air Control System. By the end of 1990, the System was multinational. As the Commander in Chief Central Command noted in a message dated 26 December,

> We have firmly integrated the multinational forces into our overall command and control structure. U.S. and Saudi air defense forces have recently formed a combined control and reporting center (CCRC) for the Northeastern Sector of Saudi Arabia. Syrian, Egyptian, and French liaison officers maintain 24 hour contact with their air defense (AD) forces through U.S.-supplied communications equipment located in the CCRC .... A secondary communications channel has been established from the CCRC through the U.S. Air Support Operations Center to our Tactical Air Control Parties located with each nation's forces.[177]

There was even a plan to use U.S. AWACS to alert Israel in case Iraq's air force tried to strike at Israeli targets through Jordan.[178]

Setting up an effective Tactical Air Control System, however, did not come cheap. By the beginning of Desert Storm, all of the Air Force's Airborne Battlefield Command and Control Center aircraft were under CENTAF's command.[179] At that time, CENTAF had 6 of the 8 available EC-130 COMPASS CALL electronic warfare aircraft, 3 of the 5 deployed Air Support Operations Centers, 2 of the 5 deployed Control and Reporting Centers, both of the developmental E-8A JSTARS aircraft, and 124 of the 184 deployed Tactical Air Control Parties.[180] The European Command sent 25 percent of its intelligence manpower to CINCCENT and most of its tactical communications to Saudi Arabia or to Proven Force

---

[177](S) Msg, 2115Z 26 Dec 1990, from USCINCCENT, to AIG 904, subj: SITREP, Section 5, "Commander's Evaluation."

[178](S) Memo, to Lt Col Stanfil, from Lt Col McCormick, subj: "Air Defense Warning to Israel, 30 Jan 1991.

[179](S) Msg, 2244Z, 15 Jan 1991, from Joint Staff, Washington, to USCINCCENT, CC-J3, subj: "Airborne Relay Command and Control Units."

[180](S) Memo, "Gen McPeak's Speech to National Defense University (NDU) Input," from CSS-Tactical Control Duty Officer, to XOXO, 14 Feb 1991.

in Turkey.[181] Finally, the Strategic Air Command committed all available RC-135V RIVET JOINT aircraft, which were national assets, under Joint Chiefs' control, to the theater.[182]

Tactical Air Command Manual 2-1, *Tactical Air Operations*, defines the Tactical Air Control System as a "system for planning, directing, coordinating, and controlling theater air operations."[183] In Operation Desert Shield, that system was put together piecemeal. Yet it was operating as a whole system in a month and was multinational by the end of December 1990. Giving it that capability, however, depleted the command and control units in the United States and Europe and left the United States with no effective tactical air command and control reserve. Overall, however, the story of the development of the Tactical Air Control System in the theater is noteworthy because of both its complexity and its success. The latter enabled General Horner, the first Joint Force Air Component Commander, to bring the full weight of coalition air power to bear on the forces of Iraq.

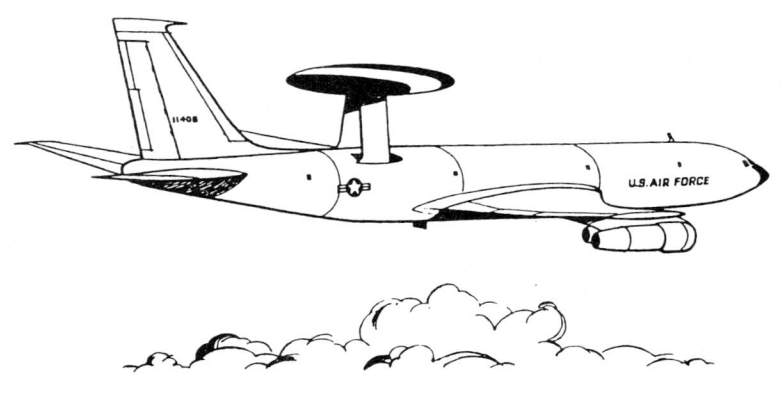

---

[181](S) Msg, from Gen Galvin, to Gen Powell, subj: "Status of USEUCOM Forces Following Deployment to SWA," 2034Z, 20 Feb 1991.

[182]Robert S. Hopkins, III, "Ears of the Storm," *Air Force Magazine*, Vol. 75, No. 2 (Feb 1992), p 42.

[183]TAC Manual 2-1, "Tactical Air Operations," HQ Tactical Air Command, Langley AFB, VA, Aug 1991, p 5-9.

5

The CENTAF TACC

Air Force Manual 1-1 states that a Tactical Air Force Commander should have one centralized control point from which to direct his forces.[1] The Tactical Air Control System (TACS) provides this capability through the Tactical Air Control Center (TACC), which is the highest operational element of the Tactical Air Control System and serves as the operations center for all air activity within the Tactical Air Control System's area of responsibility.[2] As such, the Tactical Air Control Center plans, coordinates, and directs the tactical air effort and supervises all tactical air control functions.[3] In theory, the center is a staff organization working for the Director of Operations (DO) and the Director of Intelligence (IN), both of whom report to the Air Component Commander.[4] The TACC, as envisioned and initially established in the theater by U.S. Central Command Air Forces (CENTAF), mirrored what had been prescribed in CENTAF Regulation 55-45.[5] This chapter will describe the CENTAF Tactical Air Control Center's initial organization, its functions, and the evolution of those functions.

---

[1] Department of the Air Force, *Basic Aerospace Doctrine of the United States Air Force*, AFM 1-1, 16 Mar 1984, see esp. pp 4-1, 4-2. The revised AFM 1-1 makes essentially the same argument. See Department of the Air Force, *Basic Aerospace Doctrine of the United States Air Force*, AFM 1-1, Volume I, Mar 1992, p 18; Department of the Air Force, *Basic Aerospace Doctrine of the United States Air Force*, AFM 1-1, Volume II, "Essay W: Organizing to Win," Mar 1992.

[2] (S/NF) Department of the Air Force, Multi-Command Manual (MCM) 3-1, *General Planning and Employment Considerations*, Volume I, 19 Dec 1986, p 4-1.

[3] The TAC Regulation 55-45 stated that "as the Commander's operation center/command post, the TACC provides the facility and personnel necessary to accomplish the planning, directing and coordinating of tactical air operations." TACR 55-45, *Tactical Air Force Headquarters and the Tactical Air Control Center*, 8 Apr 1988.

[4] The TACC also supports the Joint Force Air Component Commander when, as in the Gulf War, the air component commander is appointed as the JFACC.

[5] USCENTAF Regulation 55-45, *United States Central Command Air Employment Planning Process*, 27 Jun 1990, p 2-2. The TACC in theater also was similar to the generic TACC prescribed by HQ TAC.

The Initial CENTAF TACC

The Tactical Air Control Center as envisioned and initially established in the theater by Central Command Air Forces mirrored what had been prescribed in CENTAF Regulation 55-45,[6] published on 27 June 1990, just over a month before the Iraqi invasion of Kuwait. In addition, Central Command Air Forces exercised this Tactical Air Control Center organization during the exercise Internal Look in July 1990. The Tactical Air Control Center comprised four major staff divisions: Combat Plans, Combat Intelligence, Combat Operations, and the Enemy Situation Correlation Division. These divisions supported two functional areas (operations and intelligence) and time periods (future plans and current operations). The Combat Plans Division built plans for future operations (seventy-two hours into the future) based upon intelligence support provided by the Combat Intelligence Division. Ongoing operations were monitored and controlled by the Combat Operations Division, supported by the Enemy Situation Correlation Division. Liaison elements such as the Army's Battlefield Coordination Element (BCE) and the Naval Amphibious Liaison Element (NALE) were included in the TACC to coordinate operations. Figure 15 illustrates this relationship.[7]

The Combat Plans Division and the Combat Operations Division were organizationally subordinate to the Deputy Chief of Staff, Operations. The Director of Combat Intelligence (DCI) reported to the Deputy Chief of Staff, Intelligence and directed the activities of the Combat Intelligence Division, the Enemy Situation Correlation Division, and the All-source Intelligence Center. The Tactical Air Control Center also included a Director of Air Defense (DAD), responsible directly to the Director of Operations and Joint Force Air Component Commander (JFACC). In addition to these functions, the initial CENTAF organizational structure included an Airlift Control Center (ALCC) commanded by the Commander, Airlift Forces (COMALF), and a group of Strategic Forces Advisors (STRATFOR), commanded by a STRATFOR Commander. Figure 16 displays

---

[6]USCENTAF Regulation 55-45, *United States Central Command Air Employment Planning Process*, 27 Jun 1990, p 2-2. The TACC in theater also was similar to the generic TACC prescribed by HQ TAC in Tactical Air Command Regulation 55-45, 8 Apr 1988.

[7]TACR 55-45, *Tactical Air Force Headquarters and the Tactical Air Control Center*, 8 Apr 1988.

the CENTAF organizational structure, in its entirety, as it appeared on 24 August 1990.

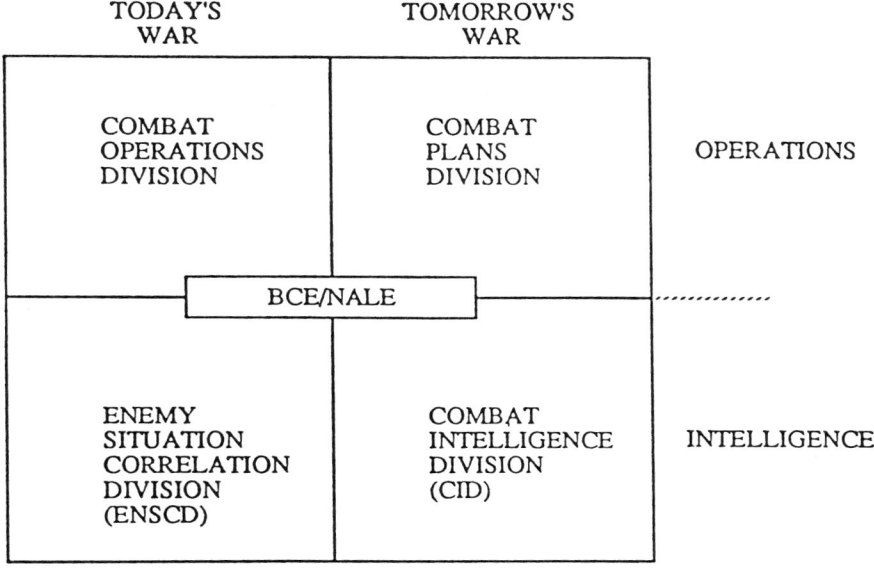

Figure 15
Tactical Air Control Center Divisions

The following sections describe the functions and duties of the CENTAF Tactical Air Command Center divisions and offices.

Combat Plans Division

The Combat Plans Division planned for the employment of assigned forces in future Air Tasking Order (ATO) periods, that is, tomorrow's war. This division, staffed by officers and technicians experienced with the tactical weapon systems employed, tried to ensure that planning included, for example, appropriate force packaging, efficient use of electronic combat assets, and air-to-air refueling support.[8] The planning contained,

---

[8]TACR 55-45.

Figure 16
CENTAF Organizational Structure

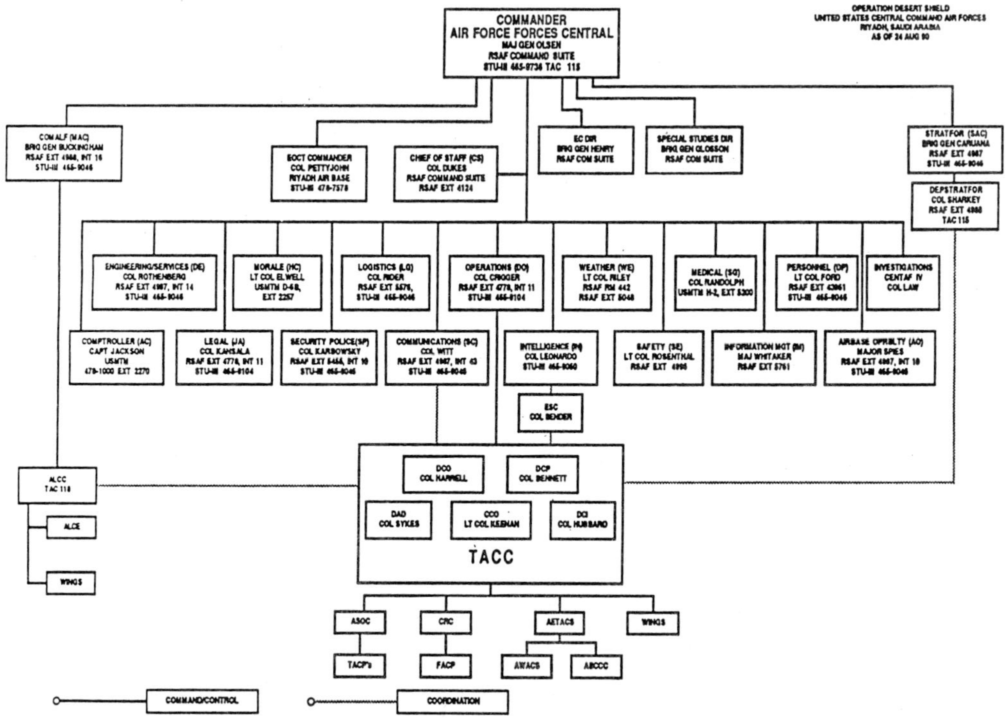

in addition to unit tasking, unique or recently changed control instructions and directives[9] and was disseminated to all concerned in the form of an Air Tasking Order.[10] To accomplish this task the Combat Plans Division was organized into several divisions. As shown in Figure 17 the four major functional divisions were the Combat Operations Planning Division (COPD), the Fighter Plans Division, the Special Support Division, and the TACS Division. Two specialized functions also were included in the Combat Plans Division: the ATO Division (or the CAFMS Division) and the Airborne Control Element (ACE) Coordinator.[11]

The Combat Operations Planning Division received and disseminated the commander's guidance letter and oversaw the joint targeting process, but its main function was to ensure the accomplishment of the planning process for the production of a flyable Air Tasking Order. To do this, the Division had three functional branches and a planning staff: the Employment Plans Branch, the Long Range Plans Branch, the Night Targeting Branch, and the Combat Planning Staff (COPS).[12] The Combat Planning Staff, working with other component and allied liaison officers,

---

[9]For example, rules of engagement, the airspace structure and control procedures included in an Airspace Control Order and search and rescue information are examples of types of information normally included in a tasking order. Special instructions to units and rules of engagement were published separately with daily updates.

[10]In general, the size or scale of the operation governs the means of ATO dissemination. A limited operation might require a simple ATO transmitted verbally. An operation with a large number of units at diverse locations would require a large ATO constructed specifically for the unique aspects and size of the operation. An ATO format also can be altered with changes to the air commander's objectives. Modern, automated systems have improved the speed of development and transmission of an ATO significantly. One secondary requirement for the ATO is that it must be able to be developed, published, and disseminated manually should the automatic equipment fail. This places a premium on having enough trained personnel in a TACC. They serve as a manual back-up to an increasingly automated process. See TACR 55-45, *Tactical Air Force Headquarters and the Tactical Air Control Center*, 8 Apr 1988.

[11](S) USCENTAF *Combat Plans Handout*, Oct 1990.

[12]USCENTAF Regulation 55-45, *United States Central Command Air Employment Planning Process*, 27 Jun 1990.

Figure 17
Four Major Functional Divisions of the Combat Plans Division

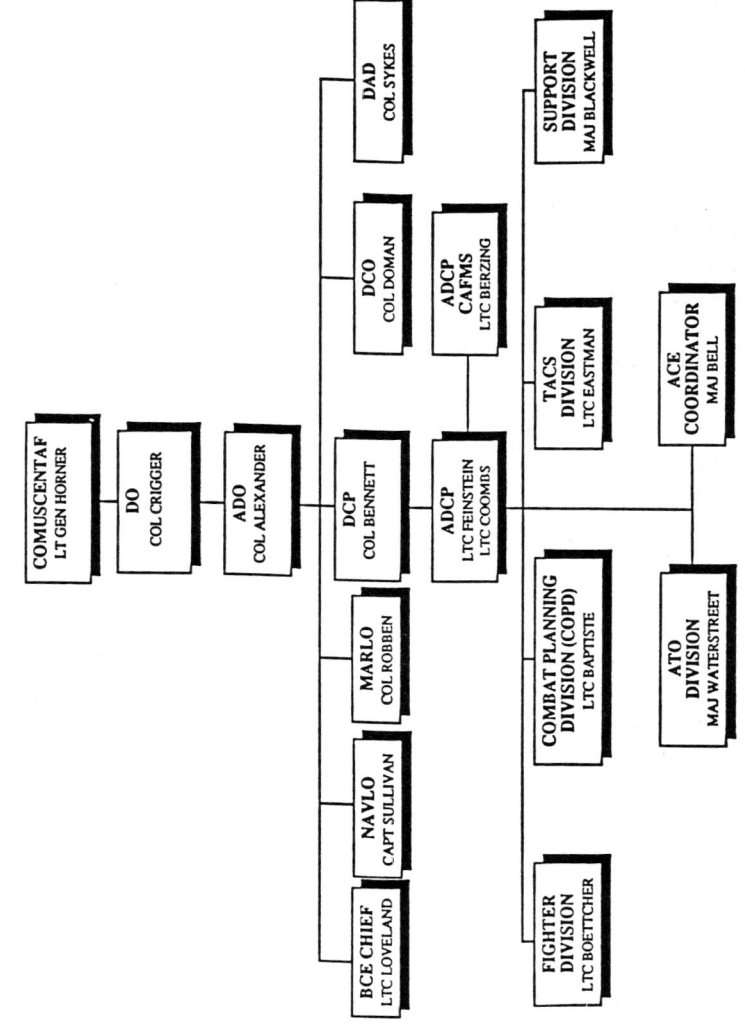

was responsible for developing the initial plans for the use of airpower in defense of Saudi Arabia. This arrangement is illustrated in Figure 18.[13]

Fighter Plans Division

Once the Combat Operations Planning Division staff finished the planning for an Air Tasking Order period, the Fighter Plans Division completed the final coordination. Fighter Plans was composed of working sections representing all the forces being tasked by the ATO, including liaison officers from other U.S. Services and coalition nations. Fighter Plans Division "fraggers" worked closely with (a) the Special Support Division to develop air refueling tanker schedules and coordinate electronic combat, search and rescue (SAR), and special operations forces (SOF), (b) the TACS Division's Airspace Branch to produce the Airspace Control Order (ACO),[14] and (c) the Combat Intelligence Division to coordinate enemy order of battle and intelligence collection management.[15]

ATO Division

The completed and coordinated Air Tasking Order was passed to the Air Tasking Order Division, where it was typed into the Computer Assisted Force Management System (CAFMS) and broadcast to the various units and agencies. The CENTAF Air Tasking Order cycle and the equipment used to disseminate the completed ATO will be examined in greater detail below.

Combat Operations Division

The Combat Operations Division was the CENTAF Tactical Air Control Center's second major element. The Combat Operations Division

---

[13](S) *USCENTAF Combat Plans Handout.*

[14]The ACO was included in the ATO as part of the Special Instructions, which included communication information, rules of engagement, and search and rescue procedures.

[15]The Combat Plans Division cannot adequately plan and task any air operation without the Combat Intelligence Division providing the necessary information and analysis to (a) identify targets, (b) estimate threats (ground-to-air, as well as air-to-air), and (c) assess damage from strikes.

**Figure 18
Combat Planning Staff Works With Others
To Develop Air Tasking Orders**

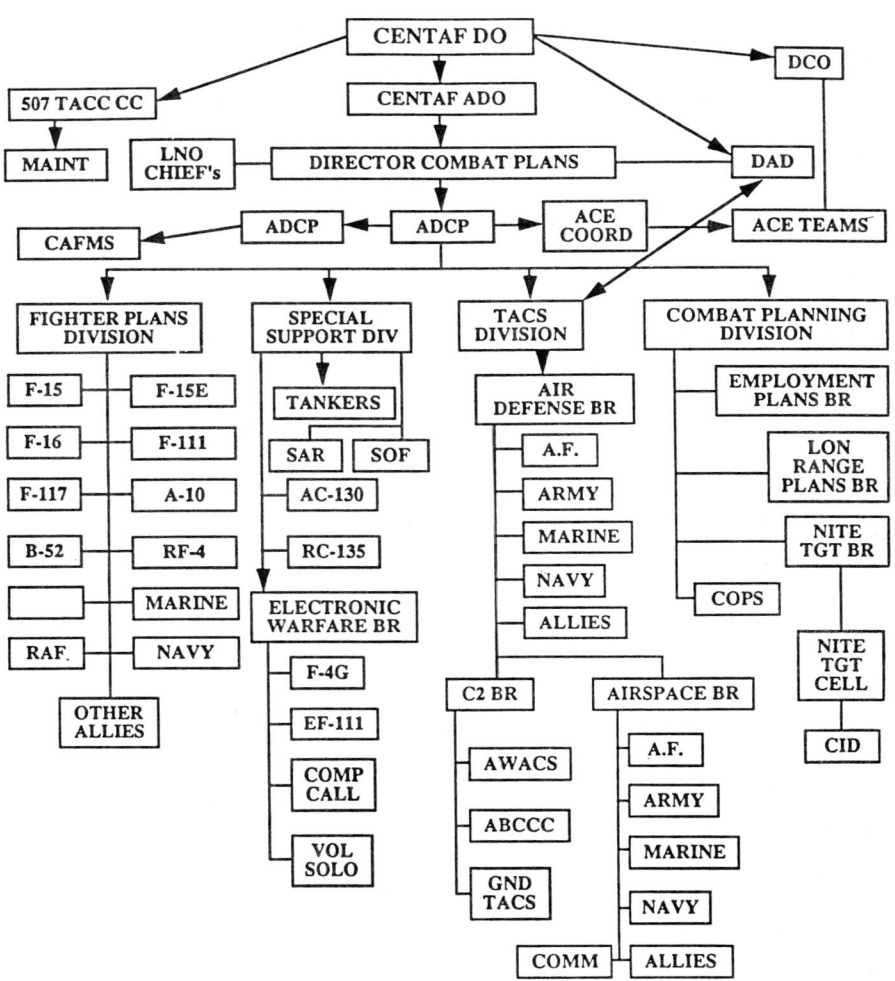

138

provided real-time central control, coordination, and integration of ongoing air operations for the air commander.[16] In doing so, its chief responsibility was to execute the Air Tasking Order, but it also approved and implemented changes to the Order,[17] monitored the conduct of the air campaign, and managed all tasked assets through the Fighter Duty Officers assigned to the Tactical Air Control Center.[18] Combat Operations Division officers managed the displays and information readouts presented to senior battle staff during their duty period. Figure 19 shows the organization of the Combat Operations Division as it existed in Riyadh.[19] Figure 20 displays the physical layout and organization of the Combat Operations Division (the "bubble") as it was finally set up in the basement of the Royal Saudi Air Force headquarters.[20] As envisioned by CENTAF, the Joint Force Air Component Commander and Director of Operations were to rely upon the Combat Operations Division to "fight" the air campaign.

Director of Air Defense

Within the Tactical Air Control Center, the Director of Air Defense was responsible to the CENTAF Director of Operations for the combined interoperability with, and integration of, U.S. forces and host nation(s)'

---

[16]USCENTAF Regulation 55-45, *United States Central Command Air Employment Planning Process*, 27 Jun 1990.

[17](U) The Combat Operations Division was assigned responsibility for the next day's ATO ten hours prior to the ATO effective time.

[18](U) For example, Combat Operations monitored the communications links with airborne assets such as the Airborne Battlefield Command and Control Center (ABCCC) and Airborne Warning and Control System (AWACS) aircraft. The total air situation display was monitored by the Combat Operations Division and adjustments were made to the air order of battle based upon the recommendations of its personnel.

[19]Memo, Charles H. Shipman, Lt Col, USAF, Director, Manpower and Organizations, USCENTAF to A/MO, 26 Mar 1991, subj: HQ USCENTAF Desert Storm Organization Structure. Although this chart described the organizational structure used during the war, this structure had been established during Desert Shield.

[20]Briefing, 9th AF Commander, USCENTCOM, Operation Desert Storm Hogwash, Maxwell AFB, AL, 12 Jul 1991.

**Figure 19
Combat Operations Division In Riyadh**

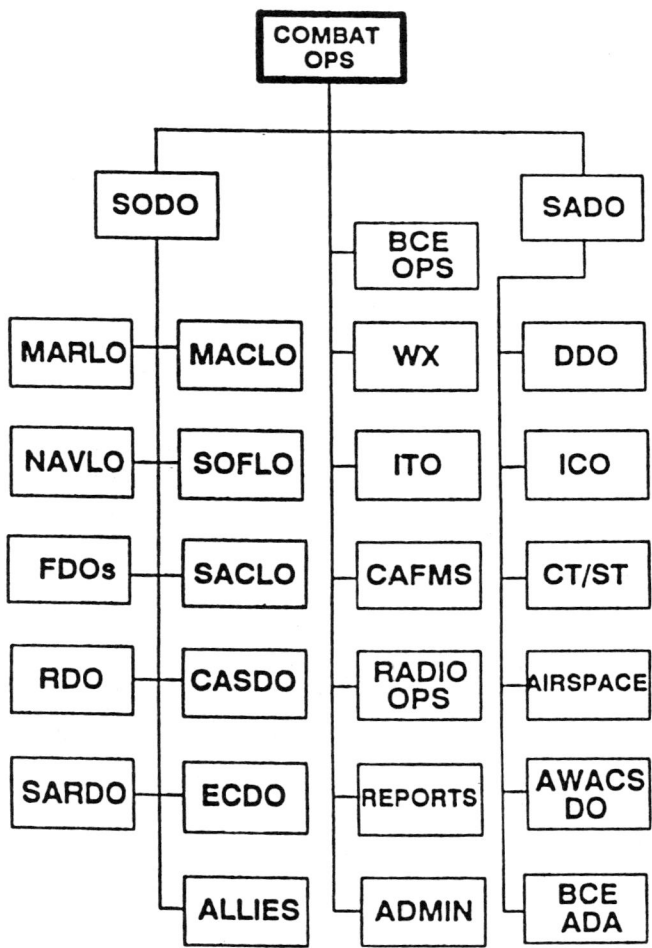

**Figure 20
Combat Operations**

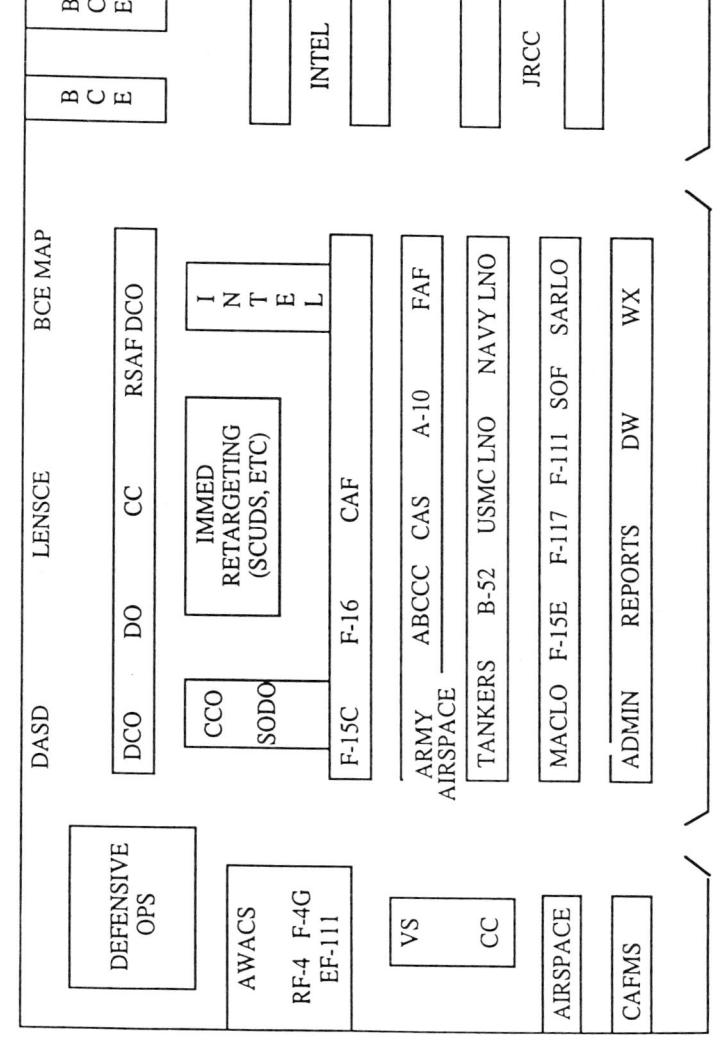

air defense systems, forces, and airspace procedures and facilities.[21] Hence, the Director of Air Defense occupied a critical position in the Tactical Air Control System. He negotiated the agreements that covered the airspace structure, air traffic control procedures, command and control procedures and instructions, combined rules of engagement, and safe passage and minimum risk routing procedures. The monumental job of the Director of Air Defense was further compounded by the ever increasing number of forces arriving in theater.

Intelligence Support to the TACC

Intelligence representation in the Tactical Air Control Center came under the direction of the Deputy Chief of Staff for Intelligence through the Director of Combat Intelligence to the Combat Intelligence Division and the Enemy Situation Correlation Division. The primary duty of the Combat Intelligence Division was to provide pertinent and timely intelligence in support of air campaign planning and execution.[22] Inherent in the Division's activities was the task of maintaining the flow of intelligence information among the Combat Planning Staff, Combat Plans Division, and the Enemy Situation Correlation Division. The Director of Combat Intelligence also oversaw the operations of the Enemy Situation Correlation Division, which had three primary functions: (a) providing combat intelligence to the TACC Combat Operations Division, which could change the execution of the air plan, (b) providing near-real-time, all-source intelligence relevant to the Tactical Air Control Center's other functions and reviewing and validating targets prior to plan execution,[23] and (c) managing the flow of intelligence information and staff into the center from the Combat Intelligence Division, collection systems, and other intelligence organizations.[24] Figure 21 represents the Intelligence

---

[21]USCENTAF Regulation 55-45, *United States Central Command Air Employment Planning Process*, 27 Jun 1990.

[22]*Ibid.*

[23]*Ibid.*

[24]For example, intelligence information and staff coming into the TACC included battle damage assessments, intelligence systems operators and target collections, and administration representatives. See TACC Mission statements, USCENTAF/HO TO USCENTAF/PA, 27 Feb 1991.

Figure 21
Prewar Plan of Intelligence Organization to Support TACC

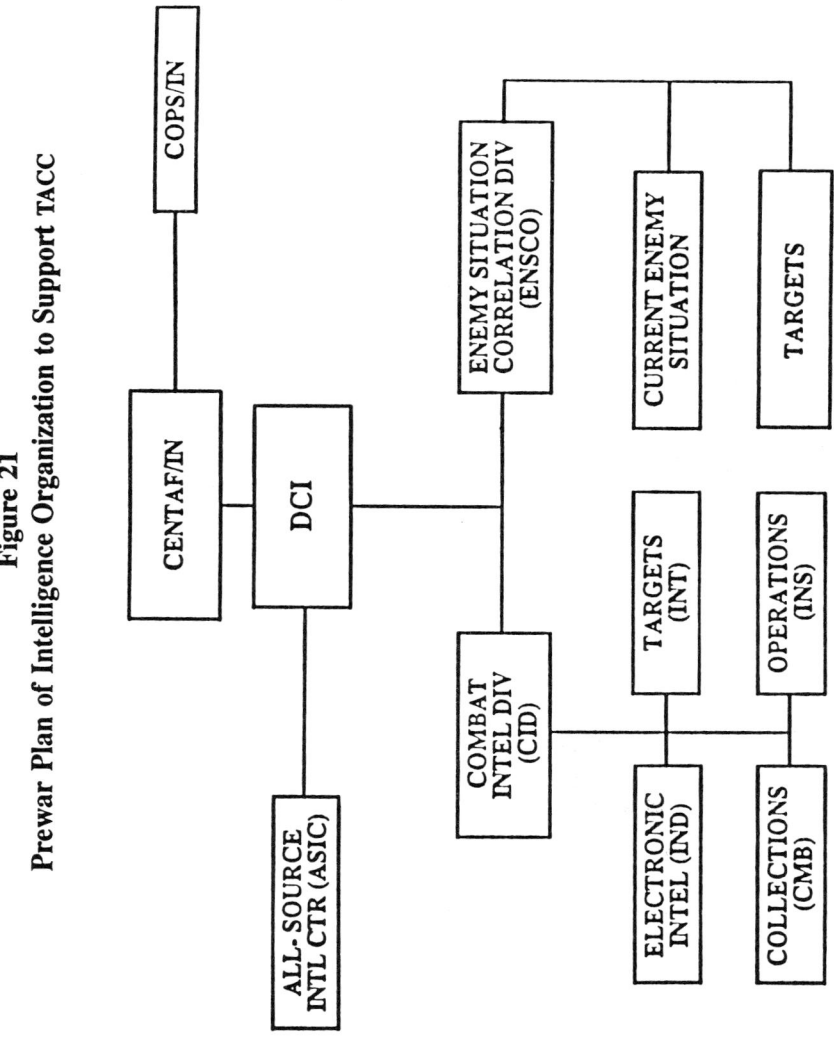

Organization as it was envisioned in prewar planning to support the TACC.[25]

A note is necessary concerning the organizational relationship between the Tactical Air Control Center's intelligence and combat plans and operations components. Unlike the Combat Plans Division and the Combat Operations Division, the Combat Intelligence Division and the Enemy Situation Correlation Division worked for the CENTAF Deputy Chief of Staff, Intelligence–not for the CENTAF Director of Operations. Thus, although intelligence analysts were tasked to support the Director of Operations's activities, their organizational chain of command led to Intelligence. This arrangement created a potential for conflict in the way intelligence personnel responded to taskings from Combat Plans or Combat Operations.[26]

Development of the CENTAF Air Tasking Order Process

The Tactical Air Control Center, as well as the entire Tactical Air Control System, is tied together by the Air Tasking Order. This Order promulgates the air campaign plan developed by the Combat Plans and Combat Intelligence Divisions and transmits the plan throughout the TACS. The Air Tasking Order, however, is not itself a plan; it is the means by which tasks are communicated to the applicable units. The Air Tasking Order is a message containing most pertinent information about flight operations during a specific period.[27] It usually contains takeoff times for all aircraft under the control of the issuing commander,[28] air

---

[25] USCENTAF Regulation 55-45, *United States Central Command Air Employment Planning Process*, 27 Jun 1990.

[26] For example, In Oct 1990, Brig Gen Glosson noted that Intelligence organizations were not supporting operations planners. He argued that one reason for this failure was that "unlike the remainder of our profession, [Intelligence] works truly for someone else other than the commander on the scene." (S) Intvw, TSgt Theodore J. Turner, USCENTAF History Office with Brig Gen Buster C. Glosson, 14th Air Division (P) Commander and Director, USCENTAF Campaign Plans, 18 Oct 1990.

[27] U.S. forces do not always train and use a standard ATO format. For example, where U.S. forces are involved in operations with allied nations–e.g., NATO–different ATO formats are used. ATOs are issued daily and, most often, cover twenty-four hours.

[28] The Air Component Commander or Joint Air Component Commander may not control all air assets in theater. Specifically, the Marine and Naval commanders may retain a significant portion of their air assets for use by their Service. In this case, the ATO may contain only those air forces allocated by the Service component to the air

refueling times and locations, and targets and times over targets (TOT) for a specific period. In addition, the Order often contains daily updates to the Special Instructions (SPINS) and Airspace Control Order (ACO), which tell the pilots the procedures to be followed en route.[29]

Central Command Air Forces used the format published by the Joint Tactical Command, Control and Communications Agency for its Air Tasking Order.[30] Mission orders were arranged first by organizations, for example, tactical fighter wings or squadrons and Navy CVs, and then in order of times over targets. Figure 22 reproduces a page from an Air Tasking Order from Desert Shield.[31] The description of each mission is formatted. The first line details mission data, including:

- a unique alphanumeric mission identifier for the aircraft described in the mission order;

- an alphabetic package code which referred to all missions taking part in a particular launch—not all aircraft in a single package would be assigned to attack the same target;

- the flight leader's call sign—other aircraft would take the flight leader's name but be distinguished from the flight leader by succeeding numbers;

- the number and type of aircraft in the mission;

---

commander.

[29] *Joint User Handbook for Message Text Formats*, Joint Tactical Command, Control and Communications Agency, 1 Sep 1988.

[30] *Joint User Handbook for Message Text Formats*, Joint Tactical Command, Control and Communications Agency, 1 Sep 1988. However, U.S. forces do not always train and use a standard ATO format. For example, where U.S. forces are involved in operations with allied nations—e.g., NATO—different ATO formats are used. ATOs are issued daily and, most often, cover twenty-four hours.

[31] (S) Air Tasking Orders, Desert Shield, 30 Nov 1990, GWAPS, CSS Safe 6.

Figure 22
Page From Air Tasking Order

```
                    PENTAGON
               OPERATIONS DIRECTORATE

IMMEDIATE/ROUTINE                    ZYUW RHIUFMA4679 3341315
O R 301300Z NOV 90 ZFF-1
FM HQ USCENTAF FWD//HQ RSAF OPERATIONS//
TO AIG8589
RUFTLEA/20TFW RAF UPPER HEYFORD UK//CC//
RUFLEPA/20TFW DEPLOYED INCIRLIK AB TU//CC//
RUHGPEM/435ALCE DET ONE DEPLOYED//

          SECTION 1 OF 37
OPER/OPERATION DESERT SHIELD//
MSGID/ATOCONF/USCENTAF-CBT PLAS//
NARR/USCENTAF/RSAF DESERT SHIELD ATO G DAY C+116 01 DEC 90
THE FOLLOWING WILL SERVE AS A TEMPORARY KEY TO ALL SETS CONTAINED
WITHIN THE AIR TASKING ORDER.  ANY FIELDS THAT DO NOT CONTAIN DATA
WILL BE REPLACED WITH A HYPHEN.
```

[DELETED]

```
ALL FIELDS ARE ACCOUNTED FOR UNTIL THE LAST MANDATORY FIELD.
ALL TRAILING OPTIONAL FIELDS WITHOUT DATA ARE DROPPED.//
PERID/ 010100Z/TO:020300Z//
AIRTASK/UNIT TASKING//
TASKUNIT/   C41//
MSNDAT/2703/ZN/BADMAN 03/1A-6E/GINT/
MSNLOC/
AMPN/ REMARK IDENTIFIER(S): A E G
      COMMENTS: 24 HOUR STRIKE ALERT//
MSNDAT/
MSNLOC/
AMPN/
```

```
MSNDAT/                          [DELETED]
MSNLOC/
AMPN/
```

```
NARR/ UNIT REMARKS:       C41
UNIT REMARKS A
SEE TANKER SPINS FOR AAR INFORMATION.
UNIT REMARKS E
CONTACT EAST AWACS FOR DIRECT CONTROL, USE EAST COMM PLAN.
UNIT REMARKS G
CONTACT GULF WHISKEY.
...........................................................
//
```

[DELETED]

```
*** AF SECTION MESSAGE ***

DISTRIBUTION                                               3
ACTION                                    (A)
INFO   XO(1) CSS VIA XOXO(1) FILE CY(1)
AF SECTION MESSAGE (1)
                                  TOTAL COPIES REQUIRED    3

          MCN=90334/21951   TOR=90334/1348Z  TAD=90334/1348Z  CDSN=MAD271
*AIR FORCE MESSAGE*                                            PAGE 1 OF  2
                                                               301300Z NOV 90
                                                               SECT 01 OF 37
```

- an abbreviation identifying mission type, for example, "INT" for interdiction;

- a field to indicate alert status;

- two fields to indicate the required ordnance loadout; and

- two fields to provide Identification Friend or Foe squawks in Modes II and III.

The second line lists either target location (TGTLOC) for strike missions or mission location (MSNLOC) for nonstrike missions. This line includes fields for the following data:

- time on target (TOT);

- time off target (TFT);

- target identification–normally a basic encyclopedic number, or BEN–sometimes a short description;

- target type (seldom used);

- aimpoints or designated munitions point of impact (DMPI); and

- the request number for targets requested from field forces–for example, army or marines–for tactical air strikes.

The data fields for aerial refueling, intra-theater airlift, mission support (for example, ABCCC and AWACS), and reconnaissance missions are similar to those described above. Task unit entries end with remarks which add instructions related to special instructions, detailed aimpoints, or command and control.

Upon arrival in theater, CENTAF priorities included bedding down the deploying forces and developing a plan to defend Saudi Arabia. The

Combat Planning Staff[32] assumed the task of assembling a coherent plan for Saudi Arabia's defense. The focus of that initial planning effort was the use of air power to interdict and destroy Iraqi ground forces while coalition ground forces moved to defensive positions.[33] By late August, Central Command Air Forces was publishing two distinct Air Tasking Order products: (a) the daily Air Tasking Orders, which assigned tasks such as training and ground/airborne alert commitments and (b) the ATO B for D-Day, which included the tasks inherent in the developing plan for the defense of Saudi Arabia. The daily Air Tasking Orders detailed the ground and airborne alert commitments, air refueling activity, and airlift within the theater. Each Air Tasking Order identified alphabetically (ATO B, ATO C, ATO D, etc.), was superseded every day by a new Order with the subsequent alphabetic designation. The first daily Air Tasking Order published by CENTAF staff in the theater was ATO B, published on 12 August 1990.[34]

The Air Tasking Order continued to expand and develop as the coalition grew and more U.S. and allied forces became available. By late August, CENTAF also began publishing *daily training* in the ATO. Greater training requirements led to increases in the size and complexity of the ATO. CENTAF adjusted the designation sequence for subsequent Air Tasking Orders once the alphabetic designation reached ATO Z on 26 September 1990, or C+50.[35] The designation of the ATO for 27 September did not revert to the beginning of the alphabet; the designation for 27

---

[32] As illustrated in Figure 18, the Combat Plans Division hierarchy had several levels. The COPS (along with Employment Plans Branch, Long Range Plans Branch, and Night Targeting Branch) was under the Combat Planning Division, which, in turn, was a major element in the Combat Plans Division.

[33] The first Air Tasking Order published on 12 Aug 1990 gives an example of the tasking given to the units in these early days of the deployment. The F-15Es (from the 4th TFW) were assigned to assume ground alert loaded with an "equal mix of SCLS and load maximum number of aircraft and place on 30min GND alert. Be prepared to counter an Iraqi invasion of SA. Plan for 4 ship int msns, max sortie surge rates." (S) (HQ USCENTAF FWD msg 12040Z Aug 1990, Operation Sandwedge ATO-B, GWAPS Microfilm Roll Number 23969, Frame Number 400.

[34] (S) USCENTAF msg 120404Z Aug 1990, Operation Sandwedge ATO-B, GWAPS Microfilm Roll Number 23969, Frame Number 400.

[35] (S) USCENTAF msg 251350Z Sep 1990, USCENTAF ATO-Z, C+50, 26 Sep 1990, GWAPS CSS Safe 7, folder "Desert Shield Air Tasking Orders (ATOs)," 16-30 Sep 1990.

September (or C+51) was ATO F.³⁶ CENTAF continued to use the alphabetic identifiers F through Z for the daily Orders until the air campaign began on 17 January 1991.

The daily Air Tasking Order designation was changed to avoid confusion with the second ATO: ATO B for D-Day. Unlike the daily ATO, ATO B for D-Day included specific taskings, targets, missions, and procedures that would be executed should Saudi Arabia be attacked by Iraqi forces.³⁷ Throughout the fall and early winter of 1990 ATO B for D-Day was updated and published several times. The last versions of ATO B for D-Day reflected the tasking inherent in the Combined Operations Plan for the defense of Saudi Arabia published on 29 November 1990.³⁸

The Special Instructions, published in the Daily Air Tasking Order, solved a critical problem facing CENTAF Forward staff when they arrived in theater, that is, there were no standing airspace plans, search and rescue procedures, or communications procedures. Negotiations had not been completed among the various countries and agencies on such issues as training ranges and routes, safe passage procedures across national borders, and air refueling procedures.³⁹ Negotiations on these issues had to be accomplished while the forces deployed and the coalition was formed. As agreements were reached and plans developed, the Special Instructions published in the Daily ATO and D-Day ATO grew in size and

---

³⁶(S) USCENTAF msg 261205Z Sep 1990, USCENTAF ATO-F, C+51, 27 Sep 1990, GWAPS CSS Safe 7, folder "Desert Shield Air Tasking Orders (ATOs)," 16-30 Sep 1990.

³⁷In Nov 1990, Lt Col David A. Deptula, the chief air planner for the CENTAF Special Planning Group, noted that the "D-Day Plan was a required contingency plan for when the folks got over here in the event Saddam rolled over the border. . . . [T]here had to be a defensive plan." See (S) Intvw TSgt Theodore J. Turner, USCENTAF History office with Lt Col David A. Deptula, Chief Air Planner, USCENTAF Special Planning Group, 1 Nov 1990.

³⁸To avoid confusion caused by changes in unit taskings copies of ATO-B for D-Day were destroyed as new versions were published. The final version of ATO-B for D-Day was published on 17 Dec 1990. This version of the ATO illustrates the final development of the defensive air taskings supporting the Combined OPLAN for the defense of Saudi Arabia. (GWAPS Microfilm Roll Number 23974, Frames 3930-1128.)

³⁹In other theaters (e.g., Europe/NATO), procedures and agreements have been negotiated and put "on the shelf" for possible use. Refinements of existing procedures and agreements take place through live flying and command post national and multinational exercises.

complexity. By late September 1990, the Special Instructions had grown to include the following ten separate sections:[40] General Information, Electronic Combat Information, Communications Plan, Safe Passage Procedures, Command and Control, Search and Rescue Procedures, Rules of Engagement, Target Guidance, Air-to-Air Refueling Tanker Information, and the Airspace Control Order. Each Special Instructions section contained information critical to the execution of tasking contained in the Air Tasking Order. Daily training and staff practice refined the Instructions so that key matters (such as supporting airspace structure, and command and control procedures) were fully developed and coordinated when the strategic air campaign began.

Figure 23 illustrates the planning cycle (to publish the Air Tasking Order) initially established by Central Command Air Forces in Saudi Arabia. The CENTAF staff planned to use this cycle in the event they would execute the D-Day ATO. The cycle to plan, produce, and execute an Order was spread over three days, or seventy-two hours.[41] Initially, the ATO execution period covered a twenty-four hour period from 0100Z through 0059Z the next day.[42] Action on each Air Tasking Order cycle began at 0900Z (1200L)[43] with a meeting of the Combat Planning Staff. Immediately following that meeting, the Joint Target Coordination Board convened to discuss targeting strategy, deconfliction, and sortie apportionment. Between 1030Z and 1130Z, the ATO Guidance Letter[44] and

---

[40]For example, see (S) Msg, CENTAF FWD/HQ RAF Operations to Subordinate Units, 260815Z Sep 1990, subj: Special Instructions, USCENTAF ATO Master Weekly SPINS, 27 Sep through 3 Oct 1990.

[41]Occasionally the cycle is referred to as thirty-six or forty-eight hours long. The difference is simply where one starts and stops the clock. For example, if measured from the first hour rather than the last hour of the twenty-four hour ATO period, the cycle is forty-eight hours.

[42]Ltr, Col James C. Crigger, Deputy Chief of Staff, Operations, CENTAF, to ARCENT/G3, MARCENT/C3, NAVCENT/N3, RAF/LNO, RAF, subj: Air Tasking Order (ATO) Nominations, 3 Sep 1990.

[43]Riyadh local time, e.g., 1200L, is derived by adding three hours to Zulu time, e.g., 0900Z.

[44]The Guidance Letter is issued by the JFACC but is based upon guidance from the Theater Commander.

**Figure 23
Proposed Sorties Apportionment**

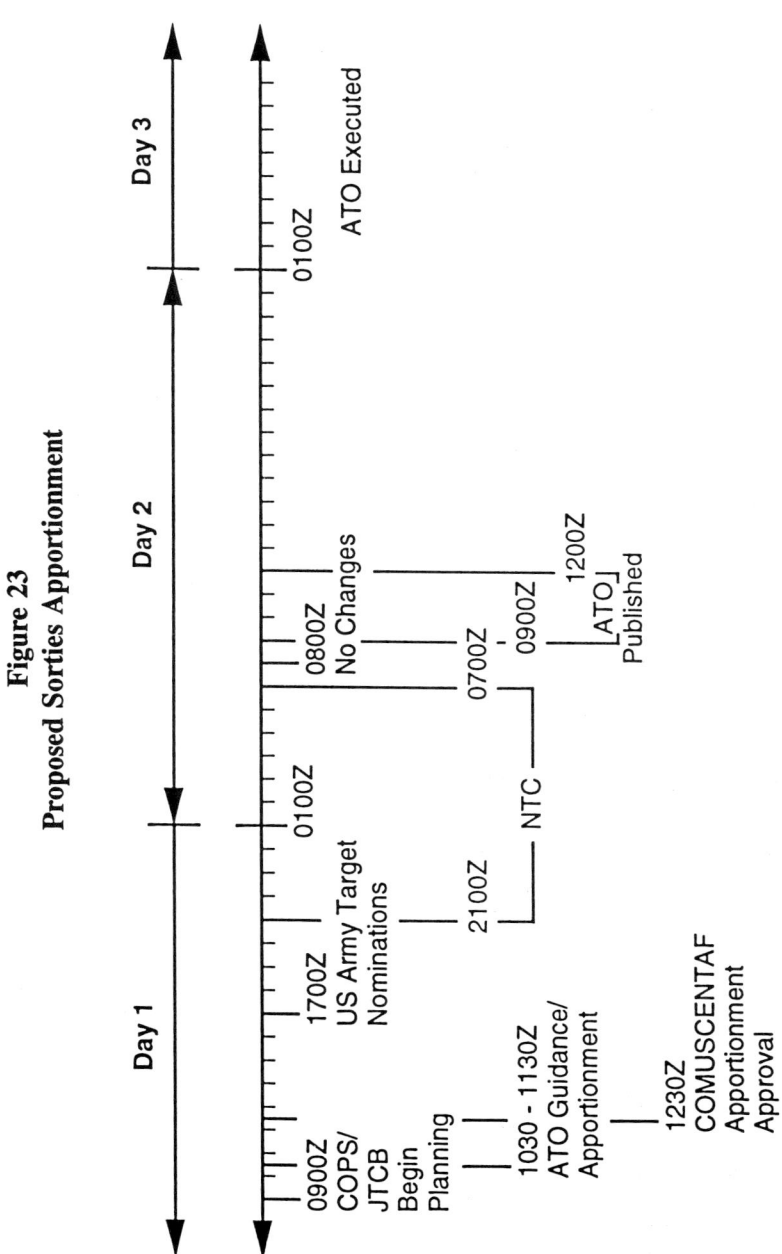

apportionment[45] briefing for the Deputy Chiefs of Staff were prepared. At 1230Z the COMUSCENTAF (Central Command Air Forces Commander) apportionment meeting was held, at which the Commander approved the ATO Guidance Letter and transferred the apportionment to the Commander in Chief, Central Command. Between 1300Z and 1400Z, information was prepared for the night targeting cell. U.S. Army target nominations were due at 1700Z; they were merged, ranked, and forwarded to the intelligence and targeting specialists. Intelligence specialists validated each target, gathered the required mission planning data, and weaponeered[46] each target for a suggested mix of aircraft and weapons.[47] This process was completed by 2100Z, when the sortie allocation process began. The night targeting cell,[48] working between 2100Z and 0700Z, produced a proposed sortie allocation by using the Commander's apportionment guidance, combined with munitions and weapon system capability.[49]

---

[45] Apportionment is a statement of the level of effort which is to be given to missions. For example, fifteen percent counterair, forty-three percent interdiction, two percent strategic offense, and forty percent planned CAS.

[46] Weaponeering "is the process of determining the quantity of a specific type weapon required to achieve a specified level of damage to a given target, considering target vulnerability, weapon effects, munitions delivery errors, damage criteria, probability of kill, weapon reliability, etc. When the objective of force employment is to employ lethal force against a target, targeteers use a variety of weaponeering methodologies to determine expected damage levels. These weaponeering methodologies include both nonnuclear and nuclear weaponeering techniques. Common to both methodologies is aimpoint selection and weapons effects analysis." Department of the Air Force, *An Introduction to Air Force Targeting*, AF Pamphlet 200-17, 23 Jun 1989, p 21.

[47] Targeteering is a complex and difficult subject to master. According to AFP 200-17, the targeteer must understand "doctrine; strategy; operational plans and planning cycles (both ours and the enemy's); weapons systems and tactics; research and development processes; mapping, charting, and geodesy; quantitative and qualitative analytical techniques; physics; and structural engineering." Targeting involves integrating "intelligence threat information, the target system, and target characteristics with operations data on friendly force posture, capabilities, weapons effects, objectives, rules of engagement, and doctrine." See Department of the Air Force, *An Introduction to Air Force Targeting*, AF Pamphlet, 23 Jun 1989, pp 8-9.

[48] The Night Targeting Cell, a component of the Night Targeting Branch, was located in the Combat Planning Division. See Figure 18.

[49] There are differences between the times setting deadlines for actions between the letter sent by Col Crigger, DCS/O (to ARCENT, MARCENT, NAVCENT, RAF, and RSAF) and the USCENTAF/RAF procedures handout published one month later. (S) See the USCENTAF/RAF, *Desert Shield Combat Plans Handout*, Oct 1990. See also Ltr, Col James C. Crigger, Jr., Deputy Chief of Staff, Operations, CENTAF, to ARCENT/G3, MARCENT/C3, NAVCENT/N3, RAF/LNO, RAF, subj: Air Tasking Order (ATO) Nominations, 3 Sep 1990.

This proposed sortie apportionment was submitted to the CENTAF Commander by 0630Z on day 2. Once he approved the Air Tasking Order, it was passed to the fighter division where it was completed and prepared for transmission to the units. The final proof of the fighter part of the ATO was released at 0700Z. At 0800Z, no further changes were accepted to the day's Order, and it was published between 0900Z and 1200Z. Upon receipt of the ATO, the units would plan their missions and begin execution at 0100Z, day 3–the start of the next Air Tasking Order execution period.[50]

Once H-hour of the particular ATO was reached, control of it was turned over to the Combat Operations Division, with intelligence support from the Enemy Situation Correlation Division. If the Joint Force Air Component Commander wanted to change a mission at this point, the Combat Operations Division would notify the specific unit and the other agencies or units associated with that mission. For example, if the Commander directed a change in takeoff time of a strike mission, the unit flying the strike mission and the escort aircraft units, the refueling aircraft, and the air defense system would have to be notified.

Over time, the Computer Assisted Force Management System became the primary means to distribute the Air Tasking Order within the theater. Initially, however, the CAFMS was not established widely, and the first ATOs were distributed by a variety of other means, including the use of STU-IIIs and modems, backed up by Saudi secure FAX machines and a Saudi secure logistics management network.[51] Although Central Command Air Forces

---

In the September letter, Col Crigger notes that the then-current ATO cycle covered "a twenty-four hour period from 0100Z through 0059Z the next day." He added that target submission times were largely driven "by the limited communications connectivity throughout the theater which increases ATO transmittal/distribution time." The *Desert Shield Combat Plans Handout* describes the planning process with greater detail. There are two key differences between the Crigger letter and the *Combat Plan Handout*. The first difference is the deadline for submission of target nominations from the components. The Crigger letter specified that target nominations were due at 1300Z; the *Combat Plans Handout* specified 1700Z. Second, the Crigger letter set the ATO publishing period at 1200Z to 1500Z; the *Combat Plans Handout* set the publishing period from 0900Z to 1200Z.

[50]Ltr, Col James C. Crigger, Jr., Deputy Chief of Staff, Operations, CENTAF, to ARCENT/G3, MARCENT/C3, NAVCENT/N3, RAF/LNO, RAF, subj: Air Tasking Order (ATO) Nominations, 3 Sep 1990.

[51]Briefing, "Air Tasking Order (ATO) Preparation and Composite Force Packaging," nd.

staff realized that the information transfer situation would improve over time, they feared that the limited ATO distribution system would become saturated rapidly. A backup to the electronic system was needed should it break. To solve this problem, on 21 August 1990, the CENTAF Director of Operations, Col. James C. Crigger, Jr., requested that C-21 aircraft be made available to fly the Order to several bases.[52] Aircraft courier flights continued throughout the war and were considered the backup should the ATO transmission system fail.[53] Aircraft courier flights were also used to provide the ATO to naval carrier task forces.[54]

---

[52] Ltr, Col James C. Crigger, Jr., Director of Operations, CENTAF FWD, to COMALF, ALCC, subj: C-21 Taskings, 21 Aug 1990.

[53] Use of the CAFMS entailed risks concerning reliability, or "back-up," and transmittal. First, if the system were disabled or shut down for even a short period of time–a few hours–it would have been impossible for the ATO to be distributed throughout the theater within an acceptable period of time. Second, the size of the document generated difficulties in transmitting the ATO electronically to Air Force (and Navy) units.

[54] In 1989, there was an Air Force-Navy initiative to install CAFMS on the USS MT WHITNEY in support of Operation Solid Shield. The test was supported by a SHF SATCOM link through the Norfolk Naval Ground Station. The link supported successfully a 1,000 sortie ATO and the transfer of more than 100 messages between 507 TACCS (located at Shaw AFB, SC) and the USS MT WHITNEY. However, the lessons learned from this installation were not applied–CAFMSs were not installed on carriers, training did not continue, and neither the Air Force nor the Navy expressed a desire to put CAFMS on other ships.

During Desert Shield and Desert Storm, the JFACC was required to support six carrier fleets and forty-two additional remote terminal users. Typical organizational problems in disseminating the ATO were compounded by procedural and mechanical limitations. Navy personnel were not trained to use or maintain CAFMS. There had been no pre conflict training, there had been no exercises, nor had the lessons of the USS MT WHITNEY in Solid Shield 89 been applied. Mechanical obstacles included an insufficient quantity of equipment initially deployed to support the size of the campaign, the communications links were incapable of supporting a very large daily ATO, uninterrupted WWMCCS links were unreliable and unable to transmit the ATO, and the deployed carriers failed to dedicate a SHF SATCOM link to support receiving the ATO.

During Desert Shield, the Navy tried at least five ways to receive the ATO: AUTODIN (too slow), WWMCCS (ATO too long, satellite link unreliable), PC transfer to Pentagon then forwarded to FLTCOMM (too slow), software conversion program developed to put ATO in Navy message format–Janap 126–then paper tape was cut on CAFMS and passed to Navy over FLTFLASH (too slow), use of S-3 aircraft to hand carry the ATO. The final solution–use of S-3 aircraft–proved the fastest and most effective. Briefing, Maj Whitehurst, TAC/DOYY, HQ TAC, subj: USAF/USN ATO Interface, nd. See also (S) Center for Naval Analyses, *Desert Storm Reconstruction Report*, Volume VIII: *C³/Space and Electronic Warfare* (Alexandria, VA, 1992), p 1-13; (S) Center for Naval Analyses, *Desert Storm Reconstruction Report*, Volume II: *Strike Warfare* (Alexandria, VA, 1991), p 2-16;

Summary

Moving, modifying, manning, and managing the military organization created to defend Saudi Arabia and reclaim Kuwait was difficult. This chapter reviewed and described the organization of the CENTAF Tactical Air Control Center in Riyadh. The role of this chapter was not merely to provide a description of the CENTAF process for planning and exercising command and control over forces. The chapter also set the stage for a detailed description of how the special offensive planning organization was created, grew, and assumed central importance in the command and control of U.S. and allied air forces.

Briefing, "Air Tasking Order (ATO) Preparation and Composite Force Packaging," nd. See (S) Chapter 3 for a discussion of the JFACC's role in dealing with the CENTAF-NAVCENT communications problems.

6

The Black Hole and Its Impact

Almost immediately after the invasion of Kuwait, planning began at the Air Staff to develop a strategic air campaign against Iraq.[1] Under the direction of Col. John A. Warden, III, Deputy Director for Warfighting, HQ USAF/XOXW, the concept of an offensive, strategic air campaign was developed, briefed to a variety of audiences, and taken to the theater.[2] The development of this plan influenced the ongoing planning process at Central Command Air Forces (CENTAF) and affected the make-up of the developing theater command and control system. In particular, this chapter will examine the Special Planning Group, also known as the "Black Hole," which was established outside of the CENTAF Tactical Air Control Center (TACC) organization and assigned the task of expanding and completing the Air Staff concept for a strategic air campaign plan. We also will analyze the relationship among the Black Hole, the CENTAF TACC, and intelligence organizations. Finally, we will describe the CENTAF TACC reorganization, which (as offensive action approached) combined the Black Hole with the Tactical Air Control Center planning staff.

Black Hole Origins

On 19-20 August 1990, Colonel Warden and several of his staff briefed their strategic campaign plan, "Instant Thunder," to key members

---

[1] On 10 Aug 1990, Gen Schwarzkopf called Gen Powell to ask that Air Force planners begin work "on a strategic bombing campaign aimed at Iraq's military." H. Norman Schwarzkopf with Peter Petre, *It Doesn't Take a Hero* (New York, 1992), p 313. In addition, see (S) Hist, 9th AF/USCENTAF (David L. Rosmer), *9 AF/CENTAF in Desert Shield: The Initial Phase*, Aug 1990, 10 Jan 1992, p 13; see also GWAPS *Planning* report.

[2] Work on the offensive air concept began at the request of Gen H. Norman Schwarzkopf in a telephone conversation with Vice Chief of Staff Gen John M. Loh (on 5-6 Aug 1990). Col Warden and a group of staff officers were sent to Riyadh by Gen Schwarzkopf on 19 Aug. Before going to Saudi Arabia, Warden had briefed Gen H. Norman Schwarzkopf, Gen Colin Powell, Gen Alfred M. Gray (USMC Commandant), and Adm Frank B. Kelso (Chief of Naval Operations).

of the Central Command (CENTCOM) and CENTCOM Air Force staffs in Saudi Arabia. Gen. Horner, acting as Commander in Chief, Central Command (Forward), was dissatisfied with the plan because it ignored the large number of Iraqi forces on the Saudi border.[3] Brig. Gen. Buster C. Glosson, who had been assigned to the Joint Task Force Middle East aboard the USS *LaSalle*, saw the Instant Thunder briefing and volunteered to oversee the development of a strategic–offensive–air campaign against Iraq.[4] Three key members of Warden's team were asked to stay in Saudi Arabia to become the nucleus of a planning team (that came to be) called the Black Hole. In addition to the three Air Staff officers who remained in the theater, people from the Central Command Air Forces staff, other Services, and coalition partners, as well as officers from the deploying units and Tactical Air Command headquarters, were detailed to man the select planning group.[5] This group was organized into a Special Studies

---

[3] According to Lt Gen Horner, Col Warden was unable to answer practical questions about the disposition of forces or effective responses to potential Iraqi actions. (S) Intvw, Barry Barlow, Richard G. Davis, and Perry Jamieson with Lt Gen Charles A. Horner, 9th AF Commander, 4 Mar 1992.

[4] (S) Intvw, Richard G. Davis, Perry Jamieson, and Barry Barlow with Lt Gen Charles A. Horner, Commander, 9th AF, 4 Mar 1992; (S) Intvw, TSgt Theodore J. Turner, CENTAF History Office with Brig Gen Buster C. Glosson, 14th AD (P) Commander and Director, USCENTAF Campaign Plans, 17 Oct 1990; (S) Intvw, Thomas A. Keaney, Mark D. Mandeles, Williamson Murray, and Barry Watts with Lt Col David A. Deptula, SAF/OSX, 20-21 Dec 1991. Lt Col Deptula served as the Chief Air Planner, Special Planning Group, CENTAF FWD, during Operation Desert Shield/Storm.

[5] In Oct 1990, Brig Gen Glosson recalled that his first action was to ensure he: had an expert in building ATOs, a person that was very familiar and had built numerous OP Orders, a person that had been involved in execution planning, to include the entire gamut from the SEAD aspects, to munitions, to weapons systems . . . including the timing, AWACS, tankers, RIVET JOINT, and all the support elements. Once I got those requirements covered from Ninth Air Force staff, I asked each of the units that were going to be participating to provide two people. The reason I got two people is I let the unit commander decide who he sent and I figured that there would never be a situation where a person would select the exact people that I would–so out of the two people I would get at least one that I could hang onto for a while. (S)Intvw, Tsgt Theodore J. Turner, CENTAF/HO with Brig Gen Buster C. Glosson, 14th AD (P) Commander and Director, USCENTAF Campaign Plans, 17 Oct 1990.

Division aligned under Maj. Gen. Thomas R. Olsen, acting CENTAF Forward Commander.[6] The 24 August 1990, CENTAF Forward organizational chart illustrates this relationship (see Figure 24).[7] Because of the political sensitivities concerning planning offensive operations against Iraq, access to the Special Studies Division (the Black Hole) work areas was tightly controlled.[8] Only a select group of planners directly involved with the development of the campaign and the senior staff were allowed into the planning area, or even had knowledge of their activities.[9] Very few members of the CENTAF Combat Plans Division and Combat Operations Division were granted access. No mention of the concept would be made until the developing coalition was ready to accept such a plan.[10]

---

[6]On 6 Aug 1990 Gen Schwarzkopf and Lt Gen Horner, among others, accompanied the Secretary of Defense to Saudi Arabia for discussions with the Saudi Arabian government. After gaining Saudi Arabian approval for the deployment of U.S. forces to the Kingdom Gen Schwarzkopf returned to the United States leaving Lt Gen Horner in the Kingdom as CINCCENT Deployed. On 8 Aug 1990 Maj Gen Thomas R. Olsen arrived in Riyadh, Saudi Arabia with the first contingent of U.S. Air Force, CENTCOM (i.e., CENTAF) personnel to set up the headquarters of CENTAF Forward. The job of establishing the CENTAF TACC in the theater fell to Maj Gen Olsen as the acting CENTAF Commander FWD. Gen Olsen continued to act as COMUSCENTAF (FWD) and Gen Horner as CINCCENT (FWD) until 24 August 1990 when Gen Schwarzkopf returned to the theater. At this time Gen Horner took up the duties of COMUSCENTAF.

[7]Under Title V, which includes chart CENTAF Organizational Chart, CENTAF Microfilm record, GWAPS.

[8](S) Intvw, Thomas C. Hone, Mark D. Mandeles, and Maj Sanford S. Terry with Col Paul Dordal, Joint Staff, Operations Directorate (J-3), Joint Operations Division, EUCOM/CENTCOM Branch, 9 Jan 1992. [DELETED] As a result of political sensitivities and security concerns, initial offensive planning was conducted on a unilateral basis by a small group of USCENTCOM, USCENTAF, and Air Staff planners. These efforts were extremely sensitive [DELETED]. (S/NF) AAR CENTCOM J-5, Plans, 5 Mar 1991, p 9.

[9]Even some officers assigned to work on the strategic air campaign did not immediately have access to the Instant Thunder plan. Cdr Donald W. McSwain recalled that he and the other naval officer assigned to the Black Hole, Cdr Maurice Smith, were read into part of Instant Thunder on 23 Aug–they received the rest of the briefing later. (S) Intvw, Mark D. Mandeles and Maj Sanford S. Terry with Cdr Donald W. McSwain, CNO Op 741, 21 Apr 1992.

[10]See (S) GWAPS *Planning* report.

Lt Col Ben Harvey, Col John Warden, Lt Col David Deptula, and Lt Col Ron Stanfil enroute to Riyadh to brief Instant Thunder to Gen Horner.

In the initial days of August 1990, the prime tasks facing Central Command Air Forces staff were bedding down deploying air forces and developing a plan to defend Saudi Arabia.[11] Tactical forces were unprepared to apply the full range of combat power immediately after initial deployment–unit deployments were made before support aircraft, command, control, communications and intelligence packages, and preferred munitions arrived.[12] In the meantime, however, as early as 8 August 1990, elements of the CENTAF staff also began to develop offensive

---

[11](S) Hist, 9th AF/USCENTAF (David L. Rosmer), *9AF/CENTAF in Desert Shield: The Initial Phase*, Aug 1990, 10 Jan 1992, p 63.

[12](S/NF/WNINTEL/NC/ORCON) Briefing, HQ TAC, "Desert Storm Lessons Learned" in USAF Desert Shield/Desert Storm Hot Wash, 12-13 Jul 1991, Maxwell AFB, AL.

Figure 24
CENTAF Forward Organization

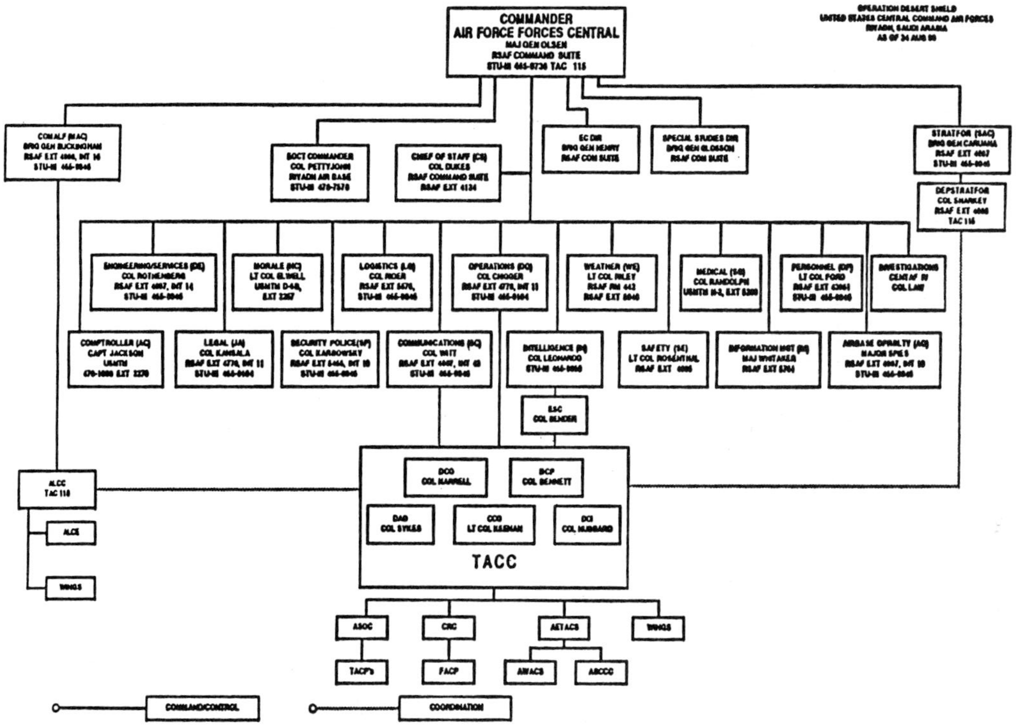

options against Iraq.¹³ The earliest offensive concept was called the "punishment ATO [Air Tasking Order]."¹⁴ The concept was limited in scale and not designed to be an integrated strategic air campaign, involving simultaneous attack on geographically dispersed targets to cripple the ability of Iraq to wage war. It did include an option to attack deep, strategic targets in Iraq. CENTAF officers also began developing an Iraqi target catalog.¹⁵

Yet, the primary focus of CENTAF's Combat Plans Division was different from that of the Black Hole. General Glosson and his staff developed a plan which diverged from official Army and Air Force thought about the concept of air-land battle. The Black Hole's plan was based upon the concept of strategic airpower as a complete, independent force on the battlefield. The resulting campaign plan was consistent with the nucleus of the Instant Thunder plan. Instant Thunder proposed that a major, if not deciding, factor in forcing nation-states to surrender was precise, over-

---

¹³At the end of Feb 1990, during its annual Southwest Asia Symposium, CENTAF revealed publicly that it was refocussing attention on Iraq. (S) MR, David L. Rosmer, Chief, USCENTAF/9th AF History Office, subj: Notes from the Third Annual USCENTAF Symposium on Southwest Asia, Conducted at Shaw AFB, SC, 28 Feb - 1 Mar 1990; (S) *9AF/CENTAF in Desert Shield: The Initial Phase*, p 13.

Other organizations which also developed offensive options included HQ TAC. In early Aug 1990, TAC developed a plan beginning "with demonstrative attacks against high value targets . . . [and then] escalat[ing] as required until all significant targets are destroyed. . . . This strategy allows time and opportunity for Hussein to reevaluate his situation and back out while there is something to save." (S) See fax from Brig Gen Griffith, TAC/XP to Maj Gen Alexander, AF/XOX, 11 Aug 1990. "CENTCOM Air Campaign Plan," GWAPS, CHSH-14.

¹⁴The D-Day ATO, rather than the punishment ATO, would have been employed if the Iraqis had crossed the border into Saudi Arabia. See (S) *Planning* report.

¹⁵This work was based on then-recent CENTCOM studies of Iraqi military capabilities, including (S) USCENTCOM, Security Environment 2000, A CENTCOM View, 21 May 1990, p III-3; (S) RAdm Grant Sharp, The Sharp Report, Planning for the Gulf War, 3 Dec 1991, p 5. Ninth TIS targeteers completed a target study of Iraq on 15 Jun 1990–six weeks before Iraq invaded Kuwait. The 9th TIS target study contained 183 Iraqi and 35 Kuwaiti targets. See (S) *Planning* report.

whelming aerial attack against "centers of gravity": key political, industrial, economic, social, and military institutions or systems.[16]

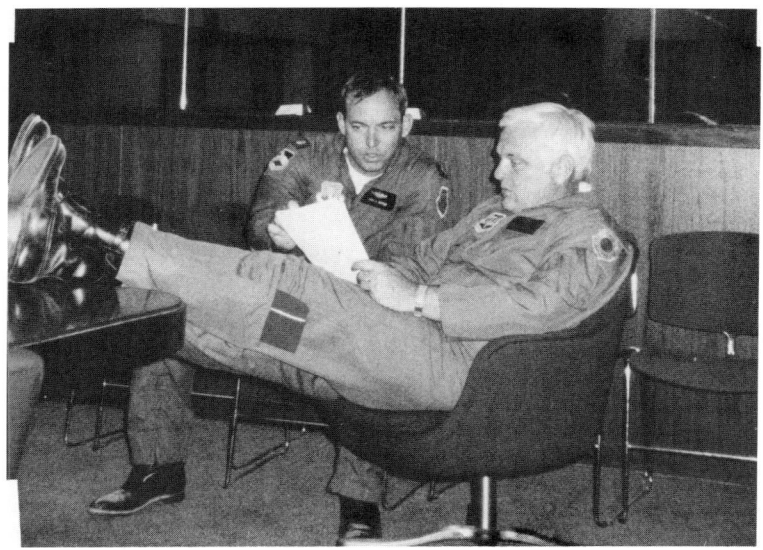

Lt Col Deptula reviewing attack plan for Gen Glosson.

Around 23 August, staff officers selected to serve in the Black Hole began adapting the Instant Thunder plan to theater conditions. This attack plan was not a full Air Tasking Order, such as those produced by CENTAF's Combat Plans Division. There was not enough time or resources to employ a "business as usual" approach to building an ATO. Instead, the attack plan matched available air assets with priority targets to achieve "maximum strategic impact." On 29 August, the Black Hole's first fully

---

[16] See (S) GWAPS *Planning* report for discussion of the goals of the Black Hole's strategic air campaign plan.

coordinated Air Tasking Order (based on the attack plan) was published,[17] and it was the basis of the plan that was executed on 17 January 1991.[18] Over time, the number of targets grew from 84 to 712.

Background on how the Black Hole (a) developed the Master Attack Plan (MAP), (b) transformed the MAP into a flyable Air Tasking Order, and (c) issued the ATO is necessary to explain the role of that group in the theater command and control system, and especially the Tactical Air Control Center.[19] As noted above, the Black Hole initially was isolated from the TACC's other divisions for reasons of operational security. In late August 1990, the Black Hole consisted of approximately thirty planners (listed in Figure 25) headed by General Glosson.[20] Of these planners, joint and allied representation was provided by two U.S. Navy commanders,[21] one U.S. Army lieutenant colonel,[22] and one British Royal Air Force wing commander.[23] Only a few U.S. Air Force Intelligence officers were assigned to the group.[24] Glosson selected operations

---

[17](S) Briefing, Lt Col Deptula, SAF/OSX, Instant Thunder (Offensive Campaign Phase I) Planning Assessment–24 Sep 1990, Presentations to SECAF and XOXW, nd [Briefing presented upon return from first trip to Saudi Arabia, late Sep 1990.]

[18](S) Intvw, CMSgt John Burton, HQ TAC History Office with Lt Gen Charles A. Horner, Commander, 9th AF, nd [Mar 1991].

[19]The TACC was located at CENTAF Headquarters in Riyadh.

[20]The list is neither official nor exhaustive. It is based on the recollections of several officers who were assigned to the Black Hole.

[21]Cdr Donald W. McSwain and Cdr Maurice Smith.

[22]Lt Col William Welch.

[23]Wing Commander Mick Richardson.

[24]Air Force intelligence community representation included Lt Col Robert Kershaw and Capt John Glock. It also should be noted that not every intelligence officer who was "read-in" to the Instant Thunder plan on 20 August remained to help the planning effort. Five intelligence officers received the briefing in August–Capt John Heidrick, Capt John Glock, Capt Jay Bachhuber, Capt Tim Carver, and Capt Tom Clemmons. The day after the briefing, Heidrick became ill and did not return to the Special Planning Group. Clemmons went home (to the U.S.) and did not return until late September. Memo, Capt John Glock to Lt Col Daniel Kuehl and Lt Col Sanford S. Terry, GWAPS, subj: Intelligence personnel in the Black Hole, 18 Aug 1992.

Figure 25
"Black Hole" Strategic Air Campaign Planners*
Involved from August and September 1990

Brig Gen Buster C. Glosson**	Director, Campaign Plans
Brig Gen Larry Henry[a]	Director, Electronic Combat
Lt Col Dave Deptula[b]**	Chief Attack Planner
Lt Col John Turk[c]	Air-to-Air
Lt Col Rodger Greenawalt	Gen Glosson Exec
Lt Col Bob Kershaw	Intelligence Representative
Wg Commander Mick Richardson	RAF Representative
Commander "Duck" McSwain***	Persian Gulf Representative (A-6)
Commander "Fast Eddie" Smith***	Red Sea Representative (F/A-18)
Lt Col Bill Welch	Army Representative
Lt Col Bert Pryor	AWACS Planner
Lt Col Jim Pritchett	Tanker Planner
Major Bob Eskridge**	F-117 Representative
Major Scott Hente	Tanker Planner
Major John Kinser	Air Command Element
Major Mike Oelrich	Electronic Combat
Major Jefferey L. "Oly" Olsen	USMC Representative (F/A-18)
Major Gary Alexander	Electronic Combat
Major John Sweeney[d]	ATO Process
Major Dave Waterstreet	ATO Process
Captain Bill "Burners" Bruner**	NBC/Scud Planner
Captain Jim Hawkins	B-52 Planner
Captain Eric Holdaway	ELINT/SIGINT Representative
Captain Kirby Lindsey	Logistics Representative
Captain Randy O'Boyle	SOF Representative
Captain Rolf "Bugsy" Siegel	USMC Representative
Captain John Glock	Intelligence Planner/BDA
Major Al Vogel	AWACS Representative
Major Harry Heintzelman	Law of Armed Conflict

Onboard October and November 1990

Brig Gen Glen Profitt[e]	Electronic Combat
Colonel Bob Osterloh	Assistant Plans Division Chief
Major Abdulhameed Alqadhi	RSAF Representative
Major Dave Karns	B-52 Planner

Major Ernie Norsworthy	F-16 Planner
Major Mark "Buck" Rogers	Assistant Attack Planner
Major F. T. Case	Models and Analysis
Captain Mike "Cos" Cosby	Mission Support System
Capt Turki Bin Bandar Bin Abdul Aziz	RSAF Representative
Flight Leftenant Callum Steel	RAF Intelligence

Onboard January 1991

Colonel Anthony J. Tolin	Chief, Plans Division
Lt Col Sam Baptiste[e**]	Director, KTO Planning Cell
Lt Col Phil Faye	OCA Planner
Lt Col Steve Head	Intelligence Planner
Lt Col Rick Lewis	Special Assistant Glosson
Major Charley Allan	Models & Analysis
Major Michael "Chip" Setnor	F-117 Representative
Major Cliff Williford	F-111 Representative
Major Gary Green	F-15E Representative

* Only includes Strategic Air Campaign planners in Riyadh – does not include planners involved from CHECKMATE in Pentagon nor all those associated with KTO or defensive planning.

** USAF Fighter Weapons School Graduate, compilation based on memo, Charles H. Shipman, Director, Manpower & Organization, USCENTAF to 9th AF/MO, HQ TAC/XPM, subj: HQ USCENTAF Desert Storm Organization Structure, 26 Mar 1991.

*** Naval Strike Warfare Center (also known as "Strike U") graduate.

[a] Original EC Chief Planner – departed for new assignment in November 1989.

[b] In January 1991 became Director, Iraq/Strategic Target Planning Cell.

[c] In January 1991 became Assistant Director, Iraq/Strategic Target Planning Cell.

[d] In January 1991 became Assistant Director, KTO Planning Cell.

[e] Replaces Brig Gen Henry.

[f] Prior to January 1991 was responsible for defensive planning on CENTAF/DO staff.

planners on the basis of their experience and knowledge in their respective weapon systems.²⁵ Very few of the CENTAF staff had access to the Black Hole.

Knowledge of the Black Hole's first Air Tasking Order (29 August), known as ATO-1, was kept strictly within "need to know" channels but included the most senior Central Command Air Force officers.²⁶ ATO-1 was not published or transmitted through the CENTAF's normal ATO distribution system, the basis of which was the Computer Assisted Force Management System (CAFMS). Instead, ATO-1 was written on personal computers in the Black Hole, printed after normal working hours on the CENTAF ATO Division printers, and hand carried, along with the latest version of the Master Attack Plan, to "trusted agents"²⁷ in each of the

---

²⁵In Oct 1990, Brig Gen Glosson described his concerns on staffing in an interview with the CENTAF history office. See (S) Intvw, TSgt Turner with Brig Gen Glosson, 17 Oct 1990.

Brig Gen Anthony J. Tolin, the Chief of CENTAF's Plans Division (beginning Jan 1991), pointed out two reasons Brig Gen Glosson staffed his group primarily from outside 9th AF/CENTAF. First, the 9th AF staff was fully employed–doing the day-to-day administration of U.S. and allied air assets in theater. Second, although there were some good people in 9th AF, (Glosson and others believed) the overall quality of the staff was not high. Tolin also believed that General Russ, TAC Commander, told Lt Gen Horner that Horner could borrow any TAC officer for wartime duty. Intvw, John F. Guilmartin, Jr., with Brig Gen Anthony J. Tolin, Commander, 57th Fighter Wing, 30 Jan 1992.

A Navy member of the Black Hole reported that he asked that particular officers (by name) be assigned to the Black Hole. He knew these officers from previous assignments. (S) Intvw, Mandeles and Maj Terry with Cdr McSwain, 21 Apr 1992.

²⁶Col Ryder and Col Crigger were read-in on the strategic plan very early. General Thomas R. Olsen knew about the plan from the beginning. Brig Gen Glosson briefed selected members of the CENTAF staff on the strategic air campaign about the third week of September, so that they could start studying how to operate when the plan was executed. (S) Intvw, Brig Gen Glosson, 20 Oct 1990.

²⁷There were at least two "trusted agents" in each wing: the wing commander and the chief of weapons (who also may have led the wing mission planning cell). In some wings, e.g., the F-117A's 37th TFW, there may have been one more trusted agent. In the case of the 37th TFW, the additional trusted agent was the chief of intelligence.

wings and organizations throughout the theater.[28] ATO-1 was classified Top Secret, Limited Distribution; copies of ATO-1 and its associated Master Attack Plan were destroyed as they were superseded.[29] Hence, copies of the earliest ATO-1s no longer exist.[30]

In the meantime, Central Command Air Forces published two distinct Air Tasking Orders through open channels. These ATOs were the daily ATO and ATO B for D-Day.[31] The majority of officers believed they would execute the CENTAF ATOs; they knew nothing of the strategic air campaign, as embodied in ATO-1, until the decision had been made to execute an offensive operation against Iraq.

The few liaison officers assigned to both the Black Hole and Combat Plans Division ensured that CENTAF's daily and D-Day ATO Special Instructions[32] reflected the requirements of the Black Hole's strategic air campaign. Once a requirement was identified by the Black Hole planning staff, liaison officers would carry that requirement to the CENTAF Combat Operations Planning Division, where it was put into the CENTAF's ATO

---

[28]For example, see the message sent, on Department of the Air Force, USCENTAF (Shaw AFB) stationery, from Brig Gen Glosson to Col Hal Hornburg, commander of the 4th TFW. Brig Gen Glosson added a handwritten note to the bottom of the message: "Please annotate the ATO to reflect your desired munitions and provide estimated results with the data available." (S) Msg, Brig Gen Glosson, CENTAF to Col Hornburg, 4th TFW, Thumrait, subj: Offensive Air Campaign (Desert Storm), 29 Aug 1990. See also (S) briefing, Lt Col Deptula, SAF/OSX, Instant Thunder (Offensive Campaign Phase I) Planning Assessment–24 Sep 1990, Presentations to SACAF and XOXW, nd [Briefing presented upon return from first trip to Saudi Arabia, late Sep 1990.]; (S) Intvw, Lt Col Terry with Lt Col Eskridge, GWAPS, 10 Aug 1992.

[29](S) Intvw, Lt Col Terry with Lt Col Eskridge, GWAPS, 10 Aug 1992.

[30](S) Briefing, Lt Col Deptula, SAF/OSX, Instant Thunder (Offensive Campaign Phase I) Planning Assessment–24 Sep 1990, (S) Intvw, Lt Col Terry with Lt Col Eskridge, GWAPS, 10 Aug 1992; (S) Intvw, TSgt Turner, CENTAF History Office with Brig Gen Glosson, 14th AD(P) Commander and Director, USCENTAF Campaign Plans, 20 Oct 1990.

[31]See (S) Chapter 5.

[32]For example, the Special Instructions sections on airspace procedures and communications plan were written to reflect the Black Hole's strategic air campaign. (S) Intvw, Lt Col Terry with Lt Col Eskridge, GWAPS, 10 Aug 1992.

Special Instructions.³³ Training needed to prepare units for specific missions in support of the strategic air campaign was also entered into the Air Tasking Order in this way. For instance, if a mass launch were planned for the strategic air campaign Black Hole planners would get that tactic included in training tasked in the daily ATO.³⁴ Thus, the units were able to prepare for the eventual strategic air campaign without knowing such a campaign would be waged.³⁵

The establishment of the Black Hole created a second (and ad hoc) planning effort–parallel to the formal CENTAF planning effort. The relative importance of each to the objectives of Commander in Chief, Central Command changed over time. In the first few weeks of the deployment, CENTAF and CENTCOM staff worked feverishly to develop plans to defend Saudi Arabia. This planning effort would have been critical if, in mid-August 1990, Iraq had continued its aggression and violated Saudi territory. Every day the Iraqis delayed invading Saudi Arabia increased the likelihood that the Black Hole's campaign plan would be executed. General Horner believed–very early in Desert Shield–that the Black Hole's strategic air campaign would be executed.³⁶ His recollection is supported by the direction given to Brigadier General Glosson to have the

---

[33] For example, when an air refueling track was needed to support the strategic air campaign, that requirement was passed to the Combat Operations Planning Division by one of the tanker planners in the Black Hole. The Division would build the track, coordinate the airspace, and publish these instructions as part of the Airspace Coordination Order in a CENTAF ATO.

[34] Many of the Black Hole planners were "dual hatted." Thus, they were able to have the unit suggest a tactic, e.g., a mass launch, which would then be included in the daily training ATO, say, for every Friday. In this way, the requirements of the strategic planners became a routine part of the weekly training.

[35] [DELETED] In like manner, Operation Desert Triangle–which involved F-14 flights in Saudi Arabia along the Iraqi border–was facilitated by being included in the daily training ATO. Desert Triangle included EA-6Bs to record Iraqi responses. [DELETED] (S) Intvw, Cdr McSwain.

[36] By mid-September, Generals Powell and Schwarzkopf had decided that should there be any conflict, the Air Force's response would be the offensive air campaign. In Gen Horner's words, "I think anybody would have come to that conclusion." See (S) Intvw, Barry Barlow, Richard G. Davis, Perry Jamieson with Lt Gen Horner.

Black Hole campaign ready by 15 September 1990, only six weeks after Iraq's invasion of Kuwait.[37]

Implications of the Black Hole: Plans, Process, and Authority

The two planning staffs employed different approaches to the development of their respective campaign plans. In planning for the immediate defense of Saudi Arabia, Central Command Air Forces staff saw their efforts as part of a joint campaign. Missions were divided into roles of Battlefield Air Interdiction (BAI), Close Air Support (CAS), Air Interdiction (AI), Offensive Counter Air (OCA), and Defensive Counter Air (DCA). Doctrine on air-land battle provided the context for plans devoted to offensive operations against Iraq. Many targets were common to the planning efforts of both CENTAF and the Black Hole,[38] but the main focus of the CENTAF Combat Plans Division effort was the combined arms campaign for the defense of Saudi Arabia. Tremendous effort was expended in CENTAF and CENTCOM developing the Combined Operations Plan for the Defense of Saudi Arabia, published on 9 December 1990. The ATO B for D-Day was an integral part of that operation. In contrast, the Black Hole focused upon offense–to devise a plan to achieve national and military objectives, to *win* the war, through air power alone; that is, to make the ground campaign unnecessary.[39]

In addition to the different planning foci, the processes used to plan in CENTAF and the Black Hole were distinct. CENTAF staff used proce-

---

[37](S) Intvw, Brig Gen Glosson, 17 Oct 1990.

[38]Forty-six percent of the targets planned for D-Day–based on the 16 Jan 1991 Master Attack Plan–were on the 15 Jun 1990 CENTAF target list. Forty-four percent of CENTCOM's 27 Jun 1990 joint target list were integrated into the 6 Jan 1991 MAP. See (S) GWAPS *Planning* report. See also the discussion of target set growth in (S) GWAPS *Operations and Effectiveness* volume.

[39]As with the similar efforts of Checkmate theoreticians, it is still an open question whether Black Hole officers correctly identified Iraqi "center[s] of gravity"–those targets which could disable the ability of Iraq to wage war. It is clear that Col Warden's prediction that Iraq would surrender after six days of bombing (in clear weather) did not come to pass–after more than forty days of bombing. Certainly, those forty days of bombing were equivalent to more than six days of clear weather bombing. See also (S) GWAPS *Planning* report for discussion of warfighting objectives of air power theoreticians.

dures and expertise developed through numerous joint exercises. The most recent of these joint exercises was Internal Look 90, a Joint Warfare Center controlled exercise (focusing on the defense of Saudi Arabia), which had just been completed.[40] In the main, the CENTAF planning effort had some Central Command involvement, especially in the intelligence area. CENTAF staff allocated assets based upon the Commander in Chief's guidance and apportionment. Target priorities were established by the intelligence analysts and updated daily. In mid-September, approximately one month after the Joint Targeting Coordination Board (JTCB) had been established, target allocations and Service requests were discussed at the board with the other components. The importance or authority of the Board is questionable as it was staffed with relatively low-ranking officers: a Marine lieutenant colonel, an Army captain and an Air Force captain.[41] However, the JTCB could have conducted joint oversight of the target selection process. All nominated targets were validated by trained targeteers and weaponeers for the proper mix of aircraft and weapons.

Black Hole planning resulted in a Master Target List and Master Attack Plan, but development of these and the subsequent Air Tasking Order was not "joint" in the same way as the CENTAF effort. Black Hole operations planners made target nominations and sortie allocations. The planners assigned to the Black Hole from the other Services and allies provided some oversight of the effort, but there was no formal Joint Targeting Board or "joint" staff review.[42] General Glosson, as the director of the Black Hole, answered directly to the Joint Force Air Component Commander and Commander in Chief, Central Command. The combination of overwhelming Air Force representation in the Black Hole

---

[40](S) After Action Report, HQ USCENTCOM, Operation Desert Shield/Operation Desert Storm, 15 Jul 1991; Intvw, (S) Maj Leary, Mandeles, Lt Col Terry with Lt Col Ross Dickinson, Joint Warfare Center, 8 May 1992.

[41](S) Intvw, Lt Col Frank D. Kistler, Mark D. Mandeles, Maj Sanford S. Terry with Capt John Glock, SAC/IN, 30 Jan 1992. Capt Glock was one of the SAC augmentees sent to CENTAF in Aug 1990 and was one of the first intelligence planners assigned to the Special Planning Division.

[42]Individual planners assigned to the Black Hole had varying amounts of interaction with their units and Services, but there was no formal process of briefing or describing the status of the planning effort to commanders outside of the CENTCOM organizational hierarchy.

with compartmentalization of the planning effort reduced the amount of interaction and coordination with Central Command and component staffs.

Intelligence Planning and Support

The Black Hole and CENTAF Deputy Chief of Staff, Intelligence had different perspectives on the amount of time it took to put together targeting materials. To plan, intelligence analysts and targeteers rely on an extensive supply of data, for example, in the form of target pictures and mensurated coordinates. Yet, the intelligence community had not devoted a lot of resources to Iraq, and the necessary data were unavailable. CENTAF staff did not deploy with the types of target materials needed to support the planning effort for the strategic air campaign. In addition, intelligence and Black Hole officers applied different criteria–measures of effectiveness–to evaluate the purpose and outcome of attacks. Intelligence officers train to determine a particular level of target destruction. Formulae and weapons data found in the Joint Munitions Effectiveness Manuals (JMEMs) and data on specific aircraft capability and weapons loads form the basis of targeteering–determining the number and type of weapon needed to achieve a desired probability of kill.[43]

In contrast, the Black Hole officers, under pressure to put together a viable campaign quickly, did not have time to wait while the intelligence community gathered hard data, studied and assimilated it, and produced target planning materials. This caused operations planners enormous frustration. When their initial requests for support came up short, either because of lack of data or because of a difference of opinion on what was needed, the operations planners quickly turned away from relying on the CENTAF intelligence community for any meaningful help in building the campaign and relied on their own experience and training.[44]

The few Intelligence officers assigned to the Black Hole expected to employ standard formulae and procedures to analyze each target selected for the air campaign. In contrast to this approach, the strategic air

---

[43] See (S) GWAPS *Weapons, Tactics, and Training* report for a discussion of weaponeering and targeteering.

[44] (S) Intvw, Brig Gen Glosson, 18 Oct 1990.

campaign entailed (a) attack against an entire target base simultaneously and (b) use of different damage criteria. General Glosson's planners abandoned absolute target destruction in favor of functional effect.[45] Glosson explained his perceptions about this basic difference in an interview shortly after the cease fire:

> The intelligence community gets too hung up at the local level on data and not information. They're too concerned about how to tabulate every piece of data that we get. They are too concerned about making sure that a certain level of destruction is reached on a target that corresponds to some preconceived notion or JMEM. One 2,000 bomb in a center of a building (if it explodes inside), even if the building on the exterior remains intact, means that the mission is probably 100% accomplished . . . . Some level of operational understanding must be present as a base.[46]

In Glosson's opinion, the use of stealthy, precision systems such as the F-117 also negated the need for the standard intelligence analysis of targets. The capabilities of precision-guided munitions, as General Glosson argued, were not reflected accurately in Joint Munitions Effectiveness Manuals. For example, to achieve a desired level of destruction or probability of kill of a facility, JMEMs calculations might require five F-111s carrying nonprecision weapons. Black Hole planners, however, believed an adequate functional effect could be achieved by a single F-111F delivering a precision-guided munition.[47] In addition, Colonel Deptula believed, given the training and experience of officers in the Black Hole, they could targeteer without support from the traditional intelligence system. In retrospect, Deptula noted:

---

[45](S) Intvw, Keaney, Mandeles, Murray, Watts with Lt Col Deptula; (S) Intvw, Office of Air Force History with Lt Col Deptula, SAF/OSX, 8 Jan 1992.

[46](S) Intvw, Brig Gen Glosson, 6 Mar 1991.

[47]Yet, the majority of weapon platforms in the theater were not precision weapon carriers but "dumb" bomb carriers. When employing dumb bombs, JMEMs calculations give the planner an analytical tool with which to evaluate the effectiveness of his desired weapon and aircraft against a particular target. See also (S) Intvw, Keaney, et al., with Lt Col Deptula, 20 Dec 1991.

Relying on my weapons school background–familiar with the aircraft capabilities, and familiar with the types of weapons and their associated effects–combined with knowing the desired effects to be achieved on the targets from our strategy, I could pretty much come up with a force package to go against a particular group of targets to achieve a respectable amount of damage or to have the desired impact we want to achieve.[48]

This perspective led some planners to believe that they could plan an air campaign successfully without dedicated targeteering and weaponeering organizational support.[49]

The rift between the planners and the intelligence community was widened by "turf battles" between key intelligence officers and operations planners.[50] Three examples illustrate the range of encounters. The first example began in late August and reached its climax in September. It concerns the difficulties the 37th Tactical Fighter Wing had in receiving intelligence information critical to planning missions. The F-117 mission planners needed specific photographic data to plan an attack,[51] but Central Command Air Forces/Intelligence did not provide such data to the F-117 wings. When the 37th Tactical Fighter Wing could not get the required imagery from theater intelligence sources, its commander, Col. Alton C. Whitley, coordinated with Headquarters, Tactical Air Command to find and supply the needed data.[52] Colonel Whitley also addressed the difficulty of getting information from CENTAF Intelligence on two separate

---

[48](S) Intvw, Tsgt Turner with Lt Col Deptula, 1 Nov 1990.

[49]Weaponeering and target development was accomplished by officers assigned to the Black Hole, as were intelligence analysis of information, order of battle development, target selection and validation, and situation updates. These tasks also were being accomplished by the formal intelligence system, but only in support of the CENTAF planning process. Those performing weaponeering and targeteering in the Black Hole were not trained in those military occupational specialties. (S) Intvw, TSgt Turner, with Lt Col Deptula; (S) Intvw, Capt Glock, 30 Jan 1992.

[50](S) Background Paper, Observations of the Air Campaign against Iraq, Aug 90 - Mar 91, Lt Col Deptula, 29 Mar 1991.

[51](S) Intvw, Maj Heston, 16 Oct 1992.

[52](S) Msg, 37th TFW(Deployed)//CC//, 101916Z Sep 90, subj: Situation Update (personal for Col Crigger).

occasions in messages to Col. Crigger, then CENTAF Director of Operations.[53] When the situation did not improve, Colonel Whitley took his complaint to General Glosson.[54]

In a message sent to Glosson on 13 September 1990, Colonel Whitley contended that the information his wing needed to plan missions was available in the CENTAF Sensitive Compartmented Information Facility (SCIF). Tactical Air Command had forwarded the information to the 37th Tactical Fighter Wing through appropriate intelligence channels. Yet, CENTAF's Director of Intelligence Col. John A. Leonardo, Jr., withheld the information from the wing. One of Colonel Whitley's wing personnel assigned to support Col. Leonardo, MSgt. Marvin Short, was ordered to leave the target materials needed by the 37th TFW unopened in the SCIF.[55] Whitley added that one of his pilots, Maj. Robert D. Eskridge,[56] had been threatened by Colonel Leonardo; unless the wing stopped requesting information, he would "pull the plug" on that 37th TFW's Tactical ELINT (electronic intelligence) Processor.[57] [DELETED] Colonel Leonardo was replaced shortly after this incident. The second example concerns disagreements over the simple numbering or cataloging of targets. The intelligence community identified targets with a Basic Encyclopedia Number (BEN). Lieutenant Colonel Deptula, the Black Hole's Chief Planner, wanted to employ a different numbering system for targets on the Master Attack Plan. His system used an abbreviation based upon the type of target and a number (for example, Strategic Air Defense target number 4 was designated SAD04). This approach made it easier for the operation planners to work with and manipulate packages in the Master Attack Plan during the planning, and later, execution phase of a

---

[53](S) *Ibid*; (S) Msg, 37th TFW(Deployed//CC, 112030Z Sep 90, subj: Required Intelligence Support (personal for Col Crigger).

[54](S) Msg, 37th TFW(Deployed)//CC//, 131400Z Sep 90, subj: Intelligence Support (personal for Brig Gen Glosson).

[55](S) Msg, 37th TFW(Deployed)//CC//, 101916Z Sep 90, subj: Situation Update (personal for Col Crigger).

[56]Maj Eskridge also was assigned to the Special Planning Division–the Black Hole.

[57][DELETED]

campaign.[58] The intelligence community insisted on using Basic Encyclopedia Numbers. As Capt. John Glock, one of the intelligence officers assigned to the Black Hole, explained,

> It's not that we couldn't [use the Black Hole's target identification system]. It's just that we recognize that anything that you are going to do within the intelligence community–if you are going to want any sort of support for target materials or anything–else you are going to have to use those basic encyclopedia numbers.[59]

The planners in the Black Hole used their own numbering system primarily, and the intelligence (especially the targeteering) community continued to use its own.[60] Efforts were made to use both numbering systems simultaneously, but the use of two distinct numbering systems was a source of contention (and sometimes confusion) throughout the entire operation.[61]

The final example of conflict between intelligence and operations planners concerns the effects the physical arrangement of office space had on the nature of staff interaction. Initially, Central Command Air Force intelligence personnel worked in the Air Combat Operations Center located in the basement of the Royal Saudi Air Force Headquarters. Once established, the Black Hole staff operated out of a conference room on the third floor of the same building. This room was outgrown rapidly; there was insufficient space to store the types of target and planning materials needed to plan the air campaign and still have room to work. General Glosson recognized the difficulty in working in small and cramped quarters and proposed that a planning tent be set up in the

---

[58](S) Intvw, Keaney, et al., with Lt Col Deptula, 20 Dec 1990; (S) Intvw, TSgt Turner with Lt Col Deptula, 1 Nov 1990.

[59](S) Intvw, Capt Glock, 30 Jan 1992.

[60](S) Intvw, Keaney, et al., with Lt Col Deptula, 20 Dec 1991.

[61]During Desert Shield and Desert Storm, Black Hole planners used both target identification systems in the MAP. But mistakes in matching the two systems introduced confusion into the tasking and assessment of missions. The units were unsure which targets to attack. The planners were unsure whether targets had been attacked. See the case studies in (S) Chapter 2 and 7.

Electronic Security Command facility.[62] Intelligence personnel assigned to the Black Hole moved into this facility almost immediately. The operations planners remained in the conference room on the third floor of the Saudi Air Force building.

The physical arrangement of the work space impeded cooperation between intelligence staff and the Black Hole. To get materials or information, planning staff had to depart the Saudi Air Force building, walk across a parking lot and through a hole that had been knocked in the wall around the United States Military Training Mission compound, pass a Saudi guard, walk through the Training Mission compound and, finally, pass through the guard post controlling entry to the SCIF. This journey is illustrated in Figure 26.

Enforcement of security regulations with a SCIF further exacerbated coordination difficulties. When Electronic Security Command personnel were the main users of the SCIF, the Black Hole operational planners were granted ready access–regardless of whether they had an Sensitive Compartmented Information (SCI) clearance. However, by mid-October, when CENTAF Intelligence had left the basement and moved to the SCIF, entry rules were enforced rigorously.

Unescorted entry to the SCIF was granted only to those with an appropriate SCI clearance, and those without an SCI clearance had to be escorted. Most Black Hole operations planners did not have SCI clearances, thus reducing their interaction with intelligence staff. This situation continued after the Black Hole moved (in late October) from the third floor conference room to the basement of the Saudi Air Force building.

These three examples only outline the range of "turf" conflicts between key operations planning and intelligence officers during Desert Shield. The effect of these conflicts was to reduce the amount of those

---

[62]This facility was placed on the soccer field of the U.S. Military Training Mission compound next to the RSAF headquarters. Originally, this facility was designed to be a SCIF to support RC-135 operations in the theater. The Special Access Required tent for the Special Planning Division was set up in the SCIF around 22 Aug 1990. See (S) Intvw, Capt Glock, 30 Jan 1992.

Figure 26
Relationship of Saudi Air Force Building to SCIF

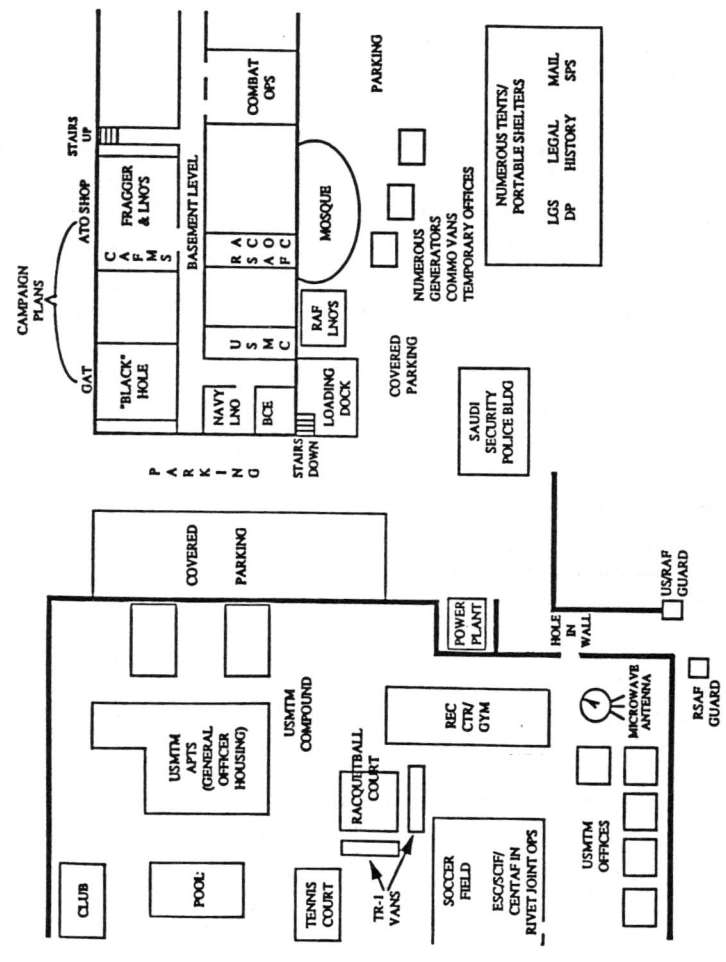

kinds of coordination and interaction needed to plan and execute an air campaign using the formal CENTAF organization.

Interpersonal Relationships

One of the biggest problems faced by deployed personnel was how to respond and adapt to changes in deployment plans. Habits and personal relationships enhanced the cohesion and interaction of the staffs during the first hectic days of Desert Shield. These habits and relationships had been established in a variety of ways–through participation in exercises and in the course of previous assignments. For example, most of the CENTAF staff who deployed early in Desert Shield had just participated in Internal Look 90 (including the augmentees from supporting commands such as the Strategic Air Command), so they were familiar with each other (and staff functions) when they began the Desert Shield deployment on 7 August 1990.[63] In addition, key CENTAF personnel had held their positions for several years, allowing close working relationships with other officers to develop. Such longstanding relationships helped establish and run the new organization in Saudi Arabia. Staff officers

---

[63]Internal Look 90 (IL-90), a USCENTCOM sponsored and conducted command post exercise, was designed to enhance readiness of USCENTCOM and subordinate commands. IL-90 represented the first time commanders and staff set up bare base headquarters using real-world bare base equipment and tactical communications in a simulated wartime environment to counter an Iraqi invasion of the Arabian peninsula. Previous exercises addressed the "Defense Guidance" scenario to counter a Soviet invasion of Iran. USCINCCENT draft OPLAN 1002-90 provided the framework for the exercise. IL-90 was divided into three phases conducted at Duke Field (Florida), Hurlburt Field (Florida), and Fort Bragg (North Carolina). In Phase I (the deployment), held between 9 and 19 July, exercise forces moved from home stations to exercise locations and established command, control, and communications facilities. Phase II (employment), held between 20 and 28 July, involved three parts. First, a two-day STAFFEX (20-21 July) checked communications and validated C^2 procedures and organization. Second, from 23 to 25 July, events simulated days D+8 through D+10 of draft OPLAN 1002-90 (i.e., delay/interdiction operations). An eighteen-hour pause followed this period during which computer simulations were reprogrammed and staff graphics were adjusted to facilitate transition from delay to defend. From 26 to 28 July, events simulated days D+18 through D+20 of draft OPLAN 1002-90 (i.e., defend operations). Phase III emphasized redeployment. The redeployment began on 29 July with the departure of main bodies and concluded on 4 August when the last trail party departed the exercise area. See (S) After Action Report, HQ USCENTCOM, Operation Desert Shield/Operation Desert Storm, 15 July 1991; (S) Brief, "USCENTAF Internal Look 90," nd.

were comfortable with their own roles and duties and understood the capabilities and weaknesses of other officers and the various staff agencies. Augmentees from outside the CENTAF staff were brought into an organization with a well-defined purpose and structure.

Unlike those assigned to Central Command Air Forces, personnel in the Black Hole could not rely on common expectations, built through participation in command post exercises, to help plan the strategic air campaign. Yet, other factors affected the capability to plan. First, there was very specific mission guidance. Second, the organization was small, which enhanced the formation of personal relationships. Third, the tight security of the planning group and the perceived critical nature of their task helped create an *esprit de corps*. Finally, since they came from a variety of backgrounds and assignments, Black Hole officers also could employ personal contacts with a variety of agencies outside CENTAF organization. Contacts with Air Staff officers, for example, helped set up critical information channels to intelligence agencies. Some members of the Black Hole were U.S. Air Force Fighter Weapons School graduates, which opened up links in the world of tactics and weapons employment.[64] For example, planning for the use of tanker assets would have been extraordinarily difficult without the Strategic Air Command tanker planners assigned to the group, who used their experience and contacts to overcome information and analysis gaps.[65]

Beginning in August 1990, informal communications channels connected several levels of the Black Hole with disparate parts of the U.S. defense establishment outside the Central Command area of responsibility. Examples of informal communications channels include Brigadier General Glosson receiving target (and other) information from Rear Admiral McConnell in Washington,[66] Lieutenant Colonel Deptula

---

[64] Most of the key individuals in the Black Hole were USAF Fighter Weapons School graduates, including Brig Gen Glosson, the Director of Campaign Plans, Lt Col Deptula, Chief Attack Planner and later, Director of the Iraq Planning Cell, Lt Col Sam Baptiste, Director of the KTO Planning Cell.

[65] For the previous ten years, SAC tankers had been assigned to refueling operations in Operation Elf One. See (S) Chapter 4 for discussion of Elf One.

[66] (S) Intvw, Brig Gen Glosson, 6 Mar 1991.

receiving similar information from the Air Staff's Checkmate,[67] and Cdr. Roy Balaconis (with the Black Hole's TLAM cell) organizing an informal network to employ and evaluate the effectiveness of the Tomahawk Land Attack Missile.[68] Yet, these informal communications channels or organizations were not always able to link information users with appropriate information provides. A Navy staff officer who served in the Black Hole evinced surprise upon learning, after the war, that four naval officers (from OP-741) worked in Checkmate. He claimed that he would have used them to provide another source of data and information.[69]

Over time, the informal communications channels and networks increased in number, compensating for "disconnects" between the Black Hole and official–CENTAF–organization (and its formal procedures), or for the key planners' perceptions that CENTAF staff could not perform the appropriate analysis.[70]

---

[67](S) Intvw, TSgt Turner, with Lt Col Deptula; (S) Intvw, Keaney, et al., with Lt Col Deptula, 20 Dec 1991; (S) Intvw, Keaney, et al., with Lt Col Deptula, 21 Dec 1991; (S) Intvw, Hone and Mandeles with Lt Col Deptula, 2 Jan 1992.

[68]In this case, the impetus for establishing an informal network came from an officer assigned to the Joint Staff. In Dec 1990 Cdr Roy Balaconis was reassigned to Washington from the Persian Gulf. Before being reassigned, Balaconis developed a number of personal contacts with middle-level officers at CINCCENT and NAVCENT. In Washington, Balaconis was assigned to the Joint Staff's Operations Directorate (J-3), headed by Lt Gen Thomas W. Kelly. [DELETED] See (S/NF) Briefing, J-3, Joint Operations Division, "Tomahawk: Employment and Effectiveness During Desert Storm," 13 Feb 1992; (S) Intvw, Cdr McSwain, 21 Apr 1992.

[69](S) Intvw, Cdr McSwain, 21 Apr 1992.

[70]In this respect, Secretary of the Air Force Donald Rice noted:

I think when you look at what was involved in planning the strategic air campaign it is wholly unrealistic to expect that it could have been done out in Riyadh. The resources that the Checkmate operation were able to pull together that in many cases involved accessing things that probably could only have been accessed in Washington or through contacts that had to be made in Washington, you just couldn't have done that out in the field. That's not to say they couldn't have planned some level of strategic air campaign plan out there but a lot of the details about how the telephone system worked . . . [lot of details that we got on the actual construction and layout of the buried bunkers, and command and control centers, and special facilities in the key Iraqi buildings, and in the palaces, and all kinds of things of that sort, . . . the Checkmate operation [obtained this information] through intelligence sources. I

The relationship between General Glosson and Rear Admiral Michael McConnell[71] further illustrates the importance of the informal communications channels to those planning the air campaign and building the Master Attack Plan. As noted above, Glosson decided that little usable information would be forthcoming from interaction with the CENTAF/CENTCOM intelligence agencies.[72] To compensate, Glosson and the other planners in the Black Hole established an extensive intelligence network through informal contacts with the Defense Intelligence Agency (DIA), Central Intelligence Agency (CIA), Checkmate (AF/XOXWF), and individuals at the

---

don't see how that level of stuff ever could have been done out in Riyadh. . . . [T]he work that was done in Checkmate was always . . . passed at the colonel or lieutenant colonel level.

Intvw, (S) Lt Col Suzanne Gehri, Lt Col Edward Mann, and Lt Col Richard Reynolds with Dr. Donald Rice, Secretary of the Air Force, 11 Dec 1991.

[71] RAdm Michael McConnell was JCS J2 and Deputy Director of the Defense Intelligence Agency.

[72] In an interview conducted in mid-October 1990, Brig Gen Glosson reported "a total breakdown in intel's ability to support our effort." (S) Intvw, TSgt Turner with Brig Gen Glosson, 18 Oct 1990. Later, Glosson added that his conversations with RAdm McConnell compensated for the failures of the local intelligence organization. In Glosson's words:

The most difficult aspect of prosecuting this war from my standpoint was the ability to keep your arms around intelligence and have data transformed into information in a timely fashion. That did not happen at the local level during this war. If it had not been for my personal friend, Admiral McConnell, who is the number three guy in DIA, I shudder to think of some of the mistakes we would have made. The shortcomings that I have just described in intelligence would have resulted in a ten-fold size problem, if not for the information passed directly from Admiral McConnell. I can't put enough importance on that one point in the prosecution of this war. Had it not been for that man's willingness to ensure that we had the best information as fast as possible, we would have had numerous embarrassing moments and we would have lost a lot more lives. We would have actually looked inept at times due to a lack of intelligence.

(S) Intvw, MSgt Turner with Brig Gen Glosson, 6 Mar 1991. We examine CENTAF/IN officers' perceptions of this relationship in (S) Chapter 8, "BDA and the Command and Control of the Air Campaign."

MAJCOMs.[73] This informal network extended to the wings deployed in theater. The STU-III (secure telephones) allowed planners the capability to talk and receive information and intelligence from sources worldwide without having to rely on hard copy messages sent through the military message traffic system. The Black Hole planners perceived that a large percentage of target information and target intelligence they used came through these informal sources.[74]

The working relationship between Glosson and McConnell began when Glosson returned to the United States in October 1990 to brief the President and the Chairman of the Joint Chiefs of Staff on the air campaign. Glosson's frustration with the intelligence community had reached the "breaking point." At the direction of Secretary of Defense Richard B. Cheney, Glosson spoke with McConnell, and the beginning of a modus operandi was established.[75] As the war progressed, Glosson and McConnell spoke more frequently. Eventually, they talked two or three times a day.[76] McConnell gave Glosson direct intelligence information about Iraqi forces and kept him informed about decisions and decision makers in Washington. Glosson, in turn, passed information from McConnell to General Schwarzkopf–helping to keep CINCCENT "ahead"

---

[73](S) Intvw, Thomas C. Hone (and other GWAPS) with Maj Gen Glosson, 9 Apr 1992.

[74]Target information and intelligence includes identification of new targets and proving proper target coordinates or characteristics. There is no formal GWAPS database detailing, by source, the intelligence information used by Black Hole planners (Black Hole planners did not construct such a database either). Hence, planners were able to give (and we can report) only subjective estimates of the sources and importance of target information and intelligence. See (S) Intvw, TSgt Turner with Lt Col Deptula, 1 Nov 1990; (S) Intvw, Keaney, et al., with Lt Col Deptula, 20 Dec 1991; (S) Intvw, Keaney, et al., with Lt Col Deptula, 21 Dec 1991; (S) Intvw, Richard G. Davis, Perry Jamieson, and Diane T. Putney with Brig Gen Glosson, SAF/LL, 12 Dec 1991.

[75]It is not entirely clear from the interviews how or when Glosson and McConnell met. The two might have met casually during the summer–a few months earlier. (S) Intvw, GWAPS staff with Brig Gen Glosson, 9 Apr 1992. In February 1992, RAdm McConnell recalled that he first met Brig Gen Glosson in October 1990. McConnell saw that Glosson was "Mr. Decisionmaker," and therefore sought him out to offer his personal help. (S/NF/WNINTEL) Intvw, Ronald Cole and Diane T. Putney with RAdm Michael McConnell, DIA, 5 Feb 1992.

[76]McConnell recalled that in December a secure telephone (STU-III) was installed at home in his bedroom. It was used very frequently during the first two weeks of Jan. (S/NF/WNINTEL) Intvw, Ronald Cole and Diane T. Putney with RAdm Michael McConnell, DIA, 5 Feb 1992.

of policy concerns or questions from Washington.⁷⁷ Schwarzkopf wanted to keep contacts outside the theater to a minimum–especially in the planning and execution of the air campaign–but he permitted the Glosson-McConnell link because of its usefulness.⁷⁸

Brigadier General Glosson claimed to have contacts in the White House who informed him of discussions and concerns that would be addressed to the Commander in Chief, Central Command.⁷⁹ Glosson was able to use this information to alert General Schwarzkopf to impending questions or issues. Glosson was also well acquainted with Secretary Cheney. This relationship began when Glosson was the Deputy Assistant Secretary of Defense for Legislative Affairs.⁸⁰ Cheney and Glosson talked on the telephone several times during the planning phase of the strategic air campaign and met occasionally. This interaction gave Glosson an opportunity to promote his ideas and strategy for the air campaign.

Glosson's personal contacts extended to senior leaders of Arab regimes; he repeatedly referred to his "royal friend" in interviews. This individual kept Glosson informed on issues and concerns being expressed by senior Arab leaders. Although Glosson was only a brigadier general, he had greater access to information and to senior national leaders than individuals of higher rank and authority.⁸¹

Informal intelligence links also developed at the staff level. Raw intelligence data and other types of planning information passed between

---

⁷⁷McConnell recalled that while he sent much material to Brig Gen Glosson, he also sent copies of that material to CINCCENT and the JFACC. (S/NF/WNINTEL) Intvw, RAdm McConnell, 5 Feb 1992.

⁷⁸(S) Intvw, Keaney, et al., with Brig Gen Glosson, 9 Apr 1992.

⁷⁹Glosson did not name his White House contacts. (S) Intvw, GWAPS staff with Glosson, 9 Apr 1992. In a separate interview, Glosson declared that his name was on a very short information routing list: "I've got sheets of paper I can show you, and the sheets of paper say: President of the United States, Vice President, Secretary of State, Secretary of Defense, Schwarzkopf, and Buster Glosson. I can show you those pieces of paper." (S) Intvw, Davis, et al., with Maj Gen Buster C. Glosson, 12 Dec 1991.

⁸⁰Glosson held this position from Sep 1988 until Jul 1990.

⁸¹Some officers on Glosson's staff also had greater access to information and to senior national leaders than individuals of higher rank and authority. Lt Col David A. Deptula, Glosson's chief planner, was assigned to CENTAF from the Secretary of the Air Force's staff policy group (SAF/OSX). As a consequence, Deptula had a direct connection with the Secretary of the Air Force, Donald Rice.

members of the Black Hole and the Air Staff at the Pentagon. The Air Staff, through Air Force Checkmate, provided a variety of services to Black Hole planners in a fraction of the time it would have taken the formal intelligence system. Checkmate officers developed relationships at the staff officer level with individuals and offices in all the major intelligence organizations: DIA, CIA, the National Security Agency, and the Joint Chiefs of Staff. Air Staff action officers were assigned to the intelligence agencies to help gather information needed by the planners in Checkmate and in the theater. As a result of these informal relationships, intelligence information was passed from the intelligence agency to the user quickly and with no intervening processing by the organized intelligence system in theater.[82]

The CENTAF Reorganization

In December 1990, General Horner reorganized Central Command Air Forces' organizational structure and staff. His stated purpose in this reorganization was to "strengthen and standardize our organizational alignment."[83] Horner's CENTAF planning staff reorganization was preceded by a critical decision related to organizational structure. On 5 December 1990, the 14th and 15th Air Divisions(P) were created, bringing to four the number of provisional air divisions.[84] The strategic [the 17th Air Division(P)], and airlift forces [the 1610th Airlift Division(P)] had already been organized into Provisional Air Divisions on 24 August 1990[85] and 31 October 1990, respectively.[86] The 14th AD(P) was now established and given operational control (OPCON) of all the tactical fighter units in the theater. The 15th AD(P) was formed with operational control of electronic combat, command and control, and reconnaissance assets.[87] Each air division was assigned a different level of command authority.

---

[82](S) Lt Col Deptula, "Observations on the Air Campaign, Aug 90-Mar 91," 29 Mar 1991.

[83](S) Msg, COMUSCENTAF to AIG 10322, 120600z Dec 90; (S) Intvw, Barlow, et al., with Lt Gen Horner, 4 Mar 1992.

[84]Msg, COMUSCENTAF to AIG 10322, 120600z Dec 90, subj: USCENTAF Organization Structure.

[85]Headquarters Strategic Air Command, Special Order GB-084, 24 Aug 1990.

[86]Headquarters Military Airlift Command, Special Order GA-11, 31 Oct 1990.

[87]HQ Tactical Air Command, Special Order GB-14, 5 Dec 1990.

The authority exercised by each air division commander tells much about the execution of the air campaign.[88]

Under the previously existing command relationship, the 17th AD(P) and the 1610AD(P) had no direct operational authority over deployed forces.[89] Tasking and execution authority were held by Central Command Air Forces or commanders outside the theater. With the reorganization, the 14AD(P) and 15AD(P) commanders got operational control of their assigned assets.[90] Operational control gave each air division commander much greater flexibility in directing how the assets assigned to that division would execute each tasking. In effect, the reorganization transformed brigadier generals assigned staff functions within CENTAF (Brigadier Generals Glosson and Profitt) into commanders having warfighting command authority.[91] Of the four air division commanders, the reorganization had the greatest implications for General Glosson. As 14th AD(P) Commander, he had operational control of all fighter and attack aircraft. Every U.S. Air Force aircraft with the capability to put ordnance on a target, with the exception of the B-52, came under operational control and command authority of Brigadier General Glosson.

After he had reorganized the air division structure, General Horner turned his attention to the CENTAF planning staff. The role played by Combat Plans changed due to the decisions to prosecute the offensive air campaign as visualized by the Black Hole. Officers in Combat Plans had

---

[88] For example, the Strategic Air Command passed to USCINCCENT OPCON of B-52s deployed in support of Operation Desert Shield/Storm. OPCON of SAC air refueling and reconnaissance assets remained with the SAC numbered air force, 8th or 15th Air Force. TACON of air refueling assets was passed to COMUSCENTAF as the JFACC. TACON of SAC reconnaissance assets was passed to the 17th AD(P) commander. (Msg CINCSAC to 8th AF, 15th AF, 3d AD, 7th AD, 14th AD, 17th AD(P), 4300d BMW(P), 24 1900Z Aug 90, subj: Command relationships of SAC Forces Supporting Desert Shield.) OPCON of in-theater airlift assets was given to USCINCCENT. USTRANSCOM maintained OPCON of strategic airlift. All other Tactical Air Force units deployed to the USCENTCOM area of responsibility were assigned Combatant Command (COCOM) to USCINCCENT. (Msg, Chairman, Joint Chiefs of Staff, 222335Z Oct 1990, Operation Desert Shield Command Relationships.) USCENTAF then exercised OPCON of the deployed tactical forces. See Appendix 4 for detailed discussion of command relationships.

[89] Although, the 17th AD(P) had TACON of reconnaissance assets.

[90] Headquarters Tactical Air Command, Special Order GB-14, 5 Dec 1990.

[91] See Appendix 4 for discussion of the difference between staff and command authority.

planned for the defense of Saudi Arabia; its efforts had resulted in numerous Operations Orders and the subsequent Air Tasking Orders that supported these plans. The efforts of the smaller Black Hole centered on building a plan to conduct a true strategic attack against an enemy's infrastructure and leadership.

On 17 December 1990, General Horner created the Campaign Plans Division by combining the planning staffs of the Black Hole and the Combat Plans Division. Campaign Plans replaced Combat Plans in the CENTAF Tactical Air Control Center organizational hierarchy. All functions falling under Combat Plans Division such as the Combat Operations Planning staff, Tactical Air Control System (TACS) Division, and Computer Assisted Force Management System (CAFMS) Division were integrated into the new Campaign Plans. Figure 27 displays the relationships among planners before the reorganization.[92] Figure 28 illustrates the relationships after this reorganization.[93] The functions of the Special Support Division, TACS Division, Fighter Plans Division, and CAFMS Branch now came under the ATO Division. The Airborne Command Element (ACE) Division and the Liaison Division remained basically intact. The Combat Operations Planning Division (COPD) became the nucleus of the Kuwait Theater of Operation (KTO) Cell within the Guidance, Apportionment, and Targeting (GAT) Division, and the Black Hole became the Iraq Cell in the GAT. In addition, the GAT included nuclear, biological, chemical/Scud, ground, and air liaison cells.[94]

---

[92](S) USCENTAF *Combat Plans Handout*, Oct 1990. See (S) Chapter 5 for a full discussion of the CENTAF planning staff.

[93](S) USCENTAF *Combat Plans Handout*, Jan 1991.

[94]In March 1992, Lt Gen Horner recalled that the reorganization occurred because of "evolutionary" changes taking place rather than a "thought-out process." In Horner's words,

> The evolution was this: You had Jimmy Crigger running the day-to-day operations for Desert Shield. The TACC was doing the day-to-day operations to include the defensive planning and execution. Then you had the Black Hole; well, the Black Hole *became* [emphasis on tape] the plans function as we shifted from defense to offense, so we always kept this residual defense plan, but it sort of shrunk down to the tail. Buster is doing all the planning, and because of the secrecy–because we did not want to jeopardize diplomacy–Jimmy's guys were never really directly involved in Buster's–the Black Hole–thing. So the natural evolution is that you go ahead and make the Black Hole the Plans, and

Figure 27
Relationship Among Planners Before Reorganization

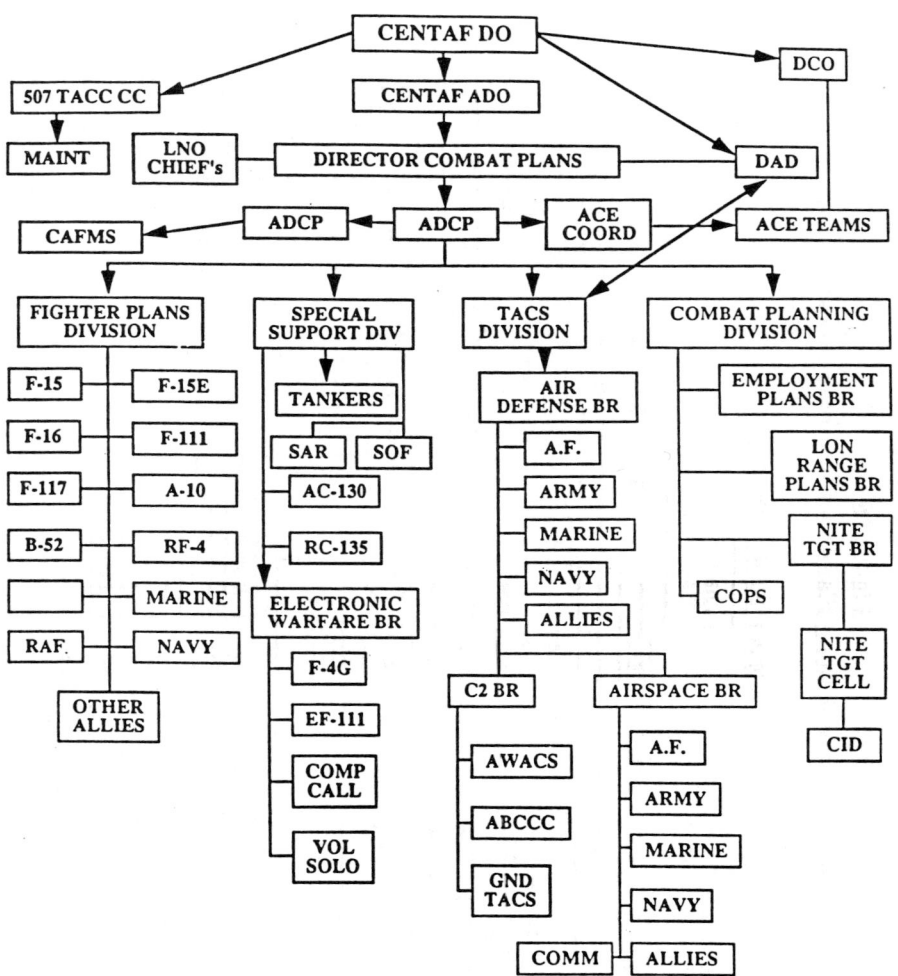

Figure 28
Relationship Among Planners After Reorganization

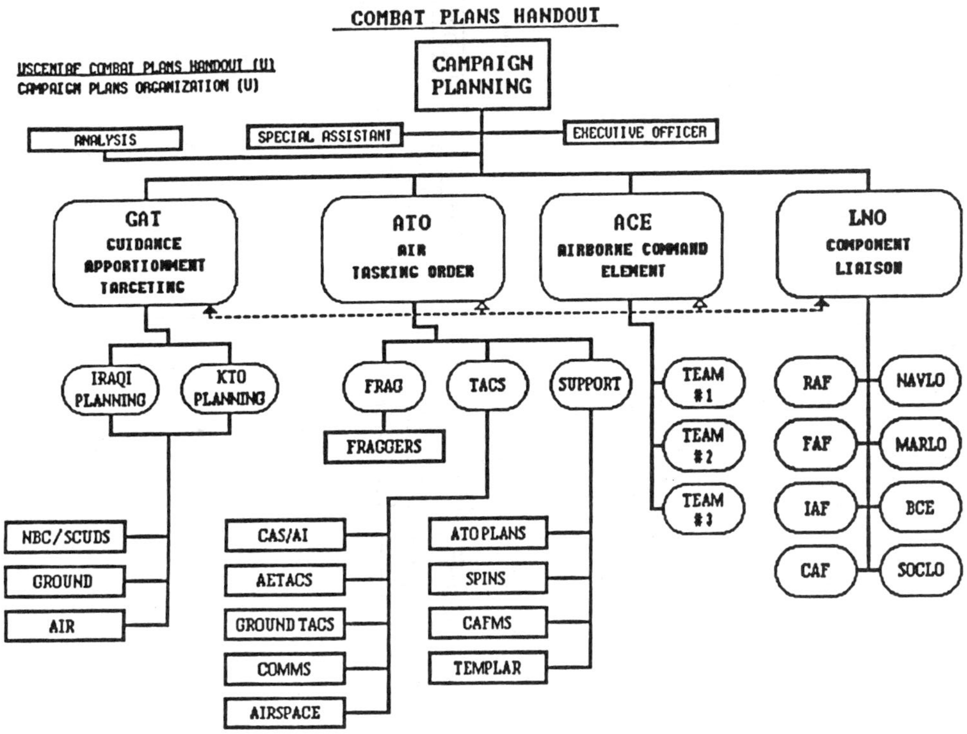

The December Reorganization's Organizational Context

After the December 1990 reorganization, General Horner continued his established pattern[95] of dealing primarily with problems relating to his nstitutional role as Joint Force Air Component Commander.[96] Once the decision had been made to employ an offensive plan against Iraq, many issues were raised by flag-level officers of other Services and countries directly to General Horner, rather than through Col. James Crigger, Jr., the CENTAF Director of Operations Director of Operations. With hindsight, Maj. Gen. Corder argued that Horner, overwhelmed by matters he did not have the time to handle, brought Corder to Saudi Arabia to be CENTAF DO, replacing Colonel Crigger.[97] General Corder believed one of

---

> in the reorganization, we just took the residual–Sam Baptiste and the guys who were in Ops–and pushed them in with the Black Hole guys, and said, 'Now you are Combat Plans.'

(S) Intvw, Barlow, et al., with Lt Gen Horner.

[95] See (S) Chapter 3.

[96] (S) Intvw, GWAPS with Maj Gen John A. Corder, Deputy Commander for Operations, USCENTAF (November 1990 to March 1991), 18 May 1992. Corder's view is supported by Brig Gen Glosson's report in an October 1990 interview. Glosson remarked that Horner "has given me total freedom and has not put any constraints on us as far as trying to militarily develop the best strategic air campaign that we can possibly develop. I have had no meddling and no tinkering at all." (S) Intvw, TSgt Turner with Brig Gen Glosson.

Gen Horner–as JFACC–also was able to take a more philosophical view of day-to-day operations than others. For example, as the battle of Khafji was developing, Horner received a frantic telephone call from a Saudi commander pleading for B-52 bombers to attack the Iraqis. Gen Horner answered,

> Khalid, you are going to get more air than you have ever seen in your life. He said, 'I've got to have air!' I said, 'Khalid, trust me. You are going to get a lot of air, more air than you need.' He said, 'Are you sure?' I said, 'Khalid, *trust me.* You are going to get a lot of air.' He said, 'Okay.' Then this little devil that lives in all of us said, 'Khalid, I want you to keep one thing in mind, though.' 'What's that?' I said, 'Your ass is in Khafji. My ass is in Riyadh.' (Laughter)

(S) Intvw, Barlow, et al., with Lt Gen Horner.

[97] Corder noted that Crigger had been doing a "superb" job as DO, an opinion echoed by Gen Horner. (S) Intvw GWAPS with Maj Gen Corder, 18 May 1992; Gen Horner called Crigger "one of the real heroes." Horner believed that Crigger was disappointed

his main tasks was to relieve Horner of having to divert attention from more important institutional matters. In addition, Corder believed Horner wanted him to oversee (but not control) the actions of Brigadier Generals Glosson, Profitt, Caruana, and Tenoso.[98]

General Corder also saw a key task in melding together the Guidance, Apportionment, and Targeting staff with the CENTAF staff. Combining the two staffs was deemed necessary in order to prepare the third day's (and subsequent day's) Air Tasking Order.[99] As the interaction among events, differing interpretations of tasks, and personalities played out, taking charge of the Tactical Air Control Center as Director of Operations proved quite difficult. This situation seems to have been acceptable to General Horner,[100] who, like many commanders and senior executives, managed tasks by channeling his subordinates' competition.[101]

The Revised Air Tasking Order Development Process

General Horner created Campaign Plans in the Tactical Air Control Center reorganization. This agency made slight changes to the Air Tasking Order planning cycle. Three ATOs were still prepared at any given time. Our description of the planning process, and the changes to it, begins with the creation and uses of the Master Attack Plan.

The Master Attack Plan was a command and control planning innovation developed by the chief Guidance, Apportionment, and Targeting planner to help focus planning efforts on simultaneous and relentless

---

upon being replaced by Corder. Yet, according to Horner, Crigger "said, 'fine,' saluted, and kept on working and doing things. He had every right to pout, piss, and moan; be mad, angry, and down-hearted; but he is a soldier. He really is a great guy." (S) Intvw, Barlow, et al., with Lt Gen Horner.

[98]In Gen Corder's words, one duty was to "chase after" the Air Force brigadier generals working for Horner. (S) Intvw, Maj Gen Corder.

[99](S) Intvw, Maj Gen Corder.

[100]For example, Horner noted that "sometimes John Corder and Buster Glosson would get into it a little bit. Sometimes I would let them fight each other, and then sometimes I would get them both so mad at me that they were buddies and fighting me. That's the way it works . . . . " (S) Intvw, Barlow, et al., with Lt Gen Horner. Maj Gen Corder also described several situations in which Horner managed through competition between Glosson and Corder. (S) Intvw, Maj Gen Corder.

[101]For example, see Richard E. Neustadt, *Presidential Power* (New York, 1960).

attack against targets critical to supporting the Iraqi war machine, relationships among targets to be attacked, and operational-level effects.[102] The Master Attack Plan was crucial to the planning process,[103] both as a means to facilitate the planning process and as a tool to centralize authority in the hands of the planners. The impetus for creating this new planning tool was in the tasks performed and approach to campaign planning taken by the Black Hole.[104] In retrospect, Major General Corder argued that "he who controls the target list"–and the sequence in which targets are attacked–"controls the war."[105] Of course, this aphorism makes sense only if the units can–and do–execute the tasks assigned to them. In any event, he who controls the target list certainly controls the planning process. Black Hole planning was facilitated by its own target list, the Master Target List.

The Master Attack Plan Document

The Master Attack Plan was assembled prior to the Air Tasking Order. Mediated by the target planning worksheets, the Attack Plan formed the basis of the Air Tasking Order. The ATO was simply an administrative vehicle to (a) transfer the daily plan to the wings and (b) provide call signs, times on targets, and other detailed information required for the execution of the plan.[106] Those working in Guidance, Apportionment, and Targeting viewed the Master Attack Plan as a significant tool for planning an air campaign. In their view, the existence of the Master Attack Plan made processing an Air Tasking Order much more than simply matching a ranked target list with air assets. Lieutenant Colonel Deptula noted that, with the MAP, the GAT had a "coherent plan that was thought out on the basis of the kind of effect we wanted to achieve on an individual basis, not simply matching a list of targets to a

---

[102] Target Planning Worksheets (TPWs), an existing planning tool, were used to transfer information from the MAP to the ATO. The existence and use of TPWs was an important carryover from earlier or past procedures. The TPWs supplied a familiar form for the presentation and transmission of objectives and information. Deptula noted that doing away with TPWs would have risked failures in transfer of information from the MAP to the ATO. (S) Intvw, Keaney, et al., with Lt Col Deptula, 20 Dec 1991; (S) Intvw, Office of Air Force History with Lt Col Deptula, 20 Nov 1991.

[103] However, the three-day planning cycle was not new.

[104] (S) Intvw, Keaney, et al., with Lt Col Deptula, 20 Dec 1991.

[105] (S) Intvw, Maj Gen Corder.

[106] (S) Intvw, GWAPS with Lt Col Deptula, 21 Dec 1991.

bunch of assets or servicing the target list mentality."[107] After the war, General Horner recalled he viewed the MAP as a "distillation" of the Air Tasking Order.[108]

Lieutenant Colonel Deptula led the effort to assemble the Master Attack Plan. Deptula's typical workday ran from 0630 to 2400 or 0100. Figure 29 depicts the anticipated planning cycle.[109] His day began with morning meetings, including the Combat Operations shift changeover briefing (sometimes termed the JFACC Staff meeting) attended by CENTAF staff officers. Horner would be briefed on the previous night's activities and lay out the Central Command Commander in Chief's analysis of the situation. Then Horner would dismiss the big meeting and convene a battle staff meeting with all the two-star generals and intelligence and planning officers. This meeting would include a long discussion based on the Defense Intelligence Agency information that had arrived the night before. At the end of the meeting, Horner would present his guidance. Deptula would then assemble the GAT staff to pass out the information received from the battle staff meeting, lay out the direction for the day's work, and be briefed by Maj. "Buck" Rogers on the previous night's changes. The weather staff officer would contribute a weather forecast.

---

[107](S) Intvw, Office of Air Force History with Lt Col Deptula, 20 Nov 1991. In addition, Deptula proposed a simple measure to improve the process: put the master attack list on a simple interactive database with multiple screens. The database must be capable of being updated with bomb damage assessment, additional intelligence information, and new targets. During the war, updating the MAP was accomplished by hand.

[108](S) Intvw, Barlow, et al., with Lt Gen Horner.

[109](S) Briefing, Lt Col Deptula to Gulf War Air Power Survey, "The Air Campaign: Planning and Execution," 26 Nov 1991.

Figure 29
Anticipated Planning Cycle

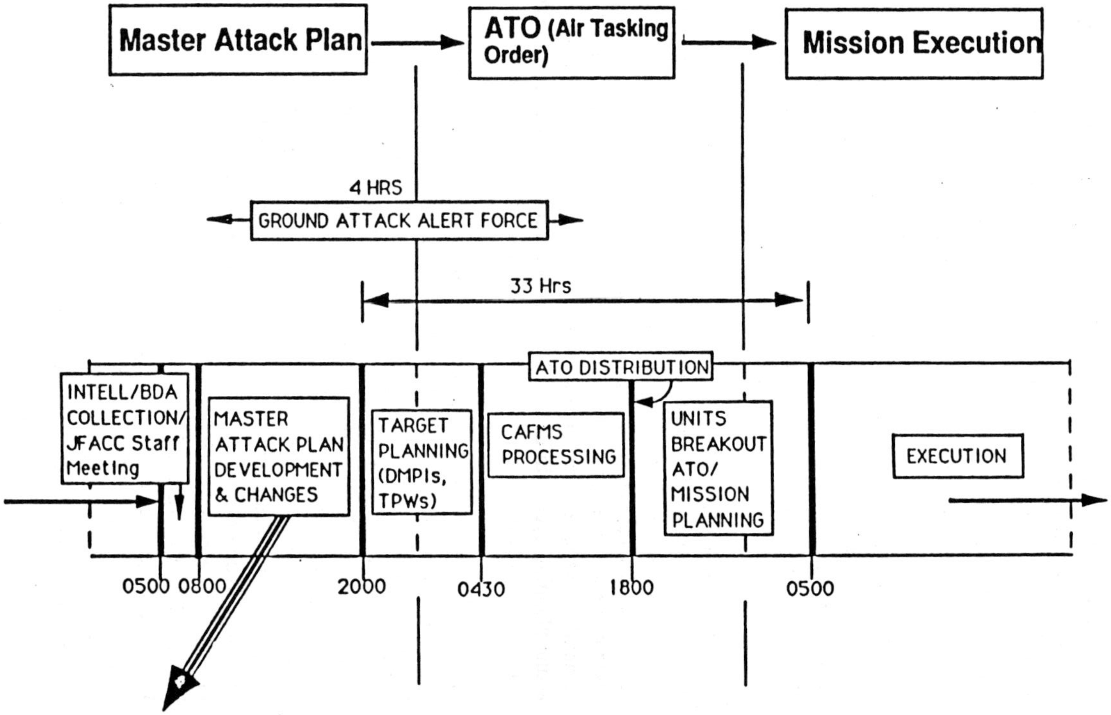

Then, around 1000, Horner would come in to talk[110] about the specific attacks planned for that day and night.[111] In the meantime, the weapons

---

[110]Horner described his morning stroll, stopping to talk with Deptula (about targets two days in advance), Lt Col Sam Baptiste, Army Lt Col Jack Welch (who picked Army targets), and staff in the Scud room. In Horner's words, "That [walk] became more of a daily operation rather than the planning thing. All we could do was just put forces up and do the best we could." In the afternoon, Horner and Glosson would brief Schwarzkopf, who would only change attacks against Army divisions. (S) Intvw Barlow, et al., with Lt Gen Horner.

[111](S) Intvw, Keaney, et al., with Lt Col Deptula, 20 Dec 91. Horner said he went to the Black Hole around 0900 to ask about targets two days from now. (S) Intvw Barlow, et al., with Lt Gen Horner. Brig Gen Tolin recalled that Gen Horner would stop by at "mid-day." Intvw, John F. Guilmartin, Jr., with Brig Gen Anthony J. Tolin, 30 Jan 1992.

As noted in Chapter 1, the chief problem in relying on interviews conducted some time after an event is that memories fade. This is not an issue of truthfulness, but does raise a concern about the verisimilitude of accounts based solely on interviews. In many cases, the discrepancies among accounts may not matter; for example, the apparent disagreement above about when Gen Horner went to the Black Hole to discuss targeting. In another example, there appears to be a disagreement concerning the start time of the actual planning cycle. In Lt Col David A. Deptula's 15 Oct 1991 presentation, (S) "The Air Campaign: Planning and Execution," he included a chart showing the planning cycle starting at 0800 local time. (Lt Col David A. Deptula, Chief Planner, CENTAF Special Planning Group [Desert Shield], Director, Strategic Target Planning Cell [Desert Storm], (S) "The Air Campaign: Planning and Execution," presentation given to the Defense Science Board's Sub Panel on Air Operations, 15 Oct 1991.) In a later version of this briefing, given to GWAPS on 26 Nov 1991, Deptula changed the briefing slide to show a 0500 planning cycle start time. He also added a JFACC Staff Meeting somewhere between 0500 and 0800. (Lt Col David A. Deptula, Chief Planner, CENTAF special Planning Group [Desert Shield], Director, Strategic Target Planning Cell [Desert Storm], (S) "The Air Campaign: Planning & Execution," presentation given to the Gulf War Air Power Survey, 26 Nov 1991.) The USCENTAF (S) Combat Plans Handout dated Jan 1991 showed the ATO cycle starting with a 1000 CC (Gen Horner) discussion with the GAT. The Warrior briefing, (S) "Air Tasking Order (ATO) preparation and Composite Force Packaging," given to the CSAF and to GWAPS by Lt Col Sam Baptiste, Chief of Weapons and Tactics at 9th AF HQ, did not give any specific time frame for the start of the planning process. The script of the briefing only states that the "initial planning for an ATO period began in GAT with Guidance from four primary sources . . . ." (Lt Col Sam Baptiste, Chief of Weapons and Tactics, 9th AF HQ, "Air Tasking Order [ATO] Preparation and Composite Force Packaging," Project Warrior briefing given to Gulf War Air Power Survey, 9 Mar 1991. Note, this briefing focuses on the actual timing of the planning process when the CENTAF staff began the construction of the ATO Document itself).

systems specialists were collecting and assimilating the bomb damage assessment[112] and talking to units about the previous night's efforts.[113] The information from the units was used to update the target list "scorecard"–the list used to monitor progress in achieving the air campaign objectives. Glosson would arrive at the GAT around 1200L. A Joint Target Coordination Board (JTCB) meeting was held each day at about the same time to rank target nominations from Army, Navy, Marine, and coalition representatives. Deptula and Glosson would examine the scorecard and go over near-term campaign objectives. Glosson would talk with Rear Admiral McConnell, and based upon McConnell's newest intelligence updates, Glosson would adjust the Master Attack Plan currently under development. Glosson and Deptula would then walk over to Combat Operations, where they would review the Air Tasking Order being executed; based upon the most current information, they might direct changes to the current Order.[114] They also would review "tomorrow's attack plan," the Air Tasking Order being assembled from the targeting planning worksheets, for possible changes. After Deptula and Glosson's review of changes to the current and next day's ATO, the planning staff would perform an overall quality control check.[115] By late afternoon, Guidance, Apportionment, and Targeting had produced a draft Master Attack Plan that contained the targets, times over targets, and types of aircraft tasked against each specific target.

Given these various accounts, it is difficult to say when planning for a particular ATO cycle actually started. Yet, the disconnect between the other sources is probably not critical to understanding the process. Planning started in the GAT when the GAT planners arrived at work.

[112]The presence of the weapon system experts in the Black Hole was very helpful. Deptula noted that these weapon system representatives provided feedback and input for the particular weapons systems, and they represented their units. They would tell Deptula if there were "something stupid in the . . . package." Intvw (S), Office of Air Force History with Lt Col David A. Deptula, SAF/OSX, 20 Nov 1991.

[113]This last step of collecting information from the units was a "work around of Intel." Black Hole officers could not wait for the ranked target nominations list (which normally arrived between 1400 and 1600L). (S) Intvw, Office of Air Force History with Lt Col Deptula, SAF/OSX, 29 Nov 1991.

[114]Three ATOs were prepared at any given time. The planning process began with the GAT working on the "day after tomorrow" ATO. The MAP would be used to develop the ATO. Concurrently, the GAT would develop the USCENTAF/CC Guidance Letter, which detailed the level of effort and emphasis for the planning cycle in progress for the units and CENTAF Staff.

[115](S) Intvw, Office of Air Force History with Lt Col Deptula, SAF/OSX, 20 Nov 1991.

Target nominations came in to the Targeting cell at all times of the day. Deptula recalled that he had to find time to add these targets to the Master Attack Plan. In the meantime, Deptula built the MAP for the "day after tomorrow" using CINCCENT guidance and information from the daily 1900L component commanders meeting.[116] Glosson would return to Guidance, Apportionment, and Targeting around 2000L and review the "day after tomorrow's" Master Attack Plan with Deptula, who would give it to the night targeting cell to create target planning worksheets.[117] The transfer of this information to the night targeting cell completed the target planning.

Intelligence and operations planners examined each target to select actual impact points for the weapons, build force packages, assign mission information such as call signs and mission numbers, and do a "sanity check" on the plan as it then stood. At 0430L hours, the information was forwarded to the ATO division in the form of target planning worksheets.[118] The ATO Division's fraggers completed the final coordination. By 1400L each day, all inputs from fraggers and others were due to operators, who completed the process of building the Air Tasking Order and transmitted it to the units by 1800L.

Superficially, this Air Tasking Order development cycle was similar to the cycle used by the Combat Planning Division for several months in planning the D-Day ATO and daily training ATOs. However, there were three differences; two major and one minor. Because of these differences, the reorganized ATO cycle altered the process of identifying, ranking, and assigning targets. The first major difference concerned the joint nature of air mission planning. During Desert Shield, the CENTAF Combat Planning Division had employed a rudimentary "joint" planning process when it planned for the defense of Saudi Arabia; a Joint Target Coordination Board had worked with Central Command Intelligence and the other components to list and rank targets. After the reorganization, a joint planning process was used only on Kuwaiti theater of operations targets to identify Army-nominated targets in the preparation of the

---

[116] Brig Gen Glosson also attended these meetings. (S) Intvw, Office of Air Force History with Lt Col Deptula, 20 Nov 1991.

[117] Intvw, (S) Office of Air Force History with Lt Col Deptula, 20 Nov 1991.

[118] Briefing, Lt Col David A. Deptula to Center for Strategic and International Studies, "Lessons Learned: The Desert Storm Air Campaign," Apr 1991.

battlefield. The joint planning process was used mainly on targets in the Kuwaiti theater.[119]

In contrast, the planning process in the Iraq Cell did not rely principally on information generated "jointly." Members of the Iraq cell briefly reviewed the ranked target list produced by CENTAF and CENTCOM intelligence and other Services but relied more on information from other sources to plan.[120] The Guidance, Apportionment, and Targeting cell operations staff selected, ranked, and analyzed targets and assigned assets against specific targets. There was little intelligence review of selected targets. As noted above, weaponeering, designated munitions point of impact selection, force packaging, and discussion of suppression of enemy air defense support and enemy threats were accomplished by the operations planners and the one or two intelligence officers assigned to the night shift. The Joint Munitions Effectiveness Manual process was seen as too unwieldy. The CENTCOM Joint Targeting Coordination Board did not review target nominations generated by the GAT.[121]

The second major–and critical difference is that in the Central Command Air Forces planning process, no changes were accepted after 0800Z on Day 2.[122] The revised planning process established after the December CENTAF reorganization did not include such an injunction. Changes could be made at any time.

The third, and minor, difference due to the reorganization was a shift in the effective ATO period from 0100Z - 0059Z to 0200Z - 0159Z. This

---

[119]Intvw, (S) Thomas C. Hone, Lt Col Frank D. Kistler, Mark D. Mandeles, and Maj Sanford S. Terry with Brig Gen Richard I. Neal, USMC, 17 Jan 1992. Brig Gen Neal was Deputy J-3, CENTCOM during the Gulf War.

[120]Briefing, "Air Tasking Order (ATO) Preparation and Composite Force Packaging," nd [1991].

[121]However, Gen Schwarzkopf and Gen Horner were fully aware of, and in agreement with, the target selections. Prior to the war, Schwarzkopf and Horner approved Special Planning Group plans and targets lists. With the onset of the war, Gen Horner or Gen Glosson would brief the target selection for the next ATO at every 1900L CENTCOM staff meeting. Target priorities would be discussed at that meeting. This discussion ensured that the overall CINC priorities were met. However, as the ground war approached, components wanted to have a greater voice in target selection. Also see Intvw, (S) Brig Gen Neal.

[122]See (S) Chapter 5, p 5-28.

shift gave units more time to plan individual mission sorties[123] and provided a more useable night tasking window for special aircraft, such as the F-117. These three changes played a significant role in how the air campaign was executed.

While the Master Attack Plan helped Guidance, Apportionment, and Targeting officers focus their planning efforts, it also disrupted established procedures. In theory, the GAT officers would look at a seventy-two hour period encompassing Day 1 to Day 3 of the Air Tasking Order planning cycle. The role played by the GAT in this cycle would be concentrated on preparing the strategic guidance–the Master Attack Plan–for the attacks to be conducted on Day 3 (the "day after tomorrow"). The ATO Division would put together the Air Tasking Order for Day 2 of the planning cycle ("tomorrow")–collating information and guidance to remove conflicts among times over target. The Combat Operations Division would monitor "today's" execution of the Air Tasking Order (Day 1) and incorporate target changes based on new intelligence or bomb damage assessment into the ATO being executed. However, this theoretical picture did not describe what actually happened. The GAT officers operated independently of CENTAF staff officers; their actions were not circumscribed by CENTAF procedures for organizing and issuing the Air Tasking Order.

It is not clear if General Glosson purposely set out to change the planning cycle or whether the ultimate form of the planning cycle–as practiced in Desert Storm–was the outcome of other actions. It is clear, however, that Glosson believed he could receive bomb damage assessment a lot faster than the process promised and hence respond more flexibly and rapidly to a dynamic combat situation. This belief played a large role in how General Glosson led the planning effort during Desert Storm.[124] Between October and December 1990, briefings were presented to senior civilian and military leaders, including President Bush, which contained a slide stating that bomb damage assessment would be used to

---

[123]Briefing, "Air Tasking Order (ATO) Preparation and Composite Force Packaging," nd [1991].

[124]In Chapter 7 we will show that one result of the GAT's independence was the circumvention of the forty-eight to seventy-two hour planning process, primarily for targets in Iraq.

plan Day 3 attacks against targets previously hit.[125] This timetable could be met only if the planners expanded their responsibilities beyond Day 1 and Day 2 and assumed the responsibility for execution of the Day 3 (or current) Air Tasking Order. We will discuss this point in detail in the next chapter.

Summary and Review

In this chapter, we described how the Black Hole (a) developed the Master Attack Plan, (b) transformed the MAP into a flyable Air Tasking Order, and (c) published the ATO. We also showed how the Tactical Air Control Center developed in ways far different from its paper line diagram description or from the generic model suggested by Tactical Air Command Regulation 55-45 or USCENTAF Regulation 55-45.

The reorganization of CENTAF's planning staff put the former Black Hole staff firmly in charge of the air campaign planning effort. General Glosson was named Chief, Campaign Plans—complementing his authority as 14th AD(P) Commander. Glosson now controlled the entire planning and execution effort.[126] The leader of the most critical element of Guidance, Apportionment, and Targeting, Lieutenant Colonel Deptula of the Iraq Cell, had contributed to the offensive plan from the beginning. The GAT's KTO Cell was led by Lieutenant Colonel Baptiste. While Baptiste had access to the strategic air campaign early in Desert Shield, he was deeply involved in the daily training and D-Day Air Tasking Orders—not in the planning for the strategic air campaign. With the reorganization, there would be no more duplicate Air Tasking Orders, no more separate ground and air campaigns, and no question of planning and execution authority. The driving focus of the Black Hole—the strategic air campaign against Iraq—became the focus of the CENTAF staff as a whole.

---

[125] Intvw, Brig Gen Tolin. In contrast to Brig Gen Tolin's recollection, Deptula recalled that Black Hole officers planned to begin making adjustments as BDA began to arrive. (S) Intvw, Office of Air Force History with Lt Col Deptula, 20 Nov 1991; (S) Intvw, GWAPS with Lt Col Deptula; 20 Dec 1991.

[126] Gen Glosson, as the chief of Campaign Plans or as 14th AD(P) Commander, was subordinate to Gen Horner. Glosson as chief of Campaign Plans also worked for the CENTAF DO, Maj Gen John A. Corder. As the chief planner Glosson was a staff officer and had no command authority at all over the execution of the ATO. However, as an air division commander he had command authority over those assets assigned him, and was responsible to the JFACC for execution of taskings given to his units via the ATO.

Participants in the planning process ascribe great importance to the reorganization. Lieutenant Colonel Deptula believed that the centralization of authority in Glosson's hands was a key to the overall success of the air campaign. According to Deptula,

> This arrangement was highly successful in facilitating the execution of the air war. There was no misunderstanding or dilution of intent of the plan between the planner and those executing the plan because the same individual was in charge of both. Highly effective in concept as well as in actual implementation.[127]

If Deptula is correct, this arrangement integrated or merged two distinct chains of command below, rather than at, the position of Joint Force Air Component Commander (Lieutenant General Horner)—and allowed Brigadier General Glosson to control the planning and execution process in the Tactical Air Control Center.

Looking ahead to Desert Storm, the integration of planning and execution authority in General Glosson's hands may have had consequences beyond promises of reducing "misunderstanding" between the "planner and those executing the plan." Unit-level representatives cited in the *Tactical Analysis Bulletin* 91-2[128] suggest that Glosson's proclivity to make changes, in the context of centralized planning and execution authority, caused confusion in executing the Air Tasking Order.[129] The F-16/F-111 case study in Chapter 7 illustrates this situation. In addition, back-channel communications, informal links between Riyadh and Washington, and reliance on past friendships and confidences created a situation in which the strategic air campaign could be planned in an environment free of traditional "staff" thinking and parochial constraints.

Yet, there may have been significant "costs" to the reorganization. Not least of these was the willingness of GAT officers during Desert Shield (and

---

[127] Lt Col Deptula, (S) "Observations on the Air Campaign, Aug 90-Mar 91, 29 Mar 1991.

[128] (S) USAF Tactical Fighter Weapons Center, *Tactical Analysis Bulletin*, Volume 91-2, Jul 1991.

[129] (S) That is, Gen Glosson provided verbal guidance directly to the combat wings in the field. Lt Gen Horner understood that Glosson was calling the units to order changes in the ATO before launch. However, Horner believed that the changes ordered by Glosson did not have a detrimental impact on the war effort. (S) Intvw, Barlow, et al., with Lt Gen Horner.

later, during Desert Storm) to make decisions on the basis of little, or poorly understood, data and information. Theater intelligence officers believed that information received through informal channels by the Black Hole from the Air Staff was "non validated."[130] In addition, the information came from up to four different sources,[131] making it even more difficult–under strict time constraints–to array and analyze information in a coherent fashion. Because of the capability to pass classified information over the STU-III, target information could be accessed as quickly and easily as a phone call to senior-level officials in Washington, D.C. The theater intelligence community could not keep up with the very short lag times between the development of a target idea in Washington, D.C. [DELETED] and transmission of that information to the GAT. None of this target information passed through the CENTCOM CCJ2 and CENTAF target intelligence organizations for analysis and further target development.

The reorganization also did not reintegrate theater intelligence agencies into the campaign planning process. Theater intelligence planners contended that targets were attacked unnecessarily because of the way information entered the Guidance, Apportionment, and Targeting cell. Intelligence officers argued that targets selected and struck often (a) did not meet Commander in Chief, Central Command targeting objectives, (b) did not have the appropriate preparatory analysis to identify aim points and desired mean points of impact, and (c) bypassed standard target material production.[132] Indeed, initially the GAT did not employ a data management system to track and catalog the rapidly arriving intelligence inputs and targets nominations. Eventually, Guidance, Apportionment, Targeting Cell officers managed the variety of target information they received by developing a target nomination worksheet. The worksheet gave structure to the information coming from CENTAF/IN, TACC Combat Operations, DIA, CENTCOM J2, JCS J2, Checkmate, USSOCOM, [DELET-

---

[130] To targeting officers, this relationship between Black Hole and Air Staff officers was a major source of irritation. See, for example, (S) JULLS Report Number 50641-13128 (00066), USCENTAF Special Planning Group, Impact on Targeting, submitted by CCJ2-SG, 15 Jul 1991.

[131] Gen Glosson and the GAT received target information from Checkmate, DOD-JIC, and CENTCOM.

[132] (S) JULLS Number: 50641-13128 (00066), submitted by CCJ2-SG, Capt M. Menke, 15 Jul 1991.

ED].¹³³ Anyone with a contact in the GAT could supply intelligence or nominate a target. New information arriving in the GAT was reviewed, added to the Master Target List, and marked for action.

The number of personnel in the Desert Storm Tactical Air Control System eventually reached almost 5,000, excluding those at the tactical airbases.¹³⁴ The geographic spread, number of interactions, and number of occupational specializations combined to form a very complex organizational architecture to support the Joint Force Air Component Commander. And this organizational complexity partly accounts for difficulties encountered in devising and executing the air campaign. The institutional context in which planning was conducted to establish command and control of a large and diverse air force generated tension and conflict between formal organization (that is, CENTAF) and ad hoc organization (the Black Hole). Officers created informal communications channels to deal with that conflict or to get information more quickly.¹³⁵ These informal channels also compensated for the confusion caused by abandonment of existing deployment plans.

---

¹³³Intvw (S) Lt Col Frank D. Kistler and Mark D. Mandeles with Maj Gen Thomas R. Olsen, USAF (ret), formerly Deputy Commander CENTAF, 9 Mar 1992. For example, see (S) Msg, M. P. C. Carns, Lt Gen, USAF, JCS/DJS (signed by M. McConnell) to CENTCOM///J2/J3//INFO CENTAF//DO/INTACC/INT//, 131535Z Feb 91, subj: Israeli Proposed Scud Targets in Western Iraq.

¹³⁴(S) Intvw Donald A. Kellum with Col John Duane, Commander, 507th Air Control Wing, 14 Jun 1992.

¹³⁵For example, information about air campaign planning activities in Riyadh flowed to Washington. Lt Col Deptula and Maj Mark "Buck" Rogers provided Lt Col Paul Dordal, who worked on the Joint Staff, such information. (S) Intvw, Thomas C. Hone, Mark D. Mandeles, and Maj Sanford S. Terry with Col Paul Dordal, Operations Directorate (J-3), Joint Operations Division, EUCOM/CENTCOM Branch, 9 Jan 1992. The Secretary of the Air Force, Donald Rice, also received information from Lt Col Deptula (who was assigned to USCENTAF from SAF/OSX) during both Desert Shield and Desert Storm. The communications were primarily "back channel." See, for example, (S) Memo Lt Col Deptula to Secretary Rice, subj: Feedback from SECDEF/CJCS Meeting with CINC and Component Commander, 9 Feb 1991.

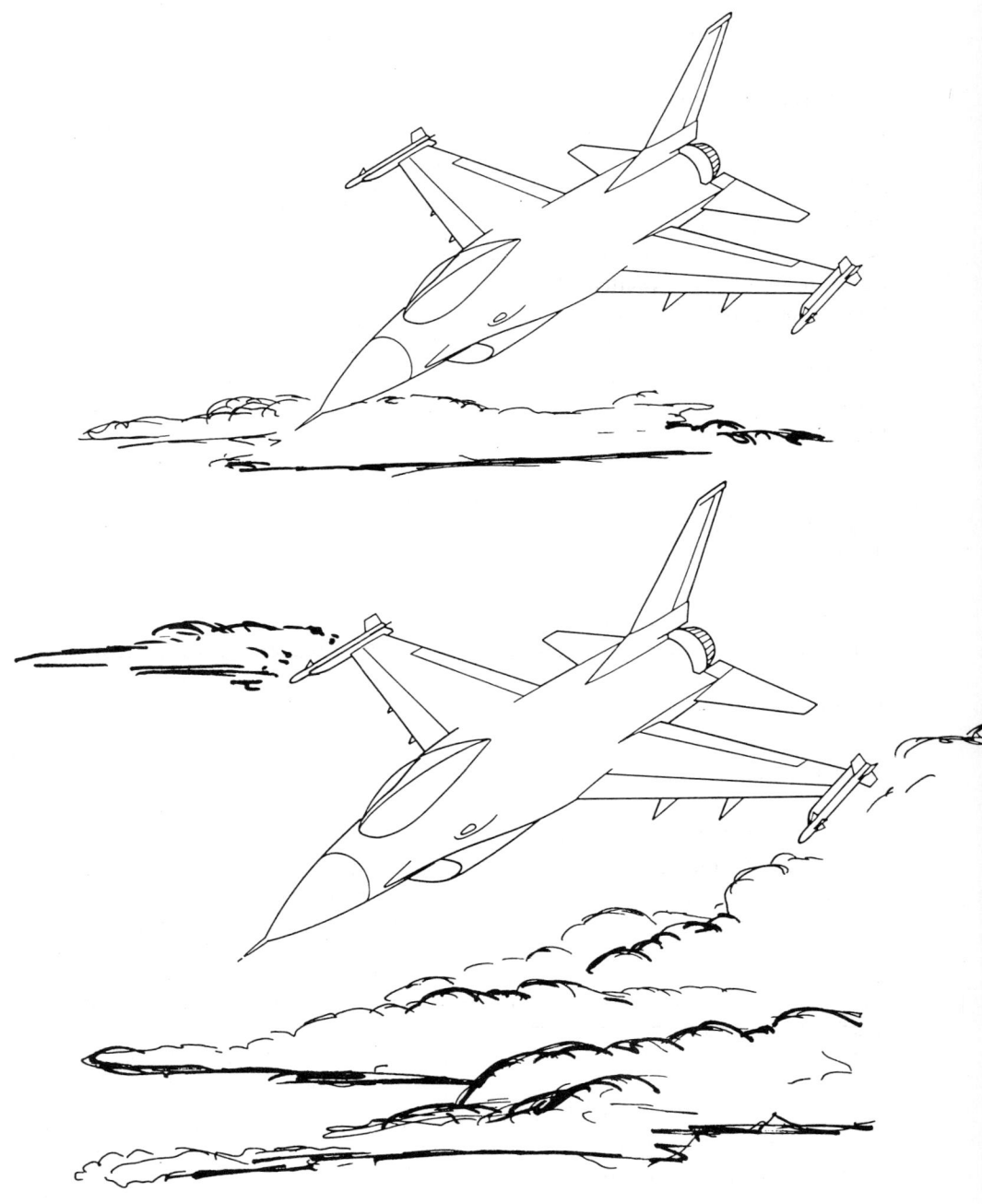

7

The TACC and GAT in Desert Storm

In previous chapters we examined the responsibilities and tasks of officers at different organizational levels of U.S. Central Command Air Forces. In Chapter 3, we analyzed the types of problems faced by Lt. Gen. Charles A. Horner as he managed the diverse activities of many different offices and performed the institutional role of the Joint Force Air Component Commander. In Chapters 4 and 5, we described selected key components of the CENTAF Tactical Air Control System (TACS) and the organization of the CENTAF Tactical Air Control Center (TACC). In Chapter 6, we surveyed the origins and evolution of the Black Hole during Desert Shield. These chapters show that the organization conducting the war was very complex, replete with sometimes cross-cutting formal lines of authority, ad hoc organizations, and informal communications channels.

Chapter 7 deals with the relationship between centralized control (and planning conducted) in Riyadh and decentralized execution of the Air Tasking Order (ATO) by the wings. The context for this analysis is in the coordination among officers assigned to the formal organization (CENTAF) and those comprising the war's critical ad hoc organization–the Black Hole. The December 1990 CENTAF reorganization placed the Black Hole within CENTAF's Guidance, Apportionment, and Targeting group (GAT).[1] In this chapter we will examine the role of the Master Attack Plan (MAP) in the three-day ATO planning cycle as we compare the command and control of the first three days of the air campaign[2] with subsequent days.[3]

---

[1] As described in Chapter 6, the "Black Hole" was the popular name given to the staff function of developing an offensive plan against Iraq. The Special Planning Group was among its many official names. The official name of the Black Hole changed several times. In previous chapters, we used the name "Black Hole" to refer to the group of officers led by Brig Gen Buster C. Glosson, who developed the offensive plans during Desert Shield and Desert Storm. With the December 1990 CENTAF reorganization, the chief reason to disguise the presence and function of the Black Hole ceased. The organization acquired a new name, the Guidance, Apportionment, and Targeting Division, or GAT. In this chapter we will use the name GAT to refer to the planning division as it existed after the December 1990 reorganization.

[2] The ATOs for the first two days and the MAP for the third day of the air campaign were completed during the five months of Desert Shield.

We will also survey Desert Storm command and control in the context of (a) adjustments to bad weather, (b) the Scud hunt, and (c) Intelligence support.

Chapter 7 also approaches the task of describing how the air campaign was executed from an unorthodox angle. Rather than viewing government agencies from the "top-down," that is, in terms of their structure, purposes, and resources,[4] we supplement the recollections of the chief planners devising and executing the air campaign with a view from the units–the "bottom-up."[5] The contrast between top-down and bottom-up analyses also will help explain the differences between building and executing an Air Tasking Order for a "dynamic" and "static" environment.

Operation of the GAT

During Desert Shield, a period of about five months, Days 1 and 2 of the air campaign were "fully scripted," and the Master Attack Plan for Day 3 was prepared.[6] In putting together the MAP for the first two days, the choice of targets and attacking aircraft was considered carefully.[7] General Horner thought the resulting offensive air plan was "too precise." Horner would have been happy with about half of the objectives the

---

[3] The planning for subsequent days of the air campaign was conducted in parallel with ongoing combat operations.

[4] Of course, this approach has been applied in most studies of command and control. For example, see C. Kenneth Allard, *Command, Control, and the Common Defense* (New Haven, 1990); Martin Blumenson and James L. Stokesbury, *Masters of the Art of Command* (Boston, 1975); Thomas P Coakley, ed, *C³I: Issues of Command and Control* (Washington, DC, 1991); Martin Van Creveld, *Command in War* (Cambridge, 1985).

[5] The difference between "top-down," and "bottom-up" approaches to understanding organizational behavior is explained by James Q. Wilson in *Bureaucracy: What Government Agencies Do and Why They Do It* (New York, 1989).

[6] GAT planners assembled the Master Attack Plans for Days 1 and 2, transformed them into ATOs, printed the ATOs for Days 1 and 2, and sent these to the wings via courier. GAT planners also put together a MAP for Day 3. Under the logic of the planning process–on Day 1 of the air campaign–the GAT would begin working on the Day 4 MAP, and the ATO Division (using Target Planning Worksheets generated from the Day 3 MAP) would begin constructing the Day 3 ATO.

[7] For a discussion of how rules of engagement regarding legal targets were written, see (U) GWAPS Volume III, *Support*, Chapter 4.

Black Hole planners tried to achieve on the first two days.[8] Horner was correct in his view that many strike, refueling, support, and reconnaissance operations (for example, suppression of enemy air defenses, electronic warfare support, and tankers) were tightly coupled. Each mission was linked closely to other missions or support activities. A change to one mission cascaded through the plan, affecting the other missions and multiplying the number of departures from the original plan.[9] The complexity of this script or plan was so great that the air campaign planners were surprised there were not about four to five midair collisions with tankers that first day.[10] Implications of the Air Tasking Order's great complexity were evident for at least a month before combat began. Maj. Gen. John A. Corder noted that even during December 1990, when a few changes were made to the Master Attack Plan, it would take a week to address the effects of those changes in other parts of the plan.[11]

In Horner's view, it was necessary to prepare the planners for the effects of Murphy's Law. He believed that detailed war planning was more appropriate for nuclear warfare and explicitly drew the comparison between conventional and nuclear war planning in cutting off the GAT's preparation of ever more Master Attack Plans and Air Tasking Orders in advance of actual combat. In contrast to nuclear planning, conventional warfare planning must be flexible. In Horner's words,

---

[8] Deptula reported the conversation in interviews conducted after the war. (S) Intvw, GWAPS with Lt Col David A. Deptula, SAF/OSX, 20 Dec 1991. When questioned on this vignette by Air Force historians, Horner did not remember the conversation, but believed he might have made that argument to Deptula. (S) Intvw, Barry Barlow, Richard G. Davis, and Perry Jamieson with Lt Gen Charles A. Horner, Commander, 9th AF, 4 Mar 1992.

[9] (S) Intvw, GWAPS with Lt Col David A. Deptula, SAF/OSX, 21 Dec 1991; (S) Intvw, Office of Air Force History with Lt Col Deptula, 20 Nov 1991.

[10] Intvw, Office of Air Force History with Lt Col Deptula, 20 Nov 1991; (S) Intvw, GWAPS with Lt Col Deptula, 20 Dec 1991. Lt Col James Philips noted, "God had to have been with us 'cause we didn't have a midair. We knew we were going to have one and we didn't. It was so congested. We attempted to control it, but it was so congested, and some of the people didn't play by the rules." (S) Intvw, Jacqueline R. Henningsen, HQ SAC, DCS/Plans & Resources with Maj Scott Hente, HQ SAC/DOO, Maj John Heinz, HQ SAC/DOO, Lt Col James Philips, HQ SAC/DOO, and Lt Col James Schroder, 99th Strategic Weapons Wing, 11 Mar 1991.

[11] (S) Intvw, GWAPS with Maj Gen John A. Corder, Deputy Commander for Operations, USCENTAF (Nov 1990 to Mar 1991), 18 May 1992.

conventional war [is a matter of] action/reaction a lot, and you have got to be able to capitalize on mistakes the enemy makes . . . . So what I wanted [the GAT planners] to do, I did not want them to become so enthralled with preplanning that they were unable to react when the war started. That is why I would never let them do a full-day third-day ATO. I wanted them immediately to start–and you saw the perfection of the first two-day plan, and then you saw them kind of drop off in terms of really good planning for about three or four days until they learned how to do chaos war, and then they suddenly became very good again.[12]

Table 7 illustrates the key planning cycle activities and products that the Campaign Plans (which contained the GAT and the ATO Division) and Combat Operations Divisions were designed to accomplish as combat began on Day 2.[13]

When the air campaign began, the GAT officers believed they were the only ones who understood the logic and contents of the campaign plan[14]–such as the relationship among objectives, target sets, and weapons in-theater. The GAT planners' belief probably was reinforced on Day 2 by witnessing the rampant confusion in the ATO Division as officers attempted to translate the Day 3 Master Attack Plan into an Air Tasking Order.[15] In an interview conducted after the war, Corder recalled he

---

[12](S) Intvw, Lt Gen Charles A. Horner, 4 Mar 1992.

[13]This table is based on a slide in a briefing prepared by Lt Col David A. Deptula. Briefing, Lt Col David A. Deptula, SAF/OSX, subj: "The Air Campaign: The Planning Process," rev 3, nd [1992].

[14](S) Intvw, GWAPS with Lt Col Deptula, 20 Dec 1991. (U) When Lt Col Mark "Buck" Rogers reviewed the command post exercises held on 6 and 13 January 1991, he also noted that only he, Lt Col Deptula, and Brig Gen Glosson had a thorough understanding–in terms of theory and practice–of the air campaign. Lt Gen Horner was comfortable with the plan but did not have the level of understanding of the other three. This perception was confirmed by the 13 January exercise, which was a "dry run" of transforming the Day 3 MAP into the ATO. One "lesson" of this exercise was that either Rogers or Deptula had to be in the GAT at all times. (S) Intvw, Lt Col Frank D. Kistler and Mark D. Mandeles with Lt Col Mark "Buck" Rogers, SAF/LL, 31 Jan 1992.

[15]Maj Gen Corder noted that the officers working in the ATO Division were unable to complete the ATO on time. Corder sent only partially completed ATO to the wings. See (S) Intvw, GWAPS with Maj Gen John A. Corder, 18 May 1992.

Table 7
**Planned Activities: Day 2 of the Air Campaign in
Directorates for Campaign Plans and Combat Operations**

Organization	GAT (Guidance, Apportionment, Targeting)	ATO (Air Tasking Order)	OPS (Combat Operations)

Product	o Master Attack Plan
	o Guidance Letter
	o Target Planning Worksheets
	o Change Sheets
		o ATO (CAFMS)
		    - Add detail (callsigns, squawks, SPINS, etc.)
		    - Airspace deconfliction
		    - Tanker tracks
		o ATO transmission
			o Execution Management
			    - Coordination
			    - Immediate Taskings
			    - Changes

Focus	Planning: Day 4	Processing: Day 3	Execution: Day 2

believed in mid-January that Glosson would send GAT staff to help assemble the ATO when the war began. Glosson did not. CENTAF staff quickly found itself, in Corder's words, "discombobulated," trying to coordinate varied and manifold details of operations. And, the task took much longer than anticipated: nine to ten hours instead of two to three. On the second day, at 1800L, the third day's ATO was to have been generated. At 2200L, only about thirty or forty percent of the ATO had been generated, including some of the critical strike packages. At this point, Corder decided to send the ATO–as it stood–to the wings. For various reasons, including tanker availability, a sizable portion of the planned strike packages were cancelled.[16]

At this time, instead of exclusively preparing the MAP for Day 4, the GAT officers started to assume responsibility for some of the functions

---

[16](S) Intvw, GWAPS with Maj Gen Corder, 18 May 1992. (U) The sortie change data indicate only a small number of cancellations (approximately 35) and a moderate number of additions (about 100). The cancellations Corder describes probably never were entered into the ATO sent to the wings. These missions were rolled over into later versions of the MAP and ATO.

envisioned for other Tactical Air Control Center divisions. They began monitoring the execution of the Day 1 and 2 ATOs (the function of Combat Operations) and making changes to Day 3 while that ATO was being prepared for publication by the ATO Division.[17]

As shown in Chapter 6, CENTAF officers before the reorganization were restricted from making changes to their plan after 0800Z of the second day in the three-day ATO planning cycle.[18] The revised planning cycle instituted after the reorganization contained no such rule. In effect, GAT planners were able to change, without justification to another staff element or senior officer, the planned targets and time over targets after the ATO itself should have been completed. As Desert Storm began, the absence of an outside (the GAT) restriction on making ATO changes also altered the relationship between the separate Campaign Plans and the Combat Operations divisions. GAT officers assumed not only some of the duties of the other division within Campaign Plans, the ATO Division, but also some of the duties of Combat Operations in monitoring and executing the current day's ATO. In effect, the separate functions of planning and execution were combined in one office. The GAT's influence expanded to cover a wider share of command and control for the air campaign. Figure 30 illustrates a GAT planner's postwar view of how the GAT came to control planning and ATO execution over the full three-day planning cycle.[19] The ability of GAT planners to make changes at any point in the ATO planning cycle resulted in a marked departure from how this process had been visualized in Desert Shield.

How to Assess the Command and Control of the Air Campaign

One way to assess the effectiveness of command and control is to examine changes and adjustments made to a plan after it had been released as an Air Tasking Order. Two types of questions pertain to ATO

---

[17]See (S) Chapter 4 for discussion of the functions of the TACS.

[18]See also (S) Chapter 5.

[19]This figure is a slide in a briefing prepared by Lt Col David A. Deptula. (S) Briefing, Lt Col Deptula, SAF/OSX, subj: "The Air Campaign: The Planning Process," rev 3, nd [1992].

**Figure 30
Reality: Timeline**

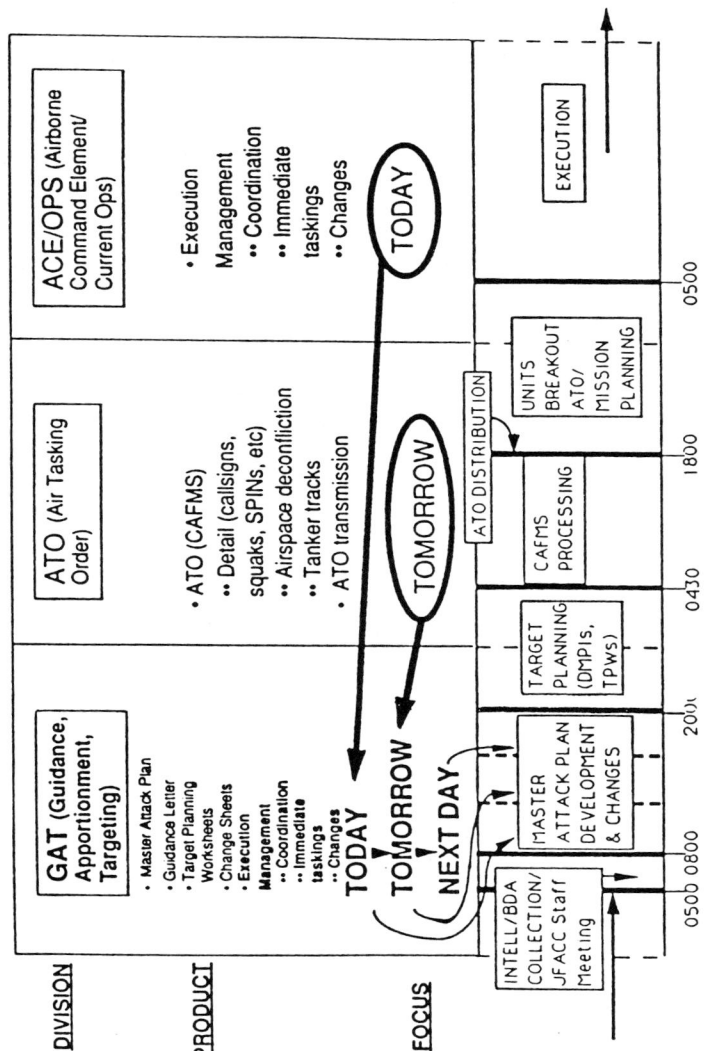

changes in the "chaos war" of Desert Storm. First, there is the general question: What do planning changes—ATO changes—measure? Second, there are the specific questions about planning and execution during Desert Storm. Did the changes reflect something wrong with the planning process? Did the changes reflect recent information about the target? Did they merely reflect the "responsiveness" and "flexibility" inherent in airpower? Can we distinguish changes which have no effect on ultimate campaign goals from those changes which have a positive effect on campaign goals? Answers to these questions will have to await a fuller examination of Desert Shield and Desert Storm records. However, we will try to provide a context in which to evaluate them.

ATO Changes

Changes made to the Air Tasking Order reflect on the planning and execution aspects of command and control.[20] The GAT planners made changes to the ATO under the assumption that those changes would improve the effectiveness of the air campaign. Yet, in terms of planning, ATO changes may reveal problems in the quality and timeliness of information used to make decisions. GAT officers planned and made comparisons among strike options despite uncertainty about the future (outcomes of planned strikes) and about the present (outcomes of strikes which had already taken place). In terms of execution, the way the GAT officers chose to handle uncertainty—making last-minute changes at the Combat Operations Division and at the wings instead of feeding the changes into the end of the three-day planning process—further reduced the quality of information GAT officers worked with. The case study later in this chapter illustrates pitfalls in the assumption that last-minute changes would help achieve campaign goals; the ATO changes introduced yet another source of uncertainty for GAT planners and units to work with.

Table 8 contrasts Days 1, 2, and 3 planned sorties with the total number of sorties changed and the number of timing and target changes made to the ATO. There were no changes for Day 1 and only a small number of changes on Day 2. On these days the units executed the ATO essentially as written by GAT planners, and they saw little reason to order changes.

---

[20]"ATO changes" refer to changes made by GAT officers to targets, times over targets (TOTs), support packages, and so on. The term does not include those situations, for instance, where the pilot had to abort the mission after launch (e.g., because of an equipment malfunction), or where the target could not be found or seen.

Table 8
Planned Sorties versus ATO Changes
Days 1, 2, and 3[21]

	Sorties Planned	Timing & Target Changes	Total Sorties Changed
Day 1	2,759	0	0
Day 2	2,900	16	68
Day 3	2,441	112	449

The first two days of the air campaign had gone well. Day 3, however, was very troublesome to all concerned–for example, many sorties were cancelled from the ATO because of tanker nonavailability,[22] or tankers were not in the right places. On Day 4, the ability to match tanker and support aircraft with strike aircraft in the ATO declined further. The problem with the tankers was traced to the continued attempt to plan, over a short period of time, a tight schedule linking strike aircraft with tankers.[23] Over the five months of Desert Shield, the use and placement of tankers had been planned carefully for the first two days of combat. As Brig. Gen. Patrick P. Caruana put it, "we had [the initial plan worked out] down to the minute."[24] General Glosson admitted a planning shortfall on this matter.[25] He solved the problem by changing the goal of

---

[21]Sources: GWAPS Composite Sorties Database and TACS Change Log.

[22]Tanker aircraft were not listed in the Black Hole's MAP. Instead, tanker tracks and assignments were added by officers in the ATO Division, who, during the initial days of the air campaign, had little understanding of the MAP or its components.

[23](S) Intvw, Jacqueline R. Henningsen, DCS/Plans & Resources, HQ SAC with Brig Gen Patrick P. Caruana, Commander, 42d Air Division, SAC, 13 Mar 1991.

[24](S) Ibid.

[25](S) Intvw, MSgt Theodore J. Turner, USCENTAF, History Office with Brig Gen Buster C. Glosson, Director, USCENTAF Campaign Plans, 6 Mar 1991. (U) Brig Gen Caruana noted that after the start of Desert Storm it came "almost as a shock" to the planners that tankers comprised a limiting factor in air operations. (S) Intvw, Brig Gen Patrick P. Caruana.

tanker planning. Rather than tasking tankers to particular sorties or packages, planners placed tankers in particular tracks: areas, orbits, and altitudes. One effect of this change was to reduce by twenty to forty the planned number of tankers employed every day.[26]

The much larger number of changes on and after Day 3, illustrated by the tanker example above, reflects a major shift in the planning and execution processes. The process of planning the subsequent days of the war has been called "the dynamic planning process."[27] Changes were made on a nearly "constant basis." A key GAT planner argued that there was a reason for every target change, although the planners did not have the time to record all the reasons.[28] The process had dynamic results. Table 9 presents number of changes to the daily ATO–Day 1 through Day 43 of the air campaign–based on nine sources (that is, additions and cancellations).[29]

---

[26] The number of tankers tasked fell from a range of 270 to 290 a day to about 250 tankers. Maj Gen Corder recalled he told Glosson the problem with tankers was that there was no flexibility in tanker use. Corder's solution was to plan for the use of a proportion of the fleet and to use the rest to fill in on emergency bases. (S) Intvw, Maj Gen John A. Corder, Brig Gen Caruana also argued that he solved the problem by not "fragging" more than 265-275 tanker sorties per day, which gave them the flexibility to add approximately 25 sorties to fill in for trouble spots. (S) Intvw, Brig Gen Patrick P. Caruana, Commander, 42d Air Division, SAC, 13 Mar 1991.

[27] (S) Intvw, Office of Air Force History with Lt Col Deptula, 20 Nov 1991.

[28] (S) Intvw, Office of Air Force History with Lt Col Deptula, 8 Jan 1992.

[29] The numbers of sorties planned per day are taken from the GWAPS Composite Sorties Database. These daily totals include both combat and support aircraft. The numbers of sorties changed were compiled from the TACS change log and the CAFMS Database. Changes for both combat and support aircraft were totaled.

All data on the types of changes made to the planned sorties comes from the entries in the TACS Change Log. This log was initiated to monitor and track the changes submitted to the TACS. Record-keeping improved during the course of the war. Initially, changes were logged as they were received–leading to mixed days and making it more difficult to assign a sequential change number. For example, the fourth change received for ATO D would be entered as change D04. The data for the ATO C through E are mingled. Beginning with ATO F, log book sheets were reserved for specific days.

Log entries included the change number, mission number(s) or package(s), time on target, package, type of change, remarks, tanker (a "check mark" if applicable), AWACS (a "check mark" if applicable), and the initials of the log keeper. Additional information was added on aircraft type and the number of aircraft to some records. This happened more frequently towards the last half of the war.

By correlating dates and mission numbers with entries in the CAFMS Database, it was possible to fill in much of the missing information on the number and type of aircraft changed. The mission planning guide had some information linking mission numbers with aircraft types. When specific data could not be located, the number and type of aircraft were estimated based on the package, mission number, and information on aircraft tactics (e.g., F-14 normally fly as pairs under a single mission number, tankers, and individual mission numbers).

This process does not yield a precise count of the numbers of sorties changed per day. It does provide the best estimate possible based on the available data. Note, it may make more sense to refer to the change data in terms of the nearest ten changes to avoid the appearance of having more precision than can be justified.

Table 9
ATO Changes, Day 1-Day 43[a]

ATO Day	Scud Hunt Change or Addition[b]	Non-weather Target Change[c]	Timing Change[d]	Other Change[e]	Addition[f]	Weather Change[g]	Other Cancellations[h]	Maintenance Cancellation[i]	Operational Cancellation[j]	Totals
1	0	0	0	0	0	0	0	0	0	0
2	0	14	2	3	20	29	0	0	0	68
3	28	76	36	120	105	47	29	0	8	449
4	12	116	57	95	225	109	129	0	70	813
5	74	124	83	89	91	395	63	8	48	975
6	12	50	62	109	208	26	56	4	25	552
7	2	168	43	244	129	71	12	0	18	687
8	13	123	86	162	66	0	63	11	20	544
9	0	80	41	87	126	76	83	0	38	531
10	40	50	52	143	158	0	43	2	38	526
11	10	104	67	106	165	85	48	4	15	604
12	4	68	67	71	116	0	41	0	0	367
13	10	11	70	57	66	0	6	0	0	220
14	0	82	240	48	158	4	37	0	8	577
15	0	142	139	73	80	0	109	0	0	543
16	0	309	106	58	36	0	9	0	0	518
17	8	163	51	125	87	47	7	0	0	488

Table 9
ATO Changes, Day 1-Day 43[a]

18	0	179	76	151	82	0	23	0	3	514
19	73	165	108	114	88	0	100	0	2	650
20	0	159	144	166	47	0	51	0	4	571
21	0	82	169	220	90	0	41	0	10	612
22	76	71	127	110	88	0	87	0	2	561
23	0	191	102	28	74	0	30	0	8	433
24	48	133	62	70	15	0	37	0	12	377
25	34	65	34	153	80	0	56	0	4	426
26	0	79	50	119	109	0	16	0	7	385
27	0	172	23	76	65	0	27	5	0	363
28	14	166	158	183	108	0	118	0	0	747
29	19	161	79	137	53	0	28	0	10	488
30	0	62	80	67	98	0	29	1	0	336
31	10	203	39	124	81	23	47	0	2	530
32	0	147	133	81	54	134	11	1	4	564
33	0	162	42	80	67	0	9	0	9	369
34	14	178	85	95	92	0	49	0	4	517

Table 9
ATO Changes, Day 1–Day 43[a]

35	0	194	132	109	58	67	65	0	4	629
36	0	45	41	64	50	10	48	0	2	260
37	2	347	107	69	76	0	57	0	9	667
38	16	147	68	361	116	0	30	0	7	745
39	2	277	73	141	147	26	52	0	0	718
40	0	196	107	165	146	39	76	0	9	738
41	25	218	89	150	325	64	34	0	0	905
42	7	327	97	272	129	0	149	0	0	981
43	0	59	123	58	87	0	61	0	6	394
Totals	**553**	**5,865**	**3,550**	**4,953**	**4,261**	**1,252**	**2,066**	**36**	**406**	**22,942**

[a] Source: GWAPS Composite Sorties Database, TACS Change Log.
[b] Sorties diverted to Scud hunt, or new sorties added to hunt Scuds.
[c] Changes to mission target for any reason other than weather.
[d] Changes to time over target, or air refueling control time (ARCT).
[e] Changes to mission numbers, call signs, tanker assignments, and unspecified changes.
[f] New sorties.
[g] Target changes, timing changes, mission adds, and cancellations caused by bad weather at the base or target area.
[h] Unspecified cancellations.
[i] Cancellation because aircraft required maintenance.
[j] Crew rest, aircraft unavailable, tanker unavailability.
[k] Most of these changes were to SPINS; some changes were to Tomahawk Land Attack Missile.

Figure 31 plots the number of planned (ATO) sorties against the number of sorties changed (as counted in the TACC log).[30] This figure shows that (after Day 2) GAT planners made an average of more than 500 changes each day. Examination of the planned sorties versus ATO timing

---

[30]Beginning with the ATO for Day 2 of Desert Storm, officers in the TACC logged ATO change requests to monitor and better organize the change process. As Deptula noted above, not all changes were entered onto the change sheets. The use of the telephone resulted in many verbal change requests.

Changes were recorded for ATOs designated C through Z (covering Days 2 through 24) and ATOs A through S (covering Days 25 through 44). The hand-written record is the best available source of the number and type of changes processed for each ATO and is the basis for the change data presented in this report.

Change numbers were assigned in the log with an alpha-numeric designator. For example, change D-42 was the forty-second change received for ATO D. Date-time groups for the change or the affected mission were not recorded, but page numbers could be used to assign changes to the appropriate ATO D. Changes for the first ATO C through E appear to have been entered as they arrived, since changes for ATOs D and E were mixed in with changes for ATOs C and D. Beginning with ATO F (Day 5), specific pages were reserved for each ATO, probably to make it easier to assign consecutive page numbers–there were a few errors in change numbers for the first three ATOs.

The TACC log book was organized into column for the change number, mission number(s) effected, TOT, package number, type of change (add, change, cancel), remarks, check marks for tankers and AWACS coordination, and initials (probably the person making the entry). The columns are not complete for all entries. Additional information on the type of aircraft affected was often included. The number of sorties was included less often. The number of logged changes varied from a low of 19 for Day 2 (ATO C) to a high of 158 for Day 39–the first day of the ground campaign. Eighty to 100 changes were common until the last 10 days of the war, when the number increased to the 130-150 range.

To better interpret the impact these changes had on the TACC and the execution of the ATO, the data in the change log were correlated with the Composite Sorties Database to get more information about the number and type of aircraft changed and the type of changes made. Then these augmented log data were categorized by type of change and summed by day to create daily totals of the number of sorties changed. The categories used are the following: sorties changed or added for Scud hunting; sorties added; weather-related additions or target changes; timing changes; target changes; other changes; weather cancellations; maintenance cancellations; operational cancellations; and other cancellations. Changes to the Special Instructions (SPINS) section of the ATO and changes to the Tomahawk Land Attack Missile missions were logged but not used in this analysis.

Figure 31
Planned Sorties (ATO) versus Sorties Changed (TACC Change Log)

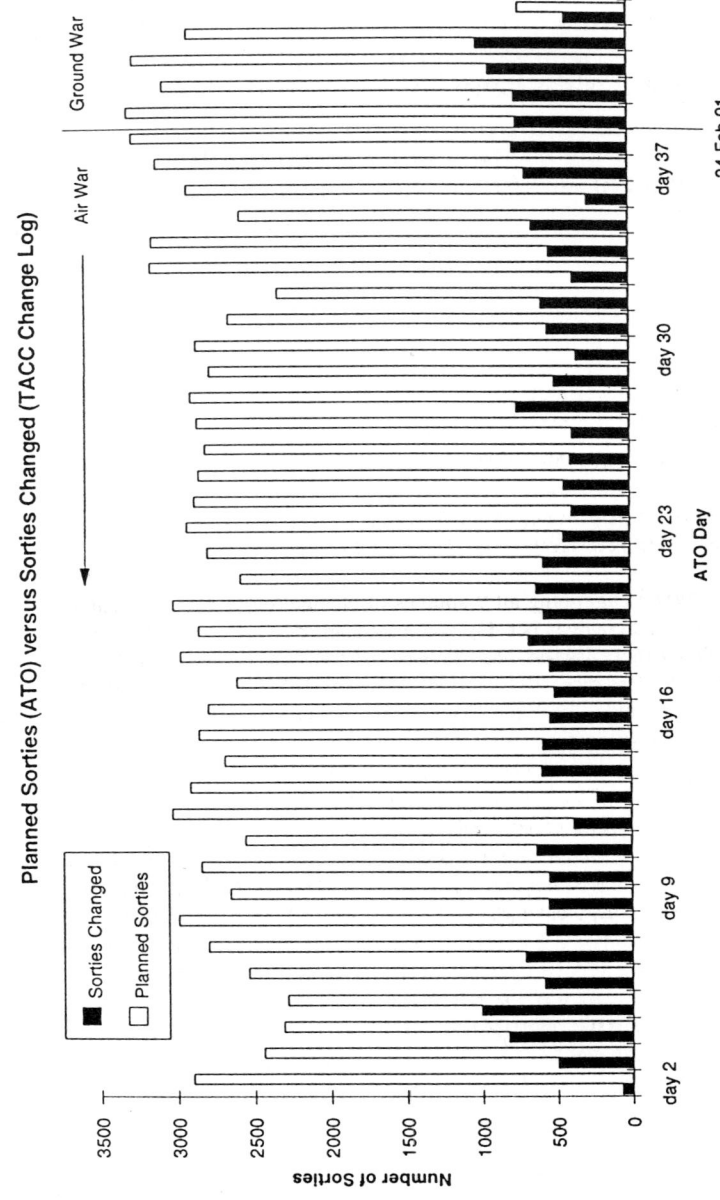

and target changes shows a great deal of variability.[31] The cause of this variability is not readily apparent. Not all changes to a plan, the ATO, will have the same impact on the overall execution of that plan. Specifically, target changes, timing changes, and major changes to complex mission scenarios will have a greater impact on current operations than changes based on weather, maintenance availability, or crew rest. Figure 32 presents this same information as a comparison of the sorties changed as a percentage of the sorties planned each day.

After the war, senior GAT planners recalled expecting grave coordination problems after Day 2. The CENTAF planning system was established to support a maximum of 2,400 sorties a day.[32] By Day 10,

---

[31] We began this analysis with Day 6, rather than Day 3, because many changes (on Days 3, 4, and 5) were made due to bad weather and learning how to work within the three-day ATO planning cycle. We stopped analysis at Day 39 because many ATO changes were made to accommodate the ground campaign.

When examining all 9 sources of change to the ATO (see Table 9), there is a mean of 518 ATO changes per day and a standard deviation of 129. If the number of changes made by GAT planners had "leveled off," we should see a much smaller standard deviation–a lot less dispersion around the mean. When examining only 2 key sources of ATO changes (timing and target changes) over the same Day 6 through Day 39 period, the same wide dispersion appears. The average number of timing and target changes is about 226, with a standard deviation of 91. Again, if the number of timing and target changes made by GAT planners had leveled off, we should see much less variability. Due to the time limit on this project, we did not correlate the variability in daily ATO changes with factors such as the quantity and quality of intelligence information received (on a particular day) from Washington, Scud launches, or personnel fatigue. One explanation for the variability in ATO changes which also can not be rejected is that the frequency and tempo of changes ordered by GAT officers early in the air campaign induced a cycle of other changes over several days. Since the planning and execution of the ATO cycle involved overlapping activities, the ATO planning process was unable to reach some sort of steady state. This issue regarding the implications of constant changes made in a process is similar to one described by W. Edwards Deming. See "On Some Statistical Aids Toward Economic Production," *Interfaces*, Vol. 5 (August 1975), pp 1-15.

[32] Soon after the end of the war, Glosson noted that the system should have supported between 1,500 and 2,000 sorties a day, with a maximum of 2,400 sorties. The maximum number of sorties run in an exercise was 2,400. (S) Intvw, MSgt Theodore J. Turner with Brig Gen Glosson, 6 Mar 1991. The system was overloaded by the attempt to generate and transmit more sorties than appropriate to the number of terminals in theater.

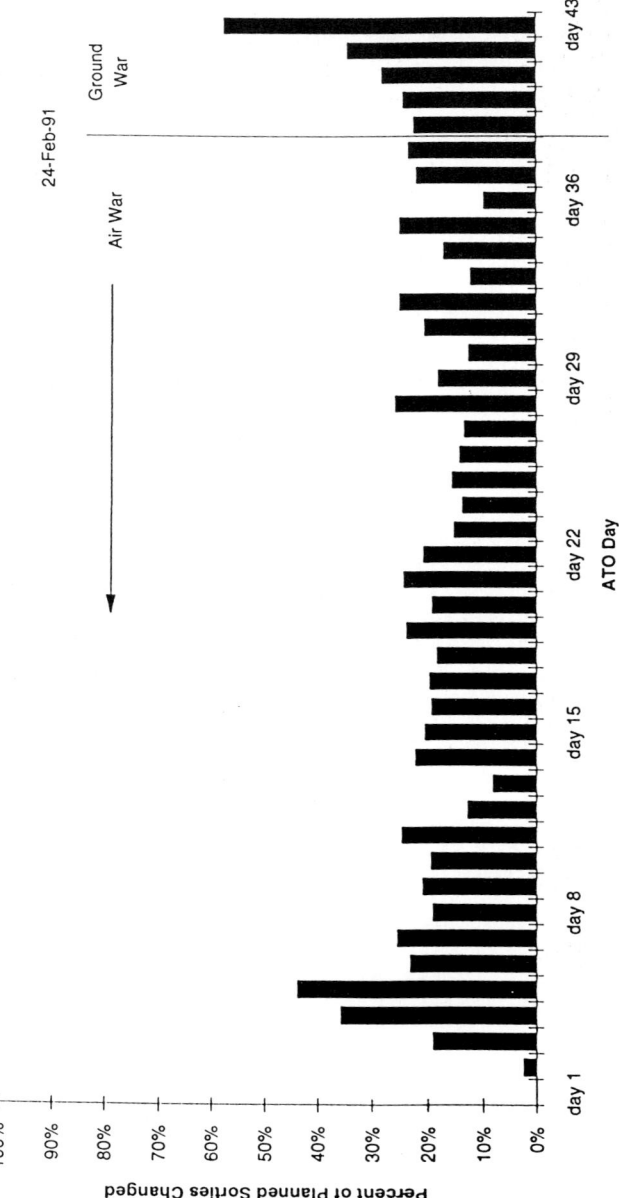

Figure 32
Sorties Changed as a Percentage of Sorties Planned

222

Brigadier General Glosson was asking for more than 3,000 sorties a day.[33] In Glosson's words,

> They had never experienced anything like that. And as a result, it was just overwhelming. It took us almost half of the war to get the ATO out at a time that was acceptable to me. That being about 1500 to 1700. For the first three weeks, the ATO would be published somewhere between 1800 and 2100.[34]

Strategic and KTO planning cell chiefs, Lt Cols Deptula and Baptiste, discuss air allocation during planning session

Changing the ATO while it was being coordinated, and especially after it had been released to the wings, increased the complexity and fragility of the process. To compensate for late changes to the Master Attack Plan, the GAT would often call the wings and tell them what the first two or three hours of the Air Tasking Order were going to be, so they could plan

---

[33] An alternate interpretation of Deptula and Glosson's expectations of coordination problems would include mentioning that the GAT did not "use" the CENTAF system to generate the air plan. Thus, it did not matter that the CENTAF system was designed to handle up to 2,400 sorties. Was victory dependent upon generating 3,000 sorties a day? Could we have won the air war by flying fewer than 2,400 sorties per day?

[34] (S) Intvw, MSgt Theodore J. Turner with Brig Gen Buster C. Glosson, 6 Mar 1991.

their missions.[35] Glosson admitted that he did not realize at the time that the size and complexity of the ATO had driven the Computer Assisted Force Management System (CAFMS) software near to exceeding its capability.[36] In particular, according to Lt. Col. David A. Deptula, Glosson expected package and mission commanders to exercise tactical initiative, that is, to find their own tankers or to make major in-flight adjustments.[37] And planning and intelligence officers at the squadrons did coordinate operations.[38] This coordination was made possible by the possession of STU-IIIs (secure telephones) and other means of reliable, secure communication at the wing level.[39]

---

[35]RAND analysts, Leland Joe and Dan Gonzales, noted some undesirable consequences of last-minute changes upon the units.

> [S]ome changes to the ATO were made very close to mission execution. In these cases, the necessary target graphics for the delivery of precision munitions were sometimes not available. In addition, many of the target changes did not specify desired mean points of impact (DMPIs), leaving the choice up to the wing. Since the wings were not equipped to handle these functions, or did not have necessary target graphics available, the 9th TIS at the TACC in Riyadh frequently became involved in picking DMPIs and providing target graphics material. The latter could involve the Defense Mapping Agency facility in St. Louis, which kept a library of mapping materials. If necessary data [were] available at DMA, mensurated coordinate data could be provided to the TACC within a few hours.

(S/NF) Leland Joe and Dan Gonzales, *Command and Control, Communications, and Intelligence in Desert Storm Air Operations*, WD(L)-5750-AF (Santa Monica: RAND Corporation, Feb 1992), pp 30, 32.

[36](S) Intvw, MSgt Theodore J. Turner, with Brig Gen Buster C. Glosson, 6 Mar 1991.

[37](S) Intvw, GWAPS with Lt Col Deptula, 20 Dec 1991.

[38]For example, F-111F units communicated directly with F-15E and F-117 units to conduct their own bomb damage assessment. These communications "prevented striking hardened targets that had previously been hit by other PGM units." (S) USAF Tactical Fighter Weapons Center, *Tactical Analysis Bulletin*, Volume 91-2, Jul 1991, p 7-3. Other interviews with wing-level operations officers complements the assessment reported by *TAB*, 91-2. (S) Intvw, Thomas C. Hone with Maj John Nichols, 401st TFW during Desert Storm, 20 Jul 1992; (S) Intvw, Mark D. Mandeles and Lt Col Sanford S. Terry with Maj Robert J. Heston, 37th TFW (P), Director of Intelligence (during Desert Shield/Desert Storm), 16 Oct 1992.

[39](S) Intvw, Maj Robert J. Heston, 16 Oct 1992.

It appears that Guidance, Apportionment, and Targeting officers did not anticipate the need to develop specific procedures to mitigate ATO change coordination problems.[40] As the war progressed, the GAT-CENTAF coordination problems had several sources. First, General Glosson believed putting together the ATO was an administrative function which could have been accomplished very easily with the "latest state-of-the-art computer support and a few sergeants. I didn't need all those officers in there that didn't understand that all they were doing was a mechanical cookbook process."[41] Second, as Major General Corder noted, the physical separation of the GAT from the ATO Division made face-to-face interaction less likely. Third, the first time CENTAF officers putting together the ATO ever saw the type of GAT "inputs" that would be used for the campaign was on the first day of the air campaign–when GAT officers submitted target planning worksheets comprising the third day's attack packages.[42]

Weather-Related ATO Changes

A major cause of changes unrelated to organizational and planning factors within the CENTAF staff was weather. Figure 33 shows the number of changes blamed on weather.[43] On Day 4, about 100 sorties were changed due to various weather problems. Day 5 saw the most weather-related changes of the war: approximately 400. After the first week,

---

[40]On 6 and 13 January 1991, the GAT held planning exercises which tested the ATO building process for the Day 3 ATO. The exercise did not include participation of the other Divisions in the TACC. (S) Intvw Lt Col Mark B. "Buck" Rogers; (S) Intvw, GWAPS with Maj Gen John A. Corder, 18 May 1992.

[41](S) Intvw, Richard G. Davis, Perry Jamieson, and Diane T. Putney with Lt Gen Buster C. Glosson, 12 Dec 1991.

[42]Corder recalled that "in the first couple, three days, [Brig Gen] Buster [C. Glosson] would come down and see what was going on. He'd see this chaos [in the TACC] . . . . He thought . . . [an] inept bunch of people [in] the TACC were trying to run the thing." (S) Intvw, GWAPS with Maj Gen John A. Corder, 18 May 1992.

[43]As noted in footnote 19, all data on the types of changes made to the planned sorties come from the entries in the TACS Change Log. Figure 33's weather-related changes includes "weather additions and target changes" and "weather cancellations" due to bad weather at the base or target area. See Table 9.

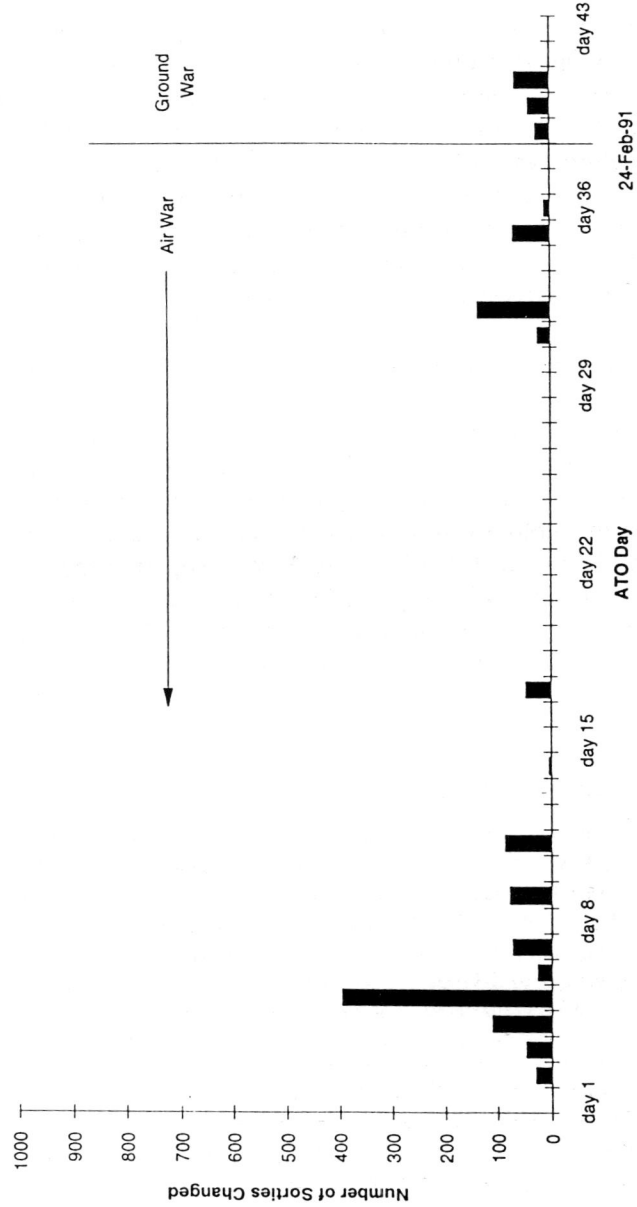

**Figure 33
Sum Weather-related Changes**

weather-related changes did not seem to cause major perturbations in the planning process. One explanation for this is that planners used the weather forecasts to avoid assigning targets in areas having forecasts of bad weather (especially in Iraq).[44]

While Air Tasking Order changes are an imperfect measure of effectiveness of the ATO planning process, they may be used to assess how well the process communicated the intent of the campaign planners to the flying units, and how well the flying units understood that tasking. As the preceding pages illustrate, ATO changes, changes made to the tasking given to a unit after an ATO had been published, comprised a significant percentage of the total number of sorties flown during the air campaign. The impact of those changes, as a measure of the command and control process, is discussed in the next section.

Centralized Planning, Decentralized Execution

From the onset of hostilities, the duration of the war was a major uncertainty for air campaign planners. Initially, Glosson feared the air campaign would not be allowed for more than a few days.[45] Hence, his direction to Deptula was to hit every strategic target in Iraq as quickly as possible. The objective of the Guidance, Apportionment, and Targeting planners was to use every sortie available to hit the most important targets, across all target categories, every day.[46] This attitude was reflected in the willingness to (a) concentrate planning attention on platforms

---

[44] See (S) Volume III, *Support*, Chapter 5.

[45] (S) Intvw, GWAPS with Lt Col Deptula, 21 Dec 1991. (U) We also should note that although Soviet Secretary General Mikhail Gorbachev offered political support to the coalition, there were concerns that the Soviets simultaneously were pursuing other agenda. For example, five days after the start of the air campaign, Soviet officials were still attempting to broker peace. (Andrew Rosenthal, "Bush Demands Iraq Start Pullout Today Despite Its Assent to 3-Week Soviet Plan," *The New York Times*, 23 Jan 1991, p 1.) These Soviet efforts continued. On 29 Jan 1991, a joint statement by Secretary of State James Baker, III and Soviet Foreign Minister Alexander Bessmertnykh asserted a cease fire was possible. (Bill Nichols and Johanna Neuman, "U.S. Soviet Cease-fire Plan Offered," *The Washington Times*, 30 Jan 1991, p 1.) On 11 Feb 1991, Soviet envoy Yevgeny Primakov arrived in Baghdad to discuss a possible ceasefire with President Saddam Hussein. (Rick Atkinson, "Bush: No Immediate Plan to Start Ground War, U.S. Will Rely 'For a While' on Air Power Against Iraqis," *The Washington Post*, 12 Feb 1991, p 1.)

[46] (S) Intvw, GWAPS with Lt Col Deptula, 21 Dec 1991.

capable of delivering precision-guided munitions[47] and (b) call wing operations officers directly with instructions about new or different targets. For example, when the weatherman came in to the GAT and said the weather was bad over Baghdad that night, Glosson would tell Deptula to come up with "thirty-four more new targets for the [F-]117s, and add jokingly 'Oh, by the way, you have twenty minutes.'"[48]

From his position as planner and commander, Glosson did not

> consider changes to the ATO a problem. In other words, you make changes to the ATO based on intelligence. You make changes to the ATO based on weather, which caused more changes than anything else. The way the ATO process is set up, if you lose a target to weather you have the choice of rolling them back in two days later or making a change to the next day's ATO. An aircrew flying to the same target that you planned to fly the night before is not a difficult task. Although on paper it may seem that it's a little more ratcheting. The key is to make the change early, then the impact on the aircrew is minimum.[49]

---

[47] Although the MAP included targets for Proven Force, Proven Force did not employ aircraft capable of delivering PGMs. (Proven Force was not initially in the ATO.) This may account for the GAT allowing Proven Force a good deal of discretion in planning and execution. During the first weeks of the war, Deptula gave Proven Force officers "mission-oriented" orders, that is, they were given a list of targets in a geographic area and left to work out their own strike plans, tankers, coordination, deconfliction. In effect, Proven Force had its own route package–despite Gen Horner's great antipathy for the route package system employed in Vietnam. [(S) Intvw, Barlow, et al., with Lt Gen Horner. Brig Gen Glosson also expressed great resolve to avoid the types of mistakes made in Vietnam. (S) Intvw, Msgt Theodore J. Turner, with Brig Gen Glosson, 6 Mar 1991.] Latitude line 34 north was used to deconflict operations. Eventually, Horner told Deptula to control Proven Force operations. To do so, Deptula had a target book, with which he would compare Proven Force target nominations with his own guidance. Deptula made no change in Proven Force plans when there was agreement between Proven Force target nominations and GAT targeting guidance. Deptula assumed the Proven Force planners knew their weapons systems and their geographical area better than he did, so he allowed Proven Force officers to specify the numbers and types of aircraft going into their strike packages. [(S) Intvw, GWAPS with Lt Col Deptula, 20 Dec 1991; (S) Intvw, Office of Air Force History with Lt Col Deptula, 29 Nov 1991; (S) Intvw, Lt Col Mark "Buck" Rogers, 31 Jan 1992.]

[48] Sometimes the twenty-minute deadline was used as a joke to emphasize the tempo of operations. (S) Intvw, Office of Air Force History with Lt Col Deptula, 20 Nov 1991.

[49] (S) Intvw, MSgt Turner with Brig Gen Glosson, 6 Mar 1991.

Gen Glosson, Col Tolin, and Lt Col Deptula discuss attack plan while Maj Ernie Norsworthy works on F-16 issue.

Glosson's position on ATO changes was partly a result of his view about the nature of war. For Glosson, war is a problem in

> managing chaos. That doesn't mean you don't plan, that doesn't mean you don't try to make everything as predictable as possible, but it's just not that way. There are other people that refer to this as the fog of war. You cannot let yourself get to the point where you are so predictable that everything is just like a cookbook. That's how you get people killed, that's how you lose.[50]

But Glosson's position on ATO changes also reflected a lack of appreciation for the results last-minute ATO target or timing changes had on the rest of ATO and on the people putting the ATO together.[51] In addition,

---

[50] (S) Intvw, MSgt Turner with Brig Gen Glosson, 6 Mar 1991.

[51] (S) Intvw, Brig Gen Caruana, 13 Mar 1991. (U) However, on many occasions, Brig Gen Glosson asked his staff in the GAT whether the ATO changes he ordered were proving a too difficult task on the units. (S) Intvw, Mark D. Mandeles and Lt Col Sanford S. Terry with Lt Col Robert D. Eskridge, 15 Dec 1992.

other senior planners also did not appreciate the effects changes (to a tightly scheduled plan) had on the units.[52] The planners made procedural changes when the changes ordered by senior planners threatened to thoroughly disrupt the conduct of the air campaign, as with tankers during Days 3 through 7.[53]

According to the units, ATO changes were a major source of mission planning instability.[54] Unit-level officers also believed that the planners did not appreciate the effects last-minute ATO changes had on their ability to strike targets. For example, the F-15E community wrote:

> Time needed to plan air interdiction missions is critical. Aircrews need to have ATO changes at least six hours prior to take-off in order to plan interdiction package missions properly. On several occasions ATO changes were received with little or no time to plan, brief, and upload the appropriate munitions. Aircrews became less effective in executing interdiction missions when there was insufficient planning time. Changes to the ATO should be the exception, and changes that are not time critical should be incorporated in the follow-on ATO.[55]

---

[52] Col Anthony J. Tolin admitted that late ATO changes were a significant problem for the wings—"the people on the end of the whip." That is, he recognized the difficulties incurred for the units when a late ATO change also required new target study, weapon changes, and new packaging to get to new targets. However, he explained it was important to not waste sorties by attacking targets that had just been destroyed. Intvw, John F. Guilmartin, Jr. with Brig Gen Anthony J. Tolin, Commander, 57th Fighter Wing, 30 Jan 1992.

[53] Brig Gen Caruana noted that tanker planners had to insert themselves more forcefully into the planning process. It was only after "strict controls" were placed on the number of tanker sorties which would be planned that the dynamic combat situation was managed better. (S) Intvw, Brig Gen Caruana.

[54] (S/NF/WN/NC) USAF Tactical Fighter Weapons Center, *Tactical Analysis Bulletin*, Volume 91-2, Jul 1991.

[55] (S/NF/WN/NC) *Ibid*, p 3-11.

Officers from the F-117 community reviewing the war reiterated the F-15E officers' position.⁵⁶ In sum, they noted that

> the amount of changes that were made in the ATO daily became almost overwhelming. . . . While we were able to accept changes later (up to step time), the planning of the missions suffered and protection of the F-117A suffered. Greater than four line changes became dangerous as deconfliction and threat avoidance were hurriedly accomplished. Rigid rules need to be established at the TACC to prohibit last minute changes.⁵⁷

Officers from the F-111 community echoed the views expressed above. They stated that the

> CENTAF planning cell [GAT] would call directly to a unit with tasking that the TACC was unaware of, thus making coordination extremely difficult. Tasking should have gone through TACC to ensure proper support packaging. Instead individual units were forced to initiate, develop and procure support.⁵⁸

Planning officers, who also understood the difficulty of keeping track of operations when many last-minute changes were made to the Air Tasking Order, complained during Desert Storm about people making last-minute changes without acknowledging the way those changes would effect the rest of the plan. In some cases targets would be abandoned in favor of a "hot biscuit"–a (perishable) high-value mobile target.⁵⁹

As noted in Chapter 6, one implication of consolidating planning and command authority at Brigadier General Glosson's level was that he could easily change the ATO after it had been distributed to the wings.⁶⁰

---

⁵⁶Regarding changes, the F-117 community stated "make them early, concise and coordinated or don't make them at all. We tended to reduce our sortie effectiveness when the changes came in late." (S/NF/WN/NC) *Tactical Analysis Bulletin*, Jul 1991, p 5-5.

⁵⁷(S/NF/WN/NC) *Tactical Analysis Bulletin*, Jul 1991, p 5-8.

⁵⁸(S/NF/WN/NC) *Ibid*, p 7-4.

⁵⁹(S) Intvw, Thomas A. Keaney, Mark D. Mandeles, Williamson Murray, and Barry Watts with Lt Col David A. Deptula, SAF/OSX, 20 Dec 1991.

⁶⁰Glosson, as Director of the newly formed Campaign Plans, was subordinate to Corder, the Director of Operations. However, Glosson, as an Air Division commander, was directly responsible to Horner through a separate chain of command. Corder, as DO, concerned himself with the organization and process necessary to produce a daily combat

Table 10 displays planned sorties against timing and target changes, the types of changes most likely to cause problems for a unit. While the ATO changes may be broken down into distinct classes for analysis, the classes are not equal in importance. When evaluated in terms of their effect on the wings, target changes and timing changes caused the most disruption. A single target or timing change created the need to recoordinate or resynchronize with other strike and support sorties and tankers. In addition, these changes affected crew rest and maintenance cycles. Target changes also created new opportunity costs for mission planners as the last-minute demand for target descriptions and imagery crowded out activities in the planning cycle.

Target changes,[61] timing changes, sorties added, and other changes (including unspecified changes and changes to callsigns, tankers, weapons loadouts, mission numbers, and number of sorties per mission) account for the bulk of the ATO changes. Of these, target changes (excluding weather-related target changes) is the largest category with a median of 145 changes per day, and 4 days where the number of target changes ranged from 275 to 347. In all, approximately 23,000 ATO changes were processed during the Gulf War. More than 5,800 of these were target changes, and 3,500 were timing changes. Together, these two categories accounted for more than 40 percent of the ATO changes.[62]

---

tasking, the ATO. Glosson, as chief campaign planner and air division commander, oversaw the **development and execution** of the air campaign. The combination of line and staff authority in the person of Glosson seemed to be acceptable to Horner, but created conflict with Corder. (See (S) Chapter 6.)

[61]Target changes include switching one target for another, and adding or changing secondary targets. Some target changes included TOT changes, but were counted only as a target change. Timing changes are made to TOT and air refueling control time (ARCT). They varied in duration from twenty minutes to several hours.

[62]These numbers raise a critical issue in understanding the logic of the air campaign plan. If one of the prime purposes of the air campaign was to attack the Iraqi ability to understand what was happening to them and to defend against attack, then attention to absolute physical destruction of targets–as the intelligence community recommended and the GAT planners rejected–was unnecessary. After the start of the war, Glosson and Deptula argued, it was more important to keep the Iraqi military confused and disorganized by a relentless and constant attack. Yet, if functional degradation was of overriding importance, then was it necessary to have so many last-minute target and timing changes? The new target could easily have been added to the third day of the planning cycle.

Table 10

**Sorties Planned, Sorties Changed, Target and Timing Changes
Day 1 through Day 43**

ATO Day	Sorties Planned	Total Sorties Changed	Target Changes	Timing Change	Sum Timing and Target Changes
day 1	2,759	0	0	0	0
day 2	2,900	68	14	2	16
day 3	2,441	449	76	36	112
day 4	2,311	813	116	57	173
day 5	2,286	975	124	83	207
day 6	2,539	552	50	62	112
day 7	2,803	687	168	43	211
day 8	2,990	544	123	86	209
day 9	2,657	531	80	41	121
day 10	2,844	526	50	52	102
day 11	2,555	604	104	67	171
day 12	3,031	367	68	67	135
day 13	2,914	220	11	70	81
day 14	2,691	577	82	240	322
day 15	2,859	543	142	139	281
day 16	2,796	518	309	106	415
day 17	2,607	488	163	51	214
day 18	2,972	514	179	76	255
day 19	2,856	650	165	108	273
day 20	3,019	571	159	144	303
day 21	2,581	612	82	169	251
day 22	2,798	561	71	127	198
day 23	2,929	433	191	102	293
day 24	2,883	377	133	62	195
day 25	2,854	426	65	34	99
day 26	2,808	385	79	50	129

Table 10 (cont'd)

Sorties Planned, Sorties Changed, Target and Timing Changes
Day 1 through Day 43

ATO Day	Sorties Planned	Total Sorties Changed	Target Changes	Timing Change	Sum Timing and Target Changes
day 27	2,863	363	172	23	195
day 28	2,906	747	166	158	324
day 29	2,778	488	161	79	240
day 30	2,868	336	62	80	142
day 31	2,656	530	203	39	242
day 32	2,332	564	147	133	280
day 33	3,158	369	162	42	204
day 34	3,149	517	178	85	263
day 35	2,580	629	194	132	326
day 36	2,919	260	45	41	86
day 37	3,119	667	347	107	454
day 38	3,279	745	147	68	215
day 39	3,309	718	277	73	350
day 40	3,073	738	196	107	303
day 41	3,271	905	218	89	307
day 42	2,911	981	327	97	424
day 43	723	394	59	123	182
Total	116,818	22,942	5,865	3,550	9,415

Source: GWAPS Composite Sorties Database and TACS Change Log.

Analysis of the distribution of the target and timing changes indicates that they were at their lowest levels during the first two weeks of the war, and they appear to be independent of the number of sorties planned. They did not peak on the same days. The number of target and timing changes combined per day tended to remain below 350 changes and did not exceed approximately 450 changes.[63] It is not clear whether the desire to attack as many targets as possible–as quickly as possible–accounted for more wasted sorties than would have occurred had changes been rolled into the ATO for the "day after tomorrow."[64] In the view of one GAT planner

> in retrospect, and it's . . . the point some of us were making at the time, 'Look, if you just let us execute as planned then we roll what we didn't do today, no we will skip and leave tomorrow alone–that's already planned–the guys are out there working on it' . . . drove the one set of team guys nuts, because they and the [F-]111s were on the short string all the time and had to respond to almost hourly changes.[65]

Comparing the air campaign's command and control of Days 1 and 2 with that of the subsequent days is somewhat like comparing night and day. Days 1 and 2 were largely programmed, or "scripted." Critical or difficult decisions about operational performance were irrelevant to the planning process. Measures of effectiveness–either functional degradation or absolute physical destruction–did not play a large role in near real-time operational assessments. The script for Days 1 and 2 would have been played out, largely as written, even if there had been several midair tanker collisions or other problems. The planners decided what was important (that is, which targets), and the planners decided the appropriate sequencing of actions to attack the targets. In addition, this plan or script was written over a fairly long period of time, and the planning cell offi-

---

[63] The data do not permit an answer to the question of whether we reached limits of the capacity to make changes.

[64] It is important to note that errors in a plan vary in significance, and only those errors that singly or in combination affect key functions should be inhibited. It may not be reasonable, wise, or possible to detect every potential error. Planners should be attuned to finding and correcting those errors which are critical to mission success. In this context, faced with the prospect of stopping the air campaign on a moment's notice, Deptula recalled the choice was made to try to identify and correct all potential errors and to order last-minute changes. (S) Intvw, Office of Air Force History with Lt Col Deptula, 20 Nov 1991.

[65] (S) Intvw, Office of Air Force History with Lt Col Deptula, 20 Nov 1991.

cers essentially were able to choose with whom they would interact outside the planning cell. Together, these factors made the decision problem for the planners clear and well-structured and the process manageable.

Command and control of the subsequent days of the air campaign was an entirely different matter. Assessment of the results of strikes became very important as a guide for future strikes. Now, the GAT had to interact and coordinate planning and assessments with a far larger group of officers and agencies, some of whom were purposefully uncooperative.[66] But even for those officers and agencies which tried to cooperate with the GAT, coordination was not easy. Knowledge of which organizational procedures applied to what situation was not distributed evenly throughout USCENTAF. GAT officers invented ad hoc procedures, further complicating coordination with those trying to apply established process and rules of procedure. Now, the viewpoints and concerns of various senior leaders in the United States and Central Command became factors to consider every day in planning and executing Air Tasking Orders.[67] Now, the vast number of aircraft available to be used and the short time available to plan greatly increased the difficulty of planning. Together, these factors made the decision problem for the planners muddy and ill-structured and the process difficult to manage. The GAT planners tried to adjust to this new situation by working even harder and by transforming what they could do–for example, ordering changes directly to units–into what they should do.

The tendency to transform what could be done into what should be done was evident at other levels of CENTCOM too. There was a pronounced tendency of CENTCOM Headquarters staff and leaders to try to influence planning in ongoing dynamic engagements. Corder and Brig. Gen. George K. Muellner described just such a situation. In the early

---

[66] See (S) Chapter 6 for a discussion of how personality and bureaucratic conflicts impeded cooperation. This discussion is amplified in (S) Chapter 8, where we discuss more fully problems in supplying and integrating bomb damage assessments during Desert Storm.

[67] For example, Gen Schwarzkopf described several broad cases in which senior leaders (and others) working in Washington, DC exerted pressure on him. He specifically discussed Scud launches at Israel, whether enough bombing had taken place to accomplish our strategic objectives, and when to begin the ground campaign. See H. Norman Schwarzkopf with Peter Petre, *It Doesn't Take a Hero* (New York, 1992), pp 418, 430, 441-43.

days of Desert Storm, when CENTCOM staff worked only with hardcopy photos, an Army officer visiting the JSTARS Ground Support Module saw a target develop–an Iraqi convoy was moving. The Army officer took a hard copy of the imagery to CENTCOM J2. Coincidentally, while the Army officer was showing the image to Brig. Gen. Leide, Gen. Schwarzkopf walked in and saw the image. Consequently, Schwarzkopf called Horner and demanded to know what air assets were being deployed against those vehicles. Horner did not know what Schwarzkopf was talking about, and so Schwarzkopf became angry, ordered attacks against the vehicles, and offered to send the image to Horner. By the time Army officers delivered the image to CENTAF, the scene was several hours old. Corder received the assignment of resolving the issue. He asked Leide whether the targets had moved. Leide did not know. But Corder demanded the real-time information to obey Schwarzkopf's order. Corder's point was to remove headquarters staff from targeting. In the end, the headquarters involvement was unnecessary. JSTARS had already directed an attack against the convoy.[68]

A Tale of Two Packages: Day 4

The planning, tasking, and execution of two separate aircraft packages on 21 January 1991, or D+4 of the air campaign, illustrates senior leaders' beliefs of controlling the air campaign and the difficulty of dynamic planning. At least five versions of the Master Attack Plan for the D+4 Air Tasking Order were produced (containing these two packages) by 20 January at 2002L. The first package was composed of F-16s from the 363d Tactical Fighter Wing (TFW) at Al Dhafra, and the second package was made up of F-111s from the 48th TFW at Taif. The initial MAP development for this tasking began on 19 January around 0800. The effective time of this particular ATO was 20 January 2320Z to 22 January 0501Z.[69] Figure 34 presents a map showing assigned targets.

---

[68] (S) Intvw, GWAPS with Maj Gen Corder, 18 May 1992; Intvw, Thomas C. Hone, Maj Anne D. Leary, Mark D. Mandeles with Brig Gen George K. Muellner, DCS/Requirements, HQ TAC, 16 Apr 1992.

[69] (S) GWAPS, CSS Safe 6, Desert Shield 20 Jan 1991, Air Tasking Orders.

Figure 34
Map Showing Assigned Targets

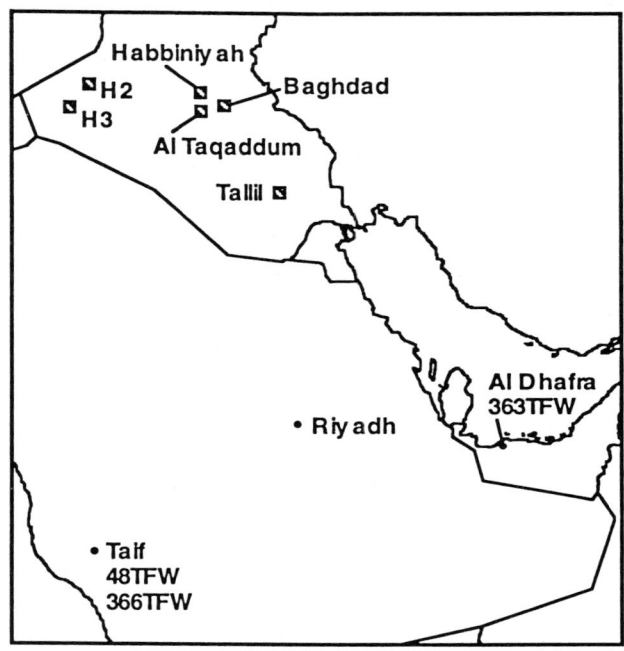

In the initial rough draft of the MAP for 21 January, a forty aircraft F-16 package from the 363d TFW wards assigned targets in the Baghdad area with a time over target at 1300-1330Z, and an eight-aircraft F-111 attack package from the 48th TFW was assigned targets in the Tallil area with a time over target at 0230-0245Z. Both packages were supported by enemy air defense suppression forces, EF-111s and F-4Gs.[70] The second version of this MAP (prepared at 19 January, 2100) was nearly identical to the first pencil draft.[71]

Comparison of the Target Planning Worksheets (TPWs) prepared to translate the draft MAPs into the ATO reveals conflicting instructions. The F-16 aircraft from the 363d TFW were called "package A." The TPW

---

[70] (S) GWAPS, BH Box 1, Folder 9, Master Attack Plan, D+4, 21 Jan 1991, 5th 24 hours.

[71] (S) *Ibid.*

listed the time on target against Baghdad area targets as 1315Z-1330Z, approximately the same time on target listed in the draft MAP. However, the number of F-16s in the package was reduced from forty to twenty-four. The TPWs tasked F-4G aircraft from the 35th TFW and EF-111 aircraft from the 366th TFW to support package A.[72]

The F-111 aircraft from the 48th TFW were called "package D." In both drafts of the Master Attack Plan (the initial pencil copy and the 2100L versions) and the corresponding Target Planning Worksheets, the F-111s were assigned targets in the Tallil area with the time on target block between 0230Z and 0245Z. The TPWs assigned the same F-4G and EF-111 mission numbers to support both the F-16s (package A) and F-111s (package D).[73] However, the number of aircraft tasked changed. During Desert Storm it was common for the same flight of F-4Gs and EF-111s to support different attack packages. In this type of situation the different package targets were near each other, and the times over targets were synchronized. In the case of the D+4 ATO, however, the targets, Tallil and Baghdad, were separated by approximately 200 miles, and the times over targets (1300Z-1330Z for package A and 0230Z for package D) were 11 hours apart. The same suppression of enemy air defense support could not have been used for both attack packages.

The D+4 Air Tasking Order instructions for package A (the 363d TFW's F-16s) were identical to the tasking in the corresponding Target Planning Worksheets. Minor errors crept into the ATO with respect to some of the support missions (for example, the TPW listed F-15C missions for escort/sweep, while none were listed in the ATO), but the essential information was the same.[74] However, part of the ATO tasking for package D (the 48th TFW's F-111s) did not match the Master Attack Plans or the Target Planning Worksheets. For example, the information for the sweep/escort support did not match the TPW. More importantly, the target in the ATO was changed to the H2 airfield.[75] No record of the reason for this change, or the change itself, can be found.

---

[72](S) Target Planning Worksheets, ATO D+4, 21 Jan 1991, HQ 9th AF/OSX, Shaw AFB, NC, Lt Col Jefferey Feinstein.

[73](S) *Ibid.*

[74](S) Desert Shield 20 Jan 1991, Air Tasking Orders.

[75](S) *Ibid.*

The Air Tasking Order was transmitted on 20 January at 1855L, shortly after the CENTAF goal of 1800L.[76] In this ATO, as in the targeting worksheets, the taskings for the SEAD support for package A (the F-16s) and package D (the F-111s) were in conflict. The tasked suppression of enemy air defenses simply could not support packages separated by widely different times and locations. The origin of the conflict between instructions contained in the Master Attack Plan and ATO may be found in the way the ATO was completed and published. Another MAP was printed at 1427L (the operator entered 20 January, 1400L into the computer file). The tasking for package A printed in this Master Attack Plan was identical to earlier Plans. The MAP still listed forty F-16s in the package instead of the twenty-four tasked in the Target Planning Work sheets and the ATO. However, changes to the package were written in pencil on the printed MAP. The F-16 package was lined out, the time on target was changed to 0400Z-0430Z, and the target changed to the H2 and H3 airfields. The tasking for package D (the F-111s) remained essentially unchanged.[77]

The next Master Attack Plan, and the first one approved (and signed) by General Glosson, was printed at 1848L. It assigned package A against the H2 and H3 airfield complexes with a change in time on target, as the penciled changes to the previous MAP indicated (forty F-16s were still listed). Package D was still tasked against the Tallil area. Pencil changes on this MAP indicate that package D was "retargeted to H2," which matched the published ATO tasking.[78]

A final Master Attack Plan, printed at 2002L and also signed by Generals Glosson and Deptula, was identical to the previous, 1848L version. Package A remained assigned against the H2 and H3 airfields. Package D still was tasked against the Tallil area targets, despite the tasking in the published ATO and the penciled change on the previous (1848L) MAP.[79]

---

[76](S) *Ibid.*

[77](S) Master Attack Plan, D+4, 21 Jan 1991, 5th 24 hours.

[78](S) *Ibid.*

[79](S) *Ibid.*

Sometime in the planning process, someone assigned packages A and D to attack the H2/H3 airfield area. This decision can be tracked using the different versions of the MAP. With respect to package A (F-16s), the change in the target area and time on target was not entered into the Air Tasking Order. It is not clear whether this change was passed to the 363d TFW via telephone. Moreover, no version of the Attack Plan registered a reduction from forty to twenty-four in number of F-16s assigned to strike the target. In contrast, the ATO assigned package D (the F-111s) to attack the H2 airfield, a target change which was not specified in the corresponding MAPs. The ATO also did not include synchronized enemy air defense suppression; this support as tasked in the ATO could not accompany both packages.

The Tactical Air Control Center change log for the 21 January Air Tasking Order included three notes which might relate to package A. The first note addressed a minor confusion concerning the sweep/escort tasking. The second note adjusted air refueling control times for the F-16 package, which could have supported the changes to the F-16s' target and time on target found in later versions of the Master Attack Plan. The third note is confusing. The Control Center change log identified the F-16 aircraft in package A by individual mission number and assigned them to strike the "C-7 Chem Prod Fac/Al Taqaddum Afld."[80] This target does not match any of the targets assigned in previous MAPs or the published ATO.

What finally happened? All twenty-four F-16s in the 363d Tactical Fighter Wing in package A successfully launched and attacked targets. However, the F-16s attacked neither the initial Baghdad area targets nor the H2/H3 airfield targets identified later in the MAP. Mission Reports obtained from the 363d TFW indicate that the unit attacked the Habbaniyah Possible Chemical Warfare Production Facility Number 2 and the Al Taqaddum airfield–targets which were approximately thirty miles west of the initial Baghdad area targets but which were in agreement with the change found in the TACC change log. All the times on targets for these attacks were in the original TOT block (1300Z-1330Z) specified in

---

[80](S) GWAPS, TACC ATO Changes, NA #370.

the first MAP and corresponding ATO.[81] The GAT planners entered some of these results into their tracking system. Eight F-16s were shown to have struck the Habbaniyah Chemical Warfare facility. Whether these were the eight F-16s from the 363d TFW is not known. The sixteen F-16s which attacked the Al Taqaddum airfield were not noted in the log.[82]

The 48th Tactical Fighter Wing's Mission Reports tell another story. The ATO assigned package D (F-111s) to targets in the H2 airfield area. Of the eight F-111s assigned these targets, only two aircraft released weapons on target. Four aircraft aborted the mission, upon AWACS direction, due to absence of tanker support. Two others aborted because of computer or inertial navigation system problems.[83] According to CAFMS data, the F-4G mission support package was aborted.[84] It is not known whether other F-4Gs provided support. The EF-111 support from the 366th TFW flew as scheduled in the ATO. It is not known where the aircraft flew.[85] And GAT planners did not know what happened either. The GAT's records show that no F-111 aircraft hit the H2 targets assigned to the F-111s in package D for that day. The log shows, however, that forty F-16s attacked that target.[86]

The Great Scud Hunt

A second issue in implementing centralized planning and decentralized execution concerns the presence of information required to make decisions. The Scud hunt demonstrates the importance–for a centralized planning office–of information and appropriate procedures to analyze it.

---

[81](S) 363d TFW Mission Reports, 211700Z, 211730Z, 211730Z Jan 1991, GWAPS Mission Database.

[82]Target Attacks By Day By Aircraft H-Hour Thru Day +32, GWAPS, Box 2, Folder 56.

[83](S) 48th TFW Mission Reports, 210415Z, 210640Z, 210850Z, 211327Z Jan 1991, GWAPS Mission Database.

[84](S) GWAPS Mission Database.

[85](S) *Ibid.*

[86]Target Attacks By Day By Aircraft H-Hour Thru Day +32, GWAPS, Box 2, Folder 56.

Beginning Day 1, sorties were planned to address the Scud launch threat.[87] Given the press coverage of Scud attacks, one might have expected a greater number of sortie changes to attack Scuds. The evidence does not seem to support this expectation. Approximately 4,750 anti-Scud sorties (see Table 11)[88] were planned between Day 1 and Day 43. Approximately twelve percent of these planned sorties were changed or added.

The number of daily Scud hunting sorties varied between 75 and 160. During Desert Storm, Iraq launched 88 missiles at Israel and Saudi Ara-

---

[87] Called Scuds, the missiles were actually "Al Husseins," Soviet designed and supplied Scud B models modified by the Iraqis. The program initially entailed cannibalizing three Scuds to produce two Al-Husseins. Two design changes are important. First, more than 1,000 kilograms of propellant were added to increase range. Second, the payload was reduced from 800 to only 190 kilograms. See W. Seth Carus and Joseph S. Bermudez, Jr., "Iraq's Al-Husayn Programme, Part I," *Jane's Soviet Intelligence Review*, May 1990, pp 204-09; W. Seth Carus and Joseph S. Bermudez, Jr., "Iraq's Al-Husayn Programme, Part II," *Jane's Soviet Intelligence Review*, June 1990, pp 242-48.

[88] The DOD's *Conduct of the Persian Gulf War*, also known as the Title V Report (April 1992, UNCLASSIFIED), lists Scud hunting sorties planned in the ATO by day—but only in chart form. The GWAPS Consolidated Sorties Database does not contain enough detail to provide a good estimate of the number of Scud-hunting sorties planned. The TACC Scud-Chasing Log included in the (S) Institute for Defense Analyses (IDA) draft report, *Desert Storm Scud Campaign* (Alexandria, VA, Apr 1992), documents the sorties generated in response to specific Scud launch threats. The IDA report identifies a total of 539 sorties for the 43 days of the air campaign.

The Scud sorties planned data presented here in chart and tabular form were taken from the Title V chart and are correct to within two sorties. The smallest unit marked on the Title V chart, Daily Total (for sorties) scale was four sorties.

The data on Scud-related sorties added or changed were taken from the TACC Change Log and correlated with the GWAPS Composite Sorties Database.

Task Force 2's launch numbers were used in this study to show the maximum amount of Iraqi missile launch activity driving the Scud hunt. The Task Force assumes that (a) these daily sortie totals reflect the final version of the ATO after changes and (b) the changes or additions for Scud hunt totals, based on the TACC Change Log, are accounted for in the Scud sortie daily totals. See (S) GWAPS Volume II, *Weapons, Tactics, and Training*.

Table 11
Anti-Scud Sorties

ATO Day	Date	Sorties Planned	Change or Addition	Scuds Launched
1	17 January	154	0	1
2	18 January	92	0	7
3	19 January	40	28	4
4	20 January	70	12	8
5	21 January	165	74	1
6	22 January	133	12	7
7	23 January	105	2	5
8	24 January	126	13	0
9	25 January	117	0	10
10	26 January	147	40	6
11	27 January	124	10	0
12	28 January	149	4	2
13	29 January	83	10	0
14	30 January	83	0	0
15	31 January	142	0	1
16	1 February	111	0	0
17	2 February	103	8	3
18	3 February	75	0	0
19	4 February	84	73	0
20	5 February	106	0	0
21	6 February	120	0	0
22	7 February	147	76	1
23	8 February	100	0	0
24	9 February	90	48	1

Table 11
Anti-Scud Sorties

ATO Day	Date	Sorties Planned	Change or Addition	Scuds Launched
25	10 February	114	34	0
26	11 February	153	0	3
27	12 February	135	0	0
28	13 February	98	14	0
29	14 February	121	19	5
30	15 February	153	0	1
31	16 February	132	10	4
32	17 February	148	0	0
33	18 February	130	0	0
34	19 February	124	14	1
35	20 February	95	0	0
36	21 February	90	0	6
37	22 February	100	2	0
38	23 February	116	16	3
39	24 February	96	2	3
40	25 February	90	0	5
41	26 February	104	25	0
42	27 February	88	7	0
43	28 February	149	0	0
TOTALS		4,753	553	88

Sources: GWAPS Composite Sorties Database and TACS Change Log.

bia. Almost 60 percent of those missiles were launched over the first 12 days of the war. The data do not show an obvious relationship between sorties and Scud launches.[89] The average daily Scud hunt represented approximately 6 percent of the average daily strike sorties. However, Generals Horner, Glosson, and others reported devoting a greater proportion of thought and attention to hunting Scuds than to other missions.[90]

The problem of defeating the Scuds after they had been launched may be divided into three parts. The first was detecting a Scud launch. Once ignited, Scud missile motors produced a visible and very hot plume, and this plume was the key to sensing Scud launches and then trying to attack the mobile transporter-launchers. The second was alerting a Patriot antimissile battery that one or more Scuds were approaching. The third was solving the Patriot's fire control problem.[91] The third piece of this problem is covered by the *Space* report.[92] The first two pieces, plus the effort to smash the mobile launchers before they could get away, are command and control topics. The paragraphs which follow detail the command and control of the Scud hunt and explain why coalition air strikes were not particularly effective against the mobile Scud launchers.[93]

Coalition air used standard reconnaissance, targeting, and attack procedures to find and then attack the Scud production and assembly

---

[89] Access to more highly classified data might show a link among Scuds launched and sorties planned or changed.

[90] (S) Intvw, Lt Gen Charles A. Horner, Commander; (S) Intvw, Davis, et al., with Lt Gen Glosson, 12 Dec 1991. There was great concern at the highest levels of U.S. government–including President Bush, Secretary of State Baker, Secretary of Defense Cheney, and Gen Powell–that the coalition would fracture if Israel attacked Iraq in retaliation. RAdm McConnell echoed this belief. (S) Intvw, Ronald Cole and Diane T. Putney with RAdm Michael McConnell, DIA, 14 Feb 1992.

[91] (S) Defense Science Board, *Lessons Learned in Operations Desert Shield & Desert Storm*, Jun 1992, p 68.

[92] See (S) *Space* report.

[93] The focus of this section is on how CENTAF dealt with the missiles, rather than on their technical performance or psychological and diplomatic effects.

areas and fixed launch sites.[94] However, finding and striking forward assembly areas logistic bases, and then the missile transporter-launchers which operated from these dispersed facilities, challenged existing techniques of command and control.[95] It also was an unsuccessful effort.[96]

The "hunt" really began as the mobile missiles were deployed, as the missiles were first fueled and the transporter-launchers then moved to the launch sites. Once at the site, a missile crew had to erect the missile, start the launch sequence, fire the missile, lower the erector, pack up, and get out. The whole cycle took less than one hour, and all of it could be (and was) done at night.[97]

Most Coalition air units lacked equipment capable of finding mobile Scud launchers unless they knew where to look beforehand.[98] That is, they had difficulty transforming successful area surveillance into effective pinpoint targeting. [DELETED] Forward Looking Infrared sensors (FLIRs) on Air Force and Navy attack planes easily spotted trucks at night. FLIR sensors were useful for short-range targeting–especially if

---

[94] The approach used by CENTAF had three parts: (a) preplanned attacks against production, storage, and fixed launch sites; (b) day and night visual searches for transporter-launchers moving to their launch sites; (c) airborne patrols to attack the transporter-launchers after they had fired their missiles. (S) TACC/CC/DO Current Ops Log, 2300Z, 27 Jan 1991, Microfilm Roll Number 0882616, CHECO.

[95] The Iraqi facilities which built Scuds were very vulnerable to conventional air attack. The fixed missile launch sites were also difficult to hide. However, the mobile launchers and the decoys, the missile assembly areas which supported them, and the logistics which sustained them were very difficult to locate (or track). Yet it was precisely these activities and areas which air forces were pressured to attack (and assumed they could find and attack) during Desert Storm.

[96] (S) Rpt, Desert Storm Scud Missile Working Group III, 30 May 1991, Defense Intelligence Agency, Washington, D.C., GWAPS New Acq. File No. 108. Also (S) *Lessons Learned During Operations Desert Shield and Desert Storm*, pp 64-74. (U) On 9 Feb 1991, for example, two F-15Es patrolling in an area from which Scuds had been fired witnessed an actual launch, but they could not locate the transporter-launcher. See the (S) TACC/CC/DO Current Ops Log, 9 Feb 1991, 0036Z, Microfilm Roll Number 0882616, CHECO.

[97] (S) *Lessons Learned in Operations Desert Shield & Desert Storm*, 8 Jun 1992, pp 64, 67.

[98] (S) *Ibid*, p 67.

cued—but not for area searches due to their narrow fields of view. Finally, special forces units sometimes found mobile Scud launchers.[99]

Sensors picked up the missiles as they began their flights: the Defense Support Program (DSP). [DELETED][100] The DSP satellite's sensors "typically detected and verified the launch. [DELETED][101]

The DSP satellites provided Space Command with observations that were then used to calculate the approximate location of the missile's launch site. Its launch time could be determined to within seconds. [DELETED][102] [DELETED][103]

Space Command and Central Command had developed a "Scud warning system" capable of alerting Patriot batteries of approaching Scud warheads by the beginning of Desert Storm.[104] [DELETED][105] The existence of this space-based warning system allowed CENTCOM's Patriot batteries to avoid staying on constant, around-the-clock alert. [DELETED][106]

[DELETED][107] [DELETED][108] [DELETED][109]

---

[99](S) *Ibid.*

[100]Also (S) Memo, "Input to Title V Final Report on the Conduct of the Persian Gulf Conflict," Air Staff (XOOSO), pp 1-2.

[101](S) *Lessons Learned in Operations Desert Shield & Desert Storm*, p 68.

[102][DELETED]

[103]Discussions with Lt Cdr R. Morgan, USN, and Col F. Herre, USAF, Space Alternate Command Center (SPACC), USSPACECOM, Falcon AFB, CO, 16 Dec 1991.

[104]See (S) GWAPS *Space* report, Chapter 5.

[105](S) Rpt, "SAC Scud Warning," GWAPS New Acq. File, No. 128.

[106]*Conduct of the Persian Gulf War*, Appendix T, pp 755-56.

[107][DELETED]

[108]In addition to TRAP, and if data were relayed from RC-135Vs in some fashion.

[109](S) Memo, "Input to Title V Final Report," p 2; also, (S) Briefing, "Air Force Intelligence Support to Air Operations: Desert Storm Examples," 26 Feb 1992, GWAPS Files.

This part of the Scud alert and hunt system was developed in early August 1990 after a Strategic Air Command (SAC) Senior Controller, Brig. Gen. K. F. Keller, commented to a young SAC watch officer in SAC's Command Center that it was "a shame" SAC strategic warning systems did not support CENTCOM. The watch officer, Capt. John Rittinghouse, volunteered to rig something up and was given permission to proceed. Rittinghouse and another young Captain, J.D. Broyles, first contacted Space Command, then CENTCOM's command center, where the senior controller said that CENTCOM welcomed their help. SAC personnel talked back and forth with CENTCOM, worked out a communications link, and then tested voice warning. Once they were satisfied with it, they added data on missile launch and trajectory.[110] Then they turned the whole set of procedures over to Space Command, whose personnel used them during Desert Storm.[111]

---

[110](S) Rpt, J. Rittinghouse and J.D. Broyles, subj: "The Development of Strategic Air Command Scud Missile Alerting Procedures Used During the Iraqi War of 1991," nd, GWAPS New Acquisition File, No. 128.

[111]The alert process resembled, in its details, that used to warn RAF squadrons of impending attacks by V-1s against England in June and July 1944. Then, the elements (air search radars, air defense coordination centers, interceptors, barrage balloons, and layered rings of antiaircraft guns surrounding prime targets) of an existing air defense system were altered from a system to defeat manned bombers to one which filtered out attacking cruise missiles. Because the numbers of V-1s sent against England (1280 fell on London alone in the month between mid-June and mid-July 1944) were high, and because the missiles approached targets like London from many angles simultaneously, the Royal Air Force's air defense system was at first overwhelmed. Single telephone lines into interceptor bases, for example, were simply too slow a means for transmitting the kinds of data needed by planes sitting on the ground who needed to get airborne and then chase down many low-flying missiles. But improved data collection and transmission, coupled with a new weapon (antiaircraft shells with proximity fuzes), allowed the defenders to reduce the V-1 from a major military threat to a minor one. Something very similar to this happened in the Gulf: sensors reporting to Space Command began a sequence of communications which alerted the point defense system (Patriot) and the units tasked with finding and striking Scud batteries. See W. F. Craven and J. L. Cate, eds, *The Army Air Forces in World War II*, Vol. III, (Chicago, 1951), pp 526- 545; see also, John Terraine, *A Time for Courage, The Royal Air Force in the European War, 1939-1945* (New York, 1985), pp 652-653.

With approximately four minutes warning, Patriot battery commanders could assign targets to appropriate fire units, assume the appropriate ATBM firing mode, and employ a firing doctrine of launching at least two—and in many cases three or four—Patriot missiles against each engageable object in order to achieve a sufficiently high probability of kill.[112] From CENTCOM's perspective, however, the real need was to find and destroy the mobile Scud launchers firing from Iraq. The key to wrecking the mobile launchers before they could escape (hide, and then reload) was fixing the location of any given mobile launcher within an area small enough to be quickly scanned by targeting sensors (for example, FLIR) carried by U.S. aircraft orbiting overhead.

The need to target the mobile launchers was well understood before Desert Storm, as was the difficulty of doing so.[113] [DELETED][114] Iraqi officers had learned to employ Scuds in ways other than according to Soviet doctrine. [DELETED][115] Uncertainty about the mobile launchers' deployments and operating patterns precluded predicting where they would hide during the day and how long they could stay in the field before having to return to a central facility for maintenance.[116]

The Defense Intelligence Agency deployed a number of National Military Intelligence Support Teams to CENTCOM Headquarters as well as to a number of component headquarters and key commands in the Gulf region. The National Military Intelligence Support Teams were tasked to expedite both collection requests and rapid and responsive results dissemination. They typically were manned by knowledgeable intelligence personnel who were equipped with secure radios, personal computers, and facsim-

---

[112](S/NF/WN) *Conduct of the Persian Gulf War*, Appendix T, pp T-199 through T-203; (S) Briefing, Lt Gen T. S. Moorman, Jr., Commander, Air Force Space Command, 16 Dec 1991, Peterson AFB, CO.

[113](S) Information Paper, "Tactical Missile Defense (TMD), Operation Desert Shield," 27 Aug 1990, CIS Folder No. 43, "Organization/Operations," CHST File, GWAPS.

[114](S) *Ibid.*

[115](S) *Ibid.*

[116](S/NF) Msg, "RII-1056, Indications of Scud Refuelings," 2 Dec 1990, DIA, CIS Folder No. 43, "Organization/Operations," CHST File, Container 34, GWAPS.

ile machines and who had been assigned accesses to secure satellite communications links for expertly requesting and receiving intelligence data. [DELETED][117] [DELETED][118] [DELETED][119] [DELETED][120] [DELETED][121]

[DELETED][122][DELETED][123]

For post-launch detection, the systems available to find and then attack mobile Scud launchers from the air simply did not have the information they needed in time to carry out their mission successfully.[124] Aircraft orbiting above likely launch areas needed fairly precise information. F-15Es, for example, needed an estimate of a launcher's location (the "launch point") [DELETED][125] The Iraqis also used decoys to deceive U.S. sensors, so that even if the area of a launch were known, it was not therefore certain that attacking aircraft would hit the Scud or the decoy.[126]

---

[117](S) Msg "Trip Report, 9-12 Oct 1990," from R. Butler to the RAND Corporation, GWAPS RAND File in New Acquisition File.

[118](S) Briefing, "NORAD/USSPACECOM Intel Support to Desert Storm," Lcdr R. Morgan, USN, 16 Dec 1991, Peterson AFB, CO.

[119](S) Msg, "Launches," from DIA to CENTAF, 7 Dec 1990, in CIS Folder 43, "Organization/Operations," CHST File, Container 34, GWAPS.

[120](S) Msg, "RII-1056, Indications of Scud Refuelings."

[121](S) Briefing, "Tactical Ballistic Missile Warning Support to Desert Storm."

[122](S) Memo, "Scud Attack Plan," nd, Document No. 42-3-6-10-5, CIS File, Folder 40, CHST Records, Container 34, GWAPS. The (S) TACC/CC/DO Current Operations Log gives several cases like that for 0036Z, 9 Feb 1991, where two F-15Es on station over a suspected Scud launch area actually witnessed a launch but could not find the launcher afterward. Microfilm Roll Number 0882616, CHECO.

[123](S) *Lessons Learned in Operations Desert Shield & Desert Storm*, p 70.

[124](S) *Ibid*, p 69.

[125](S) *Ibid*.

[126](S) Rpt, Desert Storm Scud Missile Working Group III.

Even the use of JSTARS (Joint Surveillance Target Attack Radar System) did not significantly improve the targeting of mobile Scud launchers. [DELETED][127] By the time U.S. attack aircraft received information on the launcher's location, the launcher was usually gone.

[DELETED][128]

Because mobile Scud transporter-launchers were so difficult to locate, one postwar conference concluded that "Scud CAP [combat air patrol] was flown continuously with no major success in finding launchers on a routine basis."[129] F-15Es, the mainstay of Scud combat air patrols, were sent to patrol areas of Iraq "to continuously appear to threaten potential launch sites."[130] Nothing much better could be done. As the Defense Science Board concluded in its draft report regarding post-Scud launch results, "There was no doctrine and there had been no training. Procedures and integration were ad hoc and not optimum. Information to enable successful attack could have been available with existing assets. Relatively minor changes should have made a difference." The Board also remarked that "A capability to find and destroy . . . Scuds before they launch implies hitherto unachieved integration and a new level of processing or surveillance data."[131] Put another way, the obstacles to attacking the mobile launchers were rooted primarily in the command and control procedures employed.

The process of finding and then targeting Scud mobile launchers involved a sequence of actions: (a) wide area surveillance, (b) analysis of the data from this surveillance in theater command and control centers, (c) the localization and identification of targets, (d) attack by defending

---

[127](S) *Lessons Learned in Operations Desert Shield & Desert Storm*, p 69.

[128](S) Msg, "Launches."

[129](S) Rpt, Desert Storm Scud Missile Working Group III. The (S) TACC/CC/DO Current Operations Log for 2330Z, 11 Feb 1991 notes that F-15Es which obtained the coordinates of a Scud transporter-launcher within five minutes of an actual launch were still unable to locate a target.

[130](S) Msg, Air Tasking Order, 8 Feb 1991, Section 13, Unit Remarks X, from HQ, USCENTAF, to HQ, RSAF Operations.

[131](S) *Lessons Learned During Operations Desert Shield & Desert Storm*, p 74.

forces, and (e) the assessment of the results. The Defense Science Board believed that the systems required to perform this process were available, but that they did not work together effectively enough and often enough to destroy the mobile Scud launchers.[132] A combined DIA/Defense Department working group said much the same thing–that the Scud hunters needed accurate data appropriate to their weapons and means of moving those data quickly from detection and processing systems (such as JSTARS) to orbiting attack aircraft.[133] This is a command and control problem, and it is almost precisely the same problem faced by the Air Force once it accepted the mission of finding strategic relocatable targets (mobile Soviet ICBMs) in the mid-1980s.

In the Scud hunt, wide area surveillance of launches was a success; it gave Patriot batteries sufficient warning. Unfortunately, localization and identification were not equally successful. [DELETED][134] Desert Storm revealed that information, in the right place at the right time, was the key to narrowing a search for a "stealthy" enemy. The problem of locating the mobile Scud transporter-launchers was never really solved. [DELETED][135]

The above two subsections provide only a flavor of the difficulty in (a) developing effective procedures for the employment of airpower and (b) synchronizing and orchestrating the many different aircraft into the Air Tasking Order. The problem of orchestrating so many aircraft had special implications for the planners in assessing the effects of strikes contained in ATOs just executed. The following section describes some of those implications.

---

[132](S) *Ibid.*

[133](S) Rpt, Desert Storm Scud Missile Working Group III, p 8.

[134](S/NF) Memo, "Iraqi Mobile Scud Launcher Inventory and Employment Strategy" (DIM 54-91), Defense Intelligence Agency, Feb 1991, CIS Folder No. 6, "Correlation/ Analysis," CHST File, Container 34, GWAPS.

[135](S) TACC/CC/DO Current Ops Log, 2300Z, 27 Jan 1991.

Intelligence Support for Planning and Command and Control

Lieutenant General Horner, Joint Force Air Component Commander, expected–and accepted–intelligence deficiencies. He had to decide whether to make an issue out of the allocation of intelligence resources. In his words,

> I think you are always going to have intelligence shortfalls. My criticism of Intelligence is that in peacetime it goes to Washington, and in wartime it should go to the theater. We tried to establish where it comes down in theater. The problem is, the Army overloaded it immediately with requests for stuff, so I didn't even bother; I mean, I couldn't get my foot in the door, so I just said, 'To hell with it.'[136]

[DELETED][137] [DELETED][138]

Nevertheless, planners in the Guidance, Apportionment, and Targeting cell had different notions of (a) the usefulness of intelligence support and bomb damage assessment and (b) the necessity of obtaining such support. Intelligence support and bomb damage assessment in the form of imagery was deemed critical to the efficient allocation[139] of precision-guided munitions and the types of aircraft capable of precise delivery of munitions. Given the difference between General Horner and GAT planners' views, how did the GAT planners evaluate their information resources, and how did they respond to the implications of those evaluations?

---

[136](S) Intvw, Lt Gen Charles A. Horner.

[137]See Jeffrey T. Richelson, "Volume of Data Cripples Tactical Intelligence System," *Armed Forces Journal International* (Jun 1992), pp 35-37; see also (S) GWAPS *Space* report.

[138](S/NF) Joe and Gonzales, *Command and Control, Communications, and Intelligence in Desert Storm Air Operations*, p 9.

[139]Deptula's concern for efficiency was manifested in his use of measures of effectiveness. Deptula preferred a functional measure of destruction rather than absolute measure of physical destruction. As a rule of thumb, Deptula recalled, he never put more than two GBUs on a target at any one time. This strategy allowed him to apply the aircraft and munitions to more Iraqi targets. (S) Intvw, GWAPS with Lt Col David A. Deptula, 20 Dec 1991.

The GAT's Intelligence Support Problem

From the start of the air campaign bomb damage assessment presented three types of problems to the GAT planners. The first was organizational and concerned the proper division of labor and specification of communications channels to deliver required information. The second problem involved the allocation of assets which could provide appropriate imagery or other raw data. The third problem concerned what data were available to evaluate operations.

The division of labor and communication of information within–and between–CENTAF and CENTCOM presented a difficult situation for the GAT planners. Reconnaissance needs were discussed and validated every day at 1000L at the Daily Aerial Reconnaissance Review meeting, chaired by the CENTCOM J-2. Requests for bomb damage assessment were then forwarded to agencies controlling the assets for further review and evaluation with other competing demands. This process separated the control of reconnaissance systems from the in-theater users. The sensor taskers were unaware of the rationale behind the tasking requests or of last-minute changes in attack plans. The in-theater units were unaware of which requests for coverage had been approved. As a result, CENTAF targeteers in the Tactical Air Control Center relied on in-theater reconnaissance systems for most target development.[140]

In addition, as noted above, the GAT's use of a shorter, informal planning cycle for Iraqi targets reduced the ability to coordinate with Central Command Air Forces/Intelligence (CENTAF/IN) the GAT's information requirements. CENTAF/IN generally was two to three days behind the GAT's planning cycle.[141] The implication of this time lag was that by the time CENTAF/IN had produced bomb damage assessment on a given target, the GAT already had reached a judgement about it from sources in Check-

---

[140] (S/NF) Joe and Gonzales, *Command and Control, Communications, and Intelligence in Desert Storm Air Operations*, pp 9-10.

[141] Chapter 6 showed that because of informal communications channels, the Black Hole/ GAT received critical information from Washington twenty-four to forty-eight hours before CENTAF/IN. The ability of GAT planners to receive information quicker than CENTAF/IN remained during Desert Storm.

mate, responses to direct inquires to the wings, or aircraft videotape recorder (AVTR) tapes.[142]

The second bomb damage assessment problem concerned the allocation of assets to collect data. The number of theater reconnaissance aircraft available to acquire bomb damage assessment was much smaller than the number of daily strike sorties. Hence, many strikes were not accompanied by assessment.[143] Table 12 displays the number of in-theater-based reconnaissance sorties during the war.

Coalition aircraft flew 3,236 reconnaissance-type sorties over the 43 days of the war, for an average of 75 sorties a day. Meanwhile, U.S. forces flew an average of 1,600 strike sorties each day.[144] The number of strike sorties, therefore, overwhelmed the ability of in-theater reconnaissance assets to provide a broad assessment of functional—or absolute—damage done to Iraqi targets.

---

[142](S) Intvw, GWAPS with Lt Col David A. Deptula, SAF/OSX, 20 Dec 1991; see Chapter 8, footnote 11 for description of AVTR.

[143][DELETED] See (S) Chapter 9 of this report and (S) GWAPS *Space Operations in the Gulf War*, Chapter 4.

[144]A question may be raised about the relationship drawn between reconnaissance-type sorties and attack sorties. A given attack package may contain twenty-four to thirty-six aircraft. Hence, the proper relationship may be between reconnaissance sorties and attack packages. However, at present, the data do not permit matching reconnaissance sorties with attack packages. Thus, the less precise relationship will have to suffice.

Table 12
Total Reconnaissance Sorties[145]
17 January to 28 February 1991

Reconnaissance*	Side-Looking Aperture Radar**	Observation Flight***
2,406	147	683

*Reconnaissance missions flown by U.S. A-6, A-7, EA-6B, F-14, F/A-18, P-3, RC-135, RF-4C, S-3, MH-60, and coalition RF-5, Tornado GR-1, Jaguar, Mirage F1-CR, and Mirage 2000 aircraft.

**SLAR missions flown by U.S. OV-1D and RC-12 aircraft.

***Observation flight missions flown by U.S. A-6, F-16, F/A-18, and S-3B aircraft.

The third bomb damage assessment problem was a matter of what data were needed to evaluate the effectiveness of operations. In one sense, this issue concerns whether the planners could design and incorporate feedbacks into their decisionmaking process. Feedback systems operate on the basis of a measurable or observable discrepancy between the actual and desired situation. Being able to measure the distinction between actual and desired results allows a planner to pick out errors, which he can then act to correct by changing the plan for future operations. Unfortunately, for most of the missions on the Air Tasking Order, the post-strike data and information available to the GAT were not clear enough to show GAT planners that their goals had been achieved (that targets had been degraded, damaged, or

---

[145]These data were compiled from the GWAPS Composite Sorties Database.

destroyed) so that restrikes could be scheduled.[146] Put another way, planners did not get timely theater feedback.[147]

In many respects, the sensing of error in the air campaign was quite intuitive because only imperfect information was available about many details of how the air campaign was being conducted.[148] Sometimes, figuring out what was happening, or deciding whether an error had been made, was a matter of negotiation. For example, high-speed antiradiation missile (HARM) (AGM-88) fratricide incidents illustrate how important the quality of information was for detecting errors. In one incident, a U.S. Army artillery radar was attacked by a friendly aircraft. Consequently, an order was sent to the F-4G squadrons to check their electronic warfare libraries to ensure that the signatures of U.S. artillery radars could not be read into a HARM's memory. After that order was issued, Major General Corder thought that the problem had been solved. Simultaneously, Brig.

---

[146] Given the problems encountered by planners to get appropriate information to evaluate the effectiveness of air operations, it is ironic that senior Iraqi officers assumed that the planners knew everything. [DELETED]

[DELETED]

(S/REL UK) Joint Debriefing Center, "The Gulf War: An Iraqi General Officer's Perspective," date: 910311.

[147] As the Defense Science Board observed, the lack of timely BDA was a function of poor weather; sometimes lack of external observables on the target; delays in receipt of exploited, high-resolution imagery; lack of high-quality cameras on the delivery aircraft; need for better methods of exploit and document aircraft video. Also "intelligence collection management was not tied to the attack plans, and the intelligence and planning staff were not collocated or sufficiently integrated. There were no information processing support tools to maintain the master target list and status of targets." In addition, the reconnaissance capability could not deliver the coverage or the detail needed to regularly and effectively assess the damage inflicted by the new, precision, standoff weapons. (S) *Lessons Learned During Operations Desert Shield & Desert Storm*, pp 20, 86.

[148] During an interview with Lt Col Deptula, one member of GWAPS remarked that Gen Glosson claimed that Deptula had kept the planning process "on track." Deptula noted that he constantly argued against a "sortie generation mentality." Criteria he used to do keep the planning process on track included "coherency and timing." But there were no "hard" indicators of either coherency or timing. (S) Intvw, GWAPS with Lt Col Deptula.

Gen. Profitt, as commander of the 15th AD, believed the fratricide problem could be handled by replacing HARMs with Shrikes (AGM-45) and Mavericks (AGM-65). Corder discovered the change in missile loadouts two days later; he tried to convince Profitt to reinstate the HARM, because the Shrike–a less advanced missile than the HARM–was more likely to lead to fratricide. Profitt would not reinstate the HARM. The issue was presented to Horner, who sided with Corder.[149]

Reflecting on his Gulf War experience, Major General Corder argued that people expect too much from bomb damage assessment–for example, perfect information. The call to have better BDA is used to avoid having to make difficult military judgements. In his words,

> At a certain point in time, you're going to have to stand up based on your complete understanding of all sources available . . . . If you wait . . . until you're absolutely sure . . . that the BDA problem [is] solved, you might have missed the opportunity.[150]

Within the Tactical Air Control Center, Corder had a "gross understanding" of bomb damage assessment based on Mission Reports.[151] His strategy to understand the effect of air operations had two components. First, Corder looked at the daily summaries concerning how many targets we planned to attack, how many were attacked, and how well they were hit. Second, he spoke via telephone to officers at the wing command post to get an idea of how well the attacks proceeded. He added, "the way you find out [what the strike's effects were was to] go and talk to people who are on the scene twenty-four hours a day."[152] It is not clear

---

[149]Note, Corder could not command Profitt; Profitt was responsible to Horner. (S) Intvw, GWAPS with Maj Gen John A. Corder, 18 May 1992.

[150](S) Intvw, GWAPS with Maj Gen John A. Corder, 18 May 1992.

[151]However, the ATO and MISREPs do not provide a lot of information about what the air assets were doing. The ATO was changed a great deal, even after it had been completed. Because of all these changes, MISREPs will not be linked to the ATO. For example, in many cases, "all you ever see in [MISREPs/ATO] is airplanes going to Joint STARS." (S) Intvw, GWAPS with Maj Gen John A. Corder.

[152](S) *Ibid.*

that Corder's solution to developing bomb damage assessment was superior to that of the GAT planners.

The GAT's Solution to Intelligence Support Problems

Central Command Air Forces/Intelligence took more time to develop its ranked target nomination list than the pace of dynamic planning allowed;[153] their target nominations were slow in arriving or out-of-date.[154] The Guidance, Apportionment, and Targeting cell's solution to these problems—an apparently unresponsive organization and inadequate reconnaissance assets—was to rely ever more strongly on its own intelligence acquisition and analysis system.[155] The Checkmate analyses helped GAT planners decide what targets to attack next.[156] In other words, Checkmate provided both critical information and a strategic thought process.[157]

The GAT planners also created their own tools to track bomb damage assessment information. During the early days of the war, a good deal of attention was devoted to aircraft videotape recorder film. One GAT planner recalled spending several hours a day looking at AVTR imagery from F-117 and F-111F aircraft which could provide "film" on their own strikes. Over time, this exercise convinced planners that if the weather

---

[153] (U) Deptula recalled, when the GAT planners wanted input on a particular critical or fixed target, Glosson called McConnell. McConnell forwarded the photograph in about four hours. The GAT acted on that information. Twenty-four hours later, the GAT received the same photo from CENTAF/IN, and CENTCOM/J2 provided the same photo another twenty-four hours later. (S) Intvw, Office of Air Force History with Lt Col David A. Deptula, SAF/OSX, 20 Nov 1991.

[154] [DELETED]

[155] As shown in (S) Chapter 6, planning officers in Saudi Arabia spoke with counterparts in Checkmate daily during Desert Shield to acquire information and analysis unavailable in theater. According to Deptula, the real value of Checkmate during the war was as an information fusion center. The GAT, during the war, got plenty of direct information, e.g., from Electronic Security Command. (S) Intvw, Office of Air Force History with Lt Col Deptula, 20 Nov 20 1991.

[156] [DELETED] (S) Intvw, Office of Air Force History with Lt Col Deptula, 20 Nov 1991.

[157] (S) *Ibid*; (S) Intvw, Office of Air Force History with Lt Col Deptula, 8 Jan 1992.

was acceptable, and the F-117, F-15E, or F-111F pilot said he dropped a munition on a fixed target's desired mean point of impact, it could be removed from the target list.[158]

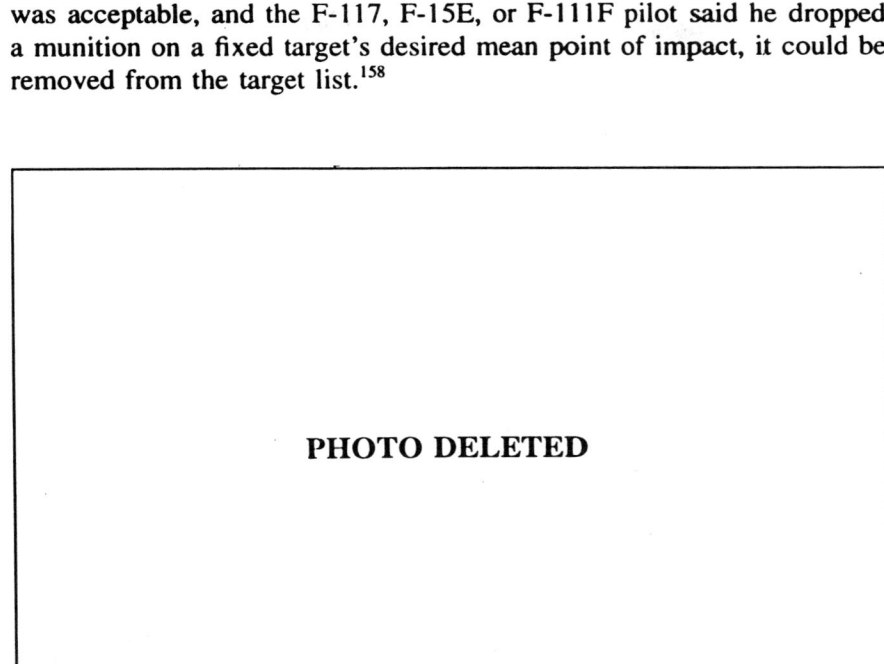

Lt Col Deptula briefing Gen Horner on Baghdad targets.

The second solution was to acknowledge the inadequacy of information and make do with the information available by using different measures of effectiveness. Since timely imagery was unavailable for most target sets, it was often not possible to determine absolute physical damage. During Desert Shield, Lt. Col David Deptula proposed using a different measure of effectiveness (MOE)—a disabling functional effect on Iraqi targets.[159] The effect MOE was not in the Instant Thunder plan.[160]

---

[158]Eventually, Deptula did not spend a lot of time examining AVTR. (S) Intvw, Office of Air Force History with Lt Col Deptula, 20 Nov 1991; (S) Intvw, GWAPS with Lt Col Deptula, SAF/OSX, 21 Dec 1991.

[159]See (S) Volume VI, *Effectiveness*, Chapter 1.

Deptula, however, proposed the MOE to General Glosson, who agreed to use it in the theater. The advantage of this MOE was that it reduced planning time–units could get their target assignments and begin to prepare force packages, mission plans, and route plans much earlier than if the planners were waiting for information indicating absolute physical destruction of targets. And, when the target materials did arrive, they were incorporated into later Air Tasking Orders as necessary.[161]

Summary and Review

To control large numbers of air sorties, the Air Force has built a very complicated organizational architecture. This architecture combines technology, compartmented information, many people having myriad occupational specialties and perspectives, sometimes conflicting organizational responsibilities, and numerous agencies–with so many linkages and pathways that naming let, alone tracing, all the connections may be impossible. Yet, as such human-organization-machine systems become more integrated and complex, more interdependent and interlocked, the probability of system failures increases. And at some point, the system may become so complicated that Gulf War-type organizational ad hoc solutions or fixes may be inadequate.

The story of the GAT during Desert Storm presents several compelling contrasts. First, building and executing an Air Tasking Order for a static environment (where the decision problem was clear and well-structured) was very different from doing the same for a dynamic environment

---

[160] Although the effect MOE was introduced to Glosson in August, it was not on any of the viewgraphs used in the briefings delivered to President Bush, Chairman Powell, General Schwarzkopf, Secretary of Defense Cheney, or the theater wing commanders during the months between October and December 1990. We cannot prove that the effect MOE was not **discussed** at these briefings. (S) Briefing, Brig Gen Buster C. Glosson, "Offensive Campaign, Phase I," to CJCS, Gen Colin Powell, 13 Sep 1990; (S) Briefing, Brig Gen Glosson, "Offensive Campaign, Phase I," to President Bush, 11 Oct 1990; (S) Briefing, Brig Gen Glosson, "Theater Campaign, Phases II & III," to CINC, Gen H. Norman Schwarzkopf, 1 Dec 1990; (S) Briefing, Brig Gen Glosson, "Theater Campaign, Phases II & III," to Wing Commanders, CENTAF, 18 Dec 1990; Briefing, Lt Gen Charles A. Horner, "Offensive Air Campaign" to Secretary of Defense Richard B. Cheney, 20 Dec 1990.

[161] (S) Intvw, Office of Air Force History with Lt Col Deptula, 29 Nov 1991.

(where the decision problem was ill-structured and less manageable). Hence, the type of ad hoc organizational fixes possible in the Gulf War may be more difficult to invent and implement in another situation. The present organizational structure is identical with the one which, as the Defense Science Board noted,

> produced the lack of readiness which characterized our posture on August 1, 1990, the lack of interoperability of the force deployed, the failure to anticipate the kind of weapons and sensor interactions which became so obviously necessary during Desert Shield, the failure to realistically exercise this contingency scenario and learn from it when it was recognized as the most probable use of military forces. It is the same structure that has consistently failed to address the identification problem in a comprehensive way, failed to create and practice concepts for BDA for the weapons and sensors which were clearly evident, and failed to anticipate the roles that space sensors, communications, and navigation systems would be required to play in this, the most likely, application of U.S. forces. . . . [T]he basic institutional processes have not changed. . . . "[162]

Second, there was a difference between what senior leaders and planners believed they could manage and the reality of this war. For example, General Horner believed he "had real-time control of the air. The only thing I didn't have real-time control of was the F-117s because when they go Stealth, they go silent, but they were generally in Baghdad anyway."[163]

Yet, the evidence shows that bomb damage assessment was often inadequate or nonexistent, and communications between the GAT and the wings were often confusing. As a result, Horner's quotations are revealing for what they show he knew about the conduct of the war effort at the unit level. Horner may have had real-time control of air at times. But those times were short. Furthermore, the control of operations exercised by the GAT planners was constrained by their lack of adequate BDA and by their conflicts with CENTAF/IN.

---

[162](S) *Lessons Learned During Operations Desert Shield & Desert Storm*, pp 61-2.

[163](S) Intvw, Lt Gen Horner, 4 Mar 1992.

In one respect, the large number of aircraft available may have been a decisive aid in avoiding critical command and control decisions. When a key GAT planner complained that some air assets were not being used to greatest effect (for example, Marine AV-8Bs), Horner responded there was no need to cause an internal squabble among the Services over doctrine. The coalition had so many aircraft in theater that it could do whatever its leaders wanted done and afford to let the Marine Corps do what it wanted to do.[164] In another context, Horner added, the reason the war was easy

> is because we weren't stressed. Let's be truthful about it. We never had to make a decision as to whether the French brigade died or the Marine brigade died or the Saudi brigade died. If we had had to make those kinds of decisions, it would have been a lot more difficult.[165]

At each level of CENTAF key and significant officers believed they were managing the chaos of war. However, when the activities of the many significant participants are pieced together, the problem is that neither planners nor General Horner, the Joint Force Air Component Commander–knew the details of what was happening in the air campaign or how well the campaign was going. Chapter 8 will examine the issue of bomb damage assessment in greater detail. The chapter describes how assessments were conducted and the implications of the assessment process for command and control. Chapter 9 will survey how significant operational decisions were made below the level of the GAT planners or the Joint Force Air Component Commander. Officers aboard airborne command and control platforms were able to manage the chaos of war and compensate for the difficulty of coordinating a large and complex Air Tasking Order.

---

[164](S) Intvw, Office of Air Force History with Lt Col Deptula, 29 Nov 1991.

[165](S) Intvw, Lt Gen Horner.

8

BDA and the Command and Control of the Air Campaign

In testifying to members of Congress, Gen. H. Norman Schwarzkopf commented at length on the intelligence support given his command during the war against Iraq.[1] General Schwarzkopf said, "We had very, very good intelligence support. We had terrific people. We had a lot of capabilities."

At the same time, however, Schwarzkopf noted that

> BDA [bomb damage assessment] . . . was one of the major areas of confusion. And I feel that was because there were many people who felt they were in a better position to judge battle damage assessment from a pure analysis of things like photography, and that sort of thing, alone, rather than allowing the theater commander . . . to apply good military judgment to what he is seeing. That led to some reports that were confusing. It led to some disagreements. As a matter of fact, it led to some distancing on the part of some agencies from the position of Central Command at the time, as to what the battle damage assessment really was . . . .

The confusion over how best to do battle damage assessment was not, according to Schwarzkopf, a minor issue. As he put it,

> There were certain very specific trigger points, to use the term, that we felt that we had to arrive at before we could successfully launch the ground campaign. And it was important that we had good analysis of how we were coming, how we were progressing towards those trigger points before we were in a position to recommend to the president of the United States that we do launch a ground campaign.

The General told Congress that he did not get that required "good analysis."

---

[1] (S) Rpt, Investigations Subcommittee, Committee on Armed Services, *Intelligence Successes and Failures in Operation Desert Shield/Storm*, House of Representatives, 102nd Congress, 2nd Session, nd.

Schwarzkopf also described in some detail what he thought his command's problem in this area was: the inability to give him, in "near real time," the information he needed at his level. In fact, he also told Congress that his component commanders had the same problem: they did not receive the intelligence they needed when they most needed it. He attributed this lack of useful intelligence to a preoccupation with "what might be called national systems which respond more to the national directive out of Washington."

In sum, General Schwarzkopf said that BDA reporting[2] complicated his ability to know whether his air forces were achieving their campaign objectives and thereby increased the risk, in his eyes, that he would order his land forces to attack at the wrong time. That is, he could not be sure of the outcome of air operations because he did not receive outcome-related information or receive it in time.

This is a very serious charge. General Schwarzkopf argued that theater-level and CENTAF intelligence organizations did not perform well despite the quality of their personnel and equipment. What hurt them, in his view, was the way intelligence gathering, analysis, and reporting was organized and managed. In this chapter, we consider Schwarzkopf's point by examining the process of producing BDA and the impact of that process on the construction and execution of the Air Tasking Order (ATO). In particular, we will explore the character of the data and information available to operations planners in the Special Studies Division [initially called the "Black Hole" and later the Guidance, Apportionment, Targeting (GAT) group] and how the management of the BDA process affected the command and control of the air campaign. Before we do that, however, we must define bomb damage assessment and explain its role in shaping the Air Tasking Order.

Why do BDA? What is it?

Bomb damage assessment is a specialized process. Its roots go back to World War II, when air commanders learned that aircrews consistently overestimated the damage they had inflicted on enemy targets.[3] The first BDA methodology was the systematic analysis of photographic reconnais-

---

[2]Reporting of BDA information should not be confused with fused intelligence.

[3]David MacIsaac, *Strategic Bombing in World War Two: The Story of the United States Strategic Bombing Survey* (New York, 1976), p 26.

sance. That now well-established methodology has been supplemented in the years since World War II by techniques which rely on other forms of intelligence, especially electronic and signals intelligence. At the same time, however, the all-weather, 'round-the-clock nature of modern tactical air warfare has prompted combat planners to demand BDA within twenty-four hours so that they can better distribute their sorties across the range of enemy targets. As more and sometimes more accurate data on damage and effects have become available, the pressure to analyze and then use the data quickly as the basis for planning has also increased.

The formal definition of bomb damage assessment is "the determination of the effect of all air attacks on targets. . . . "[4] The process of BDA attempts to determine if, first, the weapons hit their targets and then if the weapons achieved the results desired. BDA also involves estimating how long it will take enemy units to repair the damage and whether additional strikes are needed to complete the destruction of the target or impede enemy repair efforts. BDA is only one element of a larger process called "combat assessment," which estimates the overall effectiveness of an air campaign.[5] Combat assessment includes bomb damage assessment but also covers other forms of assessment, including whether attacks on physical targets have achieved psychological, social, or economic objectives.[6]

BDA analysts must have some basic intelligence about the targets of missions before the missions themselves are flown, including information on the layout and appearance of the target and the types of weapons scheduled to be used against it. Once the mission is flown, the analysts must know whether there were any changes to the planned attack. Were different munitions used? Were they dropped from an altitude different than that planned? Was the aimpoint the same as that planned? BDA analysts draw required target data from target intelligence files. They get information on planned missions from the Air Tasking Order. They rely on Mission

---

[4] JCS Pub 1-02, *Department of Defense Dictionary of Military and Associated Terms*, 1 Dec 1989. See also Tactical Air Command Regulation 55-45, *Tactical Air Force Headquarters and the Tactical Air Control Center*.

[5] Department of the Air Force, AF Pamphlet 200-17, *An Introduction to Air Force Targeting*, 23 Jun 1989.

[6] BDA should not be confused with Munitions Effectiveness Assessment. The latter is conducted by scientists and engineers concerned about the physical effects of explosives, or the reliability of sensors, or whether the tactics used on missions make the most of a system's destructive capabilities. BDA focuses on what targets are like after attack. Mission Effectiveness Assessment focuses on what weapons do to targets.

Reports for data on how missions were actually flown. Clearly, BDA is very dependent on accurate, timely data. Missing or inaccurate data at any stage of the process (from imagery of the target before attack to postattack Mission Reports) must reduce the validity of BDA.

Force-level decisionmakers[7] view BDA as a measurement stick to evaluate the success or failure of their plans. They use it to determine if a restrike is required or if the air assets under their control can be sent to another target. By contrast, the unit-level planner and aircrew (often the same people) view BDA as confirmation that the attack hit the target or as evidence that the next attack should be conducted differently. This is an important distinction. It means that the same basic information, such as photographs of a strike, will be used to answer different questions at the unit and force levels. It also means that planners at the unit and force levels will press for the BDA useful to them.

BDA must satisfy the needs of the force-level planner and the unit-level planner. To do that, it must be based on a sound methodology which answers the needs of both types of planner. It must, in short, say whether the damage criteria have been met and whether the weapon used performed as expected. Bomb damage assessment must be done from a distance, without perfect information. Yet the better the information, and the faster it reaches both force-level and unit-level planners, the better the answer to the question, "How much damage did we do?"[8] Ideally, planners will receive target damage results very soon after a strike.[9] This up-to-date information can be used within the Air Tasking Order planning cycle to tailor the air effort.

---

[7] For the purposes of this study, the term "force-level decisionmaker" refers to the planner one level up from the unit (e.g., wing). In this case, the force-level decisionmaker is the GAT planner located in the TACC.

[8] *An Introduction to Air Force Targeting*, para 9-4, 9-5, 9-6.

[9] And in some cases, BDA was in the planner's hands within an hour of a strike. For example, BDA was transferred to the Black Hole on TLAM strikes within 45 minutes of an attack. See (S) Chapter 6, footnote 68. Lt Col Deptula also recalled incidents in which RAdm McConnell was able to provide BDA within four hours of a request from Brig Gen Glosson. Needless to say, this short turn-around time was much faster than CENTAF/IN or CENTCOM J2. (S) Intvw, Office of Air Force History with Lt Col David A. Deptula, SAF/OSX, 20 Nov 1991.

What Information was Available to Build the ATO *in Desert Storm?*

Information used to assess bomb damage came in several formats during Desert Storm. Gathering that information began with the filing of In-flight Pilot Reports and post-flight Mission Reports.[10] Each report had its own key place in the BDA process. In-flight Reports were transmitted from attack aircraft at predetermined times or points following attacks on their targets. Transmissions were in the "clear" and provided unclassified information about the attack, for example, whether the mission succeeded or failed. In many cases, Airborne Command, Control, and Communications (ABCCC) or the Airborne Warning and Control System (AWACS) received and forwarded the data to Combat Operations in the Tactical Air Control Center. The In-flight Report information formed the basis for the Mission Reports, which were prepared by unit intelligence personnel immediately after each sortie was completed. Using the In-flight Report and aircraft videotape recording (AVTR),[11] or gun camera and radar film, the aircrew was debriefed. Then, the Mission Report was prepared and forwarded to the CENTAF Combat Intelligence Division.

At the direction of Brig. Gen. Buster Glosson, 14th Air Division Commander, F-117 and F-111F units prepared videotape summaries of all the aircraft videotape recordings and forwarded them to the GAT planners,[12] initially so that CENTAF would have evidence of the accuracy of the bombing of targets in Baghdad. The point was to allay speculation on the part of the news media that the attacks on Baghdad were killing civilians.[13] However, these video summaries were also a summary means–a short cut–to BDA, and GAT personnel began using them for that purpose.[14] Frequently, the aircraft videotape recorder was the only evi-

---

[10](S) Chapter 2, Figure 8, Desert Storm Mission Report.

[11]Only three types of coalition aircraft (F-117A, F-15E, F-111F) possessed AVTR systems capable of viewing and recording bomb impact on target. For example, the F-15E LANTIRN targeting pod did not go fully on-line until the middle of February 1991. With a few exceptions, up until that time the majority of AVTR inputs were from F-117A and F-111F (using the PAVE TACK pod).

[12](S) Intvw, Mark D. Mandeles and Lt Col Sanford S. Terry with Maj Robert J. Heston, the 37th TFW (P) Director of Intelligence from 9 Aug 1990 to 31 Mar 1991, 19 Oct 1992.

[13](S) Intvw, Mandeles and Terry with Maj Robert J. Heston, 16 and 19 Oct 1992; see also the section on the THREAT model in Appendix 3.

[14]See (S) Chapter 7, footnote 159.

dence reviewed within the GAT of weapon impact and detonation. Mission Reports contained the bulk of information about the effects of detonations, but the GAT planners were not addressees for Mission Reports.[15]

In addition to these unit products, GAT planners had available to them other tactical, theater[16] and national intelligence.[17] These included intercepts of Iraqi communications and signals, as well as imagery (from the visible, infrared, and radar portions of the electromagnetic spectrum). The Iraqis clearly had some idea of U.S. capabilities in these areas because they exercised careful communications discipline. They also broadcast radar signals selectively and infrequently, making it difficult for GAT planners to accurately gauge the status of many radar sites. Lt. Gen. Charles A. Horner's decision to keep Iraqi radars on CENTAF's "active" threat list until the Tactical Air Control Center had positive photographic proof that they had been destroyed kept the Constant Source database full.[18] A later section of this chapter will show why that was a problem.

Planned BDA Process: Theater

Planned Organization in Theater

U.S. Central Command's pre-Desert Shield plans for action were laid out in USCINCCENT Operation Plan (OPLAN) 1002-90 (Second Draft) of 18 July 1990. Annex B, covering intelligence, gave Central Command J-2 the responsibility for preparing guidelines for component intelligence

---

[15] The CENTAF/IN created the Address Information Group (AIG), which is the standard list of addresses for particular pieces of information. For example, the F-117A Director of Intelligence did not address MISREPs to the GAT because the GAT was not on the AIG. He did talk with the FIDO in the TACC and members of the GAT to describe the outcome of his unit's missions. Yet, their conversation did not include all data on the mission, and the extent of communication between the GAT and other unit-level intelligence officers is not known. See (S) Intvw, Maj Robert J. Heston, 16 and 19 Oct 1992.

[16] As illustrated in (S) Chapter 7, Table 11, U.S. and Allied forces flew an average of seventy-five reconnaissance type intelligence collection missions each day between 17 Jan and 28 Feb 1991.

[17] [DELETED] See (S) Task Force III's *Space Operation in the Gulf War*, Chapter 4; (S) Ltr, [DELETED], USAF, Chief, Target Intelligence Division, Office for Global Analysis, DIA to Col Emery M. Kiraly, Executive Director, GWAPS, subj: Gulf War Air Power Survey, 2 Dec 1992.

[18] (S) Intvw, Thomas C. Hone, GWAPS with Maj Lewis Hill, USAF, GWAPS, 5 Nov 1992.

organizations and control over any contacts between those organizations and intelligence organizations outside the theater.[19] This concept gave CENTCOM J-2 the responsibility for managing all the intelligence functions supporting the theater. CENTCOM J-2, however, did not have the personnel required to monitor the component and national intelligence collection systems, let alone the expertise to direct the thousands of specialists in all the supporting intelligence organizations.[20]

In the area of overhead imagery, for example, Operation Plan 1002-90 assigned CENTCOM J-2 "overall responsibility."[21] To exercise that responsibility, CENTCOM J-2 planned to establish a Collection Management Office, and the latter, located in the Joint Intelligence Center, would "compile all collection activities . . ." in the theater.[22] The plan was that each component would set up its own Collection Management Office and send a representative to sit on the Daily Aerial Reconnaissance and Surveillance conference chaired by the CENTCOM J-2 Collection Management Office. The daily conferences would serve as the means of passing CENTCOM guidance to the component intelligence organizations and, more importantly, as the forum where the components would make their specific requests known to Central Command.[23]

[DELETED][24]

[DELETED][25] [DELETED][26] [DELETED][27]

---

[19](S/NF) USCINCCENT OPLAN 1002-90 (Second Draft), 18 Jul 1990, Annex 7 to Annex B (Intelligence), pp B-7-1 and B-7-2.

[20](S) *Intelligence Successes and Failures in Operations Desert Shield/Storm*, p 5. The April 1990 *Staff Directory* for the Headquarters, U.S. Central Command lists approximately 150 personnel in CENTCOM J-2.

[21](S/NF) OPLAN 1002-90 (Second Draft), 18 Jul 1990, Annex 7 to Annex B, p B-7-3.

[22](S/NF) *Ibid.*

[23](S/NF) *Ibid*, p B-7-2.

[24][DELETED]

[25](S/NF) *Ibid*, p B-7-5.

[26](S/NF) *Ibid*, p B-7-3.

[27](S/NF) *Ibid*, p B-7-4.

U.S. Central Command Air Forces planned to have intelligence personnel participate actively in constructing the Air Tasking Order,[28] assessing the results of missions flown, and determining long-range plans beyond the routine ATO cycle. Intelligence was to be an active participant in each and every phase of the ATO production process. Unfortunately, Central Command Air Forces did not have enough intelligence personnel to fulfill this major responsibility. In addition, the intelligence personnel who did deploy worked in different locations, which hindered mutual support.[29] Their separation was made all the worse by a lack of sufficient secure communications links that otherwise would have allowed them to communicate directly and quickly with the GAT planners.

Planned Theater Intelligence Organizational Relationships

In addition, the Tactical Air Control Center did not function as planned after CENTAF deployed. For example, USCENTAF Regulation 55-45 called for the CENTAF Target Intelligence Division to become a branch of the Combat Intelligence Division of the Tactical Air Control Center and support the Combat Plans Division. Intelligence personnel also were assigned to the Enemy Situation Correlation Division (ENSCD), where they supported the Combat Operations Division. Figure 35 illustrates the organizational arrangements proposed by Regulation 55-45.

According to planning done before Desert Shield, CENTAF's Targets Division (INT) would comprise three sections: Target Nominations Branch (INTN), Combat Assessment Branch (INTA),[30] and ENSCD.[31] Under the plan, target analysts working in the Target Nominations Branch were supposed to nominate specific targets for strikes they believed would fulfill the commander's guidance and Central Command's campaign objectives. Each Target Nominations Branch analyst was supposed to be assigned to a specific aspect of the air campaign (that is, offensive counter air, air interdiction, command and control) to identify, weaponeer, and rank targets and target types for attack. In the plan, these analysts were

---

[28] USCENTAF Regulation 55-45, *Air Employment Planning Process*, 27 Jun 1990, p 3-3.

[29] See (S) Chapter 6.

[30] INTN and INTA supported the CID and Combat Plans.

[31] ENSCD supported the Combat Operations Division.

supposed to help the Combat Operations Planning Staff develop the Air Tasking Order.

Figure 35
Theater Intelligence Organizational Relationships

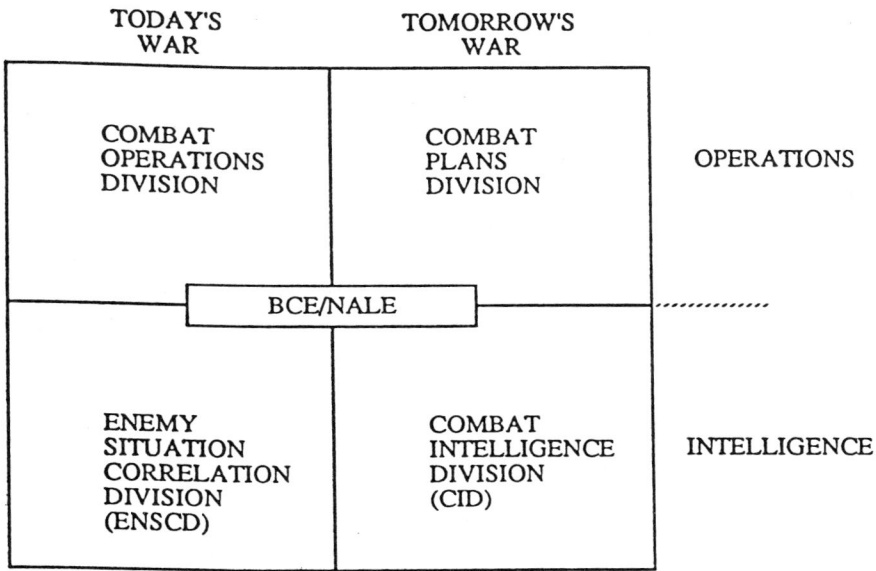

In the pre-Desert Shield plan, analysts in the Combat Assessment Branch were given responsibility for monitoring the current status of targets. In that capacity, they would alert the Target Nominations Branch to targets which had to be reattacked. In addition, Combat Assessment analysts would produce an Air Combat Assessment report documenting the effectiveness of combat operations, enemy reconstitution capabilities, and the reliability of coalition weapon systems.

According to the plan, the Enemy Situation Correlation Division target analysts would nominate near real-time targets. They would search for high-value, fleeting targets for attack by alert or diverted aircraft, then monitor the execution of the Air Tasking Order to determine which targets had been attacked. Then they would pass this information back to the Target Nominations Branch.³² The ENSCD was the third organization within the Tactical Air Control Center that needed accurate and up-to-date BDA, because, in the prewar plan, it supported Combat Operations in executing "today's" war.

The Intent of USCENTAF Regulation 55-45

USCENTAF Regulation 55-45 specified that targeting guidance from the Commander in Chief Central Command and the Commander of the Central Command Air Forces be applied to the selection and ranking of targets through the Joint Targeting Coordination Board using the Daily USCENTAF Guidance Letter.³³ Regulation 55-45 anticipated a continual interaction between operations and intelligence analysts.³⁴ In the prewar plans, the Combat Assessment Cell was given the responsibility for supporting this interaction by maintaining a list reflecting the status of previously fragged targets. This list–the strike history–was the point of reference to which all parties using bomb damage assessment in the Tactical Air Control Center were, in the plan, supposed to refer.³⁵

BDA Collection Management

The success of this organization for the provision and analysis of bomb damage data depended on the timely inputs made by the collection managers assigned to the Combat Assessment Cell. Figure 36 illustrates the planned flow of requests made by collection managers to Central Command, national, and tactical theater assets. Collection managers would be responsible for providing the Chief of Targets and senior weapons and tactics officers with reports needed on each target nominated for reattack.³⁶ CENTAF Combat Assessment Cell collection managers were expected to review and approve the collection requirements presented by all CENTAF's air units. In this capacity they were to ensure that requests for intelligence were properly integrated, reviewed, and, where possible, satisfied from information already available in the Tactical Air Control

---

³²*Air Employment Planning Process*, p 2-3.

³³*Ibid*, p 3-12.

³⁴*Ibid*, p 3-3.

³⁵*Ibid*, p 3-4.

³⁶*Ibid*.

Center. If the center did not have the needed data, these managers were supposed to make sure they were collected.[37]

Under the plan, the collection managers had very critical responsibilities. They were expected to remain aware of new or changing collection opportunities while ensuring that Tactical Air Control Center personnel were apprised of the total collection potential. To do this, they would have to work with operations and target intelligence personnel to ascertain if collection requests had been satisfied. At the same time, they were supposed to remain aware of the capabilities of Air Force, national, and other Services' collection resources. The latter could be tasked through a request made by the CENTAF representative on the USCENTCOM/J2C collection management board.[38] Unfortunately, of the five CENTAF personnel eventually assigned as collection managers, only two had had limited experience working in that position.[39] In addition, Central Command had rated all component staffs as marginal in planning and managing the production of their requirements for intelligence support.[40] As a result, CENTAF collection managers evidently lacked the ability to use effectively the intelligence information management systems with which the component commands deployed.

---

[37] *Ibid*, p 5-9.

[38] *Ibid*, Chapter 5.

[39] USCENTCOM, *Baseline Assessment Document–Third Edition (BAD-3) for the Theater Intelligence Architecture Program (Final)*, 12 Sep 1990, p 4-5. There is no way to determine by position and AFSC that people assigned to particular functions within CENTAF Collection Management were properly trained for their job and had the background to support collection efforts. It is also impossible to determine where these individuals were assigned before the war and whether they were logically assigned based on experience.

[40] *Baseline Assessment Document–Third Edition (BAD-3) for the Theater Intelligence Architecture Program*, p 4-5.

**Figure 36
Collection Management
Flow of Requests to CENTCOM, National and
Tactical Theater Assets**

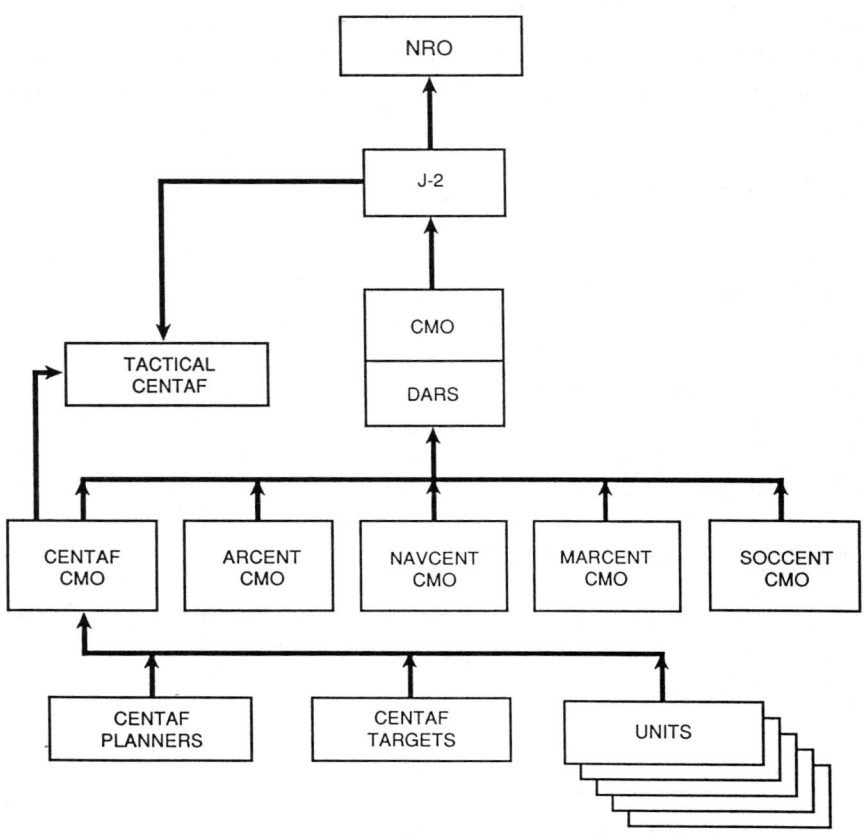

The Importance of the Combat Assessment Cell

Planning for BDA focused on the Combat Assessment Cell, which was subordinate to the Chief of Targets. The Combat Assessment Cell was formally assigned the responsibility for analyzing the cumulative effects of bombing and for preparing estimates of how long it would take the Iraqis to repair the damage. CENTAF Regulation 55-45 specified that the Combat Assessment/BDA Cell was to pass pertinent information to both the Enemy Situation Correlation Division and the Combat Intelligence Division's target developers.[41]

In the plan, the Combat Assessment/BDA Cell received a hard copy Air Tasking Order and then posted BDA to it. In addition, its personnel were supposed to prepare periodic target summaries using the BDA data collected through all the means, photographic and otherwise, available to the theater. Based on its findings this Cell was to provide collection requirements to the collection managers and present daily BDA/ combat assessment briefings to the Commander of the Central Command Air Forces.[42]

The Flaws in Precrisis Plans

However, for all of the regulations and operations plans, an architecture for the collection and dissemination of bomb damage assessment did not exist in Central Command or its components.[43] The architecture was only a concept; it did not describe a working system. General intelligence guidelines specifying which agencies reported "what" and "to whom" were in place, but an operative and cohesive mechanism for tracking, collating, and disseminating BDA had to be created once personnel were in place.[44] As the Center for Naval Analyses put it, "The theater BDA process suffered from a cold start, in which the lack of adequate procedures, practice, and manpower were felt."[45]

Unit support, collection, and production were ill-defined, or, in some cases, defined just prior to deployment. One USCENTAF officer noted in an after action report that "when we deployed we would have had trouble

---

[41]*Air Employment Planning Process*, Chapter 5.

[42]*Ibid.*

[43]*Baseline Assessment Document–Third Edition (BAD-3) for the Theater Intelligence Architecture Program*, pp 5-1 - 5-7.

[44]SSgt William K. Sherwood, 12TIS NCOIC, Weaponeering, Trip Report - Operation Desert Shield/Storm, 10 May 1991. We should add, the troubles experienced in Internal Look 90 were not attributed to the organization of intelligence support. Intvw, Maj Anne D. Leary, Mark D. Mandeles, Lt Col Sanford S. Terry with Lt Col Ross Dickinson, Joint Warfare Center, 8 May 1992.

[45]Frank Schwamb, et al., (S) *Desert Storm Reconstruction Report, Vol. II: Strike Warfare, Center for Naval Analyses* (CRM 91-178), Oct 1991, p 3-3.

running a major exercise much less conducting a war."[46] In fact, any exercise, conducted anywhere by U.S. forces prior to Desert Storm, would probably have revealed that collecting and processing BDA in adequate quantity and quality just was not likely.[47] Given the fact that it would always be under great pressure to produce results quickly, the exercise Control Cell would probably make up the results that the senior staff wanted. The fact that it was difficult to duplicate realistic BDA inputs and demands under extreme time pressure in peacetime exercises inhibited effective, realistic planning.[48]

An Effort to Develop Theater-Level BDA Software

CENTAF did make an effort in the year before the war to take advantage of computer capabilities to develop and produce bomb damage assessment to support the Air Tasking Order generation process. An intelligence augmentee to CENTAF apparently was assigned responsibility to modify existing software for this purpose. The new software was

---

[46](S) AAR, USCENTAF/IN After Action Report and Lessons Learned, 25 Mar 91, from Col [no first name] Rauschkolb, to Col [Christopher L.] Christon (CENTAF/IN), with 17 Attachments.

[47]BDA during any phase of an exercise, in both quantity and quality, is inadequate. Within the artificialities of an exercise targeting and intelligence will always give the appearance of working as expected. One of the problems is that intelligence is often included more for the operations staff than for training of intelligence personnel. It is rare that new targets are interjected to reflect the increased attention from the national intelligence community. Collection management also suffers. It does not get sufficient exercise in performing its function, especially within the parameters required by the operators. There is little Air Force-wide training for theater-level assets. Rarely is anyone concerned with checking that a tasked unit in fact has the target materials required to fly a mission. Also the intelligence dissemination process is not sufficiently tasked. Component-level exercises tend to support the decision makers. However, during these exercise crises much of the effort is directed down to the operational units–units which are almost always simulated and very undemanding.

[48]SSgt Sherwood, Trip Report - Operation Desert Shield/Storm, 10 May 1991. SSgt Sherwood noted:

> I mentioned we exercised this plan [BDA] successfully during Exercise IMMINENT THUNDER. The measure of success has to be qualified, because the key factor of having a database with the targeting and mission data readily available and formatted at the start of each ATO day was simulated. This simulation was approved at the time, because the actual ATO database, ATO Bravo . . . had been 'hand-poked' into the computers, but follow-on ATOs were to be generated automatically using a computer system called TEMPLAR.

ready in time for testing during the exercise Imminent Thunder, which was held two months before Operation Desert Storm began. The BDA program itself was a database of all of the targets in the Air Tasking Order, with BDA data fields added. The goal was to create a baseline database with all of the Air Tasking Order data in place before any of the BDA reports rolled in.

This database could be entered into a computer by hand. It could also be created using an electronic ASCII file transfer from the Computer Assisted Force Management System, which Tactical Air Control Center personnel thought they would use (if war came) to build the Air Tasking Order. By using the ATO data from CAFMS, the BDA Cell would automatically tie all of the targets to the aircraft assigned to strike them, and have times over targets, mission numbers, call signs, and targeting data as well.

The point was to prepare a database which presented as complete a picture of the air war as possible. It had to be done with a stand-alone program because of the inherent limits of the CAFMS software. These limits forced developers in CENTAF to take data generated by CAFMS and translate them into an ASCII file format, placing them on floppy disks. The data could be used to build a separate but representative database for actual correlating target/mission data with BDA. Databases from three different systems had to be tied together if a total "target picture" were to exist. General Horner approved an effort to develop this database.[49]

The plan was to process bomb damage assessment using three separate computer workstations. This would allow three people to use information in the BDA database simultaneously, thereby expediting the handling of incoming message traffic. At the first workstation, an operator correlated Mission Reports and In-flight Reports (first-phase BDA) to the targets assigned in the Air Tasking Order. At the second workstation, another operator would enter BDA collected from national assets (second- and third-phase BDA). At the third workstation, the operator–a combat assessments officer–could analyze the available BDA and then recommend whether to nominate a target for another strike.

---

[49] SSgt Sherwood, Trip Report - Operation Desert Shield/Storm. The problem with CAFMS was that targeting information was never standardized, e.g., target coordinates could be expressed in different formats.

BDA inputs also were to be "fused" (that is, merged with other types of intelligence data) and then passed to Central Command, where a BDA cell would estimate general attrition trends. At the beginning of each ATO day, a cumulative strike history, with BDA and real-time mission and targeting data, could be analyzed, and new BDA could be entered quickly into the database to update the target record.[50]

The plan was to take bomb damage assessment collected from national assets and transfer it from the second workstation, via a floppy disk, to the first workstation, where it could be read into the master database. The first workstation would do all the reporting. The purpose of this system was to take advantage of the ease with which data in a digital format can be analyzed and displayed.[51] The process by which CENTAF's Air Tasking Order was assembled in 1990 still involved a lot of pen-and-pencil work. If BDA were to be posted and transferred by pen and pencil, the ATO process would become less responsive to changes in targets. Unfortunately, the CENTAF BDA analysis system was not problem-free by January 1991. Moreover, Guidance, Apportionment, and Targeting cell planners did not know about this system, and so they put together one of their own after the beginning of Desert Storm.[52]

Planned BDA Process: Washington

Organization in Washington

The Joint Staff understood that Central Command was responsible for conducting reconnaissance in-theater. Components and supporting commands would produce their own required intelligence or get assistance from CENTCOM.[53] The Chairman of the Joint Chiefs was prepared to direct the allocation of strategic reconnaissance assets in response to Commander in Chief, Central Command requirements. CENTCOM, for example, had to be given the authority to direct the U-2/TR-1s used in the theater, and CENTAF directly controlled only its RF-4s.

---

[50] SSgt Sherwood, Trip Report - Operation Desert Shield/Storm.

[51] *Ibid.*

[52] *Ibid.* See also (S) Chapter 7.

[53] JCS Publication 3-56.1, Chapter IX, Volume II, pp B-20, B-21.

[DELETED]⁵⁴ [DELETED]⁵⁵

As Central Command forces deployed to the Persian Gulf area, the 480th Tactical Intelligence Group, out of Langley AFB, Virginia, analyzed reconnaissance imagery and produced targeting materials for use in the theater. [DELETED] In pre-Desert Shield plans, requests to DIA for imagery were supposed to come through USCENTCOM J-2 collection managers, who were given the responsibility for reviewing and ranking requests from the deploying components.⁵⁶

How Did GAT Planners Actually get BDA?

The Basic Problem

Guidance, Apportionment, and Targeting planners requested that BDA be produced as soon as possible after each strike.⁵⁷ Had it been produced as planned, BDA would have been used in the Air Tasking Order planning cycle. GAT planners attempted every day during Desert Storm to get such imagery. In fact, the ATO Planning Guidance identified a need for imagery "against any target struck on previous air task orders which [had] either not yet been covered or inadequately covered for bomb damage

---

⁵⁴*Ibid*, pp 10-16.

⁵⁵*Ibid*, p 16.

⁵⁶(S) *Desert Storm After Action Report*, from Lt Col Sterne, Lt Col Byrd, Maj Massey, 7 Mar 1990 (sic); see also (S) Lt Col Bondzeleske, Weapon Effects Officer DX-5 (AF/XOXWD), *After Action Report*, 18 Mar 1991; see also, (S/NF/WN) Capt Steve Hedger, AFIA/INKS, *Point Paper on BDA Imagery Exploitation*, 21 Sep 1990; and see also (S) DX BDA CON OPS, 11 Sep 1990–the latter two are filed in CHST 51-12; see also (S) *Checkmate BDA Team – Daily Tasks (As of 26 Jan 91)*, from Lt Col Allan W. Howey, Deputy, Checkmate BDA Team; see also (S) *DIA's Bomb Damage Assessment (BDA) Process* briefing [CHST 51-10], with note from Lt Col Ben Harvey to Colonel Warden "here's updated BDA brief–recommend we get on LGEN Adam's calendar this week."

⁵⁷*Air Employment Planning Process*, p 3-12; see also ATO Planning Guidance for D+3 - 33 and D+35 - 43 (reel number 23978, frames 936-1080). Besides the usual distribution to the commanders copies were provided to USCENTAF/IN, Combat OPS, SAC Director, SAC Planners, ESC, RSAF, RAF, US Navy, US Marine Corps, BCE, Canadian LNO, French LNO and outside of USCENTAF it was provided to USCENTCOM J2/J3/C3I. See also Master Attack Plans for Days D+15 (pages 2,4,5) D+19 (reel number 23674, pp 7-8). In each case RF-4Cs and RF-5s were tasked to provide reconnaissance in the KTO, some specifically against bridges.

assessment purposes."[58] GAT planners felt so strongly about this matter that they did not change the "Collection Management Guidance" for the duration of Desert Storm.

However, CENTAF collection managers had to satisfy both unit- and force-level requests for BDA.[59] As noted in a report prepared by the Assistant Secretary of Defense (for Command, Control, Communications and Intelligence), several factors kept the collection managers from satisfying both these "clients." First, the concept of the air campaign (and how the campaign changed over time) was not clearly briefed to the collection managers. Second, some collection managers, rather than being centrally located in the Tactical Air Control Center, were not in the Center or were moved several times. Only in the third week of Desert Storm were all the collection managers finally linked up with the imagery analysts in the Tactical Air Control Center they were supposed to be working with all along.[60] Third, the different imagery and intelligence collection units working for Central Command were not practiced in putting the theater command's plan into effect in realistic exercises. Their relationships with each other were never well defined.[61]

These problems placed CENTAF collection managers at a disadvantage in what turned out to be a competition for the attention of Central Command. CENTCOM J-2 decided which component requests for intelligence data would be satisfied first. As a result, CENTAF's requests were often not satisfied on time to meet the needs of the Air Tasking Order planners

---

[58](S) ATO Planning Guidance for D+3 - 33 and D+35 - 43 (reel 23978, frames 936-1080), Collection Management Guidance in Priority Order. Besides the usual distribution to the commanders copies were provided to USCENTAF/IN, Combat OPS, SAC Director, SAC Planners, ESC, RSAF, RAF, US Navy, US Marine Corps, BCE, Canadian LNO, French LNO and outside of USCENTAF it was provided to USCENTCOM J2/J3/C3I. See also Master Attack Plans for Days D+15 and D+19 (reel 23674, pp 2-8). In each case RF-4s and RF-5s were tasked to provide reconnaissance in the KTO. Some of those missions were against bridges.

[59][DELETED]

[60](S) Intelligence Program Support Group, Office of the Assistant Secretary of Defense (Command, Control, Communications and Intelligence), *Operation Desert Shield/Desert Storm Intelligence Dissemination Study–Final Report*, Appendix L–CENTAF, 28 May 1992.

[61]*Baseline Assessment Document–Third Edition (BAD-3) for the Theater Intelligence Architecture Program (Final)*, pp 4-11, 4-12.

or the unit-level planners.[62] Put another way, the availability of BDA to CENTAF was hampered by the implementation of CENTCOM's precrisis intelligence concept and by a lack of practice on the part of the collection managers working in or for the Tactical Air Control Center.

For example, the Iraqi Air Defense Operations Center in Baghdad was a very high-priority target when the air war commenced on the night of 16/17 January 1991. Consequently, two F-117As were assigned to attack it. The Air Defense Center ceased to be a target when GAT planners decided that postmission pilot debriefs and cockpit video footage showed that all bombs had hit on, or extremely close to, their desired mean points of impact and had properly detonated. This is the kind of assessment which GAT planners wanted to be able to make for all targets.

Unfortunately, different types of targets require different types of BDA. For example, analysts could usually decide whether point targets such as Baghdad Air Defense Operations Center were destroyed or nonfunctional by examining a few images. The same sort of analysis did not work for Republican Guard divisions entrenched in or near Kuwait. Air operations against them were essentially attritional and—hopefully—cumulative, with no particular aimpoint being of higher priority until ground operations were imminent. Under these circumstances, it was difficult to decide, just from aerial photographs, whether any given Republican Guard unit was capable of fighting effectively.

Without bomb damage assessment, GAT planners considered all targets as still functional, still dangerous. Imperfect knowledge about the effectiveness of strikes led to unnecessary restrikes, the waste of munitions, and to placing crews and equipment unnecessarily at risk. Unnecessary restrikes also kept GAT planners from allocating aircraft and munitions to other targets. The planners did not correct this situation because they did not know where and how to obtain all the BDA they needed. In accordance with regulations, the daily ATO Planning Guidance letter

---

[62] This was not just a problem for CENTAF; it also effected NAVCENT. According to an analysis done by the Center for Naval Analyses, BDA was such a scarce resource during Desert Storm that many targets assigned to the Navy's carrier battle groups in the Red Sea and Persian Gulf were not adequately covered. See Frank Schwamb, et al., (S) *Desert Storm Reconstruction Report, Vol. II: Strike Warfare*, pp 3-19 and 3-20.

stated, in general terms, those requirements.[63] The problem was that the requirements were often not met.

Collection Systems That Were Employed

By the time the war started, Central Command had established U-2R[64] and TR-1[65] in the theater.[66] [DELETED][67] Strategic Air Command imagery interpreters were able to analyze Senior Year Electro-optical Reconnaissance System (SYERS) film,[68] and produce imagery interpretation reports. [DELETED][69] [DELETED][70]

[DELETED][71]

Table 13 lists the major theater imagery exploitation systems supporting CENTAF targeting and possessing the ability to support Desert Storm BDA operations by October 1990.[72]

---

[63](S) Intvw, Lt Col David A. Deptula. Deptula noted that the Guidance Letter also was used to provide information to the people putting together the ATO.

[64]The Lockheed U-2R is considered a national, rather than tactical, intelligence asset. The planes can be outfitted with either cameras or equipment, depending on the nature of a particular mission.

[65]The TR-1 is an updated version of the U-2, but considered a tactical, instead of national, intelligence asset.

[66](S/NF/WN) Robert J. Butler, *Intelligence Support for BDA and Targeting in Operation Desert Storm*, RAND WD(L)-5633-1-AF (Santa Monica, Nov 1991). (S/NF/WN) See also (S) Leland Joe and Dan Gonzales, *Command and Control, Communications, and Intelligence in Desert Storm Air Operations*, RAND WD(L)-5750-AF (Santa Monica, Feb 1992). See also CENTCOM, *Desert Shield Chronological list of events – Aug 90 - Apr 91*.

[DELETED]

[67][DELETED]

[68](S/NF) SYERS is an electro-optical sensor. [DELETED]

[69](S/NF/WN) Robert J. Butler, *Intelligence Support for BDA and Targeting in Operation Desert Storm*.

[70](S/NF/WN) *Command and Control, Communications, and Intelligence in Desert Storm Air Operations*.

[71](S/NF/WN) *Intelligence Support for BDA and Targeting in Operation Desert Storm*.

[72](S/NF/WN) *Ibid*. (S/NF/WN) See also Project Air Force Assessment of Operation Desert Shield: *Volume II, The Buildup of Combat Power*–Technical Appendices, pp 171-76, 197-99.

Table 13
Imagery Exploitation and Production In-theater (October 1990)

[DELETED]

Table 14 depicts the disposition of U.S. intelligence sensors available to the theater as of 20 January 1991.[73]

Table 14
Areas of Sensor Commitment

[DELETED]

By mid-January 1991, JSTARS (Joint Surveillance Target Attack Radar System) and RF-4s with long-range oblique photographic, side-looking, and forward-looking panoramic cameras were based in the theater. These assets were complemented by additional Strategic Air Command TR-1s with ASARS-II and by British Jaguars and Tornados with side-looking IR sensors and long-range oblique photography. TARPS (tactical air [photographic] reconnaissance pod system) for the F-14 were deployed on aircraft carriers employed in Desert Storm. The Royal Saudi Air Force RF-5E aircraft rounded out the tactical reconnaissance force for Central Command.

Processing Collected Data

As additional assets became available the need for more personnel and equipment to exploit, produce, and disseminate images grew pressing. DIA, CENTCOM, and CENTAF tried to address these needs collectively with the formation of a Joint Imagery Production Center (JIPC–pronounced "gypsy").[74]

The JIPC was created from existing assets. It had key elements: [DELETED], a mobile intelligence processing element from the 9th Remote

---

[73] Source: (S/NF) HQ USAF/INX, OADR.

[74] (S) *Operation Desert Shield/Desert Storm Intelligence Dissemination Study–Final Report*, Appendix L–CENTAF, p 4-11.

[DELETED]

Tracking Station at Beale AFB, and a joint imagery exploitation cell with 200 imagery interpreters from several organizations. This organization was fully operational by 10 January 1991 and capable of producing 1,700 prints per day. By 15 January, the JIPC was exploiting [DELETED] imagery and U-2 camera film brought by courier daily from Taif to Riyadh.[75]

The JIPC had trouble starting up because it was created ad hoc in the theater. Getting organized, combined with the increasing demand for imagery by operational users, kept the JIPC from meeting user demands and made the component staffs extremely unhappy. For example, the JIPC was designed to support CENTAF with liaison to CENTCOM. The JIPC's role later changed to CENTCOM support, with the primary user being the U.S. Army.[76]

The original concept also called for the JIPC to process one to two U-2 missions per week. This task was expanded to daily mission processing, which placed a greater demand on JIPC personnel than they were able to satisfy. In addition, the JIPC was also directed to play a major role in the bomb damage assessment process for the Commander, Central Command, which meant that half of the interpreters who had been available to process reconnaissance were instead doing target analysis.[77] By the end of Desert Storm, the JIPC had processed 1.3 million feet of U-2 imagery and produced over 53,000 selected prints.[78]

---

[75](S/NF/WN) *Intelligence Support for BDA and Targeting in Operation Desert Storm.*

[76](S/NF/WN) *Ibid*, p 15. See also USCENTAF/IN, Msg dtg 050726Z Feb 1991, subj: Unit Imagery Distribution.

CENTAF/IN acknowledges the need for timely premission imagery in this message. CENTAF/IN personnel concentrated on those units going to the KTO and attacking the Republican Guard units. The initial intent was to provide (a) RF-4 imagery from the JIPC and (b) U-2R mosaics, which would require assembly at the unit. CENTAF/IN attempted to complete work on one Iraqi division each day. The information would be distributed via C-21 from the JIPC at Riyadh, or from Shaikh Isa.

[77](S/NF/WN) *Intelligence Support for BDA and Targeting in Operation Desert Storm*, p 15.

[DELETED]

[78](S/NF) *DCS/Intelligence Operation Desert Shield/Storm After Action Report–Executive Edition*, 30 Aug 1991, p 9.

[DELETED]⁷⁹ [DELETED]⁸⁰ [DELETED]⁸¹

CENTCOM finally accepted the creation of the JIPC in time to assist the Desert Storm air operation with imagery support. However, CENTCOM's slow organizational response to the dynamics of the deploying (Desert Shield) force intelligence requirements resulted in a delay in the improvement of the quality and quantity of intelligence available to theater commanders. CENTCOM never recovered from this delay.⁸²

The Role of the Defense Intelligence Agency (DIA) in BDA

DIA Analysis of Satellite Data

[DELETED]⁸³ [DELETED]⁸⁴

---

⁷⁹[DELETED]

⁸⁰(S) *Intelligence Successes and Failures in Operation Desert Shield/Storm*, p 4.

⁸¹(S) *Ibid*, p 7.

⁸²The Center for Naval Analyses (CNA) discovered that Navy carrier battle staffs often pressed for permission to schedule second strikes on targets while the TACC was still waiting for data from CENTCOM and national sources. As the CNA analysis put it, the "BDA system" just could not keep pace with "the dynamic strike campaign." See (S) *Desert Storm Reconstruction Report, Vol. II: Strike Warfare*, p 2-19 and p 3-25.

⁸³DIA's Technical Program Office passed structural analyses of hard targets to Checkmate. (S/NF) Ltr, [DELETED] to Col Kiraly, subj: GWAPS, 2 Dec 1992.

⁸⁴(S) *Desert Storm After Action Report*, 7 Mar 1990 (sic); see also (S) Lt Col Bondzeleske, *After Action Report*, 18 Mar 1991; see also, (S/NF/WN) Capt Hedger, *Point Paper on BDA Imagery Exploitation*, 21 Sep 1990; and see also, (S) DX BDA CON OPS, 11 Sep 1990–the latter two are filed in CHST 51-12; see also (S) *Checkmate BDA Team – Daily Tasks (As of 26 Jan 1991)*, from Lt Col Howey; see also (S) DIA's "Bomb Damage Assessment (BDA) Process" briefing [CHST 51-10].

[DELETED]⁸⁵

Air Staff Cooperation with DIA

DIA's concept of operations was based on the premise that theater assets would focus on tactical targets in the Kuwait Theater of Operations, while national assets would concentrate on strategic targets in Iraq. DIA itself would be the lead agency for strategic BDA. DIA asked the staff of the operations deputy to the Chief of Staff of the Air Force for help in the BDA process.[86] Checkmate, an Air Staff group, was given this responsibility. The group had already shifted its activities from wargames and simulations to joint air campaign planning. Checkmate's Air Force personnel were augmented by Army, Navy, and Marine Corps officers.[87]

Liaison with intelligence agencies was provided by DIA, Central Intelligence Agency, and National Security Agency liaison personnel, who worked next to Checkmate's space in the Pentagon. This Joint Intelligence Center evolved into a BDA collection cell at the onset of hostilities.[88] During the first stage of imagery analysis, the Checkmate cell was involved deeply in the BDA process. An open-line consultation was conducted around-the-clock. During the second stage, Checkmate provided one Air Force analyst to the DIA cell, and Air Force weapon system experts were on call. During stage three, Checkmate also provided an

---

[85](S) Thomas P. Christie, John N. Donis, and Gregory A. Corliss, *Desert Storm Strategic Air Campaign Bomb Damage Assessment (BDA)*, Institute for Defense Analyses Document D-1088, Jan 1992. See also (S) *Desert Storm After Action Report*, 7 Mar 1990 (sic); see also (S) Lt Col Bondzeleske, *After Action Report*, 18 Mar 1991; (S/NF/WN) see also Capt Hedger, *Point Paper on BDA Imagery Exploitation*, 21 Sep 1990; and see also, (S) DX BDA CON OPS, 11 Sep 1990–the latter two are filed in CHST 51-12; see also (S) *Checkmate BDA Team – Daily Tasks (As of 26 Jan 1991)*, from Lt Col Howey, Deputy, Checkmate BDA Team; see also (S) DIA's "Bomb Damage Assessment (BDA) Process" briefing [CHST 51-10].

[86](S) *Ibid.*

[87]See (S) Chapter 6; Volume V, *Plans and Strategy*.

[88](S/NF/WN) See footnote 85.

analyst, while weapon system experts and planners were on call for more in-depth consultation.[89]

The DIA-Directed BDA Process in Washington

[DELETED][90]

[DELETED]

[DELETED][91]

In DIA's view, bomb damage assessment support to Central Command provided timely assessments of attack results on selected strategic targets which facilitated in-theater retargeting and restrike decisions. In addition, DIA was able to answer basic questions about strike results such as whether the target was hit or what functional or structural damage was achieved.[92]

The Split Between GAT Planners (Black Hole) and CENTAF/IN

The antipathy between Brigadier General Glosson and his GAT planners, on the one hand, and the intelligence analysts assigned to CENTAF on the other could not have been more unfortunate, especially given the overabundance of data flowing to the theater from Washington. It merits attention in this volume because it shows how the best intentions of qualified, motivated personnel can be overcome by organizational arrangements which, at first, appear to be benign.

As noted earlier, General Glosson viewed the theater force-level (TACC) intelligence organization as unresponsive to his and his planners'

---

[89](S/NF/WN) *Ibid.*

[90](S/NF/WN) See footnote 85.

[91](S/NF/WN) *Ibid.*

[92](S/NF/WN) See footnote 85.

needs.⁹³ The intelligence personnel, by contrast, did not know during Desert Shield that Glosson and his staff would plan the actual air war, and they apparently found the Black Hole's requests for information both a surprise and a burden. In an understandable reaction, Glosson created his own intelligence network using personal contacts in Washington, D.C., and selected individuals on the CENTAF staff who willingly kept him informed on BDA issues.⁹⁴ The Task Force could not identify all the individuals in this network, but the network did exist, and Glosson apparently felt that he had no choice but to organize and then use it.

However, many CENTAF intelligence personnel resisted supporting General Glosson even after he and his staff emerged from their "Black Hole" and became the Guidance, Apportionment, and Targeting cell. Once Desert Storm commenced, most of the force-level analysts remained in their special SCIF (facility for compartmented information). Hence there were two "camps"–the GAT and the force-level analysts, each in its own special, secure area, and each suspicious of the other. One consequence of this mutual suspicion was that CENTAF/IN officers did not begin filling information requests until Black Hole leaders invited more targeting officers into the planning process.⁹⁵ Even then, intelligence support

---

⁹³See (S) Chapters 6 and 7; also (S) Intvw, Lt Col Frank D. Kistler, Mark D. Mandeles, Maj Sanford S. Terry with Capt John Glock, ACC/INT, Langley AFB, VA, 30 Jan 1992. During the August 1990 period, Glock admitted, "we really weren't in any way responsive to them (Black Hole), in fact, at one point, [Lt] Col [David A.] Deptula was asking for a chart or trying to do something, and I told him we don't work for you."

⁹⁴As (S) discussed in Chapters 6 and 7; see also (S/NF/WN) BDA Tapes, Black Hole Working Materials folder from Riyadh [NA-317]; Memo, Lt Cdr Muir (Special Navy briefer attached to CENTAF/IN) to Brig Gen Buster C. Glosson, Commander 14th AD(P), 20 Feb 1991. Memo states ready access to RF-4 BDA photography of bridges, direct discussion with DIA concerning bridges, and "I will task national systems through the collection management process."

⁹⁵In their after action report, the targeting cell complained bitterly about their credibility with the planning staff and the fact there were direct feeds to Brig Gen Glosson with no info copies to them. They went so far as to admit that the planning staff gave little consideration to their "limited ability to support rapidly changing target lists." They also identified the fact that senior intelligence targets people never attended meetings to discuss target selection until one of them had been assigned to work airfields 14 days into the war. (S) AAR, USCENTAF/IN After Action Report and Lessons Learned, 25 Mar 1991, from Col [no first name] Rauschkolb to Col [Christopher L.] Christon

to the planners may have been grudging.⁹⁶ Another consequence was that GAT planners did not ask for BDA in the right way. For example, their daily guidance letters repeated the same requests over and over, when in fact the force-level intelligence analysts needed to know what the planners' priority was for BDA.

BDA analysts work best when information about targets (which installation and which aimpoint, for example) and weapons is included in the Air Tasking Order and its subsequent changed versions. Unfortunately, force-level BDA analysts received only pieces of the ATO, and subsequent changes were often not provided.⁹⁷ The many changes made by the GAT over secure phone lines to the wings were also not sent to analysts in the combat assessment cell. Because there was only (at best) a loose infor-

---

(CENTAF/IN), INT Attachment.

⁹⁶For example, targeteers pointed out that GAT planners requested imagery through CENTAF/IN. However, the planners were told no imagery was available. Later, planners discovered that the imagery had never been ordered. Intelligence collection efforts began on future attack plans around Day 16 of the war–after intelligence officer augmentees were assigned to the airfield attack team. (S) USCENTAF/IN After Action Report and Lessons Learned, 25 Mar 91, from Col Rauschkolb to Col Christon, INT Attachment.

⁹⁷*DCS/Intelligence Operation Desert Shield/Storm, Executive Edition*, pp 24, 25, 27.

The CJCS requested any tactical BDA results to "enhance total campaign assessment." In addition, the message stated: "To facilitate complete, efficient planning and solve demands for information contained in the ATO, request confirmation of the Strategic Target List by category, and submission of critical BDA facts by target and electronic transmission of the ATO via AUTODIN message system." (S) CJCS Msg 190447Z Jan 1991, subj: Transmitting Air Tasking Order (ATO).

After the first week of combat, staff in theater and Washington complained about incomplete BDA information. A JCS message stated, in part, that " . . . despite the absence of key target information" identifying critical items needed as "designated weapons, desired damage, DMPI, etc" the system providing BDA and status of targets is working. Except for the first day of combat "information necessary to conduct BDA has been limited." All Washington agencies, including Joint Staff and DIA "separately and in concern," have "addressed the need for the information to all levels of CENTCOM and CENTAF repeatedly since last October." A FLASH message has produced limited response in the form of a partial target data base. The only other data received are from a partial ATO faxed 3-4 hours prior to execution. "Of the information needed for BDA, that partial ATO contains only type of aircraft, time over target, and target name, BE, or coordinate." (S) CJCS/J2J Msg, 242256Z Jan 1991 (subj is unknown).

mation link between force-level planners and BDA analysts, planning decisions were made on the basis of incomplete and imperfect information.

The effect of this lack of adequate information on operations can be seen in the employment of B-52s. Table 15 shows the B-52 munitions expended against ground targets during the war.[98] It was nearly half the total tonnage.

Table 15

Total Air Force Munitions Expenditure versus B-52 Munitions Expenditure
(in tons)

Total USAF*	Total B-52**	Percentage B-52/Total Air Force
55,856	25,635	46%

* Munitions included are: Mk-20, CBU-89, CBU-52/58/71, CBU-87, GBU-10/I-2000, GBU-12, GBU-15, GBU-24/I-2000, GBU-27, GBU-28, Mk-84, Mk-82, M-117, UK 1000, and CALCM.

** Munitions included are: CBU-52/58/71, CBU-87, CBU-89, M-117, Mk-82, UK 1000, and CALCM.

Strategic Air Command imagery interpreters in Omaha were familiar with the fixed installation targets assigned to the B-52s, but they did not have access to the complete Air Tasking Order every day or to a comprehensive strike history (none was kept). Consequently, they were not alerted ahead of time to strikes by other aircraft on the installations

---

[98]Data derived from DOD, *Conduct of the Persian Gulf War* (Washington, DC, Apr 1992) and GWAPS Missions Database.

covered by the B-52s, and they did not receive changes to the B-52 portion of the ATO because the changes were passed directly to units in Diego Garcia, Spain and the United Kingdom via telephone. Other changes were radioed directly to the aircraft enroute to the target by Strategic Air Command Advance Liaison personnel. This mattered because approximately forty percent of B-52 missions experienced basic target changes.[99] The fact that the B-52 imagery interpreters did not know precisely what their bombers had struck and whether other aircraft had attacked the same targets made it difficult to draw sound inferences of when damage was inflicted and by what aircraft.[100]

Yet a third negative consequence of the separation between the GAT and CENTAF/IN was that the GAT planners did not understand that their operator-designed target numbering system confused and frustrated the force-level intelligence analysts supporting the Tactical Air Control Center.[101] When the GAT planners used their own target numbering system to identify targets for the units, they made it very difficult for the force-level intelligence analysts to track the air campaign by referring to a master list of targets. Moreover, because GAT planners relied on their own numbering system, unit targeting officers were forced to contact CENTAF targets for information. The latter, in turn, took matters up with GAT planners, who often wondered why targeting officers could not keep

---

[99] Background Paper, Maj Lewis Hill, USAF, GWAPS, "BDA, Reporting, Targeting, and the Database," draft, Sep 1992.

[100] General Accounting Office analysts argued after the war that SAC imagery analysts could not tell B-52 mission planners whether the bombers were dropping their bombs in an inaccurate but consistent way (and hence in a way that could be corrected). According to the GAO analysts, there was a systematic error, and it was not corrected until the last days of the war. If true, this claim would have an important implication: that only about twenty percent of the unguided bombs dropped by the B-52s (or ten percent of all Air Force munitions expended) were aimed accurately. See "Operation Desert Storm: Limits on the Role and Performance of B-52 Bombers in Conventional Conflicts," General Accounting Office, draft (Washington, DC, nd), pp 3, 57.

[101] Lt Col Deptula claimed that he invented the Black Hole's target numbering system. (S) Intvw, GWAPS with Lt Col Deptula, SAF/OSX, 20 Dec 1991.

track of the air campaign.[102] A forced collocation of Operations and Intelligence might have set it right.

The direct "feeds" of information from Washington to the GAT also blocked the efforts of force-level intelligence analysts to provide useful inputs to the planning process. Text, STU-III secure voice transmissions, and information gathered by the National Military Intelligence Support Terminals network (even though it was located in the SCIF) were not provided as information copies to CENTAF intelligence. The direct communication between General Glosson and RAdm. McConnell, which the force-level intelligence analysts were not party to, worsened the situation for two reasons. First, it encouraged Glosson to talk directly to Washington as often as he could. Second, it stifled the ability of the intelligence analysts attached to the Tactical Air Control Center to produce BDA. What they did produce appeared less than adequate when Glosson compared it to what he was getting from Washington. As a result, targets chosen by GAT personnel "often did not meet CINCCENT objectives [and] had inappropriate aim points. . . . "[103]

Consequences for Pilots and Aircrew

Theater- and national-level intelligence support during Desert Shield and Desert Storm often failed to meet pilots' expectations.[104] Target

---

[102](S) USCENTAF/IN After Action Report and Lessons Learned, from Col Rauschkolb to Col Christon, INT Attachment, p 3-8.

[103](S) JULLS Long Report submitted by Capt M. Menke - CCJ2-SG, JULLS Number: 50641-13128 (00066), p 119 (U). " . . . [T]his unofficial operator/agency targeting process produced targets that: (a) often did not meet CINCCENT objectives; (b) had inappropriate aim points selected; and (c) by-passed the target material production, weaponeering, and precise coordinate mensuration processes. The requisite check against the no-fire target list was also bypassed." He goes on to say that because of this nonstandard ATO construction procedure the CINCCENT's targeting objectives weren't met, which resulted in restriking targets unnecessarily.

[104]As the Center for Naval Analyses (S) *Desert Storm Reconstruction Report Vol. II: Strike Warfare* observed, "Initial BDA information was so poor that fraggers were unable to track whether ATO-scheduled targets had in fact been struck or whether the strike had been diverted . . . or canceled altogether. . . . " See p 3-19, (S) CNA CRM 91-178, Oct 1991. The point is that the lack of timely, adequate BDA had an effect which cascaded through the whole mission planning process, from the TACC to both Air Force

materials were distributed unevenly, and there were no qualified targeting officers in some units.[105] There appeared to be several reasons for these problems. First, the different levels of theater command and control had different BDA needs. CENTCOM's needs, for example, were different from those of the GAT planners in the Tactical Air Control Center, yet the same basic in-theater processing system tried to support both. Second, the center itself was not designed to support the units. That role was given to Central Command Air Forces/Intelligence. But CENTAF/IN was not working hand-in-glove with the GAT planners, so many Air Force units, responding to the Air Tasking Order, were not receiving the BDA support they needed (or thought they needed). Finally, GAT planners had not participated in the operations planning for Desert Shield, yet that planning is what guided the use of the many imagery generating systems (such as the U.S. Marine Corps unmanned aerial reconnaissance vehicles) available to coalition forces.

Pilots and aircrew may have believed that force-level intelligence officers were unaware of their requirements and unable to ensure that sufficient amounts of targeting materials would be available to conduct unit missions.[106] The apparent result of this absence of critical information was a number of unnecessary reattacks. Despite a huge effort to produce and then distribute imagery and other aids to targeting, pilots and aircrew criticized national-, theater-, and force-level intelligence support (from premission target photos to postmission BDA) throughout Desert Storm.[107]

Differences Between Plans and Reality: The Consequences

Organizational: The Proliferation of Targeting Cells

In mid-December 1990, as the bulk of CENTCOM planning shifted from defensive to offensive actions, CENTAF's duplicative planning cells

---

and Navy wings.

[105]Maj Hill, "BDA, Reporting, Targeting, and the Database."

[106](S) USAF Tactical Fighter Weapons Center, *Tactical Analysis Bulletin*, Volume 91-2, Jul 1991, pp 7-8.

[107](S) *Ibid*, p 3-10.

295

for defensive and offensive operations were merged.[108] CENTAF became responsible for battle damage assessment of strategic targets in Iraq and of interdiction targets along the lines of communication from Iraq to Kuwait. Central Command's Army Component was responsible for assessing damage to Iraqi ground forces in Kuwait, and its staff produced lists of ground targets in the Kuwaiti theater of operations.[109] By this time, CENTAF had three targeting/BDA support cells in operation.

One targeting/BDA cell was in the Tactical Air Control Center, located in the Royal Saudi Air Force Headquarters. CENTAF targeteers in this cell supported the TACC combat operations staff by receiving and keeping track of Mission Reports and information transmitted over the phone concerning recent strikes.[110] The second CENTAF BDA cell operated in a SCIF on the U.S. Military Training Mission soccer field adjoining the Saudi Air Force Headquarters compound.[111] This combat assessment cell received all transmitted intelligence reports, made target recommendations, and produced an Air Combat Assessment Summary. The Summary was the "fused" report of the evidence (including bomb damage assessments) of the results of the air campaign to date. It was distributed both to the wings and to the Joint Force Air Component Commander. CENTAF Intelligence officers had designed the combat assessment cell to be the center of BDA activities.[112] The third CENTAF cell was created by GAT planners, who established their own BDA process when they did not get the information they wanted from the Tactical Air Control Center or combat assessment cell analysts.[113]

---

[108] See (S) Chapter 6.

[109] [DELETED]

[110] (S) AAR, USCENTAF/IN After Action Report and Lessons Learned. See also Chapter 6.

[111] (S) AAR, USCENTAF/IN After Action Report and Lessons Learned.

[112] Maj Hill, "BDA, Reporting, Targeting, and the Database."

[113] Analysts with the Center for Naval Analyses argued in (S) *Desert Storm Reconstruction Report, Vol. II: Strike Warfare* that there were too many BDA databases being analyzed in too many places at the same time. One consequence was that "intelligence support to the Navy officers assigned to help select and schedule targets was an *ad hoc* affair." See p 3-2 of (S) CNA CRM 91-178, Oct 1991.

Methodological: Videotapes as a BDA Tool

During Desert Storm, GAT planners could get videotapes (AVTR) from F-117, F-111F, and F-15E units (sometimes as quickly as four hours) before any other imagery was available.[114] As Col. Anthony J. Tolin noted, this AVTR information permitted planners to send a "sortie on to some other bridge" instead of wasting a sortie on that same bridge."[115] But AVTR film was not a panacea for planners. Electro-optical imagery systems mounted on the aircraft delivering munitions were often blanked out by the flash of their weapons. In addition, poor weather sometimes blocked or obscured targets from aircraft videotape equipment. Finally, A-10 and F-16 AVTRs tape the HUD, or heads-up display, that is projected on the pilot's winsdscreen. In these cases, the weapon release but not weapon impact is recorded. Other aircraft, such as the B-52, do not have an AVTR. In cases such as these, planners had to decide whether to order a second strike right away or wait for a fuller intelligence assessment based on data from a variety of sources, including satellites.

The Relationship Between Organization and Information

At the force level, the CENTAF BDA plan was scrapped at the last minute for two reasons. First, the computer system for matching BDA with the Air Tasking Order–described earlier in this chapter–never became fully operational. Second, CENTAF/IN did not have enough trained personnel to do BDA.[116] This would not have been a problem if the computer-based system had worked, but it did not, leaving a pile of work in the hands of a few individuals.

CENTAF/IN bomb damage assessors realized forty-five minutes after H-hour that there were serious problems with the BDA software they were trying to use. To compensate, they consolidated the three BDA workstations into one. They also rewrote the system's data entry programs so

---

[114](S) Intvw, Maj Robert J. Heston, 16 and 19 Oct 1992. See also Maj Hill "BDA, Reporting, Targeting, and the Database."

[115](S) Intvw, John F. Guilmartin, Jr. with Brig Gen Anthony J. Tolin, Commander 57th Fighter Wing, 30 Jan 1992.

[116]SSgt Sherwood, Trip Report - Operation Desert Shield/Storm.

that all the information needed could be handled at this one station. The USCENTAF BDA Cell released an Air Combat Assessment Summary from this location every twelve hours. An additional report, released every three to four hours, provided interim BDA information. These interim reports were disseminated by hand throughout USCENTAF.[117]

This minimally capable BDA process required two people per shift to correlate manually 1,500 messages a day, or more than one per minute. BDA information gleaned from these messages was then typed into the BDA program. One week into the war, targets personnel began producing strike history files and consolidating the twelve-hour summaries into one product. About this time, operators of this one BDA terminal became aware of DIA's second- and third-stage BDA analyses arriving in theater.[118]

The apparent inability of BDA analysts to catch up to operations once the air campaign began led GAT personnel to make their own damage assessments. However, as CENTAF Director of Combat Intelligence, Col. Jeffery Hage, noted, GAT officers had little Tactical Air Control Center experience. This relative lack of experience led GAT officers to misuse theater intelligence assets available for validating targets.[119] Two examples illustrate the problem. First, an inadequate understanding of weapons effects by one GAT planner (with a primary air-to-air background) caused him to set laser-guided I-2000 penetrator bombs (with delayed fuzes) against bridge spans.[120] Unfortunately, these weapons caused only minor damage because they punched through the decks of the bridges and exploded harmlessly beneath them.[121] The resulting unsuccessful strikes were wasted sorties; reattacks brought unnecessary risk to aircrews.

---

[117] *Ibid.*

[118] *Ibid.*

[119] See also (S) Chapters 6 and 7; (S) USCENTAF/IN After Action Report and Lessons Learned; (S) After Action Report by Col Jeffrey M. Hage, CENTAF Director of Combat Intelligence.

[120] A targeteer, using the Joint Munitions Effectiveness Manual (JMEM), can give the mission planner a choice of aircraft and weapons optimized for the target.

[121] (S/NF/WN) *Tactical Analysis Bulletin*, Volume 91-2, Jul 1991, pp 7-6, 7-11, 7-12.

The second example concerns assignment of the desired mean points of impact, or DMPIs.[122] The GAT planners made a conscious decision to permit some wings (for example, the 37th TFW) to select DMPIs for their assigned targets. This decision made good use of the targeting and BDA expertise in the F-117 wing, but in some other wings there was a substantial lack of expertise to perform this task. Permitting wings to assign DMPIs further complicated the national- and force-level BDA analysts' efforts to assess damage because they did not know the DMPIs chosen by wing officers. In addition, no wing-level organization possessed a complete database of enemy installations. For instance, no wing-level targeteer possessed details on the internal construction of Iraqi hardened underground facilities. This situation apparently forced many wing targeteers to contact the CENTAF targeting cell for information.[123]

It often took several days to get BDA from the Joint Imagery Production Center.[124] This delay contributed to inadequate force-level BDA analysis and led Central Command to order unnecessary restrikes.[125] The delay in getting information from the JIPC was partly due to an oversight in prewar planning; it was not intended to be involved in the BDA process. By the second day of the air war, however, BDA imagery production accounted for almost half of the laboratory's select print effort. Normally, the JIPC would send such developed imagery to the units assigned bombing missions in the Air Tasking Order, but the fact that it often took a relatively long time for the GAT to complete daily Master Attack Plans meant that the JIPC often did not know in time which wings were to get the imagery available. The scope of the air campaign against

---

[122] The desired mean point of impact (DMPI) is the intended point which the bomb or munition should hit. Setting the DMPI is especially important for hardened targets, where the targeteer wants the explosive to go through armor or concrete before detonation. Setting the DMPI properly is equally important where the target is soft or spread out. A high explosive can shatter an antenna, but it needs to be placed where the blast pressure from its detonation is the greatest. Hence the need to train specialists in the methods of determining proper DMPIs.

[123] (S) Intvw, Maj Heston, 19 Oct 1992.

[124] Lt Col F. L. Talbot, USAF, *CENTAF Intelligence Targets Division After War Report*, 18 Mar 1991, p 20; see also (S/NF) Defense Science Board, *Lessons Learned During Operations Desert Shield and Desert Storm*, Draft, Jun 1992.

[125] (S) USCENTAF/IN After Action Report and Lessons Learned, INT Attachment.

Iraq just compounded this problem. Delays in getting the proper and needed BDA to the wings just added to the task of covering all the important targets with the necessary quantity and type of ordnance. BDA problems made it harder to put together an Air Tasking Order that reflected the Commander in Chief's guidance, and lapses in the ATO just made accurate BDA that much harder to achieve. It was a vicious circle.

The Central Command Air Forces/Intelligence after action report asked and answered the key question: "Were we organized right to go to war? The answer is a resounding no!"[126] The CENTAF/IN's most critical failure was its inability to provide bomb damage assessment for the Guidance, Apportionment, and Targeting cell.[127] The CENTAF after action report concluded that probably the major reason for that failure was the physical separation of Intelligence from the GAT in its special access space, as well as security barriers to entry into the intelligence SCI Facilities.[128]

CENTAF intelligence also failed to fuse aircrew Mission Reports.[129] At the unit level, debriefing and Mission Report preparation proved to be the biggest time consumer, second only to target database management and threat updates.[130] However, at the CENTAF level, strike results provided in Mission Reports were not considered credible without national or tactical reconnaissance. Moreover, most of the Mission Reports were never passed from the theater to agencies such as the CIA and DIA. The ingrained flexibility within tactical combat units was the key to surmounting this underutilization. Units used secure telephones as work-arounds to share the necessary information to accomplish mission planning.[131]

BDA analysts themselves misinterpreted precision-guided munitions weapon effects and, consequently, mission success. In World War II,

---

[126](S) USCENTAF/IN After Action Report and Lessons Learned, with 17 Attachments.

[127](S) *Ibid.* See also (S) Chapters 6 & 7.

[128](S) USCENTAF/IN After Action Report and Lessons Learned.

[129](S/NF/WN) *Tactical Analysis Bulletin*, Volume 91-2, Jul 91, p 11-8.

[130](S/NF/WN) *Ibid*, pp 7-8, 7-9.

[131](S) Intvw, Maj Heston, 16 and 19 Oct 1992.

shortfalls in the photographic evidence of BDA were of little importance. The unguided weapons dropped on targets typically resulted in widespread damage in and around the desired aimpoints. Strategic targets, such as factories or railyards, were either heavily damaged or partially damaged, or even missed altogether, and photographic interpreters were able to distinguish among levels of damage because of the homogenous nature of the explosives, the aiming methods, and the reliance on cumulative effect to assess destruction.

However, precision weapons permit functional targeting, in which destruction of one node accomplishes the mission with no mass destruction. In an attack with precision munitions on a hardened shelter, for example, unless the contents of the shelter explode violently, a post-attack photograph would show only a small entry hole. There might be little evidence of damage inside the shelter. Classic photo-interpretation would describe the target as slightly damaged. However, AVTR tape, capturing the impact of the weapon, might show the weapon exploding (and modern weapons generally do)[132] and any secondary explosion venting out doors and ventilators. Unfortunately, most BDA photos, and many AVTR tapes, simply do not capture entry holes or indications of secondary explosions.[133] BDA methodology has been evolving as both weapons and reconnaissance technologies have evolved. Unfortunately, most of the Tactical Air Control Center's personnel involved in damage assessment were not current in this evolving technology.

Use of national asset capabilities enables the definition of more precise target sets and thus allows greater compliance with national policy and the laws of armed conflict. However, CENTAF could not adequately implement these requirements during an air campaign conducted at so rapid a pace because the Tactical Air Control Center lacked automated access to the requisite information. Targeteers in the theater were more dependent on

---

[132] Approximately fifteen to twenty percent of bombs dropped during WW II did not explode. And this figure is not unusual–even for unguided weapons manufactured quite recently.

[133] The aspect of angle of BDA photos can be crucial. Photos taken from straight overhead may miss a bomb hole caused by a weapon with a shallow-angle flight path. Similarly, if the photo is taken from the side of the target, an entrance hole on the far side will be invisible to the interpreter.

national systems because Central Command did not have at its disposal a variety of tactical reconnaissance systems. Yet targeteers in the theater found their access to national systems blocked or impeded. In addition, some intelligence information collected by national assets was either not sent to the theater or not released below the general officer level.[134]

Despite these organizational obstacles, many wings were able to get the information they needed by communicating directly with other units. During Desert Storm, many squadrons were sent to bomb airfields and told to choose their own mean points of impact. After the first two nights it became necessary for the 4th Tactical Fighter Wing(P), 37th TFW(P), and 48th TFW(P) to maintain duplicate photos and maps reflecting the DMPIs each had struck or would strike.[135] Without this type of management, pilots discovered–after their weapons had been released–that the desired mean point of impact they were to attack had been hit earlier. For the wings, preventing unnecessary target restrikes required numerous hours on the telephone and continuous coordination.

The units literally were swamped by the growth in the threat database. It grew beyond their ability (in terms of time and manpower) to manage because there was not enough tactical or national BDA imagery to confirm many kills and so remove enemy targets from the active list. What the wings needed from the Tactical Air Control Center was a continually updated list of targets based upon comprehensive combat assessment. When they did not get it, units demanded copies of each other's Mission Reports. They tried to validate their databases based on actual threat emissions picked up by aircraft radar warning receivers and often not displayed by Constant Source. Wing mission planners and intelligence officers used this technique to get a better, although not totally comfortable, feeling as to what threats were active in a particular target area on a given day.

Tactical Air Control Center and wing personnel managed to put together a BDA process that "worked," but it did not work the way it was

---

[134]*Tactical Air Force Intelligence Desert Storm Lessons Learned Conference, Final Report,* Jan 1992, p 49.

[135](S) Intvw, Maj Heston, 19 Oct 1992.

supposed to. GAT planners and their counterparts in the wings had to perform extraordinary feats of informal coordination each night.¹³⁶ But it was not enough to satisfy users. Consider the testimony of General Schwarzkopf to the investigations subcommittee of the House Armed Services Committee, cited at the beginning of this chapter. After listening to that testimony and weighing the available evidence, the subcommittee noted that

> BDA is now neither art nor science. The operations and intelligence communities will undoubtedly bicker for years over *post factum* calculations. The arguments will be useful if they help these two communities devise a doctrine for tactical BDA so that commanders in the future can be better served.¹³⁷

Summary and Review

The national intelligence community appeared unfamiliar with or unresponsive to the intelligence needs of the warfighting commanders.¹³⁸ There also were substantial shortfalls in the management, fusion, and application of tactical intelligence. [DELETED] When that information was not forthcoming ("CENTAF was perhaps the worst offender in this regard."¹³⁹), lower level units created their own informal networks to get whatever current information they could. Higher level staffs were often not informed of this, which meant that, at times, higher level staffs (such as CENTAF) and unit staffs did not share the same sense of how the air campaign was going.

---

¹³⁶They were not alone. A similar problem afflicted personnel in Proven Force. As two members of the latter pointed out, "one could more easily detect 'battle damage' inflicted upon beleaguered BDA analysts by frustrated senior staff than the genuine destruction visited upon the Iraqi enemy by coalition airpower." Maj J. M. England and MSgt M. G. Rolirad, both of ECJ2-T, HQ USEUCOM, "Battle Damage Data Base to the Rescue (Almost)," in *Target Director's Update*, Edition No. 15 (Aug 1991), p 11.

¹³⁷(S) Committee on Armed Services, Report on *Intelligence Successes and Failures in Operation Desert Shield/Storm*.

¹³⁸(S) *Ibid.*

¹³⁹(S) *Ibid.*

The real source of this problem was a lack of prewar training at headquarters and between headquarter staffs and the units. CENTAF intelligence staff, for example, had not trained to support an air campaign with such a high sortie rate. They also were not prepared to assess the effects of the strikes of so many different kinds of offensive air units. CENTAF intelligence staff had trained to support the Ninth Air Force, not the multi-Service, multinational air armada which was eventually pulled together under Lieutenant General Horner's leadership. Because the command and control (including computer hardware and software) of tactical air forces was different in each theater, it was not possible for assessment personnel from other theaters to jump right in and augment CENTAF BDA specialists. The supply of the right kinds of BDA simply could not keep up with the demand.[140] There were not enough trained specialists who had worked together, and the automated systems they used were not tied together effectively.

---

[140] MAJCOM Commanders' "Hot Wash," Maxwell AFB, 12-13 Jul 1991, 9th AF briefing slide 5, Section 19.

9

The Airborne TACS at War

The airborne portion of the Tactical Air Control System consisted of AWACS, JSTARS, ABCCC, RIVET JOINT aircraft, and forward air controllers. This chapter will focus primarily on the use of AWACS, ABCCC, and JSTARS as command, control, communications and coordination systems.

[DELETE] During Desert Shield and Desert Storm, RIVET JOINT aircraft were controlled by the Strategic Air Command, and the ways in which they work are classified at a level above that which the Task Force wished to use in this study. Thus, we will state here only that RIVET JOINT provided real-time intelligence coverage.

AWACS, Airborne Command, Control, and Communications (ABCCC), and the Joint Surveillance and Target Attack Radar System (JSTARS) were employed to bring order to the confusion and chaos of the pace of action during Desert Storm. Just how these systems and their crews did that will be the subject of the sections which follow.

AWACS

By the beginning of Desert Storm, the 552d Airborne Warning and Control Wing had eleven AWACS aircraft and nineteen crews in Saudi Arabia, three aircraft and five crews at Incirlik, Turkey, and two other aircraft with their crews as a reserve at Mildenhall, England.[1] On the night of 16 January 1991, U.S. and Saudi AWACS aircraft followed first-strike coalition aircraft to patrol orbits near the border with Iraq. Figure 37 illustrates the four U.S. and one Saudi orbit.[2] The airborne U.S.

---

[1] (S) Briefing, Capt Ted Robertson, USAF, 552d ACW/DOW, subj: "AWACS Involvement in Combat Airspace Management During Desert Storm," Jun 1991. (U) There also was another AWACS plane and crew in reserve at Tinker AFB, Oklahoma.

[2] (S) Briefing, Capt Robertson, "AWACS Involvement in Combat Airspace Management During Desert Storm."

spare covered the other three AWACS when any one of them left station (for example, for refueling or maintenance). The Saudi AWACS was the final air defense shield and was positioned in an orbit over Riyadh. It also maintained communications with the Tactical Air Control Center (TACC) at Central Command Air Forces (CENTAF).[3] [DELETED][4] The three U.S. Air Force and NATO AWACS based at Incirlik allowed a single aircraft to be on station around the clock to watch Turkish airspace.

Figure 37
U.S. and Saudi AWACS Orbits Near the Border with Iraq

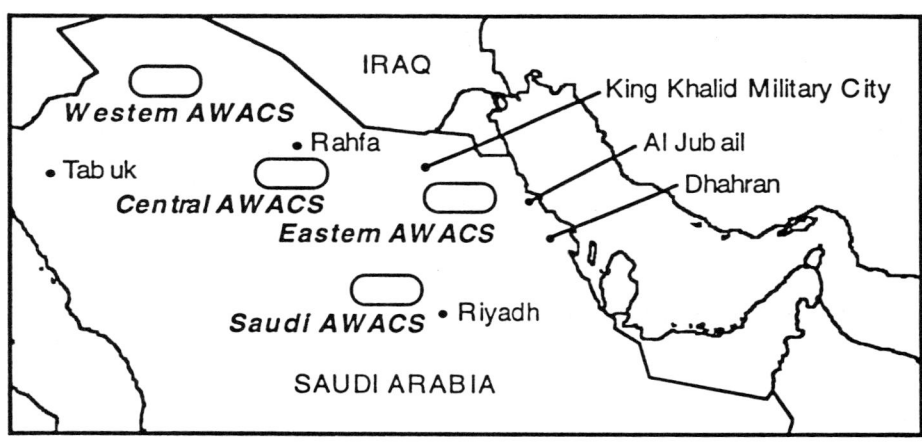

The Air Tasking Order (ATO), the key air mission control document for the combat wings, was also the basis for the effectiveness of AWACS. An AWACS Tactics Planning Cell in the TACC represented the AWACS Wing, and its members helped develop the Air Tasking Order. If the 552d's Mission Planning Team at Riyadh found any problems with the

---

[3](S) Memo, Capt Guy Cafiero, USAF, 552d ACW to Task Force 4, GWAPS, subj: E-3 Employment Desert Storm, 1992. (U) Note: the Royal Saudi Air Force had five E-3A AWACS aircraft.

[4](S/NF) Multi-Command Manual (MCM) 3-1, Volume XV, *Tactical Employment, AWACS*, 1 Mar 1992.

daily ATO (such as a conflict in radio frequencies assigned two different flights of aircraft), they called their colleagues in the Tactics Planning Cell in the Tactical Air Control Center. If there were no conflicts, the Mission Planning Team would use the Computer Assisted Force Management System (CAFMS) to obtain from the Air Tasking Order the information that the AWACS crews needed to predict the arrival of friendly aircraft in their patrol zones.[5] Boeing Military Aircraft Company personnel aided the Mission Planning Team in compiling and printing the time-line charts and combat air patrol summary sheets given to the AWACS crews during their preflight briefings.[6]

[DELETED][7] [DELETED][8]

[DELETED][9]

The three forward AWACS aircraft performed several important functions. First, they stood watch to alert combat air patrol fighters if Iraqi aircraft approached the Saudi border. Second, the AWACS monitored coalition strike flights as they moved from friendly to hostile airspace and re-

---

[5](S) Memo, Capt Cafiero, GWAPS, E-3 Employment Desert Storm, 1992. (U) The memo includes copies of some of the strike package work sheets prepared for the AWACS crews.

[6](S) Memo, Capt Guy Cafiero, USAF, 552d ACW to Task Force 4, GWAPS, subj: Air Tasking Order Execution, 1992. (U) The strike package time-line charts, read from left to right, showed which flights of which aircraft would enter the radar coverage of all three AWACS forward zones, and–most importantly–when. Using such charts, AWACS controllers could anticipate the arrival and departure of friendly aircraft in their areas. The time-line charts were supplemented by illustrations of CENTAF air refueling tracks and of strikes against enemy targets. The CAP summary sheets contained data on radio callsigns and mission times and tracks for combat air patrol fighters (USAF, Saudi, Canadian, USN, and RAF).

[7](S) Memo, Capt Guy Cafiero, USAF, 552d ACW to Task Force 4, GWAPS, subj: Concept of Operations [during Desert Storm], Launch/Recovery of E-3, MCC/AC G Crew, 1992.

[8](S) Memo, Capt Guy Cafiero, USAF, 552d ACW to Task Force 4, GWAPS, subj: Typical Sortie, 1992. [DELETED]

[9](S) Memo, Capt Guy Cafiero, USAF, 552d ACW to Task Force 4, GWAPS, subj: E-3 Radar Detection, 1992.

turned. Third, the E-3s kept track of so-called "high value assets," such as electronic warfare planes. Finally, AWACS crews assisted search and rescue efforts and special operations forces. The AWACS mission was always to counter enemy attacks while simultaneously preventing fratricide.[10]

Soon after the beginning of Desert Storm, AWACS was also assigned the mission of monitoring aerial refuelings. In November, Central Command Air Forces had laid out a complex pattern of aerial refueling orbits for use by aircraft on missions against Iraqi targets.[11] The primary means of controlling the refueling process was a schedule and a series of tanker orbits at different altitudes. In effect, tanker tracks were stacked at 1,000-foot intervals like the layers of a cake. This procedural solution (used effectively during Southeast Asia air operations in the late 1960s and early 1970s) to the problem of mating tankers with refueling aircraft worked well the first two days of the air war.

Then, bad weather forced aircraft seeking tankers to climb for better visibility. In addition, the amount of time needed to translate the target planning worksheets into the Air Tasking Order kept many units from receiving the ATO until late in their mission planning cycles, so aircraft needing fuel were often not sure precisely where they would find their assigned tankers.[12] The resulting confusion left senior Tactical Air Control Center officers with no choice but to have AWACS air controllers coordinate aerial refueling, though they were not "responsible for routing [civilian and airlift] . . . air traffic over the Arabian Peninsula during operations."[13]

---

[10](S) Briefing, Capt Robertson, "AWACS Involvement in Combat Airspace Management During Desert Storm."

[11](S) Paper, "Tanker Anchors," Tactics Planning Cell, TACC, CENTAF, Nov 1990, Task Force 4 AWACS File, GWAPS.

[12](S) 28th AD, Desert Shield/Desert Storm Lessons Learned, nd [ca 1992]. See also Chapter 7.

[13](S) Memo, Capt Guy Cafiero, USAF, 552d ACW to Task Force 4, GWAPS, subj: Airspace Management, 1992.

[DELETED]¹⁴ [DELETED]¹⁵

[DELETED]

[DELETED]¹⁶ [DELETED]¹⁷

[DELETED]¹⁸ [DELETED]¹⁹

[DELETED]²⁰ [DELETED]²¹,²²

The need to track and keep in contact with numbers of flights and many different kinds of aircraft kept AWACS crews busy. By the end of January 1991, an AWACS combat airspace management crew normally consisted of one "high value" air asset controller (for example, for control of EC-130H COMPASS CALL electronic jamming aircraft), one tanker controller, two controllers to watch strike packages, one controller each for defensive and offensive counterair, one more to check every aircraft in the E-3's assigned zone of radar coverage, and–finally–a Mission Crew Commander. East and west AWACS E-3s also carried Navy liaison officers.

---

[14](S) Memo, (Col B. R. Witt, USAF, DCS, Comm-Computer Systems) USCENTAF/SC to TACCS/CC and others, subj: Communications Test Results–TACC- AWACS UHF TACSAT, 27 Oct 1990.

[15](S) Ltr, CENTAF/SCOO, subj: GATR Site Procedures for Airborne Users, 21 Jan 1991.

[16]Something like this had been done in Southeast Asia in 1968-69, when the Marine Corps linked Navy and Air Force air surveillance systems.

[17](S) Briefing, Carrier Airborne Early Warning Weapons School (CAEWWS), subj: "Desert Shield/Storm E-2 Lessons Learned, 9 Oct 1991." See the section on "Data Link."

[18](S) *Ibid*. See the section on "E-2/E-3 Operations."

[19](S) 28th AD, Desert Shield/Desert Storm Lessons Learned, nd [ca 1992]. Also, "Desert Shield/Storm E-2 Lessons Learned" 9 Oct 1991, p 3, in Task Force 4 AWACS File.

[20](S) 28th AD, Desert Shield/Desert Storm Lessons Learned, nd [ca 1992], see especially "US Navy/AWACS Operations."

[21](S) SMSgt Vincent C. Presley, *The 28th Air Division/552 Air Control Wing History 1991-92*, draft, Chapter II, pp 26-29.

[22](S) *Ibid*, Chapter II, p 29.

The back-up E-3 carried an Airborne Command Element (of three or four personnel, headed by a senior officer), which coordinated communications among the orbiting E-3s and assumed control of the whole AWACS formation if contact with the Tactical Air Control Center were lost.[23]

Given the scale of the air offensive against Iraq and its forces in Kuwait, AWACS crews were kept very busy.[24] The speed with which coalition forces gained air superiority over Iraq reduced the pressure on AWACS crews to monitor Iraqi airborne threats. However, the Commander in Chief's decision to use coalition airpower to isolate and then pound Iraq's forces in Kuwait meant that "The most concerted airspace management effort was kill box deconfliction."[25]

Beyond the Fire Support Coordination Line, aircraft attacking ground targets were to operate in "kill zones" (later called "kill boxes"). Central Command Air Forces divided the Kuwait theater into 30 by 30 nautical mile squares. Entry of strike aircraft into the airspace of these squares beyond the Fire Support Coordination Line was monitored and controlled by AWACS (and sometimes ABCCC or JSTARS) crews. The attacking aircraft were then handed over to either the ABCCC or JSTARS for actual targeting and control. The success of kill box missions depended on close "coordination between [sic] AWACS, ABCCC, the aircraft involved in targeting, a Marine Direct Air Support Center (DASC) and finally the ground commander."[26] The sheer volume of coalition air action meant that the risk of fratricide was high. In one case, "an F-16 flight was cleared by the ACE [Airborne Command Element] to dump weapons inside the F-15E kill box. The weapons fell between the F-15E's during

---

[23](S/NF) Multi-Command Manual (MCM) 3-1, Vol XV, *Tactical Employment, AWACS*, 1 Mar 1991, pp 3-16 to 3-18. Also (S) Memo, Capt Guy Cafiero, USAF, 552d ACW to Task Force 4, GWAPS, subj: Weapons Director Functions, 1992.

[24](S) Briefing, Capt Robertson, "AWACS Involvement in Combat Airspace Management During Desert Storm." (U) Capt Robertson also noted that each AWACS tanker controller managed, on average, "15 tankers at any given time." (P 5 of text accompanying slides.)

[25](S) Briefing, Capt Robertson, "AWACS Involvement in Combat Airspace Management During Desert Storm," p 8.

[26](S) *Ibid.*

The long-range air search radar in the AWACS could operate on six frequencies.

their attack run."[27] As a result, the TACC Director of Combat Operations informed all AWACS Airborne Command Elements, all ABCCC aircraft, and both JSTARS planes that "No controlling agency will direct non-scheduled flights into an active kill box . . . without Tactical Air Control Center/ Display Console Operator (Grouch) approval."[28] In this case, "Grouch" was aptly named. Kill box deconfliction will be dealt with more in the next section of this chapter, which covers the Airborne Battlefield Command, Control and Communications system.

[DELETED][29] [DELETED][30]

The AWACS story during Desert Shield/Desert Storm was not without flaws. Minor problems arose that, while not seriously hampering operations, tended to cause friction within the command and control system.

---

[27]Ltr, Col Michael F. Reavey, Director Combat Operations (Night), CENTAF to: ACE/ABCCC/JSTARS, subj: Control of Kill Box Airspace, 20 Feb 1991.

[28]*Ibid.*

[29](S) Ltr, Lt Gen Charles A. Horner, Commander to ACE Directors, subj: Tactical Operation Notes, nd [ca Jan 1991].

[30](S) Memo, To US AWACS, subj: Link Fact Sheet-Turkey AWACS, 4 Feb 1991.

Confusion over the role of the Airborne Command Element[31] and training of Element personnel onboard the AWACS, nonstandard fighter check in procedures, misunderstanding of who controlled what in the kill boxes (especially late in the air campaign), and using the AWACS as an air refueling control agency are examples of some of these minor, but nevertheless important, problem areas.[32]

Overall, the AWACS effort in Desert Storm was impressive. During the 5 months of Desert Shield, AWACS E-3s based in Saudi Arabia flew 397 sorties for a total of 5,052 flying hours. During Desert Storm, the Saudi-based E-3s flew 356 sorties for a total of 5,028 hours in the air. AWACS flying as part of Proven Force logged almost 518 hours in the air during Desert Storm.[33] The "surge" for Desert Storm is clear from the figures on E-3 operations. The busiest flying month during Desert Shield was December, when the E-3 AWACS flew over 1,085 hours. In January, however, the aircraft were in the air approximately 2,500 hours; in February, the comparable figure was 2,300 hours.[34] The Proven Force AWACS assisted in the destruction of 6 Iraqi aircraft; the Saudi-based AWACS helped shoot down 38 Iraqi aircraft (of the 41 shot down).[35] Saudi-based E-3s even planned and executed missions over Iraqi territory in an effort to cut off the Iraqi aircraft that fled to Iran.[36]

ABCCC

I had an Army target I wanted to hit . . . . No Air Force air was available . . . . The weather was bad over Kuwait City, so the Marines

---

[31]The Airborne Command Element, working on the AWACS, is the direct link to the JFACC. See Chapter 4.

[32](S) USAF Tactical Fighter Weapons Center, *Tactical Analysis Bulletin*, Volume 91-2, Jul 1991, pp 2-1, 3-10, 4-9, 11-10, 11-15.

[33](S) Memo, Capt Guy Cafiero, GWAPS, subj: E-3 Employment Desert Storm, 1992.

[34](S) 28th AD, Desert Shield/Desert Storm Lessons Learned, "Numerical Statistics for E-3 Aircraft," nd [ca 1992].

[35](S) SMSgt Presley, *The 28th Air Division/552 Air Control Wing History 1991-92*, Chapter III, p 56.

[36](S) Ltr, Maj Kevin Dunleavy, 552d ACW/DOW, Tactics Planning Cell, CENTAF, subj: Central E-3 Operations North of Saudi-Iraqi Border, nd [Dec 1990].

found me a six-ship of A-6s loaded up. And so now you have an Army target, off the Army target list, struck by Navy A-6s, scrounged up by the Marine [liaison officer] via an Air Force Command & Control platform. And if that ain't purple, I don't know what is.[37]

This quotation illustrates the "good news" and the "bad news" of the air-to-ground campaign, which was monitored and often controlled by ABCCC air crews with the cooperation of Army, Marine Corps, and Navy personnel. The air-to-ground portion of the Tactical Air Control System was joint and multinational, and it was largely successful. But getting there—making the coordination work day after day—was difficult; it demanded constant vigilance, and even real diplomacy, on the part of the air- and ground-based elements of the Tactical Air Control System charged with the responsibility for pulling it off.

With the concept of a Joint Force Air Component Commander in place, the Tactical Air Control Center was nominally in control of the air-to-ground campaign, especially before the ground assault began on 24 February. Yet Lieutenant General Horner was well aware of the concerns of the theater ground commanders that air strikes against entrenched Iraqis might not be sufficiently under their control.[38] His plan for coordinating air action against the Iraqi army was based upon the previously discussed concepts of the kill zone and the Fire Support Coordination Line. The CENTAF Air Support Operations Centers (there was one with the XVIII Airborne Corps and another with Saudi forces) would activate and deactivate the boxes, and the crew in the ABCCC would clear "push close air support" attack aircraft into and out of them. The Director of the ABCCC Battlestaff was also responsible, under guidance from the Operations Deputy at the Tactical Air Control Center, for shifting air from interdiction in the kill zones to support of hard-pressed ground units.[39]

---

[37](S) Intvw, Maj Anne D. Leary, Mark D. Mandeles, and Lt Col Sanford S. Terry with Capt Randall A. Soboul, USA, Maj Michael S. Mathews, USAF, and Maj Wiley L. Hill, USAF, 7th Airborne Command and Control Squadron, Keesler AFB, MS, 7 May 1992.

[38] See (S) Chapter 3.

[39](S) USCENTCOM, *Concept of Operations: Tactical Air Request Net, CAS, Interdiction and ABCCC, Desert Shield,* 9 Sep 1990, paras 3.a, 3.d, and 3.h.

Attack air sorties were to be allocated among kill boxes based on targeting decisions made after consultation between the Army's Battlefield Coordination Element in the TACC and the TACC's Air Force planners and targeteers. The Fire Support Coordination Line was to be the dividing line between close air support sorties and Air Interdiction sorties. Close air support sorties would have to be cleared with Tactical Air Control Parties or with forward air controllers. Interdiction sorties would be flown as part of an orchestrated effort directed by the Commander in Chief and implemented through the Joint Force Air Component Commander and the Air Control Center (and through the TACC's extension, the ABCCC).

General Horner had already chosen to apply a "push close air support" concept to any operations against Iraqi forces. CENTAF would put the aircraft in the air. Ground units would ask their associated Tactical Air Control Parties (or Marine Air/Naval Gunfire Liaison Companies) for support. These requests would be passed to Air Support Operations Centers, which would organize them, set priorities among them, and then turn the list of targets over to the ABCCC. The Director, Airborne Battlestaff was authorized to assign available attack planes to targets.[40] Marine Corps ground units were to work within their own system; if they needed more help than organic air could provide, they were to contact their Direct Air Support Center, which would then talk to the orbiting ABCCC. If the ABCCC needed Marine aviation, it could call the Marine Corps Tactical Air Control Center or the Direct Air Operations Center.[41]

Ground commanders were unhappy with this arrangement. It was not the arrangement Army units had worked out with the Air Force in Europe, and it also was not what the Marine Corps usually did. The division commanders under Lt. Gen. Franks, commander of the VII Corps, openly opposed it.[42] They wanted to "own" the airspace in front of their divisions. That way, the corps would have a "free hand in artillery fires

---

[40](S) *Ibid*, paras 2.a. and 2.c.

[41](S) *Ibid*, para 2.e.

[42]See (S) Chapter 3.

as well as air defense."⁴³ Their opposition to giving the TACC control over the air bombardment of enemy ground units was not based on Service parochialism. They simply did not feel secure working with a set of procedures that had not been tested in combat. They also did not know how they would direct their own artillery fire effectively if they could not also direct their own air support.⁴⁴

The use of the Fire Support Coordination Line to coordinate air operations against ground targets caused, according to an official source, "more confusion and concern than any other" among Army VII Corps division commanders.⁴⁵ The latter saw the Line as a device that would restrict their movements instead of bring them the close air support they would need once the ground war started. General Horner worried about the possibility of ground forces moving beyond the Line without coordination,⁴⁶ and hence beyond the area where close air support was tightly controlled from the ground.⁴⁷

The abundance of airpower (including attack helicopters), coupled with the Army's concern that it be applied intelligently and flexibly, placed the Airborne Command, Control, and Communications crews on the spot. ABCCC crews were the contact point between two command and control systems. The first collected and filtered planned Army air support requests from the corps' targeting cells through the corps' commands to Army Central Command and then to the Battlefield Coordination Element. The most important of these requests would be placed into the Air Tasking Order, and ABCCC crews would carry this list of anticipated

---

⁴³(S) After Action Review, 8th Air Support Operations Group (ASOG), Operations Desert Shield/Storm, 6 Dec 1991, p 3.

⁴⁴(S) *Ibid*, p 9.

⁴⁵(S) *Ibid*, p 7.

⁴⁶Intvw, Robert L. Mandler with Col Michael F. Reavey, 21 Dec 1991.

⁴⁷At 0200Z on 26 Feb 1991, for example, the western ABCCC discovered in a message from a VII Corps artillery commander that lead elements of the VII Corps were at least two hours ahead of where they were supposed to be. The TACC and Battlefield Coordination Element were not aware of the precise location of the VII Corps. (S) 7th Air Command and Control Squadron (7th ACCS)/TACC Liaison Officer's Log, 26 Feb 1991.

strikes with them on their daily missions. The second command and control system reached from the Tactical Air Control Parties with the Army's maneuver units to the Air Support Operations Centers at corps level. This system brought more immediate requests to the ABCCC, via radio. If a conflict existed between what was planned and what was asked for, the Director, Airborne Battlestaff on the ABCCC made the call.[48]

The hitch in this "balancing act" was that how the Director, Airborne Battlestaff made his decision depended on the information he received from his own crew, other parts of the Tactical Air Control System (especially the Tactical Air Control Center and the Air Support Operations Center), and the strike pilots (who were a key source of intelligence on Iraqi dispositions and movements).[49] Army planners understood this and tried to use it to their advantage. For example, the TACC target list given to west ABCCC aircrew on 16 January 1991 did not include interdiction targets in the order that they were given in Army Central Command's "Deep Operations" target nominations worksheet.[50] The TACC's target priorities (which supposedly reflected the Commander in Chief's guidance) were not the same as the Army's. Yet an Army liaison officer was part of the crew of the ABCCC. His job was to recommend to the Director, Airborne Battlestaff the tradeoffs (if any) to be made between planned attacks and attacks made in response to last-minute requests from Tactical Air Control Parties. The Army liaison officer was, in effect, another link with the attacking aircraft, and Army corps' targeting cells tried to divert attack sorties to "pop-up" targets through him.[51]

Put another way, ABCCC controllers were under pressure from multiple sources simultaneously. They had the Air Tasking Order in front of

---

[48](S) Log, 7th ACCS (ABCCC)/TACC Liaison Officer Log, 14 Feb 1991, after 0710Z, put it very well: (U) "The DABS must consider all variables and decide what will be the appropriate balance between diverting everything and diverting nothing."

[49] 602d Tactical Air Control Wing, Deputy Commander for Operations LL, Desert Storm Conference, Detachment 7, Fort Bliss, TX, nd.

[50](S) "Target Worksheet," 1320Z, 16 Jan 1991; (S), USARCENT Deep Operations, "Target Nominations Worksheet," 1341Z, 16 Jan 1991.

[51](S) After Action Review, 8th ASOG, Operations Desert Shield/Storm, 6 Dec 1991, p 9.

them. They were supposed to facilitate its implementation. At the same time, they were supposed to stay in touch with the Air Support Operations Centers and the Tactical Air Control Parties. The east ABCCC, with a Marine liaison officer on board, was supposed to clear air attacks through the Marine Corps Direct Air Support Center. There was often a conflict between what was planned and what the ground units wanted.

On 25 January, for example, the deputy director of combat operations in the TACC told the west ABCCC not to authorize changes in the targets planned without his approval.[52] On 1 February, the duty officer in the 7th Air Command and Control Squadron (supporting the TACC) told CENTAF that "everybody [sic] is now running their own little war, sometimes in the same place. It's going to get dangerous if somebody doesn't figure a way to get all C^3 [command, control, and communications] assets integrated."[53] General Horner asked his deputy for operations to "Please get to bottom of this."[54] Horner could not orchestrate a systematic campaign against Iraqi ground forces if his Tactical Air Control Center could not be sure just where strikes were going or what effect they were having once they bombed their targets.

General Horner's command and control problem with respect to air-ground operations had two parts. The first has already been discussed: ABCCC crews were often subject to a number of simultaneous demands for air support, and they were sending aircraft to targets in ways which the TACC often could not follow. The second cause of confusion regarding just who was in charge was the inability of ABCCC crews to communicate with the aircraft they were supposed to be directing and monitoring.

[DELETED][55] [DELETED][56]

---

[52](S) Log, 7th ACCS (ABCCC)/TACC Liaison Officer Log, 0750Z 25 Jan 1991.

[53](S) Msg, 7 ACCS Deployed, DO to USCENTAF, DO 0230Z 1 Feb 1991, Microfilm Roll Number 23986, Frames 962-966, GWAPS.

[54]Horner's handwritten comments are on the message.

[55](S) Log, 7th ACCS (ABCCC)/TACC Liaison Officer Log, 22 Jan 1991.

[56](S) Memo, CAS/ABCCC AI Coordinators to A/CC, 22 Feb 1991, subj: ABCCC and AWACS Communications Survey, p 1, Microfilm Roll Number 26399, Frames 957-962, GWAPS.

ABCCC crews, the contact point between two command and control systems, were sometimes flown on EC-130s.

[DELETED]⁵⁷ [DELETED]⁵⁸

ABCCC crews were supposed to be traffic cops and data gatherers. They were to check strike aircraft into and out of kill boxes and gather data from the egressing aircraft about the locations and conditions of targets. In fact, they became battle managers, picking and choosing among targets even before the ground war began on 24 February. Army and Marine Corps liaison officers on the ABCCCs reviewed their component target lists, the target lists given them by the TACC staff, and requests for support from ground units and made judgments about which targets aircraft were to be assigned.⁵⁹ That ABCCC aircrews became battle managers was not a prob-

---

⁵⁷(S/NF/WN) USAF Tactical Fighter Weapons Center, *Tactical Analysis Bulletin*, Volume 91-2, Jul 1991, pp 11-6, 11-7.

⁵⁸(S) Log, 7th ACCS (ABCCC)/TACC Liaison Officer Log, 3 Feb 1991.

⁵⁹(S) Intvw, Leary, Mandeles, and Terry with Capt Soboul, USA, Maj Mathews, USAF, and Maj Hill, USAF.

lem so long as (a) the TACC could track what targets were hit and (b) strike aircraft did not stack up waiting for target coordinates within kill boxes while the ABCCC liaison officers discussed with the Director, Airborne Battlestaff what to do. At times, however, the TACC lost track of what was happening, because aircraft had problems checking in with ABCCC and acquiring targets.

On 3 February, for example, on orders from General Horner, special F-16 "killer scouts" began working with the ABCCCs. Two of these F-16s were assigned to orbit over selected Iraqi divisions. They were given the mission of selecting targets; the ABCCCs would relay the target coordinates to waiting attack aircraft and then pick up the reports from the attackers as the latter left the area.[60] Poor communications with the ABCCC aircraft frustrated this innovation.[61] ABCCC crews thought at the time that their HAVE QUICK radios were being jammed inadvertently by EC-130H COMPASS CALL electronic warfare aircraft, but the evidence did not fully support their suspicions.[62] Horner was concerned enough about the problem to demand a solution.[63]

On 7 February, as a short-term measure, the Tactical Air Control Center limited the number of A-10s in any kill box at any given time to two 2-ship flights.[64] This caused A-10s flying missions against kill box coordinates to stack up, so the TACC advised the west ABCCC to divert the surplus A-10s to other targets.[65] On 8 February, the TACC/Director of Operations (DO) ordered the ABCCC and AWACS wings to develop potential solutions in time for a 13 February meeting.[66] The solutions they came up with were both technical and procedural.

---

[60](S) Log, 7th ACCS (ABCCC)/TACC Liaison Officer Log, 1521Z, 3 Feb 1991.

[61](S) *Ibid*, 0315Z, 5 Feb 1991.

[62](S) *Ibid*, 0951Z, 6 Feb 1991, and 7 Feb (no time given).

[63](S) *Ibid*, 1510Z, 7 Feb 1991.

[64](S) *Ibid*, 1710Z, 7 Feb 1991.

[65](S) *Ibid*, 2330Z, 7 Feb 1991.

[66](S) Memo, Lt Col R. Duncan, USAF, Combat Plans, TACS Division, to CENTAF/DO, subj: Utilization of AWACS Aircraft by ABCCC Battle Staff, 8 Feb 1991, Microfilm Roll Number 23654, Frames 639-640 and 650-656.

On 13 February, for example, the TACC/DO decided that, until the ground war began, VII Corps would not get an immediate response to its requests for air interdiction.[67] The point was to cut down on the number of communications to the ABCCC. The next day, TACC/DO ordered the ABCCC crews not to divert "priority" missions in the Air Tasking Order.[68] On 17 February, the TACC/DO ruled that attack aircraft flying strikes against certain kill boxes could not drop their ordnance unless they first checked in with either AWACS or ABCCC.[69] These solutions appear to have helped, but the problems had made ground commanders cautious. The 1st Armored Division, for instance, "never simultaneously employed [close air support] aircraft, artillery, and attack helicopters in the same target area—not because the assets were not available, but because of the coordination difficulties involved."[70]

ABCCC and the Marine Corps

Marine officers rode the east ABCCC aircraft; they acted much like the Army liaison officers—checking aircraft into and out of kill boxes, responding to requests for immediate support from the ground, and supporting the Marine Corps Direct Air Support Center. Because the Marines had their own system of air support,[71] they had at first resisted the kill box concept. During the air campaign, however, the Marine Direct Air Support Center assumed de facto control over entry into the kill boxes in front of U.S.

---

[67](S) *Ibid*, 0200Z, 13 Feb 1991.

[68](S) *Ibid*, 0710Z, 14 Feb 1991.

[69](S) *Ibid*, 1838Z, 17 Feb 1991.

[70](S) After Action Review, 8th Air Support Operations Group (ASOG), Operations Desert Shield/Storm, 6 Dec 1991, p 5.

[71]USMC aircraft, before making a strike, would check in with their Tactical Air Command Center. The Center would pass them to the USMC Tactical Air Operations Center to see if there were any potential conflicts with other flights. The Tactical Air Operations Center would then shift control to the Direct Air Support Center (which was sometimes airborne) for any last minute mission update. The DASC would then contact the ABCCC and tell the latter that USMC planes were heading for a kill box. Coming back from a mission, control was passed back through the same organizations. Background Paper, Deconfliction of Air Within the MARCENT Area of Responsibility, nd.

Marines Central Command forces.⁷² Indeed, the Direct Air Support Center's influence was so great that the Eastern Area Command told Central Command Air Forces in January that "they did not feel confident that their air support needs would be met by USMARCENT in a high paced, limited air asset action."⁷³

That fear turned out to be unjustified, but Marine liaison officers on the east ABCCC did relish the opportunity to direct the airplanes of other Services. Working with their own Direct Air Support Center, these Marine liaison officers directed A-10s against Iraqi units in Kuwait, relayed information from a remotely piloted vehicle (drone) to help battleships *Wisconsin* and *Missouri* bombard shore targets, and even coordinated B-52 strikes.⁷⁴

As far as the Marine liaison personnel were concerned, work on an ABCCC was just an opportunity to grab attack aircraft looking for action.⁷⁵ On 25 February, for example, "the USMC representative onboard ABCCC requested and received permission to control the roads running North out of Kuwait City."⁷⁶ On 27 February, the Marine Corps liaison was busy finding ways to circumvent the TACC's policy of restricting the number of attack flights working a kill box at any given time.⁷⁷

---

⁷²(S/NF) Briefing, MARCENT, Desert Storm, MARCENT Command Brief, 28 Mar 1991.

⁷³(S) Memo, Lt Col R. E. Duncan, USCENTAF Combat Plans, TACC, TACS Division, to DCP, DCO, ADO, DO, subj: CAS Trip Report, 24 Jan 1991, Microfilm Roll Number 23654, Frames 574-575, GWAPS.

⁷⁴(S) Chronology, ABCCC *Marine Liaison Team Det Chronology*, (7th ACCS, 5 Mar 1966), pp 10-11.

⁷⁵(S) *Ibid*, p 13.

⁷⁶(S) *Ibid*, p 14.

⁷⁷(S) *Ibid*, p 15.

Tactical Air Control Parties

Anyone familiar with the history of close air support in past wars[78] will know what it was like for the Tactical Air Control Parties: communications problems, vehicle problems, problems just getting food and shelter and keeping warm and dry.[79] They had to stay with the Army units they were assigned to support. As in past wars, many of the vehicles which carried them were unarmored, and Control Party personnel were wounded by enemy fire. The brackets holding their radios were often not strong enough or could not withstand vehicle vibration. The vehicles (especially the Army's high-mobility multi-purpose wheeled vehicle, or HMMWV) often did not produce enough electric power to sustain communications equipment.

On the positive side, however, the Tactical Air Control Parties had Global Positioning Satellite receivers, which they found "invaluable."[80] They also praised communications with AWACS and ABCCC and coordination with "Fast FAC" F/A-18Ds.[81] Though the Army's aviation brigades of attack and assault helicopters did not range out in front of their armored divisions, as they had planned to do in a war with the Warsaw Pact in Europe, they nevertheless apparently benefitted from having Party liaison.[82] Air Force Tactical Air Control Party personnel also noted the importance of the training they received during the months before Desert Storm.[83]

---

[78] Benjamin Franklin Cooling, ed, *Case Studies in the Development of Close Air Support* (Washington, DC, 1990).

[79] All these problems are documented in the Desert Storm lessons learned conferences held by the 602d Tactical Air Control Wing, Deputy Commander for Operations.

[80] (S) Briefing, Maj Miles Batt, USA, USAF AGOS/SAJ, subj: Desert Storm, Presentation to Maj Anne D. Leary, Mark D. Mandeles, and Lt Col Sanford S. Terry, 8 May 1992. (The briefing was prepared upon Maj Batt's return to the U.S. from Kuwait.)

[81] (S) *Ibid.* See also 602d Tactical Air Control Wing, Deputy Commander for Operations LL, Desert Storm Conference, Lessons Learned, Detachment 1-2, "Historical Input," 24 Feb 1992.

[82] (S) *Ibid.*

[83] 602d Tactical Air Control Wing, Deputy Commander for Operations LL, Desert Storm Conference, Detachment 7, Fort Bliss, TX, nd, p 3.

The 8th Air Support Operations Group, however, noted that the problem of fratricide, once the Army units it supported moved against the enemy, was never overcome. Despite the use of orange markers, Global Positioning Satellite receivers, signal mirrors, dedicated forward air controllers, and Tactical Air Control Parties, there was no guaranteed way of avoiding attacks on friendly forces. "The problems in friendly vehicle identification at night were enormous, and in most cases insurmountable. As a result, night [close air support] sorties flown during the ground offensive were all employed well forward of the FLOT (Forward Line of Troops)–5 Km or more."[84]

Matters were even more hectic for the Air Support Operations Center and the ten Tactical Air Control Parties which supported the Northern Area Command (which mixed Saudi, French, Syrian and Egyptian forces). Air Force personnel put their close air support communications together "with bits and pieces from all tactical commands."[85] As their Air Support Operations Center struggled to get the Air Tasking Order daily ("CAFAMS [sic] is slooooow"),[86] they relied on Army Special Forces personnel to keep them in contact with the Arab units, most of whom had little or no experience working with attached or supporting fixed-wing aviation.

ABCCC Performance

An Air Force major, part of an Airborne Command, Control, and Communications crew, told interviewers an interesting story. During a postmission brief, an A-10 pilot cursed ABCCC for not having a target for him. The major asked the pilot why he had the problem. The pilot answered, "Well, I checked in and they acted like they didn't know who I was." The major then asked the pilot what frequency he used to check in. The pilot responded with the AWACS frequency and callsign. When informed of his mistake, the A-10 pilot said, "AWACS, ABCCC, what the

---

[84](S) After Action Review, 8th Air Support Operations Group (ASOG), Operations Desert Shield/Storm, 6 Dec 1991, p 11.

[85]602d Tactical Air Control Wing, Deputy Commander for Operations LL, Desert Storm Conference, Lessons Learned, 23 TASS, Davis-Monthan AFB, AZ, p 1.

[86]*Ibid.*

hell is the difference?"[87] Maybe this instance highlights one of the major problems that the ABCCC faced during the war; the level of knowledge was unequal between the ABCCC controllers and the attack pilots they were to control.

[DELETED][88] [DELETED][89] [DELETED][90]

The Joint Surveillance Target Attack Radar System (JSTARS)

In Desert Storm, JSTARS stole the show. Anyone who has seen the JSTARS moving target indicator radar displays, for example, of the Iraqi retreat from Kuwait City, will know why. Indeed, the screen images can be saved, combined, and then run sequentially, and the effect is magical. The enemy's forces deploy, scatter, and then regroup right in front of the viewer's eyes. JSTARS is visual; it shows you where your enemy is and what he's doing now. It should not surprise anyone that JSTARS was in great demand during Desert Storm.

Operations

JSTARS missions began on 14 January.[91] Each E-8 aircraft flew in random mission tracks within an assigned operating area.[92] Flights were scheduled in the Air Tasking Order. From its orbit, the JSTARS aircraft

---

[87](S) Intvw, Leary, Mandeles, and Terry with Capt Soboul, USA, Maj Mathews, USAF, and Maj Hill, USAF.

[88](S) After Action Review, 8th ASOG, Operations Desert Shield/Storm, 6 Dec 6 1991, p 1.

[89](S) Intvw, Leary, Mandeles, and Terry with Capt Soboul, USA, Maj Mathews, USAF, and Maj Hill, USAF.

[90]602d Tactical Air Control Wing, Deputy Commander for Operations LL, Desert Storm Conference, Detachment 7, Fort Bliss, TX, nd, p 6.

[91](S) Msg, Maj Gen John A. Corder, USCENTAF/DO to USCINCCENT//CCJ2//CCJ3, 222030Z Jan 1991, subj: Joint Stars Operations.

[92]USCENTAF, Employment Concept, Joint Surveillance and Target Attack Radar System (JSTARS), nd, Microfilm Roll Number 10238, Frames 523-32, GWAPS.

could pick up moving targets. The aircraft's synthetic aperture radar could be applied to any spot within its area coverage to detect stationary objects.[93]

(S) The crew would usually find moving objects. They also looked for signs of stationary targets that merited examination with the synthetic aperture radar. If they found any indicators of potential targets, they contacted strike aircraft, ABCCC, or the Tactical Air Control Center. [DELETED][94] [DELETED][95]

Yet, ground commanders were quick to realize what it could give them, and they competed among themselves to gain coverage for their fronts. Before JSTARS missions, the ground component commanders would submit target coordinates for the one JSTARS platform flying at any given time to examine. Once in the air, the JSTARS crew found itself under siege from ground commanders who communicated with the E-8 through their Ground Support Modules.[96] As Brig. Gen. George K. Muellner, JSTARS commander during Desert Storm, recalled in an interview, "every night we'd get into a battle. . . . the VII Corps wanted to run it his way, and MARCENT wanted to run it their way."[97] Central Command tried to meet all the requirements placed on JSTARS, but, as Muellner observed later, "there was NOBODY [emphasis his] early on to say, 'Hey, we've looked at your requirements.'"[98]

The solution to this problem of setting priorities came when General Schwarzkopf's deputy, Lt. Gen. Calvin Waller, held daily meetings to set

---

[93](S/NF/WN) Briefing, Col George Muellner, Col Martin Kleiner, Col Harry Heimple, Col Mendel Solomon, Col Royce Grones, subj: Joint STARS–Support of Desert Shield, nd, Microfilm Roll Humber 10238, Frames 443-475, and Microfilm Roll Number 10211, Frames 179-223, GWAPS.

[94](S) Briefing, Maj J. Coates, 12th Tactical Intelligence Squadron, subj: Joint STARS–Desert Storm, 4-6 Jun 1991, Microfilm Roll Number 26572, Frames 1823-1847, GWAPS.

[95]Intvw, Thomas C. Hone, Maj Anne D. Leary, Mark D. Mandeles with Brig Gen George K. Muellner, DCS-Requirements, HQ TAC, 16 Apr 1992.

[96]*Ibid.*

[97]*Ibid.*

[98]*Ibid.*

JSTARS was in great demand during Desert Storm due to its moving target indicator displays.

JSTARS coverage, to decide where the JSTARS would fly.[99] Before that time, JSTARS spent a great deal of time hunting Iraqi Scud missiles from one or both of its western orbits. By 28 January, for example, the Air Tasking Order was designating certain aircraft as "Scud CAP" [combat air patrol]. These planes flew orbits over suspected Scud launch sites and were at the call of the JSTARS E-8.[100] "And that was a prime irritant to the ground component commanders."[101]

JSTARS worked better when its radars were applied to Iraqi ground units. Even then, however, Colonel Muellner found that his crews had to do much of their own analysis. Maj. Gen. Corder, General Horner's deputy for operations in the Tactical Air Control Center, helped the JSTARS crews obtain color printers for their display consoles. The crews would mark the color output to show enemy movement and give it the TACC's intelligence personnel. With Corder's approval and the help of

---

[99]*Ibid.*

[100]7th ACCS/TACC Liaison Officer Log, 0200Z 28 Jan 1991.

[101]Intvw, Hone, Leary, and Mandeles with Brig Gen Muellner.

Brig. Gen. Kenneth Minihan, intelligence deputy at the Tactical Air Command, and Army Lt. Gen. John Yeosock, Muellner and his subordinates put together a joint "planning and exploitation cell" in time for the ground war.[102]

Once the air war began, JSTARS personnel discovered that Airborne Command, Control, and Communications and Marine Corps Direct Air Support Center personnel had problems knowing how to interpret dynamic, real-time targeting data. They would direct attack aircraft to where an enemy target had been and not to where it would soon be–even though JSTARS provided "velocity vectors." To improve their understanding and confidence, Muellner had a Director, Airborne Battlestaff from an ABCCC and some of his subordinates fly with a JSTARS; he did the same with Direct Air Support Center personnel. This seemed to work.[103]

[DELETED][104]

JSTARS was involved successfully in the defeat of the Iraqi force that attacked Khafji. The system also detected the "mother of all retreats" from Kuwait City on 25 February and directed (with the East ABCCC) the air interdiction attacks on the traffic fleeing from the city. During Desert Storm, JSTARS flew 49 combat sorties over 535 hours. The two E-8s located over 1,000 important targets and controlled over 750 attack sorties. The two aircraft were available 85 percent of the time; the radars were up 80 percent of the time. Contractor support in the theater contributed significantly to the system's success.[105]

The Aerial TACS in Action–An Assessment

The technical sophistication of the airborne elements of the Tactical Air Control System should not obscure the performance of its human operators. AWACS, RIVET JOINT, ABCCC, and JSTARS put in long, stress-filled hours;

---

[102] *Ibid.*

[103] *Ibid.*

[104] [DELETED]

[105] (S/NF/WN) See footnote 97.

327

those personnel had to bring great concentration to their jobs. The enemy did not help. Iraqi aircraft rehearsed threatening passes against RIVET JOINT and AWACS aircraft during Desert Shield.[106] Fighters held them off; all airborne TACS assets (except forward air controllers) were "high value air assets" and were protected accordingly, but the threat of destruction was present nonetheless. The work of these airborne command and control platforms showed that flying command stations could carry the 'round-the-clock air battle to the enemy and even coordinate night air/ground operations against hostile forces.

---

[106]Robert S. Hopkins, III, "Ears of the Storm," *Air Force Magazine*, Feb 1992, pp 41-43.

10

Conclusion

In an interview after the war, Lt. Gen. Charles A. Horner characterized himself and his fellow Gulf War senior commanders (including Gen. H. Norman Schwarzkopf) as good, competent professionals, but certainly not as heroes or military geniuses.[1] He was trying, in an offhand way, to explain that the success of U.S. forces was due as much to their planning, their training, their systems, and their top-to-bottom professionalism as it was to the skill of their theater commanders. Put another way, the "depth" of U.S. command and control (broadly defined) meant that any well-trained, professional team of American leaders, commanding an above-average force, could spectacularly outperform the best team of leaders Iraq could put in the field.

Why this should have been so is what this report has been all about. After all, it is not as though everything went smoothly for American and coalition command and control. Missions sometimes did not go as planned, as several of the examples from Chapter 7 show.[2] There were also disagreements among senior commanders about how best to use the air units available to the coalition, about which aircraft and sorties belonged in the Air Tasking Order, and, once the ground war started, about which commanders had the authority to adjust the Fire Support Coordination Line. Finally, there were cases in which the Tactical Air Control Center staff misunderstood what was happening in the air campaign. Victory was not automatic. To see Desert Storm as an inevitable walkover would be wrong.

---

[1] (S/NF) Intvw, Barry Barlow, Richard G. Davis, Perry Jamieson with Lt Gen Charles A. Horner, Commander, 9th AF, 4 Mar 1992. See also H. Norman Schwarzkopf with Peter Petre, *It Doesn't Take a Hero* (New York, 1992).

[2] The Scud Hunt, for example, was clearly unsuccessful tactically. However, to the extent that it persuaded Israeli leaders and population that the United States was serious about combatting the Scud threat and therefore contributed to keeping Israel out of the war, the Scud Hunt was a strategic success.

Some of these problems would have arisen anyway, no matter who the U.S. and coalition commanders were. On the one hand, the difference between the Air Force and the Marine Corps over the authority of the Joint Force Air Component Commander (JFACC), for example, had not been resolved when Iraq invaded Kuwait (see Appendix 2). Schwarzkopf, Horner, and the other component commanders had to settle the disagreement during Desert Shield through discussions and negotiations. Because the authority of the JFACC was a matter of importance to all the component commanders, those negotiations continued on tacitly into Desert Storm. Some problems, on the other hand, can be traced directly to the personalities of the commanders involved. For example, the domination of the Air Tasking Order process during Desert Storm by the Guidance, Apportionment, and Targeting cell (GAT), described in Chapter 7, was one consequence of Brig. Gen. Buster C. Glosson's strong personality and aggressive leadership style. Clearly, people are at the heart of the Tactical Air Control System (TACS), and their perceptions and personalities cannot be ignored when considering the effectiveness of any TACS in any particular conflict.

The Importance of Effectiveness (or Outcomes)

But effectiveness is the concern of this report–whether the TACS used the great resources placed at its disposal effectively, in spite of the problems always inherent in commanding forces during a war. Chapter 1 of this report argued that there was a connection between how well a military organization perceived and then solved its command and control problems and challenges, and how well it performed in war. As noted in Chapter 1, military organizations experience their most important reality (war) only infrequently. Most of the time, military organizations can only simulate war through practice exercises and in training. As a result, war usually brings many surprises, and military organizations–which are, after all, composed just of people, with the limitations of people–must try to anticipate those surprises and cope with them. Military organizations that cannot cope with the unexpected lose wars.

How simple yet how frustrating this situation is. Because war is full of surprises, military leaders must try to create and maintain command and control systems (composed of personnel, procedures, and equipment) that can adapt to the unexpected by sensing, analyzing, and then solving the problems which the surprises endemic to war create. But there is no way to know for sure in peacetime that the command and control which performs well during exercises will respond equally well to the confusion, uncertainty, and stress of wartime operations.

To use the terms introduced in Chapter 1, impressive peacetime outputs are no guarantee of successful wartime outcomes. However, because individuals and organizations focus in peacetime so much on output, senior leaders must monitor the people (in organizations) they lead so as to detect and then, if necessary, correct any focus on outputs which obstructs the achievement of the proper outcomes. This is not easy.

Consider the Tactical Air Control Center during Desert Storm. The GAT was focused on outcomes. Central Command Air Forces/Intelligence (CENTAF/IN) did not, apparently, grasp the concept of operations, which stressed outcomes over outputs. The two organizations, which should have worked closely together to help produce Air Tasking Orders, did not work well together at all. General Glosson pushed ahead anyway (see Chapter 7), handing his GAT planners CENTAF/IN's responsibilities and using his authority as 14th Air Division(P) Commander to communicate directly with the wings under his command. Glosson monitored the situation and then took "corrective" action, but was it the right action? And, given the pace of the air war, how could Glosson know whether his action was right or not until some time after the conflict had ended?

One reason why the personnel in the GAT found it difficult to work with the other organizations within the Tactical Air Control Center during Desert Storm was because the members of the GAT had been cut off from the routines maintained within the Center during Desert Shield. Isolated unavoidably as they secretly planned for an offensive air campaign, the members of the GAT developed a shared concept of operations–an outcome concept–which other parts of the Tactical Air Control Center did not. General Glosson shared this concept. Furthermore, he had developed "special" sources of intelligence information, and the fact that he had access to "inside" information gave him and his subordinates in the GAT confidence that they could achieve victory even without the support they felt they deserved from CENTAF/IN.

The friction between the GAT and CENTAF/IN shows why the distinction between outputs and outcomes is important: because organizations will tend, even in war, to produce those outputs developed during peacetime training. One reason this happens is because there are two types of rationality in the minds of command and control personnel during a conflict. The first focuses on outcomes; those who are "rational" in this way feel that whatever outputs do not contribute to victory are simply wasted effort. Those who define "rationality" in output terms, however, fear that deviating from the routines which produce "proper output" will only lead to organizational confusion and chaos. Both views make some "sense," and knowing that both do allows those interested in bettering command and control to compare and tradeoff the advantages of each position, and that is the first step toward setting command and control systems on a sensible foundation.

Command and Control: What Does It Mean?

There are many obstacles to effective command and control of air forces across a whole theater, despite decades of research, development, and innovation in the field of command and control. In World Wars I and II, an air commander could often do little more than send his aircrews off and then pray for their safe return. Now, the aircrews, in concert with systems such as AWACS, ABCCC, and JSTARS[3] can implement a concept of operations developed by senior commanders and consult both with those commanders and with one another while the operation is in progress. The potential this mode of command gives to air units is tremendous. The whole air campaign, including air-to-air engagements and air-to-ground attacks, can be directed from the air itself, and elements of the campaign, such as interdiction, can be modified in real time to suit a changing situation.

However, the problems of coordination and problem-solving this advanced system of command and control creates are enormous. Innovation has come hand-in-hand with increasing complexity, and the latter has required the users of this increasingly complex system to learn to coordi-

---

[3] AWACS: Airborne Warning and Control Systems; ABCCC: Airborne Command, Control, and Communications; JSTARS: Joint Surveillance Target Attack Radar System.

nate even more of their actions with one another. Where this lesson has not been learned—as when GAT personnel feuded with their counterparts in CENTAF/IN—the system has not worked as anticipated. Where the lesson has been learned—as in the operations of AWACS and ABCCC aircraft—there has been a great payoff.

There has been a revolution in the command and control of air operations in recent years. That revolution has two sides. The first side is technological: advanced electronics and high-technology command and control systems can be made to support command and control of high-volume, sophisticated air operations. The second side is social: the "professional" Services have learned to use these systems. In terms of outputs and outcomes, the Services, through simulations and realistic exercises, have developed organizational "outputs" that are closely suited, even in peacetime, to giving them the situational "outcomes" that they must have to be victorious. There has been, in short, a fruitful interaction between maturing systems and the people who train to use them.

This interaction, however, was supplemented during Desert Shield and Desert Storm by a shared commitment among senior commanders to avoid the apparent mistakes of the past. Lieutenant General Horner might well have made his motto a defiant, "No more Vietnams." In the terms used in this report, he thoroughly rejected any approaches to being the JFACC that he thought were too focused on outputs instead of outcomes. In pushing and prodding the Tactical Air Control Center and his air units to face and solve problems, he promoted an ethic of leadership which was outcome oriented. Horner consciously chose to err on the side of stressing outcomes because of his sense of what had been the mistakes of the air war against North Vietnam. It is this aggressive outcome-oriented approach that characterizes the story of USAF theater-level and unit-level command and control during Desert Shield and Desert Storm.

Despite the revolution in the technology of command and control, Desert Storm was much like past air campaigns. Commanders' personalities clashed, communications sometimes failed, and informal and ad hoc organizations sprang up to deal with real or perceived problems that existing organizations could not deal with. At times, aircraft dropped bombs where they should not have; at other times, they kept dropping bombs where they no longer needed to. Precrisis intelligence was skimpy. Wartime intelligence fell on the theater like an avalanche. Intelligence staff fought with planners, and operators cursed both. Nothing **new** here; nothing **unexpected** here. Nothing here suggests that problems are unresolvable, either. The record of Desert Storm, however, suggests that these traditional problems of command and control may never be totally overcome before a conflict actually begins.

Key Findings

1. From the perspective of command and control, the primary obstacle faced by the commanders of coalition Air Forces during Desert Storm was not Iraqi resistance but organizational problems within the Tactical Air Control System itself. Chief among these was the unanticipated growth in the responsibilities of the Guidance, Apportionment and Targeting division of the operations directorate of the Tactical Air Control Center. Given the authority to develop daily attack plans and promulgate operational direction of the air campaign in December 1990, the GAT quickly took control of the entire Air Tasking Order generation process. In doing this, it exercised responsibilities which had been formally assigned to other divisions under the operations directorate of the Tactical Air Control Center. The GAT also took over much of the intelligence directorate's function and even conducted its own bomb damage assessments.

2. Because the other personnel manning the Tactical Air Control Center had not trained for this change, and because GAT personnel could not do well all the duties they had assumed, the Air Tasking Order process itself lost efficiency quickly. For example, changes issued to the Air Tasking Order after it had been published comprised a significant percentage of the total number of sorties flown after the first two days of the air war. The wings kept pace with the many changes through frequent, secure conversations with members of the Tactical Air Control Center.

3. The Guidance, Apportionment, and Targeting division was just one of many important ad hoc command and control organizations. Another was the network of communications established among ABCCC and AWACS crews, Tactical Air Control Parties accompanying U.S. ground forces, and "Fast FAC" forward air controllers as they worked to send coalition strike aircraft against the Iraqi army deployed and dug in

opposite coalition forces in Saudi Arabia. The fact that there were many, unanticipated ad hoc organizations was significant.

4. The ad hoc organizations were supported by great numbers of relatively easy-to-use secure communications devices, particularly the ubiquitous Secure Telephone Unit (STU-III). These secure transmitters and receivers, working through satellite links, allowed personnel in Saudi Arabia to communicate easily and often with one another and with Washington. The volume of this communication nearly overwhelmed the communications equipment and personnel assigned to the theater, and the nature of much of the communication changed the character of command and control. For example, Brigadier General Glosson, head of the GAT, and RAdm. Michael McConnell, deputy director of the Defense Intelligence Agency in Washington, talked frequently on the phone. McConnell passed sensitive information to General Glosson–information which Glosson used to compensate for what be believed were weaknesses in the workings of the Tactical Air Control Center's intelligence directorate.

5. The rapid pace (or velocity) of the air campaign, coupled with the ability of new sensors such as JSTARS to monitor enemy movements in real time, outran the procedures by which the theater-wide Air Tasking Order was constructed and then disseminated. As General Glosson recognized, the ATO process was archaic. It depended on a lot of paper-and-pencil work and could not keep up with needs of units for planning materials such as accurate and timely bomb damage assessments and estimates of enemy movement at night (which JSTARS provided).

6. Decisionmakers at various levels of the Tactical Air Control System often did not get the information they needed to direct the air campaign or did not get that information on time, despite all the technological innovations (such as satellite communications) which had been introduced in the years before Desert Shield and Desert Storm. For example, the Tactical Air Control Center lacked a process for developing timely bomb damage assessments for the air campaign's planners. Faced with no information or delayed information, campaign planners called directly to sources in Washington or used videotapes sent by wings whose planes were flying strike missions. Once planners obtained information, however, they often did not use it effectively because they were not fully trained in its interpretation.

7. The existence of many ad hoc command and control organizations increased the impact of individual personalities. Because information such as bomb damage assessment was often lacking, individuals who could get it or get it faster gained influence over the direction of the air campaign. The networks these individuals created to gain information were usually based on informal contacts that grew out of past associations. For example, GAT personnel with Fighter Weapons School training reached out to other graduates. In the ad hoc organizations, these contacts based on past associations took the place of the standard operating procedures and routines that linked personnel in formal organizations. (See Chapters 6 and 7.)

8. The JFACC's role was a difficult one to fill. Lieutenant General Horner had to deal with the Commander in Chief, the coalition air commanders, the other Services, and the Tactical Air Control System, which was his primary tool for managing the air campaign. Horner chose to focus his attention outside the TACS, leaving its day-to-day management to his deputies. He managed the TACS "by exception," intervening only when he believed it was necessary.

9. Centralized direction of a theater-wide air campaign is possible. During Desert Storm, the lack of common procedures, training, equipment, and software among the Services was a major obstacle to effective centralized command and control.

10. Command and control of air operations was often exercised from airborne platforms such as AWACS, ABCCC, and JSTARS. These platforms gave the Tactical Air Control System substantial reliability. Because AWACS, ABCCC, and JSTARS had related or overlapping capabilities, however, personnel manning them had to develop means of coordinating their operations. Put another way, redundancy had a high coordination "cost."

11. U.S. Air Force and Navy problems in the area of command and control were caused by a lack of compatibility of communications and tasking systems and by insufficient joint training in command and control.

12. The ad hoc Scud warning system worked well. The ad hoc mobile Scud/launcher localization and targeting procedures did not work

effectively. The former was effective while the latter was not because the equipment for actually targeting the mobile Scud launchers was inadequate for the task (though, because it was all that was available, it had to be used).

13. Communications barely kept up with the deployment of air forces during Desert Shield, and only strenuous efforts kept the communications "system" in the Gulf from collapsing.

14. The months of training during Desert Shield were valuable because they gave the many individuals manning the various elements of the Tactical Air Control System time to focus on the specifics of a campaign against Iraqi forces. Chapter 9, for example, noted how important it was for Air Force liaison officers working with Army ground units to put their training and equipment to the test in prewar exercises, and Chapter 3 showed that it took time for all the air units in the coalition to become accustomed to working from the Air Tasking Order.

Lieutenant General Horner, and the many air units under his control, did win an overwhelming victory, despite fears–expressed in the press and privately within the government before Desert Storm–that they would win only at great cost. The magnitude of that victory, however, was due in a substantial way to a very effective combination of training, tactics, and equipment. This was a revolution in the relationship of peacetime outputs to wartime outcomes. In plain language, training was more realistic. The Gulf War also showed that the scope and tempo of operations upon which an air commander can act has increased. However, technological and organizational innovations to solve old command and control problems have created new problems of coordination and problem-solving for command and control. The events of the Gulf War also suggest, however, that these new problems can–and will–be solved.

Appendix 1

Definition of Terms

administrative control - (DOD, NATO) Direction or exercise of authority over subordinate or other organizations in respect to administrative matters such as personnel management, supply, services, and other matters not included in the operational missions of the subordinate or other organizations. (JCS Pub 1-02)

airborne battlefield command and control center - (DOD) A United States Air Force aircraft equipped with communications, data link, and display equipment; it may be employed as an airborne command post or a communications and intelligence relay facility.

air command - (DOD) A major subdivision of the Air Force; for operational purposes, it normally consists of two or more air forces. (JCS Pub 1-02)

air defense - (DOD) All defensive measures designed to destroy attacking enemy aircraft or missiles in the earth's envelope of atmosphere, or to nullify or reduce the effectiveness of such attack. (JCS Pub 1-02)

air ground operations system - (DOD, NATO) An Army/Air Force system providing the ground commander with the means for receiving, processing, and forwarding the requests of subordinate ground commanders for air support missions and for the rapid dissemination of information and intelligence. (JCS Pub 1-02)

airspace management - (DOD) The coordination, integration, and regulation of the use of airspace of defined dimensions.

air support operations center - (DOD, NATO) An agency of a tactical air control system collocated with a corps headquarters or an appropriate land force headquarters, which coordinates and directs close air support and other tactical air support. (JCS Pub 1-02)

allocation - (DOD) The translation of the apportionment into total numbers of sorties by aircraft type available for each operation/task. (JCS Pub 1-02)

apportionment - (DOD, NATO) The determination and assignment of the total expected effort by percentage and/or by priority that should be devoted to the various air operations and/or geographic areas for a given period of time. (JCS Pub 1-02)

area air defense commander - (DOD) Within an overseas unified command, subordinate unified command, or joint task force, the commander will assign overall responsibility for air defense to a single commander. Normally, this will be the Air Force component commander. Representation from the other Services' components involved will be provided, as appropriate, to the area air defense commander's headquarters. (JCS Pub 1-02)

area command - (DOD, NATO) A command which is composed of those organized elements of one or more of the armed Services, designated to operate in a specific geographical area and placed under a single commander. (JCS Pub 1-02)

basic encyclopedia - (DOD) A compilation of identified installations and physical areas of potential significance as objectives for attack. (JCS Pub 1-02)

bomb damage assessment - (DOD) The determination of the effect of all air attacks on targets (e.g., bombs, rockets, or strafing). (JCS Pub 1-02)

call sign - (DOD, NATO) Any combination of characters or pronounceable words that identify a communication facility, a command, an authority, an activity, or a unit; used primarily for establishing and maintaining communications. (JCS Pub 1-02)

chain of command - (DOD, NATO) The succession of commanding officers from a superior to a subordinate through which command is exercised. (JCS Pub 1-02)

change of operational control - (DOD) The date and time (Coordinated Universal Time) at which the responsibility for operational control of a force or unit passes from one operational control authority to another. (JCS Pub 1-02)

close air support - (DOD, NATO) Air action against hostile targets which are in close proximity to friendly forces and which require detailed integration of each air mission with the fire and movement of those forces. (JCS Pub 1-02)

Combatant Command (command authority) - (DOD) Non-transferable command authority established by title 10, United States Code, section 164, exercised only by commanders of unified or specified combatant commands. Combatant Command (command authority) is the authority of a Combatant Commander to perform those functions of command over assigned forces involving organizing and employing commands and forces, assigning tasks, designating objectives, and giving authoritative direction over all aspects of military operations, joint training, and logistics necessary to accomplish the missions assigned to the command. Combatant Command (command authority) should be exercised through the commanders of subordinate organizations; normally this authority is exercised through the Service component commander. Combatant Command (command authority) provides full authority to organize and employ commands and forces as the CINC considers necessary to accomplish assigned missions. Also called COCOM. (JCS Pub 1-02)

command - (DOD) **1.** The authority that a commander in the military Service lawfully exercises over subordinates by virtue of rank or assignment. Command includes the authority and responsibility for effectively using available resources and for planning the employment of, organizing, directing, coordinating, and controlling military forces for the accomplishment of assigned missions. It also includes responsibility for health, welfare, morale, and discipline of assigned personnel. **2.** An order given by a commander; that is, the will of the commander expressed for the purpose of bringing about a particular action. **3.** A unit or units, an organization, or an area under the command of one individual. **4.** To dominate by a field of weapon fire or by observation from a superior position. (JCS Pub 1-02)

command - (Combined) Command is the authority and responsibility for effectively using available resources and for planning the controlling, organizing, directing, coordinating, and employment of military forces for the accomplishment of assigned missions. It also includes responsibility for health, welfare, morale, and discipline of assigned personnel. (Combined OPlan)

control - (DOD) **1.** Authority which may be less than full command exercised by a commander over part of the activities of subordinate or other organizations. **2.** In mapping, charting, and photogrammetry, a collective term for a system of marks or objects on the earth or on a map or a photograph, whose positions or elevations, or both, have been or will be determined. **3.** Physical or psychological pressures exerted with the intent to assure that an agent or group will respond as directed. **4.** An indicator governing the distribution and use of documents, information, or material. Such indicators are the subject of intelligence community agreement and are specifically defined in appropriate regulations. (JCS Pub 1-02)

control and reporting center - (DOD) An element of the U.S. Air Force tactical air control system, subordinate to the tactical air control center, from which radar control and warning operations are conducted within its area of responsibility. (JCS Pub 1-02)

coordinating authority - (DOD) A commander or individual assigned responsibility for coordinating specific functions or activities involving forces of two or more Services or two or more forces of the same Service. The commander or individual has the authority to require consultation between the agencies involved, but does not have the authority to compel agreement. In the event that essential agreement cannot be obtained, the matter shall be referred to the appointing authority. (JCS Pub 1-02)

daily intelligence summary - (DOD) A report prepared in message form at the joint force component command headquarters that provides higher, lateral, and subordinate headquarters with a summary of all significant intelligence produced during the previous 24-hour period. The "as of" time for information, content, and submission time for the report will be specified by the joint force commander. (JCS Pub 1-02)

D-day - (DOD) 1. The unnamed day on which a particular operation commences or is to commence. An operation may be the commencement of hostilities. a. The date of a major effort. b. The execution date of an operation (as distinguished from the date the order to execute is issued); the date the operations phase is implemented, by land assault, air strike, naval bombardment, parachute assault, or amphibious assault. The highest command or headquarters responsible for coordinating the planning will specify the exact meaning of D-day within the aforementioned definition. If more than one such event is mentioned in a single plan, the secondary events will be keyed to the primary event by adding or subtracting days as necessary. The letter "D" will be the only one used to denote the above. The command or headquarters directly responsible for the execution of the operation, if other than the one coordinating the planning, will do so in light of the meanings specified by the highest planning headquarters. 2. Time in plans will be indicated by a letter that shows the unit of time employed and figures, with a minus or plus sign, to indicate the amount of time before or after the referenced event; e.g., "D" is for a particular day, "H" for an hour. Similarly, D + 7 means 7 days after D-day, H + 2 means 2 hours after H-hour. If the figure becomes unduly large, for example, D-day plus 90, the designation of D + 3 months may be employed; i.e., if the figure following the letter plus a time unit (D-day, H-hour, etc.) is intended to refer to units of time other than that which follows the letter, then the unit of time employed with the figure must be spelled out.

direct air support center - (DOD) A subordinate operational component of a tactical air control system designed for control and direction of close air support and other tactical air support operations, and normally collocated with fire-support coordination elements.

draft plan - (DOD, NATO) A plan for which a draft plan has been coordinated with the other military headquarters (and agreed upon by those headquarters) and is ready for coordination with the nations involved, i.e., those nations who would be required to take national actions to support the plan. It may be used for future planning and exercises and may form the basis for an operational order to be implemented in time of emergency.

exercise - (DOD, NATO) A military maneuver or simulated wartime operation involving planning, preparation, and execution. It is carried out for the purpose of training and evaluation. It may be a combined, joint, or single Service exercise, depending on participating organizations.

fire support coordination line - (DOD, NATO) A line established by the appropriate ground commander to insure coordination of fire not under his control but which may affect current tactical operations. The fire support coordination line is used to coordinate fires of air, ground, or sea weapons systems using any type of ammunition against surface targets. The fire support coordination line should follow well-defined terrain features. The establishment of the fire support coordination line must be coordinated with the appropriate tactical air commander and other supporting elements. Supporting elements may attack targets forward of the fire support coordination line, without prior coordination with the ground force commander, provided the attack will not produce adverse surface effects on, or to the rear of, the line. Attacks against surface targets behind this line must be coordinated with the appropriate ground force commander. Also known as FSCL.

forward air controller - (DOD) An officer (aviator/pilot) member of the tactical air control party who, from a forward ground or airborne position, controls aircraft in close air support of ground troops.

ground liaison officer - (DOD) An officer trained in offensive air support activities. Ground liaison officers are normally organized into parties under the control of the appropriate Army commander to provide liaison to Air Force and naval units engaged in training and combat operations.

intelligence - (DOD) The product resulting from the collection, processing, integration, analysis, evaluation, and interpretation of available information concerning foreign countries or areas.

intelligence cycle - (DOD) The steps by which information is converted into intelligence and made available to users. There are five steps in the cycle:

a. **planning and direction** - Determination of intelligence requirements, preparation of a collection plan, issuance of orders and requests to information collection agencies, and a continuous check on the productivity of collection agencies.

b. **collection** - Acquisition of information and the provision of this information to processing and/or production elements.

c. **processing** - Conversion of collected information into a form suitable to the production of intelligence.

d. **production** - Conversion of information into intelligence through the integration, analysis, evaluation, and interpretation of all source data and the preparation of intelligence products in support of known or anticipated user requirements.

e. **dissemination** - Conveyance of intelligence to users in a suitable form.

joint force air component commander - (DOD) The joint force air component commander derives his authority from the joint force commander, who has the authority to exercise operational control, assign missions, direct coordination among his subordinate commanders, and redirect and organize his forces to ensure unity of effort in the accomplishment of his overall mission. The joint force commander will normally designate a joint force air component commander. The joint force air component commander's responsibilities will be assigned by the joint force commander (normally these would include, but not be limited to, planning, coordination, allocation, and tasking based on the joint force commander's apportionment decisions). Using the joint force commander's guidance and authority, and in coordination with other Service component commanders and other assigned or supporting commanders, the joint force air component commander will recommend to the joint force commander apportionment of air sorties to various missions or geographic areas. (JCS Pub 1-02)

joint task force - (DOD) A force composed of assigned or attached elements of the Army, the Navy or the Marine Corps, and the Air Force, or two or more of these Services, that is constituted and so designated by the Secretary of Defense or by the commander of a unified command, a specified command, or an existing joint task force.

link - (DOD, NATO) In communications, a general term used to indicate the existence of communications facilities between two points.

National Command Authorities - (DOD) The President and the Secretary of Defense or their duly deputized alternates or successors. Commonly referred to as NCA.

operational command - (Combined) Operational control is having the full authority to organize and employ the units/forces as the commander in operational control considers necessary to accomplish the assigned missions. Operational control does not, in and of itself, include authority for logistics matters, administration, discipline, internal organization, or unit training. (Combined OPlan)

operational control - (DOD) Transferable command authority which may be exercised by commanders at any echelon at or below the level of combatant command. Operational control is inherent in Combatant Command (command authority) and is the authority to perform those functions of command over subordinate forces involving organizing and employing commands and forces, assigning tasks, designating objectives, and giving authoritative direction necessary to accomplish the mission. Operational control includes authoritative direction over all aspects of military operations and joint training necessary to accomplish missions assigned to the command. Operational control should be exercised through the commanders of subordinate organizations; normally this authority is exercised through the Service component commanders. Operational control normally provides full authority to organize commands and forces and to employ those forces as the commander in operational control considers necessary to accomplish assigned missions. Operational control does not, in and of itself, include authoritative direction for logistics or matters of administration, discipline, internal organization, or unit training. Also called OPCON. (JCS Pub 1-02)

operational control authority - (DOD, NATO) The naval commander responsible within a specified geographical area for the operational control of all maritime forces assigned to him and for the control of movement and protection of all merchant shipping under allied naval control. (JCS Pub 1-02)

reporting post - (DOD, NATO) An element of the control and reporting system used to extend the radar coverage of the control and reporting center. It does not undertake the control of aircraft.

rules of engagement - (DOD) Directives issued by competent military authority which delineate the circumstances and limitations under which forces will initiate and/or continue combat engagement with other forces encountered.

search and rescue - (DOD, NATO) The use of aircraft, surface craft, submarines, specialized rescue teams, and equipment to search for and rescue personnel in distress on land or at sea.

sortie - (DOD, NATO) In air operations, an operational flight by one aircraft.

specified command - (DOD) A command that has a broad continuing mission and that is established and so designated by the President through the Secretary of Defense with advice and assistance of the Joint Chiefs of Staff. It normally is composed of forces from but one Service. (JCS Pub 1-02)

supported command and supporting command - Support is the action of a force that aids, protects, complements, or sustains another force in accordance with a directive requiring such action, or a unit in battle such as aviation, artillery, or naval gunfire used as a support for infantry, or an element of a command that assists, protects, or supplies other forces in combat. Unless limited by the establishing directive, the commander of the supported force will have the authority to exercise general direction of the supporting effort. General direction includes the designation of targets or objectives, timing and duration of the supporting action, and other instructions necessary for coordination and efficiency. Normally, the supporting commander will be permitted to prescribe the tactics, methods, communications, and procedures to be employed by elements of the supporting force. (JCS Pub 0-2)

tactical air control center - (DOD, NATO) The principal air operations installation (land or ship based) from which all aircraft and air warning functions of tactical air operations are controlled.

tactical air control party - (DOD, NATO) A subordinate operational component of tactical air control system designed to provide air liaison to land forces and for the control of aircraft.

tactical control - (DOD, NATO) The detailed and, usually, local direction and control of movements or maneuvers necessary to accomplish missions or tasks assigned. (DOD Note: Also called TACON.) (JCS Pub 1-02)

tactical control - **(Combined)** Tactical control is the detailed direction and control of movements or maneuvers necessary to accomplish missions or tasks assigned. (Combined OPlan)

time on target - (DOD) 1. Time at which aircraft are scheduled to attack/photograph the target. 2. The actual time at which aircraft/photograph the target. 3. The time at which a nuclear detonation is planned at a specified desired ground zero.

unit - (DOD, NATO) 1. Any military element whose structure is prescribed by competent authority, such as a table of organization and equipment; specifically, part of an organization. 2. An organization title of a subdivision of a group in a task force. 3. A standard or basic quantity into which an item of supply is divided, issued, or used. In this meaning, also called "unit of issue." **4.** With regard to reserve components of the Armed Forces, denotes a Selected Reserve unit organized, equipped and trained for mobilization to serve on active duty as a unit or to augment or be augmented by another unit. Headquarters and support functions without wartime missions are not considered units.

unified command - (DOD) A command with a broad continuing mission under a single commander and composed of significant assigned components of two or more Services, and which is established and so designated by the President, through the Secretary of Defense with the advice and assistance of the Joint Chiefs of Staff, or, when so authorized by the Joint Chiefs of Staff, by a commander of an existing unified command established by the President. (JCS Pub 1-02)

zulu time - (NATO) Greenwich Mean Time.

References

Joint Pub 1-02, *Department of Defense Dictionary of Military and Associated Terms*, 1 December 1989 (JCS Pub 1-02)

Joint Chiefs of Staff Publication 0-2, *Unified Action Armed Forces (UNAAF)*, 1 December 1986; Change 1, 21 April 1989. (JCS Pub 0-2)

Combined OPlan for Offensive Operations to Eject Iraqi Forces from Kuwait, 17 January 1991. (Combined OPlan)

Appendix 2

The Origins of the JFACC

This appendix briefly describes the history of Air Force experience with theater control of air resources (or the lack thereof) in World War II, Korea, and Vietnam. It also summarizes the development of the Joint Force Air Component Commander (JFACC) concept in the 1980s. The actions of officers in the different Services responsible for planning and executing the air campaign in the Gulf War cannot be understood without also considering the origins of the ideas, attitudes, and command philosophies that each Service brought to the crisis. In particular, the Air Force held a position about the control and use of air power across a theater that had its origin in previous wars. In addition, the actions of air officers in the Air Force, Navy, and Marine Corps were shaped by the formal negotiations and discussions which had taken place among the Services as the JFACC concept was developed in the 1980s. Hence this appendix can serve a detailed prologue to the events of Desert Shield and Desert Storm.

A Brief History of the Theater Command of Air Forces

The idea that separate air forces in a theater of war should be under the control of one air officer can be traced back to World War II, when it was possible for the first time for air commanders to actually plan theater-wide air campaigns. The concept of theater-wide command was expressed clearly in War Department Field Manual FM 100-20 of 21 July 1943:

> The inherent flexibility of air power is its greatest asset. This flexibility makes it possible to employ the whole weight of the available air power against selected areas in turn; such concentrated use of the air striking force is a battle winning factor of the first importance. Control of the available air power must be centralized and command must be exercised through the air force commander if this inherent flexibility and ability to deliver a decisive blow are to be fully exploited.[1]

---

[1] War Department Field Manual FM 100-20, *Command and Employment of Air Power*, 21 Jul 1942 (Washington: GPO, 1944), p 2.

This approach to air operations, though not implemented fully in World War II (nor later in Korea or Vietnam), became the ideal for Army Air Corps officers, and that ideal was handed on to their successors in the independent Air Force.

An illustration from World War II, however, reveals some of the problems inherent in implementing the concept and suggests why its first serious test had to wait for the Gulf War. The illustration is the command of Allied air forces before and during the invasion of Normandy in June 1944. Gen Eisenhower, the theater CINC, had command of the expeditionary armies and the tactical air forces supporting them. He also had a nominal command of both American and British heavy bombers, and could, if necessary, divert them from their primary mission of bombing Germany to support the Allied armies. However, even though Eisenhower's chief deputy was Arthur Tedder, a British Royal Air Force Air Chief Marshall, there was no overall air commander for the theater. Instead, there were two strategic air force commanders (one U.S., the other British) and one expeditionary air force leader (Air Chief Marshall Trafford Leigh-Mallory of the Royal Air Force). This arrangement forced the three senior air commanders to negotiate the allocation of aircraft between tactical and strategic missions, and dragged Eisenhower and Tedder into any conflicts among them.[2]

Air Corps aviation commanders, basing their position on this – and similar – cases, argued after World War II for a separate military Service (called the U.S. Air Force) and, then, *Air Force* control over both strategic and theater air assets.[3] Their position was that Eisenhower's problem before Normandy (and later, too) was that he didn't really have an air deputy with the experience to control all theater air forces. They argued during and after the war that creating a separate and equal aviation Service would provide the kind and level of leadership able to serve effectively in a theater air commander's position. By the beginning of the Korean War in the summer

---

[2]W.A. Jacobs, "The Battle for France, 1944," in *Case Studies in the Development of Close Air Support*, ed by B.F. Cooling (Washington: Office of Air Force History, 1990).

[3]The similar cases were (a) the appointment of Air Marshall Tedder as commander of *allied* air forces in the Mediterranean in 1943, (b) Gen George Kenney's service as Gen MacArthur's air deputy – where he planned missions for Army *and* Navy aircraft – in the Southwest Pacific Area, (c) the combined efforts of Army, Navy, and Marine Corps aviation in the Guadalcanal campaign of 1942-43, and (d) the combination of tactical Army and Marine Corps aviation during the conquest of Okinawa in 1945.

of 1950, the founders of the Air Force had gained independence for their Service. They had also gained independent control of strategic air units, but they had not been installed as theater air commanders.

They would not be given formal command of theater aviation during the Korean War, either. In June 1950, the President, responding to the emergency in Korea, designated Gen. Douglas MacArthur, commander of the U.S. Far East Command, as both U.S. theater commander and commander of United Nations forces. MacArthur was supposed to have a joint staff, but in fact he had "continued his World War II practice of maintaining a theater staff that was joint and unified only in name. . . ."[4] Lt. Gen. George Stratemeyer, USAF, commanding the Air Force units based in Japan, Guam, and the Philippines (the Far East Air Forces), was almost immediately faced with a call, from the Navy theater component commander, for "exclusive use" of the skies over much of northwest Korea.[5]

From that moment, and then through most of July 1950, Stratemeyer and his staff waged a quiet, persistent bureaucratic battle to place control over all theater air (allied as well as U.S. Navy) in his hands or in those of his operational subordinate commanders. Despite the fact that Stratemeyer was not close personally or organizationally to General MacArthur, he and his deputies were, to a great degree, successful. By mid-July 1950, they had (a) pulled control of tactical theater air operations from MacArthur's headquarters staff, (b) successfully delegated that control to Stratemeyer's Fifth Air Force in Korea, (c) forced MacArthur to recognize Stratemeyer as senior theater air commander, and (d) reached at least an accommodation with the Navy over the issue of unified control of theater air assets. By the end of that month, Stratemeyer had also gained de facto control over the theater-level air targeting committee which advised General MacArthur. Yet MacArthur had refused to appoint the Air Force component commander the theater air commander, and there the matter rested throughout the Korean War, much to the irritation of Stratemeyer and his successor, Lt. Gen. O. P. Weyland.

---

[4]B. F. Cooling, ed, *Case Studies in the Development of Close Air Support* (Washington: Office of Air Force History, 1990), p 358.

[5]The story of Lt Gen Stratemeyer's efforts is taken from R.F. Futrell, *The United States Air Force in Korea, 1950-1953* (Washington: Office of Air Force History, U.S. Air Force, 1983).

The U.S. Air Force did not want the control of theater air forces in Southeast Asia to be divided and dispersed among different commands and among the Services. Vietnam was not supposed to be, in command terms, another Korea. Unfortunately, that is precisely what it was. In 1965, for example, the Military Assistance Command, Vietnam (MACV) was responsible for all military operations in South Vietnam. The commander, 2d Air Division was the Air Force component commander under the commander, MACV. The latter reported to the theater commander, the Commander in Chief, Pacific (CINCPAC). However, the commander of the Navy's carrier Task Force 77, which operated in the Gulf of Tonkin, also reported to CINCPAC, but through the commander, 7th Fleet and then through the Commander in Chief, Pacific Fleet (CINCPACFLT).

On paper, it looked like Air Force and Navy air operations could be coordinated by CINCPAC, the overall theater commander. In fact, however, the commander, MACV reported directly to the Joint Chiefs of Staff and to the President. Moreover, CINCPAC's air component commander (Commander, Pacific Air Forces, or CINCPACAF), was neither the theater air commander nor CINCPAC's principal air advisor. When U.S. planes began bombing North Vietnam in earnest in 1965, representatives of the 2d Air Division from MACV and of Carrier Task Force 77 formed the Rolling Thunder Coordinating Committee to apportion Navy and Air Force strikes. The Committee chose to divide North Vietnam into six geographic areas, called "route packages," and three were assigned to the Navy, two to the Air Force, and the sixth was shared. In effect, the local air commanders, with the approval of CINCPAC, set up separate Air Force and Navy air wars.

As the Air Force effort in both South and North Vietnam increased in 1966, the 2d Air Division was superseded by the 7th Air Force, with headquarters in Saigon. By then, there were at least three air wars in Southeast Asia, with no overall commander. The commander, MACV "essentially ran air operations within South Vietnam, using the Commanding General, Seventh Air Force, as his Deputy COMUSMACV for Air. . . ."[6] Commander, MACV also directed the interdiction bombing of the Ho Chi Minh Trail in Laos, though his planned strikes had first to be cleared with the U.S. ambassador there, who was using air in a variety of

---

[6]G. A. Cosmas, "General Westmoreland and Control of the Air War," in *Command and Control of Air Operations in the Vietnam War*, Colloquium on Contemporary History, 23 Jan 1991 (Washington: Naval Historical Center, Navy Department), p 30.

ways to support elements of the Laotian population that were resisting the North Vietnamese.

CINCPAC, as the senior theater commander, was officially responsible for the air war against North Vietnam, and the commanders of the Seventh Air Force and the 7th Fleet took orders from him through their component commanders (CINCPACAF and CINCPACFLT, respectively). But it was the President and his advisors (especially the Secretary of Defense) who really directed the Rolling Thunder campaign against North Vietnam; the theater commander (CINCPAC) was only nominally in charge. In addition, B-52s of the Strategic Air Command (SAC) that flew combat missions in the theater remained under SAC's control, even when they attacked targets in South Vietnam (where MACV furnished the bombers with their target coordinates). Finally, Marine Corps aviation in South Vietnam, under the command of the III Marine Amphibious (later Expeditionary) Force, flew close air support missions under the direction of Seventh Air Force after 1966.

This dispersion of authority over air operations resulted from and added to inter-Service conflict and disputes among the various air commanders within the theater. In 1965, for example, the commander, MACV challenged the authority of CINCPAC, the theater commander, to direct the bombing of North Vietnam. He took his case right to the Joint Chiefs of Staff, who sided with CINCPAC. The commander, MACV however, still controlled close air support missions in South Vietnam through (after 1966) Seventh Air Force and III Marine Expeditionary Force. Despite requests from the commander, Seventh Air Force that he unite the theater air effort under one air officer, CINCPAC refused to appoint a subordinate theater air manager. The message in all this was clear: authority over air assets was dispersed and therefore negotiable. As a result, when the commander, Seventh Air Force tried to take command of the 1st Marine Air Wing in January 1968, the Commandant of the Marine Corps fought the effort all the way to the President, who decided in favor of the commander, Seventh Air Force.[7]

Managing the multiple air wars in Southeast Asia remained a matter of negotiation among the theater commander and the local commanders

---

[7]*Ibid*, p 31. For more on command and control in Southeast Asia, see "Command, Control and Communications Structures in Southeast Asia," Vol. I, Monograph I of *The Air War in Indochina*.

through operations Linebacker I and Linebacker II (the bombing of Hanoi) in 1972. The pattern had been set in 1965, with the creation of the Rolling Thunder Coordinating Committee, and only the pressure of events forced the Services to set aside their resistance to effective joint coordination of air action. Lt. Gen. John Vogt, Seventh Air Force Commander (April 1972-September 1973) during Linebacker I and II (spring of 1972 through December), noted in an interview with Air Force researchers that the close cooperation between officers of his staff and their counterparts in the Army's Air Operations Section in Saigon was due to the fact that many staff officers had been sent home before the North Vietnamese launched their attack on the South.[8] It was a matter of collocated staffs short of personnel having to improvise, and not the result of having a joint staff structure or command.

Indeed, local Navy, Air Force, and Marine air commanders had learned to coordinate their actions *despite* the lack of a joint command. Perhaps the major reason why local and theater commanders did not resolve their inter-Service differences by developing an effective joint command was the involvement of senior civilians in Washington in day-to-day operations. That involvement encouraged local and theater commanders to appeal their differences to Washington, which encouraged the civilians to intervene even more. The chain of command was so loose and confused that there was a kind of bargaining free-for-all, where different field commanders worried about their informal ties to influential civilian bureaucrats in Washington.[9]

This unfortunate situation actually helped hinder the resolution of a major problem in the technology of the command and control of air operations. One reason why Navy officers in Southeast Asia resisted Air Force efforts to create a single theater-wide air manager was because the control of many air sorties required "extremely high information flows" that existing Air Force Tactical Air Control Centers (TACCs) could not handle.[10] The Navy's position was that no one TACC could really plan the whole air battle in the theater, despite advances in ground-to-air communications and in the means of handling large amounts of data (that is,

---

[8] Intvw, Office of Air Force History with Lt Gen John W. Vogt, Bolling AFB, Washington, DC, 31 Jan 1986, p 15.

[9] The negative effects of all this essentially political activity are explored in Martin Van Creveld's *Command in War* (Cambridge, MA: Harvard Univ. Press, 1985), Chap. 7.

[10] "Command, Control and Communications Structures in Southeast Asia," p 146.

with computers). As one Air Force study noted, the Navy was close to the truth: "the introduction of automation has resulted in the essentially independent growth of a multitude of C3 automated systems which have become interconnected through a series of ad-hoc arrangements."[11] In effect, the Navy's argument *against* the Air Force position that there should be a single manager for air at the theater level was that the Air Force was making essentially a case based on faith and not upon what existing technology in the existing organization could do.

The Air Force position, by contrast, was that improvements in the technology of command and control, especially automated tactical displays, effective radio links between attacking flights and surveillance aircraft, and integrated radar track data from ground and airborne radars, had in fact made it possible for commanders in ground command centers to monitor and direct complex air actions.[12] The Navy, so the argument ran, had not kept up with the evolution of Air Force command and control in the theater. By the end of 1968, the Air Force operated in Southeast Asia airborne communications relay aircraft and other planes performing the early warning mission. Air Force units had also (a) installed a system (codenamed SEEK DATA) which automated mission reports and threat intelligence, (b) linked Air Force tactical communications with Navy and Marine Corps tactical data displays through the USMC's air operations center, and (c) developed a secure voice communications net.[13] The Air Force position was that these systems were the ones essential to a functioning Tactical Air Control System. The Navy did not agree. Where the Air Force saw evolution toward a coherent system, the Navy saw confusion.

In World War II, theater control of air operations was essentially a matter of allocating responsibility for types of targets, as when General Eisenhower ordered his strategic air commanders to bomb railroad yards. By 1968, however, the Air Force was in the process of developing near

---

[11]*Ibid*, p 151.

[12]Rpt, Lt Col R. M. Burch, *Command and Control, 1966-1968*, Project CHECO, HQ PACAF, Directorate, Tactical Evaluation, CHECO Division, Office of Air Force History, Washington, DC.

[13]*Ibid*, p 35. In 1967-68, the 7th Air Force linked its EC-121 radar surveillance and early warning aircraft with its Airborne Battlefield Command, Control and Communications planes and its Tactical Air Control Center in Saigon. The purpose was to allow the TACC to shift strikes in support of ground forces from one region in South Vietnam to another, adjacent region if the ground situation changed.

real-time control of air operations through its Tactical Air Control Center, so that an aviation commander on the ground could, in theory, direct flights of aircraft across much of North and South Vietnam. By 1972, during Operations Linebacker I and II, signals intelligence personnel were able to alert U.S. units flying in North Vietnamese airspace that enemy fighters were taking off to attack them.[14] Did this ability to exploit the enemy's communications *and* provide that critical intelligence to friendly aircraft in time for them to intercept the enemy mean that a theater air commander could direct sorties as well as allocate them to mission categories? The answer was not clear in 1972, but most of the systems which now make up a Tactical Air Control System were present in *at least* rudimentary form.

Veterans of Rolling Thunder such as Lt. Gen. Charles Horner and his senior operations deputy during Desert Storm, Maj. Gen. John Corder, carried some lessons away from their experience. They had worked within an evolving theater air control and surveillance system, but they had also experienced the negative consequences of a divided theater command structure. As a result, they were firmly committed to having an Air Force officer as theater air commander in a setting like that in Vietnam. A second lesson was the need to oppose the kind of negotiating with officials in Washington that had characterized the control and command of air forces during Rolling Thunder. Added to these lessons was a confidence that central command of theater-wide air forces from multiple Services was organizationally and technically possible.

The Emergence of the JFACC Concept in the 1980s

Two issues came together during the early years of the Reagan Administration. The first, pushed by Congress and accepted by the White House, was an effort to give the theater commanders more say in the development of strategic plans and Service programs. The second, fostered by the House and Senate Armed Services Committees, aimed at increasing the effectiveness of joint operations and the authority of joint commands and led eventually to the Goldwater-Nichols act (the Department of Defense Reorganization Act of 1986). A spin-off of these two

---

[14]This was "Teaball," a ground control intercept facility which first went into operation in August 1972 and gave U.S. pilots real-time warning of North Vietnamese MiG interceptor attacks. See Rpt, M. F. Porter, *Linebacker: Overview of the First 120 Days*, Project CHECO, 27 Sep 1973, HQ PACAF, Directorate of Operations Analysis, Office of Air Force History, Bolling AFB, Washington, DC, pp 68–69.

issues was growing support among the Services themselves for the concept of a joint theater air commander.

In 1982, the Joint Chiefs established a Joint Doctrine Pilot Program, inviting submissions from the unified and specified commanders. Three years later, the Commander in Chief of the European Command (CINCEUR) formally submitted to the Chiefs a joint doctrine for theater counterair operations. One element of this proposed doctrine was the concept of the Joint Force Air Component Commander, an officer appointed by the theater or Joint Force Commander to plan and coordinate a jointly fought air campaign.[15] On 21 February 1986, the Chiefs approved CINCEUR's proposal as JCS Publication 26, *Joint Doctrine for Theater Counterair Operations*.

In a message communicating their decision, the Chiefs noted that "The Joint Force Air Component Commander's responsibilities will be assigned by the Joint Force Commander (normally these would include, but not be limited to, planning, coordination, allocation and tasking based on the Joint Force Commander's Apportionment decision)."[16] In the same message, the Chiefs also confirmed the policy, expressed in an "Omnibus Agreement," which governed the command and control of Marine Corps tactical aviation:

> The Marine Air-Ground Task Force (MAGTF) Commander will retain operational control of his organic air assets. . . . The MAGTF Commander will make sorties available to the Joint Force Commander, for tasking through his Air Component Commander, for air defense, long-range interdiction and long-range reconnaissance. Sorties in excess of MAGTF direct support requirements will be provided to the Joint Force Commander. . . .[17]

The decision of the Joint Chiefs to grant authority to theater commanders to create a joint air component commander was balanced against the demand of the Marine Corps that its Air-Ground Task Force aviation not be removed from the control of MAGTF commanders.

---

[15]Msg, from Chairman, Joint Chiefs of Staff; subj: "Joint Doctrine for Theater Counterair Operations," 4 Mar 1986, p 1.

[16]*Ibid*, p 2.

[17]*Ibid*, p 2.

This balance was not stable, despite the Chiefs' attempt to make it so. For example, JCS Publication 26 (now 3-01.2, *Joint Doctrine for Theater Counterair Operations*), issued 1 April 1986, contained both the description of the Joint Force Air Component Commander's responsibilities *and* the statement from the Omnibus Agreement that the Marine Air-Ground Task Force commander would "retain operational control of his organic air assets." However, the publication also said that, "Normally, the [JFACC] will be the Service component commander who has the preponderance of air assets to be used and the ability to assume that responsibility." The key phrase was "ability to assume." The Marines would later argue that no Air Force JFACC really had the ability to assume responsibility for controlling the aviation side of Marine combined arms operations. The Air Force would respond that the Marine air-ground perspective, though valid for them, should not be allowed to threaten the unity of a theater air campaign.

JCS Publication 26, however, did not cover just airborne counterair operations. It also covered ground-based air defenses, dividing air defense systems into those "organic" to ground units and those under the operational control of the Area Air Defense Commander (who was also, normally, the JFACC).[18] In addition, Publication 26 gave the Area Air Defense Commander responsibility for promulgating, under the theater commander's guidance, "weapons control procedures" for *all* ground-based air defense systems.[19] Finally, JCS Publication 26 gave the JFACC the responsibility for recommending the apportioning of air forces and for actually allocating the "air sorties apportioned to perform counterair operations by the joint force commander. . . ."[20]

In August 1986, the Joint Chiefs issued Joint Publication 12, "Tactical Command and Control Planning Guidance and Procedures for Joint Operations,"[21] as part of the process of explaining the methods by which the JFACC's responsibilities would be implemented. Joint Publication 12 defined terms such as "apportionment" and "allocation" and noted that "The actual allocation of those air sorties apportioned by the JTF Com-

---

[18] JCS Pub 26, *Joint Doctrine for Theater Counterair Operations*, 1 Apr 1986, p III-5.

[19] *Ibid*, p III-5.

[20] *Ibid*, p III-6.

[21] JCS Pub 12 (now Pub 3-56.24), *Tactical Command and Control Planning Guidance and Procedures for Joint Operations, Joint Interface Operational Procedures (JIOP) Message Text Formats*, 1 Aug 1986.

mander to support the JTF as a whole will be prescribed by the Joint Force Air Component Commander (JFACC). . . ."[22] Publication 12 also defined the "air tasking cycle," and it defined the product of the cycle as "an intra-Service Air Tasking Order."[23] It also specified that the JFACC would coordinate close air support operations when the "supporting Service component cannot satisfy the supported Service component's requirements. . . ."[24]

Publication 12 also exempted Army helicopters from the JFACC's control. By definition, they did not fly sorties, and they did not "perform the functions of close air support, escort, or airlift."[25] The Army thought of its helicopters the way the Marine Corps thought of its fixed-wing aviation – as "organic" to a "combined arms team" and therefore normally "controlled by the Army Component Commander."[26] However, if another Service wanted Army helicopter support, it would have to pass its request through the JFACC, the JFACC would have to "validate" the request, and, if the request were approved by the joint force commander, the JFACC would "task the Army to perform the mission via an Operations or Fragmentary Order." That done, the requesting Service would work directly with the Army component commander to work out the details of Army helicopter support.[27]

Joint Publication 12 also specified in some detail the procedures that the Services would follow to work within what it called an "air tasking cycle."[28] Clearly, the JFACC could not serve as the coordinating and planning agent for the theater or joint force commander if there were no common standard among the Services for requesting air missions and for planning and tasking them. The level of detail in Joint Publication 12 was put there to satisfy that need and indicates that the commitment to the JFACC concept by the Chiefs was serious. The major issues – including the status of Army helicopters and the relationship between the Marine Corps and the JFACC – were addressed in detail, and the policies and

---

[22] *Ibid*, Vol. IV, Part V, p III-45.

[23] *Ibid*.

[24] *Ibid*, p III-46.

[25] *Ibid*, p III-47.

[26] *Ibid*.

[27] *Ibid*, p III-48.

[28] *Ibid*, pp III-48-50.

procedures laid out in Joint Publication 12 were consistent with the guidance that the Joint Chiefs had promulgated the previous April in Joint Publication 26.

In 1987, the Joint Staff modified JCS Publication 1, *Dictionary of Military and Associated Terms*, to include, for the first time, a definition of the Joint Force Air Component Commander and his responsibilities. The latter included "planning, coordination, allocation and tasking based on the joint force commander's apportionment decision."[29] It looked like the promise of effective theater control of air power was being realized at last. However, in June 1988, JCS Test Publication[30] 3-03.1, *Follow-On Forces Attack*, listed the responsibilities of the JFACC only as coordinating and deconflicting the joint air interdiction effort. The Air Force officially differed (as it had every right to do) with that language, preferring *planning*, as well as coordinating and deconflicting.[31] That change would have brought Test Publication 3-03.1 into line with joint test publication 3-04, *Joint Maritime Operations (Air)*, of 1 May 1988, where the JFACC's responsibilities were given as including, but not limited to, "planning, coordination, allocation, and tasking based on the [Joint Force Commander's] apportionment decision."[32]

According to officers on the Air Staff, the JFACC concept was first tested in exercise Ocean Venture-88 (May 1988) by the staff of the Atlantic Command. The Commander, Twelfth Air Force served as the JFACC, and he used an air tasking order to allocate USAF and Navy sorties (in excess of fleet air defense requirements) among close air support and interdiction missions.[33] However, representatives of the Fleet Marine Force, Atlantic and of the Tactical Air Command and the Twelfth Air Force were subsequently unable to agree completely on a concept of operations for the

---

[29] JCS Pub 1 (now JCS Pub 1-02), 1 Jun 1987, *Department of Defense Dictionary of Military and Associated Terms*, p 201.

[30] JCS publications move through a definite sequence of drafting and approval, starting with an "initial draft," then becoming a "formal draft," then being circulated and applied as a "test publication," and then, finally, gaining formal approval as a "joint publication."

[31] JCS Test Publication 3-03.1, *Follow-On Forces Attack*, 16 Jun 1988, p III-7. The Air Force's "Difference of Opinion" is in Appendix B, p 1.

[32] JCS Test Publication 3-04, *Joint Maritime Operations (Air)*, 1 May 1988, p III-5.

[33] Point Paper, subj: Joint Force Air Component Commander (JFACC) and JFACC Implementation, 13 Oct 1989, XPJD/47567; plus discussions with officers in USAF XOXD, the Pentagon.

JFACC that would apply to the next year's joint exercise. Yet that exercise (already given the name "Solid Shield") had been scheduled as a test of Joint Test Publication 3-04, *Joint Maritime Operations (Air).*

Despite Air Force objections, the exercise was run with a "JFACC Concept of Operations," which specified that the "JFACC will execute air operations using sorties made available by air capable component commanders . . . in accordance with [the commander, joint task force's] apportionment decisions."[34] From the perspective of participating Air Force officers, this concept of operations was too limited. Their argument was that it left the JFACC too dependent upon the "air capable" component commanders, thereby violating the spirit (if not the letter) of the Joint Chiefs' message of 4 March 1986 ("Joint Doctrine for Theater Counterair Operations").[35]

Because there was still no agreement among the Air Force, the Navy, and the Marine Corps about the proper scope of the JFACC's authority, the Commanding General of the Marine Corps Combat Development Command issued a letter (dated 9 March 1989) which attempted to define the proper relationship between the JFACC and the Marine Air-Ground Task Force Commander.[36] The letter reaffirmed the Marine Corps' commitment to the authority of the Marine Air-Ground Task Force Commander *and* to the JFACC concept. However, it also argued that (a) the JFACC was not directly in the chain of command, (b) the JFACC was not empowered to command "forces other than those organic to him as a Service component commander," and (c) the JFACC had "no inherent authority to exercise" operational control of air forces.[37] The letter also recognized, however, that the precise authority of the JFACC was "subject to interpretation."[38]

The letter proposed to clarify the interpretation by arguing, first, that "operational control" meant "possession of assets," so that operational

---

[34]Msg, Commander Second Fleet, 181542Z, Feb 1989.

[35]Point Paper, subj: Joint Force Air Component Commander (JFACC) and JFACC Implementation, pp 4-5.

[36]Ltr, from Commanding General, Marine Corps Combat Development Command, subj: The Joint Force Air Component Commander and Command and Control of Marine Air-Ground Task Force Aviation, 9 Mar 1989, Quantico, VA.

[37]*Ibid*, p 6.

[38]*Ibid*.

control lay only in the hands of the Marine Air-Ground Task Force Commander. Second, that the authority to task assets was de facto the authority of operational control. However, because the JFACC did not have operational control over Marine air assets, he could not task them. Third, what he could do was task those sorties which, by the Omnibus Agreement, the Marine Air-Ground Task Force Commander was pledged to offer to the Joint Force Commander.[39] These sorties were not excess, however, because they were "distinct contributions to the overall joint force effort. . . ."[40] With this argument, the letter proposed to dismiss the objection Air Force officers had raised to the JFACC concept of operations used during exercise Solid Shield.

While the Services were trying to clarify the meaning of the JFACC concept, CENTAF was responsible for preparing, for CENTCOM, an operations plan. OPlan 1021-88, dated 30 May 1989, drew its terms and its concept of authority from the newly revised or written JCS documents, such as JCS Publication 1-02, *Dictionary of Military and Associated Terms*.[41] 1021-88 made the Commander, Central Command Air Forces the Joint Force Air Component Commander, the Area Air Defense Commander, the Airspace Control Authority, and the Coordinating Authority for Interdiction. As JFACC, the Commander, CENTAF was given the authority to plan, coordinate, allocate, and task air sorties in accordance with the theater commander's guidance. The JFACC was also given the responsibility for recommending to the theater commander the proper apportionment of sorties among the various kinds of missions, such as close air support. The other component commanders were given the right to forward their own apportionment recommendations, but the Plan specified that "such separate recommendations should be the exception, not the rule, in that such recommendations are contrary to the fundamental principle of a JFACC."[42]

Once the theater commander had apportioned the sorties on a percentage basis among the required mission types, the JFACC was responsible for allocating the sorties among the aviation units which were under the

---

[39] *Ibid*, pp 6-7.

[40] *Ibid*, p 4.

[41] (S) COMUSCENTAF OPlan 1021-88, Annex C, Appendix 16, "Joint Force Air Component Commander (JFACC) Functions," p C-16-1.

[42] (S) OPlan 1021-88, p C-16-3.

operational control of the theater commander. The Marine component commander retained "allocation and tasking responsibility for direct support."[43] However, as area air defender, the JFACC was responsible for airspace control.[44] Navy air defense in CENTCOM's Area of Responsibility was to be "integrated with the JFACC land-based or airborne air defense C2 network."[45] Planning for offensive counterair operations, under the theater commander's guidance, was also the JFACC's responsibility.[46]

In the mission area of interdiction, the JFACC's powers were limited. OPlan 1021-88 specifically noted that

> . . . COMUSCENTAF has the responsibility for coordinating the interdiction effort of all components and the authority to require consultation among the components, but does not have the authority to compel agreement.[47]

At the same time, the JFACC was given the responsibility for planning, coordinating, and deconflicting "the execution of the overall theater air interdiction campaign."[48] That there might be a conflict between "coordinating" and "planning" a theater-wide air campaign was not lost on the Air Staff in the Pentagon.[49] The problem for them – and for the Commander, CENTAF – was that the scope of the JFACC's powers was still being negotiated at the Service level.

In August 1989, for example, the Tactical Air Command responded to the Marine Corps letter of the previous March.[50] TAC's difference with the Marine Corps was clear from the initial paragraphs of that response: "The JFACC will plan the joint air operations campaign to exploit the

---

[43](S) *Ibid.*

[44](S) *Ibid.*

[45]*Ibid*, p C-16-5.

[46]*Ibid.*

[47]*Ibid*, p C-16-12.

[48]*Ibid.*

[49]Memo, subj: Review of Proposed USCINCCENT OPlan 1002-90, from XOXW to XOXX, Headquarters, U.S. Air Force, 14 May 1990, GWAPS Files.

[50]TAC/XPJ Proposal: Joint Force Air Component Commander (JFACC) Concept of Operations, 29 Aug 1989, TAC HQ, Langley AFB, VA.

capabilities of air power in support of joint force objectives. . . .[51] The JFACC has authority to allocate and task sorties flown by air forces assigned to or supporting the joint force. . . .[52] The JFC and the JFACC must evaluate and assess the impact of air action on both the enemy and friendly forces. This assessment serves as a basis for subsequent decisions regarding the employment of air power."[53] If the Marines saw the JFACC as a kind of traffic cop, coordinating overlapping air efforts, the Air Force, by contrast, saw the JFACC as the chief air planner and the joint force commander's chief air deputy.

This was a very real difference. It mattered in Desert Shield and Desert Storm because it had not been officially resolved by August 1990. Hence it formed a backdrop to the actions of Lt. Gen. Charles Horner, USAF, the Joint Force Air Component Commander during these operations, and to those of the Navy and Marine Corps component commanders. The Air Force position, forcefully presented in the TAC paper of August 1989, was that the JFACC, the component commander with the preponderance of combat air assets in the theater, was responsible for directing the theater-wide air effort. The Marine Corps and Navy were not committed to this position, had not trained for it, and had not purchased the equipment (such as the Computer Assisted Force Management System terminals) required to implement it effectively.[54]

Though the Service chiefs had formally accepted the concept of the JFACC in 1986, they had also endorsed the Omnibus Agreement, which the Marine Corps had steadfastly held on to as protection against the possible loss of "organic" aviation during a combat operation. The concerns of the Marine Corps go back to the 1930s, when the Fleet Marine Force was created to conquer Japanese-held islands as part of a U.S. offensive against Japan in the Western Pacific. At that time, the Navy had assured Marine Corps commanders that Navy carrier aviation would provide Marine ground troops with adequate close air support. Marine Corps leaders did not accept the Navy's assurances and fought –

---

[51]*Ibid*, p 1.

[52]*Ibid*, p 2.

[53]*Ibid*, p 6.

[54]One problem for the Navy was that the software for CAFMS differed from theater to theater, so that terminals configured to work with CENTCOM would not, apparently, automatically work in the Pacific.

successfully – for the expansion and modernization of their own air arm.⁵⁵ Since 1947, Marine Corps operations had been based on the assumption that "organic" aviation would sustain Marine ground units engaging the enemy. Marine Corps combined arms combat organization and training was based upon "organic" air.

So it was almost inevitable that, after 1986, as the specifics of the JFACC concept were worked out through exercises and JCS joint publication reviews, Marine Corps and Air Force officers would disagree. That they disagreed about the JFACC's authority, however, should not obscure areas where they came together. Both Services, for example, agreed that the JFACC was responsible for setting up systems for air traffic control and area air defense during joint operations. Both Services also agreed that the JFACC, *in coordination with the component commanders*, would make air apportionment recommendations to the theater or joint force commander. Navy, Air Force, and Marine air commanders under the Commander in Chief, Central Command had also agreed that their air planning would be done using the Air Force Air Tasking Order Process, and that the JFACC had the authority to make changes in the ATO when the situation necessitated it.⁵⁶ Where their parent Services disagreed the most was over the air component commander's authority when he acted as JFACC.

Central Command's Operations Plan 1002-90 reflected this disagreement. It gave the JFACC responsibility for (a) "Planning, coordination, allocation, and tasking based on USCINCCENT apportionment decisions," (b) "Recommending to USCINCCENT apportionment of theater air sorties," (c) coordinating with the component commanders "to ensure integration of air operations," (d) "Integration of supporting maritime air resources through" the Navy component commander, (e) area air defense, (f) airspace control, and (g) conduct of "counterair, close air support, and interdiction operations."⁵⁷ These responsibilities were given as tasks.

The potential for conflict between the JFACC and the component commanders was contained in them. How, for example, could the JFACC

---

⁵⁵"Procurement of Airplanes for Fleet Marine Force," *Hearings before the General Board of the Navy*, 22 Sep 1938, p 175, National Archives.

⁵⁶(S) OPlan 1021-88, p C-16-13 and p C-16-14.

⁵⁷(S/NF) USCINCCENT OPlan 1002-90, Outline Plan, HQ, US Central Command, 16 Apr 1990, pp 23-25.

conduct operations if his powers were only to coordinate separate Service efforts? And what was the status of Commander, CENTAF's OPlan 1021-88 under the new CINCCENT OPlan 1002-90? How could the JFACC be held accountable for tasks if his office did not have the authority to compel the component commanders to accept his guidance? These questions were a very important part of the background to the JFACC's actions during Desert Shield and Desert Storm.

Appendix 3

Use of C3 Modeling Aids to Prepare for and Predict War

"Never has a war been so programmed, so modeled. I guarantee it."
Brig. Gen. Buster C. Glosson[1]

It might be more accurate to say that some of the command and control for Desert Storm was more programmed, more modeled than command and control in any previous air war. As Chapters 7 and 8 show, a lot of what happened in the Tactical Air Control Center (TACC) and in the Tactical Air Control System (TACS) during Desert Storm was improvised. Nevertheless, models were used, and this appendix will illustrate how software models were employed (in Washington and in theater) during Desert Shield and Desert Storm and suggest when and why they were employed successfully.

Such models were developed because experience with operations research during World War II convinced military officers that specialists trained in the techniques of modeling and simulation could contribute to the solution of complex military problems.[2] The faith in the utility of models and simulations as aids in making decisions in the areas of development and operations grew during the postwar years, and all the Services trained and hired professionals skilled in the use of such techniques.

The limited range of topics operations researchers were asked to consider during Desert Shield/Desert Storm continued the pattern of

---

[1] Cited in Tony Capaccio, "Computer Runs Honed Attacks on Nuclear, Chemical Sites," *Defense News*, 5 Aug 1991, p 3.

[2] Jacob A. Stockfisch, former Asst. Secretary of the Army for Research and Development, showed in his book, *Plowshares into Swords* (New York, 1973), p 189, that operations research (or operations analysis) helped allied military leaders figure out how best to use the weapons they had and also how to avoid pouring money into projects that would have little payoff during the war.

constraining such specialists to analyses that would not call into question the authority exercised by operational commanders. The decision tools and models used by operations researchers in the Persian Gulf War reduced the anxiety of the senior leadership about tactics and force mixtures but did not alter the basic conception of how to wage the air campaign. The range of topics and issues considered was limited to those for which the operators running the Black Hole needed answers.

Modeling and Decision Aids in the Theater

Operations researchers brought several models to Saudi Arabia that helped operators understand the implications of tactical- and theater-level force packaging decisions. One theater-level force packaging model was C3ISIM, a hybrid monte carlo or deterministic simulation developed for the U.S. Army Missile Command by Teledyne Brown Engineering. C3ISIM was developed to study alternative command and control structures needed to defeat the tactical ballistic missile threat in central Europe.[3] However, the model's information needs were severe, and the relevant data were not readily available.

Characteristics of C3ISIM

On the one hand, several features of the C3ISIM model facilitated its choice as a decision tool. First, a unique feature of C3ISIM was that the command, control, and communications (C^3) capabilities of real systems were modeled with a high degree of accuracy, which made the model a desirable tool for assessing attacks against a Soviet-style integrated air defense system. Second, the model's high-resolution graphics output allowed an analyst to view a battle from high above, synchronize activities to an elapsed time clock, and replay a mission. In effect, the model permitted an operations planner to see the strengths and weaknesses of a plan as the planned operation unfolded. On the other hand, C3ISIM required many detailed data inputs, such as radar frequencies, antenna gains and transmit power levels, positions of air defense systems and waypoints of all aircraft, and probabilities of kill for every missile and bomb against

---

[3]C. Bradford Cooper, "Extended Air Defense Simulation (EADSIM) History," unpublished, nd.

a variety of targets. In August 1990, "much of the necessary data were missing," and the modeling team responsible for running C3ISIM had no experience building such a large scenario.[4]

Use of C3ISIM

On 4 or 5 August 1990, armed with a terrain map of Iraq and Defense Intelligence Agency (DIA) enemy order of battle, Air Force Studies and Analysis Agency (AF/SAA) analysts began—on their own initiative—to look at how C3ISIM[5] could be used to analyze the air defense networks in Saudi Arabia and Iraq.[6] On 25 August, three weeks after AF/SAA analysts began using C3ISIM to analyze air defense networks, Maj. Gen. Minter Alexander, Air Force Director of Plans (AF/XOX), asked Maj. Gen. George Harrison (Director of AF/SAA) to estimate the attrition incidental to the campaign being drafted in Checkmate. AF/SAA's Theater Force Directorate conducted three analyses to answer Alexander's request. The first analysis provided a "quick and dirty" answer to AF/XOX within one week by using a spread sheet model and attrition estimates generated from a previous AF/SAA study effort. The second analysis employed AF/SAA's theater-level campaign model, TAC Thunder, to look at attrition levels for a ten- to fourteen-day campaign and a thirty-day campaign. The results of this work were submitted to the Concepts Analysis Agency as input to a ground warfare model.[7] The third analysis used the unproven C3ISIM model to examine the first twenty-four hours of the allied air attack plan. The C3ISIM model was well suited for a detailed, mission-level study. It

---

[4]Frederic T. Case, *Analysis of Air Operations During Desert Shield/Desert Storm* (USAF Studies and Analysis Agency, Washington, DC, Nov 1991), p 2.

[5]In the late 1980s, Teledyne Brown Engineering Company developed C3ISIM, a hybrid monte carlo/deterministic simulation, for what was then the US Army Missile Command. Currently, the US Army Strategic Defense Command manages the model. The model was conceived as a tool to study alternative command and control structures needed to defeat the tactical ballistic missile threat to Central Europe. Several names have been associated with the C3ISIM model. It also has been known as TMD C3ISIM, and as the Extended Air Defense Simulation – EADSIM. Case, *Analysis of Air Operations During Desert Shield/Desert Storm*, pp vii, 1-2.

[6]Intvw, Mark D. Mandeles and Jim Vernon with Lt Col Frederic T. Case, Air Force Studies and Analyses Agency, 30 Mar 1992.

[7]*Ibid.*

played out engagements between fighters and surface-to-air missiles and fighters. It accounted for the effects of centralized command and control centers. Furthermore, a graphic playback of the results was used to examine the progress of the simulated battle as it unfolded.[8]

During September and early October, AF/SAA analysts collected a great deal of data necessary to give validity to the model's calculations; they then developed a prototype model of the air campaign. Developing and running of the prototype model revealed that it was difficult to feed into the model both enemy sensor locations and the C^3 network that tied those sensors together.[9] In addition, the model simplified emissions control of friendly or enemy radar systems by having them radiating at all times. This simplification precluded modeling an effective IADS where normally the radars are off the air. The model also did not account for confusion at the command nodes; instead, it assumed a near-perfect level of performance at enemy command centers. Finally, the model assigned a single value to the outcome of missiles fired or shots taken but did not consider speed, altitude, or aspect angle of the missile engagement.[10]

While still stationed in the Pentagon, AF/SAA analysts did not have access to the details of the Guidance, Apportionment, and Targeting cell's (GAT's) Master Attack Plan, which they needed in order to conduct a thorough analysis.[11] AF/SAA analysts therefore simplified their working assumptions. They assumed that Iraq's air force would not pose an early threat. Fuel consumption rates and the probabilities of kill for Iraqi optically guided antiaircraft artillery were not modeled. In addition, the attacking aircraft were started and stopped at their air refueling drop-off

---

[8]*Ibid*; Case, *Analysis of Air Operations During Desert Shield/Desert Storm*, p 1.

[9]Case, *Analysis of Air Operations*, p 2.

[10]*Ibid*, p 3.

[11]The structure of the Master Attack Plan is well-suited to providing needed information for the modelers. The MAP is essentially a list of attack packages. The list details the target(s), the programmed time-over-target, and the number and type of aircraft scheduled to attack that target. In addition, the MAP is tied together by mission numbers and package identifiers. See Chapter 6.

points in northern Saudi Arabia, and no estimates were made of operational losses within the attack plan.[12]

The simulation was run in order to estimate red and blue losses. The model allowed analysts to trace the effect of attrition on different force levels, attack strategies, and targeting tactics. It also identified, based on targeting strategy, which threat surface-to-air missile was most lethal. The basic scenario was run ten times. The average blue attrition rate was about four percent of the force involved in the attack. This result was very close to the first, one-week, "quick-and-dirty," AF/SAA study effort. The highest loss rates were experienced by the packages tasked to attack heavily defended areas without sufficient suppression of enemy air defense (SEAD) support.[13] The ability to do this sort of analysis, though not used in the first stages of Desert Shield, was helpful later, after mid-September, to GAT planners. It allowed them to experiment with different force packages and tactics without at the same time showing the coalition's hand to the Iraqis.

Use of Modeling and Decision Aids in C^3 Preparation for War

During the first week of October, AF/SAA analysts briefed the model results through the AF/SAA chain of command. By mid-October, Major General Alexander and Maj. Gen. Charles A. May, Jr. (Assistant DCS/P&O) had heard the briefing. On 15 October, a message was sent to Brig. Gen. Buster C. Glosson offering the model, a team of four analysts, and equipment. In part the message stated:

> AF/SA has developed a computer analysis capability which has use in developing and evaluating air operations . . . the model was excellent for that analysis, but has potential for many other applications such as designing a SEAD campaign, identifying attrition 'hot spots,' or finding vulnerability in the Iraqi IADS.[14]

---

[12] Case, Analysis of Air Operations During Desert Shield/Desert Storm, p 4.

[13] *Ibid*, pp 4-5.

[14] Msg, Maj Gen Alexander to Brig Gen Buster C. Glosson, 15 1715Z Oct 1990.

Glosson answered positively. On 16 October, AF/SAA began planning to deploy to Riyadh.[15]

On 21 October, the first two (of four AF/SAA) analysts arrived in Riyadh. Upon arrival, they briefed both Brigadier General Glosson and Brig. Gen. Larry Henry (CENTAF chief of Electronic Combat) on the prototype model and plans to model the Air Tasking Order (ATO). The ATO analysis would support Glosson, while the SEAD analysis would support Henry. Glosson asked for a quick assessment of operations plans and alternative courses of action. Unfortunately, working conditions for computer modeling were difficult. The day before, a GAT operations planner had plugged a coffee pot into an open socket, which caused a circuit breaker to pop. As a result, half of the computers and all cooling fans in the GAT lost power. Within two days of seeing that conditions in the Black Hole were not optimal for the computing equipment, the AF/SAA analysts requested, purchased locally, and then installed a 10,000 watt transformer with four 20 ampere circuits. On 26 October, the computer system was running.[16]

In the meantime, the primary analysis task was to acquire and convert allied mission data into C3ISIM format. Two difficulties in this stage of work were the volatility of the daily ATO and the layout of the threat. There was no automated input into C3ISIM of either the missile order of battle or electronic order of battle, and AF/SAA analysts could not keep up with the changes. They employed a simplification in order to gain experience with the model: the date of the plan and the threat were frozen. Results of runs of the order of battle at a particular date were summarized, and subsequent attention was devoted to the changes that had occurred since the dates were fixed. The threat database problem remained throughout the stay in Saudi Arabia.[17]

On 12 November, AF/SAA analysts began their first executable runs, based on the ATO dated 9 November. By this time, the team had become

---

[15]Msg, Brig Gen Buster C. Glosson, 18 1205Z Oct 1990; Case, *Analysis of Air Operations During Desert Shield/Desert Storm*, p 5.

[16]Case, *Analysis of Air Operations*, p 6.

[17]*Ibid*, p 7.

established as a working part of the planning cell. These runs covered the first three hours of real time (from H-hour minus one to H-hour plus two) but required almost eight hours to execute on the computer. Two executions of the model were conducted each day, and a total of nine runs of the model were made. The model confirmed previously identified dangerous areas in Iraq and helped to recommend ways to deal with them.[18] AF/SAA analysts showed that one to two A-6s were being lost in attacks on targets in downtown Baghdad. The threat array was formidable and could not be suppressed sufficiently. In the next update to the plan, the A-6s were no longer conducting attacks in downtown Baghdad. In another example, the model showed that point area defenses in western Iraq were able to shoot down F-15Es using low-altitude tactics against Al Hussein missile sites. An alternative tactic was suggested by the Black Hole's F-15E mission planner: ingress at low altitude to surprise the air defenses, then pop-up above the air defense sites' maximum engagement altitude to deliver ordnance. In future executions, this change resulted in no F-15E losses. The results were briefed on 18 November.[19]

The task for the next model update was to examine as much as possible the first day's attacks. The modelers had to develop a methodology to account for losses incurred by the Iraqi air defenses and include these losses in a defensive force for the next wave of attacks. The scenario was run nine times, and after group discussion among the EC planners and analysts, two distinct second-wave threat laydowns were developed. The same process was used to produce third-wave laydowns, based on the outcomes of the second-wave attacks.[20] The analysis of the first day's attacks was limited by significant simplifications. The C3ISIM model did not include the air-to-air threat; programmers were unable to emulate the employment tactics they suspected the Iraqis would use. Programmers also lacked a critical factor for modeling–parametric data for fuel flows for coalition and Iraqi aircraft.[21]

---

[18]Navy officers already had argued that the dense AAA threat in downtown Baghdad made an attack with A-6s too costly. (S) Intvw, Mark D. Mandeles and Sanford S. Terry with Cdr Donald W. McSwain, CNO OP-741E, 21 Apr 1992.

[19]Case, *Analysis of Air Operations*, pp 8-9.

[20]*Ibid*, p 9.

[21]*Ibid*, p 9.

A forecast for the outcome of the first twenty-four hours was produced using the Air Tasking Order and threat laydown of 5 December. Shortly after this analysis had been completed, additional forces were programmed into theater and the size and scope of the ATO began to grow. In the meantime, the AF/SAA team began another analysis task–to examine the first night's congestion during air refueling operations. This analysis was completed in early January.[22]

On 28 December, Brigadier General Glosson requested an analysis of air refueling operation for night one. Operations planners in the GAT were concerned about the possibility of mid-air collisions.[23] In the meantime, AF/SAA analysts met with C3ISIM software engineers from Teledyne Brown to draft and rank modifications to the model. Delivery of the modifications to Riyadh took a lot of time–almost as much time as it took to develop, code, and test the software modification. The delivery problem was solved by establishing a defense data network channel between Huntsville, Alabama and Riyadh. Code modifications were transferred electronically from the computer host in Huntsville to Riyadh. Without this electronic connection, the code corrections and modifications would not have been delivered in time to be used. The modified code was delivered and used to complete the air refueling analysis.[24]

On 12 January 1991, the air refueling analysis was completed. Maj. Scott Hente, an architect of the air refueling plan noted:

> ... we thought we had done it [the air refueling scheduling plan] right and your analysis confirmed our suspicions ... it raised our confidence level and confirmed our gut feel ... we knew it would be congested and your analysis helped confirm that we were within acceptable limits.[25]

After completing the analysis of air refueling, AF/SAA analysts returned to the attrition modeling for the ATO as it existed on 13 January.

---

[22] *Ibid*, pp 9-10.

[23] (S) Intvw, MSgt Theodore J. Turner with Brig Gen Buster C. Glosson, 6 Mar 1991.

[24] Case, *Analysis of Air Operations During*, p 11.

[25] *Ibid*.

They were ready to begin iterative runs when the execution order was received and attrition estimates were no longer needed.[26] By this time, it was clear that C3ISIM was unusable for real-time operations planning unless major productivity enhancements were made.[27] By mid-January, C3ISIM was not able to model each day's activity; the daily ATO was very complex, and changes were frequent and numerous. Once Desert Storm began, AF/SAA analysts looked for other tasks which did not involve the entire scenario, for example, analyses of aircraft losses by region, and the effects of tactics against a specific target or larger areas. AF/SAA analysts also continued their attrition analysis.[28]

Modeling and Decision Aids in Washington

During the first week of September 1990, AF/XOXW called upon Human Systems Division (HSD) of Air Force Systems Command to assess potential noncombatant casualties resulting from attacks on selected Baghdad military targets in support of the CINCCENT. This request for support was in response to the President's goal of minimizing noncombatant casualties.[29] HSD/YAO had been studying the effects of air-delivered munitions on personnel in structures and thus was best able to address the President's concerns.[30] The study employed a computer-based model, Threat Related Attrition System (THREAT), to produce recommendations regarding specific weapons, delivery platforms, tactics, and rules of engagement to minimize noncombatant casualties.

The analysis focused only on casualties resulting from weapon system malfunction or human error. It is important to note that this analysis

---

[26]*Ibid*, p 10.

[27]*Ibid*, p 12.

[28]*Ibid*, p 14.

[29]Intvw, Mark D. Mandeles with Col Thomas G. Smogur and Dr. James M. Whitehead, 14 Apr 1992. Gen Glosson stated that only F-117s were used to attack targets in Baghdad because of the goal of minimizing collateral casualties. See (S) Intvw, MSgt Theodore J. Turner with Brig Gen Buster C. Glosson, 6 Mar 1991.

[30](S) Final Report, J. M. Whitehead, T. G. Smogur, R. J. Casey, S. Harris, M. A. Stika, and M. J. Fertal, *THREAT Model Application (Final)* (BDM/MCL-91-0016-TR), 31 Aug 1991, p 2.

would not have been possible without the presence of a large quantity of empirical research—for example, operational follow-on test and evaluation reports and contractor reliability studies—which formed critical databases.[31] Six issues were examined, including what might happen to civilians if and when weapons aimed at a target in fact hit something else, and the minimum and maximum number of civilian casualties resulting from sustained attacks on Baghdad.

The study was conducted on-site at AF/XOXW during the last week of September and first week of October 1990. The analysis produced recommendations regarding the specific weapons, delivery platforms, tactics, and rules of engagement to mitigate the risk of noncombatant casualties in Baghdad. Upon completion, the study results were briefed to the National Command Authority,[32] to key members of the Air Staff,[33] and to theater planners. On 14 November 1990, Col. John A. Warden III sent the briefing and related material to Brigadier General Glosson.[34] Warden claimed that the analysis showed how noncombatant casualties could be minimized with careful "pre-mission planning to avoid misdesignation of targets (the principal driver of noncombatant casualties) and the employment of suitable aircraft and weapons systems."

Unfortunately, a lack of understanding of how the air war was in fact being fought in real time undermined the ability of planners to use models to correct their errors. At the national level, for example, preventing errors

---

[31] Intvw, Col Smogur and Dr. Whitehead. The BDM report lists some of the studies used to build the THREAT system databases. See Dr. Whitehead, et al., *THREAT Model (Final)* report.

[32] Intvw, Col Smogur and Dr. Whitehead; see also Bob Woodward, *The Commanders* (New York, 1991), p 341, which describes a 1 Dec 1990 Joint Staff presentation to President Bush. General McPeak cites figures and issues taken from the THREAT analysis.

[33] There were approximately eight briefings to key individuals on the Air Staff. See, for example, the following, all given by Col Thomas Smogur, AFSC/HSD: (S) Briefing to AF/XOXW, 19 Oct 1990; (S) Briefing to Maj Gen Alexander, 23 Oct 1990; (S) Briefing to Col Blackburn, AF/IN, 25 Oct 1990; (S) Briefing to Lt Gen J.V. Adams, 25 Oct 1990; (S) Briefing to Gen John Loh and Maj Gen R.M. Alexander, 26 Oct 1990. See also Dr. Whitehead, et al., *THREAT Model (Final)* report, pp 29, 72-118.

[34] (S) Memo, Col John A. Warden III to Brig Gen Buster C. Glosson, subj: Briefing—Noncombatant Casualties in Iraq, 14 Nov 1990.

(that is, causing civilian casualties) had to wait until the errors themselves were made, which meant that the Chairman of the Joint Chiefs, the Secretary of Defense, and the President could do little more than restrict the types of targets selected. This is exactly what they did after the 12 February 1990 Al Firdes bunker strike. At the theater-level, misdesignation of targets was inevitable once errors were introduced into target selection and mensuration through clerical mistakes and through the use of different notation systems (worldwide geodetic system or relational mapping).

Three "quick-and-dirty" analyses followed the initial analysis of casualties in Baghdad. In the first, THREAT was used to assess Iraqi claims about the number of civilian casualties from the 12 February strike on a hardened bunker in Baghdad. The second case concerned questions about the relation between the number of personnel wounded in action (WIA) and the number killed in action (KIA), and the need to extrapolate from numbers of WIAs reported to be treated at hospitals near an air attack to the numbers of KIA that might have been associated with that attack. The third case involved the Iraqi-launched Al-Hussein missile that hit a hangar near Dhahran Air Base, killing and injuring many U.S. Army troops. This incident provided an opportunity to assess the credibility of THREAT Facility model results against the actual number of casualties caused by a missile.[35]

Summary and Review

Proponents of computer-based modeling often assume that more and better equipment would solve all problems. They promise computer systems that will remove the organization from the vagaries of judgmental decision and place its decision process on a more "rational" basis.[36] AF/SAA analysts did *not* make this assertion; they did not promise more than they could deliver. The limitations of this type of computer model in a fluid, rapidly changing environment grew to be well understood by

---

[35](S) Dr. Whitehead, et al., *THREAT Model (Final)* report, p 30.

[36]Russell Stout, Jr., *Management of Control? The Organizational Challenge* (Bloomington, 1980), p 90.

modelers and their commanders.[37] In addition, senior Desert Storm leaders constrained the uses of computer-based decision aids by asking narrow questions and by retaining a healthy skepticism regarding the answers they received and the usefulness of those answers.[38]

---

[37](S) EOTR, Maj Gen George B. Harrison, Commander, Air Force Studies and Analyses Agency, 12 Nov 1991, p 3; Lt Col David A. Deptula noted that C3ISIM was helpful in some planning but was not critically valuable. Intvw, Thomas A. Keaney, Mark D. Mandeles, Williamson Murray, and Barry Watts with Lt Col David A. Deptula, SAF/OSX, 21 Dec 1991.

[38]For example, civilian modelers, asking broad questions, supplied predictions which were orders of magnitude higher than what transpired. Unconstrained use of such models by commanders (or civilian leaders) could have seriously distorted military policy. For example, Joshua Epstein, a political scientist at the Brookings Institution, used a computer model to determine that American casualties would range between 3,344 and 16,059. Epstein briefed these results widely to high-level civilian and military audiences, including the JCS. See Jacob Weisberg, "Gulfballs: How the Experts Blew It, Big-Time," *The New Republic*, 25 Mar 1991, p 18.

Appendix 4

Gulf War Command Arrangements

An understanding of the formal organization of the allied forces in the Persian Gulf War is fundamental to an understanding of how decisions were made and how the war was prosecuted. As shown in this report, the war effort was in large part driven by informal relationships and ad hoc organizations. However, the formal structures bestowed upon the leaders the authority to institute ad hoc organizations or use the informal communications channels to influence the actions of the formal. The formal structures provided the framework upon which relationships were later built. In addition, the formal structure provided the foundation to which individuals turned to resolve questions of authority.

There are three elements of command relations that together describe the formal structure of any military organization. The first element is the division of labor represented by the organizational chart.[1] The second concerns functional relationships among organizational units; for example, a tactical reconnaissance squadron has a specific function which is different from that of a tactical airlift wing. The third element of command relationships is the type of authority one level in the organization has over another.

We must begin with a few words about semantics. The terms "command" and "control" and adjectives such as "operational" and "tactical," as in "operational control," have very specific meanings when used in the context of command relationships. These terms, and others that will be described in detail later, give or constrain an individual's specific (often legal) authority. Other terms do not imply specific types of legal authority but simply refer to organizational structures in total or to individuals within the formal structure. For this purpose, we will use

---

[1] The organizational chart of lines and boxes, typical of military (and civilian) organization shows the formal organization structure: who works for whom and which units are subordinate or superordinate.

the terms "line of authority" or "organizational structure" when referring to a hierarchy of superordinates and subordinates without reference to specific types of authority.

During the Gulf War there was no single formal line of organizational authority from the President to the pilot in the cockpit, but rather several lines of different types of authority, some overlapping, some parallel. The following paragraphs describe three lines of authority: (a) the "Service Organization," the formal structure through which each of the military Services (Air Force, Navy, Marine Corps, and Army) manage their peacetime functions, (b) the "Unified Combatant Command," which combines elements of two or more of the Services to conduct joint operations, and (c) the "Joint Task Force Organization," created by Gen. H. Norman Schwarzkopf to facilitate the accomplishment of his specific mission.

The Service Organization

As Commander of the Ninth Air Force, Lt. Gen. Charles A. Horner was part of a line of authority which ran from the President through the U.S. Air Force organizational structure. Referred to as the "Service" chain of command, each of the Services has lines of authority that tie it together. See Figure 38.

Air Force lines of authority begin with the President under constitutional authority granted the Commander in Chief in Article II, Section 2. This authority then flows through the Secretary of Defense[2] to the Secretary of the Air Force as the head of the Department of the Air Force. Under Section 8013, Title 10, United States Code, the Secretary is responsible for "all affairs of the Department of the Air Force," including recruiting, organizing, supplying, equipping (including research and development), training, servicing, mobilizing, demobilizing, administering, maintaining, and the construction, outfitting, maintenance, and repair of military equipment, buildings, structures, and facilities.[3]

---

[2]The Secretary of Defense's authority will be described below.

[3]Title 10, United States Code (10 USC), *Armed Forces*; Subtitle D, Air Force; Chapter 803, Department of the Air Force; Section 8013, Secretary of the Air Force.

**Figure 38
The Service Chain of Command**

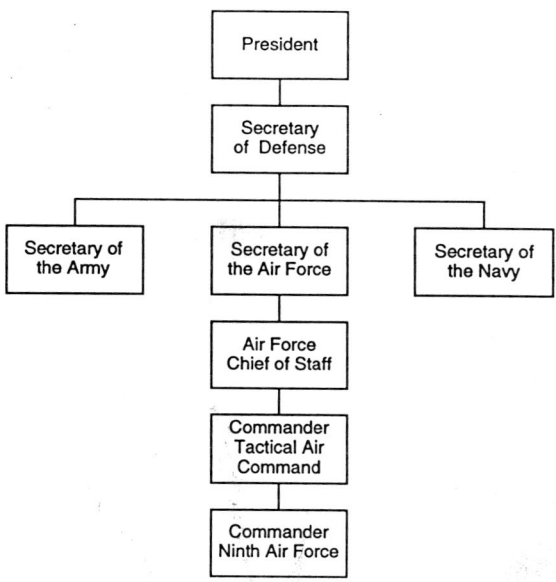

The Air Force Chief of Staff is appointed by the President to "transmit the plans and recommendations of the Air Staff to the Secretary [of the Air Force] and advise the Secretary with regard to such plans and recommendations" and "after approval . . . by the Secretary, act as the agent of the Secretary in carrying them into effect . . . ."[4] In addition, the Chief of Staff will "exercise supervision . . . over such of the member and organizations of the Air Force as the Secretary determines. . . ."[5] In practice this means that the commanders of Air Force major commands (MAJCOMs) such as the Tactical Air Command.[6] Military Airlift Com-

---

[4] *Ibid*, §8033, para (a)(2)(d)(2) and (a)(2)(d)(3).

[5] *Ibid*, para (a)(2)(d)(4).

[6] The organizations described herein are those organizations in existence at the time of the Gulf War. The Air Force reorganization of 1992 has changed many of these MAJCOMs.

mand, and U.S. Air Forces in Europe work[7] for the Chief of Staff, who, in turn, works for the Secretary of the Air Force. Basically, the Chief of Staff is an advisor to the Secretary of the Air Force; he provides trained and equipped forces to the combatant commanders for employment in combat but is not a commander and does not have "command" authority over the employment of forces in combat.

The Tactical Air Command (TAC), headquartered at Langley AFB, Virginia, had three subcommands, or numbered air forces. The commander of TAC exercised "command" authority over the members of these subcommands. One of these was the Ninth Air Force stationed at Shaw AFB, South Carolina. The commander of the Ninth Air Force, General Horner, exercised command over those units assigned to the Ninth Air Force. As "commanders" with "command authority" the Commander of the Tactical Air Command and the Commander of Ninth Air Force have the

> authority and responsibility for effectively using available resources and for planning the employment of, organizing, directing, coordinating, and controlling military forces for the accomplishment of assigned missions.[8]

Command authority also includes legal authority under the Uniform Code of Military Justice; for example, the authority to convene a court-martial.[9] In addition, these commanders are responsible for health, welfare, morale, and discipline of assigned personnel.

This Service chain from the President through the Secretary of the Air Force and the Chief of Staff, through the commanders of Air Force major commands and numbered air forces, down through the commanders

---

[7]Most of the Air Force MAJCOM commanders also "work for" commanders of unified commands; for example, the Commander in Chief of the U.S. Air Forces in Europe reports to both the Chief of Staff and the Commander in Chief of U.S. European Command. In reference to the Gulf War, as we shall discuss later, the Service chain of command and the unified chain of command come together with the commander of 9th AF instead of at the MAJCOM level.

[8]Joint Publication 1-02, *Department of Defense Dictionary of Military and Associated Terms*, Dec 1989. (JCS Pub 1-02) See also Volume IV, Appendix 1, "Glossary."

[9]10 USC, Chapter 47.

of wings, groups, and squadrons, to the individuals assigned to the organizations includes "administrative control." That is, the

> [d]irection or exercise of authority over subordinate or other organizations in respect to administrative matters such as personnel management, supply, services, and other matters not included in the operational missions of the subordinate or other organization.[10]

That portion beginning with the commanders of major commands down to the squadron commanders also includes, as their titles indicate, command authority. That is:

> ... the authority and responsibility for effectively using available resources and for planning the employment of, organizing, directing, coordinating, and controlling military forces for the accomplishment of assigned missions. It also includes responsibility for health, welfare, morale, and discipline of assigned personnel.[11]

The Unified Combatant Command Organization

In addition to the Service organization structure, Title 10 also legislated the establishment of "unified combatant commands . . . to perform military missions."[12] While the Service structures are focused on providing administrative, logistical, and training support to combat forces, the combatant command structure[13] is focused on combat employment of those forces. The unified commands comprise military units designated by the four Services. See Figure 39.

---

[10]*Ibid.*

[11]JCS Pub 1-02.

[12]10 USC, §161, para (a).

[13]For the purposes of this report, the terms "combatant command," "unified command," and "unified combatant command" are synonymous. At the time of the Gulf War there were eight unified combatant commands: U.S. European Command (USEUCOM), U.S. Southern Command (USSOUTHCOM), U.S. Pacific Command (USPACOM), U.S. Special Operations Command (USSOCOM), U.S. Transportation Command (USTRANSCOM), U.S. Space Command (USSPACECOM), U.S. Atlantic Command (USLANTCOM), and U.S. Central Command (USCENTCOM).

Figure 39
The Unified Combatant Command Organization

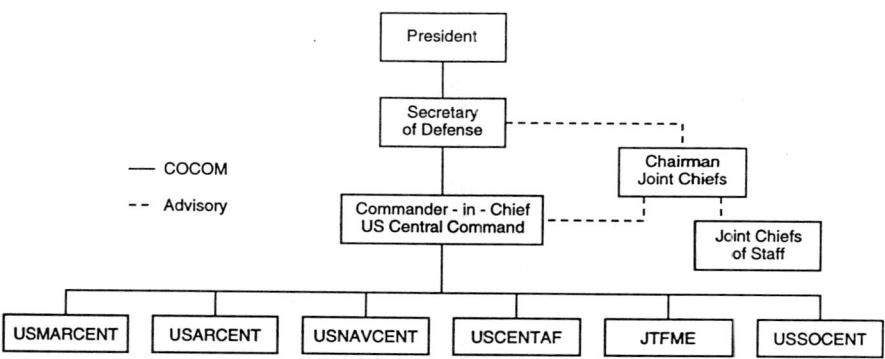

The combatant command structure begins, as the Service structure, with the constitutional authority of the President, but unlike the Service structure, the line of authority goes through neither the Service Secretary nor the Chief of Staff. "Unless otherwise directed by the President, the chain of command to a unified . . . combatant command runs—(1) from the President to the Secretary of Defense; and (2) from the Secretary of Defense to the commander of the combatant command."[14]

The Goldwater-Nichols Reorganization Act of 1986[15] clarified the extent of authority to be exercised by the commanders of the unified commands and the authority the combatant commander over the Service components of their command. This authority, called combatant command (COCOM) authority,[16] gave General Schwarzkopf, Commander in Chief of the U.S. Central Command (USCINCCENT), authoritative direction over his

---

[14] 10 USC, §162, para (b).

[15] Public Law 99-433, 1 Oct 1986.

[16] 10 USC, §164.

command, including all aspects of military operations, joint training, and logistics. COCOM authorizes the combatant commander to prescribe the chain of command within his command and to organize the command and its forces as he considers necessary to accomplish the missions assigned by the Secretary of Defense and the President. While unit administration, support, and discipline are a Service Secretary responsibility, COCOM gives the combatant commander coordination and approval authority over those aspects affecting the accomplishment of his mission. Because of the Service responsibilities for administration and support, unified commands normally maintain a peacetime organizational structure which parallels the Service structure as did Central Command. That is, the day-to-day functions of the forces are managed by the Service components.

Unlike most unified commands, the Air Force headquarters designated as Central Command's Air Force component was not a major command. Instead, it was a level of command below the major command–the numbered air force.[17] Thus, General Horner was appointed both the Commander of U.S. Central Command Air Forces (the Air Force component to USCENTCOM) and Commander, Ninth Air Force (a command echelon below the Tactical Air Command major command). In addition, the members of General Horner's staff functioned as both a numbered air force staff and as the staff of the Air Force component to a unified command.

U.S. Central Command also was unique in that it had no air forces, other than the Air Force component command (CENTAF) headquarters staff assigned to the unified command in peacetime.[18] The Air Force units apportioned for use by Central Command in event of war came, as planned, from other unified and specified commands or U.S.- based forces assigned to the Tactical Air Command. Most of the forces tasked were not assigned to USCINCCENT prior to deployment. Hence, the deployment orders issued by the Chairman, Joint Chiefs of Staff on behalf of the Secretary of Defense and the operations orders published by USCINCCENT specified USCINCCENT's level of authority over the deploying

---

[17]U.S. Southern Command, headquartered in Panama, also has a numbered air force as its Air Force component command.

[18]For example, U.S. European and Pacific Commands have Air Force fighter aircraft assigned and stationed within their area of responsibility during peacetime.

forces. Generally, all unified commanders would transfer combatant command[19] of forces to USCINCCENT as those forces entered USCINCCENT's area of responsibility (Southwest Asia).[20] Forces to be employed by USCINCCENT but stationed outside USCINCCENT's area of responsibility were "CHOP'ed" (Change of Operational Control) to USCINCCENT. Thus forces were placed under the operational control[21] of USCINCCENT, allowing General Schwarzkopf to task the units. In October, the Chairman of the Joint Chiefs of Staff, after consultation with the Joint Chiefs, sent a message to all the combatant commanders clarifying these relationships.

---

[19]Combatant command authority is the nontransferable command authority established by Title 10, United States Code, Section 164, exercised only by commanders of unified or specified combatant commands involving organizing and employing commands and forces, assigning tasks, designating objectives, and giving authoritative direction over all aspects of military operations, joint training, and logistics necessary to accomplish the missions assigned to the command. Combatant command, usually exercised through the Service component commander, provides full authority to organize and employ commands and forces as the CINC considers necessary to accomplish assigned missions. Also called COCOM. See Appendix 1.

[20]There were a few exceptions to the norm of transferring COCOM of deployed forces to USCINCCENT. USCINCTRANS transferred OPCON of theater airlift assets and retained control of strategic (intertheater) assets (C-141 and C-5 aircraft). CINCSAC passed OPCON of all deployed B-52 and any CONUS based B-52 tasked to support Desert Shield to USCINCCENT; however, SAC refueling assets (KC-135 and KC-10 aircraft) remained under the operational control of 8th Air Force, 15th Air Force, and 17th Air Division (all SAC organizations).

[21]Operational control is the transferable command authority which may be exercised by commanders at any echelon at, or below, the level of combatant command. OPCON is inherent in Combatant Command and is the authority to perform those functions of command over subordinate forces involving organizing and employing commands and forces, assigning tasks, designating objectives, and providing authoritative direction necessary to accomplish the mission. OPCON includes authoritative direction over all aspects of military operations and joint training necessary to accomplish missions assigned to the command. OPCON, usually exercised through the Service component commanders, provides full authority to organize commands and forces to employ those forces as the commander in operational control considers necessary to accomplish assigned missions. OPCON does not include authoritative direction of logistics, administration, discipline, internal organization, or unit training. See Appendix 1.

(1) Tactical Air Force units deployed to the USCENTCOM AOR are reassigned COCOM to USCINCCENT unless COCOM was or is specifically designated to another command in the Deployment Order.

(2) CINCSAC B-52s supporting Desert Shield are attached OPCON to USCINCCENT. CINCSAC support assets (such as tanker aircraft) will be provided in support of or TACON to USCINCCENT, as directed by Deployment (Air Tasking) Orders.

(3) When directed, USTRANSCOM airlift personnel and assets are attached OPCON to USCINCCENT.[22]

The Joint Task Force Organization

The Commander in Chief of U.S. Central Command recognized as early as 1988 that the peacetime, Service-oriented organizational structure would not satisfy the wartime needs of the combatant commander. Therefore, the USCINCCENT Operational Plan (OPlan) 1002-88 reorganized the air power elements of the Central Command under a single individual called the "Joint Force Air Component Commander."[23] This functional organization of air forces was carried forward in the 1990 draft version of USCINCCENT OPlan 1002 and all the post 2 August 1990, Desert Shield and Desert Storm plans.

As the Joint Force Air Component Commander (JFACC), General Horner was responsible for:

(1) planning, coordinating, allocating, and tasking [of air assets] based on USCINCCENT apportionment decisions,

(2) recommending to USCINCCENT apportionment of theater air sorties to various missions or geographic areas in coordination

---

[22](S) Msg, CJCS to combatant commanders, 222335Z Oct 1990, subj: Operation Desert Shield Command Relationships.

[23]Chapter 3 contains a detailed description of the Joint Force Air Component Commander; a history of the JFACC concept is in Appendix 2.

with COMUSARCENT, COMUSMARCENT, COMUSNAVCENT, COMSOCCENT, and other commanders supporting USCENTCOM as appropriate, and

(3) direct coordination with COMUSARCENT, COMUSMARCENT, COMSOCCENT, COMUSNAVCENT, COMJTFME and supporting forces to ensure integration of air operations within USCINCCENT's concept of operations.[24]

In order to accomplish this, the Joint Force Air Component Commander was given specific authority over elements of both U.S. and allied forces. First, as the Ninth Air Force Commander and Commander of U.S. Central Command Air Forces, General Horner already had authority over U.S. Air Force forces, as described in the previous two sections; therefore, as Joint Force Air Component Commander, he was not given any additional authority over the Ninth Air Force. As the JFACC, however, he was given additional authority over Naval and Marine air units.

It is important to note that General Horner did not have a joint air forces staff; that is, he had no staff comprising members of each of the Services to support his role as Joint Force Air Component Commander. Instead, he relied upon his Air Force staff (USCENTAF/Ninth Air Force staff) supplemented by "liaison officers" from the other Services as well as representatives from the Military Airlift Command and Strategic Air Command to augment the Tactical Air Control Center staff.

In order to ensure that the joint air forces could safely execute the air campaign plan, General Horner was also appointed the Area Air Defense Commander and Airspace Control Authority.[25] As the former, he was responsible for defense of the airspace over friendly forces, a task which included ensuring that enemy air forces could not successfully attack friendly ground forces and that friendly air forces could safely transit

---

[24](S) Msg, USCINCCENT to Joint Staff, et al., 101100Z Aug 1990, subj: USCINCCENT Order for Operation Desert Shield.

[25]*Combined OPlan for Offensive Operations to Eject Iraqi Forces from Kuwait*, 17 Jan 1991, designated the Commander of Royal Saudi Air Forces as the Airspace Control Authority; however, there is no indication that there were any changes in policy or procedures with this appointment.

friendly airspace without being attacked by their own air defense assets. Also as Area Air Defense Commander, Horner established procedures for and "adjust[ed] weapons control status"[26] of the air defense radar network, airborne and ground alert air defense aircraft, and the friendly surface to air missile units.[27] As the Airspace Control Authority, General Horner was responsible for establishing effective airspace control procedures; that is, basic air traffic control procedures.

There were actually two joint task forces conducting combat operations during Desert Storm: Central Command and the Joint Task Force Proven Force, under combatant command of and established by Gen. Galvin, Commander in Chief U.S. European Command (USCINCEUR), on 21 December 1990.[28] The mission of the Joint Task Force was to:

> Develop a substantial joint and combined combat capability in Turkey to deter hostilities in Southwest Asia. In the event of hostilities and with permission of Turkish government, coordinate and conduct military operations in response to mission tasking from USCINCCENT.[29]

The initial Operations Order also included a simple statement of the relationship between the Commander of the Joint Task Force (CJTF), USCINCEUR, and USCINCCENT.

> USCINCCENT is supported commander. USCINCEUR is supporting commander. USCINCEUR will exercise OPCON over component forces through CJTF PROVEN FORCE. CJTF PROVEN FORCE is assigned TACON [tactical control], in direct support, to USCINCCENT for mission specific tasking and/or geographic area of responsibil-

---

[26] *Ibid.*

[27] JFACC authority did not include land-based, short-range air defense or point air defense system which remained under the OPCON of their respective component commanders.

[28] (S) Msg, USCINCEUR/ECJ3 to USEUCOM Components and USCINCCENT/J3, 210745Z Dec 1990, Msg ID: Order/USCINCEUR/001/Dec. Final version of USCINCEUR Order 001 was transmitted at 231243Z Dec 1990.

[29] *Ibid*, para 2.

ity [AOR] within CENTCOM AOR as mutually agreed between CJTF and USCINCCENT. Component commanders provide forces TACON to CJTF PROVEN FORCE for operations in Turkey and/or CENTCOM AOR. CIA, DIA, and NSA are supporting agencies.[30]

Some explanation is required to understand the ground-rules (as stated in this Operations Order) under which the Joint Task Force was operating. The relationships embodied by USCINCCENT being the supported commander, USCINCEUR being a supporting commander, and the Central Intelligence Agency, the Defense Intelligence Agency, and the National Security Agency being supporting agencies simply restate the relationships established by the Secretary of Defense in deploying the U.S. Central Command to Southwest Asia.[31] As "supported commander," USCINCCENT was given the authority to designate targets or objectives, set the timing and duration of supporting actions, and establish "other instructions necessary for coordination and efficiency" of operations.[32] As detailed in the *Unified Action Armed Forces*, "[t]he supporting commander has the responsibility to ascertain the needs of the supported force and take such action to fulfill them as is within existing capabilities, consistent with priorities and requirements of other assigned tasks."[33]

By not delegating operational control, General Galvin retained the authority to organize and employ Joint Task Force forces, assign tasks, designate objectives, and give "authoritative direction necessary to accomplish the mission."[34] There are two reasons the Commander in Chief, Europe would want to retain operation control of forces deployed to JTF Proven Force rather than delegate this authority below the unified command level as is common practice. First, as a "supporting commander," USCINCEUR was responsible for USEUCOM's support to Central Command; by retaining OPCON, he could ensure the link between USCINCCENT and

---

[30] *Ibid*, para 5A1.

[31] (TS) Msg, CJCS to USCINCCENT et al., 070050Z Aug 1990.

[32] JCS Pub 0-2, *Unified Action Armed Forces (UNAAF)*, 1 Dec 1986 (Change 1, 21 Apr 1989), p 3-18.

[33] *Ibid*, pg 3-19.

[34] JCS Pub 1-02, *Department of Defense Dictionary of Military and Associated Terms*, 1 Dec 1989.

Commander, Joint Task Force. If General Galvin had delegated operational control to Maj. Gen. Jamerson, the commander of Proven Force, Jamerson could, in theory, establish objectives and conduct operations independent of USCINCCENT. Second, at the time the Joint Task Force was established, there was a large Iraqi ground force deployed along the Iraq-Turkey border. If Iraqi forces had attacked Turkey, NATO might have been called upon to take action to defend Turkey, and General Galvin would have needed the JTF forces.

By assigning tactical control of JTF Proven Force forces to the Commander of the Joint Task Force, Jamerson was given the "local direction and control of movements or maneuvers necessary to accomplish missions or tasks assigned"[35] by USCINCCENT, or if necessary, USCINCEUR as the holder of operational control.

---

[35] *Ibid.*

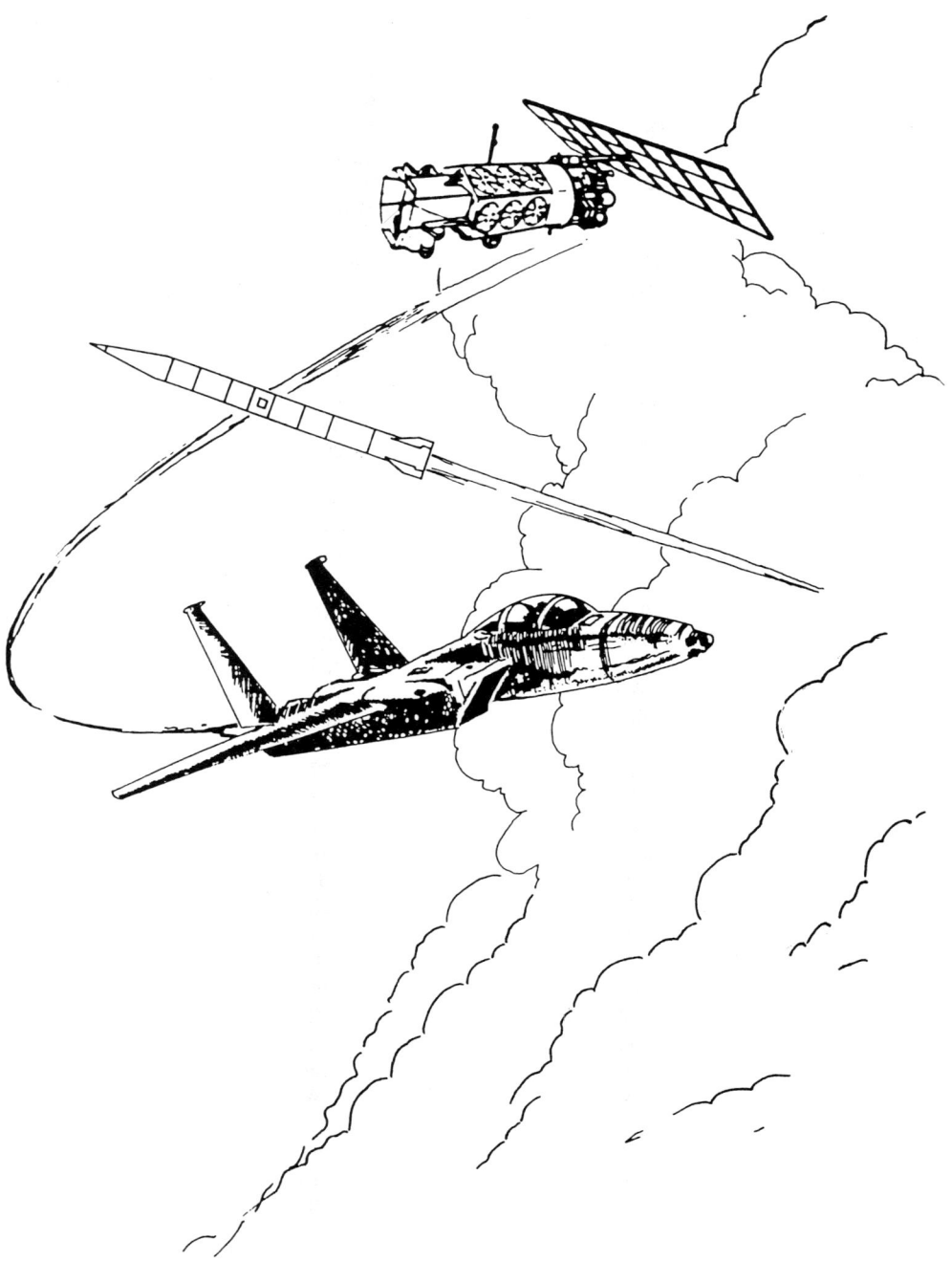

Index

A

A-6 165, 258, 312, 374
A-7 258
A-10 296, 323, 319, 321A-7 258
AADC 50
ABCCC 2, 32, 39, 41, 77, 81-83, 85, 86, 89, 90, 99, 100-102, 106, 118, 139, 147, 269, 305, 310-323, 325-327, 332, 334, 336
Abdulhameed Alqadhi 165
ACCS 99, 100, 314-319, 321, 325
ACE 83, 95, 135, 187, 310, 311
ACO 137, 145
ad hoc organization 203, 205
ADA 81
AEGIS 117, 126
AGM-45 259
AGM-65 259
AGM-88 259
air campaign 4-8, 42, 49, 52, 53, 56-60, 62-67, 69-72, 74, 75, 77, 98, 127, 139, 142, 144, 149, 150, 157-159, 162, 163, 165-169, 171-174, 176, 179-186, 190, 192, 193, 195-197, 199-201, 203, 205-210, 212-214, 221, 225, 227, 230, 232, 235-237, 243, 256, 259, 262, 265-267, 272, 282, 288, 293, 296, 297, 299, 301, 303, 311, 320, 329, 331, 332, 334, 335, 336, 351, 359, 360, 365, 370, 372, 390
air combat assessment summary 296, 297
air defense 8, 30, 47, 50, 52, 81, 83, 86, 94, 96, 115, 119-124, 129, 132, 139, 142, 153, 175, 198, 238, 239, 241, 250, 283, 305, 314, 339, 340, 359, 360, 362, 364, 365, 367, 370, 371, 373, 374, 390
air division 70, 94, 144, 185, 186, 200, 213, 214, 232, 269, 309, 312, 331, 354, 388

Air Force Logistics Command 91
Air Force Systems Command 104, 275, 377, 376
air interdiction 65, 101, 102, 169, 230, 272, 313, 319, 327, 362, 365
Air National Guard 109
air order of battle 139
air power 2, 40, 52, 71, 74, 88, 90, 130, 148, 170, 193, 195, 227, 270, 351, 362, 366, 389
air refueling 15, 17, 30, 83, 124, 133, 137, 145, 148-150, 168, 186, 218, 232, 241, 307, 311, 372, 375, 376
Air Staff 115, 157-159, 180, 181, 185, 202, 249, 288, 362, 365, 377, 383
air superiority 73, 309
Air Support Operations Center 2, 79-82, 86, 88, 89, 92, 99, 100, 101, 102, 106, 115, 116, 119, 129, 313, 315, 316, 323, 339
air tasking order (see also ATO) 6, 13, 15, 17-22, 29-31, 34, 35, 39-41, 46, 52, 53, 56, 57, 59, 65, 69-71, 75, 82, 86, 87, 90, 95, 96, 100, 101, 108, 115, 116, 117, 123, 124, 133, 135, 137, 139, 144-146, 148-150, 152, 153, 155, 163, 164, 167, 168, 171, 191-193, 195, 196-201, 205-210, 212, 223, 227, 231, 237, 239-241, 253, 254, 258, 263, 265, 266, 268, 272, 273, 277-282, 291, 292, 294, 297, 299, 306-308, 315, 316, 320, 323-325, 329, 330, 334, 335, 336, 361, 362, 367, 373, 375
Airborne Command and Control Squadron 99, 100, 312
airborne early warning 309
Airborne Warning and Control System 2, 83, 85, 89, 139, 269
aircraft availability 36
airfields 24, 25, 49, 92, 108, 122, 240, 290, 301

395

airspace control order 124, 135, 137, 145, 150
airspace coordination order 168
Al Dhafra 113, 237
Al Firdos 68
Al Hussein 374
Al Taqaddum 241, 242
Al-Hussein 378
al-Mofadi Talal 45
al-Rasheed 45
Alexander, Maj Gen 162, 165, 227, 371, 373, 377, 378
Allan, Charles 166, 281
antiaircraft artillery 123, 372
ARCENT 104, 105, 150, 152, 153
ARCT 218, 232
area air defense commander 50, 340, 360, 364, 390
area of responsibility 41, 82, 89, 131, 180, 186, 320, 342, 365, 387, 388, 391
ARM 367
Army Air Corps 352
Army Air Forces 250
Arthur, Stanley 55-58, 352
artillery 39, 81, 123, 259, 314, 320, 347, 372
ASARS 285
assumptions 4, 212, 367, 372
ATC 125, 127
Atlantic Command 362, 385
ATO (see also air tasking order) 8, 13, 15, 17, 19, 21, 24, 27-30, 32, 33, 35, 37, 41, 46, 48, 52, 53, 56, 57, 59, 64-66, 70, 87, 97, 117, 133, 135, 137, 139, 144, 145, 148, 149, 150, 152-155, 158, 162-165, 167, 168, 169, 170, 187, 191, 192, 195, 196, 197-201, 205, 206, 208-210, 212-214, 216, 219-221, 223-225, 227-232, 235, 237, 238-243, 254, 260, 266, 269, 272, 278-284, 291, 292, 294, 299, 306, 308, 335, 367, 373, 374, 375, 376
ATO bravo 278

ATO change 21, 219, 225, 230
AUTODIN 107, 116, 154, 291
automated installation file 10
AV-8Bs 264
AWACS 2, 32, 39, 41, 48, 74, 77, 80-86, 89, 90, 92, 94-98, 102, 104, 106, 107, 114, 115, 118, 119, 120, 123, 128, 129, 139, 147, 158, 165, 214, 219, 242, 269, 305-312, 317, 319, 320, 322, 323, 327, 332, 334, 336
Aziz, Tariq 44, 46, 166

B

B-52 13-15, 165, 186, 190, 291-293, 296, 321, 355, 388
bad weather 8, 206, 218, 221, 225, 227, 308
Bahrain 93, 111
BAI 169
Baker, James 227, 246
Baptiste, Sam 8, 15, 17, 180, 188, 195, 200, 223
basic encyclopedia 26, 340
battle damage 34, 142, 265, 295, 302
Battle of Khafji 190
battlefield air interdiction 65, 169
Battlefield Coordination Element 8, 64, 65, 82, 87, 90, 99, 100, 132, 313-315
BCE 8, 82, 87, 132, 281, 282
BDA (see also bomb damage assessment) 41, 63, 165, 182, 200, 259, 260, 263-270, 274, 276-303
beddown 41
Behery, Ahmed Ibrahim 43, 45, 47, 48, 68
BEN 10, 147, 159, 175, 281
Bin Abdul Aziz 44, 46, 166
Bin Bandar 166
Black Hole 8, 26, 66, 70, 72, 157-159, 162-165, 167-177, 180-183, 185-188, 192, 195, 196, 200, 202, 203, 205, 207, 213, 256,

266, 268, 289, 290, 293, 370, 373, 374
Blackburn, Col 378
Blue Ridge 55, 56
Boeing 707 102
bomb damage assessment (see also BDA) 10, 21, 38-40, 193, 196, 199, 224, 255-258, 260, 261, 264-268, 274, 277-283, 286, 288, 289, 299, 335, 340
Boomer, Walter 51, 59, 73
bridges 281, 282, 290, 298
briefing 8, 15, 17, 41, 52, 61, 63, 65, 66, 72, 75, 92, 96, 97, 103, 107, 108, 110, 112-114, 116, 118, 124, 139, 152, 153-155, 158-160, 164, 168, 171, 181, 193, 195, 197-199, 208, 210, 249-251, 262, 277, 281, 288, 303, 305, 307, 309, 310, 320, 322, 324, 325, 373, 377, 378
Bruner, William 165
Bush, George 199, 227, 247, 262, 377

C

C3 119, 120, 150, 152-154, 316, 357, 369, 370, 372, 373
C3I 42, 52, 99, 206, 281, 282
C3IC 46
C3ISIM 370, 371, 374-376, 379
C-5 94, 388
C-21 108, 154, 286
C-130 86
C-141 94, 108, 388
cable news 75
Cable News Network 75
CAFMS 15, 17, 31, 36, 55, 116, 117, 135, 137, 153, 154, 167, 187, 209, 214, 215, 224, 242, 279, 307, 366
Cairo East 127
CALCM 292
Callum Steel 166
CAP 98, 253, 307, 325
Carns 203
carrier 53, 55, 56, 116-118, 125, 154, 173, 283, 285, 287, 309, 354, 367
carrier battle groups 283
Caruana, Patrick 70, 191, 213, 214, 229, 230
CAS (see also close air support) 60, 79, 99, 101, 152, 169, 313, 317, 321
casualties 68, 376-379
CBU 292
CBU-52 292
CBU-87 292
CBU-89 292
CCRC 129
CENTAF 8, 13, 17, 37, 41, 42, 48, 50-53, 56, 59, 65, 66, 70, 71, 73, 97, 99-101, 105, 107-109, 111-113, 116-118, 120, 121, 124, 125, 128, 129, 131, 132, 133, 134, 137, 139, 144, 147, 148-150, 152-155, 157-164, 166-174, 176, 179-182, 184-187, 190, 191, 193, 195, 196-200, 202, 203, 205, 209, 210, 221, 223, 225, 231, 237, 240, 247, 251, 256, 261, 262, 264, 266, 268-270, 272, 274, 275, 276, 278-280, 282, 283, 285, 286, 289-291, 293-301, 303, 306-308, 311-313, 316, 319, 331, 332, 364, 365, 368, 373, 387
CENTAF intelligence 172, 174, 176, 182, 202, 256, 261, 264, 266, 268, 270, 278, 286, 289, 290, 293, 294, 296, 297, 299, 303, 331, 332
CENTAF rear 109
CENTCOM (see also Central Command) 41, 45, 46, 48, 50, 55, 56, 60-64, 66, 71, 73, 91, 103, 105-107, 109, 111-113, 118, 128, 157, 159, 162, 169-171, 182, 198, 202, 203, 236, 237, 249, 250, 251, 256, 261, 268, 271, 276, 280, 282-287, 291, 294, 295, 364-366, 391
Center for Naval Analyses 154, 277, 283, 287, 294, 296

397

centers of gravity 163
Central Command (see also
   CENTCOM) 10, 15, 17, 19, 31, 45,
   46, 48, 51, 53, 55, 56, 77, 86, 87,
   91, 94, 95, 97, 99, 100, 102,
   104-114, 116, 118, 119, 124, 125,
   128, 129, 131, 132, 135, 139, 142,
   144, 145, 148, 150, 152, 153, 157,
   158, 160, 167-171, 174, 176, 180,
   184, 185, 186, 193, 197, 198, 202,
   205, 236, 249, 256, 260, 265, 271,
   272, 274, 275, 277, 280, 281, 282,
   284-286, 289, 294, 295, 299, 301,
   306, 308, 310, 315, 320, 325, 331,
   358, 364, 367, 368, 385-387, 389,
   390, 391, 392
Central Intelligence Agency 71, 182,
   185, 288, 300, 391
Chairman of the Joint Chiefs of Staff
   6, 50, 183, 388
Chairman, Joint Chiefs of Staff 107,
   186, 359, 387
Checkmate 166, 170, 181, 182, 185,
   202, 256, 261, 281, 287, 288, 371
chemical 8, 26, 27, 29-31, 57, 187,
   241, 369
chemical warfare 26, 27, 29-31, 241
Cheney, Richard 43, 44, 183, 184,
   247, 262
Chief of Naval Operations 157
Chief of Staff 1, 45, 103, 104, 109,
   132, 142, 144, 150, 152, 153, 157,
   171, 288, 383, 384, 386
CID 272
CINCCENT 41, 43, 45, 48, 49, 51,
   59, 129, 159, 181, 183, 184, 197,
   294, 368, 376
CJCS 203, 262, 291, 388, 391
close air support 43, 50, 52, 60, 64,
   65, 68, 79, 80, 88-90, 100-102, 106,
   169, 313, 314, 322, 323, 339, 341,
   343, 344, 352, 353, 355, 361, 362,
   364, 367
CNA 287, 294, 296
coalition 1, 2, 7, 42, 43, 46, 48, 50,
   63, 64, 69, 71, 72-74, 83, 96, 98,
   100, 110, 111, 119, 123, 124, 127,
   130, 137, 148, 149, 158, 159, 196,
   227, 247, 248, 257, 258, 264, 269,
   273, 294, 302, 305, 307, 309, 310,
   329, 333-336, 373, 375
COCOM 186, 341, 386-388
COMALF 108, 132, 154
combat air patrol 15, 56, 95, 125,
   307
combat intelligence division 132,
   137, 142, 144, 269, 272, 277
combat operations planning staff 187,
   273
combat planning staff 135, 138, 142,
   148, 150
combat search and rescue 50
combined control and reporting center
   129
combined OPLAN 149, 342, 345,
   347, 349, 390
command and control 1-7, 41, 56, 57,
   70, 74, 75, 77, 79-85, 87-90, 92,
   99-102, 105, 107, 112, 113, 122,
   129, 130, 139, 142, 147, 150, 155,
   157, 164, 181, 182, 185, 191, 203,
   205, 206, 210, 212, 224, 227, 235,
   236, 247, 248, 253-256, 264-266,
   272, 284, 294, 303, 311, 312, 314,
   315, 316, 318, 327, 329-337, 339,
   354-357, 359, 360, 363, 369, 370,
   371
command post exercise 179
command, control and communication
   32
communications security 118
Compass Call 129, 309, 319
computers 74, 110, 112, 167, 251,
   278, 357, 373
Congress 45, 55, 84, 265, 266, 358
Constant Source 270, 302
contingency plan 87, 149
COPD 135, 187
COPS 124, 135, 148, 318
Corder, John 48, 49, 59, 66, 190,

398

191, 190-192, 200, 207-209, 214, 225, 232, 236, 237, 259, 260, 324, 326, 358
Corps:
  VII Corps 60, 103, 105, 314, 319, 325
  XVIII Airborne Corps 64, 313
  XVIIIth Airborne Corps 99
Cosby, Mike 166
Cougill, Roscoe 112
counterair 43, 50, 52, 95, 96, 152, 309, 359, 360, 363, 365, 367
CRC 80, 81, 90
Crigger, James 66, 108, 150, 152-154, 167, 174, 187, 190, 191
critical items 291
CSS 17, 24, 29, 96, 120, 129, 145, 148, 149, 237
CW 25, 27-31

D

D-Day 52, 148-150, 162, 168, 170, 197, 200, 342, 343
D-Day plan 149
DAD 132
daily ATO 17, 52, 97, 149, 154, 168, 169, 214, 221, 283, 306, 374, 376
DASC 79, 310, 320
DCS 84, 97, 107-109, 116, 125, 127, 152, 207, 213, 237, 287, 291, 308, 325, 373
deception 3
Defense Communications Agency 113, 114, 170
Defense Intelligence Agency (see also DIA) 10, 182, 193, 248, 251, 254, 287, 334, 371, 391
Defense Mapping Agency 224
Defense Meteorological Satellite Program 128
Defense Science Board 118, 126, 195, 247, 253, 259, 263, 299
Defense Support Program 249
Department of Defense (see also DOD) 7, 45, 46, 77, 84, 110, 111, 116, 254, 267, 349, 358, 362, 384, 392
Deptula, David 8, 14, 57, 72, 75, 149, 158, 159, 163, 164, 168, 172-175, 180, 181, 183-185, 192, 193, 195, 196, 197, 200, 201, 203, 207, 208, 210, 214, 219, 223, 224, 227-229, 231, 232, 235, 240, 255, 256, 259, 261-264, 268, 284, 290, 293, 379
Desert Shield 1, 2, 5, 6, 8, 17, 24, 29, 41-43, 45, 49, 50, 53, 55, 56, 60, 61, 65, 67, 71, 73, 77, 83, 91, 92, 96, 97, 100, 103, 104, 107-111, 114-121, 124-127, 130, 139, 145, 148, 149, 152-154, 157, 158, 160, 162, 169, 170, 175, 177, 179, 186, 187, 197, 200, 201, 203, 205, 206, 210, 212, 213, 224, 237, 239, 247-249, 251-253, 259, 261-265, 271-273, 277-282, 284-287, 290, 291, 294, 297, 299, 302, 305, 308, 309, 311-314, 316, 320, 323, 324, 327, 330, 331, 333, 335, 336, 351, 366, 368-373, 388, 389
Desert Shield/Storm 158, 186, 265, 271, 277, 278, 279, 280, 287, 291, 297, 302, 309, 314, 316, 320, 323, 324
Desert Storm 1, 2, 5-8, 13, 21, 37-39, 41, 42, 45, 48, 49, 52, 53, 55, 56, 58, 60, 61, 62, 65-69, 71, 72, 83, 97, 99, 101, 103, 107-111, 113, 114, 116, 117-119, 124-127, 129, 139, 154, 160, 166, 168, 170, 175, 179, 181, 197, 199, 201-203, 205, 206, 210, 212, 213, 219, 224, 231, 236, 237, 239, 243, 247, 248-256, 259, 263, 264, 269, 277-288, 290, 293-296, 299, 301, 305-312, 315, 320, 322-327, 329-331, 333, 335, 336, 351, 358, 366, 368-373, 376, 379, 389, 390
desired mean point of impact 261,

298, 301
Dhahran 92, 93, 96, 108, 112, 120, 378
DIA (see also Defense Intelligence Agency) 182, 183, 185, 202, 247, 251, 254, 270, 281, 285, 287-291, 297, 300, 371, 391
Dickinson, Ross 170, 277
Diego Garcia 292
Direct Air Support Center 99, 100, 102, 106, 310, 313, 316, 320, 321, 326, 327, 343
director of air defense 132, 139, 142
Divisions:
  1st Armored Division
DMA 224
DMPI 147, 291, 298
doctrine 79, 86, 87, 103, 128, 131, 152, 170, 250, 251, 253, 264, 302, 359, 360, 363
DOD (see also Department of Defense) 84, 94, 202, 243, 291, 339-348
drone 321
DSN 107

E

E-2 83, 309
E-3 83, 92, 94-98, 115, 123, 306, 307, 309, 311, 312
E-8 84, 324, 325, 327
EC-130 129, 318
ECM 64
EDS 61, 250
EF-111 25, 29, 30, 96, 238, 239, 242
Eglin AFB, FL 66
Egypt 127
Egyptian 127, 129, 323
Eisenhower, Dwight D. 73, 352, 357
electric 322
electronic order of battle 374
electronic warfare 70, 95, 96, 129, 154, 207, 259, 307, 319
Elf One 92, 93, 107, 180

ELINT 165, 175
Eskridge, Robert 165, 168, 174, 229
EUCOM 159, 203
Europe 86, 95, 103, 118, 125, 130, 149, 314, 322, 370, 371, 384, 392
European Command 129, 359, 384, 385, 391
exercises 4, 87, 100, 103, 105, 149, 154, 170, 179, 180, 208, 225, 278, 282, 330, 333, 336, 341, 343, 367
exploitation 281, 285, 286, 288, 326

F

F-4G 14, 25, 27, 29, 238, 239, 242, 259
F-15 29, 94, 108, 120
F-15E 21, 32-39, 41, 148, 166, 224, 230, 231, 248, 252, 253, 261, 269, 296, 311, 374, 375
F-16 165, 201, 229, 237-242, 258, 296, 310, 319
F-111 25, 28-30, 166,173, 201, 231, 237-242
F-117 165, 166, 173, 174, 199, 224, 231, 261, 264, 269, 296, 298, 377
F-117A 21, 167, 231, 269, 270, 283
FAC 25, 28, 79, 90, 102, 241, 322, 334
facsimile 6, 107, 251
FAHD 41
fax 109, 116, 125, 153, 162
Feinstein, Jeff 27, 33, 239
fire support coordination line 64, 101, 310, 313, 314, 329, 343, 344
fleet defense 56
FLIR 248, 251
fog of war 229
Fort Bragg 179
forward air control 81
France 352
Franks, Frederick 103, 105, 314
fratricide 64, 65, 72, 79, 88, 259, 260, 307, 310, 322
FSCL 64, 344

G

Galvin, John 103, 130, 391, 392
GAT 8, 10, 13, 19, 25, 27-29, 187, 192, 193, 195, 196, 198-203, 205-210, 212, 214, 219, 221, 223, 225, 228, 229, 232, 235, 236, 241, 242, 255, 256, 258, 260, 261, 263, 264, 265, 266, 268-270, 272, 281, 282, 283, 289-291, 293, 294, 296-299, 302, 330-332, 334, 335, 372, 373, 375
GBU-10 27, 30, 292
GBU-12 292
GBU-15 292
GBU-24 27, 292
GBU-27 292
GBU-28 292
GCC 120
General Accounting Office 293
Germany 352
global positioning satellite 322, 323
Glock, John 164, 165, 171, 173, 175, 176, 289
Glosson, Buster 8, 10, 17, 28, 30, 48, 49, 60, 61, 63, 66, 67, 68-72, 75, 144, 158, 162-169, 171-174, 176, 180, 182, 183, 184, 186, 190, 191, 195, 196, 197-202, 205, 208, 209, 213, 214, 221, 223-225, 227-229, 231, 232, 240, 246, 247, 259, 261, 262, 268, 269, 289, 290, 293, 294, 330, 331, 334, 335, 369, 373, 375, 377, 378
Goldwater-Nichols 358, 386
GOSC 116
GR-1 258
Griffith, Gen. 162
ground control intercept 358
ground forces 41, 51, 77, 79, 81, 86, 88, 94, 119, 148, 295, 314, 316, 334, 357, 390
ground order of battle 37
ground station 80, 103, 104, 154
ground station modules 104

Guam 116, 353
guidance, apportionment and targeting 8, 333
guidance, apportionment, targeting 68, 72, 202, 209, 266

H

H-2 24, 31
H-3 24, 26, 27, 30, 31
hardened aircraft shelter 31
HARM 259, 260
Harvey, Ben 160, 281
HAS 1-3, 5, 25, 28, 31, 40, 53, 57, 64, 74, 77, 79, 83, 128, 129, 190, 206, 214, 263, 267, 278, 291, 301, 316, 324, 329, 332, 333, 337, 342, 343, 345, 346, 357, 360, 365, 366, 369, 371, 373, 381-383, 387, 392
Have Quick 95, 114, 319
Hawk 115
helicopter 125, 315, 320, 322, 361
Henry, Larry 52, 166, 373
Hente, Scott 165, 207, 376
HMMWV 322
Holdaway 165
Horner, Charles A. 3, 5, 8, 10, 21, 41-49, 51, 52, 56-75, 77, 91, 92, 100, 104, 119, 120, 124, 130, 157-159, 164, 167, 169, 185-188, 190, 191, 193, 195, 198, 200, 201, 205-208, 228, 232, 237, 246, 247, 255, 260, 262, 264, 265, 270, 279, 303, 311, 313, 314, 316, 319, 326, 329, 330, 333, 335, 336, 358, 366, 382, 384, 387, 389, 390
House Armed Services Committee 302
Hurlburt Field, FL 179
Hussein 69, 162, 227, 374, 378

I

I-2000 292, 298
IADS 8, 372, 373

identification friend or foe 123, 147
IFF 123
Imminent Thunder 278, 279
Incirlik 305, 306
Independence 199, 353
inertial navigation system 242
infantry 60, 347
infrared 21, 37, 248, 270
infrastructure 41, 106, 110, 111, 187
INMARSAT 113
Instant Thunder 157-159, 162-164, 168, 262
Institute for Defense Analyses 243, 288
integrated air defense system 8, 370
intelligence staff 176, 303, 333
INTELSAT 113
interdiction 42, 43, 50, 52, 65, 91, 99, 101, 102, 106, 147, 152, 169, 179, 230, 272, 295, 313, 315, 319, 327, 332, 354, 359, 362, 364, 365, 368
Internal Look 132, 170, 179, 277
interoperability 139, 263
Iran 52, 92, 179, 312
Iraq cell 187, 198, 200
Iraqi air force 94
Iraqi army 2, 313, 334
Israel 129, 236, 243, 247, 329

J

J-2 105, 256, 271, 281, 282
J-3 63, 64, 159, 181, 198, 203
J-5 60, 91, 159
J-6 112, 113
Jaguar 258
Jamerson, James 392
Japan 353, 367
JCS (see also Joint Chiefs of Staff) 7, 77, 123, 124, 182, 202, 203, 267, 280, 291, 339-342, 345-349, 359, 360, 362, 364, 367, 379, 384, 385, 392
JCSE 107
JFACC (see also Joint Force Air Component Commander) 1, 41, 42, 46, 48-53, 55, 57-60, 62-65, 67, 69-75, 90, 105, 106, 131, 132, 150, 154, 155, 184, 186, 190, 193, 195, 200, 311, 330, 333, 335, 351, 358, 360, 361, 362-368, 389, 390
JFC 366
JIC 202
JIPC 286, 287, 299
JMEM 15, 172, 298
Joint Chiefs of Staff (see also JCS) 6, 17, 50, 59, 103, 107, 113, 128, 130, 183, 185, 186, 280, 346, 348, 349, 354, 355, 359, 360, 362, 363, 378, 387, 388
joint communications support element 107
Joint Force Air Component Commander (see also JFACC) 3, 21, 41, 42, 46, 48, 50-53, 55, 56, 58, 60, 62-65, 71, 73, 75, 77, 83, 87, 90, 101, 105, 130, 131, 132, 139, 153, 171, 190, 201, 203, 205, 255, 265, 296, 312, 313, 330, 345, 351, 359, 360-364, 366, 389, 390
Joint Intelligence Center 271, 288
Joint Munitions Effectiveness Manual 198, 298
Joint Operations Planning and Execution System 91
Joint Staff 53, 63, 102, 113, 129, 159, 181, 203, 280, 291, 353, 356, 362, 377, 389
Joint Surveillance Target Attack Radar System 102, 103, 324
Joint target list 170
Joint Task Force 52, 71, 86, 87, 158, 340, 345, 363, 382, 389-392
Joint Task Force Middle East 52, 158
JOPES 107
Jordan 129
JSTARS 32-41, 84, 102-106, 129, 237, 253, 254, 285, 305, 310, 311, 324-326, 325-327, 332, 335, 336

JTCB 170, 171, 196
JTF 361, 392
JTIDS 98, 114

J

KC-10 388
KC-135 388
Keller, K.F. 249
Kelly, Thomas W. 181
Khafji 190, 327
Khalid 44, 46, 48, 97, 190
KIA 378
kill box 310, 311, 319-321
kill boxes 310, 311, 313, 318, 320
killed in action 378
killer scouts 319
Kiraly, Emery 270, 287
Korean War 73, 352, 353
KTO 37, 166, 180, 187, 200, 223, 281, 282, 286
KTO cell 200
Kuwait 2, 37, 42, 46, 50, 52, 57, 59-61, 71, 74, 93, 124, 132, 155, 157, 162, 169, 187, 283, 288, 295, 309, 310, 312, 321, 322, 324, 327, 330, 349, 390
Kuwait theater of operations 37, 288
Kuwaiti 8, 14, 162, 197, 198, 295

L

Langley AFB, VA 103, 108, 109, 116, 128, 130, 281, 289, 366, 384
LANTIRN 269
leadership 10, 55, 57, 187, 303, 330, 333, 352, 370
Leonardo, Col 174, 175
Lewis, Rick, 166
Linebacker I 356, 358
Linebacker II 356
lines of communication 295
Link 11 98
logistics 39, 46, 84, 91, 104, 153, 165, 248, 341, 345, 346, 386-388

Loh, John 157, 378

M

M-117 292
MAGTF 42, 51, 359
maintenance personnel 92
major commands 183, 303, 383, 384
MAP (see also master attack plan) 10, 15, 17, 19, 30, 32, 33, 65, 164, 170, 175, 192, 193, 196, 197, 200, 205, 206, 208, 209, 213, 228, 237, 238-241, 342, 371, 372
MARCENT 52, 150, 152, 153, 320, 325
Marine Corps 42, 51, 52, 58, 60, 63, 64, 69, 83, 99, 102, 106, 115, 116, 264, 281, 282, 288, 294, 308, 312-314, 316, 318, 320, 321, 326, 330, 345, 351, 352, 355, 357, 359, 361, 362, 363, 366, 367, 382
Marine Expeditionary Force 355
marines 42, 60, 61, 105, 125, 147, 312, 320, 360, 366
mark 82 37
Marvin Short 174
MASS 168, 169, 300
master attack plan (see also MAP) 10-14, 17, 19, 21, 24, 25, 27, 28, 29-34, 49, 65, 67, 68, 164, 167, 168, 170, 171, 175, 182, 191, 192, 193, 196, 197, 199, 200, 205-209, 223, 237-241, 372
master target list 27, 171, 192, 203, 259
Mauz, Henry 52, 56
Mavericks 259
McConnell, Michael 180, 182-184, 196, 203, 247, 261, 268, 293, 335
MCM 89, 95, 131, 306, 309
McPeak, Merrill 1, 129, 377
McSwain, Donald 55, 159, 164, 165, 167, 169, 181, 374
meteorology 128
MH-60 258

403

Middle East Joint Task Force 71
Military Airlift Command 108, 185, 383, 390
MILSATCOM 114
Ministry of Defense 45
Mirage 2000 258
missile 84, 115, 117, 122, 123, 126, 181, 218, 219, 242, 243, 247-254, 259, 325, 339, 370-372, 374, 378, 390
mission report 21, 23, 30, 31, 36-41, 269, 299
MK-20 292
MK-82 292
MK-84 39, 292
mobility 82, 322
mobilization 348
Moore, Royal 42, 52, 58, 59, 61-63
moving target indicator 324, 326
MTL 27
Muellner, George 84, 103-105, 237, 324-326
munitions 13, 15, 24, 27, 147, 152, 158, 160, 167, 172, 173, 198, 224, 228, 230, 255, 261, 267, 283, 291, 292, 293, 296, 298, 300, 377
munitions storage 27
national command authorities 345

N

National Military Intelligence Support Teams 251
National Security Agency 71, 110, 111, 185, 288, 391
NATO 101-103, 111, 144, 145, 149, 306, 339-341, 343, 345-348, 392
nature of war 229
naval 42, 52, 53, 55, 56, 58, 117, 132, 144, 154, 157, 159, 166, 181, 277, 283, 287, 294, 296, 313, 342, 344, 346, 347, 354, 390
NAVCENT 52, 53, 56, 150, 152, 153, 155, 181, 283
navigation 120, 242, 263

Navy 45, 52, 53, 55, 56, 60, 69, 74, 83, 113, 115-118, 125, 145, 154, 164, 167, 181, 196, 248, 281, 282, 283, 287, 288, 290, 294, 296, 308, 309, 312, 336, 345, 351-354, 356, 357, 362, 363, 365-367, 374, 382
NBC 165
NCA 345
Nellis AFB, NV 115
network 49, 75, 83, 106, 107, 109, 111, 112, 115, 116, 126, 153, 181-183, 290, 293, 334, 365, 372, 375, 390
New York Times 227
Night Targeting Cell 13-15, 19, 152, 197
Ninth Air Force 41, 53, 56, 94, 99, 158, 303, 382, 384, 387, 389, 390
Norsworthy 165, 229
North Vietnam 52, 73, 333, 354, 355
North Vietnamese 355, 356, 358
Northern Area Command 99, 101, 323
NTC 13
nuclear 8, 13, 57, 152, 187, 207, 347, 369

O

O'Boyle, Randy 165
OCA 166, 169
Oelrich, Mike 165
offensive 60, 66, 67, 70, 73, 75, 96, 155, 157, 158, 159, 160, 162, 164, 168, 169, 170, 186, 190, 200, 205, 206, 262, 272, 295, 303, 309, 323, 331, 344, 349, 365, 367, 390
offensive counter air 169, 272
Office of the Assistant Secretary of Defense 282
"Oly" Olsen 165
Olsen, Thomas 45, 158, 159, 165, 167, 203
Oman 113
Omnibus Agreement 42, 51, 60, 359,

360, 364, 366
OPCON 185, 186, 346, 388, 390-392
operational control 42, 51, 70, 105, 185, 186, 340, 341, 345, 346, 359, 360, 363, 364, 365, 381, 388, 392
operational security 164
Operations Directorate 159, 181, 203, 333, 334
operations order (see also OPORD) 42, 43, 45, 50-52, 391
operations staff 61-63, 198, 278, 295
OPLAN 45, 71, 93, 124, 149, 179, 271, 342, 345, 347, 349, 364, 365, 367, 368, 389, 390
OPLAN 1002-90 45, 71, 93, 179, 271, 365, 368
OPORD 42, 43
order 001 391
order 003 45
order of battle 37, 137, 139, 173, 371, 374
Osterloh, Bob 165

P

Pacific Command 385
Panama 387
Patriot 115, 126, 247, 249, 250, 254
Pave Tack 269
Peace Shield 119, 120
Persian Gulf 45, 46, 56, 84, 87, 94, 107, 114, 117, 120, 165, 181, 243, 249, 250, 281, 283, 291, 369, 381
PGM 224, 228
phase I 164, 168, 179, 262
phase II 179
phase III 179
planners 8, 13, 14, 19, 21, 24, 31, 40, 65, 66, 69, 70, 74, 95, 112, 117, 126, 144, 157, 159, 164, 165, 166-169, 171-176, 180-183, 185, 187, 192, 196-198, 200, 202, 206-208, 210, 212, 213, 214, 219, 221, 227, 228, 230, 232, 235, 236, 241, 242, 254-256, 258-261, 263-270, 272, 280-283, 289-291, 293, 294, 296, 298, 302, 313, 315, 331, 333, 335, 373, 375, 378
planning 3, 7-10, 13, 15-17, 19, 21, 27-29, 32-34, 40, 42, 45, 46, 48-52, 55, 59, 60, 63, 66, 70, 75, 77, 79, 87, 89-91, 96, 97, 107, 118, 127, 130-133, 135, 137, 138, 139, 142, 144, 148, 149, 150, 152, 153, 155, 157, 158, 159, 162-164, 166-177, 180, 181, 182, 184-187, 191-203, 205, 206, 207-210, 212-215, 221, 223, 224, 225, 227, 228, 230-233, 235, 236-240, 242, 255, 256, 259, 260-262, 267, 268, 272-278, 281-283, 288, 290, 291, 293, 294, 295, 299, 300, 306, 307, 308, 312, 326, 329, 335, 341, 343-345, 351, 359-362, 365, 367, 373, 374, 376, 378, 379, 384, 385, 389
population 329, 355
Powell, Colin 6, 44, 130, 157, 169, 247, 262
preplanned close air support 88, 90, 102
president 50, 73, 183, 184, 199, 227, 247, 262, 265, 345, 346, 348, 353-355, 377, 378, 382-384, 386
Pritchett, Jim 165
Profitt, Glenn 70, 186, 191, 259, 260
Proven Force 52, 129, 228, 302, 311, 312, 390-392
Pryor, Bert 165
Punishment ATO 162
push CAS 60, 101

Q

Qatar 111
quick-reaction package 108

R

RAF 150, 152, 153, 165, 166, 250, 281, 282, 307

Rafha 120
RAND 124, 224, 251, 284
RC-135 96, 176, 258
readiness 179, 263
reconnaissance 3, 32, 41, 70, 80, 82, 96, 147, 185, 186, 207, 247, 256-259, 261, 267, 270, 271, 280-282, 284, 285, 287, 294, 300, 301, 359, 381
Reconnaissance Wing 96
reconstitution 273
recovery 307
Red Sea 165, 283
refueling 7, 15, 17, 30, 83, 90, 95, 124, 125, 133, 137, 145, 147-150, 153, 168, 180, 186, 207, 218, 232, 241, 305, 307, 308, 311, 372, 375, 376, 388
reliability 13, 152, 154, 267, 273, 336, 377
remotely piloted vehicle 321
reorganization 8, 13, 157, 185-188, 190, 191, 197, 198, 200-202, 205, 210, 358, 383, 386
Republican Guard 37, 283, 286
research and development 152, 369, 382
reserves 109
resupply 50
RF-4C 258, 281
Rice, Donald 181, 182, 184, 203
Rivet Joint 82-85, 96, 104, 130, 158, 305, 327
Rogers, "Buck" 165, 193, 203, 208, 225, 228
Rolling Thunder 73, 354-356, 358
route package 52, 228, 354
Royal Air Force 49, 164, 250, 352
Royal Saudi Air Force 8, 43, 45, 48, 107, 119, 139, 176, 285, 295, 306
RSAF 43, 47, 52, 66, 94, 109, 152, 165, 166, 176, 253, 281, 282
rules of engagement 50, 56, 57, 91, 95, 123, 124, 135, 137, 142, 150, 152, 206, 346, 377

Russ, General 167

S

S-3 154, 258
SAC 13, 171, 180, 186, 207, 213, 214, 249, 250, 281, 282, 293, 355, 388
Saddam Hussein 149, 227
SAM 8, 15, 17, 122, 166, 180, 188, 195
SAR 39, 137
SATCOM 107, 154
satellite communications 93, 106, 107, 112-114, 251, 335
Saudi Air Force 8, 43, 45, 48, 68, 107, 119, 139, 176-178, 285, 295, 296, 306
Saudi Arabia 13, 41, 43, 45, 71, 91-98, 102, 104, 107, 109-111, 113, 116, 118, 119, 124, 125, 127, 128, 129, 137, 147-150, 155, 157-160, 162, 164, 168-170, 179, 187, 190, 197, 243, 261, 305, 311, 334, 370, 371, 372, 374
Schultz, Dave 109
Schwartz, Paul 46
Schwarzkopf, H. Norman 2, 3, 5, 6, 8, 41, 42, 44-46, 49, 50, 56-64, 67, 69, 71, 73, 91, 103, 108, 124, 157, 159, 169, 183, 184, 195, 198, 236, 237, 262, 265, 266, 302, 325, 329, 330, 382, 386, 388
SCIF 174, 176, 178, 290, 293, 295
Scud 8, 10, 32, 53, 68, 113, 165, 187, 195, 203, 206, 216, 218, 219, 221, 236, 242, 243, 246-254, 325, 329, 336
Scud alert 249
Scud B 242
Scud CAP 253, 325
Scud hunt 206, 216, 218, 242, 243, 246, 247, 254, 329
Scud warning 249, 336
SEAD 25, 29, 158, 240, 373

search and rescue 39, 50, 96, 135, 137, 149, 150, 307, 346
Secretary of Defense 43, 44, 71, 159, 183, 184, 203, 247, 262, 282, 345, 346, 348, 355, 378, 382, 386, 387, 391
Secretary of State 184, 227, 247
Secretary of the Army 369
sector operations center 120
secure telephone unit 109, 334
security 71, 84, 92, 110, 111, 118, 159, 162, 164, 176, 180, 185, 261, 288, 299, 391
Setnor, Chip 166
Sharp, Grant 45, 162
Shaw AFB 27, 33, 65, 66, 101, 154, 162, 167, 239, 384
SHF 107, 112, 154
SIGINT 165
signals intelligence 114, 267, 358
SITREP 129
SKYNET 113
SLAR 258
Smith, Maurice 55, 159, 164, 165
SOF 137, 165
software 55, 74, 102, 104, 107, 116, 154, 224, 278, 279, 297, 303, 336, 366, 369, 375
sortie generation 259
sortie rate 303
Southeast Asia 73, 308, 354-357
SPACC 249
space operations 112, 257
Spain 292
spare parts 106
special forces 248, 323
special instructions 124, 135, 137, 145, 147, 149, 150, 168, 219
special operations 72, 137, 307, 385
Special Operations Command 72, 385
special operations forces 137, 307
Special Planning Group 8, 149, 157, 158, 164, 195, 198, 202, 205
SPINS 145, 150, 209, 218, 219
SPOT 315, 324

stealth 264
stealthy 173, 254
strategic air campaign 150, 157, 159, 162, 163, 165, 166-169, 171, 172, 180, 181, 184, 190, 200, 201, 288
Strategic Air Command 96, 124, 130, 179, 180, 185, 186, 249, 250, 284, 285, 292, 305, 355, 390
strategic air defense 175
Strategic Bombing Survey 266
strategic level 45
strategy 51, 150, 152, 162, 173, 184, 254, 255, 260, 288, 372
STRATFOR 13, 132
STU 108-111, 153, 183, 202, 224, 293, 334
Sudayri 48, 49
Sultan 44, 46
super high frequency 107
suppression of enemy air defenses 15, 25, 27, 207, 240
surface-to-air missile 115, 372
surge 97, 98, 148, 311
SWA 130
SYERS 284
Syrian 129, 323

T

table of organization and equipment 347
TAC (see also Tactical Air Command) 1, 79-81, 83, 84, 86, 87, 99, 103, 104, 107, 108, 110, 115, 116, 120, 130-132, 154, 160, 162, 164, 166, 167, 237, 325, 366, 371, 384
TACAIR 101, 102
TACC (see also Tactical Air Control Center) 2, 8, 19, 30, 35, 36, 43, 48, 49, 59, 62, 64-66, 68, 70, 72, 74, 77, 79, 80, 83, 87, 89, 90, 94, 97, 99, 101, 106, 108, 117, 118, 120, 131, 132, 135, 142, 143, 144, 157, 159, 164, 187, 202, 205, 219, 220, 224, 225, 231, 241, 243, 247,

407

248, 252, 253, 254, 268, 270, 287, 289, 294, 295, 306, 308, 311, 313, 314, 315-321, 325, 326, 356, 357, 369
TACON 186, 347, 388, 391
TACP 79, 88
TACS 42, 65, 77, 80, 82, 83, 85, 86, 88, 90, 91, 94, 96, 101, 106, 113, 115, 119, 128, 131, 135, 137, 144, 187, 205, 210, 213, 214, 218, 225, 305, 319, 321, 327, 330, 335, 369
Tactical Air Command (see also TAC) 1, 41, 77, 79, 81, 86, 87, 94, 103, 104, 115, 116, 130, 132, 133, 158, 174, 185, 186, 200, 267, 320, 326, 363, 366, 383, 384, 387
Tactical Air Control Center (see also TACC) 2, 6, 8, 10, 19, 35, 42, 43, 48, 49, 52, 53, 62, 63, 65-67, 69, 70, 72, 74, 75, 80-83, 86-89, 92, 94-97, 100, 102, 105, 106, 108, 114, 115-118, 120, 131-133, 135, 137, 139, 142, 144, 155, 157, 164, 187, 191, 200, 201, 205, 210, 241, 256, 260, 267, 269, 270, 272, 274, 275, 279, 282, 283, 293-297, 301, 302, 306, 308, 309, 311-316, 319, 325, 326, 329, 331, 333-335, 342, 347, 357, 358, 369, 390
Tactical Air Control Party 79, 88, 322, 344, 347
Tactical Air Control System 2, 42, 51, 65, 77, 80, 84, 88, 90, 92, 96, 98, 99, 101, 106, 114, 115, 118, 119, 128-131, 142, 144, 187, 203, 205, 305, 312, 315, 327, 330, 333, 335, 336, 339, 342, 343, 347, 357, 358, 369
Tactical Air Control Wing 94, 315, 322-324
Tactical Air Operations Center 52, 115, 116, 320
Tactical Air Warfare Center 66
tactical ballistic missile 251, 370, 371
tactical control 77, 129, 347, 392

Tactical Fighter Wing 24, 29, 32, 41, 94, 174, 237, 241, 242, 301
Tactical Intelligence Squadron 325
TADIL 115
Tallil 238-240
tankers 15, 124, 158, 180, 207, 213-215, 219, 224, 228, 230, 232, 308, 309
tanks 91
TAOC 52
target list 27, 170, 171, 192, 193, 196, 198, 203, 259, 261, 290, 291, 294, 312, 315, 318
targeteering 15, 152, 172, 173, 175
TARPS 285
Tenoso, Brig. Gen. 191
TFW (see also Tactical Fighter Wing) 21, 24, 29-31, 37-40, 148, 167, 168, 174, 175, 224, 237-239, 241, 242, 269, 298, 301
The Times 27, 29, 123, 152, 239, 241
Thumrait 113, 168
time over target 37, 218, 238, 291
Tinker AFB, OK 305
TIS 162, 224
Title V 110, 159, 243, 249
TLAM 181, 268
TMD 251, 371
Tolin, 166, 167, 195, 200, 229, 230, 296
Tomahawk 181, 218, 219
TOT 10, 34, 64, 145, 147, 219, 232, 241
TR 280, 284, 285, 377
TR-1 280, 284, 285
TRADOC 86-88, 99, 103
Training and Doctrine Command 86, 87, 103
TRANSCOM 107
Turkey 52, 130, 305, 311, 391, 392
Turkish 306, 391

U

U.S. Air Force 116, 117, 159, 164,

180, 186, 306, 336, 342, 352-354, 365, 382, 389
U.S. Army 101, 118, 123, 152, 164, 259, 286, 370, 378
U.S. Central Command 45, 46, 48, 86, 87, 91, 105, 131, 205, 271, 272, 385, 386, 387, 389, 391
U.S. European Command 384, 385, 391
U.S. Marine Corps (see also Marine Corps) 51, 83, 294
U.S. Marine Corps, Central Command 51
U.S. Navy 164, 353
U.S. Pacific Command 385
U.S. Space Command 385
U.S. Special operations Command 385
U.S. Transportation Command 385
U-2 280, 284, 286, 287
UHF 97, 101, 107, 108, 114, 116, 308
ultra high frequency 107
United Arab Emirates 99, 111, 113
United Kingdom 104, 113, 259, 292
United Nations 353
United States 111
United States Air Force 79, 131, 339, 353
United States code 341, 382, 387
USAFE 125, 127
USC 382, 384-386
USCENTAF (see also CENTAF) 8, 13, 15, 19, 30, 34-36, 57, 63, 68, 87, 97, 100-102, 105-109, 114, 116, 121, 131, 132, 135, 137, 139, 142, 144, 148, 149, 150, 152, 157-160, 162, 166-168, 179, 185-187, 190, 195, 196, 200, 202, 203, 207, 213, 236, 253, 272, 274, 277, 278, 281, 282, 286, 290, 293, 295, 296-299, 308, 316, 321, 324, 390
USCENTCOM (see also Central Command) 50, 86, 105, 139, 159, 162, 170, 179, 186, 275, 281, 282, 313, 385, 387-389
USCINCCENT 37, 42, 46, 49, 50, 59, 91, 93, 102, 123, 124, 129, 179, 86, 271, 324, 365, 367, 368, 386-389, 391, 392
USEUCOM 130, 302, 385, 391, 392
USLANTCOM 385
USMC 42, 51, 52, 100, 157, 165, 198, 320, 321, 357
USN 53, 55, 56, 117, 154, 249, 251, 307
USPACOM 385
USS *Missouri* 321
USSOCOM 202, 385
USSOUTHCOM 385
USSPACECOM 249, 251, 385
USTRANSCOM 186, 385, 388
UTC 109

V

Vietnam 52, 73, 99, 228, 333, 351, 352, 354, 355, 357, 358
Vogel 165

W

Waller, Calvin 44, 59, 61, 63, 325
Warden, John 157-159, 170, 281, 378
wargames 288
Washington 48, 50, 61, 62, 87, 102, 107, 110, 114, 118, 129, 180, 181, 183, 184, 201-203, 206, 221, 227, 236, 248, 255, 256, 266, 280, 289, 290, 291, 293, 294, 322, 334, 335, 351-354, 356-358, 369, 370, 376
Washington Post 227
Waterstreet 165
weaponeering 13, 152, 172, 173, 198, 277, 294
weather 3, 8, 128, 170, 193, 206, 216, 218, 219, 221, 225-228, 232, 259, 261, 267, 296, 308, 312
Welch, W.G. 99, 164, 165, 195

409

Whitley, Alton C. 174
WIA 378
WIN 48, 51, 62, 67, 131, 170, 336
World War II 73, 118, 250, 266, 267, 300, 351, 352, 353, 357, 369
Worldwide Military Command and Control System 107
wounded in action 378

Y

Y'Blood, William T. 48
Yeosock, John 45, 46, 73, 104, 326

Glossary

AAA	Antiaircraft Artillery
AAAM	Advanced Air-to-Air Missile
AADC	Area Air Defense Commander
AAI	Air-to-Air Interrogator Set
AAV	Amphibious Assault Vehicle
AAR	After Action Report
AASLT Div	Air Assault Division (US)
AB	Air Base
ABCCC	Airborne Battlefield Command and Control Center
ABDR	Aircraft Battle Damage Repair
ABF	Advanced Bomb Family
ABFDS	Aerial Bulk Fuel Delivery System
Abn Corps	Airborne Corps (US)
AC	Active Component
ACA	Airspace Control Authority or Airlift Clearance Authorities
ACAS	Air Combat Assessment Summary
ACC	Air Component Commander or Airspace Coordination Center or Arab Cooperation Council
ACCS	Airborne Command and Control Squadron
ACE	Airborne Command Element (USAF) or Aviation Combat Element (USMC) or Air Combat Element (NATO) or Armored Combat Earthmover (US Army)
ACM	Air Combat Maneuvers

ACO	Airspace Coordination Order or Airspace Control Order
ACR	Armored Cavalry Regiment
ACV	Armored Combat Vehicle (US Army) or Air Cushion Vehicle (USN)
AD	Air Division
ADA	Air Defense Artillery
A/DACG	Arrival/Departure Airfield Control Group
ADOC	Air Defense Operations Center
ADX	Air Defense Exercise
AECC	Aeromedical Evacuation Control Center
Aegis	Ship based long-range air defense system.
AELT	Aeromedical Evacuation Liaison Team
AES	Aeromedical Evacuation Squadron
AEW	Airborne Early Warning
AFB	Air Force Base
AFCOMAC	Air Force Combat Ammunition Center
AFDIGS	Air Force Digital Graphics System
AFEWC	Air Force Electronic Warfare Center
AFGWC	Air Force Global Weather Center
AFHRA	Air Force Historical Research Agency
AFLC	Air Force Logistics Command
AFLIF	Air Force Logistics Information File
AFLMC	Air Force Logistics Management Center
AFMSS	Air Force Mission Support System
AFR	Air Force Reserve

AFSC	Air Force Systems Command or Air Force Specialty Code
AFSOC	Air Force Special Operations Command
AFSOUTH	Allied Forces, South (NATO)
AFWMPRT	Air Force Wartime Manpower and Personnel Readiness Team
AGE	Aerospace Ground Equipment
AGL	Above Ground Level
AI	Air Interdiction
AIF	Automated Installation File
AIR	Air Inflatable Retarder
AIWS	Advanced Interdiction Weapons System
ALARM	Air-Launched Anti-Radiation Missile
ALC	Air Logistics Center
ALCC	Airlift Control Center
ALCE	Airlift Control Element
ALCM	Air-Launched Cruise Missile
ALMSNSCD	Airlift Mission Schedule
ALO	Air Liaison Officer
AMI	Aeronautical Militare Italiana
AMRAAM	Advanced Medium-Range Air-to-Air Missile
AMU	Aircraft Maintenance Unit
ANG	Air National Guard
ANGLCO	Air and Naval Gunfire Liaison Company (USMC)
AO	Area of Operation
AOB	Air Order of Battle
AOR	Area of Responsibility
APC	Armored Personnel Carrier

APCC	Aerial Port Control Center
APOD	Aerial Port of Debarkation
APS	Afloat Prepositioning Ship
ARBS	Angle Rate Bombing Set (USMC)
ARC	Air Reserve Components
ARCENT	U.S. Army Forces, Central Command
AREFS	Air Refueling Squadron
ARM	Antiradiation Missiles
ARNG	U.S. Army National Guard
ARS	Air Rescue Service
ARW	Air Rescue Wing
ASARS	Advanced Synthetic Aperture Radar System
ASD(PA)	Assistant Secretary of Defense (Public Affairs)
ASD(SO-LIC)	Assistant Secretary of Defense (Special Operations and Low Intensity Conflict)
ASM	Air-to-Surface Missile
ASMA	Air Staff Management Aide (UK and Iraq)
ASOC	Air Support Operations Center (Army/USAF)
ASUWC	Anti-to-Surface Unit Warfare Commander (USN)
ATACMS	Army Tactical Missile System
ATAF	Allied Tactical Air Force (NATO)
ATC	Air Training Command (USAF)
ATGM	Anti-Tank Guided Munition
ATO	Air Tasking Order
ATTG	Automated Tactical Target Graphic

AUTODIN	Automatic Digital Network
AVCAL	Aviation Coordinated Allowance List (USN)
AVLB	Armored Vehicle-Launched Bridge
Avn Bde	Aviation Brigade (US)
AWACS	Airborne Warning and Control System
AWN	Automated Weather Network
AWS	Airborne Warning System
BAAF	Bahrain Amiri Air Force
BAI	Battlefield Air Interdiction
BARCAP	Barrier Combat Air Patrol
BAS	Basic Allowance for Subsistence
BBBG	Battleship Battle Group
BCE	Battlefield Coordination Element
BDA	Bomb Damage Assessment
Bde	Brigade (US)
BDU	Battle Dress Uniform
BE or BEN	Basic Encyclopedia (number)
BEEF	Base Engineer Emergency Force
BLT	Battalion Landing Team (USMC)
BMP	Soviet armored personnel carrier
BMS	Bombardment Squadron
BMW	Bombardment Wing
B/N	Bombardier/Navigator
BND	German Federal Intelligence Service
BTG	Basic Target Graphic
BVR	Beyond Visual Range
BW	Biological Warfare

C-Day	Deployment Day
C3	Command, Control, and Communications
C3CM	Command, Control, Communications Countermeasures
C3I	Command, Control, Communications, and Intelligence
C3IC	Coordination, Control, Communications, and Intelligence Center
C4	Command, Control, Communications, and Computers
CA	Civil Affairs
CADOB	Consolidated Air Defense Order of Battle
CAF	Canadian Air Force
CAFMS	Computer Aided Force Management System
CAFT	Center for Anti-Fratricide Technology
CALCM	Conventional Air Launched Cruise Missile
CAMS	Core Automated Maintenance System
CAP	Combat Air Patrol
CAS	Close Air Support or Combat Ammunition System
CASSUM	Close Air Support Summary
CAT	Crisis Action Team
CB	Chemical/Biological
CBU	Cluster Bomb Unit
CBW	Chemical/Biological Weapons
CCD	Camouflage, Concealment and Deception

CCIP	Continuously Computed Impact Point
CCRC	Combined Control and Reporting Center
CEM	Combined Effects Munition
CEMIRT	Civil Engineering Maintenance, Inspection, Repair, and Training
CENTAF	U.S. Air Force, Central Command
CENTCOM	U.S. Central Command
CEP	Circular Error Probable
CES	Civil Engineering Squadron
CEV	Combat Engineer Vehicle
CFT	Conformal Fuel Tank
CI	Civilian Internees
CIA	Central Intelligence Agency
CIFS	Close-In Fire Support (USMC)
CINC	Commander-in-Chief
CINCCENT	Commander-in-Chief U.S. Central Command
CINCMAC	Commander-in-Chief, Military Airlift Command
CINCSPACE	Commander-in-Chief U.S. Space Command
CINCTRANS	Commander-in-Chief, U.S. Transportation
CINCTRANSCOM	Commander-in-Chief U.S. Transportation Command
CJCS	Chairman, Joint Chiefs of Staff
CMMS	Congressionally Mandated Mobility Study
CNN	Cable News Network

COCOM	Combatant Command (Command Authority)
COMALF	Commander, Airlift Forces
COMAO	Composite Air Operation
COMMZ	Communications Zone
COMPES	Contingency Operations Mobility Planning and Execution System
COMSEC	Communications Security
COMTAC	Commander of Tactical Air Command
COMUSCENTAF	Commander, U.S. Air Force, Central Command
COMUSCENTCOM	Commander, U.S. Central Command
CNA	Center for Naval Analysis
CNO	Chief of Naval Operations
COMINT	Communications Intelligence
COMSAT	Communications Satellite
CONUS	Continental United States
COSCOM	Corps Support Command (US Army)
CPX	Command Post Exercise
CRAF	Civil Reserve Air Fleet
CRC	Control and Reporting Center
CS	Combat Support
CSAR	Combat Search and Rescue
CSG	Contingency Support Graphic
CSS	Combat Service Support
CSSA	CENTAF Supply Support Agency or Combat Service Support Area
CT	Counterterrorism
CTJTF	Counterterrorism Joint Task Force
CVBG	Aircraft Carrier Battle Group (USN)

CW	Chemical Warfare
CWEP	Conventional Weapons Enhanced Penetration
CWP	Contingency Weather Package
D&D	Decoy and Deception
DACT	Dissimilar Aerial Combat Tactics
DARPA	Defense Advanced Research Projects Agency
DAS	Deep Air Support (USMC)
DASC	Direct Air Support Center (USMC)
DCA	Defense Communications Agency
DCI	Director of Central Intelligence
D-Day	Unnamed day on which an operations begins
DDN	Defense Data Network
DF	Direction Fired or Direction Finding
DFR/ME	Defense Fuel Region, Middle East
DFSC	Defense Fuel Supply Center
DFSP	Defense Fuel Supply Point
DIA	Defense Intelligence Agency
DIS	Daily Intelligence Summary
DISA	Defense Information Systems Agency
Div	Division
DLA	Defense Logistics Agency
DLIR	Downward Looking Infrared
DMA	Defense Mapping Agency
DMDC	Defense Manpower Data Center
DMI	Directorate of Military Intelligence (Israel, Iraq, Egypt)

DMSP	Defense Meteorological Satellite Program
DMPI	Desired Mean Point of Impact
DNA	Defense Nuclear Agency
DOC	Designed Operational Capability
DOD	Department of Defense
DOE	Department of Energy
DOPMA	Defense Officer Personnel Management Act
DOS	Department of State
DOT	Department of Transportation
DOWSR	Directorate of Weather for Strategic Reconnaissance
DPA	Defense Production Act
DPG	Defense Planning Guidance
DSB	Defense Science Board
DSCS	Defense Satellite Communication System
DSFU	Desert Storm Forecast Unit
DSMAC	Digitized Scene Mapping and Correlation
DSP	Defense Support Program
EAC	Echelon Above Corps or Eastern Area Command
ECM	Electronic Countermeasures
ECS	Electronic Combat Squadron
EDS	European Distribution System
EDT	Eastern Daylight Time
ELINT	Electronic Intelligence
EMIS	Electro-Magnetic Isotope Separation

EOB	Electronic Order of Battle
EOD	Explosive Ordnance Disposal
EOGB	Electro-Optically Guided Bomb
EOTDAS	Electro-Optical Tactical Decision Aid Software
EPW	Enemy Prisoner of War
ESA	European Space Agency
EST	Eastern Standard Time
ETTF	European Tanker Task Force
EUCOM	European Command
EW	Electronic Warfare
EWO	Electronic Warfare Officer
EWWS	Electronic Warfare Warning System or Set
FAC	Forward Air Control
FAE	Fuel Air Explosive
FAF	French Air Force
FAPES	Force Augmentation Planning and Execution System
FEBA	Forward Edge of the Battle Area
FEWS	Follow-on Early Warning System
FHTV	Family of Heavy Tactical Vehicles
FID	Foreign Internal Defense
FLIR	Forward-Looking Infrared
FLOGEN	Flow Generation computer model
FLOT	Forward Line of Own Troops
FMC	Fully Mission Capable
FMF	Fleet Marine Force
FMS	Foreign Military Sales

FMSE	Fuels Management Support Equipment
FMTV	Family of Medium Tactical Vehicles
FNOC	Fleet Numerical Oceanography Center (USN)
FOL	Forward Operating Location
FORSCOM	U.S. Army Forces Command
FOSK	Follow-on Spares Kits
FOV	Field of View
FROG	Free Rocket Over Ground
FSCL	Fire Support Coordination Line
FSS	Fast Sealift Support
FTX	Field Training Exercise
G-Day	Day the ground war began
GAO	General Accounting Office
GC	Geneva Convention
GCC	Gulf Cooperation Committee
GCI	Ground Control Intercept
GCU	Guidance and Control Unit
GDSS	Global Decision Support System
GENA	Ground Air Navigation Aids radar (U.K./Saudi)
GHQ	General Headquarters (usually theater level)
GLO	Ground Liaison Officer
GMT	Greenwich Mean Time
GNA	Goldwater-Nichols DOD Reorganization Act
GOB	Ground Order of Battle
GOK	Government of Kuwait
GOSC	General Officer Steering Committee

GP	General Purpose bomb
GPS	Global Positioning System or Satellite
H-Hour	Specific time at which operations commence
HA	Heavy Armor
HARM	High Speed Antiradiation Missile
HAB	Hardened Aircraft Bunker
HAS	Hardened Aircraft Shelter
HEMTT	Heavy Expanded Mobility Tactical Truck
HET	Heavy Equipment Transporter
HF	High Frequency
HIDACZ	High Density Airspace Control Zone
HMMWV	High Mobility Multipurpose Wheeled Vehicle
HNS	Host-nation Support
HTPM	Hard Target Penetrator Munitions
HUD	Heads-Up Display
HUMINT	Human Resources Intelligence
HVAA	High Value Airborne Assets
I&W	Indications and Warnings
IAADF	Iraqi Air and Air Defense Forces
IADF	Iraqi Air Defense Forces
IADS	Integrated Air Defense System
IAEC	International Atomic Energy Commission
IAF	Italian Air Force
ICAO	International Commercial Aviation Organization

ICRC	International Committee of the Red Cross
IDF	Israel Defense Force
IFF	Identification Friend or Foe
IFR	Instrument Flight Reference
IFV	Infantry Fighting Vehicle
IIR	Intelligence Information Report or Imaging Infrared
ILM	Intermediate-Level Maintenance
ILMC	Intermediate-Level Maintenance Center
IMA	Individual Mobilization Augmentee
IMET	International Military Education and Training
IMINT	Imagery Intelligence
IMQT	Initial Mission Qualification Training
INS	Inertial Navigation System
IOC	Intercept Operations Center or Integrated Operations Center
IOT&E	Initial Operational Test and Evaluation
IP	Initial Point
IPDS	Inland Petroleum Distribution System (US Army)
IR	Infrared
IRR	Individual Ready Reserve
ISW	Integrated Strike Warfare
ITAC	Intelligence and Threat Analysis Center (US Army)
ITF	Intelligence Task Force (DIA)
IZAF	Iraqi Air Force
J-1	Manpower & Personnel Directorate (Joint)

J-2	Intelligence Directorate (Joint)
J-3	Operations Directorate (Joint)
J-4	Logistics Directorate (Joint)
J-5	Strategic Plans & Policy Directorate (Joint)
J-6	Command, Control & Communications Systems Directorate (Joint)
J-7	Operational Plans & Interoperability Directorate (Joint)
J-8	Force Structure Resource & Assessment Directorate (Joint)
JAAT	Joint Air Attack Team
JAG	Judge Advocate General
JAIC	Joint Atomic Intelligence Committee
Jaguar	Land-based ground attack aircraft
JAMPS	Joint Automated Message Program
JCEOI	Joint Communications Electronics Operations Instructions
JCMEC	Joint Captured Material Exploitation Center
JCS	Joint Chiefs of Staff
JCSE	Joint Communications Support Element
JDOP	Joint U.S./Saudi Directorate of Planning
JDS	Joint Deployment System
JFACC	Joint Force Air Component Commander.
JFC	Joint Forces Commander
JFC-E	Joint Forces Command East
JFC-N	Joint Forces Command North

JFLCC	Joint Forces Land Component Commander
JFMCC	Joint Forces Maritime Component Commander
JFSOCC	Joint Forces Special Operations Component Commander
JIB	Joint Information Bureau
JIC	Joint Intelligence Center
JIPC	Joint Imagery Production Center
JIST	Joint Intelligence Survey Team
JMCC	Joint Movement Control Center
JMEM	Joint Munitions Effectiveness Manual
JOPES	Joint Operations Planning and Execution System
JPEC	Joint Planning and Execution Community
JPTS	Jet Propellant Thermally Stable
JRC	Joint Reconnaissance Center
JRCC	Joint Rescue Coordination Center
JS	Joint Staff
JSCP	Joint Strategic Capabilities Plan
JSEAD	Joint Suppression of Enemy Air Defenses
JSIPS	Joint Service Imagery Processing System
JSOTF	Joint Special Operations Task Force
JSPS	Joint Strategic Planning System
JSTARS	Joint Surveillance Target Attack Radar System (E-8)
JTACMS	Joint Tactical Missile System
JTCB	Joint Target Coordination Board

JTF	Joint Task Force
JTFME	Joint Task Force Middle East
JTIDS	Joint Tactical Information Distribution System
JTTP	Joint Tactics, Techniques and Procedures
JULL	Joint Uniform Lessons Learned
KAF	Kuwaiti Air Force
KCATF	Kuwait Civil Affairs Task Force
KHZ	Kilohertz
KKMC	King Khalid Military City
KIA	Killed In Action
KTO	Kuwait Theater of Operations
LAMPS	Light Airborne Multi-Purpose System (USN)
LANDSAT	Land Satellite, NASA/NOAA Satellite Program
LANTCOM	Atlantic Command
LANTIRN	Low Altitude Navigation and Targeting Infrared System for Night
LAV	Light Armored Vehicle
LCAC	Air Cushioned Landing Craft
LCC	Land Component Commander
LDGP	Low Drag General Purpose bomb
LENSCE	Limited Enemy Situation/Correlation Equipment
LG	Logistics
LGB	Laser Guided Bomb
LGGAIR	Logistics Airlift
LIATE	LANTIRIN Intermediate Automatic Test Equipment

LOC	Lines of Communication
LOS	Line of Sight
LOTS	Logistics Over the Shore
LRC	Logistics Readiness Center (USAF)
LRI	Long Range International
LVS	Logistics Vehicle System
MAC	Military Airlift Command
MACCS	Marine Air Command and Control System
MACG	Marine Air Control Group
MAG	Marine Airlift Group
MAGTF	Marine Air Ground Task Force
MAIRS	Military Airlift Integrated Reporting System
MAJCOMS	Major Commands
MAP	Master Attack Plan
MARCENT	U.S. Marine Corps, Central Command
MARDIV	Marine Division
MASF	Mobile Aeromedical Staging Facility
MASS	MICAP Asset Sourcing System
MAW	Marine Aircraft Wing
MCI	Ministry of Culture and Information (Iraq)
MCM	Mine Countermeasures or Multi-Command Manual
MEB	Marine Expeditionary Brigade
Mech Div	Mechanized Infantry Division
MEF	Marine Expeditionary Force
MEL	Mobile Erector-Launcher used for mobile missiles

METS	Mobile Electronic Test Set
METSAT	Meteorological Satellite
MEU	Marine Expeditionary Unit
MHE	Materiel Handling Equipment
MIA	Missing In Action
MIF	Maritime Interdiction Force
MICAP	Mission Critical Parts or Mission Capable or Mission Capability Limiting
MILCON	Military Construction
MILSATCOM	Military Satellite Communications
MILSTAR	Military Strategic and Tactical Relay System
MIO	Maritime Intercept Operations
MIPE	Mobile Intelligence Processing Element
MIS	Military Intelligence Study
MISREP	Mission Report
MLRS	Multiple Launch Rocket System
MLV	Memory Loader Verifier
MOBREP	Manpower Mobilization and Accession Status Report
MOD	Ministry of Defense
MODA	Ministry of Defense and Aviation (Saudi Arabia)
MOPP	Mission Oriented Protective Posture
MPES	Medical Planning and Execution System
MPF	Maritime Prepositioning Force
MPS	Maritime Prepositioning Ships
MRE	Meals Ready to Eat

MRR	Minimum Risk Route
MRS	Mobility Requirements Study
MSC	Military Sealift Command
MSE	Mobile Subscriber Equipment
MSI	Multi-Spectral Imagery
MSK	Mission Support Kits
MTACC	Marine Tactical Air Command Center
MTI	Moving Target Indicator
MTL	Master Target List
MTMC	Military Traffic Management Command
NAC	Northern Area Command
NALE	Naval Amphibious Liaison Element
NATO	North Atlantic Treaty Organization
NAVCENT	U.S. Navy, Central Command
NAVEUR	Naval Forces, Europe
NAVSTAR	Navigational Satellite Timing and Ranging
NBC	Nuclear, Biological, and Chemical
NCA	National Command Authorities
NCTR	Noncooperative Target Recognition
NDRF	National Defense Reserve Fleet
NDS	NPIC Data Systems
NF or NOFORN	Not Releasable to Foreign Nationals
NGB	National Guard Bureau
NGFS	Naval Gunfire Support
NIE	National Intelligence Estimate
NMAC	Near Mid-Air Collision
NMCS	Not Mission Capable Supplies

NMCM	Not Mission Capable Maintenance
NMIC	National Military Intelligence Center
NMIST	National Military Intelligence Support Teams
NOAA	National Oceanographic and Atmospheric Administration
NOB	Naval Order of Battle
NODDS	Naval Oceanographic Data Dissemination System
NPIC	National Photo Interpretation Center
NSA	National Security Agency
NSC	National Security Council
NTC	Night Targeting Cell (in GAT)
NVG	Night Vision Goggles
O&M	Operations and Maintenance
OAS	Offensive Avionics System
OASD/(DR&E)	Office of the Assistant Secretary of Defense (Defense Research & Engineering)
OASD/(SO/LIC)	Office of the Assistant Secretary of Defense (Special Operations/Low Intensity Conflict)
OB	Order of Battle
OCA	Offensive Counter Air
OCP	Observation Command Post
OICC	Operational Intelligence Crisis Center
OP	Observation Post
OPAIR	Opposing Air
OPCON	Operational Control
OPDS	Offshore Petroleum Distribution System (USN)

OPEC	Organization of Petroleum Exporting Countries
OPLAN	Operation Plan
OPORD	Operation Order
OPSEC	Operational Security
OSD	Office of the Secretary of Defense
OSI	Office of Special Investigations (USAF)
OSP	Operational Support Package
PACOM	Pacific Command
PA	Public Affairs
PAO	Public Affairs Officer
PCITF	Positive Combat Identification Task Force
PGM	Precision Guided Munitions
PIN	Primary Identification Number
PLO	Palestine Liberation Organization
PLS	Palletized Loading System
PLV	Program Loader Verifier
PMC	Partially Mission Capable
PMEL	Precision Measurement Equipment Laboratory
PMT	Pastoral Ministry Team
PNVS	Pilot Night Vision System
POG	Psychological Operations Group
POL	Petroleum, Oils and Lubricants
POMCUS	Pre-positioning of Material Configured to Unit Sets
POW	Prisoner of War
PREPO	Pre-positioned

PSYOP	Psychological Operation
PSYOPS	Psychological Operations
PTAS	Provisional Tactical Airlift Squadron
QEAF	Qatari Emiri Air Force
QRCT	Quick Reaction Communications Terminal
R&D	Research and Development
R&M	Reliability and Maintainability
RADIC	Rapidly Deployable Integrated Command and Control system
RAF	Royal Air Force (U.K.)
RAFVR	Royal Air Force Voluntary Reserve
RAM	Radar Absorptive Material
RC	Reserve Component
RCAF	Royal Canadian Air Force
RCC	Rescue Coordination Center or Revolutionary Command Council (Iraq)
RDAF	Royal Dutch Air Force
RDF	Rapid Deployment Force or Radio Direction Finding
RDIT	Rapid Deployment Imagery Terminal
RDJTF	Rapid Deployment Joint Task Force
Red Horse	Rapid Engineer Deployable, Heavy Operational Repair Squadron, Engineer
REMIS	Reliability and Maintainability Information System
RFI	Request for Information
RFMD	RED FLAG Measurement Debriefing
RGFC	Republican Guard Force Command (Iraq)
RIBS	Readiness in Base Services

RJAF	Royal Jordanian Air Force
RLT	Regimental Landing Team (USMC)
RO/RO	Roll On/Roll Off
ROE	Rules of Engagement
ROTHR	Relocatable Over-The-Horizon Radar
RPV	Remotely Piloted Vehicle
RRF	Ready Reserve Force or Ready Reserve Fleet
RSADF	Royal Saudi Air Defense Force
RSAF	Royal Saudi Air Force
RSLF	Royal Saudi Land Force
RTNEPH	Real-Time Nephanalysis
RW	Reconnaissance Wing
RWR	Radar Warning Receiver
S&TI	Scientific and Technical Intelligence
SA	Selective Availability
SAAF	Saudi Arabian Armed Forces
SAC	Strategic Air Command
SAG	Saudi Arabian Government or Surface Action Group (USN)
SAM	Surface-to-Air Missile
SAMAREC	Saudi Arabian Marketing and Refining Company
SANG	Saudi Arabian National Guard
SAR	Search and Rescue
SAS	Special Air Service (U.K.)
SATCOM	Satellite Communications
SBS	Special Boat Service (U.K.)
SBSS	Standard Base Supply System

SCUD	Soviet surface-to-surface missile
SCI	Sensitive Compartmented Information
SCIF	Sensitive Compartmented Information Facility
SEAD	Suppression of Enemy Air Defenses
SEAL	Sea Air Land
SECDEF	Secretary of Defense
SFG	Special Forces Group
SFW	Sensor Fuzed Weapon
SHAPE	Supreme Headquarters, Allied Powers, Europe
SHF	Super High Frequency
SIDS	Secondary Imagery Dissemination System
SIGINT	Signals Intelligence
SINCGARS	Single Channel Ground/Airborne Radio Subsystem
SIOP	Single Integrated Operations Plan
SITREP	Situation Report
SLAM	Standoff Land Attack Missile
SLAR	Side-Looking Airborne Radar
SLOC	Sea Lines of Communications
SMESA	Special Middle East Shipping Agreement
SNIE	Special National Intelligence Estimate
SOAF	Sultanate of Oman Air Force
SOC	Sector Operations Center (Air Defense) or Special Operations Command
SOCCENT	Special Operations Command, Central Command

SOCOM	Special Operations Command
SOF	Special Operations Forces
SOFA	Status of Forces Agreement
SOG	Special Operations Group
SOS	Special Operations Squadron
SOW	Special Operations Wing
SPACC	U.S. SPACECOM Space Control Center
SPEAR	Strike Projection Evaluation and Anti-Air Warfare Research (USN)
SPINS	Special Instructions
SPOT	French Satellite Probatoire d'Observation de la Terre
SRBM	Short-range Ballistic Missile
SRP	Sealift Readiness Program
SRW	Surveillance and Reconnaissance Wing
SSA	Selective Service Act
SSM	Surface-to-Surface Missile
STAMP	Standard Air Munitions Package
STGP	Special Tactics Group (USAF)
STON	Short Ton (2,000 pounds or 0.9 metric tons)
STPJ	Special Tactic Paramedics (USAF)
STRAPP	Standard Tank, Rack, Adapter, and Pylon Package
STRATFOR	Strategic Forces Advisors
STU	Secure Telephone Unit
SURVIAC	Survivability and Vulnerability Information Analysis Center
SWA	Southwest Asia

SYERS	Senior Year Electro-Optical Reconnaissance System
TAC	Tactical Air Command
TACAIR	Tactical Air
TACC	Tactical Air Control Center
TACON	Tactical Control
TACP	Tactical Air Control Party
TACS	Tactical Air Control System
TACSAT	Tactical Satellite
TADIL	Tactical Digital Information Link or Tactical Data Interface Link
TAF	Tactical Aircraft Forces
TAG	Tactical Airlift Group
TAIRCW	Tactical Air Control Wing
TALD	Tactical Air-Launched Decoy
TALO	Theater Airlift Liaison Officer
TANKREP	Tank Killer Report
TAOC	Tactical Air Operations Center (USMC)
TARCAP	Target Combat Air Patrol
TARPS	Tactical Air Reconnaissance Pod System
TAW	Tactical Airlift Wing
TAWC	Tactical Air Warfare Center
TBM	Tactical Ballistic Missile
TCN	Transportation Control Number
TDA	Tactical Decision Aid
TEL	Transporter-Erector-Launcher
TEMPER	Tent Expendable Modular Personnel
TER	Triple Ejector Rack

TERCOM	Terrain Contour Matching
TFS	Tactical Fighter Squadron
TFW	Tactical Fighter Wing
TIALD	Thermal Imaging and Laser Designating
TIARA	Tactical Intelligence and Related Activities
TIBS	Tactical Information Broadcast System (USAF)
TIROS	Television and Infrared Observation Satellites
TIS	Tactical Intelligence Squadron
TLAM	Tomahawk Land-Attack Missile
TMD	Tactical Ballistic Missile Defense
TO	Technical Order
TO&E	Table of Organization and Equipment
TOAF	Tactical Operations Area Forecast
TOT	Time Over Target
TPFDD	Time-Phased Force Deployment Data
TPFDL	Time-Phased Force Deployment List
TR	Theater Reserves
TRADOC	Training and Doctrine Command (US Army)
TRAM	Target Recognition and Acquisition Multisensor (USN)
TRANSCOM	U.S. Transportation Command
TRAP	Tanks, Racks, Adapters, and Pylons
TRG	Tactical Reconnaissance Group
TTF	Tanker Task Force
TTM	Tactical Target Material

TTP	Tactics, Techniques, and Procedures
UAE	United Arab Emirates
UAEAF	United Arab Emirates Air Force
UAV	Unmanned Aerial Vehicle
UAWS	USAREUR Automated Weather System
UCMJ	Uniform Code of Military Justice
UHF	Ultra High Frequency
UK	United Kingdom
ULN	Unit Line Number
UMMIPS	Uniform Military Management and Movement Indicator System
UN	United Nations
UND	Urgency of Need Designator
UNSC	United Nations Security Council
USACE	U.S. Army Corps of Engineers
USAF	United States Air Force
USAFE	U.S. Air Force Europe
USAFR	United States Air Force Reserve
USAR	U.S. Army Reserve
USC	United States Code
USCENTCOM	Central Command
USCG	U. S. Coast Guard
USCINCCENT	Commander-in-Chief U.S. Central Command
USCINCCENT	U.S. Commander-in-Chief, Central Command
USDAO	U.S. Defense Attache Office
USEUCOM	U.S. European Command
USG	United States Government

USIA	U.S. Information Agency
USMC	U.S. Marine Corps
USN	U.S. Navy
USNAVCENT	U.S. Navy, U.S. Central Command
USNR	U.S. Navy Reserve
USPACCOM	U.S. Pacific Command
USSOCOM	U.S. Special Operations Command
USSOUTHCOM	U.S. Southern Command
USSPACECOM	U.S. Space Command
USTRANSCOM	U.S. Transportation Command
UTC	Unit Type Code
UTE	Utilization Rate
VA	Department of Veteran's Affairs
VCJCS	Vice Chairman, Joint Chiefs of Staff
VFR	Visual Flight Reference
WAM	Wide Area Mine
WATCHCON	Watch Condition
WCDC	War Crimes Documentation Center
WFOV	Wide Field of View
WHNS	Wartime Host-Nation Support
WIA	Wounded in Action
WIN	Worldwide Military Command and Control System Intercomputer Network
WN or WNINTEL	Warning Notice: Intelligence Sources and Methods Involved
WOC	Wing Operations Center
WRM	War Reserve Material
WRSK	War Readiness Spares Kits
WSO	Weapons System Operator

WWIMS	Worldwide Indicators and Monitoring System
WWMCCS	Worldwide Military Command and Control System
WXG	Weather Group